T0359160

Enterprise Management Strategies in the Era of Cloud Computing

N. Raghavendra Rao
FINAIT Consultancy Services, India

A volume in the Advances in Business Information
Systems and Analytics (ABISA) Book Series

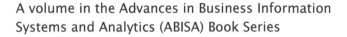

An Imprint of IGI Global

Managing Director:	Lindsay Johnston
Managing Editor:	Austin DeMarco
Director of Intellectual Property & Contracts:	Jan Travers
Acquisitions Editor:	Kayla Wolfe
Production Editor:	Christina Henning
Development Editor:	Brandon Carbaugh
Typesetter:	Cody Page
Cover Design:	Jason Mull

Published in the United States of America by
Business Science Reference (an imprint of IGI Global)
701 E. Chocolate Avenue
Hershey PA, USA 17033
Tel: 717-533-8845
Fax: 717-533-8661
E-mail: cust@igi-global.com
Web site: http://www.igi-global.com

Library of Congress Cataloging-in-Publication Data

CIP Data
Enterprise management strategies in the era of cloud computing / N. Raghavendra Rao, editor.
     pages cm
 Includes bibliographical references and index.
 Summary: "This book seeks to explore the possibilities of business in the cloud, providing a cutting-edge look at the exciting and multifaceted relationships between cloud computing, software virtualization, collaborative technology, and business infrastructure in the 21st Century"-- Provided by publisher.
  ISBN 978-1-4666-8339-6 (hardcover : alk. paper) -- ISBN 978-1-4666-8340-2 (ebook : alk. paper) 1. Information technology--Management. 2. Cloud computing. I. Rao, N. Raghavendra, 1939-

 T58.64.E676 2015
 658'.0546782--dc23

                              2015006725

This book is published in the IGI Global book series Advances in Business Information Systems and Analytics (ABISA) (ISSN: 2327-3275; eISSN: 2327-3283)

British Cataloguing in Publication Data
A Cataloguing in Publication record for this book is available from the British Library.

All work contributed to this book is new, previously-unpublished material. The views expressed in this book are those of the authors, but not necessarily of the publisher.

For electronic access to this publication, please contact: eresources@igi-global.com.

Advances in Business Information Systems and Analytics (ABISA) Book Series

Madjid Tavana
La Salle University, USA

ISSN: 2327-3275
EISSN: 2327-3283

MISSION

The successful development and management of information systems and business analytics is crucial to the success of an organization. New technological developments and methods for data analysis have allowed organizations to not only improve their processes and allow for greater productivity, but have also provided businesses with a venue through which to cut costs, plan for the future, and maintain competitive advantage in the information age.

The **Advances in Business Information Systems and Analytics (ABISA) Book Series** aims to present diverse and timely research in the development, deployment, and management of business information systems and business analytics for continued organizational development and improved business value.

COVERAGE

- Performance Metrics
- Business Systems Engineering
- Geo-BIS
- Data Governance
- Business Information Security
- Business Process Management
- Data Management
- Data Strategy
- Information Logistics
- Business models

IGI Global is currently accepting manuscripts for publication within this series. To submit a proposal for a volume in this series, please contact our Acquisition Editors at Acquisitions@igi-global.com or visit: http://www.igi-global.com/publish/.

Titles in this Series

For a list of additional titles in this series, please visit: www.igi-global.com

Handbook of Research on Organizational Transformations through Big Data Analytics
Madjid Tavana (La Salle University, USA) and Kartikeya Puranam (La Salle University, USA)
Business Science Reference • copyright 2015 • 561pp • H/C (ISBN: 9781466672727) • US $245.00 (our price)

Business Technologies in Contemporary Organizations Adoption, Assimilation, and Institutionalization
Abrar Haider (University of South Australia, Australia)
Business Science Reference • copyright 2015 • 337pp • H/C (ISBN: 9781466666238) • US $205.00 (our price)

Business Transformation and Sustainability through Cloud System Implementation
Fawzy Soliman (The University of Technology, Australia)
Business Science Reference • copyright 2015 • 300pp • H/C (ISBN: 9781466664456) • US $200.00 (our price)

Effects of IT on Enterprise Architecture, Governance, and Growth
José Carlos Cavalcanti (Federal University of Pernambuco, Brazil)
Business Science Reference • copyright 2015 • 307pp • H/C (ISBN: 9781466664692) • US $195.00 (our price)

Technology, Innovation, and Enterprise Transformation
Manish Wadhwa (Salem State University, USA) and Alan Harper (South University, USA)
Business Science Reference • copyright 2015 • 378pp • H/C (ISBN: 9781466664739) • US $195.00 (our price)

Analytical Approaches to Strategic Decision-Making Interdisciplinary Considerations
Madjid Tavana (La Salle University, USA)
Business Science Reference • copyright 2014 • 417pp • H/C (ISBN: 9781466659582) • US $225.00 (our price)

Information Systems and Technology for Organizational Agility, Intelligence, and Resilience
Hakikur Rahman (University of Minho, Portugal) and Rui Dinis de Sousa (University of Minho, Portugal)
Business Science Reference • copyright 2014 • 355pp • H/C (ISBN: 9781466659704) • US $235.00 (our price)

ICT Management in Non-Profit Organizations
José Antonio Ariza-Montes (Loyola Andalucia University, Spain) and Ana María Lucia-Casademunt (Loyola Andalucia University, Spain)
Business Science Reference • copyright 2014 • 297pp • H/C (ISBN: 9781466659742) • US $215.00 (our price)

Security, Trust, and Regulatory Aspects of Cloud Computing in Business Environments
S. Srinivasan (Texas Southern University, USA)
Information Science Reference • copyright 2014 • 325pp • H/C (ISBN: 9781466657885) • US $195.00 (our price)

www.igi-global.com

701 E. Chocolate Ave., Hershey, PA 17033
Order online at www.igi-global.com or call 717-533-8845 x100
To place a standing order for titles released in this series, contact: cust@igi-global.com
Mon-Fri 8:00 am - 5:00 pm (est) or fax 24 hours a day 717-533-8661

Table of Contents

Section 1
Introduction and Frame Work

Chapter 1
Mouna Jouini, Institut Supérieur de Gestion, Tunisia
Latifa Ben Arfa Rabai, Institut Supérieur de Gestion, Tunisia

Chapter 2
José C. Delgado, Instituto Superior Técnico, Universidade de Lisboa, Portugal

Chapter 3
R. Todd Stephens, AT&T, USA

Section 2
Cloud Computing in Education Sector

Chapter 4
Chaka Chaka, Tshwane University of Technology, South Africa

Chapter 5
Camilius Sanga, Sokoine University of Agriculture, Tanzania
George Kibirige, Sokoine University of Agriculture, Tanzania

Chapter 12

Detailed Table of Contents

Section 1
Introduction and Frame Work

Chapter 1

Mouna Jouini, Institut Supérieur de Gestion, Tunisia
Latifa Ben Arfa Rabai, Institut Supérieur de Gestion, Tunisia

Cloud computing has recently emerged as a new paradigm of computing for hosting and delivering services over the Internet. It replaces computing as a personal commodity by computing as a public utility. It is attractive solution to business owners as it eliminates the requirement for users to plan ahead for provisioning, and allows enterprises to start from the small and increase resources only when there is a rise in service demand. However, despite the significant benefits, these technologies present many challenges including lack of security. The chapter presents an advanced survey focusing on cloud computing concept. It highlights its key concepts and presents a physical architecture of this environment. Finally, the chapter defines virtualization technology as a factor for cloud computing surge and discuses security issues that damage these systems. The aim of this chapter is to provide a better understanding of the design challenges of cloud computing.

Chapter 2

José C. Delgado, Instituto Superior Técnico, Universidade de Lisboa, Portugal

Enterprise Information Systems (EIS) are increasingly designed with cloud environments in mind, as a set of cooperating services deployed in a mix of platforms, including conventional servers and clouds, private and public. If enterprise value chains are considered, in which their EIS need to cooperate, solving all the interoperability problems raised by the need to meaningfully interconnect all these services constitutes a rather challenging endeavor. This chapter describes the concept of enterprise as a service, a collection of dynamically assembled services with a lifecycle centered on the customers, and proposes a multidimensional interoperability framework to help systematizing the various aspects relevant to interoperability. Besides lifecycle, this framework presents other dimensions, namely concreteness (with various levels of abstraction), interoperability (based on structural compliance and conformance), and concerns (to deal with non-functional aspects such as security, reliability and quality of service).

Chapter 3

This chapter will focus on building an end user service cloud catalog which will bridge the gap from the design requirements to the technology delivery organization. Once in the hands of IT, a more traditional service catalog can be used to leverage the service orchestration and delivery components. The author examines designing, building, and reviewing the impact of a more end user focused service catalog. Success will be measured by reviewing the business metrics in order to show the criticality of great design techniques and using familiar models like e-commerce.

Section 2
Cloud Computing in Education Sector

Chapter 4

Within the cloud computing ecosystem and its different permutations, there exists personal mobile cloud computing. The latter has not been covered and investigated much in relation to its affordances for higher education (HE), especially in South Africa. Thus, this chapter argues that personal mobile cloud computing can offer HE significant educational affordances in the form of cloud computing value chain. It does so by providing one South African example entailing a two-project study in the HE sector in which the cloud affordances of Twitter and Facebook were leveraged for educational purposes. Regarding Twitter, one of its affordances is that it was exploited as a cloud based virtual blackboard for a course content, thereby facilitating micro-teaching and micro-learning. Concerning Facebook, one of its affordances is that it served as a cloud based mobile computing environment in which a course-specific writing process was mounted by the instructor and participants. A collective affordance for both Twitter and Facebook was both consumerization and BYOD approaches to teaching and learning.

Chapter 5

The maturity of free and open source movement has brought a number of ICT tools. It has affected the way courses are delivered, the way contents are developed, the way data are interoperable, the way learning and teaching materials are shared, the way learners access classes and the way library resources are shared. In developing countries, several libraries are migrating into digital libraries using low cost technologies readily available due to open access, free and open source technology and e-publishing tools. Recent development of cloud computing technology provides state of art tools for libraries. It provides a common platform for easy information storage and sharing. Thus, there is lowering of the cost required to procure and manage library ICT infrastructure due to the capability of that cloud computing which allows the storage to be on a single, efficient system that saves cost and time. In developing countries where most libraries suffer from limited budgets for ICT services, it is anticipated that the future of digital libraries is on cloud libraries.

Section 3
Business Models in Cloud Computing Environment

Chapter 6

The Industrial and Business landscape is changing because of the convergence of information technology and communication technologies. This convergence is creating new types of companies competing with each other. It is not about east or west, or developed markets versus developing markets; It is all about how soon a business enterprise understands the emerging technology and adapts it into its business. It is not enough that a business enterprise understands the technology but one has to be good at thinking about the applications of the technology. Now it has become a necessity for business enterprises to manage complex and interdisciplinary requirements in their organization. This chapter explores a business model developed by a textile mill to remain competitive in global market that uses the concepts of big data, cloud computing, virtual reality, and data warehousing.

Chapter 7

The growth of the Internet has provided scope for multiple applications. Governments in both developed and developing nations have started making use of the Internet in their functioning. The idea behind these governments moving from manual work to IT enabled systems through the Internet is to improve governance. Framing policies pertaining to natural resources and managing them will not be with one department under any government. E-governance, consisting of multidisciplinary experts, is required to develop a model for natural resources management in a country. The electronic governance will help the members of the e-governance and the various departments in the government to facilitate in managing their natural resources. E-governance in the area of natural resources management in any country will be successful only when there is coordination among the various government departments. Cloud computing is economically viable for implementation of e-governance projects. This chapter suggests a conceptual model for managing natural resources and natural disaster management for a country under cloud computing environment.

Section 4
Supply Chain in Cloud Computing Environment

This paper provides an overview of the dual challenges involved in protecting intellectual property while distributing business information that will need to be readable/viewable at some point such that it can be acted upon by parties external to the organization. We describe the principles involved with developing such a system as a means to engender trust in such situations – as a deperimeterized supply chain likely acting through the Cloud – discuss the requirements for such a system, and demonstrate that such a system is feasible for written text by formulating the problem as one related to plagiarism detection. The core of the approach, developed previously, has been shown to be effective in finding similar content (precision: 0.88), and has some robustness to obfuscation, without needing to reveal the content being sought.

This chapter reviews the role of cloud computing in global supply chain, thus describing the theoretical and practical concepts of cloud computing and supply chain management (SCM); the significance of cloud computing in global supply chain; the overview of electronic supply chain management (e-SCM); and the organizational information processing theory within global supply chain. The utilization of cloud computing is necessary for modern organizations that seek to serve suppliers and customers, increase business performance, strengthen competitiveness, and achieve continuous success in global business. Therefore, it is essential for modern organizations to examine their cloud computing applications, develop a strategic plan to regularly check their practical advancements, and immediately respond to the cloud computing needs of customers in global supply chain. Applying cloud computing in global supply chain will extremely improve organizational performance and reach business goals in the digital age.

Section 5
Cloud Computing in Health Sector

Chapter 10

N. Raghavendra Rao, FINAIT Consultancy Services, India

The Health care sector needs information driven service. Information is a major resource which is important to health of individual patient and the success of hospitals. The understanding between medical professionals and software professionals can be a main force behind the design, management and use of health care data and information. Health care information systems need to move from traditional integrated database to knowledge based database. Generally, data in health care sector is available as disperse elements; when it is compiled into a meaningful pattern, then it becomes information. And as information is converted into valid basis for action, then it becomes knowledge. This chapter explains making use of the concepts such as cloud computing, pervasive computing, virtual reality along with the other collaborative technology which will facilitate to create knowledge based health care system.

Section 6
Technical Issues in Cloud Computing

Chapter 11

Dilip Kumar, National Institute of Technology, India
Bibhudatta Sahoo, National Institute of Technology, India
Tarni Mandal, National Institute of Technology, India

The energy consumption in the cloud is proportional to the resource utilization and data centers are almost the world's highest consumers of electricity. The complexity of the resource allocation problem increases with the size of cloud infrastructure and becomes difficult to solve effectively. The exponential solution space for the resource allocation problem can be searched using heuristic techniques to obtain a sub-optimal solution at the acceptable time. This chapter presents the resource allocation problem in cloud computing as a linear programming problem, with the objective to minimize energy consumed in computation. This resource allocation problem has been treated using heuristic approaches. In particular, we have used two phase selection algorithm 'FcfsRand', 'FcfsRr', 'FcfsMin', 'FcfsMax', 'MinMin', 'MedianMin', 'MaxMin', 'MinMax', 'MedianMax', and 'MaxMax'. The simulation results indicate in the favor of MaxMax.

Chapter 12

Sourav Kanti Addya, National Institute of Technology, India
Bibhudutta Sahoo, National Institute of Technology, India
Ashok Kumar Turuk, National Institute of Technology, India

The data center is the physical infrastructure layer in cloud architecture. To run a large data center requires a huge amount of power. A proper strategy can minimize the number of servers used. Minimization of active servers caused minimization of power consumption. But the maximum number of virtual machine placement will be a monetary benefit for cloud service providers. To earn maximum revenue, the CSP is to maximize resource utilization. VM placement is one of the major issues to achieve minimum power consumption as well as to earn maximum revenue by CSP. In this research chapter, we have formulated an optimization problem for initial VM placement in the data center. An iterative heuristic using simulated annealing has been used for VM placement problem. The proposed heuristic has been analysis to be scalable and the coding scheme shows that the proposed technique is outperforming traditional FFD on bin packing technique.

Preface

OVERVIEW OF CLOUD COMPUTING

The advancements in Information and Communication Technology are forcing enterprises to rethink their Business Models and strategy for their business. It has become a necessity for every enterprise to keep pace with these advancements. It is also required that executives working in the enterprises are not dispensed with for lack of knowledge regarding emerging trends. In the present business scenario success is no longer guaranteed for enterprises that have financial resources and size on their side. Smaller enterprises that are flexible are providing products or services at a faster pace and lower cost. It is also because of the advancements in internet, enterprises no longer have to hire a consultant who lives nearby. As boundaries are shrinking, the level of competition is going up. More and more competition means enterprises are chasing the same dollar. Now it has become imperative for enterprises to adapt themselves to changing market conditions and government regulations of different countries. Enterprises need to plan for their business in both domestic and international markets. The better strategy should be integrating business, the knowledge of domain experts, and emerging concepts in information and communication technology to gain competitive advantage in the global market scenario. Cloud computing facilitates to achieve the above strategy.

Cloud computing is one of the concepts among the number of other concepts provided by information and communication technology. It may be said that the concepts of cloud computing is the result of the advancements in Internet. In the present Information and Communication Technology scenario, new technologies appear at high speed in the market place and at the same speed they are disappearing. Cloud computing is predicted to have more longevity.

It is said that global virtual enterprises are gaining importance because of cloud computing. The business world is in the midst of a significant transition largely due to the emergence of global virtual teams.

The importance of cloud computing is felt in the virtual enterprises. Cloud computing provides mechanism for sharing and coordinating the use of diverse resources. This mechanism enables the creation of geographically and organizationally distributed components of virtual computing systems. Cloud computing supports virtualization in respect of applications, devices, networking, storage, and servers Further it can be said cloud computing facilitates the economies across the globe closely interconnected and integrated.

There are four components that need to be integrated under cloud computing for the development of business models for virtual organizations. They are business process, application software, system software, and infrastructure such as servers, network, and database. Adding intelligence to the process of developing new models or to existing models and their management makes lots of sense because business models need considerable expertise.

There are four cloud deployment approaches. They represent specific types of cloud environments. Each cloud environment has its own characteristics. Cloud computing is generally classified as public, private, community, and hybrid clouds.

- **Public Cloud:** This cloud infrastructure is owned by an organization selling cloud services to the general public or to a business enterprise or to a large industry group.
- **Private Cloud:** This cloud infrastructure is owned or leased by single enterprise and is operated solely for that organization.
- **Community Cloud:** This cloud infrastructure is shared by several organizations and supports a specific community.
- **Hybrid Cloud:** This cloud infrastructure is composition of two or more clouds such as private, community or public those are unique entities. They are bound together by standardized or proprietary technology that enables data and application portability.

Further the cloud environment consists of generally three core components which refer to three types of services such as Software services, Platform services and Infrastructure services. These services are generally defined as Software as a Service (SaaS), Platform as a service (PaaS), and Infrastructure as a service (IaaS). However, a number of other specialized services are available. They are 1) Storage as a service, Database as a service, Security as a service, Communication as a service, Management as a service, Integration as a service, Testing as a service. Enterprises can choose a deployment model along with a particular or combination of the various services indicated above.

Notwithstanding the benefits that cloud computing offers, there are some issues and challenges associated while implementing cloud computing concept in enterprises. They are 1) Data Management and Governance, 2) Service management and Governance product, 3) Process control and monitoring, 4) Infrastructure and system reliability and availability. These issues are addressed and they are provided solutions by the expert groups in the vendor organizations who provide the cloud computing services.

GLOBALIZATION SCENARIO

In the present global Virtual Enterprises Environment Cloud Computing provides mechanism for sharing and coordination of the use of diverse resources thus enable their creation from geographically and organizationally components of virtual computing systems. This book emphasizes that cloud computing sufficiently integrates resources to deliver desired qualities of services. Further the book indicates that cloud computing facilities support management of credentials and policies when computations span multiple enterprises, and resource management protocols. Further it supports services that support secure remote access to Computing, Data Resources, and Co-Allocation of multiple resources. This book explains that cloud computing provides solution to application virtualization, storage virtualization and server virtualization. The above solutions are mainly needed for Global Virtual Enterprises.

BENEFITS FROM CLOUD COMPUTING

Data intense applications in cloud computing environment occur in scientific and business domains. Scientists require mechanism to transfer, publish, replicate, discover, share and analyze data. Business application in domains such as financial services, research and development, and online business services need to maintain database consisting regionally or worldwide. There is a good scope for carrying out research activities for developing business models for manufacturing, healthcare, education, and government sectors.

TARGET AUDIENCES

This book offers comprehensive view of cloud computing concepts being used with collaborative technologies across multiple sectors such as Education, Health-Care, Manufacturing, Government agencies, and Business enterprises. This book would be useful as reference for research scholars, research and development departments in industries. It is also a course supplement to the students pursuing computer science and information technology related subjects. This is also a good resource for software professionals who are involved in developing business applications in cloud computing environment.

GIST OF THE CHAPTERS

The book is broadly divided under six sections covering 1) Concepts and Framework, 2) Education Sector, 3) Conceptual Business Models, 4) Supply Chain in Cloud Computing, 5) Health Sector, and 6) Technologies Issues. The contributors of this book are from academics, and professionals who are involved in research related to the concept of cloud computing and developing business models using this concept.

In the Introduction N. Raghavendra Rao explains the emergence of cloud computing, perceptions and misconceptions on cloud computing. The author narrates the working of data centers in the era when mainframe systems were popular. Further he compares data center in main frame era with global virtual data center under cloud computing environment. He expresses both are similar. The advent of internet has facilitated cloud computing supporting global virtual data centers. He has made a reference of grid computing and the reason not becoming popular even though it has almost similar features of cloud computing. He also talks about the relevance of cloud computing in the domains such as Home Sciences, Financial Services, Research Collaboration, and Government Agencies. He explains the various cost aspects in the cloud computing environment.

Mouna Jouini and Latifa Ben Arfa Rabai in their chapter, "Design Challenges of Cloud Computing" talk about the challenges that arise while designing a system under cloud computing environment they also highlight the key characteristics, cloud computing, cloud computing architecture, and core foundation capabilities. They also make a reference of user tools. They also talk about stakeholder's categories and their concerns. They explain about the security threats from the angle of host, customers, data centers, and virtual machines. They indicate handling of security requirements in cloud computing environment.

The Chapter titled "An Interoperability Framework for Enterprise Application in Cloud Environments" written by Jose C. Delgado explains a multidimensional enterprise architecture framework and multidimensional interoperability framework. The author also talks about reducing coupling in interoperability. Further the author compares with the other interoperability framework. The author observes that the world is increasingly both distributed and interconnected. The author remarks that interoperability is crucial and the existing standards are not enough to ensure enterprise information systems.

R. Todd Stephen's chapter titled "Design Considerations for a Corporate Cloud Service Catalogue" gives the background of the organization AT RT Inc. The author describes the traditional services of a cloud registry and observes there is a need for a cloud service registry built on solid usability principles that can be used by an average user. Further the author explains business oriented cloud service catalog and usability criteria for an application system. The author discusses a case study on the basis of the research conducted by a team at the author's organization. The main aim of this chapter is the author is sharing the team experience at the author's organization and the team's observations on their research project.

Chaka Chaka, author of the chapter "Personal Mobile Cloud Computing Affordability for Higher Education: One Example in South Africa" explains the concept of personal mobile cloud computing. The author observes internet service providers and social networking sites support the devices which have internet access. The author feels that personal mobile computing is not given importance in respect of higher education. In the literature review in the area of higher education sector, the author presents a brief summary and synthesis of case studies related to the use and deployment of cloud computing in the selected higher education institutions. Further the author has divided the participants in two groups who were enrolled in two different undergraduate courses at a rural university in South Africa for the research study. These two groups speak English as a second language.

Camilius Sanga and George Kibirige in their chapter "Applying KOLB Experiential Theory with Cloud Computing in Higher Educational Institutions: Tanzania" observe that free and open source software has revolutionized the entire information and communication technology. They also mention that in developing countries, several countries are converting into digital libraries using low cost technologies due to open access. They point out many libraries in Tanzania have limited budget for information and communications technology services. They also talk about new aspects of this technology in libraries. Further, they discuss the creation of cloud libraries. They highlight the challenges, opportunities and the role of cloud library. They have also presented the current status of application of information technology in the libraries in some selected Tanzania's higher learning institutions. They have stressed the importance of applying KOLB experiential learning by making use of cloud computing in relation to library.

K. Hariharnath, author of the chapter titled "Big Data in Cloud Computing Environment for Market Trends" observes the concept of big data can be made use of in the cloud computing environment for assessing market trends of the manufacturing products. The author explains a business developed by a textile mill in India applying the concepts of big data, cloud computing and virtual reality in their business model. The author gives the background of the 3G textile mills and their approach in creating a business model by them. This mill has been in the business over five decades. The unique aspect of this mill is, it is being managed by a management team who belong to three different generations. Their approach and decisions are based on their experience, business insight and education. They realized the globalization scenario is affecting their market share in the market. At the recommendations of the consultants, a business model has been designed on the basis of making use of the concepts such as Big Data, Cloud Computing and Virtual Reality. Further the author explains this business model has helped 3G Textiles to remain competitive in the global market.

N. Raghavendra Rao in his chapter titled "Cloud Computing: an Enabler in Managing Natural Resources in a Country" observes that economic development has helped to raise the standard of living and has also led to mis-management of natural resources. This has also resulted in environmental issues. The author explains the components of natural resources and human activities on natural resources. The Author talks about a model for making use of space technology and cloud computing to create a knowledge based system for natural resources. This model will mainly be useful for the various government departments which are involved in the management of natural resource and environmental issues. Further the author suggests a model for handling damages caused by natural disasters. The author stresses the major problem in the developing countries is the identification of the effects on the mismanagement of natural resources. The author feels that cloud based natural resources data model will help the government in a country to change their practices for using the natural resources.

Lee Gillam, Simon Broome, and Debbie in their chapter titled "IPCRESS: Tracking Intellectual Property through Supply Chains in Clouds" observe that document archives and systems of any organization, coherently managed or not, can contain variety of high-value information relating to collaborating and competing business, business transactions, research and development plans, market analysis and strategy. Large organizations may have such documents spread widely across numerous siloed business units, with highly evolved but desperate systems, approaches and practices. The authors indicate the lack of a readily definable organizational boundary is inherent in supply chains and becomes amplified when supply chains act through software as a service. This chapter is based on a collaborative research and development project between Jaguar Land Over, University of Surrey and Geo Lang Ltd and with funding from the UK Government backed technology strategy board for 18 months. The authors of this chapter constructed the intellectual property protecting cloud services in supply chains (IPC Press) system to address supply chains and barriers to cloud adoption related data security and resilience. They explain that IPC Press, as a project is developing a capability for tracking IP through supply chains, offering cloud services to i) Prevent IP leakage ii) Detect IP leakage or theft and iii) Identify information retention beyond allowed periods.

Kijpokin Kasemsap author of "The Role of Cloud Computing in Global Supply Chain" observes that in the global market place, internet, the low cost processing capacity open standard and loosely coupled information technology infrastructure has been widely recognized as a tremendous enabler for collaboration. The author explains the role of cloud computing in the supply chain. Further the author talks about the theoretical and the practical concept of cloud computing. The author also gives an overview of e-scms and the organizational information process theory concerning information processing requirements and information capability. The author also examines the extent to which environmental uncertainty, task uncertainty and inter organizational uncertainty effect intention to adopt cloud computing concepts in supply chain.

N. Raghavendra Rao, Author of the chapter titled "Establishing Synergy between Cloud Computing and Collaborative Technology in Medical Informatics", observes health has been concern of major importance across the globe. The kind and amount of resource available now is increasing day by day. Information technology has been the most important new resource in the present century. Emergence of new tools and devices has been helping the medical profession. The author in his chapter talks about a virtual hospital scenario in India under the cloud computing environment. Further the author explains pervasive devices and virtual reality concept can be made use with the cloud computing in virtual hospital. The author discusses three case illustrations to support his approach in making use of cloud computing with collaborative technology. In one case illustration the author talks about health care information system in the virtual hospital scenario. In another case illustration e author explains the rational method in discovering a drug under cloud computing environment. In the third case illustration, the author stresses the importance of evidence based learning by medical students across the globe under cloud computing based health care system. The author is of the opinion in the era of globalization, cloud computing along with the collaboration technology will provide a lot of scope for developing knowledge based health care models.

Dilip Kumar, Bibhudatta Sahoo, and Tarni Mandal authors of the chapter titled "Heuristic Task Consolidation Techniques for Energy Efficient CloudComputing" observe that cloud computing has emerged from the concepts of heterogeneous distributed computing, and autonomic computing. The authors say that the cloud computing environment provides high performance servers and high speed mass storage devices to manage growing demand for computations and large volume data. These resources are the major source of the power consumption in data centers including air conditioning and cooling equipment. The authors indicate that data centers are the world's highest consumers of electricity. They discuss in their chapter the resource allocation problem in cloud computing as a linear programming problem with the objective of minimizing energy consumption in computation. They have applied heuristic approach in handling the resource allocation problem.

Souravkanti Addya, Bibhudutta Sahoo and Ashok Kumar Turuk, authors of the chapter titled "Virtual machine Placement Strategy for CloudComputing Data Center" observe that cloud computing technology uses the internet and central remote servers to maintain data and application. They indicate in their chapter that the use of online resources has been on increase in the last one decade. This has resulted in the increase of servers at data centers. They explain that virtualization provides the proper resources utilization. They express that the optimum placement of virtual machine server can minimize the power consumption at data center. Further they discussed that simulated annealing optimization technique has been applied in their model for virtual machine placement strategy for cloud data center.

IMPACT OF THIS BOOK

In the technology domain developments now in process are very different from the kind of information handling systems and procedures used in the past. Cloud computing has become ubiquitous. It will provide more computation power and storage for less investment than any other current computing solution. This book mainly focuses on developing business models under cloud computing and highlights the value of cloud computing in the different sectors. Further the book talks about managing virtualization resources.

N. Raghavendra Rao
FINAIT Consultancy Services, India

Acknowledgment

At the outset, I would like to thank all the chapter authors for their excellent contributions. I would like to offer my special thanks to IGI Global for the opportunity to edit the publication.

I would like to acknowledge the role of the reviewers and editorial team for their support. Finally, I thank my wife Meera for her continuous encouragement and support in my scholastic pursuits.

N. Raghavendra Rao
FINAIT Consultancy Services, India

Introduction

BACKGROUND

Information and Communication Technologies is the Major Stimulus for changes in trade and commerce. Information and Communication Technology (ICT) Is the result of the convergence of the above technologies. Now ICT is considered as a separate discipline. ICT is advancing by delivering exponential increase in computing power and communications capabilities. Many new concepts are emerging in this discipline. Cloud computing concept is one among them. The concept of cloud computing is the result of the advancements in internet. New Technologies in ICT Scenario appear at high speed in the marketplace and at the same speed they disappear. It is predicted that cloud computing will have more longevity (Hagel, & Brown, 2010). It may be said that the cloud computing is the latest innovation that has brought computing power within the reach of every business enterprise (Linthicum, 2010).

EMERGENCE OF CLOUD COMPUTING

Emergence of cloud computing in information and communication technology is equivalent to electricity revolution of a century ago. Before the advent of electrical utilities, every business enterprise and farms produced its own electricity from their stand alone generators. After the electric grid was created, business enterprises and farms stopped their generators being used. They have started using electricity by paying a reasonable price with much greater reliability. Similar type of revolution is taking place under the cloud computing environment. The desk top and laptop centric approach of computing is likely to change. Many more pervasive devices in addition to desktop and laptop will support the use of cloud computing environment. The whole scene in cloud computing environment, access to data and software stored in the centralized servers will be through internet. This is the simplest explanation to understand the cloud computing environment.

PERCEPTIONS

There are different perceptions among people who use computing systems about and cloud computing. According to some it is to have an access to software and the stored data in the cloud environment through internet or network and making use of other associated services. Others feel that there is nothing new about this concept. According to them it is something related to modernization of the time sharing model that was used before the introduction of reasonably priced computing systems. Time sharing approach has disappeared after the development of client/server technology. This Technology has provided large amounts of computing power in the desktops.

CLOUD COMPUTING

Cloud computing is a generic term that involves delivering hosted services over the internet (Rhoton, 2010). The name cloud computing is said to have been derived by the cloud symbol that is often used to represent the internet. Another interpretation can also be given that the cloud is visible in the sky from any part of the universe. Similarly the cloud services are also available from any part of the world.

DATE CENTER AND CLOUD COMPUTING

In the early days of computing, many companies actually shared a single computer system that was located in a remote date center in their premises. The system personnel would allocate and manage the resources for each user and each application. Users could request for more computing time or less by adjusting the amount of time they utilized for sharing the services. Similarly, cloud computing offers various components from deployment models and mix and match the solutions that are sought. One can make use of a component such as storage-as-a-service from one service provider, database-as-a-service from another and even a complete application development and deployment of platform from a third service provider. It has to be remembered that cloud computing facilitates the use of different cloud computing deployment models over the internet.

All the software applications, the data, and the control resided in huge main frame computer in the date center. Access to the main frame computer by the user is via computer terminal. It was known as "work station" or" Dumb Terminal". This is because; it does not have much memory, storage space or processing power. It is a merely device that connects.

USERS OF THE MAIN FRAME SYSTEMS

The users could have an access to the main frame only when they got the permission from the information Technology staff from the data center. Information Technology staff generally were not in the habit of giving them the access instantly. It was due to processing power on a main frame computer was limited. One more reason was for not giving permission to them instantly was because two or more users could not have access to the same data at the same time. The users would depend on the information technology staff for every aspect of information at the data center. Customization of the existing reports, generating new reports, or looking at some new data was possible. It could be only as per the schedule of the data center. It might take weeks or months to comply with the requests of the users, depending on the datacenter schedule.

COLLABORATION UNDER CLOUD COMPUTING

With the growth of the use of internet, there is no need to limit group collaboration to a single enterprises network environment. Now it is possible users from multiple locations within an organization and also from multiple organizations to collaborate on business processes across business organizations and geographic boundaries. Many leading manufactures in the area of infrastructure are offering the hardware necessary to build cloud network (Hassan, 2011). Many software companies are developing cloud based applications. Cloud computing concept facilitates users of any device to have an internet feature (Jennings, 2010). These devices are mobile phones, laptops, tablets and other devices which have this facility. It needs some intelligent management to connect all these devices together and assign processing task to multitudes of users.

STORAGE OF DATA IN CLOUD ENVIRONMENT

The main use of cloud computing is for the storage of data. Data is stored in multiple servers rather than in the dedicated servers used in traditional network data storage. An end-user sees it as a virtual server. It is just a pseudo name used to refer virtual space carved out of the cloud. In reality the users' data could be stored on any one computer or more computers used to create the cloud.

RELEVANCE OF CLOUD COMPUTING TO DEVELOPERS AND END USERS

There are many benefits in cloud computing technology for both developers and end users, and infrastructure.

Developers

Cloud computing provides increased space for storage and processing power to run the applications they develop. Cloud computing also enables new ways to access information process and analyze data and connect people and resources from any location anywhere in the world. In essence it takes the lid off the box with cloud computing developers. Developers are no longer boxed in by physical constraints (Roychoudhuri, Mohapatra, & Yadav, 2014).

End Users

Any user using an application under the cloud computing environment is not physically bound to a single computer system or network. End user's application and documents can be accessed wherever the end user is on network. Data or documents hosted in the cloud always exist, no matter what happens to the end user's computer system.

INFRASTRUCTURE

Cloud computing enables more efficient sharing of the resources than in the traditional net working computing environment. Hardware need not have to be physically adjacent to a firm's office or data center. Cloud computing infrastructure can be located anywhere in the world. It will be more beneficial, if it is located in the areas where real estate and electricity costs are reasonably low. Another advantage to the business enterprises, they need not purchase the computing infrastructure for infrequent intensive computing tasks. In other words the resources are available on the cost effective basis (Reese, 2010).

CLOUD PRINTING

In the present globalization scenario many electronic devices are connected to the internet. This helps us to get information and content that matters most to us. However printers are considered as standalone devices at homes or offices connected to a computer. It is felt they are irrelevant to mobile devices. Cloud computing is providing a new printing technology. It allows users to send documents to a printer from e mail capable device irrespective of the sender's location. This concept is receiving attention from the manufacturers of computer printers.

The requirements in printing business reports are changing. Keeping pace with the requirements in the business world, manufactures of printers are adapting themselves to these changes. Some printers are being manufactured with specific features to take care of the needs of users. The main change is the addition of wireless connectivity to printers. It means a user can send from his / her system a file directly to a printer located in any part of the world.

Vishal Tripathi, Principal Research analyst at Gartner, observed "Cloud print services (CPS) are Hosted offering that enable users to print documents and other content on any digital printer, copier or multi function product that is associated with cloud services. Users create a copy with a software tool, receive or down load a document or other content and send the print job from a device of their choice to CPS provider which then routes it to a file to a cloud attached printer selected by the user".

Cloud printing will help users who want to print from their smart phones or tablets, or laptops and note books. For a mobile device it is required as an option to email a file to a printer for printing. Innovations in the area of cloud printing especially relevant to internet access are taking place. The essence of this concept is to enable printers to be accessed through cloud print services that help any application on any device to print on any printer. Cloud printing is at a nascent stage and it will take some time for adoption to pickup.

SPECTACULAR GROWTH IN INTERNET

In the early years the internet was mainly used by military and research institutions in the United States of America. Now it is being used across the globe in every activity under the sun. People prefer to be "on Internet". One of the main reasons is it is simple to use. The internet is a good example for functional freedom. In principle any node can speak as a peer to any other node as long as it obeys the rules of the TCP / IP protocols, which are strictly technical, not social or political. Internet can be compared to a human language. Nobody rents a language and nobody owns a language. It is up to an individual to learn and to speak a language. People consider internet as a similar to a language. It belongs to everyone.

ORIGINS OF CLOUD COMPUTING

The following elements can be considered as important for the origination of cloud computing.

1. **Utility Computing:** The packaging and delivery of computing resources to a computer is who pays for these resources as a metered service when needed. The objective is to use the services effectively while reducing the associated costs. The term "UTILITY" is used to compare this type of computing resource utilization and payment to those utilities such as providers of electricity or natural gas.
2. **Grid Computing:** It is a form of parallel processing conducted on a network of computers. In grid computing servers, storage and networks are combined to form powerful computing resource nodes that can be dynamically provisioned as needed (Joseph, & Fellenstein, 2004).
3. **Autonomic Computing:** The functioning of a computer system without external control is known as autonomic computing. The term "AUTONOMIC COMPUTING" is based on the autonomic nervous system of the Human Body. The Human Body controls the functions such as breathing, heart and other related functions without conscious input from the individual. The objective of autonomic computing is to have the computer perform critical and complex functions without any major Intervention by a user.
4. **Platform Virtualization:** The Logical portioning of physical computing resources into multiple execution environments including servers, applications and operating systems is known as platform virtualization. Virtualization is based on the concept of virtual machine running on physical computing platform. Virtualization is controlled by a virtual machine monitor known as a hyper vision.
5. **Software as a Service:** A software distribution and deployment model in which applications are provided to customers is considered as a service. The applications can run on the users' computing systems or the providers of web services. This provides for efficient patch management and promoters collaboration.
6. **Service Oriented Architectures:** A set of services used to communicate with each other, and their interfaces are described. Their functions are loosely coupled as to whose use can be incorporated by multiple organizations.

CLOUD COMPUTING AND THE ABOVE ELEMENTS

One has to be clear when relating the above elements in the cloud computing concept (Miller, 2009). Cloud computing is not the same as utility commuting. Cloud computing does not apply to the metered service price of utility computing. Cloud computing generally uses distributed virtualized platforms instead of centralized computing resources. Grid computing cannot be considered as equivalent to cloud computing. Grid computing does use distributed virtual machines but unlike cloud computing, these machines are usually focused on a single, very large task.

Sometimes client/server is viewed as cloud computing, with the cloud appearing in the server role. However, in the traditional client server model, the server is a specific machine at a specific location. Computation in the cloud can be based on computers anywhere, split among computers. It can use virtualized platform. It will be unknown to the user. The users know that they are accessing the resources for processing to get results.

Cloud computing is not software as service. It is because that an organization can purchase and mange a software. Generally it is run on the user's hardware or someone else's machines.

Though there is an element of virtualization in the cloud, it is generally used for operating system virtualization. It can be employed on the organization's local computers or in a data center. It cannot be said virtualization is cloud computing. Cloud computing is not the same as service oriented architecture which supports the exchange of data among different applications engaged in business processes. Although the preceding elements are not synonymous with cloud computing, depending on the implementation they can be a constituent of the cloud.

According to the EDN Article Silicon Designers view cloud computing can be considered as a hierarchy of three elements. They are (1) Computing Kernels, (2) Clusters, and (3) Systems.

1. **Computing Kernels:** Processor or groups of cores enclosed within a secure perimeter and united by a single coherent address space. This definition is general enough as it encompasses a processor in a personal computer or a large multiprocessor system.
2. **Clusters:** Groups of kernels that are connected by a private local area network and respective tasks communicate among each other over low band with links.
3. **Systems:** Clusters connect through public networks and by employing communications they cross security perimeter boundaries. These transactions are necessarily slower than inter cluster communications.

APPLICATION COSTS IN CLOUD COMPUTING ENVIRONMENT

One should know the list of costs associated in making use of the services under the cloud computing environment. The flowing costs fall under the category of application service costs (Hurwitz, Kaufman, & Halper, 2010).

1. **Server Costs:** The total annual costs for making use of a server/server for software applications are decided on the basis of type *of* applications software are run in the server.
2. **Storage Costs:** These costs relate to storing data in the server/servers.
3. **Network Cost:** This cost depends on the basis of band width requirements for accessing the system in the cloud environment.
4. **Backup and Archive Costs:** The actual savings on backup costs depend on the backup strategy when the application moves into the cloud. The same is true of archiving.

5. **Disaster Recovery Costs:** In theory, the cloud service will have its own disaster recovery capabilities, so there may be a consequential savings on disaster recovery. It will be better to assess cloud providers disaster recovery capabilities. Not all cloud providers have the same definition of disaster recovery.

6. **Data Center Infrastructure Costs:** A whole series of costs covering electricity, floor space, cooling, building maintenance and other related costs cannot be easily identified to individual application, generally it is allocated on the basis of floor space the hardware running the application occupies.

7. **Platform Costs:** Some applications only run in specific operating environments. The annual maintenance costs for the application operating environment need to be calculated. It has to be allocated as a part of the overall costs.

8. **Software Maintenance Costs (Ready Made Software):** Generally this cost element is considered to be simple because it is a part of the software's annual maintenance cost. It becomes complicated if the software license is tied to processor pricing.

9. **Software Maintenance Costs (In-House Software):** These costs are related to the software developed by cloud service providers. It can be allocated at an application level.

10. **Help Desk Support Costs:** These costs are to be considered wherever the support requirements are needed.

11. **Operational Support Personnel Costs:** There is a whole set of day-to-day operational costs associated with running any application. Some are general costs that apply to every application. They are such as staff support for everything from storage to archiving, patch management, network and security. Some support tasks may be particular to a given application such as database tuning and performance management.

12. **Infrastructure Software Costs:** A whole set of infrastructure management software is in use in any installation. Generally it is considered as an associated cost.

The total of all the elements mentioned is considered as the annual data center cost. The above elements are not exhaustive. Types of costs vary from a data center to data center.

CLOUD COMPUTING AND WEB 2.0

The terms cloud computing and web 2.0 appeared at the same point of time. Both the concepts provide the same type of features to end-users. TIME O' REILLY, the god father of web 2.0 defines it as "the network as platform, spanning all connected devices. It is said that cloud computing is about computers, web 2.0 is about people". According to TIM O' REILLY cloud computing refers specifically to the use of internet as computing platform and web 2.0 is an attempt to explore and explain the business rules of that platform. Perhaps the terms cloud computing and web 2.0 are just two different ways of looking at the same phenomenon. It needs to be understood that both cloud computing and web 2.0 offer very real benefits for all involved.

VIRTUAL COMPANY

In the earlier days managing a business mean renting an office space, arranging for a phone line and utilities, hiring staff and the other related activities. The owner / executive of a business enterprise would commute to the office in the morning and stay till in the evening. The owner / executive of the business enterprise would attend all the activities of the business during the office hours only. They would leave the work at the office and would clear the pending work on the next working day. Now the scenario has changed by internet and web base applications. Now the expensive office space is not needed. One can work for a company from the comfort of one's home over the interest. Note book computer provides the access over the internet wherever wi fi connection is available.

The real power of cloud computing is that it lets anyone run ones company's operations from anywhere (Golden, 2010). Web based applications, provide all the support one gets form highly paid employees and one office itself is in the cloud rather than in an expensive building. The cloud lets even the smallest business operate like a large enterprise over the web. It is the age of the virtual company. One should know taking advantage of all that cloud offers.

GOOGLE AND CLOUD COMPUTING

It may help to understand how one of the pioneers of cloud computing, Google perceives cloud computing. From Google's perspective, there are six key properties of cloud computing.

1. **User Centric under Cloud Computing:** Once a user gets connected to the cloud, whatever is stored there such as documents, messages, images, applications, becomes yours. In addition, not only the data is yours, but you can also share it with others. In effect, any device that accesses your data in the cloud also becomes yours.
2. **Task Centric under Cloud Computing:** Instead of focusing on the application and what it can do, the focus is on what you need and how the applications can do it for you. Traditional application word processing, spread sheets, email, and so on is becoming less important than the documents they create.
3. **Computing Power under Cloud Computing:** Connecting hundreds or thousands of computers together in a cloud creates a wealth of computing power impossible with a single desktop personal computer.
4. **Data Access under Cloud Computing:** Data is stored in the cloud; users can instantly retrieve more information from multiple repositories. Access is not restricted to a single source of data, as you are with a desktop personal computer.
5. **Intelligent Access under Cloud Computing:** With all the various data stored on the computers in a cloud, data mining and analysis are necessary to access that information in an intelligent manner.
6. **Programming under Cloud Computing:** Many of the tasks necessary with cloud computing must be automated for example to protect the integrity of the data; information stored on a single computer in the cloud must be replicated on other computers in the cloud. If that one computer goes offline, the cloud's programming automatically redistributes that computer's data to a new computer in the cloud.

BRIEF HISTORY OF CLOUD COMPUTING

Generally every new concept evolves from the combination of two or more existing concepts and cloud computing is not an exception to this.

1. **Peer-to-Peer Computing:** Under the client server technology all communications between computers has to go through the server first. The obvious need to connect one computer to another without hitting the server led to the development of peer-to-peer (P2P) computing. P2P computing defines a network architecture in which each computer has equivalent capabilities and responsibilities. This is in contrast to the traditional client /server architecture. In which one and more computers are dedicated to serving the others.

2. **Distributed Computing:** One of the most important subsets of the P2P model is that of distributed computing, while idle personal computers across a network or across the internet are tapped to provide computing power for large professor intensive projects.

3. **Collaborative Computing:** Working as a group from the early days of client /server computing through the evolution of P2P, there has been a desire for multiple users to work simultaneously on the same computer based project. This type of collaborative computing is the driving force behind cloud computing. Early group collaboration systems ranged from relatively simple (Lotus notes and Microsoft next meeting) to extremely complex (the building –Block architecture of the groove network system). Most were targeted at large corporations and limited to operation over the companies private networks.

THE GROWTH OF THE INTERNET

There has been no need to limit group collaboration as a single enterprises network environment. It is interesting to note that Google which had a collection of servers that it used to power its massive search engine which made them to think using the same computing power for web based applications. This process has provided a scope for a new level internet based group collaboration.

NETWORK IS THE COMPUTER

Sun Micro systems slogan is "The Network is the Computer". This slogan is good to describe how cloud computing works. In essence network of computers are to serve data and applications to users over the internet. The network exists in the "CLOUD" of IP addresses that is known as the internet, offers massive computing power and storage capability and enables wide scope for group collaboration. This is a simple way of explanation for working of cloud computing (Grigoriu, 2009).

RELEVANCE OF CLOUD COMPUTING IN THE BUSINESS APPLICATIONS

Many organizations have realized the importance of cloud computing in the crucial areas for their business (Buyya, & Sukumar, 2011). Some examples of major business areas where cloud computing plays an important role are given below. They are not limited to these areas

1. **Life Sciences:** For analyzing and decoding strings or Biological and Chemical information.
2. **Financial Services:** Developing complex financial models and facilitating for taking accurate decisions.
3. **Engineering Services:** In the areas of automotive and aerospace for collaborative design and data intensive testing.
4. **Research Collaborations:** Enabling analyzing data and computation for intensive research.
5. **Government:** Collaboration among the departments and other agencies for Implementation of the Government polices.

LIFE SCIENCES

Life sciences sector has been witnessing much advancement in the areas of drug treatment and drug discovery. The analytic and applying information technology concepts relating to genomic, proteomics and molecules biology provide the basis for the development of a drug and its treatment. The above requirements need an infrastructure for managing data storage, providing access to the data. Cloud computing is chosen for secure data storage, secure data access, privacy and highly flexible integrating. Life sciences can utilize the cloud computing environment to execute sequel comparison algorithms and enable molecular using the collected secured data for analysis.

FINANCIAL ANALYSIS AND SERVICES

This sector has also been witnessing much dramatic advancements in the financial analysis and financial services. Accuracy of data and faster execution are among the most salient objectives across financial communities. These objectives are now achieved by real time access to the current and historical market data. Complex financial models in the areas of financial engineering and financial derivatives are required to be developed for global financial market. Cloud computing is made use of for these models. Cloud computing provides an opportunity to create Global Virtual Financial organizations. Global Virtual Financial Organizations Facilitate the experts in the Financial sector to extend their services.

RESEARCH COLLABORATION

Research oriented organizations and universities are involved in advanced research in their respective areas. Global virtual research organizations are involved in research collaborative activities. They need volumes of data, tremendous amounts of storage space and thousands of computing processors. The cloud computing concept provides mechanisms for resource sharing by Global virtual research organizations. These organizations are constituted to resolve scientific research problem with a wide range of participants from the different parts of the world.

GOVERNMENT

Generally the data in the information systems in the Government Departments is largely unutilized by the respective departments. It is because most of the data is in standalone systems in the respective departments. E-Governance followed by many governments departments is in isolation and scattered pattern. This procedure lacks integration towards e-governance. It is easier to implement e-governance application at one location under cloud computing based architecture compared to similar application is being implemented by multiple locations. Migration to new technology is relatively easier and faster in the cloud based architecture (Krikos, 2010).

BASIS FOR CHOOSING CLOUD

One of the most important considerations in deciding which services should be placed on a cloud is cost. Critical applications that can affect an organization's mission should not be placed on the cloud. Another point to be remembered is that applications should be designed in such a way that they can be moved from one cloud provider to another. It helps to avoid being locked to a particular vendor. In addition, some laws and regulations require that critical data be kept on organization's site and under its control.

BASIC DESIGN PRINCIPLES FOR CLOUD SECURITY

Earlier days computer software had not been written with security in mind. Now security has become a primary objective (Krutz, & Vines Dean, 2010). It is because of malicious attacks against information systems. A completely secure system will exhibit poor performance characteristics or might not function at all. It is suggested that the following areas need to be given special attention (Mather, Kumaraswamy, & Latif, 2010).

1. **Handling Data:** Some data is more sensitive and requires special handling.
2. **Code Practices:** Care must be taken not to expose too much information to hackers.
3. **Language Options:** Strengths and weakness of the computer language used should be analyzed.
4. **Input Validation:** Content data entered by a user should never have direct access to a command.
5. **Physical Security of the System:** Physical access to the cloud servers should be restricted.

GRID AND CLOUD COMPUTING

It is interesting to note that the terms used in grid and cloud computing arc similar. However the early ideas associated with these terms had a slightly different angle from today's perspective. It is apt to quote the "TECHNICAL DEFINITION OF THE GRID" from IBM- GRID is the ability, using a set of open standards and protocols, to gain access to applications and data, processing power, storage capacity, and a vast array of other computing resources over the internet. A grid is a type of parallel and distributed system that enables the sharing, selection, and aggregation of resources distributed across "MULTIPLE" administrative domains based on their (Resources) availability, capacity, performance, cost, and users quality of service requirements.

Earlier grid vendors used to mention four types of grids. They are Departmental grids, Enterprise grids, Partner grids and Open grids (Plaszezak, & Wellner, 2006).

Departmental Grids

Departmental grids are installations that are allocated to one institution and usually serve one purpose. They are behind corporate firewall and therefore have minimal security requirements. Departmental grids are usually owned exclusively by one internal user group who work together closely on a project, set of related projects or business process. This is basically for resource sharing among the departments in an enterprise.

Enterprise Grids

Enterprise grid systems are owned by one organizational entity. They are used for many purposes. Enterprises grids stay behind the corporate firewall. External access is restricted. It is also restricted to one way communication. Resources themselves are never being moved out of the firewall. Enterprises grids are often deployed by enterprises who want to pool the resources previously scattered among departments.

Partner Grids

Partner grids are installations that go beyond the corporate firewall. They allow sharing of resources by several organizations. Partner grids often have peer-to-peer architectures. Partner grids are mainly for collaborating the number of participants from several enterprises.

Open Grids

It was anticipated that open grids or global grids would emerge in the grid scenario. Organizations using proprietary communication channels felt open grids would hamper the inter operability with their partners. Partner grids by nature would involve several stake holders; it might be difficult to force all of them into a single proprietary solution. The appearance of web hosting and the virtual CPU provisioning service in the market has been considered as equal to global grids or open grids.

CLOUD COMPUTING

The advancements in the area of internet, contributed to cloud computing, which has over taken global grid computing in the process. Comparison may be made in respect of certain terms used in the grid and cloud computing concepts. Partner grids can be considered as equal to community cloud. Enterprise grid is similar to private cloud. Open grid or global grid can be said to be equal to public cloud. Departmental grid and community cloud can be termed as the same. Grid computing also like cloud computing has been applied in the sectors such as life Sciences, Finance, Engineering, and Research.

PERVASIVE COMPUTING AND CLOUD COMPUTING

Pervasive computing (Burkhardt, Henn, Hepper, Rintdorff, & Schack, 2005) is a new dimension of personal computing that integrates mobile communication, ubiquitous embedded computer systems, consumer electronics and the power of the internet. Micro electronics technology offers small, powerful devices and displays with low energy consumption. Digital communication technology provides higher band width, higher data transfer rates at lower cost and worldwide roaming. Cloud computing enables delivery of business models for information technology services over the internet. Cloud computing provides an access to the data from any part of the world. Pervasive devices facilitate an access to cloud computing.

CONCLUSION

Many new concepts have been emerging in information and communication technology discipline. Close analysis of these concepts indicate many of these concepts are the extension of the existing concepts. Every new concept has an advantage over the previous concept. Sometimes two or more concepts or technologies are combined to evolve a new concept. Cloud computing is one among them. It is said that cloud computing has contributed to the success of globalization policy followed by many countries. One more interesting aspect of the cloud to computing is the emergence of global virtual enterprises. Further these enterprises are changing business landscape across the borders of the countries.

N. Raghavendra Rao
FINAIT Consultancy Services, India

REFERENCES

Burkhardt, J., Henn, H., Hepper, S., Rintdorff, K., & Schack, T. (2005). *Pervasive Computing New Delhi: Pearson Education*. Singapore: Private Limited.

Buyya, R., & Sukumar, K. (2011, May). Platforms for Building and Deploying Applications for Cloud Computing. *CSI Communications Journal, 35*(2), 6–11.

Golden, B. (June 2010). *How Cloud Computing Can Transform Business*. Boston, MA, USA: Harvard Business Review

Grigoriu, A. (2009). *The Cloud Enterprise*. Wokingham: BP Trends Publications United Kingdom.

Hagel, J., & Brown, J. S. (2010). *Cloud Computing's Stormy Future*. Boston: Harvard Business Review M A USA.

Hassan, M. Z. (2011, May). Cloud Networking. *CSI Communications Journal, 35*(2), 20–21.

Hurwitz J., Kaufman R., Bloor M, & Halper F. (2010). *Cloud Computing for Dummies*. New Delhi: Willey India Private Limited.

Jennings R. (2010). *Cloud Computing with the Windows Azure Platform*. New Delhi: Wiley India Private Limited.

Joseph, J., & Fellenstein, F. (2004). *Grid Computing New Delhi: Pearson Education*. Singapore: Private Limited.

Krikos A (2010). *Disruptive Technology Business Models in Cloud Computing*. Cambridge: MIT USA.

Krutz R. L., & Vines R. D. (2010). *Cloud Security*. New Delhi: Willey India Private Limited.

Linthicum, D. S. (2010). *Cloud Computing and SOA Convergence in your Enterprise New Delhi: Dorling Kindersley*. India: Private Limited.

Mather, T., Kumaraswamy, S., & Latif, S. (2010). *Cloud Security and Privacy*. Mumbai: Shroff Publishers and Distributors Private Limited.

Miller, M. (2009). *Under Standing Cloud Computing; Cloud Computing. New Delhi: Dorling Kindersley*. India: Private Limited.

Plaszczak, P., & Wellner, R. Jr. (2006). *Grid Computing*. New Delhi: Elesvier.

Reese, G. (2010). *Cloud Application Architectures*. Mumbai: Shroff Publishers and Distributors Private Limited.

Rhoton, J. (2010). *Cloud Computing Explained: Implementation Hand Book for Enterprises London*. Recursive Press.

Roychoudhuri, D., Mohapatra, B., & Yadav, M. (2014, February). Rationalize Your Cloud Model Using Open Source Stack. *CSI Communications Journal, 37*(11), 11–14.

KEY TERMS AND DEFINITIONS

Architecture: In information processing, the design approach taken in developing a program or system.

Batch Processing: A non interactive process that runs in queue. Early computers were capable of only batch processing.

Distributed Processing: Spreading the work of an information processing application among several computers.

Grid Computing: A step beyond distributed processing, involving large number of network computers that are harnessed to solve common problem.

Infrastructure: The fundamental systems necessary for the ordinary operation of an information technology department.

Internet: A huge computer network linking almost all the computers in the world and enabling them to communicate via standard protocols (TCP/IP) and data formats.

Interoperability: The ability of a product to interface with many other products; usually used in the context of software.

P2P: Peer to Peer networking system in which nodes in a network exchange data directly instead of going through a central server.

Protocol: A set of rules that computers use to establish and maintain communication among themselves.

Provisioning: Making resources available to users and software.

Section 1
Introduction and Frame Work

Chapter 1
Design Challenges of Cloud Computing

Mouna Jouini
Institut Supérieur de Gestion, Tunisia

Latifa Ben Arfa Rabai
Institut Supérieur de Gestion, Tunisia

ABSTRACT

Cloud computing has recently emerged as a new paradigm of computing for hosting and delivering services over the Internet. It replaces computing as a personal commodity by computing as a public utility. It is attractive solution to business owners as it eliminates the requirement for users to plan ahead for provisioning, and allows enterprises to start from the small and increase resources only when there is a rise in service demand. However, despite the significant benefits, these technologies present many challenges including lack of security. The chapter presents an advanced survey focusing on cloud computing concept. It highlights its key concepts and presents a physical architecture of this environment. Finally, the chapter defines virtualization technology as a factor for cloud computing surge and discuses security issues that damage these systems. The aim of this chapter is to provide a better understanding of the design challenges of cloud computing.

INTRODUCTION

With the advent of information technologies, society relies heavily upon software. In fact, software is found in automobiles, airplanes, chemical factories, power stations and numerous other systems in which it plays a critical role. Software or business applications need computing resources and hence important investment in IT infrastructure. The infrastructure is often very costly ranging from a small number of servers to an entire data center. However, provisioning and managing computing resources is so costly. There are three major costs: (1) capital costs, i.e., the cost of buying the hardware, software, and installation costs, (2) maintenance and operation costs, i.e., the cost of personnel to maintain the infrastructure as well as cost of power, cooling, and sever storage, and (3) additional costs, for example, to buy extra hardware and software to

DOI: 10.4018/978-1-4666-8339-6.ch001

provide high availability, reliability, scalability, and security (Minhas, 2013). This creates a high barrier in adopting software.

In contrast to traditional information technology (IT), Cloud computing, as a new technology, aims to solve many problems like problems outlined above. In fact, it provides computing resources at a low cost while at the same time freeing users from the tedious and often complex tasks of maintaining and provisioning resources (Minhas, 2013). It offers on-demand resource provisioning. It provides three types of services: Software as a Service (SaaS), Infrastructure as a Service (IaaS) and Platform as a Service (PaaS) which promise potential cost savings for businesses by offering remote, scalable computing resources. However these services benefits, migrating to a cloud computing infrastructure poses several security risks to an organization's data and customer applications (Buecker et al., 2009; Cloud Security Alliance, 2009; Hanna, 2009; Heiser & Nicolett, 2008; Subashini & Kavitha, 2010; Wooley, 2011). As an initiative to address such risks, we outline security threats in this environment and identify customer's needs on security context.

The purpose of this chapter is to give a state of the art to cloud computing technologies. In fact, we present, firstly, the basic concepts related to this term. Then, we introduce the cloud computing environment. Finally, we identify threats and security attributes occurred in this environment.

The remainder of this chapter is organized as follows:

1. In the first part we introduce and define cloud computing environments, its history and its essentials characteristics.
2. In the second part, we show motivating factors in cloud computing adoption
3. In the third part, we present essential characteristics of these systems and discus the benefits and drawbacks of public cloud services.
4. In the fourth part, we provide an overview of cloud computing environment. We introduce a detailed architecture, stakeholder's categories and services offered by cloud computing systems.
5. In the fifth part, we present an overview of virtualization technology.
6. In the sixth part, we study security issues on cloud computing systems as well as it was cited as major risk in these systems.

1. HISTORY

In the early days of computing, computer resources were a centralized organizational asset, that represents a massive investment of money, time and labor; only large organizations could afford to acquire, maintain and operate such infrastructures. With the advent of personal computers in the 1980s, the prevailing computing paradigm changed drastically: first, the low cost of personal computers opened a worldwide market of people and organizations large and small; second, this situation fostered, in turn, a large pool of talent that was able to develop and distribute PC-based applications, at the same time as it was creating a market for such applications; third, the centralized paradigm of mainframe-based computing at large organizations was progressively replaced by local area networks, linking servers and terminal computers within an organization; fourth, the pervasiveness of the internet transformed the global mass of personal computers into a massive network of nodes, sharing information, services, software, and. . . malware of all kinds (Ben Arfa Rabai et al., 2013).

Even though personal computers are fairly dependable in general, and require relatively little expertise to maintain and operate, under this computing paradigm end-users are still responsible for operating a complex machine about which they understand very little. Also, each individual computer is used a minimal fraction of the time, and typically deploys only a very small fraction of its wide range of software and hardware capabilities (Ben Arfa Rabai et al., 2013).

The idea of providing a centralized and distributed computing service dates back to the 1960s, when computing services were provided over a network using mainframe time-sharing technology. In 1966, Canadian engineer Douglass Parkhill published his book *"The Challenge of the Computer Utility"* (Papkhill, 1966), in which he describes the idea of computing as a public utility with a centralized computing facility to which many remote users connect over network. Mainframes allow multiple users to share both the physical access to the computer from multiple terminals as well as to share the CPU time. Mainframes allow an effective use of computing resources with an acceptable performance. However, mainframes were difficult to scale and provision up-front because of the high hardware costs. Indeed, users didn't have control over the performance of mainframe applications because it depended on how many users utilized the mainframe at a given moment. Thus, the introduction of personal computers that provokes a new challenge of data sharing.

With the emerging of the internet, it was introduced the client-server architecture which transformed into more complex two-tier, three-tier, and four-tier architectures. As a result, the IT infrastructure becomes very costly and difficult to manage.

Cloud computing become known, in 2006, by more people after two events. First was Google CEO Eric Schmidt's announcement, in 2006, of a new business model "Cloud Computing", which enables access to remotely hosted data and computation resources from anywhere. In the same year, Amazon.com announced one of the most important Cloud Computing services by now: the Elastic Cloud Computing (EC2) as part of the Amazon Web Services (AWS) (Han, 2009).

2. DEFINITIONS

Cloud Computing is an emerging paradigm of computing that replaces computing as a personal service by computing as a public utility. Cloud services are often compared in their nature to utility services such as gas or electricity. In fact, cloud computing services as a public utility as the use of electricity (instead of building generators) and also as the use of telecommunications service call (instead of building and working our own cell tower)

Cloud computing systems provide computing resources (such as processor compute time and data storage) on demand via a service provider rather than maintaining your own hardware and software environment. The resources are dynamically provisioned over the internet and invoices its subscribers based on the use of computing resources.

Cloud computing is a subscription-based service where you can obtain networked storage space and computer resources. We can consider, for instance, your experience with email to clarify the work of this system. Your email client, if it is Yahoo!, Gmail, Hotmail, and so on, takes care of housing all of the hardware and software necessary to support your personal email account. When you want to access your email you open your web browser, go to the email client, and log in. Thus, the most important part of the equation is having internet access. So, your email is not housed on your physical computer and you access to it through an internet connection and you can access it anywhere. If you are on a trip, at work, or down the street getting coffee, you can check your email as long as you have access to the internet. Finally, as we note, that your email is different than software installed on your computer. An email client is similar to how cloud computing works. Except instead of accessing just your email, you can choose what information you have access to within the cloud (Foster et al., 2008).

There are many definitions for Cloud computing (Vaquero et al., 2009). For example, Wong in (Wong, 2009) views Cloud computing as an "evolution of the old client/server paradigm, a transformation prompted by the ubiquitous presence of the Internet and the availability of high bandwidth connections". According to Foster et al. in (Foster et al., 2008), Cloud computing is "A large-scale distributed computing paradigm that is driven by economies of scale, in which a pool of abstracted, virtualized, dynamically-scalable, managed computing power, storage, platforms, and services are delivered on demand to external customers over the internet." The National Institute of Standards and Technology defines cloud computing as "a model grants convenient, on-demand network access to a shared pool of configurable computing resources (e.g., networks, servers, storage, applications, and services) that can be rapidly provisioned and released with minimal management effort or service provider interaction" (Mell & Grance, 2009). Moreover, Jensen et al, in (Vaquero et al., 2009), present in their paper the most available cloud computing definitions, gathered from experts, in order to get an integrative definition. They concluded that CC "is associated with a new paradigm for the provision of computing infrastructure". In (Subashini & Kavitha, 2010), Cloud computing was considered as a way to increase the capacity or add capabilities dynamically without investing in new infrastructure, training new personnel, or licensing new software. It extends Information Technology's (IT) existing capabilities.

Cloud computing is the result of Information and Communication Technology (ICT) evolution. In fact, it is based on several technologies like virtualization, distributed systems, web service service-oriented architecture, service flows and workflows and web 2.0. It conceals, as well, the complexity of the infrastructure (buying installing servers, storage, networking, and related infrastructure) from users when they used cloud computing services because users may allocate on demand the infrastructure needed. It does everything to deploy tools that can scale to serve as many users as desired. Providers allow software installation and maintenance. In addition to that, they centralize control over consumers who can access the service anytime, anywhere, can share data and collaborate more easily and keep their data stored safely in the infrastructure.

Cloud services, as indicated in figure 1, would be available to individuals and organizations, large and small, and would operate on the same pattern as other public utilities (Ben Arfa Rabai et al., 2013), namely:

- Subscribers sign up for service from a service provider, on a contractual basis.
- The service provider delivers services of data processing, data access and data storage to subscribers.
- The service provider offers warranties on the quality of services delivered.
- Subscribers are charged according to the services they use.

Cloud computing plays an important role in many recent critical applications, such as astronomy, weather forecasting, and financial applications. Since these applications process large amounts of data, cloud computing is one promising solution to handle such data. In fact, it provides the needed storage and processing equipments though clouds. It also enables users that do not have the technical expertise to support their own infrastructure to get access to computing on request.

3. CLOUD COMPUTING MOTIVATING FACTORS

A survey conducted by the Records in the Cloud (RiC) project conducted in April 2013 to 353 (Duranti, 2013) responses concluded that 57% of respondents are currently using cloud computing,

Figure 1. Structure of cloud computing environments

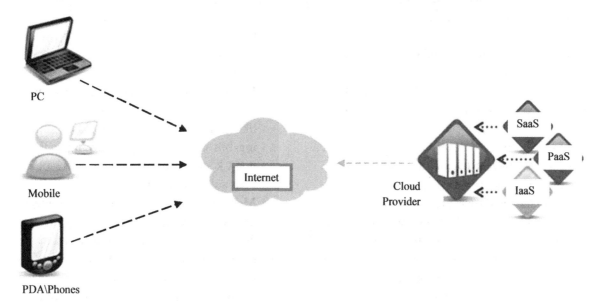

and the majority has adopted cloud computing in the last three years. Among potential users, 38% are currently considering cloud services.

The survey reveals indeed that both current and potential users are motivated by the potential to reduce costs by adopting cloud computing, but some respondents' comments reveal that this benefit may not be easy to obtain. Approximately (54%) of current users and (58%) potential users selected "reduce cost" as their primary motivation for adopting cloud computing.

The cloud computing adoption is increased last years. In fact, Cloud computing has particular characteristics that distinguish it from classical resource and service provisioning environments (Jangra, A. & Bala, R. 2011):

- Infinitely (more or less) scalable.
- Cost saving/less capital expenditure.
- Higher resource utilization.
- Business agility.
- Disaster recovery and Back up.

We can conclude hence that cost saving factor presents the main raison that encourages the various organizations for the adopting the cloud computing.

Moreover, traditional application integration technologies are performed in a rigid and slow process that usually takes a long time to build and deploy, requiring professional developers and domain experts. They are server-centric and thus do not fully utilize the computing power and storage capability of client systems. However, Cloud computing is a new infrastructure deployment environment that delivers on the promise of supporting on-demand services like computation, software and data access in a flexible manner by scheduling bandwidth, storage and compute resources on the fly without required end-user knowledge of physical location and system configuration that delivers the service.

4. KEY CHARACTERISTICS OF CLOUD COMPUTING

The National Institute of Standards and Technology (NIST) defines cloud computing by seven essential characteristics (Mell & Grance, 2009; Mell & Grance, 2011; Furht & Escalante, 2010):

- **Multi-Tenancy:** In a cloud environment, services owned by multiple providers are co-located in a single data center. The performance and management issues of these services are shared among service providers and the infrastructure provider. The layered architecture of cloud computing provides a natural division of responsibilities: the owner of each layer only needs to focus on the specific objectives associated with this layer.
- **Scalability and On-Demand Self-Service:** It provides resources and services for users on request without requiring human interaction with each service's provider.
- **Broad Network Access:** The services provided by the cloud are available over the network and accessed through standard mechanisms that promote use by heterogeneous thin client platforms (like mobile phones, laptops, and PDAs).
- **Resource Pooling:** It provides resources pooled to serve multiple clients, with different physical and virtual resources dynamically assigned and reassigned according to consumer demand. The customer generally has no control or knowledge over the exact location of the provided resources. Examples of resources include storage, processing, memory, network bandwidth, and virtual machines.
- **Rapid Elasticity:** Cloud computing systems are autonomous systems managed transparently to users. However, software and data inside clouds can be rapidly and elastically reconfigured and consolidated to a simple platform depending on user's needs. The capabilities available for rent are infinite and can be purchased in any quantity at any time.
- **Pay per Use:** Customers pay for services and capacity as they need them. In fact, like your electric bill, your cloud computing bill can be unexpectedly large if you don't keep a close watch on the resources your solutions are utilizing.
- **Measured Service:** Cloud computing resource usage can be measured, controlled, and reported providing transparency for both the provider and consumer of the utilized service. Cloud computing services use a metering capability which enables to control and optimize resource use.

There are four main factors contributing to the surge and interests in Cloud Computing (Mell & Grance, 2009; Mell & Grance, 2011):

- The rapid decrease in hardware cost versus the increase in computing power.
- The storage capacity and the advent of multi-core architecture and modern supercomputers.
- The exponentially growing data size in scientific instrumentation and Internet publishing and archiving.
- The wide spread adoption of Services Computing and Web 2.0 applications.

Therefore, we can notice that the Cloud Computing system has the main following advantages (Mell & Grance, 2009; Mell & Grance, 2011; Vaquero et al,. 2009 ; Wang et al,. 2008; Rittinghouse & Ransome, 2010):

- **Lower Cost:** Pay as you go, no hardware investments or software licenses
- **More Performance:** Processing time on demand

- **More Efficiency:** Higher usage rates of servers
- **Less Maintenance:** Someone else manages the servers and core software
- **Unlimited Storage Capacity:** Virtually unlimited computing power, bounded only by provider assets rather than by individual user assets
- **Convenience:** No need for users to be computer-savvy, no need for tech support
- **Dependability:** Provided by highly trained provider staff
- **Service Quality:** Virtually unlimited data storage capacity, protected against damage and loss.

However, the most cited possible disadvantages of cloud computing are:

- **Dependency on Internet Connectivity:** Requires a constant connection
- **Loss of Control:** The problem of someone else hosting hardware, software and data, which results in security concerns
- **Unpredictable Cost:** Pay as you go means that the cost of computing will be different every month.

5. CLOUD COMPUTING ENVIRONMENT

We present, in this section, architectural elements that form the basis for cloud computing system. Then, we try to distinguish different cloud computing actors. Finally we present services offers by this technology.

5.1 Cloud Computing Architecture

The Cloud Computing Architecture of a cloud computing system is the structure of the system which includes cloud resources, services, middleware, software components and the relationships between them. Figure 2 summarizes the proposed cloud computing architecture (Ben Arfa Rabai et al., 2013; Jouini et al 2012).

Cloud computing architecture can be divided into three parts:

- Core foundation capabilities
- Cloud services
- User tools

5.1.1 Core Foundation Capabilities

The core foundation capabilities layer provides basic building blocks to architect and enable the above layers. It includes:

- **Data Center Facilities:** This level provides information concerning the provider's data centers like location of data (hosting place), type network used to accede to it, the firewall used... This is primarily focused on helping users identify common data center characteristics that could be damaging services continuity, as well as characteristics.
- **Security and Data Privacy:** This level aims to identify security, privacy and other organizational requirements for cloud services to meet as a criterion for selecting a cloud provider. It covers security control techniques or recommendations to provide security and privacy in data and secure cloud services. It gives many procedures, policies and solutions in privacy and security requirements (authentification and authorization, privacy, certification and compliance, auditing and accounting) that are believed to have long-term significance for cloud computing (Cloud Security Alliance, 2009; ENISA, 2010).
- **Service Management and Provisioning:** Cloud monitoring and cloud service management tools allow cloud providers to ensure optimal performance, continuity

Figure 2. Cloud computing services and architecture (Ben Arfa Rabai et al., 2013)

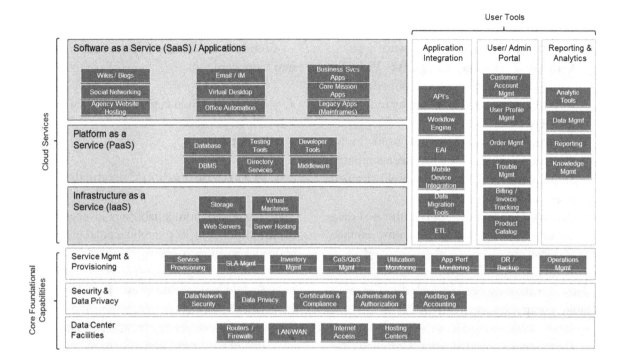

and efficiency in virtualized, on-demand environments. These tools, software that manages and monitors networks, systems and applications, enable cloud providers not just to guarantee performance, but also to better control provisioning of resources. For example, cloud monitoring tools enable cloud providers to track the performance, continuity and security of all of the components that support service delivery: the hardware, software and services in the data center and throughout the network infrastructure.

5.1.2 Cloud Services

Cloud Computing services are formed by three sub layers. We will explain more these layers in the following section.

- **Infrastructure as a Service layer (IaaS):** It is also known as the virtualization layer. It offers a pool of storage and computing resources as a service to its contracted customers on demand. This computing infrastructure is formed for instances by servers, CPUs, memories, software, and network equipment.

- **Platform as a Service (PaaS):** Provides a development and support environment for application development through the use of support tools. The purpose of the platform layer is to minimize the burden of deploying applications directly into VM containers. For example, Google App Engine operates at the platform layer to provide API support for implementing storage, database and business logic of typical web applications.

- **Software as a Service (SaaS):** Is where application services are delivered over the network on a subscription and on-demand basis. SaaS or PaaS services are often developed and provided by a third party distinct from the IaaS provider.

Compared to traditional service hosting environments such as dedicated server farms, the architecture of cloud computing is more modular. Each layer is coupled with the layers above and below, allowing each layer to evolve separately. The architectural modularity allows cloud computing systems to support a wide range of application requirements while reducing management and maintenance overheads.

5.1.3 User Tools

Cloud computing user tools helps users to accomplish their needs. We cite as tool application integration and reporting and analyzing tools.

Cloud management interfaces (for example, the Amazon admin console) provide functions allowing users to manage a cloud lifecycle. For instance, users can add new components to the cloud such as servers, storage, databases, caches, and so on. Users can use the same interface to monitor the health of the cloud and perform many other operations.

As examples of users tools, we can cite:

Jboss Enterprise Middleware

JBoss Enterprise Middleware is the leading enterprise-class open source software used to build, deploy, integrate, orchestrate, and present web applications and services in a service oriented architecture (SOA). These software products are used by end-users to create applications, integrate applications, data and devices, and automate business processes.

These solutions offer customers stability and open source innovation. Using JBoss Enterprise Middleware, customers can:

- Decrease development complexity
- Improve inadequate end-user experience
- Resolve business process friction
- Enable unparalleled flexibility
- Significantly lower total cost of ownership

Eucalyptus Entreprise Edition

Eucalyptus Enterprise Edition (Eucalyptus EE) enables customers to implement on-premise cloud computing with Eucalyptus, the most popular open source private cloud software, and vSphere, VMware's industry-leading virtualization platform. Eucalyptus EE support is the only on-premise cloud computing solution available today for customers, providing a robust, affordable cloud computing solution that leverages their investment in VMware technologies.

Eucalyptus Enterprise Edition is built on Eucalyptus. Eucalyptus is the acronym for Elastic Utility Computing Architecture for Linking Your Programs To Useful Systems. Eucalyptus enables pooling compute, storage, and network resources that can be dynamically scaled up or down as application workloads change. Eucalyptus Systems announced a formal agreement with AWS in March 2012 to maintain compatibility. It is an open source software infrastructure for implementing on-premise cloud computing using an organization's own information technology (IT) infrastructure, without modification, special-purpose hardware or reconfiguration. Eucalyptus turns data center resources such as machines, networks, and storage systems into a cloud that is controlled and customized by local IT. Eucalyptus is the only cloud architecture to support the same application programming interfaces (APIs) as public clouds, and today Eucalyptus is fully compatible with the Amazon Web Service cloud infrastructure.

5.2 Stakeholder's Categories

Cloud providers and consumers are the two main entities in CC system (Huth & Cebula, 2011).

Cloud providers can be devided into three classes of stakeholders, namely: the service provider, the corporate or organizational subscribers, government subscriberd and the individual subscribers:

- **The Service Provider:** Is an external enterprise or organization that offers cloud services to its customers. The providers host and manage the underlying infrastructure and offer different services (SaaS, PaaS, IaaS) to the consumers, the service brokers or resellers. Cloud brokers and resellers plays the same role as "Cloud providers" in certain contexts. We can cite as exemples of cloud providers Amazon, Google, IBM, Microsoft and Sun Microsystems, that establish new data centers for hosting cloud computing applications in various locations around the world in order to provide redundancy and ensure reliability in case of site failures.
- **The Corporate or Organizational Subscribers:** Are multiple organizations (governments …) that access the infrastructure based on similar needs. The cloud consumers access to different type of services (SaaS, PaaS, IaaS) through Internet-based interfaces (like a browser)
- **The Individual Subscribers:** Are persons that are customers of a cloud. The cloud consumers access to different type of services (SaaS, PaaS, IaaS) through Internet-based interfaces (like a browser).

5.3 Cloud Computing Services

Cloud computing providers can offer services at different layers of the resource stack (see figure 3), simulating the functions performed by applications, operating systems, or physical hardware. The most common approach (Mell & Grance, 2009 ; Mell & Grance, 2011 ; Vaquero et al,. 2009) defines cloud computing services as three layers of services which provide infrastructure resources, application platform and software as services to the consumer.

5.3.1 Infrastructure as a Service (IaaS)

The Infrastructure as a service layer was based on virtualization technology and provides the basic computing infrastructure of servers, processing, storage, networks and other fundamental computing resources where the consumer is able to deploy and run arbitrary software, which can include operating systems and applications. The consumer does not manage or control the underlying cloud infrastructure but has control over operating systems, storage, deployed applications and possibly limited control of select networking components (Mell & Grance, 2009).

The main purpose of IaaS is to avoid purchasing, housing and managing the basic hardware and software infrastructure components, and instead obtain those resources as virtualized objects controllable via a service interface (which reduces hardware costs).

Customers are allocated computing resources in order to run virtual machines consisting of operating systems and applications.

5.3.2 Platform as a Service (PaaS)

Platform as a Service adds a higher level to the cloud infrastructure by providing a platform upon which applications can be written or deployed. These service providers offer, in this layer, application programming interfaces (APIs) that enable developers to exploit functionality over the Internet rather than delivering complete applications. It delivers development environments to programmers, analysts and software engineers as a service. PaaS gives end users control over application design, but does not give them control over the physical infrastructure (Rittinghouse & Ransome, 2010).

The main purpose of PaaS is to reduce the cost and complexity of buying, housing and managing

Figure 3. Cloud computing presented as a stack of service

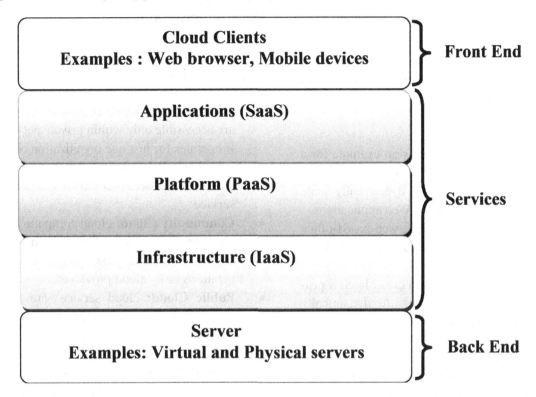

the underlying hardware and software components of the platform, including any needed program and database development tools (Meiko et al., 2009). PaaS gives end users control over application design, but does not give them control over the physical infrastructure.

5.3.3 Software as a Service (SaaS)

Software as a Service provides the consumer with typical software applications that run over the cloud computing infrastructure. SaaS delivers applications through a web browser to thousands of customers rather than installed on their computer. The end user does not exercise any control over the design of the application, servers, networking, and storage infrastructure.

The main purpose of SaaS is to reduce the total cost of hardware and software development, maintenance and operations. All these services

offer scalability and multitenancy. In addition, they are self-provisioning and can be deployed through public cloud deployment modules.

Examples of these three modes of Cloud Computing are shown in Table 1.

Table 1. Examples of the three delivery services of cloud computing

Layer	Examples
Software as Service (SaaS)	Facebook, Gmail, Google Apps
Platform as Service (PaaS)	Amazon Web services, Windows Azure
Infrastructure as Service (IaaS)	Amazon EC2, Xen SalesForce.com

Examples

Amazon's Elastic Compute Cloud (EC2) is a prominent example for an IaaS offer. It offers the user a virtual server, with the CPU, memory, storage, operating system and hypervisor or system monitoring software included (Furht & Escalante, 2010).

- **Google App Engine:** Is an example for a Web platform as a service (PaaS) which enables to deploy and dynamically scale Python and Java based Web applications.
- **Google Apps:** Provides web-based office tools such as e-mail, calendar, and document management.
- **Rackspace Cloud:** Is a cloud IaaS. It provides users with access to dynamically scalable computing and storage resources, as well as third-party cloud applications and tools
- **Salesforce.com:** Is a cloud SaaS. It provides a full customer relationship management (CRM) application
- **Zoho.com:** Is a cloud SaaS. It provides a large suite of web-based applications and it is used often by organizations.

Cloud service models describe how cloud services are made available to clients. Figure 3 illustrate that cloud computing service models have synergies between each other and be interdependent, like PaaS that dependent on IaaS because application platforms require physical infrastructure. In cloud computing system, we focus on three main parts as shown in Figure 3: the front end, the back end connecting to each other through the Internet and the cloud services.

There are many new and emerging technologies which adopted by for cloud computing systems. One such enabling technology for cloud computing is virtualization. In the next section, we provide a brief overview of virtualization.

5.4 Cloud Computing Deployment Models

Cloud computing may be deployed on four types of cloud (Mell & Grance, 2011):

- **Private Cloud:** Cloud computing services are accessible only within private network. It operates for just one organization or one subscriber. It provides a full control over data, security, access control and quality of service.
- **Community Cloud:** cloud computing services are offered to a limited number of organizations. It may be managed by organizations or by cloud providers.
- **Public Cloud:** cloud services are available to publicity and computing resources are provisioned over the internet to its subscribers (any organizations can use it).
- **Hybrid Cloud:** it combines several cloud types (more than one) that stay unique entities but are bound together by proprietary technology that enables data and application portability (like cloud bursting for load balancing between clouds).

NIST has also defined the cloud deployment models, which include public, private, hybrid, and community clouds as shown in figure 4. An example of a public cloud model is Google Docs, where the application and data are stored in Google's data center somewhere.

6. VIRTUALIZATION TECHNOLOGIES

Cloud computing shares many aspect with several technologies like grid computing, virtualization, utility Computing, autonomic Computing:

Figure 4. NIST cloud models

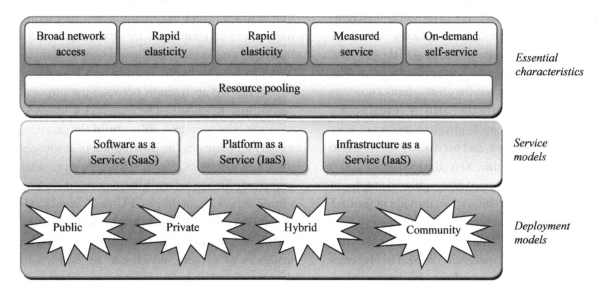

- **Grid Computing:** It involves a network of computers that are utilized together to gain large supercomputing type computing resources. Using this network of computers large and complex computing operations can be performed. In grid computing these networks of computers may be present in different locations.
- **Utility Computing:** It defines a "pay-per-use" model for using computing services. In utility computing, billing model of computing resources is similar to how utilities like electricity are traditionally billed.
- **Autonomic Computing:** Originally coined by IBM in 2001, it aims at building computing systems capable of self-management, i.e. reacting to internal and external observations without human intervention in order to overcome the management complexity of today's computer systems.

After presenting a quick overview of most technologies adopted by cloud systems, we will detail virtualization technology at the rest of this section. In fact, cloud computing leverages virtualization technology to achieve the goal of providing computing resources as a utility.

Virtualization concept has been around in some form since 1960s (for example in IBM mainframe systems). Since then, the concept has matured considerably and it has been applied to all aspects of computing, memory, storage, processors, software, networks, as well as services that IT offers (Sahoo et al., 2010).

Virtualization was defined by Vaughan-Nichols in (Vaughan-Nichols, 2008) as "Technology that lets a single PC or server simultaneously run multiple operating systems or multiple sessions of a single OS. This lets users put numerous applications and functions on a PC or server, instead of having to run them on separate machines as in the past". Virtualization can be defined as a technology such that there is a software abstraction layer between the hardware and operating system and applications running on top of it. This software abstraction layer is called Virtual Machine Monitor (VMM) or Hypervisor.

Virtualization or Machine virtualization is a technique that allows the resources of a physical machine to be shared among multiple partitions known as virtual machines (VMs). Each virtual machine runs an independent (possibly different) operating system and the associated set of applications. The hypervisor manages the physical resources and provides a mapping between the physical resources and the abstractions known as virtual devices (Liu et al., 2010). A virtual device corresponding to each physical resource, e.g., CPU, disk, memory, and network, is exported to every virtual machine. Xen (Barham et al., 2003) and VMware (VMware) are popular examples of virtual machine monitors. We provide in figure 5 an overview of machine virtualization.

Thus, virtualization architecture provides this illusion through a hypervisor/VMM. The Hypervisor is software layer which:

- Allows multiple Guest OS (Virtual Machines) to run simultaneously on a single physical host.
- Provides hardware abstraction to the running Guest OSs and efficiently multiplexes underlying hardware resources.

Virtualization allows abstraction and isolation of lower level functionalities and underlying hardware. This enables portability of higher level functions and sharing of the physical resources. Virtualization technologies rely on a hypervisor to provide the abstraction between the physical and virtual machines. The hypervisor interacts with the hardware and software in the physical world and manages the distribution of resources to virtual machines. So, the hypervisor provides everything the virtual machine requires, including virtual networks, memory, CPU, and virtual hardware. This level manages the physical resources and allows sharing of their capacity among virtual instances of servers, which can be enabled or destroyed on demand.

6.1 Virtualization in the Cloud

Virtualization simplifies the process of sharing computer resources. Cloud computing needs to be able to share resources in order to improve efficiency and reduce costs. This makes the two

Figure 5. Virtualization architecture (Minhas, 2013)

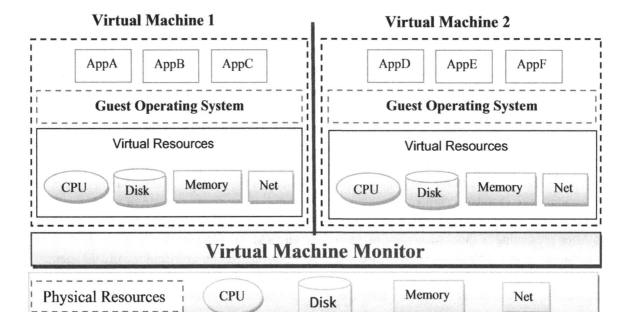

technologies a natural fit to work together. Virtualization increases the efficiency of hardware utilization, while cloud adds a layer of management so that VMs care be created, scaled and torn down as required. This is why a majority of today's cloud solutions are built on virtualization technology.

The behind of cloud computing high performance is a virtualized infrastructure. Virtualization has been in data centers for several years as a successful IT strategy for consolidating servers. Used more broadly to pool infrastructure resources, virtualization can also provide the basic building blocks for your cloud environment to enhance flexibility.

IaaS is the virtualized, multitenant infrastructure that underpins your cloud and enables multiple applications for business groups across the enterprise to share. IaaS is built and delivered using a set of technologies that start with virtualization as the basic building block. A cloud management platform enables you to run a multitenant environment using the resources from the virtual infrastructure and security technologies at every level.

Virtualizing storage and networks is emerging as a general strategy. In fact, results from a Gartner survey of 505 data center managers worldwide reports that planned or in-process virtualization of infrastructure workloads will increase from approximately 60 percent in 2012 to almost 90 percent in 2014 (Gartner, 2013).

For example, in the IaaS Amazon's Elastic Computing Cloud (EC2), the cloud provider manages and operates a pool of possibly tens of thousands of interconnected machines. Users can rent out as much computing power as they need from this pool of resources. In Amazon's EC2, this is made possible by the use of virtualization. Users are provided access to virtual appliances that come in varying sizes in terms of physical resources allocated (e.g., CPU, memory), allowing users to choose a size depending on their resource needs. By exploiting virtualization, cloud providers are able to achieve higher resource consolida-

tion, better resource utilization, and flexibility in provisioning and managing computing resources (Minhas, 2013).

Applications, services and basic functions provided in a Cloud Computing system are based on the Virtual resources which are abstracted from Physical Resources, for example Ben Arfa Rabai et al., 2013):

- Virtual physical resources, such as V-CPUs, V-Storages, V-Networks.
- V-Networks can be further divided into V-Routers, V-Switches,
- V-Firewalls, VPNs, V-Interfaces, V-Links based on physical Router/ Switch.

Virtualization uses the hypervisor or virtual machine monitor which (Mell & Grance, 2009):

- Enables guest operating systems (OSs) to run in isolation of other Oss
- Run multiple types of Oss.
- Increases utilization of physical servers.
- Enables portability of virtual servers between physical servers.
- Increases security of physical host server.

One of the most important and heavily relied technology in cloud computing is Virtualization (Liu et al., 2010). The reason for using virtualization is reduced cost and better monitoring. Virtualization allows (Menken & Blokdijk, 2009; Sahoo et al., 2010):

- **Easier Manageability:** Whole network can be monitored and managed form a single point. Administrators manage and monitor the whole group of computers in a network from a single physical computer.
- **Availability:** One can keep the virtualized instances running even if the node needs to be shut down for maintenance purposes. This can be done by migrating the virtual-

ized instances to other machines and later migrating them back to the computer without closing the instance.

- **Scalability:** Administrator can easily add a new node with basic installation to contribute with the existing virtual machines to provide the services. So as the company expands the cluster will also expand.

- **Increased Security:** The information and applications can be put in different virtual machines (separate entities) on a single physical machine. If a virus comes in it will not affect the whole computer because it will reside only in the one VM and other VMs will not be affected thus delivering the services.

- **Reduced Costs:** Costs are reduced in the sense that less hardware, less space and less staffing requirements. Network costs are also lowered as less switches, hubs and wiring closets are required.

7. SECURITY IN CLOUD COMPUTING ENVIRONMENT

Cloud Computing offers all the advantages of a public utility system, in terms of economy of scale, flexibility, convenience but it raises major issues, not least of which are: loss of control and loss of security. We show in this section security challenges in cloud environment. We conducted, then, a systematic literature review to identify its information security threats and identify security requirements applicable in the cloud computing.

7.1 Security Challenges in Cloud Computing System

Security is one of the most challenging research works in cloud computing system because users secrete are by providers who try to protect the data from other outside source. In fact, the use of cloud computing technology carries some risks along

with its many rewards, not least of which are the loss of control and the loss of security (Hanna, 2009; Subashini & Kavitha, 2010; Wooley, 2011; Xuan et al., 2010; Rittinghouse & Ransome, 2010; Vouk, 2008; Ben Arfa Rabai et al., 2013; Jouini et al 2012). Indeed, by trusting its critical data to a service provider (externalization of service), a user (whether it be an individual or an organization) takes risks with the availability, confidentiality and integrity of this data: availability may be affected if the subscriber's data is unavailable when needed, due for example to a denial of service attack or merely to a loss; confidentiality may be affected if subscriber data is inadvertently or maliciously accessed by an unauthorized user, or otherwise unduly exposed; integrity may be affected if subscriber data is inadvertently or maliciously damaged or destroyed.

In addition to that, security is cited as the major issues for this environment by many surveys. For example, figure 6 shows a survey recently conducted by IDC enterprise. The survey was applied on 244 IT executives/CIOs and their line-of-business (LOB) colleagues to gauge their opinions and understand their companies' use of IT cloud services. So, Security ranked first as the greatest challenge or issue of cloud computing (Meiko et al., 2009 ; Subashini & Kavitha, 2010; Xuan et al., 2010 ; Kenneth Kofi, 2010 ; Rittinghouse & Ransome, 2010).

The sections below highlight security issues and threats related to cloud computing technology and their potential risks. Then, we determine the security requirements for CC environments.

7.2 Security Threats on Cloud Computing Environment

Virtualization, which is the software layer that emulates hardware to increase utilization in large datacenters, is one of the main components of a cloud computing system (Ibrahim et al., 2010), but it causes major security risks. In fact, ensuring that different instances running on the same

Figure 6. Results of IDC survey ranking security challenges (Rittinghouse & Ransome, 2010)

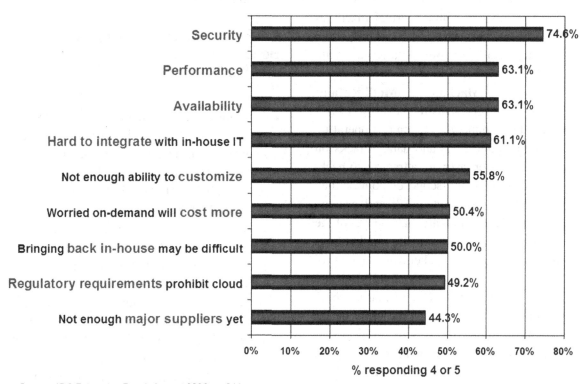

Q: Rate the challenges/issues ascribed to the 'cloud'/on-demand model
(1=not significant, 5=very significant)

Source: IDC Enterprise Panel, August 2008 n=244

physical machine are isolated from each other is a major task of virtualization. Therefore, a cloud computing system is threatened by many types of attacks including security threats between the subscriber and the datacenter, the hypervisor and the VMs and between the VMs themselves (Wooley, 2011; Jouini et al 2012; Ben Arfa Rabai et al., 2013). We consider the security threats that are most often cited in relation with cloud computing system (Cloud Security Alliance, 2010; Ibrahim et al., 2010; Subashini & Kavitha, 2010 ; Wayne & Timothy, 2011; Wooley, 2011; Jouini et al 2012; Ben Arfa Rabai et al., 2013).

Computing is based on virtualization technology that may causes major security risks which can be classified into three categories. Each of these types of attacks is examined in more detail below (Jouini et al 2012; Ben Arfa Rabai et al., 2013):

- Security threats originating from the host (hypervisor).
- Security threats originating from the VMs.
- Security threats originating between the customer and the data center.

7.2.1 Security Threats Originating from the Host (Hypervisor)

- **Monitoring Virtual Machines from Host:** Monitoring the VM from the hypervisor software is an important part of managing and controlling the VMs. Hypervisor is software that controls the layer between the hardware and the operating systems. The system administrator or other authorized user can make changes to the components of one or more virtual machines (VMs) which generates a security risk (Jouini et al 2012; Ben Arfa Rabai et al., 2013).

- **Virtual Machine Modification:** Hypervisor represents the next lower layer of software under the customer's operating system, applications and data. Attacks on the hypervisor layer are attractive to hackers because of the scope of control they can gain if they can install and execute their malicious software on this layer of the VM software. Compromising the hypervisor means that an attacker can take control of that layer and all of the hosted virtual machines that are hosted on that machine Jouini et al 2012; Ben Arfa Rabai et al., 2013).

- **Threats on Communications between Virtual Machines and Host:** In cloud computing system, all communications must pass through the hypervisor to all of the hosted VMs and at this point an attacker can inject malicious software in an attempt to eavesdrop or gain control over any or all of the systems. However, the worst case occurs when the hypervisor is compromised by malware, since this puts all the VMs that are being hosted on that machine at risk for security breaches (Wooley, 2011; Jouini et al 2012; Ben Arfa Rabai et al., 2013)).

- **Placement of Malicious VM Images on Physical Systems:** The attack known as cloud malware injection involves creating a malicious virtual machine image and then places that image into the hypervisor so that it is treated like a legitimate system in a collection of virtual machines. If this is successful, then the malicious virtual machine image is allowed to run the adversary's code (Ibrahim et al., 2010; Wooley, 2011; Jouini et al 2012; Ben Arfa Rabai et al., 2013).

7.2.2 Security Threats Originating Between the Customer and the Datacenter

- **Flooding Attacks:** Flooding attacks consist of overloading the server hosting services with an enormous number of requests for data processing (Wooley, 2011; Jouini et al 2012; Ben Arfa Rabai et al., 2013).

- **Denial of Service (DoS):** The denial of service attack is a critical problem for virtual machines (VMs) used on cloud components. In fact, it indicates that the hypervisor software is allowing a single VM to consume all the system resources and thus starving the remaining VMs and impairing their function (Jouini et al 2012; Ben Arfa Rabai et al., 2013).

- **Data Loss or Leakage:** The threat of data compromise increases because of the architectural or operational characteristics of the cloud environment (user's data is stored outside the enterprise boundary, by the service provider). Data loss may be caused operational failures, insufficient authentication or authorization, deletion or alteration of records without a backup of the original content, jurisdiction and political issues, disasters, inconsistent use of encryption and software keys. Thus, intrusion of data can be done either by hacking through the loop holes in the application or by injecting client code into the system (Jouini et al 2012; Ben Arfa Rabai et al., 2013).

- **Malicious Insiders:** This threat is amplified for consumers of cloud services by the convergence of information technology (IT) services combined with a general lack of transparency into provider process and procedure. Such threats include fraud, sabotage and theft or loss of confidential information caused by trusted insiders. The impact that malicious insiders can have on an organization is considerable, given their level of access and ability to infiltrate organizations and assets like brand damage, financial impact and productivity losses (Cloud Security Alliance, 2010; Jouini et al 2012; Ben Arfa Rabai et al., 2013). .

- **Account, Service and Traffic Hijacking:** Attack methods such as phishing, fraud and exploitation of software vulnerabilities still achieve results. Cloud solutions add a new threat: If an attacker gains access to your credentials, they can eavesdrop on your activities and transaction, return falsified information and redirect your clients to illegitimate sites allowing them to compromise the confidentiality, integrity and availability of those services (Cloud Security Alliance, 2010; Jouini et al 2012; Ben Arfa Rabai et al., 2013).

- **Abuse and Nefarious Use of Cloud Computing:** Cloud computing providers offer their customers an unlimited compute, network and storage capacity coupled with a week registration process where anyone with a valid credit card can register and immediately begin using cloud services. Cloud computing providers are so being under attack due to the weakness of their registration systems which let to spammers, malicious code authors and other criminals to perform their activities easily. We can site also as threats, zeus botnet, trojan horses (Cloud Security Alliance, 2010; Jouini et al 2012; Ben Arfa Rabai et al., 2013).

- **Insecure Application Programming Interfaces:** Cloud computing providers expose a set of software interfaces or APIs that customers use to manage and interact with cloud services. These interfaces must be designed to protect against both accidental and malicious attempts to circumvent policy. Reliance on a weak set of interfaces and APIs exposes organizations to a variety of security issues related to confidentiality, integrity, availability and accountability. This category includes Anonymous access and/or reusable tokens or passwords threat, clear-text authentication or transmission of content threat, inflexible access controls or improper authorizations threats, unknown service or API dependencies (Cloud Security Alliance, 2010; Jouini et al 2012; Ben Arfa Rabai et al., 2013).

7.2.3 Security Threats Originating from the Virtual Machines

- **Monitoring VMs from Other VMs:** One of the security risks encountered when using virtual machines is the lack of guaranteed isolation of the application and data when a shared resource such as memory space is utilized by multiple VMs. Cloud computing servers can contain tens of VMs and these are vulnerable to attack whether they are active or not. VMs that are active are vulnerable to all of the security attacks that a conventional physical service is subject to. However, once a VM has been compromised by an attack on other VMs residing on the same physical server, they become all vulnerable to the same attack due to the fact that each machine shares memory, disk storage, driver software and hypervisor software (Ibrahim et al., 2010; Jouini et al 2012; Ben Arfa Rabai et al., 2013).

- **Virtual Machine Mobility:** Virtual machines (VMs) which are disk images hosted in a hypervisor platform are easily copied or transferred to other locations. The ability to move and copy VMs poses a security risk because the entire system, applications and data can be stolen without physically stealing the machine (Wooley, 2011; Jouini et al 2012; Ben Arfa Rabai et al., 2013).

- **Threats on Communications Between Virtual Machines:** VMs are allowed to communicate with other VMs running on the same physical equipment using channels such as the shared clipboard functions. When sharing resources such as memory, real or virtual network connections, between VMs can introduce possible security risks for each machine because there is the possibility that one or more of the VMs has been compromised by malicious programs (Ibrahim et al., 2010; Wooley, 2011; ; Jouini et al 2012; Ben Arfa Rabai et al., 2013).

We can classify these threats into three categories according to their origins as it is shown in table 2.

7.3 Security Requirements on Cloud Computing Environment

Information security encompasses three basic security attributes namely confidentiality, availability and integrity (Allen et al., 2008). Besides these three fundamental attributes, non-repudiation and accountability, authentification, authorization, identification and privacy (Firesmith, 2004; Allen et al., 2008).

As security requirements for cloud computing systems, we consider the security concerns that are most often cited in connection with cloud computing (Krutz & Vines, 2010 ; Cloud Security Alliance, 2009; Hanna, 2009; Subashini & Kavitha, 2010 ; Wooley, 2011; ENISA, 2010), namely: availability, integrity, confidentiality. We further refine this classification by considering different levels of criticality of the data to which

these requirements apply (Jouini et al 2012; Ben Arfa Rabai et al., 2013).

7.3.1 Availability

Availability refers to the subscriber's ability to retrieve his/ her information when he/she needs it. Un-availability may be more or less costly depending on how critical the data is to the timely operation of the subscriber. We refine availability requirement by considering different levels of criticality of the data as follow (Jouini et al 2012; Ben Arfa Rabai et al., 2013):

- **Critical Data:** This data is critical to the day-to-day (or minute-by-minute) operation of the subscriber, and any delay in making this data available is deemed disruptive to the subscriber. Example: product data for an e-commerce merchant; the merchant cannot conduct business without it, and stands to lose sales as well as customer loyalty as a result of un-availability (Jouini et al 2012; Ben Arfa Rabai et al., 2013).
- **Archival Data:** Archival data typically has two attributes that set it apart from critical data: first, it is accessed seldom; second, its access is not time-critical, i.e. delays in delivering it do not cause a great loss. In an e-Commerce application, this data could be, for example, archival order data: such data is accessed only in exceptional cases (for example: a customer has a complaint, or wants to return or exchange merchandise), not a routine operation; and when that data is needed, it is accessed off-line (for example, by staff who are handling a customer complaint), rather than as part of an interactive operation. As a result of these two attributes, unavailability of archival data carries a much lower penalty than unavailability of critical data (Jouini et al 2012; Ben Arfa Rabai et al., 2013).

Table 2. Security threats on the cloud computing environment

Attack Types	Threats
Security threats originating from the host (hypervisor)	Monitoring virtual machines from host. Communications between virtual machines and host. Virtual Machine modification. Placement of malicious VM images on physical systems.
Security threats originating from the VMs	Monitoring VMs from other VM. Communication between VMs. Virtual machine mobility
Security threats originating between the customer and the data center	Denial of service (DoS) Flooding attacks Data loss or leakage Malicious insiders Account, service and traffic hijacking Abuse and nefarious use of cloud computing Insecure application programming interfaces

7.3.2 Integrity

Integrity refers to the assurances offered to subscribers that their data is not lost or damaged as a result of malicious or inadvertent activity. Violations of integrity may be more or less costly depending on how critical the data is to the secured operation of the subscriber. We refine integrity requirement by considering different levels of criticality of the data as follow (Jouini et al 2012; Ben Arfa Rabai et al., 2013):

- **Critical Data:** This data is critical to the normal operation of subscriber functions; if this data is lost; subscribers can no longer operate normally, or can no longer operate at all. For example, if we are talking about a subscriber who is an e-Commerce merchant, critical data would be his product catalog that includes product identification, product pricing, and product availability for his merchandise (Jouini et al 2012; Ben Arfa Rabai et al., 2013).
- **Archival Data:** This data is not critical to the operation of the subscriber, in the sense that the subscriber can operate if this data is lost or damaged. We assume that if integrity is lost, subscribers are duly informed.

For example, if we are talking about a subscriber who is an e-Commerce merchant, archival data would be the file that contains customer information or (for even less critical data) or information about customer recommendations (Jouini et al 2012; Ben Arfa Rabai et al., 2013).

7.3.3 Confidentiality

Confidentiality: Confidentiality refers to the assurances offered by subscribers that their data is protected from unauthorized access. Violations of confidentiality may be more or less costly depending on how confidential the divulged data is. We refine confidentiality requirement by considering different levels of criticality of the data as follow:

- **Highly Classified Data:** Exposure of this data to unauthorized parties represents an unrecoverable loss for the subscriber, that carries a very high cost, including unquantifiable/imponderable costs (such as loss of life, mission failure, security implications, etc.). For an e-Commerce subscriber, this may represent detailed personal data of its client database; exposure of such information can lead to identity theft on a massive scale, which leads in turn to customer dissatisfaction, damaged corporate reputation, civil liability and penal lawsuits (Jouini et al 2012; Ben Arfa Rabai et al., 2013).

- **Proprietary Data:** Exposure of this data to unauthorized parties represents an important but controllable and quantifiable loss; the scale of this loss is limited by its nature (typically: financial loss) and its scale (quantifiable and recoverable). For a corporate subscriber, this may be proprietary information about its intellectual property, its products or its processes (Jouini et al 2012; Ben Arfa Rabai et al., 2013).
- **Public Data:** Exposure of this data to unauthorized parties represents a minor and recoverable loss, resulting in perhaps a slight loss of competitive advantage. For a corporate subscriber, this could be demographic information about its customer base; a competitor who gains access to that data may cancel whatever marketing advantage the data afforded the subscriber (Jouini et al 2012; Ben Arfa Rabai et al., 2013).

8. CONCLUSION

Cloud computing is rapidly changing the computing landscape by fundamentally revolutionizing the way computing is viewed and delivered to the end user. Computing is now treated as a "utility" that can be provisioned on-demand, in a cost effective manner. Cloud computing presents a paradigm shift in how we provision and manage computing resources as well as how we develop, deploy, and use software applications.

In this chapter, we have surveyed the state-of-the-art of cloud computing, covering its essential concepts, architectural designs, well-known characteristics, key technologies as well as virtualiza-

tion. We show in this chapter cloud computing systems as an emerging paradigm of computing that replaces computing as a personal commodity by computing as a public utility. Besides, this technology offers all the advantages of a public utility system, in terms of economy of scale, flexibility, convenience but it raises major issues mainly security concerns. Thus, the protection of computer systems and the integrity, confidentiality and availability of the data they contain has long been recognized as a critical issue. In addition, cyber attacks or breaches of information security appear to be increasing in frequency and few are willing to ignore the possibility that the severity of future attacks could be much greater than what has been observed to date.

REFERENCES

Allen, J. H. Barnum, S. Ellison, S. R. et al., (2008). *Software Security Engineering: A Guide for Project Managers.* Addison Wesley Professional.

Barham, P. T., Dragovic, B., Fraser, K., Hand, S., Harris, T. L., Ho, A., . . . Warfield, A. (2003). Xen and the art of virtualization. In Symposium on Operating System Principles (SOSP). 19, 20, 28

Ben Arfa Rabai, L., Jouini, M., Ben Aissa, A., & Mili, A. (2013). A cybersecurity model in cloud computing environments, *Journal of King Saud University: Computer and Information Sciences.*

Boehm, B. Huang, L. Jain, A., & Madachy, R. (2004). *The Nature of Information System Dependability: A Stakeholder/Value Approach.* USC-CSSE Technical Report.

Buecker, A., Guézo, L., Lodewijkx, K., Moss, H., Skapinetz, K., & Waidner, M. (2009). *Cloud Computing: guide de la sécurité Recommandations d'IBM pour la sécurisation de l'informatique en nuage.*

Cloud Security Alliance. (2009). *Security Guidance for Critical Areas of Focus in Cloud Computing V2.1.*

Cloud Security Alliance. (2010). *Top Threats to Cloud Computing V 1.0.*

Duranti, L. (2013). *Records in the Cloud (RiC) User Survey Report, Records in the Cloud (RiC).* Project University of British Columbia.

ENISA. (2010). *Cloud computing: Benefits, risks and recommendations for information security.* Retrieved from http://www.enisa.europa.eu/act/rm/files/deliverables/cloud-computingrisk-assessment

Firesmith, D. (2004). Specifying Reusable Security Requirements. *Journal of Object Technology, 3*(1), 61–75. doi:10.5381/jot.2004.3.1.c6

Foster, I., Zhao, Y., Raicu, I., & Lu, S. (2008). Cloud computing and grid computing 360 degree compared. *In Proceedings grid computing environments workshop: GCE 2008,* 1-10. DOI doi:10.1109/GCE.2008.4738445

Furht, B., & Escalante, A. (2010). *Handbook of cloud computing.* New York: Springer. doi:10.1007/978-1-4419-6524-0

Gartner. (2013). *Will Private Cloud Adoption Increase by 2015?* Gartner Research Note G00250893 (12 May 2013).

Grobauer, B., Walloschek, T., & Stocker, E. (2011). *Understanding Cloud Computing Vulnerabilities Security & Privacy, IEEE, 9*(2), 50–57. doi:10.1109/MSP.2010.115

Han, L. (2009). *Market Acceptance of Cloud Computing: An Analysis of Market Structure, Price models and systems management.* Retrieved from http://opus4.kobv.de/opus4-ubbayreuth/files/468/thesis_leihan.pdf

Hanna, S. (2009). *Cloud Computing: Finding the silver lining.*

Heiser, J., & Nicolett, M. (2008). *Assessing the Security Risks of Cloud Computing.* Gartner Research.

Huth, A., & Cebula, J. (2011). *The Basics of Cloud Computing.*

Ibrahim, A. S., Hamlyn-Harris, J., & Grundy, J. (2010). *Emerging security challenges of cloud virtual infrastructure.* The Asia Pacific Software Engineering Conference 2010 Cloud Workshop.

Jangra, A., & Bala, R. (2011). Spectrum of Cloud Computing Architecture: Adoption and Avoidance Issues. *International Journal of Computing and Business Research, 2*(2).

Jouini, M., Ben Arfa Rabai, L., Ben Aissa, A., & Mili, A. (2012). Towards quantitative measures of Information Security: A Cloud Computing case study. *International Journal of Cyber-Security and Digital Forensics, 1*(3), 265–279.

Kenneth Kofi, F. (2010). *Cloud security requirements analysis and security policy development using a high-order object-oriented modeling technique.* Thesis.

Krutz, R. L., & Vines, R. D. (2010). *Cloud security: A comprehensive guide to secure cloud computing.* John Wiley & Sons.

Liu, Q., Weng, C., Li, M., & Luo, Y. (2010). An In-VM measuring framework for increasing virtual machine security in clouds. *IEEE Security Privacy Journal, 8*(6), 56–62. doi:10.1109/MSP.2010.143

McCarthy, L. (2011). Adoption of Cloud Computing. Retrieved from http://askvisory.com/research/adoption-of-cloudcomputing/

Meiko, J., Jorg, S., Nils, G., & Luigi, L. I. (2009). On Technical Security Issues in Cloud Computing. *IEEE International Conference on Cloud Computing.*

Mell, P., & Grance, T. (2009). Effectively and Securely Using the Cloud Computing Paradigm. *ACM Cloud Computing Security Workshop.*

Mell, P., & Grance, T. (2011). The NIST Definition of Cloud Computing. *NIST Special Publication 800-145.* Retrieved from http://csrc.nist.gov/publications/nistpubs/800-145/SP800-145.pdf

Menken, I., & Blokdijk, G. (2009). *Cloud Computing Virtualization Specialist Complete Certification Kit - Study Guide Book and Online Course.* Emereo Pty Ltd.

Minhas, U. F. (2013). *Scalable and Highly Available Database Systems in the Cloud.* PhD thesis, University of Waterloo.

Parkhill, D. (1966). *The Challenge of the Computer Utility.* US: Addison-Wesley Educational Publishers Inc.

Rittinghouse, J. W., & Ransome, J. F. (2010). *Cloud computing: Implementation, management, and security.* Boca Raton: CRC Press.

Sahoo, J. Mohapatra, S. & Lath, R. (2010). *Virtualization: A Survey on Concepts, Taxonomy and Associated Security Issues* (pp. 222-226).

Subashini, S., & Kavitha, V. (2010). A survey on security issues in service delivery models of cloud computing. *Journal of Network and Computer Applications.*

Vaquero, L. M., Rodero-Merino, L., Caceres, J., & Lindner, M. (2009). Caceres J and Lindner M, A Break in the Clouds: Towards a Cloud Definition. *Computer Communication Review, 39*(1), 50–55. doi:10.1145/1496091.1496100

Vaughan-Nichols, S. J. (2008). Virtualization sparks security concerns. *IEEE computer, 41*(8), 13-15.

VMware. (n.d.). Retrieved from http://www.vmware.com/

Vouk, M. A. (2008). Cloud Computing: Issues, Research and Implementations. In *Proceedings of the ITI 2008 30th Int. Conf. on Information Technology Interfaces.* doi:10.1109/ITI.2008.4588381

Wang, L., Von Laszewski, G., Kunze, M., & Tao, J. (2008). Cloud computing: A Perspective study. *Proc. Grid Computing Environments (GCE) workshop.* doi:10.1007/s00354-008-0081-5

Wayne, J., & Timothy, G. (2011). *Guidelines on Security and Privacy in Public Cloud Computing.* Information Technology Laboratory.

Wong, K. (2009). Pictures in the Cloud. *Computer Graphics World, 32,* 42–47.

Wooley, P. (2011). Identifying Cloud Computing Security Risks.

Xuan, Z., Nattapong, W., Hao, L., & Xuejie, Z. (2010). Information Security Risk Management Framework for the Cloud Computing Environments. *10th IEEE International Conference on Computer and Information Technology (CIT 2010).*

KEY TERMS AND DEFINITIONS

Cloud Computing: Is a technology that allows an efficient computing by centralizing data storage, processing and bandwidth between users.

IaaS: Is physical or virtual machines and other resources (storage) offered to cloud users as a service.

Outsourcing: Is the contracting out (externalization) of a business process to a third-party.

PaaS: Is a computing platform delivered as service, including operating system, programming language execution environment, database, and web server to let customers to develop their applications.

SaaS: Is applications delivered as a service to users.

Security Risk: Is any incident that compromises the assets, operations and objectives of an organization.

Virtualization: Is a recent technology that allows abstraction and isolation of lower level functionalities and underlying hardware.

Chapter 2
An Interoperability Framework for Enterprise Applications in Cloud Environments

José C. Delgado
Instituto Superior Técnico, Universidade de Lisboa, Portugal

ABSTRACT

Enterprise Information Systems (EIS) are increasingly designed with cloud environments in mind, as a set of cooperating services deployed in a mix of platforms, including conventional servers and clouds, private and public. If enterprise value chains are considered, in which their EIS need to cooperate, solving all the interoperability problems raised by the need to meaningfully interconnect all these services constitutes a rather challenging endeavor. This chapter describes the concept of enterprise as a service, a collection of dynamically assembled services with a lifecycle centered on the customers, and proposes a multidimensional interoperability framework to help systematizing the various aspects relevant to interoperability. Besides lifecycle, this framework presents other dimensions, namely concreteness (with various levels of abstraction), interoperability (based on structural compliance and conformance), and concerns (to deal with non-functional aspects such as security, reliability and quality of service).

INTRODUCTION

A *cloud* can simply be defined as a remote platform supporting the deployment and use of computer-based resources and services, in a setting characterized by elastic, dynamic and automated resource provisioning, paid as used and managed in a self-service way (Armbrust et al., 2010).

Through virtualization, a pool of physical resources (servers, storage, networks, and so on) supports the dynamic allocation, provisioning, decommissioning and release of virtual resources, forming an apparently elastic fabric of resources that are used on demand and paid as used. However, users want the services that resources support, not the resources themselves. Resources are increasingly seen as a commodity (Carr, 2004), allowing some IT enterprises, the *providers*, to specialize in providing IT-based services and resource infrastructures cheaper, more reliably,

DOI: 10.4018/978-1-4666-8339-6.ch002

better managed, faster provisioned and in a more scalable way than any of the organizations that just require these services and resources for their business activities, the *consumers*.

This dichotomy between consumers and providers, a marriage of convenience as any outsourcing agreement, is known as *utility computing* (Brynjolfsson, Hofmann & Jordan, 2010). Providers take care of many issues on behalf of the consumers, namely expertise, risks, costs and management, in what concerns resources and generic services. Consumers still have to tackle a part of the overall solution, namely application-specific services, but they can concentrate more in their core business and less on the IT technologies that support it.

After an initial period of slow growth, in which concerns about security, privacy, performance and availability acted as inhibiting factors, cloud computing is finally blossoming. For consumers, it is now easier, cheaper, and faster to get computing resources from a cloud than by resorting to conventional IT systems and applications. In most cases, the advantages now outweigh the risks and other disadvantages. All large IT providers are now investing heavily in cloud computing.

This is clearly a market driven by providers, with consumers still cautious about the transition, but the scenario is evolving at a fast pace, both for individual and enterprise consumers. Gartner analysts forecast that the public cloud services market will grow at a compound annual growth rate (CAGR) of 17.3% over the 2014-2018 five-year period (Anderson et al, 2014, May 13). Gartner also expects that end-user spending on public cloud services will grow 19% in 2014, up to $158 billion, with annual growth rates of 45% and 33% for infrastructure (IaaS) and platform (PaaS) cloud services, respectively (Anderson et al, 2014, March 31). These rates clearly indicate a shift in spending, from traditional IT systems to cloud services.

Two relevant factors gave their contribution to the bootstrap and boom of cloud computing:

- For individual consumers, social networking and multiplatform mobility (laptops, tablets and smartphones) raised the need to store information in a server somewhere, always available to be accessed seamlessly and in a synchronized way across platforms;
- For enterprise consumers, the market pressure caused by increasing global competition and ever-shortening turnaround times, combined with a sluggish global economy, emphasized the basic principle of concentrating on core business and (dynamically) outsourcing the rest.

However, the problem that drove the appearance of the Web, interoperability, remains unsolved. The goal is to endow distributed systems with the ability of meaningfully exchanging information in interaction patterns known as choreographies. The problem, unfortunately, is even worse today than 25 years ago:

- The Web provided uniform e global access to media information and created the market, instead of reacting to it. This gave time to standards (HTTP, HTML and, later, XML) to become universally used before diversity could set in. This is why today we can use any browser to access any Web site. Even in the service realm, with either SOA or REST, the scenario is essentially standardized, although standards are not enough to ensure interoperability (Lewis, Morris, Simanta & Wrage, 2008). The usual integration problems are exacerbated by the dynamic cloud environments, in which an application can migrate, which may entail a change in the access URI or in non-functional characteristics, such as security settings, policies and quality of service;
- Cloud computing provides global access to all kinds of computer-based resources, in a very dynamic environment, but these

are more complex than simple hyperme-dia documents and, above all, the mar-ket exploded before standardization was achieved. This means that today many cloud providers offer incompatible inter-faces (Petcu, 2013), which hamper the seamless use of the various clouds and lead to provider lock-in, since the costs of changing provider are typically higher than the benefits of the optimizations stemming from the free choice of a new provider.

This chapter concentrates on the first set of problems, application interoperability in cloud environments, which also entails heterogeneity. Figure 1 illustrates a scenario that may well be applicable to many enterprises, to interconnect either subsystems of an Enterprise Information System (EIS) or complete EIS, in value chains or other cooperation agreements.

An EIS will have to deal with conventional web servers, in-house servers, several general-purpose clouds types (private, public and hybrid) and specific cloud-like systems, involving mobility (Fernando, Loke & Rahayu, 2013), sensor net-works (Potdar, Sharif & Chang, 2009) and RFID tags (Aggarwal & Han, 2013), increasingly used for supply chain control.

Taking into account that enterprises need to be cooperate and to be connected, and the exist-ing diversity of platforms and applications, any computer-based system can be considered a dis-tributed and heterogeneous cloud of clouds. Some will be more dynamic than others, but all will endure the same basic problem: how to provide enough interoperability to enable EIS to cooperate without requiring exact mutual knowledge and allowing them to evolve independently.

The main goals of this chapter are:

Figure 1. An example of a complex enterprise IT environment

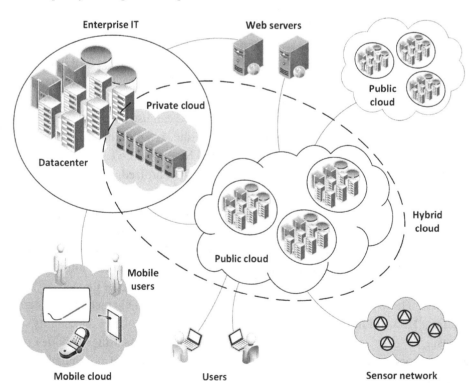

- To contribute to the field of cloud computing, in particular in the interoperability area, by analyzing several of the problems involved, especially in what concerns the design of EIS;
- To describe a multidimensional framework that explores EIS interoperability at various levels, to better dissect and understand what is involved and how this can help in systematizing methods and solutions;
- To assess the potential of structural compatibility (instead of schema sharing, used in current interoperability technologies) as a means to reduce coupling and increase adaptability, changeability and reliability, while maintaining interoperability requirements.

The chapter is organized as follows. The Background section describes some of the existing technologies relevant to the context of this chapter, followed by a discussion on how an EIS can be designed for changeability, including several variants of increasing maturity, from a traditional EIS to a more dynamic and service-based EIS. To understand better the EIS interoperability problem, a multidimensional interoperability framework is outlined, presenting several levels of abstraction of interoperability and the importance of EIS compatibility (compliance and conformance) in reducing EIS coupling without impairing interoperability. The chapter ends by comparing this framework with existing ones, outlining future directions of research and drawing the main conclusions of this work.

BACKGROUND

One of the most cited definitions of cloud computing, encompassing the characteristics described in the previous section, is given by Mell and Grance (2011), of the US National Institute of Standards and Technology (NIIST). This and other survey papers (Rimal, Choi & Lumb, 2009; Armbrust, 2010; Zhang, Cheng & Boutaba, 2010) discuss the most relevant issues involving cloud computing.

There are many providers offering cloud-based platforms services, such as big market players Amazon, Microsoft and Google, with specific systems, and other providers that have joined the open-source movement in the cloud market (Bist, Wariya & Agarwal, 2013), with cloud management platforms such as OpenStack (Jackson, 2012), CloudStack (Sabharwal & Shankar, 2013) and Eucalyptus (Nurmi et al., 2009).

Interoperability between different clouds is not easy. Standards such as OCCI (Open Cloud Computing Interface) (Edmonds, Metsch & Papaspyrou, 2011) and TOSCA (Topology and Orchestration Specification for Cloud Applications) (Binz, Breiter, Leyman & Spatzier, 2012), as well as initiatives such as the Intercloud (Demchenko, Makkes, Strijkers & de Laat, 2012), have no real impact yet on market players. Each cloud ends up having its own features and characteristics, since cloud providers need differentiation to attract customers. The dominant position of some players entitles them to define their own *de facto* standards, in particular at the API level.

Standards have been useful essentially at the lower cloud computing levels, in which the advantages of interoperability by adoption of common specifications outweigh the value stemming from differentiation (and incompatibility).

CIMI (Cloud Infrastructure Management Interface) (DTMF, 2013) is an example of such a standard, providing an API to provision and to manage resources typically found in clouds, such as virtual machines, storage volumes and networks.

CMDI (Cloud Data Management Interface) (ISO/IEC, 2012) is a SNIA (Storage Networking Industry Association) standard, adopted by ISO/IEC, which provides a RESTful API to deal with storage resources in a cloud.

OVF (Open Virtual Format) (DTMF, 2012), a DTMF standard adopted by ISO/IEC, allows applications to be packaged and deployed to virtualized systems. It is the lowest level and the most used standard in cloud computing, constituting a means to promote portability of applications between clouds.

Besides cloud API interoperability problems, applications deployed in clouds need to interact by exchanging messages and require functional and contextual interoperability, the focus of this chapter. These applications can span a wide spectrum, from high-level domains such as enterprise cooperation (Jardim-Goncalves, Agostinho & Steiger-Garcao, 2012), e-government services (Gottschalk & Solli-Sæther, 2008), military operations (Wyatt, Griendling & Mavris, 2012), healthcare applications (Weber-Jahnke, Peyton & Topaloglou, 2012), and digital libraries (El Raheb *et al*, 2011).

Several frameworks have been proposed to systematize interoperability, such as Athena (Berre et al., 2007), LCIM (Wang, Tolk & Wang, 2009), the European Interoperability Framework (EIF, 2010) and the Framework for Enterprise Interoperability (Chen, 2006). The European project ENSEMBLE embodies an effort to formulate a science base for enterprise interoperability (Jardim-Goncalves et al., 2013). A more detailed account of the existing frameworks is given in the section "Comparison with other interoperability frameworks".

Service interoperability (Athanasopoulos, Tsalgatidou & Pantazoglou, 2006) requires that interactions occur according to the assumptions and expectations of the involved applications. This involves several levels (Mykkänen & Tuomainen, 2008), such as communication protocol, message structure, data format, syntax, semantics and service composition (Khadka et al., 2011), and even non-functional and social aspects (Loutas, Peristeras & Tarabanis, 2011).

Regarding service interoperability, the world is divided into two main architectural styles: service-oriented, or SOA (Erl, 2008), and resource-oriented, or REST (Webber, Parastatidis & Robinson, 2010). SOA, usually implemented by Web Services, emphasizes behavior (although limited

to interfaces, with state and structure hidden in the implementation). REST follows the principles defined by Fielding (2000) and emphasizes structure and state, by exposing inner URIs (with interaction and application state separated and stored in the client and server, respectively, and behavior hidden in the dynamically changing structure and in the implementation of individual resources). Web Services are technologically more complex, but their model is a closer match to real world resources. REST is simpler and finer grained, but leans towards some restrictions (such as interaction statelessness) and is lower level (higher semantic gap between application concepts and REST resources), which for complex applications entails a greater effort to model, develop and maintain.

SOA and REST are not actually competitors, but rather complementary approaches, each naturally a better fit to different areas of application domains (Pautasso, Zimmermann & Leymann, 2008). Simplicity, however, is a very strong argument and most cloud management APIs now use the REST style.

DESIGNING ENTERPRISE INFORMATION SYSTEMS FOR CHANGEABILITY

As Heraclitus, an ancient Greek philosopher (Heraclitus & Patrick, 2013), once wrote, "The only thing that is constant is change". Complex systems like EIS start being changed while they are still being conceived. Therefore, an EIS must be designed primarily for changeability, throughout its lifecycle.

Figure 2 depicts a basic system lifecycle, emphasizing changeability, which can be applied to the whole EIS, as it is usually conceived today, or to any of its subsystems. The market represents the rest of the world (namely, other EIS) or the environment in which the subsystem being modeled is immersed.

Figure 2. The lifecycle of an EIS, emphasizing changeability

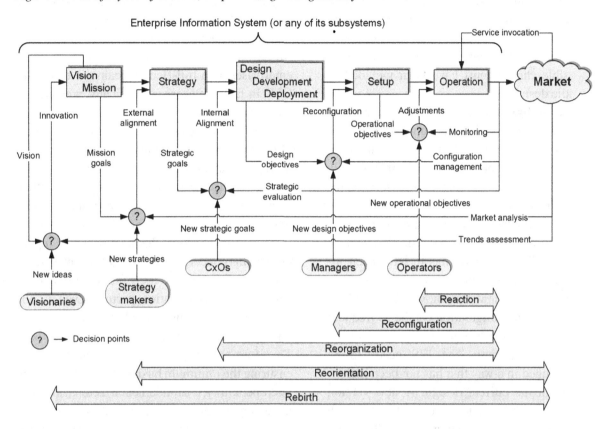

This model is maximalist, open and not prescriptive, in the sense that any EIS (or a subsystem thereof) should go through all the stages (conceptually, at least), but the level of emphasis and detail in every stage does not have to be always identical. The higher the level of the subsystem, the more important the vision and strategy will be, but it must go all the way down to operations if it is meant to work. Lower level subsystems will emphasize development and operation, but must have an underlying vision and mission as well. In the remainder of this chapter, "EIS" should be understood as the whole EIS or any of its subsystems.

Figure 2 models the lifecycle of an EIS by a pipeline of stages, each more concrete and detailed than the previous on, with several improvement loops. Each of these loops assumes that metrics (indicators) are defined so that goals and objectives can be assessed. If the difference between the desired and measured indicators is greater than some acceptable measure, the loop should be iterated to decide and implement what needs to be changed in order to improve that difference.

The inner loops deal with lower levels and greater detail, whereas outer loops deal with higher levels and less detail. Figure 2 considers the following loops (but others are possible, with a pipeline in which the stages are more detailed):

- **Reaction:** All changes involve state only, so the cost and time to detect (monitoring) and to produce a change (of state) are usually very small. The changes are very frequent and occur as a reaction to events or to foreseeable trends, in adaptive systems. This is the loop more amenable to automation. However, and not considering self-changing systems (hard to build, particularly in complex systems), every possible change must have been included in the design;

- **Reconfiguration:** Some EIS, such as in the manufacturing domain, support reconfigurability (Putnik & Sluga, 2007). This is not a new EIS, but involves more than merely changing state. Some of the subsystems will be used in a different configuration or parameterization, for example to manufacture a different product in a production line. This, however, has to have been included in the EIS design. Otherwise, we will need a new version, which is the next loop. A reconfiguration can be as frequent as its cost makes it effective;
- **Reorganization:** The EIS needs to be changed in a way that has not been included in the current design. A new version needs to be produced and deployed, which may not be completely compatible with the previous one and may imply changing other subsystems as well;
- **Reorientation:** A reorientation is a profound reorganization, as result of changes in the strategy. This usually is driven by external factors, such as evolution of competitors or customers, but can also be demanded by an internal restructuring to increase competitiveness;
- **Rebirth:** The vision and/or mission can also suffer significant changes, driven by factors such as stiff competition, technology evolution, merges/acquisitions or even replacing the person fulfilling the CEO role. This implies changes that are so profound that, in practice, it has to be rethought and redesigned almost from scratch. This loop can also correspond to a diversification of business areas, making it necessary to build a new EIS or subsystem.

Figure 2 also indicates the typical actors involved in the change/no change decision taken at the decision points (the circles with a "?"). The strategy makers vary from entrepreneurs, in small enterprises, to a full-fledged team driven by the CEO in large enterprises. Typically, a change is decided when an actor realizes that the benefit value of changing is higher than the cost value of the change implementation. Agile enterprises need low change costs (Ganguly, Nilchiani & Farr, 2009), so that changes can be frequent, either reactively (to market changes) or proactively (anticipating market trends) (Putnik & Sluga, 2007).

In the context of this chapter, Figure 2 is important in what concerns interoperability. Enterprises need to collaborate and their EIS to interoperate. Changing a collaboration partner, even if not changing anything else, most likely means changing objectives, processes, data formats, and so on. Therefore, reducing coupling between EIS, while ensuring the minimum business requirements for interoperability, is a fundamental factor in increasing enterprise agility. What this means, and how to do it, is the main goal of the interoperability framework proposed by this chapter.

THE EVOLUTION OF ENTERPRISE INFORMATION SYSTEMS

The following sections establish several possible scenarios with several types of EIS, establishing a route from a traditional EIS to the concept of what an agile EIS should be, in particular in what concerns the interaction with other enterprises and their EIS. This route can also be viewed as an agility maturity model (Imache, Izza & Ahmed-Nacer, 2012).

The Traditional Enterprise

A traditional EIS is designed and built with traditional frameworks and methods. It deals essentially with an ERP (Enterprise Resource

Planning) system, there is usually a global data model, processes are the main paradigm and reflect a repeatable workflow design, N-tier architecture is the norm, the strategy is typically oriented towards well-typified market sectors, and the goals and objectives rely essentially on past experiences and statistics as a guide for evolution.

It usually implements most of its components, with outsourcing more the exception than the norm, does not experience frequent changes, and does not deal very well with unpredictability and risk. The EIS is seen as the center of the business world, with suppliers, outsourcees and customers around it, and one of the main concerns is integration with the processes of other EIS (Chen, Doumeingts & Vernadat, 2008).

The Optimizing Enterprise

Ideally, resources should have 100% utilization, all the time. Unfortunately, customer demand is not constant and supplier capacity is limited. One solution is to own resources planned for an average customer demand, but this translates into wasted capacity when demand is lower and will not be able to satisfy customers when demand is high. Another solution is to design the EIS for dynamic, on-demand outsourcing (minimum TCO complemented with outsourcing as needed):

- When demand for a module's functionality is higher than its capacity, the requests in excess are dynamically forwarded to one or more alternative modules (with an outsourcing contract foreseeing occasional or seasonal demand);
- When the demand is lower than the module's capacity, the business model is inverted and the module can offer its excess capacity to other enterprises needing its functionality.

This way, load balancing can be achieved both at the demand and capacity ends. The load balancing between consumption and generation is automatic and dynamic, although under previously agreed contractual constraints.

The Resilient Enterprise

Any enterprise should have a backup plan in case any of its EIS modules or resources fails. Resources include humans, computers, and other equipment. Although replacing a sick person that holds specific knowledge is much more difficult than finding an alternative to a broken truck, for example, the point is that any backup plan must be built into the EIS by proper enterprise architecture design, and not dealt with only when a problem occurs. Resilience is a usual topic in IT, but sometimes enterprises tend to forget that the problem is the same in every aspect of the business (including failing suppliers, outsourcees and customers).

A typical solution for a resource failure is redundancy, either in normal use (in case of failure, only capacity is reduced) or in standby, in which case the alternative resource is only put into service when the normal one fails. In hot standby, the alternative resource exists and is reserved and ready for (almost) immediate use upon failure detection. This is generally too expensive and used only for truly critical resources. The others use warm or cold standby, in which case the situation is foreseen, what needs to be done is known but it takes increasingly longer to get the alternative solution to work. This usually implies a breach in the service provided by the failed resource, and its impact and allowed recovery time should be part of the EIS design.

The Virtual Enterprise

In industrial environments, the traditional meaning of "virtual enterprise" has been "a temporary alliance of enterprises" (Camarinha-Matos, Afsarmanesh, Garita & Lima, 1999). In more information oriented circles, Petrie and Bussler (2003) define it as "a temporary consortium of partners and services", in which services are essentially Internet-based, and take a service centric integration perspective. Grefen, Mehandjiev, Kouvas, Weichhart and Eshuis (2009) go further and use the "instant virtual enterprise" designation to emphasize the agility of a supplier network.

The meaning of "virtual enterprise" (Esposito & Evangelista, 2014) has evolved from a classical partnership of strategic outsourcing and collaboration, in a timescale of weeks to years, to a dynamic, cost optimizing service networks and collaborations, valid for a time span as small as a single business transaction.

Virtualization, through dynamic outsourcing and reconfigurability, is very important for enterprise agility. However, the automatic (or semi-automatic) design of an EIS from a market of services or processes implies a loss of design control over the outcome, unless the components comply with a general semantic framework or domain defined beforehand, to ensure their compatibility when translating goals into requirements, and component procurement and composition. That is why most of the examples in this area come from the manufacturing domain, in which the goals and requirements of a component are easier to express, and reconfigurability of the production supply chain is a fundamental objective.

The Cloud-Oriented Enterprise

Cloud sourcing (Géczy, Izumi & Hasida, 2012) is a growing trend in which outsourcing is done dynamically to cloud-based applications, typically using Web Services or a RESTful API. It is cloud computing seen from an outsourcing point of view, entailing a service delivery model characterized by the usual cloud properties:

- **Self-Service:** The customer is a heavy co-producer;
- **Automation:** The customer does not have to deal with the management of resources, provisioning of services, application patches and updates;
- **Virtualization:** The customer has no notion of where and how the service is implemented;
- **Elasticity:** The apparent service capacity shrinks or grows dynamically as the customer requires;
- **Pay-per-Use:** No investment upfront, no minimum consumption;
- **Multi-Tenancy:** The resources are shared by many customers, transparently, with security and load balancing, which reduces maximum capacity and hence the service costs.

Cloud sourcing is just a form of virtualization in service outsourcing, used as needed in a cloud bursting (Fadel & Fayoumi, 2013) fashion. An EIS must still be designed and someone has to decide which modules will be needed. Providers offer services using a utility paradigm, which means that they can offer the same service (although configurable) to any customer that wants it.

Decoupling and distributed interoperability become relevant concerns, because cloud-based services must now be designed not for a specific EIS but for a broad base of potential customers.

The Enterprise as a Service (EaaS)

This concept can be defined by the following guidelines:

- Instead of guessing what and how much the customer demand will be (introducing provisions for it in the EIS in advance), the EIS should be designed and assembled on the fly in reaction to concrete customer demand, with a high degree of customization;
- Instead of considering the EIS as part of a value chain, see it as a value creator, or an adapter between what the customer wants and what other enterprises can provide;

- Instead of seeking collaboration with other enterprises, build the EIS dynamically and virtually on top of a library of services, using outsourcing as the main organizational paradigm;
- Instead of investing a lot in defining an elaborate strategy, build the entire EIS for agility, so that strategy is easily and quickly adaptable to the fast-evolving business world.

The EaaS is a menu-based EIS, in the sense that a new, specialized and customized EIS can be built for each business transaction (or class of transactions), with lower granularity and higher agility than traditional EIS. Unlike any of the previous scenarios, outsourcing is the main service delivery mechanism of the EaaS model and is meant to be used with all service types, including human roles.

Although EaaS may seem similar to SaaS (Software as a Service), these are two orthogonal concepts. SaaS is essentially a service delivery mechanism, whereas EaaS is an EIS building paradigm. SaaS offers full applications remotely, hiding management problems, but has no idea of how an EIS should be organized, and indeed current SaaS offerings (ERPs, in particular) are not that easy to configure and to integrate with other subsystems. EaaS, on the other hand, advocates lower granularity and promotes the dynamic interoperability of services more than their static integration into an EIS. Instead of one large application, it is better to use a library of smaller, customizable services. Agile adaptability to the customer requirements is the main tenet.

Figure 3 depicts the lifecycle of the EIS of an EaaS, reflecting a changeability model more dynamic than that of Figure 2, which reflects the EIS of a traditional enterprise. Customers are at the center by design.

The EaaS model divides the EIS lifecycle into two parts, with the customer precisely at the middle. The customer is the most important actor in the lifecycle, around which everything cycles. Again, this is a maximalist model, and real cases can optimize some of the aspects. This model can be briefly explained as follows:

- **The Market Making Part:** This involves not only assessing what the customer wants but also influencing him by showing how a customized solution can solve his problems. The EaaS must make its own customers, not just wait for them to appear. It involves two loops:
  - **Reorientation:** This essentially recognizes business patterns and tries to contribute to the organization and structure of the service library, to capitalize on service reuse and minimize the customization effort and implementation time. On the other hand, the customer does not always know what exactly he needs, and the service library, based on proven business patterns, can be a precious help. In other words, it contributes to the mutual alignment between the service library and the customer needs;
  - **Rebirth:** Necessary when new technologies, innovative ideas, or competition changes appear. The EaaS develops its market vision from the gap between the customer needs and the suppliers offerings, which define the business opportunities, in particular when innovative ideas are available. Strategy, which must be light and agile, must also be attentive to competition, which has to be assumed agile as well;
- **The Service Implementation Part:** The EaaS should be able to provide a new EIS design for each customer request. Naturally, most of these requests will follow common business patterns and therefore the EIS will actually be variants of

Figure 3. The lifecycle of the EIS of an enterprise as a service

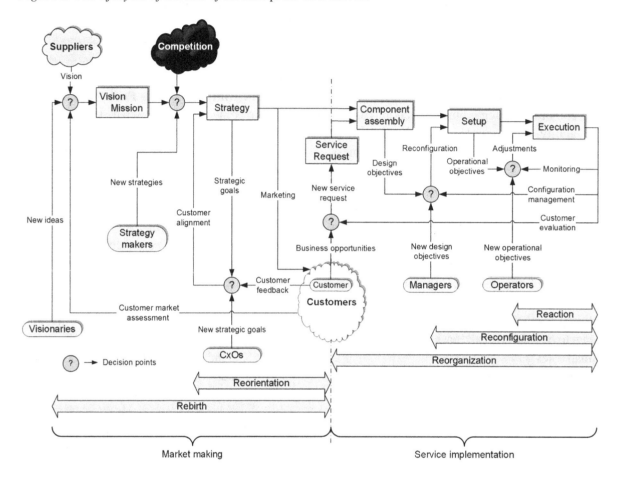

pre-established EIS, adequate to those patterns. How easy will be to adapt these patterns to concrete cases depends on how well the library is designed. This involves the following loops:

- **Reaction:** This is essentially the same as in traditional EIS, but we need to keep in mind that the EaaS must be flexible to be adaptable, which means that monitoring and control techniques may be made more specialized and adapted to each case;
- **Reconfiguration:** This is less relevant than in traditional EIS because reorganization, the next loop, becomes a feasible and more flexible alternative,

given the customization philosophy of an EaaS. Nevertheless, the EIS of an EaaS must be able to cater for situations that require frequent choice among a fixed set of configurations;

- **Reorganization:** This needs to be done in each change of pattern of customer requests. The design, development, and deployment box of Figure 2 has been replaced here by an assembly box, to make clear that this essentially involves assembling services from reusable services in the library. Adapting services and in particular developing new ones should be the exception, rather than the norm.

A MULTIDIMENSIONAL ENTERPRISE ARCHITECTURE FRAMEWORK

The customer-centric approach of the EaaS, adapting as much as possible to the customer, whatever small the business volume is, and having the production done only when the customer requires it, is a significant business paradigm shift that makes agility the most important feature, next to quality. Dividing the service lifecycle in two parts, one whose output is the library of services and the other that uses that library, helps in designing for flexibility and in promoting a wider customer base.

However, our main concern is interoperability, concerning how EIS will be able to connect and interoperate. Figures 2 and 3 express very high-level models, with not enough separation of concerns to allow us to understand what is really involved in interoperability, in its several slants and dimensions. More than a mere lifecycle, in a somewhat linear pipeline from a conceptual to an operational level, we need a multidimensional framework, in which independent dimensions can be analyzed separately.

We start by simplifying Figure 3 into two loops, which correspond to the left and right parts of Figure 3 and are depicted in Figure 4.

The *architectural loop* is inspired by the Business Motivation Model (Malik, 2009) and contemplates three main concepts, which embody three of the main questions about system development that were popularized by the Zachman framework (O'Rourke, Fishman & Selkow, 2003):

- **Motivations:** Emphasize the reasons behind the architectural decisions taken (*why* is the EIS this way), in accordance with the specification of the problem that the EIS is designed to solve;
- **Ends:** Express the desires and expectations (i.e., goals and objectives) of the stakeholders for which the EIS is relevant (*what* is the EIS trying to achieve);

- **Means:** Describe the mechanisms (i.e., actions) used to fulfill those expectations (*how* can the EIS do it).

The *fulfillment loop* in Figure 4 models subsequent stages in the lifecycle and is based on the organization adopted by classical development methods, such as the Rational Unified Process (Kruchten, 2004), eventually adapted to take into account the dynamic features of the EaaS:

- **Implementation:** Includes stages such as development, testing and deployment, but also the more dynamic features of Figure 3, such as component assembly and setup;
- **Operation:** Corresponds to executing the EIS;
- **Evaluation:** Monitors the EIS and measures indicators to assess how well the EIS meets the expectations stemming from the motivations.

The dashed arrows in Figure 4 are used to distinguish the two loops and to indicate that, in initial iterations, when details are scarce, the Means stage can loop directly to the Motivations stage. When enough detail and design decisions are reached, the lifecycle can be enlarged to encompass both loops, with Means transitioning to Implementation and Evaluation, back to Motivations if needed.

The lifecycle is just one dimension (or axis) of our architectural framework, which includes the following dimensions (or axes), depicted in Figure 5:

- **Lifecycle:** This axis is discretized into the six stages of Figure 4;
- **Concreteness:** Each stage in the lifecycle can be viewed at a very high and abstract level, or at a very detailed and concrete level. We have discretized this axis into six levels: *Conceptual, Strategic, Tactical, Pragmatic, Semantic,* and *Syntactic.* Stages of the lifecycle and their level of concrete-

Figure 4. Lifecycle of an EIS, with emphasis on separation of concerns

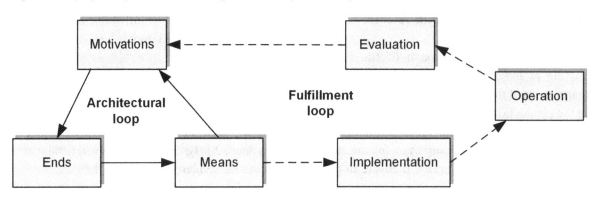

Figure 5. The axes of the architecture framework, with the front plane detailed

	Motivations	Ends	Means	Implementation	Operation	Evaluation	
Conceptual	Purpose	Vision	Mission	Model	Animation	Rationale & assessment	
Strategic	Principles, drivers & risks	Goals	Method	Design	Simulation	Strategic KPIs	Decisions
Tactical	Policies & constraints	Objectives	Plan	Blueprint	Rapid prototyping	Metrics & measurements	
Pragmatic	Patterns & exceptions	Targets & effects	Algorithm	Program	Instantiation & invocation	Monitoring & configuration	
Semantic	Concepts & ontology	Facts & assertions	Action	Operation	Verification & validation	Testing	Semiotics
Syntactic	Representation & notation	State representation	Statement	Instruction	Interpretation & execution	Profiling	

ness are orthogonal concepts. We can have the Implementation stage at a conceptual level (just ideas on how to do it) as well as the Motivations stage at a very concrete level (justification for the lowest level actions);

- **Concerns:** The focus words (*what, how, where, who, when, why*) in the Zachman framework (O'Rourke, Fishman & Selkow,

2003) are generic but do not address the entire focus range. Other questions are pertinent, such as *whence* (where from), *whither* (where to), *how much* (quantitative assessment) and *how well* (qualitative assessment). It is important to be able to express the dynamics of the EIS, its quality (how good it is, quantitatively and qualitatively) and other concerns (performance, standards, security, reliability, and so on), both functional and non-functional. This axis is discretized as needed, according to the number of concerns considered. Therefore, the framework is open-ended.

The Lifecycle and Concreteness axes form the front plane of Figure 5. Each cell, resulting from crossing the values of both axes, represents one lifecycle stage at a given level of concreteness. Each row is a refinement of the level above it, by including decisions that turn some abstract aspects into concrete ones. Each concern, functional or non-functional, represents a new plane, along the Concerns axis. We have illustrated some concerns, with plane details omitted for simplicity.

We consider the levels in the Concreteness axis organized in two categories:

- Decisions taken, which define, structure and refine the characteristics of the EIS, at three levels:
  - **Conceptual:** The top view of the EIS, including only global ideas;
  - **Strategic:** Details these ideas by taking usually long lasting decisions;
  - **Tactical:** Refines these decisions into shorter-term decisions;
- **Semiotics (Chandler, 2007):** The study of the relationship between signs (manifestations of concepts) and their interpretation (pragmatics), meaning (semantics) and representation (syntax). In this chapter, these designations correspond to the following levels:
  - **Pragmatic:** Expresses the outcome of using the EIS, most likely producing some effects, which will depend on the context in which the EIS is used;
  - **Semantic:** Specifies the meaning of the EIS, using an ontology to describe the underlying concepts;

  - **Syntactic:** Deals with the representation of the EIS, using some appropriate notation or programming language.

All the concreteness levels express a range between two opposite thresholds, also represented in Figure 5:

- **Tacit:** This is the highest level, above which concepts are too complex or too difficult to describe. It encompasses the tacit knowledge and know-how (Oguz & Sengün, 2011) of the designers of the EIS, expressing their insight and implicit expectations and assumptions about the problem domain;
- **Empiric:** The lowest level, below which details are not relevant anymore. The EIS designers just settle for something that already exists and is known to work, such as a standard or a software library.

A method will be needed to exercise the enterprise architecture framework, to navigate from the top-left cell in Figure 5 (conceptual motivations, or purpose) to the bottom-right cell (operation at the syntactic level, or interpretation & execution), with the rightmost column taking care of evaluation to decide whether to loop back for lifecycle evolution. The path taken determines the method to use. The usual approach is to follow the diagonal, more or less, reflecting the fact that advancing in the lifecycle stages also provides further detail because decisions are taken along the way, increasing the concreteness level of the design. However, other approaches are also possible, more breadth-first or more depth-first. This must be done in all concern planes. Deciding which planes to tackle first also leads to method variants. This methodology is outside the scope of this chapter.

A MULTIDIMENSIONAL INTEROPERABILITY FRAMEWORK

The framework described in the previous section details what is involved in the design of an EIS. Now we need to tackle the problem of interoperability between two interacting EIS. These can be deployed in the same cloud, in different clouds or even span several clouds. We consider services implemented by virtual resources, managed by the relevant cloud management APIs. However, bringing more than one cloud into the picture raises a cloud API interoperability problem, and different servers or cloud platforms raise portability issues.

The fundamental issue is to determine the minimum information than one needs to know about the other in order to interact in a meaningful way. This minimizes coupling (so that they can evolve as independently as possible) without hampering interoperability.

A Linearized View of Interoperability

Most interoperability technologies, such as Web Services and RESTful applications, consider only the syntactic format of messages, or at most the semantics of its terms. As Figure 5 shows, the ability to meaningfully interact involves higher levels (upper levels in the Concreteness dimension) and lifecycle stages to the left of Operation. If the Concerns dimension is taken into account, things get even more complex. For example, an interaction may fail due to excessive response times (making timeouts expire), even if functionally the design is correct.

To understand the interoperability aspect completely, we need an interoperability framework. The basic tenet is that it should be well matched to the architecture framework depicted by Figure 5. In particular, an EIS *A* should be able to interact with another *B* if each cell of the three-dimensional space (Figure 5) of EIS *A* satisfies the requirements of the corresponding cell in the three-dimensional space of EIS *B*. This is valid

even in the design stages, before Operation. For example, the motivations of *A* to send a message should match the motivations of *B* to receive it and to honor its purpose.

In practice, most of these interactions between corresponding cells are dealt with *tacitly*, not explicitly. In particular, stages to the left of Operation are usually tackled at the documentation level only. However, they are very relevant, because what happens in the design stages allows us to understand the true capabilities and limitations of interoperability solutions and technologies. Nevertheless, the Operation stage is the most visible, in terms of interoperability.

As any complex issue, interoperability may be considered at various levels of abstraction. Table 1 establishes a linearized classification of interoperability levels, with some correlation with the values in the Concreteness axis of Figure 5.

The interoperability categories in this table (first column) should be interpreted as follows:

- **Symbiotic:** Expresses the purpose and intent of two interacting EIS to engage in a mutually beneficial agreement. This can entail a tight coordination under a common governance (if the EIS are controlled by the same entity), a joint-venture agreement (if the two EIS are substantially aligned), a collaboration involving a partnership agreement (if some goals are shared), or a mere value chain cooperation (an outsourcing contract). Enterprise engineering is usually the topmost level in resource interaction complexity, since it goes up to the human level, with governance and strategy heavily involved. Therefore, it maps mainly onto the symbiotic category, although the same principles apply (in a more rudimentary fashion) to simpler subsystems;
- **Pragmatic:** The effect of an interaction between a consumer and a provider is the outcome of a contract, which is implemented by a choreography that coordinates pro-

Table 1. A linear perspective of interoperability

Category	Level	Main artifact	Description
Symbiotic (purpose and intent)	Coordination	Governance	Motivations to have the interaction, with varying levels of mutual knowledge of governance, strategy and goals
	Alignment	Joint-venture	
	Collaboration	Partnership	
	Cooperation	Outsourcing	
Pragmatic (reaction and effects)	Contract	Choreography	Management of the effects of the interaction at the levels of choreography, process and service
	Workflow	Process	
	Interface	Service	
Semantic (meaning of content)	Inference	Rule base	Interpretation of a message in context, at the levels of rule, known EIS components and relations, and definition of concepts
	Knowledge	Knowledge base	
	Ontology	Concept	
Syntactic (notation of representation)	Structure	Schema	Representation of EIS components, in terms of composition, primitive components and their serialization format in messages
	Predefined type	Primitive resource	
	Serialization	Message format	
Connective (transfer protocol)	Messaging	Message protocol	Lower level formats and network protocols involved in transferring a message from the context of the sender to that of the receiver
	Routing	Gateway	
	Communication	Network protocol	
	Physics	Media protocol	
Environmental (deployment and migration)	Management	API	Cloud environment in which each EIS is deployed and managed, and the portability problems raised
	Library (SaaS)	Utility service	
	Platform (PaaS)	Basic software	
	Computer (IaaS)	Virtual hardware	

cesses, which in turn implement workflow behavior by orchestrating service invocations. Languages such as Business Process Execution Language (BPEL) (Juric & Pant, 2008) support the implementation of processes and Web Services Choreography Description Language (WS-CDL) is an example of a language that allows choreographies to be specified;

- **Semantic:** Both interacting EIS must be able to understand the meaning of the content of the messages exchanged, both requests and responses. This implies interoperability in rules, knowledge, and ontologies, so that meaning is not lost when transferring a message from the context of the sender to that of the receiver. Semantic languages and specifications, such as OWL and RDF, map onto this category;

- **Syntactic:** Deals mainly with form, rather than content. Each message has a structure, composed of data (primitive resources) according to some structural definition (its schema). Data need to be serialized to be sent over the network as messages, using formats such as XML or JSON;

- **Connective:** The main objective is to transfer a message from the context of one EIS to the other's, regardless of its content. This usually involves enclosing that content in another message with control information and implementing a message protocol (such as SOAP or HTTP) over a communications network, according to its own protocol (such as the Transmission Control Protocol/Internet Protocol – TCP/IP) and possibly involving routing gateways;

- **Environmental:** Each EIS also interacts with the environment in which it is deployed (anew or by migration). The cloud's API and the infrastructure level that the EIS requires (existing utility services, software servers, operating system and virtual hardware, including processor types) will most likely have impact on the way EIS interact, particularly if they are deployed in (or migrate between) different clouds, from different cloud vendors. Interoperability between an application and the environment in which it is deployed is usually known as *portability* (Petcu, Macariu, Panica & Crăciun, 2013).

These levels are always present in all EIS interactions, even the simplest ones. There is always a motivation and purpose in sending a message, an effect stemming from the reaction to its reception, a meaning expressed by the message, and a format used to send it over a network under some protocol.

However, what happens in practice is that some of these layers are catered for *tacitly* or *empirically*:

- Portability is mainly dealt with in an *ad hoc* manner and usually under some form of vendor lock-in, particularly at the API level, since cloud standards are still incipient (Lewis, 2012);
- The Connective category is usually dealt with empirically, by assuming some protocol, such as HTTP or SOAP;
- Syntactic is the most used category, because it is the simplest and most familiar, with interfaces that deal mainly with syntax or primitive semantics, with data description languages such as XML and JSON;

- The Semantic category, given the increasing relevance of the Semantic Web (Shadbolt, Hall & Berners-Lee, 2006), is beginning to be explicitly addressed with semantic annotations and languages, based either on XML or JSON, but it is still largely subject to tacit assumptions, for example regarding XML's namespaces or predefined media types;
- The Pragmatic category is usually considered at the documentation level only, with many tacit assumptions, or implemented by software but without formal specification. Choreography specifications and tools to verify them are seldom used;
- The Symbiotic category is considered only with very complex EIS (such as enterprises) and in the conceptual stages of the lifecycle, again at the documentation level only. In most cases, it is simply assumed that, if an EIS exposes a service, it can be invoked regardless of motivations, purpose, or any other high-level concerns.

Another important aspect is non-functional interoperability. It is not just a question of invoking the right operation with the right parameters. Adequate service levels, context awareness, security, and other non-functional issues must be considered when EIS interact, otherwise interoperability will be less effective or not possible at all. The framework of Table 1 must be considered for each plane in Figure 5.

Finally, we must realize that all these interoperability categories constitute an expression of EIS coupling. On the one hand, two uncoupled EIS (with no interactions between them) can evolve freely and independently, which favors adaptability, changeability and even reliability (if one fails, there is no impact on the other). On the other hand, EIS need to interact to cooperate towards common or complementary goals, implying that some degree of previously agreed mutual knowledge is indispensable. The more they share with the other, the more integrated they are and the easier interoperability becomes, but the greater coupling gets.

What the interoperability framework expressed by Table 1 provides is a classification that allows us to understand better the coupling details, namely at what levels they occur and what is involved in each level, instead of having just a blurred dependency notion. In this respect, it constitutes a tool to analyze and to compare different interoperability models and technologies.

Reducing Coupling in Interoperability

Most EIS are made interoperable by design, i.e., conceived and implemented to work together, in a consumer-provider relationship. Web Services are a typical interoperability solution, in which case:

- Schemas are shared between interacting services, establishing coupling for all the possible documents satisfying each schema, even if they are not actually used;
- Searching for an interoperable service is done by schema matching with *similarity* algorithms (Jeong, Lee, Cho & Lee, 2008) and ontology matching and mapping (Euzenat & Shvaiko, 2007). This does not ensure interoperability and manual adaptations are usually unavoidable.

The interoperability concept, as defined in this chapter, introduces a different perspective, stronger than similarity but weaker than commonality (the result of sharing the same schemas and ontologies). The trick is to allow partial (instead of full) interoperability, by considering only the intersection between what the consumer needs and what the provider offers. If the latter subsumes the former, the degree of interoperability required by the consumer is feasible, regardless of whether the provider supports additional features or not. When this is true, the consumer is said to be *compatible* with the provider or, more precisely, that an EIS *A* is compatible with an EIS *B* regarding a consumer-provider relationship.

The main advantages of this are:

- Coupling is limited to the documents that actually contain the used features and not to all possible documents that satisfy the schema (reduced coupling);
- A consumer is more likely to find suitable providers based on a smaller set of features, rather than on a full schema;
- A provider will be able to serve a broader base of consumers, since it will impose less restrictions on them.

Compatibility between a consumer and a provider is known as *compliance* (Kokash & Arbab, 2009). The consumer must satisfy (*comply with*) the requirements established by the provider to accept requests sent to it, without which these cannot be validated, understood and executed.

It is important to note that any consumer that complies with a given provider can use it, independently of having been designed for interaction with it or not. The consumer and provider need not share the same schema. The consumer's schema needs only to be compliant with the provider's schema in the features that it actually uses.

Since EIS have independent lifecycles, they cannot freely share names, and schema compliance must be tested structurally, feature by feature, between messages sent by the consumer and the interface offered by the provider. This is known as *structural compatibility*.

Besides the use relationship between a consumer and a provider, the replacement relationship between two providers is also of relevance. The issue is to ascertain whether a provider *B*, serving a consumer *A*, can be replaced by another provider *Y*, such that the consumer-provider relationship enjoyed by *A* is not impaired. In other words, the issue is whether *Y* is replacement compatible with *B*.

The reasons for replacing a provider by another may be varied, such as switching to an alternative in case of failure or lack of capacity of *B*, evolution of *B* (in which case *Y* would be the new version of *B*), or simply a management decision. The important aspect to note is that, again, *Y* does not need to support all the features of *B*, but just those that *A* actually uses (partial compatibility).

Replacement compatibility between two providers is known as *conformance* (Kim & Shen, 2007; Adriansyah, van Dongen & van der Aalst, 2010). The provider must fulfill the expectations of the consumer regarding the effects of a request (including eventual responses), therefore being able to take the form of (*to conform to*) whatever the consumer expects it to be. Note that a provider may be conformant to another with respect to one consumer but not with respect to another. It all depends on the set of features used by the consumer.

Compliance and conformance are relationship properties that are not symmetric (e.g., if *A* complies with *B*, *B* does not necessarily comply with *A*) but are transitive (e.g., if *A* complies with *B* and *B* complies with *C*, then *A* complies with *C*).

Figure 6 illustrates compliance and conformance. An EIS *A*, in the role of consumer, has been designed to interact with an EIS that includes specification *B*, in the role of provider. *B* includes only the features that *A* requires and corresponds to how *A* views its provider (any other feature is irrelevant to *A*). *A* is fully compliant with *B*, in the sense that it uses only features that *B* provides, in the way that *B* expects, and *B* does not include any additional feature. At some point, *B* is replaced by an EIS *Y*, which has been designed to expect consumers that require no more features than those used by specification *X* (which is how *Y* views its consumers). Can *A* use *Y* as if it were *B*?

This depends on two necessary conditions:

- **Compliance:** *B* must *comply with X*. Since, by design, *A* complies with *B* and *X* complies with *Y*, transitiveness means that *A*

complies with *Y* and can use *Y* as if it were *B*, as it was designed for;
- **Conformance:** *X* must *conform to B*. Since, by design, *Y* conforms to what *X* expects as a provider (and the same about *B* regarding *A*), transitiveness means that *Y* conforms to what *A* expects as a provider *B* and can replace (take the form of) *B* without *A* noticing it.

Merging the Interoperability and Enterprise Architecture Frameworks

Compliance and conformance are general concepts, in terms of satisfying requirements and expectations, respectively, and can be applied to behavior, data, or any other aspect of EIS that interact, at a high level of abstraction or at a low and detailed level, as categorized by Table 1. Wherever there is a relationship, compliance and conformance are present and can explain the degree of interoperability achieved.

Figure 7 expresses this by establishing a compliance and conformance relationship (as described by Table 1 and Figure 6) between two EIS, each described by an instantiation of the enterprise architecture framework. This corresponds to adding another dimension to the framework of Figure 5.

Lower degrees of interoperability can be achieved by relaxing some of these conditions, along each of the axes. This means considering them tacitly, instead of explicitly. For example:

- **Concerns:** Not all concerns are identically relevant. Security may require fulfilling every detail, but other concerns may have fuzzier rules, such as social and cultural issues, or vary dynamically, such as quality of service (in a best effort approach) or financial conditions (with dynamic optimizations);
- **Lifecycle:** The columns Implementation and Evaluation are less relevant to interop-

Figure 6. EIS compatibility, by use (compliance, A complies with B) and replacement (conformance, Y conforms to B)

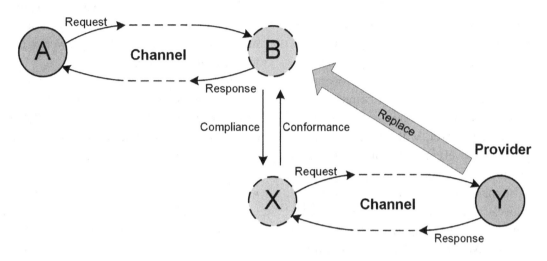

Figure 7. Complete framework, with interoperability axis (plane details omitted for simplicity)

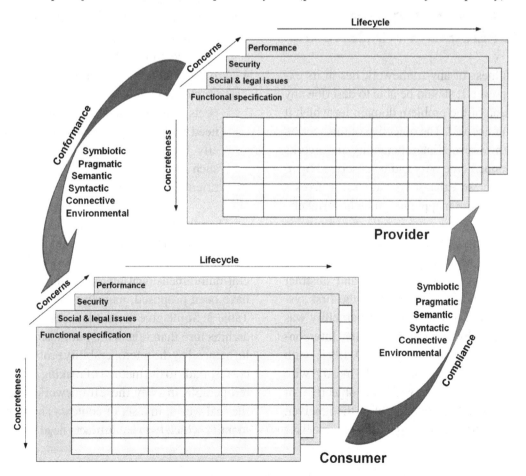

erability than the others, since different implementations can support the same operational specifications, and each interacting EIS can be evaluated separately;

- **Concreteness:** By lowering the Tacit threshold (in Figure 5) and raising the Empiric threshold, we can adjust the levels of concreteness at which interoperability is considered. The most common case in programming is to deal explicitly with the syntactic level, with some incursions into higher levels in some columns (mostly Means and Implementation). Nevertheless, it also makes sense that integration at higher levels and at lower levels uses different technologies, by using APIs that raise the empiric level and hide the details of different implementations.

COMPARISON WITH OTHER INTEROPERABILITY FRAMEWORKS

The usefulness of any framework lies in its expressive power. It should be able to describe any instantiation of the problem domain for which it has been conceived. The objective of this section is to show how several interoperability frameworks can be mapped onto ours and be described by it. Although not an exhaustive exercise, it gives a hint on how these mappings can be undertaken.

We start with the frameworks that express a linear perspective of interoperability, in the line with Table 1, which described several levels of interoperability, from high-level and abstract to low-level and concrete. One of the first systematizations of distributed interoperability was accomplished by the Open Systems Interconnection (OSI) reference model (ISO, 1994), with seven levels. This standard deals mostly with communication issues, with the objective of sending data and reproducing it at the receiver. How these data are interpreted by the receiver

and how it reacts to the data is left unspecified, encompassed by the topmost level, Application. Since interoperability must ensure not only data exchange but also meaningful use of information, this level needs to be detailed. Table 2 describes other linear interoperability frameworks, created to fulfill this purpose.

Table 2 suggests a vertical composition mechanism, in which each level is composed of artifacts in the levels below it. However, the following difficulties arise in these frameworks, caused by the existence of only one dimension:

- Composition alone is not sufficient to describe completely each level in terms of the artifacts in lower levels, particularly in the higher levels (social, cultural, ethical, legal, etc.);
- Not all interoperability levels are dealt with at the same time. Some are more dynamic and pertain to operation time, whereas others are more static and must be dealt with at conception or design time;
- An EIS is not a monolithic artifact with a single facet. It has several slants and aspects, under which interoperability may need differentiated treatment. This is usually the case of non-functional aspects, such as reliability, security, and context-oriented behavior.

These interoperability frameworks are simple but limited, when trying to cater for this diversity and variability. To overcome these problems, several multidimensional interoperability frameworks have been proposed, namely those described in Table 3. Some give more relevance to enterprise architecture than others do, but most are heavily influenced by the interoperability problem, which corresponds to the method of making two EIS interoperable. In a way, these frameworks start from the real world, in a set of contexts and domains, identify which types of artifacts need to be made

Table 2. Comparison between several linear interoperability frameworks (referred to by acronym and/ or first author)

OSI (ISO, 1994)	C4IF (Peristeras, 2006)	Lewis (2008)	Stamper (1996)	LCIM (Wang, 2009)	EIF (2010)	Monfelt (2011)
Application	Collaboration	Organizational	Social world	Conceptual	Political	SWOT
						Cultural
						Ethical
					Legal	Legal
			Pragmatic	Dynamic	Organizational	Managerial
				Pragmatic		Organizational
	Consolidation	Semantic	Semantic	Semantic	Semantic (includes syntactic)	Adaptation
						Application
Presentation	Communication	Syntactic	Syntactic	Syntactic		Presentation
Session						Session
Transport		Machine	Empirics	Technical	Technical	Transport
Network	Connection					Network
Link						Link
Physical Medium			Physical world			Physical Medium

interoperable and conceive an architectural space of dimensions oriented towards the problems to be solved in those contexts and domains.

Our approach is different, guided by the following principles:

- To consider the interoperability a generic system problem, context and domain independent, but contemplating interacting systems of arbitrarily high complexity, such as enterprises;

- To introduce real world contexts and domains as instantiations of the generic interoperability problem, using the provisions of the framework (dimensions, namely Concerns) to solve a given problem;

- To separate the framework (the organization and classification scheme of the various aspects of the enterprises that are relevant to interoperability) from the method (the plan to make two or more

enterprises interoperable). In this chapter we focus on the framework, although the method is briefly mentioned in section "A multidimensional enterprise architecture framework";

- To elect the enterprise architecture as the foundation ground for interoperability, by starting with a set of orthogonal dimensions, as illustrated by Figure 5, with lifecycle stages and levels of concreteness as the main structuring guidelines;

- To organize interoperability as a mapping from one EIS to another, as expressed by Figure 7. In other words, each interoperability issue arises from the need to relate the corresponding issues of two interacting enterprises;

- To separate what is relevant to the interoperability mechanism proper, in a domain independent way (which corresponds to understanding the intent, content and trans-

Table 3. Several multidimensional interoperability frameworks

Framework	Dimensions	Description
SOSI (Morris et al, 2004)	Operational	Issues between existing systems that need to interoperate, such as lack of information and non-intuitive user interfaces
	Programmatic	Interoperability between computer applications and solutions
	Constructive	Architectural issues such as data schema interoperability
AIF, ATHENA Interoperability Framework (Berre *et al*, 2007)	Conceptual	Integration models at the levels of enterprise/business, process, service and information/data
	Application	Methodology with methods to support the development of interoperability projects
	Technical	Implementation basis around technologies such as BPEL, Web Services and XML
FEI, Framework for Enterprise Interoperability (ISO, 2011), based on (Chen, 2006)	Concerns	At the levels of business, processes, services and data
	Barriers	Difficulties in making systems interoperable (conceptual, technological and organizational)
	Approach	Plan to overcome the barriers. Can be organized in three ways: • Integrated (a common format is used by all systems); • Unified (common goals and semantic mapping); • Federated (common goals and ontology are possible, but each system must adapt to others dynamically, without any imposed model).
ULS Interoperability Framework (Ostadzadeh & Fereidoon, 2011)	Abstract	Six classical questions of the Zachman framework (O'Rourke, Fishman & Selkow, 2003), in the interoperability context: what, how, where, who, why, when
	Perspective	Layered interoperability concerns (contextual, conceptual, logical, physical and out-of-context)
	Barriers	Considers the dimensions of SOSI (Operational, Constructive and Programmatic) as barriers and extends them with cultural barriers
ENSEMBLE European Project (Agostinho, Jardim-Goncalves & Steiger-Garcao, 2011)	Domains	Interoperability problem space: social, applied and formal sciences
	Areas	Scientific areas underlying interoperability: data, process, rules, objects, software, cultural, knowledge, services, social networks, electronic identity, cloud and ecosystems
	Elements	Scientific interoperability elements: semantics, models, tools, orchestration

fer mechanism of a message, as well as the reaction of the interlocutor, in the context of a generic transaction), from what is domain specific (such as social, cultural, ethical and legal issues);

• To separate the roles of consumer and provider in an interaction, which discriminates compliance from conformance, instead of considering generic, symmetric relationships;

• To include interoperability issues between and EIS and its deployment platform, namely in terms of portability and cloud API management diversity.

Under these principles, the mapping of the interoperability frameworks of Table 2 in our framework is done essentially in the following way:

• OSI (ISO/IEC, 1994), C4IF (Peristeras & Tarabanis, 2006), Lewis (2008) and LCIM (Wang, Tolk & Wang, 2009) have a straightforward mapping, essentially one-to-one at the lower levels and with our framework detailing the higher levels in these frameworks. In the case of LCIM, the Dynamic level corresponds roughly to the Symbiotic category in Table 1 and the Conceptual level, dealing with documentation, is mapped onto the left side of the Lifecycle-Concreteness plane of our framework, in which the EIS is designed and models and documentation are produced;

- In the framework of Stamper (1996), there is a good mapping to our framework up to the Pragmatics level. The Social world level is mapped onto a plane in the Concerns axis of our framework;
- The political and legal levels in the European Interoperability Framework (EIF, 2010) are also mapped onto planes in the Concerns axis;
- A similar mapping is done in the case of the framework of Monfelt (2011). The Legal, Ethical and Cultural levels are mapped onto planes in the Concerns axis. The SWOT analysis (Strengths, Weaknesses, Opportunities, and Threats) actually belongs to the method, not the framework, and entails performing the analysis in the context of several Concerns planes.

The mapping of the multidimensional frameworks of Table 3 can be done in the following way:

- The SOSI framework (Morris *et al*, 2004) includes the lifecycle dimension, which can be easily mapped onto the Lifecycle dimension in our framework;
- In the ATHENA framework (Berre *et al*, 2007), the conceptual integration, with the levels of enterprise/business, process, service and information/data, has a straightforward mapping onto our interoperability layers, in Table 1. The application and technical integrations, however, involve activities that are best mapped onto the method, not the framework;
- In the framework proposed by Chen (2006), the concerns dimension (business, processes, services, and data) correspond to our interoperability dimension and are mapped onto levels in Table 1. The other

dimensions, the barriers to overcome and the approach taken fit better the method than the framework. Nevertheless, there is an interesting mapping from the types of approach to the higher levels of our interoperability dimension, in Table 1. These types are integrated (a common format is used by all systems), unified (common goals and semantic mapping) and federated (there may be common goals and ontology, but each system must adapt to others dynamically, without any imposed model). These can be mapped onto interoperability profiles and therefore be described by the framework prior to exercising the method;

- The framework of Ostadzadeh & Fereidoon (2011) is based on an enterprise architecture framework, like our own. The Zachman questions map partly onto the Lifecycle stages (Motivations is why, Ends is what, Means is how) and partly onto the Concerns axis (who, where and when). The layered interoperability concerns (contextual, conceptual, logical, physical and out-of-context) map directly onto our interoperability levels in Table 1 and the remaining dimension is identical to SOSI (expressing the lifecycle), with the addition of a cultural aspect, which we map onto a Concerns plane.;
- The project ENSEMBLE (Agostinho, Jardim-Goncalves & Steiger-Garcao, 2011) follows a methodology to establish a scientific base for enterprise interoperability, rather than an interoperability framework. In this respect, the ENSEMBLE's approach is complementary to ours, coming from the opposite direction. Essentially, it adopts a top-down approach by gathering information on the real world domains that pose interoperability problems and then deriving the scientific base to solve them. Our approach, bottom-up, entails establishing a rationale for what interoperability is, as

a universal concept relating entities of any level of complexity and domain, and deriving a generic framework that allows us to structure and to organize the aspects in real world interoperability problems, as a tool that can be a precious aid in solving them.

FUTURE RESEARCH DIRECTIONS

Compliance and conformance are basic concepts in interoperability and can be applied to all domains and levels of abstraction and complexity. Although work exists on its formal treatment in specific areas, such as choreographies (Adriansyah, van Dongen & van der Aalst, 2010), an encompassing study needs to be conducted on what is the exact meaning of compatibility (compliance and conformance) at each of the interoperability levels of Table 1. Their formal definition, across all levels, needs to be made in a systematic way, building on previous work.

Cloud interoperability (Loutas, Kamateri, Bosi & Tarabanis, 2011) is a huge problem with increasingly importance. Cloud providers favor standardization but not homogeneity, since they need differentiation as a marketing argument. A study needs to be carried out on the suitability of compliance and conformance as a partial interoperability solution in cloud computing, namely in concerns cloud management APIs.

The interoperability framework presented in this chapter needs to be improved and made more complete, namely in the Concerns axis, to include relevant concerns such as security and common domain-specific aspects and problems, such as those uncovered by other frameworks and those being systematized by ENSEMBLE (Agostinho, Jardim-Goncalves & Steiger-Garcao, 2011).

The method to exercise the framework needs to be specified and structured in a systematic way, with a comparative case study regarding other interoperability methods being used today, namely those that are part of specifications promoted by

relevant bodies, such as the European Interoperability Framework (EIF, 2010) or standardized, such as the Framework for Enterprise Interoperability (Chen, 2006). As noted above, several multidimensional frameworks include parts of a method, for which currently there is no mapping in our proposal.

CONCLUSION

The world is increasingly both distributed and interconnected. Interoperability is crucial and standards are not enough to ensure cooperation between EIS (Lewis, Morris, Simanta & Wrage, 2008). In the case of cloud computing, standardization is yet to become a reality, with each large cloud provider offering its own cloud management API.

In an attempt to shed light into the problem, providing a classification structure to organize interoperability concerns, several interoperability frameworks have been proposed, both one-dimensional and multidimensional. However, their approaches fall short of providing a truly systematic organization of the problem. Most of the proposals tackle the problem of integrating existing EIS and not the general problem of how to conceive them so that they are prepared for interoperability from the start.

This chapter has presented a generic multidimensional interoperability framework, conceived with the purpose of providing a systematic way to organize and structure the various aspects that interoperability entails, with orthogonality of concepts, domain independence, large-scale complexity and extensibility as the main goals, which have been pursued along the following guidelines:

- **Orthogonality:** By considering multiple dimensions, each for an aspect or concern orthogonal to others, with all combinations valid and, as a whole, able to support a wide spectrum of applications;

- **Domain Independence:** By basing the framework on dimensions with universal applicability (such as lifecycle, level of concreteness and layers of interoperability), with domain dependent aspects as part of a concerns dimension, orthogonal to the others;
- **Large-Scale Complexity:** By contemplating not only recursive system composition (any system is a composition of other systems) and but also very complex aspects, up to the tacit, human level of understanding and reasoning;
- **Extensibility:** By allowing new concern planes and the promotion of a concern to a full dimension, if its relevance and applicability breadth justifies it.

The approach taken is generic and bottom-up, from universal architectural concepts to domain and context dependent concerns, as a complement to the more common approach, application-driven and top-down. For example, the European Interoperability Framework (EIF, 2010) has been conceived specifically for e-Government level services. The advantage of the bottom-up approach is that it leads to an open-ended framework, with a universal core that can then be instantiated and extended at will and as required in each context and domain.

REFERENCES

Adriansyah, A., van Dongen, B., & van der Aalst, W. (2010). Towards robust conformance checking. In M. Muehlen & J. Su (Eds.), *Business Process Management Workshops* (pp. 122–133). Berlin, Germany: Springer.

Aggarwal, C., & Han, J. (2013). A Survey of RFID Data Processing. In C. Aggarwal (Ed.), *Managing and Mining Sensor Data* (pp. 349–382). New York, NY: Springer US. doi:10.1007/978-1-4614-6309-2_11

Agostinho, C., Jardim-Goncalves, R., & Steiger-Garcao, A. (2011). Using neighboring domains towards setting the foundations for Enterprise Interoperability science. In Callaos, N. et al. (Eds.) *International Symposium on Collaborative Enterprises in the Context of the 15th World-Multi-Conference on Systemic, Cybernetics and Informatics* (pp. 258-264, vol. II). Winter Garden, FL: International Institute of Informatics and Systemics.

Anderson, E., ... (2014, March 31). *Forecast: Public Cloud Services, Worldwide, 2012-2018, 1Q14 Update. Document ref. G00263153*. Stamford, CT: Gartner. Retrieved May 31, 2014 from https://www.gartner.com/doc/2696318

Anderson, E., ... (2014, May 13). *Forecast Analysis: Public Cloud Services, Worldwide, 1Q14 Update. Document ref. G00261940*. Stamford, CT: Gartner. Retrieved May 31, 2014 from https://www.gartner.com/doc/2738817/forecast-analysis-public-cloud-services

Armbrust, M., Stoica, I., Zaharia, M., Fox, A., Griffith, R., Joseph, A. D., & Rabkin, A. et al. (2010). A View of Cloud Computing. *Communications of the ACM, 53*(4), 50–58. doi:10.1145/1721654.1721672

Athanasopoulos, G., Tsalgatidou, A., & Pantazoglou, M. (2006). Interoperability among Heterogeneous Services, in *International Conference on Services Computing* (pp. 174-181). Piscataway, NJ: IEEE Computer Society Press.

Berre, A. et al.. (2007). The ATHENA Interoperability Framework. In R. Gonçalves, J. Müller, K. Mertins, & M. Zelm (Eds.), *Enterprise Interoperability II* (pp. 569–580). London, UK: Springer. doi:10.1007/978-1-84628-858-6_62

Binz, T., Breiter, G., Leyman, F., & Spatzier, T. (2012). Portable cloud services using Tosca. *IEEE Internet Computing*, *16*(3), 80–85. doi:10.1109/MIC.2012.43

Bist, M., Wariya, M., & Agarwal, A. (2013). Comparing delta, open stack and Xen Cloud Platforms: A survey on open source IaaS. In KalraB. GargD.PrasadR.KumarS. (Eds.) *3rd International Advance Computing Conference* (pp. 96-100). Piscataway, NJ: IEEE Computer Society Press. doi:10.1109/IAdCC.2013.6514201

Brynjolfsson, E., Hofmann, P., & Jordan, J. (2010). Cloud computing and electricity: Beyond the utility model. *Communications of the ACM*, *53*(5), 32–34. doi:10.1145/1735223.1735234

Camarinha-Matos, L., Afsarmanesh, H., Garita, C., & Lima, C. (1999). Hierarchical Coordination in Virtual Enterprise Infrastructures. *Journal of Intelligent & Robotic Systems*, *26*(3/4), 267–287. doi:10.1023/A:1008137110347

Carr, N. (2004). *Does IT matter?: information technology and the corrosion of competitive advantage*. Boston, MA: Harvard Business Press.

Chandler, D. (2007). *Semiotics: the basics*. New York, NY: Routledge.

Chen, D. (2006). Enterprise interoperability framework. In MissikoffM.De NicolaA.D'AntonioF. (Eds.) *Open Interop Workshop on Enterprise Modelling and Ontologies for Interoperability*. Berlin, Germany: Springer-Verlag.

Chen, D., Doumeingts, G., & Vernadat, F. (2008). Architectures for enterprise integration and interoperability: Past, present and future. *Computers in Industry*, *59*(7), 647–659. doi:10.1016/j.compind.2007.12.016

Demchenko, Y., Makkes, M., Strijkers, R., & de Laat, C. (2012). Intercloud Architecture for interoperability and integration. In *4th International Conference on Cloud Computing Technology and Science* (pp.666-674). Piscataway, NJ: IEEE Computer Society Press. doi:10.1109/CloudCom.2012.6427607

DTMF. (2012). *Open Virtualization Format Specification*. Document Number: DSP0243, version 2.0.0. Portland, OR: Distributed Management Task Force, Inc. Retrieved May 30, 2014 from http://www.dmtf.org/sites/default/files/standards/documents/DSP0243_2.0.0.pdf

DTMF. (2013). *Cloud Infrastructure Management Interface (CIMI) Model and REST Interface over HTTP Specification*. Document Number: DSP0263, version 1.1.0. Portland, OR: Distributed Management Task Force, Inc. Retrieved May 30, 2014 from http://www.dmtf.org/sites/default/files/standards/documents/DSP0263_1.1.0.pdf

Edmonds, A., Metsch, T., & Papaspyrou, A. (2011). Open Cloud Computing Interface in Data Management-Related Setups. In S. Fiore & G. Aloisio (Eds.), *Grid and Cloud Database Management* (pp. 23–48). Berlin, Germany: Springer. doi:10.1007/978-3-642-20045-8_2

EIF. (2010). *European Interoperability Framework (EIF) for European Public Services, Annex 2 to the Communication from the Commission to the European Parliament, the Council, the European Economic and Social Committee and the Committee of Regions 'Towards interoperability for European public services*. Retrieved May 30, 2014 from http://ec.europa.eu/isa/documents/isa_annex_ii_eif_en.pdf

El Raheb, K. et al.. (2011). Paving the Way for Interoperability in Digital Libraries: The DL.org Project. In A. Katsirikou & C. Skiadas (Eds.), *New Trends in Qualitive and Quantitative Methods in Libraries* (pp. 345–352). Singapore: World Scientific Publishing Company.

Erl, T. (2008). *SOA: Principles of Service Design.* Upper Saddle River, NJ: Prentice Hall PTR.

Esposito, E., & Evangelista, P. (2014). Investigating virtual enterprise models: Literature review and empirical findings. *International Journal of Production Economics*, *148*, 145–157. doi:10.1016/j.ijpe.2013.10.003

Euzenat, J., & Shvaiko, P. (2007). *Ontology matching.* Berlin, Germany: Springer.

Fadel, A., & Fayoumi, A. (2013). Cloud Resource Provisioning and Bursting Approaches. In Takahashi S. Lee R. (Eds.) *14th ACIS International Conference on Software Engineering, Artificial Intelligence, Networking and Parallel/Distributed Computing* (pp. 59-64). Piscataway, NJ: IEEE Computer Society Press.

Fernando, N., Loke, S., & Rahayu, W. (2013). Mobile cloud computing: A survey. *Future Generation Computer Systems*, *29*(1), 84–106. doi:10.1016/j.future.2012.05.023

Fielding, R. (2000). *Architectural Styles and the Design of Network-based Software Architectures.* Doctoral dissertation. University of California at Irvine, CA.

Ganguly, A., Nilchiani, R., & Farr, J. (2009). Evaluating agility in corporate enterprises. *International Journal of Production Economics*, *118*(2), 410–423. doi:10.1016/j.ijpe.2008.12.009

Géczy, P., Izumi, N., & Hasida, K. (2012). Cloudsourcing: Managing Cloud Adoption. *Global Journal of Business Research*, *6*(2), 57–70.

Gottschalk, P., & Solli-Sæther, H. (2008). Stages of e-government interoperability. *Electronic Government. International Journal (Toronto, Ont.)*, *5*(3), 310–320.

Grefen, P., Mehandjiev, N., Kouvas, G., Weichhart, G., & Eshuis, R. (2009). Dynamic business network process management in instant virtual enterprises. *Computers in Industry*, *60*(2), 86–103. doi:10.1016/j.compind.2008.06.006

Heraclitus., & Patrick, G. (Eds.). (2013) The Fragments of Heraclitus. New York, NY: Digireads.com Publishing.

Imache, R., Izza, S., & Ahmed-Nacer, M. (2012). An enterprise information system agility assessment model. *Computer science and information systems*, *9*(1), 107-133.

ISO. (2011). *CEN EN/ISO 11354-1, Advanced Automation Technologies and their Applications, Part 1: Framework for Enterprise Interoperability.* Geneva, Switzerland: International Standards Office.

ISO/IEC. (1994). *ISO/IEC 7498-1, Information technology – Open Systems Interconnection – Basic Reference Model: The Basic Model, 2nd edition.* Geneva, Switzerland: International Standards Office. Retrieved May 31, 2014 from http://standards.iso.org/ittf/PubliclyAvailableStandards/index.html

ISO/IEC. (2012). *Information technology -- Cloud Data Management Interface (CDMI). ISO/IEC Standard 17826:2012.* Geneva, Switzerland: International Organization for Standardization.

Jackson, K. (2012). *OpenStack Cloud Computing Cookbook.* Birmingham, UK: Packt Publishing Ltd.

Jardim-Goncalves, R., Agostinho, C., & Steiger-Garcao, A. (2012). A reference model for sustainable interoperability in networked enterprises: Towards the foundation of EI science base. *International Journal of Computer Integrated Manufacturing*, 25(10), 855–873. doi:10.1080/0 951192X.2011.653831

Jardim-Goncalves, R., Grilo, A., Agostinho, C., Lampathaki, F., & Charalabidis, Y. (2013). Systematisation of interoperability body of knowledge: The foundation for enterprise interoperability as a science. *Enterprise Information Systems*, 7(1), 7–32. doi:10.1080/17517575.2012.684401

Jeong, B., Lee, D., Cho, H., & Lee, J. (2008). A novel method for measuring semantic similarity for XML schema matching. *Expert Systems with Applications*, 34(3), 1651–1658. doi:10.1016/j. eswa.2007.01.025

Juric, M., & Pant, K. (2008). *Business Process Driven SOA using BPMN and BPEL: From Business Process Modeling to Orchestration and Service Oriented Architecture*. Birmingham, UK: Packt Publishing.

Khadka, R., ... (2011). Model-Driven Development of Service Compositions for Enterprise Interoperability. In van Sinderen, M., & Johnson, P. (Eds.), Enterprise Interoperability (pp. 177-190). Berlin, Germany: Springer-Verlag. doi:10.1007/978-3-642-19680-5_15

Kim, D., & Shen, W. (2007). An Approach to Evaluating Structural Pattern Conformance of UML Models. In *ACM Symposium on Applied Computing* (pp. 1404-1408). New York, NY: ACM Press. doi:10.1145/1244002.1244305

Kokash, N., & Arbab, F. (2009). Formal Behavioral Modeling and Compliance Analysis for Service-Oriented Systems. In F. Boer, M. Bonsangue, & E. Madelaine (Eds.), *Formal Methods for Components and Objects* (pp. 21–41). Berlin, Germany: Springer-Verlag. doi:10.1007/978-3-642-04167-9_2

Kruchten, P. (2004). *The rational unified process: an introduction*. Boston, MA: Pearson Education Inc.

Lewis, G. (2012). The Role of Standards in Cloud-Computing Interoperability, *Software Engineering Institute*, Paper 682. Retrieved May 30, 2014 from http://repository.cmu.edu/sei/682

Lewis, G., Morris, E., Simanta, S., & Wrage, L. (2008). Why Standards Are Not Enough To Guarantee End-to-End Interoperability. In NcubeC. CarvalloJ. (Eds.) *Seventh International Conference on Composition-Based Software Systems* (pp. 164-173). Piscataway, NJ: IEEE Computer Society Press. doi:10.1109/ICCBSS.2008.25

Loutas, N., Kamateri, E., Bosi, F., & Tarabanis, K. (2011). Cloud computing interoperability: the state of play. In LambrinoudakisC.RizomiliotisP. WlodarczykT. (Eds.) *International Conference on Cloud Computing Technology and Science* (pp. 752-757). Piscataway, NJ: IEEE Computer Society Press. doi:10.1109/CloudCom.2011.116

Loutas, N., Peristeras, V., & Tarabanis, K. (2011). Towards a reference service model for the Web of Services. *Data & Knowledge Engineering*, 70(9), 753–774. doi:10.1016/j.datak.2011.05.001

Malik, N. (2009). Toward an Enterprise Business Motivation Model. *The Architecture Journal*, 19, 10–16.

Mell, P., & Grance, T. (2011). The NIST definition of cloud computing. Special publication 800-145, *National Institute of Standards and Technology*. Retrieved May 30, 2014 from http://csrc.nist.gov/publications/nistpubs/800-145/SP800-145.pdf

Monfelt, Y., Pilemalm, S., Hallberg, J., & Yngström, L. (2011). The 14-layered framework for including social and organizational aspects in security management. *Information Management & Computer Security*, *19*(2), 124–133. doi:10.1108/09685221111143060

Morris, E., ... (2004). *System of Systems Interoperability (SOSI): final report. Report No. CMU/SEI-2004-TR-004*. Carnegie Mellon Software Engineering Institute. Retrieved May 31, 2014 from http://www.sei.cmu.edu/reports/04tr004.pdf

Mykkänen, J., & Tuomainen, M. (2008). An evaluation and selection framework for interoperability standards. *Information and Software Technology*, *50*(3), 176–197. doi:10.1016/j.infsof.2006.12.001

Nurmi, D. et al.. (2009). The eucalyptus open-source cloud-computing system. In CappelloF. WangC.BuyyaR. (Eds.) *9th IEEE/ACM International Symposium on Cluster Computing and the Grid* (pp. 124-131). Piscataway, NJ: IEEE Computer Society Press.

O'Rourke, C., Fishman, N., & Selkow, W. (2003). *Enterprise architecture using the Zachman framework*. Boston, MA: Course Technology.

Oguz, F., & Sengün, A. (2011). Mystery of the unknown: Revisiting tacit knowledge in the organizational literature. *Journal of Knowledge Management*, *15*(3), 445–461. doi:10.1108/13673271111137420

Ostadzadeh, S., & Fereidoon, S. (2011). An Architectural Framework for the Improvement of the Ultra-Large-Scale Systems Interoperability. In ArabniaH.RezaH.DeligiannidisL. (Eds.) *International Conference on Software Engineering Research and Practice* (pp. 212-219). Athens, GA: CSREA Press.

Pautasso, C., Zimmermann, O., & Leymann, F. (2008). Restful web services vs. "big'" web services: making the right architectural decision. In *International conference on World Wide Web* (pp. 805-814). ACM Press.

Peristeras, V., & Tarabanis, K. (2006). The Connection, Communication, Consolidation, Collaboration Interoperability Framework (C4IF) For Information Systems Interoperability. *International Journal of Interoperability in Business Information Systems*, *1*(1), 61–72.

Petcu, D. (2013). Multi-Cloud: expectations and current approaches. In *International Workshop on Multi-cloud Applications and Federated Clouds* (pp. 1-6). New York, NY: ACM Press. doi:10.1145/2462326.2462328

Petcu, D., Macariu, G., Panica, S., & Crăciun, C. (2013). Portable cloud applications—from theory to practice. *Future Generation Computer Systems*, *29*(6), 1417–1430. doi:10.1016/j.future.2012.01.009

Petrie, C., & Bussler, C. (2003). Service agents and virtual enterprises: A survey. *Internet Computing*, *7*(4), 68–78. doi:10.1109/MIC.2003.1215662

Potdar, V., Sharif, A., & Chang, E. (2009). Wireless sensor networks: A survey. In AwanI.YounasM. HaraT.DurresiA. (Eds.) *International Conference on Advanced Information Networking and Applications Workshops* (pp. 636-641). Piscataway, NJ: IEEE Computer Society Press. doi:10.1109/WAINA.2009.192

Putnik, G., & Sluga, A. (2007). Reconfigurability of manufacturing systems for agility implementation, part I: requirements and principles. In Cunha, P., & Maropoulos, P. (Eds.), Digital Enterprise Technology: Perspectives and Future Challenges (pp. 91-98). New York, NY: Springer Science+Business Media.

Rimal, B., Choi, E., & Lumb, I. (2009). A taxonomy and survey of cloud computing systems. In KimJ. (Eds.) *Fifth International Joint Conference on INC, IMS and IDC* (pp. 44-51). Piscataway, NJ: IEEE Computer Society Press. doi:10.1109/NCM.2009.218

Sabharwal, N., & Shankar, R. (2013). *Apache Cloudstack Cloud Computing*. Birmingham, UK: Packt Publishing Ltd.

Shadbolt, N., Hall, W., & Berners-Lee, T. (2006). The semantic web revisited. *IEEE Intelligent Systems*, *21*(3), 96–101. doi:10.1109/MIS.2006.62

Stamper, R. (1996). Signs, Information, Norms and Systems. In Holmqvist, B., Andersen, P., Klein, H. and Posner, R. (Eds.), Signs of Work (pp. 349–397). Berlin, Germany: de Gruyter.

Wang, W., Tolk, A., & Wang, W. (2009). The levels of conceptual interoperability model: Applying systems engineering principles to M&S. In Wainer, G., Shaffer, C., McGraw, R. & Chinni, M. (Eds.), *Spring Simulation Multiconference* (article no.: 168). San Diego, CA: Society for Computer Simulation International.

Webber, J., Parastatidis, S., & Robinson, I. (2010). *REST in Practice: Hypermedia and Systems Architecture*. Sebastopol, CA: O'Reilly Media, Inc. doi:10.1007/978-3-642-15114-9_3

Weber-Jahnke, J., Peyton, L., & Topaloglou, T. (2012). eHealth system interoperability. *Information Systems Frontiers*, *14*(1), 1–3. doi:10.1007/s10796-011-9319-8

Wyatt, E., Griendling, K., & Mavris, D. (2012). Addressing interoperability in military systems-of-systems architectures. In BeaulieuA. (Ed.) *International Systems Conference* (pp. 1-8). Piscataway, NJ: IEEE Computer Society Press.

Zhang, Q., Cheng, L., & Boutaba, R. (2010). Cloud computing: State-of-the-art and research challenges. *Journal of Internet Services and Applications*, *1*(1), 7–18. doi:10.1007/s13174-010-0007-6

ADDITIONAL READING

Adamczyk, P., Smith, P., Johnson, R., & Hafiz, M. (2011). REST and Web services: In theory and in practice. In E. Wilde & C. Pautasso (Eds.), *REST: from research to practice* (pp. 35–57). New York, NY: Springer. doi:10.1007/978-1-4419-8303-9_2

Amundsen, M. (2012, April). From APIs to affordances: a new paradigm for web services. In *Proceedings of the Third International Workshop on RESTful Design* (pp. 53-60). ACM Press. doi:10.1145/2307819.2307832

Bravetti, M., & Zavattaro, G. (2007). Towards a unifying theory for choreography conformance and contract compliance. In LumpeM. Vanderperren W. (Eds.) *6th International Symposium on Software Composition* (pp. 34-50). Berlin, Germany: Springer. doi:10.1007/978-3-540-77351-1_4

Bravetti, M., & Zavattaro, G. (2009). A theory of contracts for strong service compliance. *Journal of Mathematical Structures in Computer Science*, *19*(3), 601–638. doi:10.1017/S0960129509007658

Castillo, P. et al.. (2013). Using SOAP and REST web services as communication protocol for distributed evolutionary computation. *International Journal of Computers & Technology*, *10*(6), 1659–1677.

Diaz, G., & Rodriguez, I. (2009). Automatically deriving choreography-conforming systems of services. In *IEEE International Conference on Services Computing* (pp. 9-16). Piscataway, NJ: IEEE Computer Society Press.

Dillon, T., Wu, C., & Chang, E. (2007). Reference architectural styles for service-oriented computing. In LiK. (Eds.) *IFIP International Conference on Network and parallel computing* (pp. 543–555). Berlin, Germany: Springer-Verlag. doi:10.1007/978-3-540-74784-0_57

Ehrig, M. (2007). Ontology alignment: bridging the semantic gap (Vol. 4). New York, NY: Springer Science+Business Media, LLC.

Erl, T. (2005). *Service-oriented architecture: concepts, technology and design.* Upper Saddle River, NJ: Pearson Education.

Erl, T., Balasubramanians, R., Pautasso, C., & Carlyle, B. (2011). *Soa with rest: Principles, Patterns & Constraints for Building Enterprise Solutions with REST.* Upper Saddle River, NJ: Prentice Hall PTR.

Fielding, R. (2008). REST APIs must be hypertext-driven. *Roy Fielding's blog: Untangled.* Retrieved May 30, 2014 from http://roy.gbiv.com/untangled/2008/rest-apis-must-be-hypertext-driven

Fielding, R., & Taylor, R. (2002). Principled Design of the Modern Web Architecture. *ACM Transactions on Internet Technology, 2*(2), 115–150. doi:10.1145/514183.514185

Gray, N. (2004). Comparison of Web Services, Java-RMI, and CORBA service implementations. In SchneiderJ.HanJ. (Eds.) *The Fifth Australasian Workshop on Software and System Architectures* (pp. 52-63). Melbourne, Australia: Swinburne University of Technology.

Graydon, P., Habli, I., Hawkins, R., Kelly, T., & Knight, J. (2012). Arguing Conformance. *IEEE Software, 29*(3), 50–57. doi:10.1109/MS.2012.26

Greefhorst, D., & Proper, E. (2011). *Architecture principles: the cornerstones of enterprise architecture.* Berlin, Germany: Springer-Verlag. doi:10.1007/978-3-642-20279-7

Haslhofer, B., & Klas, W. (2010). A survey of techniques for achieving metadata interoperability. *ACM Computing Surveys, 42*(2), 1–37.

Henkel, M., Zdravkovic, J., & Johannesson, P. (2004). Service-based Processes–Design for Business and Technology. In *International Conference on Service Oriented Computing* (pp. 21-29). New York, NY: ACM Press.

ISO/IEC/IEEE. (2010). *Systems and software engineering – Vocabulary. International Standard ISO/IEC/IEEE 24765:2010(E)* (1st ed., p. 186). Geneva, Switzerland: International Organization for Standardization.

Jardim-Goncalves, R., Grilo, A., Agostinho, C., Lampathaki, F., & Charalabidis, Y. (2013). Systematisation of Interoperability Body of Knowledge: The foundation for Enterprise Interoperability as a science. *Enterprise Information Systems, 7*(1), 7–32. doi:10.1080/17517575.2012.684401

Jardim-Goncalves, R., Popplewell, K., & Grilo, A. (2012). Sustainable interoperability: The future of Internet based industrial enterprises. *Computers in Industry, 63*(8), 731–738. doi:10.1016/j.compind.2012.08.016

Laitkorpi, M., Selonen, P., & Systa, T. (2009). Towards a Model-Driven Process for Designing ReSTful Web Services. In *International Conference on Web Services* (pp. 173-180). Piscataway, NJ: IEEE Computer Society Press. doi:10.1109/ICWS.2009.63

Läufer, K., Baumgartner, G., & Russo, V. (2000). Safe Structural Conformance for Java. [Oxford, UK: Oxford University Press.]. *The Computer Journal*, *43*(6), 469–481. doi:10.1093/comjnl/43.6.469

Li, L., & Chou, W. (2010). Design Patterns for RESTful Communication. In *International Conference on Web Services* (pp. 512-519). Piscataway, NJ: IEEE Computer Society Press.

Li, W., & Svard, P. (2010). REST-based SOA Application in the Cloud: A Text Correction Service Case Study. In *6th World Congress on Services* (pp. 84-90). Piscataway, NJ: IEEE Computer Society Press. doi:10.1109/SERVICES.2010.86

Loreto, S., & Romano, S. (2012). Real-time communications in the web: Issues, achievements, and ongoing standardization efforts. *IEEE Internet Computing*, *16*(5), 68–73. doi:10.1109/MIC.2012.115

Mooij, A., & Voorhoeve, M. (2013). Specification and Generation of Adapters for System Integration. In van de Laar, P., Tretmans, J. & Borth, M. (Eds.) Situation Awareness with Systems of Systems (pp. 173-187). New York, NY: Springer. doi:10.1007/978-1-4614-6230-9_11

Ostadzadeh, S., & Fereidoon, S. (2011). An Architectural Framework for the Improvement of the Ultra-Large-Scale Systems Interoperability. In *International Conference on Software Engineering Research and Practice*. Las Vegas, NV.

Pautasso, C. (2009). RESTful Web service composition with BPEL for REST. *Data & Knowledge Engineering*, *68*(9), 851–866. doi:10.1016/j.datak.2009.02.016

Popplewell, K. (2011). Towards the definition of a science base for enterprise interoperability: A European perspective. *Journal of Systemics, Cybernetics, and Informatics*, *9*(5), 6–11.

Severance, C. (2012). Discovering JavaScript Object Notation. *IEEE Computer*, *45*(4), 6–8. doi:10.1109/MC.2012.132

Shadbolt, N., Hall, W., & Berners-Lee, T. (2006). The semantic web revisited. *IEEE Intelligent Systems*, *21*(3), 96–101. doi:10.1109/MIS.2006.62

Sheth, A., Gomadam, K., & Lathem, J. (2007). SA-REST: Semantically interoperable and easier-to-use services and mashups. *IEEE Internet Computing*, *11*(6), 91–94. doi:10.1109/MIC.2007.133

Upadhyaya, B., Zou, Y., Xiao, H., Ng, J., & Lau, A. (2011). Migration of SOAP-based services to RESTful services. In *13th IEEE International Symposium on Web Systems Evolution* (pp. 105-114). Piscataway, NJ: IEEE Computer Society Press. doi:10.1109/WSE.2011.6081828

Uram, M., & Stephenson, B. (2005). Services are the Language and Building Blocks of an Agile Enterprise. In N. Pal & D. Pantaleo (Eds.), *The Agile Enterprise* (pp. 49–86). New York, NY: Springer. doi:10.1007/0-387-25078-6_4

Villegas, D. et al.. (2010). The role of grid computing technologies in cloud computing. In B. Furht & A. Escalante (Eds.), *Handbook of Cloud Computing* (pp. 183–218). New York, NY: Springer US. doi:10.1007/978-1-4419-6524-0_8

KEY TERMS AND DEFINITIONS

Compliance: Asymmetric property between a consumer *C* and a provider *P* (*C* is compliant with *P*) that indicates that *C* satisfies all the requirements of *P* in terms of accepting requests.

Conformance: Asymmetric property between a provider *P* and a consumer *C* (*P* conforms to *C*) that indicates that *P* fulfills all the expectations of *C* in terms of the effects caused by its requests.

Consumer: A role performed by a resource A in an interaction with another B, which involves making a request to B and typically waiting for a response.

Distributed Interoperability: Interoperability between systems that have independent lifecycles. This means that they can evolve (to a new version) without having to change, to suspend or to stop the behavior or interface of the other. Distribution does not necessarily imply geographical dispersion.

Enterprise Architecture Framework: Set of guidelines, best practices, and tools to analyze, to classify, to structure and to describe the architecture of an enterprise.

Interoperability Framework: Set of principles, assumptions, rules, and guidelines to analyze, to structure and to classify the concepts and concerns of interoperability.

Interoperability Method: Set of steps to be taken to derive an interoperable enterprise architecture from an initial problem statement or from an already existing enterprise. This is used typically in conjunction with an interoperability framework.

Interoperability: Asymmetric property between a consumer C and a provider P (C is compatible with P) that holds if C is compliant with P and P is conformant to C.

Lifecycle: Set of stages that a system goes through, starting with a motivation to build it and ending with its destruction. Different versions of a system result from iterations of these stages, in which the system loops back to an earlier stage so that changes can be made.

Provider: A role performed by a resource B in an interaction with another A, which involves waiting for a request from A, honoring it and typically sending a response to A.

Chapter 3
Design Considerations for a Corporate Cloud Service Catalog

R. Todd Stephens
AT&T, USA

ABSTRACT

This chapter will focus on building an end user service cloud catalog which will bridge the gap from the design requirements to the technology delivery organization. Once in the hands of IT, a more traditional service catalog can be used to leverage the service orchestration and delivery components. The author examines designing, building, and reviewing the impact of a more end user focused service catalog. Success will be measured by reviewing the business metrics in order to show the criticality of great design techniques and using familiar models like e-commerce.

ORGANIZATION BACKGROUND

AT&T Inc., together with its subsidiaries, provides telecommunications services to consumers, businesses, and other providers worldwide. The company's Wireless segment offers wireless voice and data communication services, such as local wireless communications services, long-distance services, and roaming services. This segment also sells various handsets, wirelessly enabled computers, and personal computer wireless data cards; and accessories, including carrying cases, hands-free devices, batteries, battery chargers, and other items. This segment sells its products through its own stores, or through agents or third-party retail stores. Its Wireline segment provides data services comprising switched and dedicated transport, Internet access and network integration, U-verse services, and data equipment; businesses voice applications over IP-based networks; and digital subscriber lines, dial-up Internet access, private lines, managed Web-hosting services, packet services, enterprise networking services, and Wi-Fi services, as well as local, interstate, and international wholesale networking capacity to other service providers. This segment also offers voice services, such as local and long-distance, calling card, 1-800, conference calling, whole-sale switched access, caller ID, call waiting, and voice mail services; and application management,

DOI: 10.4018/978-1-4666-8339-6.ch003

security services, integration services, customer premises equipment, outsourcing, government-related services, and satellite video services. The company was formerly known as SBC Communications Inc. and changed its name to AT&T Inc. in November 2005. AT&T Inc. was founded in 1983 and is headquartered in Dallas, Texas.

BACKGROUND INFORMATION

The background section is going to take a look at several different areas of the technology spectrum as they relate to this research chapter. We will begin by taking a look at basics of cloud computing and the impact this technology is having on the businesses. Next, the chapter will review a few of the usability frameworks and design considerations that can impact the utility of the application itself. Finally, we will review the traditional cloud service registry and the basic functional requirements needed by large organizations.

Cloud Computing Overview

In many ways, cloud computing offers up an alternative to the infrastructure ownership paradigm that is so prevalent today. Business and Information Technology organizations assumed they needed dedicated computers and software for their business needs. Over time this methodology creates infrastructure that has a lower utilization rate and limits the flexibility that is needed in today's rapidly changing environment. Cloud computing comes into focus only when you think about the core business drivers within Information Technology today. Some of these requirements include ways to increase capacity or add capabilities on the fly without investing in new infrastructure, training new personnel, or licensing new software. Cloud computing encompasses any subscription-based or pay-per-use service.

The service models of Infrastructure as a Service (IaaS), Platform as a Service (PaaS) and Software as a Service (SaaS) have generally become well accepted, as well as the notions of public, private and hybrid clouds. Some authors have suggested a further division of IaaS to include Hardware as a Service (Haas), Data as a Service (DaaS) and Communication as a Service (CaaS). (Butrico, M., Silva, D., & Youseff, 2008). SaaS may be the most common Cloud technology that you have used in the past. Take for example, Turbo Tax that runs in the cloud and you simply interact with the software via your computer. Nothing is actually stored on your computer and you can access the information from any device. PaaS is a little more complicated since it focuses its attention on the development of applications. Salesforce.com is an example of a company providing PaaS where you can develop applications on their platform that interact with the core Salesforce application and data. Here, the cloud service is a development platform. The final area is IaaS in which the infrastructure for your application is a cloud utility. By infrastructure, we mean databases, servers, power, and network equipment is provided for you for a utility fee. You have no long term commitment and you can simply pay for the computing service based on your usage. For instance, a cloud provider might also host its own customer-facing services on cloud infrastructure. From a hardware provisioning and pricing point of view, three aspects are new in cloud computing. The appearance of infinite computing resources available on demand, quickly enough to follow load surges, thereby eliminating the need for cloud computing users to plan far ahead for provisioning. The elimination of an up-front commitment by cloud users, thereby allowing companies to start small and increase hardware resources only when there is an increase in their needs (Armbrust, Fox, Griffith, Joseph, Katz, Konwinski, Lee, Patterson, Rabkin, Stoica, & Zaharia, 2010.)

Like any emerging paradigm of information technology, cloud computing present several research challenges that need to be addressed. While the literature reporting research challenges in cloud computing is growing quite fast, there has not been much attention paid to identify and report software engineering related challenges for designing, developing, and deploying solutions for cloud computing. We have observed that while several dozens of cloud based services are being offered, the landscape is still fragmented and there are no comprehensive guidelines for designing, developing and deploying solutions to leveraging cloud computing. Moreover, we have also observed that there is hardly any guidance available for migrating existing systems to cloud computing in terms of software engineering aspects (Babat & Chauhan, 2011).

Usability and Design Standards

The idea of usability as a key theme in the Human-Computer Interaction (HCI) literature is not new. Research in this area has been reviewed for several decades now. The basic idea is that study of human factors is a critical component in all software applications. The main goal of HCI is to propose and review techniques, methods, and guidelines associated with designing better and more usable interfaces. Research of web site usability, application usability, and now mobile interfaces all share a common goal which is to provide a better end user experience. Some research focuses on the existence or non-existence of specific functional components. Other research reviews the environment based on the emotions of the end user as well as the ability to provide a positive or negative experience. This chapter is going to focus time and energy on the functional and design elements of a web application.

The goal of this chapter is to ask the question does usability have an impact on a cloud registry environment. Can you apply usability principles to a cloud registry environment and see an improvement in end user engagement? First, we need to define what usability actually is or is not. The importance of usability is well documented. Lecerof and Paterno (1998) defined usability to include

the concepts of relevance, efficiency, user attitude, learnability, and safety. The ISO organization defines usability as the extent to which a product can be used by specified users to achieve goals with effectiveness, efficiency, and satisfaction within a pattern of contextual use (Karat, 1997). Usability is the broad discipline of applying sound scientific observation, measurement, and design principles to the creation and maintenance of web applications in order to bring about the greatest ease of use, ease of learnability, amount of usefulness, and least amount of discomfort for the humans who use the application (Pearrow, 2000). All of these definitions focus on the ability of the user to leverage the application for value creation.

There are various schools of thought on which design elements make a successful web site. Scanlon, Schroeder, Snyder, and Spool (1998) collected qualitative and quantitative data on key design factors, which included: searching, content, text links, images, links navigation, page layout, readability, graphics, and user's knowledge. Each of these design elements makes an important contribution to a successful website. Websites are built to provide information or sell a product or service. Experts indicate that usability is about making sure that the average person can use the site as intended. Well-chosen names, layout of the page, text, graphics, and navigation structure should all come together to create instantaneous recognition (Krug, 2000). Becker and Mottay (2001) developed a usability assessment model used to measure a user's experience within a web environment. The authors defined eight usability factors, which included page layout, navigation, design consistency, information content, performance, customer service, reliability, and security. Usability and design can play an important role within the electronic commerce market. Design consistency has been defined as the key to usability (Nielsen, 1998). Karvonen (2000) reported that experienced users admitted to making intuitive and emotional decisions when shopping online. Some users simply stated, "If it looks pleasant then I trust it". Even if developing trust is not that simple, the research clearly shows how important design is in the area of trust.

There are a variety of web design elements that can have a positive impact on a website's image, effectiveness, and trustworthiness. Design elements like well-chosen images, clean and clear layout, careful typography, and a solid use of color can create an effective site. In addition, a solid navigation structure and continuity in design can provide the user with the control and access required within an electronic commerce interface (Andres, 1999). Although, design elements may take on the form of a visual cue, the true value comes from a combination presentation, structure, and interactivity. A solid website is a collaboration of design, content, usability, and a back end system that is integrated into the processes of the business (Veen, 2001). Krug (2000) defines a set of tools as location indicators, which are design elements of the site that tells the user where they are. This can be in the form of a page name, header, sitemap or page utility. The page utility should be used within a list type program, which allows the user to know where they are within the list of elements. Indicators like "Page 1 of 12" can be extremely helpful informing the user of their location. Nielsen (2000) describes the need for the user to know where they are, where they have been and where they can go.

Usability is increasingly recognized as an essential factor that determines the success of software systems. Practice shows that for current software systems, most usability issues are detected during testing and deployment. Fixing usability issues during this late stage of the development proves to be very costly. Some usability-improving modifications such as usability patterns may have architectural implications. We believe that the software architecture may restrict usability. The high costs associated with fixing usability issues during late-stage development prevent developers from making the necessary adjustments for

meeting all the usability requirements (Bosch, J., Folmer, E., & Gurp, J., 2004).

Traditional Services of a Cloud Registry

A cloud service registry may also be known as a metadata repository in that it does not contain the actual service but the associated metadata describing that service. The external service registries store and maintain various types of service specifications for a certain service including structural specifications represented in WSDL, behavioral specifications represented in BPEL4WS, quality specification represented in different XML-based schema, and context specification represented in specific XML-based ontologies (Dooley, Spanoudakis, & Zisman, 2008).

The automated provisioning of services in cloud computing presents several challenges to any organization. Users can request virtual machines from cloud infrastructure providers, but these machines have to be configured and managed properly. This article describes an architecture that enables the automated deployment and management of the virtual infrastructure and software of services deployed in the cloud. The architecture takes a template description of a service, which encapsulates requirements, options, as well as behavior for a collection of resources and orchestrates the provisioning of this service into a newly created set of virtual resources. The template is used for integrating the deployment and reconfiguration behavior of a service in which logical components are described along with options to scale them and appropriately change their configuration. Services are described through a set of components, which can easily be mapped and remapped to dynamically created resources, letting services take full advantage of flexible cloud resources (Kirschnick, J., Alcaraz Calero, J., Wilcock, L. & Edwards, N., 2010). The implementation of a cloud service catalog can provide some simplifications for the end user where the complexity of the cloud environment is hidden.

With cloud computing, service providers enjoy greatly simplified software installation and maintenance and centralized control over versioning and offload these problems to cloud computing provider The diversity of the services hosting on the infrastructures or platforms provided by clouds brings a challenge: how to discover the most suitable service cater to the discovery request of service consumer which includes functional requirements and nonfunctional requirements (Chen & Li, 2010). Much has been written in the literature about automatic discovery based on functional requirements. However, most early implementations of cloud computing rarely review the catalog from an end user perspective. In this perspective, the service catalog is an integral and critical component of the cloud computing architecture. By reviewing the landscape of vendor offerings, most service registries focus on the service orchestration or deployment automation of the services. Unfortunately, the usability of these applications are poor and can only be used with extensive training. The gap in the architecture is having the ability for the traditional information worker to review and order services. The cloud services approach focuses on a positive user experience while shielding the user from the complexity of the underlying technology. Each cloud service progresses through a well-defined life cycle: The cloud service provider defines the cloud services to be offered and exposes them via a service catalog; service requesters instantiate the services, which are managed against a set of service-level agreements; and finally the cloud service is destroyed when it is no longer needed (Breiter, G., & Behrendt, M., 2009).

Research Review

Based on the research provided in this chapter, there is a need for a cloud service registry build on solid usability principles that can be used by the average end user. From the traditional services research section, we see a very complex cloud registry design is used in today's solutions. This makes sense when you think about the main requirement of automation and integration. However, business users that leverage this type of registry find very difficult to understand and a lot of training is required in order to be able to perform even the simplest of functions. When users want cloud services provided in a seamless and clear understanding way, traditional design is flawed.

BUSINESS ORIENTED CLOUD SERVICE CATALOG

During the latter part of 2009 and early 2010, the AT&T cloud program interviewed a collection of information technology professionals on what they would like to see in a cloud service catalog. The results of this interview and documentation of business requirements provided a different set of needs than the one's traditionally found in the information technology area. In this case project managers, business users, and architectural planners wanted to focus more on the service catalog functions provided by the application. The following is a result of the documented business requirements needed by this group of users:

- The users wanted a single location to get cloud services regardless if those services were virtualized cloud environments or dedicated hardware.
- The users wanted to be able to filter and sort services based on their needs.
- Users wanted to be able to view the detailed specifications of the cloud services.
- The users wanted to be able to get a price based on the quantity of services ordered.
- The users wanted to be able to get a total price for all the services ordered.
- The users wanted to be able to complete the order with a one button click.

- The users wanted to be able to do duplicate an order as well as change it.

From these business requirements we can see that the end-user is more focused on features and functionality versus the integration of backend systems. That is to say that while information technology focuses on integration and orchestration, the end-user was more concerned about what services were available, how they can get them, and how fast they can get a functional environment up an operational. The overall goal of the information technology department is to move to a much more seamless environment. An environment that is customer focused and one that can fulfill the needs of the customer as quickly as possible. By leveraging this type of cloud service registry, the end-user has the ability to fulfill those obligations and get their cloud infrastructure configured ordered configured set up and completed within days or even hours.

Business Layer of the Cloud Service Catalog

Figure 1 provides an overview of the business requirements presented in the prior section. The left side of the diagram is the information technology administration area while the right side represents the business functions associated with the information worker. The middle section represents the cloud service catalog which integrates with the service orchestration application. The service catalog acts like an ordering platform for cloud services and any specific conditions associated with the services themselves. With the service catalog, we can leverage the system for demand management as well as a governance platform for controlling the services available and service level agreements. Starting with the left side, there are many administration type functions that a cloud service catalog could perform. The first box represents the service inventory which is the inventory of IaaS, SaaS, and PaaS services

that the end user can order. These services can be bundled in order to build a complete vertical environment designed for the specific business need. The specification section is the detailed service information that can be used to describe the service. This content would include sizing information, various pricing models and a variety of categorical classifications. The metadata of the service could be segmented into the database or included in the more detailed specification. There is really no limit to the information that can be captured and then shared back to the end user. Even obscure information like service retirement data, transactions processed, or frequency of use could be leveraged by the end user to decide on a particular service.

With all of this metadata, the service catalog can leverage this information to provide functional services which create a better end user experience. Everything from search to service classifications, the catalog can make it easy to locate and procure the cloud services. Other features such as notifications, sorting, and bundling can extend the service catalog's utility to the community. Specifications may also include sizing options and any custom configurations are available. Specifications are usually more detailed documentation for the service which include usage rates, pricing, and service level agreements.

Metrics have always been an important part of information technology. Unfortunately for the most part, metrics are an afterthought of the project or application itself. The natural progression of a system that moves from innovation, incubation, and migration (or the SDLC of choice) is to eventually measure the impact and value-add to the business. Some metrics are simply irrelevant to the cloud work being done or do not have a direct impact on the long term success of the program. Information gets gathered, but no action is taken as a result. Take a look at the performance metrics in the service catalog and ask yourself, "When was the last time we took an action, based on this number?" Many times metrics are used as

Figure 1. Cloud registry functionality structure

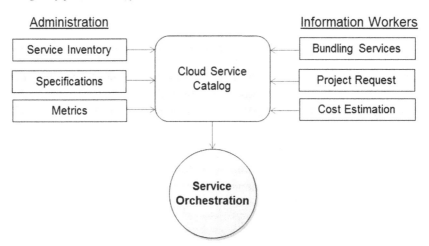

a weapon against the staff member. Dr. Edward Deming often said, "We need to drive fear out of the workplace" but most performance measurement systems do exactly the opposite. Two key categories of metrics include content and usage based metrics. Content metrics describe what information we have inside the repositories. Without considering how the data is used; content focuses on the what. Perhaps the most obvious example of content metrics is the service count. A service count sounds like a simple concept except for fact that there are multiple methods for defining what classifies as a service. We can measure the breath and scope of these service metadata elements for each object type as well as the percentage of completeness for the model itself. Some objects may have an extended meta-model with 20 metadata elements while others may only contain only a few. The number of attachments is another measurement that we can take on a specific asset. The thinking here is that objects that have extended unstructured documentation are better understood than those with only a few attachments. Examples of attachments could include service level agreements, service models, user guides, installation instructions, etc. The relationship is another content metric that most implementations fail to measure. Relationships between service assets

can follow into a wide variety of classifications: assimilation, classification, semantic, and activity based. The most obvious relationship between assets is the assimilation relationship which basically states that one asset is directly, systematically, and purposefully related to another. The classification relationship is a basic domain based relationship. The activity base relationships are created by reviewing the usage metrics which in turn create relationships like "Most Popular" or "Top Ten Downloads". Content metrics should be captured on a monthly basis and evaluated by utilizing trend analysis software which evaluates the information over an extended period of time. Ideally, the process of collection should be automated and have the ability to capture at any point in time. What growth percentage should be applied to the content metrics? Again, long term success is not defined by the explosion of growth in the first year but by the subsequent 3-5 years. The other key metric is usage. Remember, you can have all of the content in the world but without usage you haven't done much more than build a nice inventory. Usage is the key to delivering long term value-add to the organization. The first usage metric class is focused on the user. Many web based applications utilize three high-level classifications for user traffic. A "hit" is each individual file sent to a browser by the web server. A "page view" can be described as each time a visitor views a webpage on your site, irrespective of how many hits are generated. Web pages are comprised of files. Every image in a page is a separate file. When a visitor looks at a page (i.e. a page view), they may see numerous images, graphics, pictures etc. and generate multiple hits. For example, if you have a page with 10 pictures, then a request to a server to view that page generates 11 hits (10 for the pictures, and one for the html file). A page view can contain hundreds of hits. This is the reason that we measure page views and not hits. Additionally, there is a high potential for confusion here, because there are two types of 'hits'. The hits we are discussing in this article are the hits recorded by log files, and interpreted by log analysis. A second type of 'hits' are counted and displayed by a simple hit counter. Hit counters record one hit for every time a webpage is viewed, also problematic because it does not distinguish unique visitors. The third type of class is a visitor which is a human being, and their actions are 'human' events, because only humans navigate the internet. We can also track the length of time a person stays on the service catalog, what time of day is most popular, and which day compromises the heaviest traffic. These time based metrics are important to ensure the repository is up and operational 100% of the time, especially during high traffic periods. Now, if we move away from the user and focus the attention on the actual page or artifact, other metrics provide insight. We can tell which of the asset pages is viewed the most and which artifact has the highest download rate. These simple metrics may alter the way you present artifacts and even generate new classifications. Having links on the repository that represent "Most Popular", "Most Downloaded" or "Latest Additions" add value to the metadata environment. These classifications are defined as usage based classifications. In other words, the use of the repository actually defines the classification of the assets. Assuming your repository has some advanced features, you can

measure how many subscriptions per asset you have, how many transactions may be processed by the component, or what is the reuse level within the application. Remember, you can generate any number of metrics but we should only focus on the ones that can generate action, support the expansion of the brand, and help managers understand the environment.

On the information worker side, we start with the idea to bundle services together. We could bundle the services based on size; such as a large server collection. Users may also bundle services associated with the business function. For example a business unit that needs a Web server might select a small database with a couple Web server applications on top these bundling type activities to be preconfigured. Another function of bundling service is the idea of associating orders with past orders. This would allow the end-user to duplicate or replicated an order for a future application or project. The second area, project requests, would allow for things such as project approval, verification a budget, and executive oversight that would be required. The final area would include the cost estimation with service pricing. An end user can get a cost estimate which they can then take back to their business unit to gain approval. The lower circle in figure 4 indicates the need for the catalog to integrate with service orchestration piece of the infrastructure. Service orchestration is the applications that will create the virtual environments.

Design and Implementation of the Framework

With a general understanding of cloud computing and the need for a end user focused service catalog, we need to focus our attention to the design elements that can be used to improve the overall end user experience. This section will review the usability criteria that can be used to enhance the usability of the application or service registry.

USABILITY CRITERIA FOR APPLICATION SYSTEMS

Criteria for evaluating the usability of cloud registry systems should follow similar usability issues with traditional web applications and business systems. A common set of criteria needs to be developed which could be used across all cloud registry applications. Singh and Wesson (2009) provide some of the common usability criteria including the following items:

- Ease of use
- Usefulness
- Task Support
- Navigation
- Guidance
- Flexibility
- Image Design
- Customization
- Memorability Accuracy and Completeness
- Learnability
- Performance and Stability
- Visual Appeal
- System Reliability
- System Responsiveness
- UI Presentation
- Output Presentation

In order to simplify the research, this chapter will condense the list into five basic categories of usability constructs in order to evaluate improvements made on the cloud registry application. These will include the following:

- Visual Appeal of the application and cloud registry functionality.
- System Performance of the cloud registry tool.
- Ease of Use which will include the concepts of customization and navigation.
- Learnability of the cloud registry application.

- Task Support which includes workflow, form management, and basic cloud registry functionality.

The aim of this chapter is to propose a set of characteristics that are specific to cloud registry applications. This is necessary to address the inconsistent engagement of most cloud registry environments. The following sections will look at these five criteria and how they can be applied to cloud registry environments. In order to measure usability, we will define a set of heuristics or descriptors to manage the improvements. This will allow us to define specific criteria that can be evaluated in order to show the improved usability. Based on the criteria we can then measure the improvements in the cloud registry environment.

Visual Appeal

Visual appeal is a phrase used for application components that impact the presentation of information. Many technical solutions focus on putting as much information on the screen as possible with little regard to how that presentation provides context and meaning. Visual appeal includes components such as page layout, image quality, color palette, font selection, dialog boxes, controls, and form elements. Visual appeal can be reviewed by the following heuristics:

- Visual layout of the information.
- Image quality.
- Measuring the accuracy and understanding of the information being presented.
- Intuitiveness of the interface.
- Consistency of the design.

System Performance

System performance is a measurement of the how the system performs in handling the user requests. We can measure the performance by the speed by which processes requests and the number of concurrent users within a specific environment. Research suggests that performance impacts usability with a positive correlation in the areas of efficient access, search success, flexibility, understanding of content, relevant search result, and satisfaction (Janecek & Uddin, 2007). System performance can be evaluated by the following heuristics:

- Transaction processing speed.
- End user task accomplishment.
- Expected results (i.e. search results).
- Learning times.
- End user satisfaction.

Ease of Use

Perceived ease of use is the extent to which a person believes that using a technology will be free of effort. Perceived ease of use is a construct tied to an individual's assessment of the effort involved in the process of using the system (Venkatesh, 2000). Ease of use can be reviewed by the following heuristics:

- Navigation elements.
- End user task accomplishment.
- Learning times.
- End user satisfaction.
- Ability to locate specific information.
- Timeliness of information presented.

Learnability

Learnability is in some sense the most fundamental usability attribute of cloud registry applications (Nielsen, 2000). The system should be easy to learn so that the user can rapidly start getting value from the application. As Dzida, Herda, and Itzfelt (1978) reported, learnability is especially important for novice users. Learnability can be described as the amount of effort in using a new Web site and to measure how easy a site for new visitors to orient themselves and get a good over-

view of what the site offers (Jeng, 2005). Ease of use can be reviewed by the following heuristics:

- Time required to learn the application.
- Access to online help and community support.
- Ability to actively contribute to the conversation is a short period of time.
- Consistency of the design.
- Complexity of the core tasks.

Task Support

The idea of task support is an alignment between the technical world and the business environment. Does the technology support the business environment by ensuring tasks are started, completed, and communicated effectively? Task support deals with how well a product or system enables users to perform their typical tasks to achieve their goals with the product (Anschuetz, L., Keirnan, T. & Rosenbaum, S., 2002). Task support can be reviewed by the following heuristics:

- Consistent terminology is used in the application.
- Consistent use of imagery and style based on the organizational style.
- Information is real and contextual in nature.
- Confirmation of tasks.
- Tasks process support and state communication.
- Automation of redundant tasks.
- Personalization of content and context.

CASE STUDY

The research methodology was designed to provide a basis for usability along with a heuristic evaluation. The goal of the study is to demonstrate that improvements in usability will increase the usage and utility of a cloud registry environment. Usage can be defined as the number of times an end user consumes the information which is represented by the number of visits, downloading documentation and actual service orders. Utility or utilization is measured by the number of changes in the environment which come in the form of information updates. Updates can be measured by the number of adds, changes, and deletes across all of the content containers within the online environment.

Design Review

With the design information, the organization setup out to build a common cloud portal which would house information about cloud computing. This information would come in the form of written content, social media platforms, online videos, and other interactive components. The goal of the design was to increase the end user experience by implementing the usability criteria defined above. Additionally, the design would include a common cloud service catalog which would drive the deployment of cloud services throughout the enterprise.

Figure 2 provides a visual example of the home page (left) for the cloud portal as well as the on-line training page (right). The main focus of the design on the informational style pages is in the visual design, use of images, and ease of use. The rotating banner allows the cloud organization to spotlight a variety of touch points for the end user as well as enhancing the graphical user interface. Cloud users can find the latest information on the services in the catalog, a collection of training materials, access to the social media environment for the cloud organization, and access to the latest communications. The variety of information available helps the site focus on task support related to accessing cloud services as well as other features of a cloud environment. Additional integration elements, such as RSS, are present to allow for information exchange with different tools such as native RSS readers, outlook, and web browsers. Users also have the ability to subscribe for email alerts in the social media environment which

provides a greater sense of integration. By making the site easy to use and ensuring a consistency in design, we address many of the learnability issues related to internally developed web applications.

Figure 3 contains the actual service catalog (left) and the service shopping cart (right). The service catalog contains all of the PaaS, SaaS, and IaaS services available for purchase. The site provides a "Show Me" filter that allows the services to be filtered by type, category, size, and operating system. Each service contains metadata information pertaining to the actual service including category, type, operating system, size, number of CPU's, memory, storage, and cost breakdown. The service specification can be downloaded to provide a physical copy of what the end user can see on the screen. The catalog leverages the traditional shopping cart methodology which is familiar to most information technology professionals. End users can add the different services along with the quantities to the shopping cart. The catalog leverages a consistent look and feel with the rest of the site to ensure users follow a pattern of usability. Once a user has completed selecting which services they need, they can then click the shopping cart to get a final price. The right side of Figure 3 provides a visual of the shopping cart screen. The primary purpose of this screen is to provide the end-user a last chance to review the services they placed into the cart, quantities of those services they asked for as well as the pricing breakdown. The user will also be able to update the quantities of services or delete the service from the card from this particular screen.

At any point in time the end-user can return to the cloud service inventory catalog and add additional services. As described up in the research area the ability to integrate with the backend orchestration application is critical. Up until this point we've created a very nicely designed interactive service catalog that aids the end-user in the ability to select services compare services and prices services based on their business needs. But, ultimately the best level of integration is

Figure 2. Example pages in the cloud portal

Figure 3. Service catalog and cloud service cart

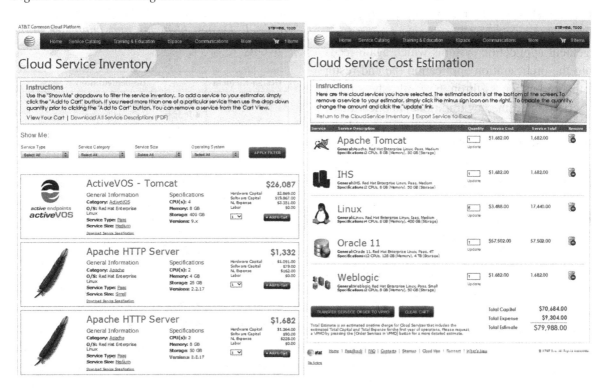

Figure 4. Linear trend lines for cloud environments

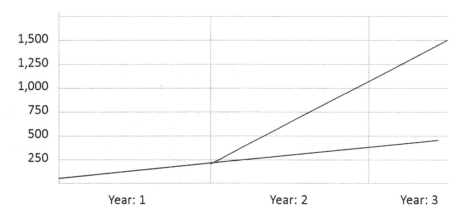

the ability to integrate the service order into the backing orchestration piece. The reason for this of course is the speed of how long it takes from when the customer decides on what services they want places the order and then that order is processed by the information technology department. Systems and applications that integrate of course will take a lot longer because it requires the need of manual processing or manual data movements. Here you can see that the application with a click of a button can simply transfer the service and service order over to the project management application systems which again feeds into the orchestration application the end result is that orders a pass-through seamlessly without any friction defined by traditional application or nonintegrated applications. Table 1 provides a more detailed review of the specific design elements defined in the background section and the actual implementation of the cloud portal.

Review Impact of a Functional Business Cloud Service

The main research question was to determine if these design elements can make a difference to the number of services or quantity of cloud environments that are being built? While the cloud program was operational for 12 months prior to

the implementation, the correlation of impact may be elusive. Take a look at Figure 4 where the cloud environments have been charted with a resulting linear trend line. The base metric was the actual number of cloud environments constructed. During the first full-year about 240 cloud environments were created by the deployment teams. We have taken the first 12 months of cloud deployments and mapped that along a linear progression. The

Table 1. Design elements and implementation tracking

Design Element	Implementation
Visual Appeal	• Overall Design of the Portal • Professional Cloud Images • Consistency of Design
System Performance	• Build upon SharePoint Infrastrucure • Leverage XML Data Exchange • Local JQuery • Responsive Design for Mobile Devices
Ease of Use	• Leverage Shopping Cart Patterns • Consistent Navigation • Feedback • Integrated Shopping Cart Inventory
Learnability	• Online Help • Social Media Community for Support • Visual Progression for Online Orders • Saving Cloud Service Cart
Task Support	• Order Confirmations • Email Confirmations • Consistent Use of Cloud Related Images • Site Map for all Cloud Resources

lower line or black line, in Figure 4, shows this trend as well as the estimated environments for three years out. As an example by the end of the second year an estimated 350-400 cloud environments should have been built. By the end of the third year, we should have upwards of 500 cloud environments constructed.

The second trend line (red) starts the environment calculation after the cloud portal was implemented; after the first 12 months of deployment. Notice that by the end of the second year, we exceeded 1,000 environments and by the third year, we exceeded 1,500. Clearly, the introduction of the cloud portal and service catalog influenced the number of environments constructed during the second and third years. This indicates that the ability to integrate the end-user business requirements as well as getting cost estimations actually makes it easier to do business with the cloud environment. This translates into more cloud environments and more conversions to the cloud infrastructure. The two trend lines indicate a divergence between the original estimate and the new trend line. By the end of year three, this difference was upwards of 700 sites.

Now the question that remains, what would have the infrastructure growth had been if this education portal, information design elements and integration had not taken place. Clearly they would be some element of growth because as with all programs early in their nature may or may not take off that will eventually continue to move forward. That is to say that the assumptions on the linear trend line may not have continued but more of an exponential growth would be seen. However, with the limited amount of data and not having a comparison environment, we have to assume the increase in environments is influenced by the ease of use as well as the information presented in the portal.

Based on subject matter expert interviews with the cloud program leadership, the cloud information portal benefited the program greatly on three different fronts. The first front was the online communications, education and training that was provided to the community. The ability to communicate the benefits of the cloud program including the cost advantages was an critical step in the deployment plan. End users needed to know what the cloud was as well as why they should migrate to this new type of infrastructure. Having the information was important but having it easy to locate and consume was just as critical. Many of the interviewees commented on how professional the application looked which in turn gave the program more credibility. This was important during the early stages when many of the automated pieces were not in place. Other comments focused on the familiarity of the end user shopping cart paradigm. Most people understand how the shopping cart works and the transition from physical goods to cloud services was relatively easy.

The second area which was aided by the design function was of course the service catalog itself. Normally services would have included a Word document to describe the specific of the service. The service catalog provided the end-user with a list of services and the ability to filter, search, and categorize them. This creates the ability to find services which increases the desire to actually move into the cloud environment. This front end environment also enables cloud service managers the ability to edit service metadata such as prices sizing configurations memory and storage very easily. This means that price shifts or price changes are automatically updated. For example a price that may change in the backend but then requires a programmer effort in order to get that price implemented. This was accomplished by leveraging feeds from the orchestration element so that the prices and quantities and sizing all always up-to-date

The final area of improvement is the ability to integrate the application with the project management systems as well as the orchestration environment. Project management here means the ability to get a budget, get approvals, and then process the order within the cloud environment. By integrating the cloud portal with the backend applications, we reduced the length of time that it took to process an order for a cloud service to drop. The next major task in the process is the ability to build the physical infrastructure. Cloud orchestration powers the self-service portals that allow end users to employ a browser interface to rapidly provision services and resources available from a catalog of standardized offerings. With orchestration software, we can streamline the process and reduce the time required to implement a cloud solution. Based on the results, the studied organization reduced the time required to build the virtual cloud environment by 85%. This decrease was in large part based on the increased integration and the automation putting both to update pricing as well as to integrate the prices into the backing orchestration applications. The largest gap in time is for the budget approvals which are still manual in that an individual must approve the order. Unlike external cloud environments that can take an order without budget approval, large organizations still have this oversight in place.

FUTURE RESEARCH DIRECTIONS

The design structure and case study introduced in this chapter provides a natural guide to future research. Typically, case studies have a much narrower domain due to the nature of business. That is to say, businesses generally do not allow for multiple iterations in order to produce a working product. Additional case studies would provide a much broader perspective and analysis which will expand the body of knowledge in this space. This chapter set out to show how solid design principles could be applied to an end user cloud service catalog. The results of which have been

positive but additional research needs to be done as cloud computing moves toward a more mature technology. The transition from an information technology perspective to one based on general knowledge workers comes with maturity of the technology itself. Therefore, additional research needs to be done to aid this transition.

CONCLUSION

Cloud computing offers several opportunities of using IT infrastructures as a utility with the possibility of scaling up or scaling down depending upon the needs an organization. However, like most of the emerging IT technologies, cloud computing has raised several technical and design challenges. The research question that this chapter wanted to address was to determine if good design based on human factors would improve the deployment of cloud services. Can we leverage other design research and improve how cloud services are defined, discovered, and selected in order to expand the value to the business? While this chapter only focused on a single implementation, it is clear that great design does help the deployment of cloud based services. From the simple education and expansion of knowledge around cloud computing to the actual ordering process, design elements improve the overall experience from the end users perspective. We have not observed much literature on software engineering aspects of developing and evolving cloud-enabled catalog systems that focus on the end user versus the core integration and orchestration tasks. During this project, we studied the common cloud portal which allowed us to test the design elements and then review the impact by the number of orders and cloud infrastructure environments. This chapter aimed at sharing our experiences and observations gained through this project and critical analysis of the literature with those who intend to move toward a more user friendly service catalog.

REFERENCES

Andres, C. (1999). *Great Web Architecture*. Foster City, CA: IDG Books World Wide.

Anschuetz, L., Keirnan, T., & Rosenbaum, S. (2002). Combining Usability Research with Documentation Development for Improved User Support. In *Proceedings of the SIGDOC*. Toronto, Canada: The Association of Computing Machinery.

Armbrust, A., Fox, A., Griffith, R., Joseph, A., Katz, R., Konwinski, A., & Zaharia, M. et al. (2010). Above the Clouds: A View of Cloud Computing. *Communications of the ACM*, *53*(4), 50. doi:10.1145/1721654.1721672

Babat, M., & Chauhan, M. (2011). A Tale of Migration to Cloud Computing for Sharing Experiences and Observations. *Workshop on Software Engineering for Cloud Computing*. Honolulu, HI: IEEE.

Becker, S., & Mottay, F. (2001, January). A global perspective on website usability. *IEEE Software*, *18*(1), 61–54. doi:10.1109/52.903167

Butrico, M., Silva, D., & Youseff, L. (2008). Toward a unified ontology of cloud computing. *Grid Computing Environments Workshop*. Austin, TX: IEEE.

Chen, H., & Li, S. (2010). SRC: A Service Registry on Cloud Providing Behavior-aware and QoS-aware Service Discovery. In *International Conference on Service-Oriented Computing and Applications*. Perth, Australia: IEEE. doi:10.1109/SOCA.2010.5707179

Dooley, J., Spanoudakis, G., & Zisman, A. (2008). Proactive Runtime Service Discovery. In *Proceedings of IEEE 2008 International Service Computing Conference*. Honolulu, HI: IEEE.

Dzida, W., Herda, S., & Itzfelt, W. (1978). User-perceived quality of interactive systems. *IEEE Transactions on Software Engineering*, *SE-4*(4), 270–276. doi:10.1109/TSE.1978.231511

Janecek, P. (2007). Faceted classification in web information architecture: A framework for using semantic web tools. *The Electronic Library*, *25*(2), 219–233. doi:10.1108/02640470710741340

Jeng, J. (2005). Usability assessment of academic digital libraries: Effectiveness, efficiency, satisfaction, and learnability. *Libri: International Journal of Libraries and Information Services*, *55*(2/3), 96–121.

Karat, J. (1997). User-centered software evaluation methodologies. In M. Helander, T. K. Landauer, & P. Prabhu (Eds.), *Handbook of Human-Computer Interaction* (pp. 689–704). New York: Elsevier Press.

Karvonen, K. (2000). The beauty of simplicity. In *Proceedings of the ACM Conference on Universal Usability*. Arlington, VA: The Association of Computing Machinery.

Krug, S. (2000). *Don't Make Me Think*. Indianapolis, IN: New Riders Publishing.

Lecerof, A., & Paterno, F. (1998). Automatic Support for Usability Evaluation. *IEEE Transactions on Software Engineering*, *24*(10), 863–888. doi:10.1109/32.729686

Nielsen, J. (1998). Introduction to web design. In *Proceedings of the SIGCHI on Human Factors in Computing Systems*. Los Angeles, CA: The Association of Computing Machinery.

Nielsen, J. (2000). *Designing Web Usability. Indianapolis, IN: New Riders Publishing. Nielsen, J. & Tahir, M. (2002). Homepage Usability: 50 Websites Deconstructed*. Indianapolis, IN: New Riders Publishing.

Pearrow, M. (2000). *Web Site Usability Handbook.* Independence, KY: Charles River Media.

Scanlon, T., Schroeder, W., Snyder, C., & Spool, J. (1998). Websites that work: Designing with your eyes open. In *Proceedings of the SIGCHI on Human Factors in Computing Systems.* Los Angeles, CA: The Association of Computing Machinery.

Singh, A., & Wesson, J. (2009). Evaluation Criteria for Assessing the Usability of ERP Systems In *Proceedings of the 2009 Annual Conference of the South African Institute of Computer Scientists and Information Technologists.* Vaal River, South Africa: The Association of Computing Machinery. doi:10.1145/1632149.1632162

Veen, J. (2000). *The Art & Science of Web Design.* Indianapolis, IN: New Riders Publishing.

Venkatesh, V. (1985). Determinants of Perceived Ease of Use: Integrating Control, Intrinsic Motivation, and Emotion into the Technology Acceptance Model. *Information Systems Research, 11*(4), 342–365. doi:10.1287/isre.11.4.342.11872

Erl, T., Puttini, R., & Mahmood, Z. (2013). *Cloud Computing: Concepts, Technology & Architecture.* Upper Saddle River, NJ: Prentice Hall.

Jaitly, A., Suri, B., & Wadhwa, B. (2014). Making sense of academia-industry gap in the evolving cloud service brokerage. In *Proceedings of the 1st International Workshop on Software Engineering Research and Industrial Practices.* New York, NY: The Association of Computing Machinery.

Kavis, M. (2014). *Architecting the Cloud: Design Decisions for Cloud Computing Service Models.* Hoboken, NJ: Wiley Publishing. doi:10.1002/9781118691779

Preece, J., Rogers, Y., & Sharp, H. (2011). *Interaction Design: Beyond Human-Computer Interaction.* Hoboken, NJ: Wiley Publishing.

Shneiderman, B., & Plaisant, P. (2009). *Designing the User Interface: Strategies for Effective Human-Computer Interaction* (5th ed.). Boston, MA: Pearson Addison-Wesley.

ADDITIONAL READING

Bouchenak, S., Chockler, G., Chockler, H., Gheorghe, G., Santos, N., & Shraer, S. (2013). Verifying cloud services: Present and future. *Operating Systems Review, 47*(2), 6. doi:10.1145/2506164.2506167

Card, S., Newell, A., & Moran, T. (1983). *The Psychology of Human-Computer Interaction.* Hillsdale, NJ: L. Erlbaum Associates Inc.

Cooper, A. (2007). *About Face 3.0: The Essentials of Interaction Design.* New York, NY: John Wiley & Sons, Inc.

KEY TERMS AND DEFINITIONS

Cloud Computing: The practice of using a network of remote servers hosted on the Internet to store, manage, and process data, rather than a local server or a personal computer.

Human-Computer Interaction (HCI): HCI (human-computer interaction) is the study of how people interact with computers and to what extent computers are or are not developed for successful interaction with human beings.

Registry: Registry acts as a core component in Service Oriented Architecture (SOA). Early SOA reference architecture named the registry as a service broker for service providers to publish service definitions, allowing service consumers to look up and directly consume the services.

Service: A cloud service is any resource that is provided over the Internet. The most common cloud service resources are Software as a Service (SaaS), Platform as a Service (PaaS) and Infrastructure as a Service (IaaS).

Service Model: Cloud computing can be divided into three service models: Software as a Service (SaaS), Platform as a Service (PaaS), and Infrastructure as a Service (IaaS). These models describe the specific function performed by the cloud service.

Service Orchestration: Application or service orchestration is the process of integrating two or more applications and/or services together to automate a process, or synchronize data in real-time. Often, point-to-point integration may be used as the path of least resistance.

Usability: Usability is a quality attribute that assesses how easy user interfaces are to use. The word "usability" also refers to methods for improving ease-of-use during the design process.

Section 2
Cloud Computing in Education Sector

Chapter 4
Personal Mobile Cloud Computing Affordances for Higher Education:
One Example in South Africa

Chaka Chaka
Tshwane University of Technology, South Africa

ABSTRACT

Within the cloud computing ecosystem and its different permutations, there exists personal mobile cloud computing. The latter has not been covered and investigated much in relation to its affordances for higher education (HE), especially in South Africa. Thus, this chapter argues that personal mobile cloud computing can offer HE significant educational affordances in the form of cloud computing value chain. It does so by providing one South African example entailing a two-project study in the HE sector in which the cloud affordances of Twitter and Facebook were leveraged for educational purposes. Regarding Twitter, one of its affordances is that it was exploited as a cloud based virtual blackboard for a course content, thereby facilitating micro-teaching and micro-learning. Concerning Facebook, one of its affordances is that it served as a cloud based mobile computing environment in which a course-specific writing process was mounted by the instructor and participants. A collective affordance for both Twitter and Facebook was both consumerization and BYOD approaches to teaching and learning.

INTRODUCTION

Cloud computing comprises an evolving ecosystem that is exponentially gaining traction in the computing ecosphere. Within this cloud computing ecosystem and its different strata, there exist both enterprise and personal cloud computing. The emerging upshot of the latter, especially among consumers, is a personal mobile cloud computing permutation. Driven largely by both major Internet corporates that provide consumer cloud computing services (e.g., Google Apps, Dropbox, SkyDrive, (see Lin, Wen, Jou, & Wu, 2013), iCloud, iTunes and YouTube) and social networking sites (e.g.,

DOI: 10.4018/978-1-4666-8339-6.ch004

Facebook and Twitter), and enabled particularly by consumerization and the practice of *bring your own device* (BYOD), personal mobile cloud computing seems to have convenient affordances to offer to higher education institutions (HEIs). Much work about the use of cloud computing in the higher education (HE) sector has been reported in some places, especially, in both the United States and the United Kingdom (Katz, Goldstein & Yanosky, 2010; Mircea & Andreescu, 2011). However, in other places such as South Africa, that is not the case. This does not necessarily imply that there is no cloud computing deployment and adoption in the HE sector in South Africa, but that there is not much documented and reported research work on the use of this variant of computing in this sector. This is even more so pertaining to the deployment of personal mobile cloud computing in the HE sector.

At the core of personal mobile cloud computing are, this chapter contends, disruptive twin trends: consumerization and BYOD. In this regard, HEIs that are willing to both *cloud compute* their academic services and operations and virtualize their information technology (IT) architectures stand a chance of leveraging affordances offered by this computing permutation, thereby assigning themselves the role of being game changers in the increasingly competitive and often cash-strapped HE sector. Against this backdrop, this chapter argues that personal mobile cloud computing can offer HE significant affordances in the overall academic cloud computing value chain. It does so by providing one South African example in the HE sector in which the cloud affordances of Facebook and Twitter were leveraged for educational purposes through an instructor's and participants' mobile phone handsets. In terms of its structure, the chapter, first, provides an overview of personal mobile cloud computing and mounts a relevant literature review. Second, it outlines a framework within which its main argument is located. Third, it presents a South African instance of the use of personal mobile cloud computing for educational

purposes in one HE institution. Fourth, the chapter presents the findings of this instance and outlines the limitations of this instance, while mapping out future research directions pertaining to personal mobile cloud computing within the HE sector.

DISRUPTIVE POST-PC TRENDS AND GAME CHANGERS

The personal computer (PC) has for a long time been the lifeline of the computing ecosystem – both the corporate and personal computing eco-systems – with the workstation and the desktop effectively being the dominant interface of this ecosystem. The PC era was, at its high water-mark, dominated by what Cheston (2012) refers to as a *bring your own* PC (BYOPC) approach to corporate IT. This development helped entrench the PC as the mother lode of many variants of computing. However, this computing trajectory has been unexpectedly upstaged by personal mobile cloud computing, consumerization and BYOD, three trends gaining popular traction that this chapter perceives as disruptive post-PC trends and game changers. Cloud computing - itself not necessarily a new trend (see Thomas, 2009) - is mostly riddled with hype and diverse definitions and views (see, for example, Alberta Education, 2012; Katz et al., 2010; McDonald, MacDonald & Breslin, 2010). As a result, an eclectic working definition is provided here which is, though not definitive, but relevant to the chapter. Therefore, cloud computing refers to a practice in which computing infrastructures, platforms and software reside in the Internet and a network of servers, and are provided as service offerings in a connected way. This network and connection of servers me-diating these service offerings within the Internet environment is metaphorically known as the cloud (McDonald et al., 2010; Mitrano, 2009; Thomas, 2009; Wang, Chen & Khan, 2014; cf. Katz et al., 2010; Kraan & Yuan, 2009; Plummer, Bittman, Austin, Cearley & Smith, 2008; Sarga, 2012).

The service offerings in question can be private, public, community, or hybrid (see McDonald et al., 2010). In this way, personal mobile cloud computing is a cloud computing variant that leverages mobility (in the form of mobile devices such as mobile phones (especially smart phones), iPads, tablets and laptops) and portability, and pervasive computing inherent in mobility. Its disruptive and game-changing nature lies in mobility, portability and ubiquity, three elements which obviate the necessity for the PC.

While consumerization as a trend is about corporates embracing and adopting web technologies for storage, collaboration and email applications (cf. Cheston, 2012) in relation to their IT needs, it is more than this corporate practice. It also entails consumer electronic devices (e.g., smart phones, iPads, tablets, virtual storages, social networking sites, instant messages and microblogs) being deployed voluntarily by end users, first, for mainstream enterprise IT purposes and, then, corporates adopting these devices for their enterprise IT needs (see Chaka, 2013a). This practice of consumers leading the way in using non-corporate devices for enterprise IT needs, and their being emulated in this practice by corporates themselves, gives rise to the concept, *consumerization*. And this is where its disruptive and game-changing disposition lies. Lastly, BYOD means precisely what this acronym stands for: it is a trend in which employees, in any company, bring personally owned mobile devices (e.g., smart phones, iPads, tablets, phablets (phone-tablet hybrids) and mini-laptops) to workplaces and use them in their daily corporate work. In so doing, employees effectively render their own devices enterprise-ready (see Burmeister, 2014). Thus, in this twin employee practices, lies not only the role of BYOD as a disruptive and game changing post-PC trend, but also that of *bring your own application* (BYOA) as a concurrent disruptive force. The different aspects of the disruptive nature of the post-PC trends and game changers are as characterized here displayed in *Figure 1*.

HIGHLIGHTS OF SOCIAL NETWORKING CLOUD COMPUTING IN THE HE SECTOR: A LITERATURE REVIEW

This section presents a brief summary and synthesis of case studies related to the use and deployment of cloud computing by selected higher education institutions (HEIs) for diverse educational purposes and for varied cloud computing affordances. Firstly, a desktop search of case studies of the use and deployment of cloud computing for teaching and learning by HEIs was conducted through the Google Scholar at different intervals from January 2014 to May 2014. Secondly, search results were screened and vetted for their relevance, informativeness, rigor and credibility in relation to the topic at hand. In the end, eight case studies were identified and selected for further scrutiny. These eight case studies were selected not for their reporting on the effectiveness or the non-effectiveness of cloud-based learning but for their highlighting the uses and applications of cloud computing for learning purposes. These case studies, then, serve as the locus of summary and synthesis for this section and as a prelude to the main case study discussed later in this chapter. The reason for a desktop search option and for not using articles in most accredited journals is that educational cloud computing is a relatively new area in the HE sector. As such, not much research work is currently available in most established academic journals as the desktop search revealed.

The first case study, conducted at two Southeastern community colleges – one rural and the other urban -in the United States (U.S.), involved about 750 students and a group of college administrators and IT support staff. However, for the purpose of this chapter, the focus will be on students' participation in the case study as this is what the chapter intends reporting about. The 750 students were enrolled in a basic computing course which was offered to them either on an online,

Figure 1. The different aspects of the disruptive nature of the post-PC trends and game changers

face-to-face or hybrid basis. Their demographic profiles were as follows: 142 of them were from a rural community college while 618 were from an urban community college; 52% of them were females and 48% of them were males; and most of them (63%) were traditional full-time degree seekers, while others were either part-time degree seekers or part-time non-degree seekers. Students' age ranged from 25 years to 55 years. Employing a technology acceptance model, this case study set out to test six hypotheses on students' perceptions of and attitudes towards the usefulness and ease of use of a cloud computing technology used at their colleges. Two of these hypotheses - hypotheses

1 and 4 - were: usefulness perceptions (1a) and ease-of-use perceptions (1b) will affect the student usage of the cloud computing tool; and student attitudes about technology will affect usefulness (4a) and ease of use (4b). Moreover, the case study utilized two methods, an online questionnaire and a focus group, to collect its data, and employed a path-analytic model to analyze this data (Behrend, Wiebe, London & Johnson, 2010).

A cloud computing used in the study was the Virtual Computing Lab (VCL) developed by a team of IT technicians at the two colleges. The platform was available to registered students for 24 hours a day, 7 days a week, who in turn could access it from their own devices, anywhere. It was deployed as a private infrastructure-as-a-service (IaaS) model that offered a wireless connection window into a computer desktop run from a remote server. In this context, the purpose of the study was to investigate factors leading to technology adoption by college students. Among other things, in relation to hypothesis 1, part 1a of it was not supported, while part 1b was supported (Behrend et al., 2010). So, this case study represents an instance in which an on-premise cloud computing platform encouraged a BYOD practice for the teaching and learning of a basic computer course.

The second case is Wakefield, Warren and Alsobrook's (2011) project. Its purpose was to employ Twitter to help support the development of a positive, online communal and social space and to facilitate student learning. It was conducted at a university in the southwest U.S. among 13 undergraduate students (7 of whom were females and 6 of whom were males) enrolled in the course, Global Policy Issues. In this case study, Twitter was employed as a communication tool for classroom discussion. The latter was a course component allotted some grading. There were three research questions the case study set out to answer:

- To what extent does the use of Twitter increase students' engagement in a course?
- To what extent does Twitter help students understand the course content and assigned readings better?
- To what extent does communication over Twitter promote social presence (interactive learning/participation/sense of being there) amongst students, and to what extent are there gender differences, if any, in this perception?

A new online survey instrument with closed and open-ended items, designed specifically for the purpose of this study, was used and administered to students at the end of a semester in a given academic year. Two of the merged findings

of this case study were as follows: students perceived Twitter as a free-flowing and interactive environment that helped them engage with one another regarding the course content; they also felt that Twitter encouraged them to engage in different types of constative communication at different times (Wakefield et al., 2011). This case study embodies elements of synchronous cloud social learning as students were able to interact with each other and with the course content in the cloud. But above all, it reflects a sense of presence learning – learning through social presence afforded by Twitter (see Chaka, 2013b, 2014a).

The third case study involved the use of five social media tools - Twitter, YouTube, Flickr, blogging and Skype - to facilitate student learning. Students had to access these social media technologies from their own mobile devices. Conducted in 2010 at a state college of medicine in the U.S., the case study had two parts and 15 fourth-year medical students as its participants. The latter had enrolled in one of the two intensive, month-long final humanities electives which they had to do after completing their medical coursework. The two electives (Creative Writing for Medicine and The Narratives of Aging: Exploring Creative Approaches to Dementia Care) were part of students' compulsory medical humanities curriculum and were designed to integrate the five social media tools in their teaching and learning delivery mode. In this regard, the main aim of this case study was to use and evaluate the integration of these five social media tools into the two electives (George & Dellasega, 2011).

The first part of the case study focused on the module, Creative Writing for Medicine, and the use of Twitter as a supplementary learning platform. Students were provided with writing prompts on Twitter by their instructor and were connected to other writing prompts from their classmates. Once they were comfortable with using this platform, their writing assignments were migrated to a shared group blog. The second part of the case study entailed the module, The Narratives of Aging:

Exploring Creative Approaches to Dementia Care, and the use of Twitter and YouTube as additional learning platforms. Two of the purposes for which YouTube was used were to: stream video clips made by Alzheimer's advocacy groups from different countries; and link students to video content of persons having dementia engaging in therapies from several countries. Finally, students designed a short video clip as part of their out-of-class group assignment that was uploaded on YouTube. In addition, Twitter was integrated into the elective to allow students to have real-time communication about their filed observations and field notes (George & Dellasega, 2011). Overall, this two-part case study enabled students to engage in: a BYOD approach to learning; real-time learning (through real-time individual writing prompts and assignments and through real-time collaboration); and a video streaming driven learning. All of this was powered through cloud-based mobile and social media technologies: the instructor could monitor students' participation and post responses to students using cloud-based social computing while, in turn, students were able to leverage personal mobile cloud computing affordances.

The fourth case study is Hershock and La-Vaque-Manty's (2012) project. This case study is about how various instructors at a U.S.'s university use cloud-based online collaboration tools (OCTs) in the respective courses that they teach. Two projects relating to utilizing such OCTs as deployed on Google Docs, are presented here. The first project concerns upper-level undergraduate Nursing students who are expected to write grant proposals to prepare themselves for independent research proposals with faculty mentors. Students are required to draft or revise certain sections of grant proposals and refine designs of their individual research proposals and their disciplinary writing skills. A students' instructor creates a Google Docs collection for weekly assignments, collating sections of grant proposals that require different skill sets and levels of conceptual mastery. Once students post their drafts to each collection,

the whole class is able to automatically view these drafts and comment on them. The instructor is also able to view and assess the extent of changes to student drafts in response to peer feedback by means of Google Docs' history revision feature (Hershock & LaVaque-Manty, 2012).

The second project involves the course, Introduction to Engineering, in which students are expected to work in teams to design, build, and trial products for given professional scenarios. Student teams have to apply course concepts to assess rival designs in relation to client-generated objectives and constraints. Nonetheless, face-to-face student discussions often result in suboptimal designs because of poor group interactions. To obviate this interactional hiccup, the instructor opted to have team discussions take place on Google Docs. Thus, tapping into Google Docs, teams are able to have synchronous, text-based online discussions in which members are geographically dispersed. In this case, students are also in a position to use the comment and chat features of Google Docs (Hershock & LaVaque-Manty, 2012). In both instances of Google Docs usage, students are able to exploit real-time affordances offered by cloud computing. That is, in both instances, students are able to engage in real-time, cloud-based online collaborative learning. For example, in the first project, not only do students engage in real-time commenting and peer feedback, but they also engage in synchronous writing. Above all, they are also subject to the instructor's synchronous monitoring and evaluation. In the second project, in addition to other highlighted affordances, students can tap into synchronous chatting.

The fifth case study is Lam's (2012) project which took place at a university in Hong Kong, China. It had 284 Hi-Diploma Program participants (who were students) from the School of Continuing and Professional Studies who were selected by means of convenience sampling. The primary objective of the case study was to develop a model of student motivation in learning with Facebook by focusing on four Facebook benefits: interaction, communication, social relationship and participation. Since Facebook was incorporated into Moodle (a learning management system), only aspects of the case study related to the use of Facebook are presented here. An arrangement was made for participants to access both Moodle and Facebook for 15 weeks in a given semester. In respect of Facebook, participants were requested to join a private study group (on Facebook) created by their instructors at the beginning of a semester. They were then required to submit their individual and group projects on the private Facebook group's wall. They also had to answer quizzes on Facebook and prepare group presentation video clips and upload them onto Facebook. In turn, instructors had to respond to student questions posted on the Facebook group promptly, update students about any new information, and provide supplementary resources using the Facebook group frequently (Lam, 2012). Here, we have Facebook being deployed as a social networking platform to enable both instructors and students to participate in a cloud-based teaching and learning, respectively. This cloud-based social computing platform offers users synchronous and asynchronous teaching and learning affordance among its other affordances.

The sixth case study is Lin et al.'s (2013) experiment that took place at a Taiwanese university and involved 70 students (38 males and 32 females) whose average age was 21 years. The main purpose of the experiment was to determine the effectiveness of a proposed cloud-based reflective learning environment on enhancing students' reflective practices and their learning performance in an industrial course on product design. The 70 students were enrolled in the Department of Industrial Education and were randomly assigned to an experimental group and a control group. The former had 35 students who used the proposed learning environment that supported their reflective learning activities; and the latter also had 35 students who underwent similar activities as the experimental group, but with the help of a discussion board and not of web applications. In view of

this, the experiment then integrated Google and Microsoft web applications as a suite of teaching and learning tools with a reflective learning environment. Google applications were meant for use by the experimental group, while the control group had to use Microsoft Office Word document to conduct and present a specific issue. Cognate Google applications used by the experimental group were: Google Plus (to facilitate reflective activities between instructors and students using this social networking application); Google Drive (to enable instructors and students to instantly edit, write down, view, and reply to reflective ideas conveyed through any PC or mobile device connected to this web-based office suite); and Google sites (to allow instructors and students to consolidate and express their reflective thoughts using this structured wiki- and webpage-creation application) (Lin et al., 2013..

Employing questionnaires, pre-test/post-test results and interviews, the experiment yielded positive results, two of which are: the proposed cloud-based reflective learning environment enabled instructors and students to engage in reflective learning activities - the environment seamlessly facilitated a student-centered learning context to help students enhance their reflection abilities; and students in the experimental group displayed higher learning motivation and reflection performance than those in the control group (Lin et al., 2013). In the main, this experiment represents one way in which freemium – not premium – cloud computing can be leveraged by instructors in the HE sectors for educational purposes.

The seventh case study pertains to Dell's 2012 (see Dell Inc., 2012) deployment of corporate cloud computing at Universidad Europea de Madrid. Attracting students around the world and offering courses spanning sports science, economics and law, Universidad Europea de Madrid is a private university servicing about 16,000 students in Spain. A majority of its students are the so-called digital natives - who are said to be familiar with the web and digital devices from an early age – and tend to arrive at Universidad Europea de Madrid with high digital expectations. In order to satisfy its IT needs and those of its students (its primary clients), Universidad Europea de Madrid has enlisted the services of Dell to help it roll out a cloud computing system that includes among other solutions, software-as-a-service (SaaS) (Dell Inc., 2012). In this instance, its business goal was to reduce IT costs and enhance online and campus-based learning, while allowing its students to use their own devices in university laboratories. In fact, at one point, it had 500 different pieces of software at 40 different laboratories that it had to constantly maintain, service and update. Therefore, there was a need for it to move to *boxless* IT. So, as part of its solutions to scale down its IT costs, it has adopted a BYOD policy, Dell cloud services and a desktop virtualization. Besides, it has adopted these cloud solutions to add value to its image so it can have a competitive edge in the HE market. As a result of all these efforts, Universidad Europea de Madrid seems to have garnered the following benefits:

- Online student numbers are set to grow by more than 100 per cent.
- Students can bring their own devices to university, boosting learning.
- Saved resources can be invested into campus facilities.
- Opening up easy and simple access to cloud computing (Dell Inc., 2012).

The eighth case study which also entails the deployment of corporate cloud computing relates to Ozyegin University (IBM, 2010). The latter is a private, non-profit university in Instabul, Turkey, that intends becoming a premier entrepreneurial research university with a stronger focus on quality teaching. Since its inception, it is experiencing an exponential growth in academic departments, research centers and student numbers. As a result, it has had pressing challenges: maintaining high-

quality educational, entrepreneurial and research standards for its growing students and faculty members; adopting fast changing technologies; and spiraling IT-related burden on faculty. In collaboration with IBM, it then embraced a cloud computing solution, and it set itself the following goals:

- Develop a new, modern curriculum with courses that make it easy for faculty to adopt emerging technologies.
- Persuade faculty members to utilize cloud computing-based software and hardware.
- Enable online and offline computer-based examinations (e.g., programming) for many students simultaneously.
- Simplify the use of high-performance computing (HPC) and distributed processing technologies for several disciplines so as to facilitate computational sciences or e-science quickly.
- Provide each registered student with a laptop (IBM, 2010).

This cloud computing roll-out process has yielded the following positives: a cloud-based finite element analysis (FEA) service has been designed and implemented for use for HPC research and teaching in different engineering departments; USB-bootable operating systems in conjunction with cloud applications are deployed to deliver custom-designed and network-controlled applications (exams and labs) to may students at the same time; and an IBM LotusLive™ collaboration suite is being rolled out so that members of the IBM Cloud Academy in Turkey can be eventually brought under one cloud universe (IBM, 2010).

Theorizing Learning within Mobile Social Networking Cloud Computing

Most learning mounted on mobile social networking occurs conversationally in the form of chatting. Such chatting – especially as deployed on

Facebook and Twitter - is mainly text-based and entails a lot of real-time texting/writing. In this way, learning delivered through social networking as an instance of cloud computing is mediated by texting or writing. As such, it needs to be theorized in line with the social networking cloud computing environment within which it takes place. One way of theorizing learning mediated through and embedded within a cloud-based personal mobile social computing provided by social networking is through an ecological framework. Grounded in the twin notion of *ecology* and *ecosystem* as conceptualized by Boylan (2004), Brooke (2009), Buck (2012) and Hodgson and Spours (2009), this framework regards learning, chatting, texting and writing on the one hand, and social networking and cloud computing on the other hand, as collectively, constituting ecologies of practices. Buck (2012), especially, posits writing as used by young adults on their mobile devices as an ecology of practice within digital environments. Employing the same analogy, in this chapter, chatting and texting enacted by young adults for purposes of learning within cloud-based mobile social networking are viewed as instances of new media writing scholarship (Brooke, 2009) occurring as part of digital literacy practices (Buck, 2012). The latter feed into ecologies of practices typifying mobile social networking and cloud computing. Moreover, in keeping with this ecological framework, both mobile social networking and mobile cloud computing are construed as enablers of real-time chat- and text-based writing and learning.

The other essential components of this framework are learners (users), mobile devices, cloud-based social networks (e.g., Facebook and Twitter) and wireless connectivity which, together, constitute a critical layer within a mobile cloud computing ecosystem. Within this ecosystem, all of these components are symbiotically interdependent: users, who in this case are learners, rely on and need mobile devices, social networks, and wireless connectivity for them to be able to access mobile cloud computing for learning purposes. In

the South African context, in particular, wireless connectivity is a critical ingredient in the mobile cloud computing ecosystem mix as broadband connectivity is expensive and, in certain cases, unreliable. Furthermore, these four components also serve as drivers and enablers of mobile cloud computing within this ecosystem. But in contrast to the other three components, learners or users hold the leverage of being actors and adopters in the overall mobile cloud computing equation. Therefore, their early or late uptake of mobile cloud computing finally determines whether they enjoy cloud affordances offered by this variant of computing earlier enough or only later on in their uptake trajectory.

Lastly, a theoretical lens through which real-time chat- and text-based writing and learning are viewed is that of socio-situated practice. The latter is articulated by Castro and Chala (2013) as a socially and culturally situated process within which writing is embedded and which determines writing as an act. According to this view, writing, as a social practice, occurs at a specific historical and temporal juncture and at a particular place in society. By extension, real-time chat- and text-based writing and learning are socio-culturally embedded in the digital life worlds of learners and mirror the lifestyles and cultures of such learners as mediated through both digital mobile devices (e.g., smart phones, iPads, tablets, phablets and mini-laptops) and the accompanying digital online environments (e.g., Facebook and Twitter). These digital online environments, in turn, mediate learners' equally digital online lifestyles and cultures.

RESEARCH METHODOLOGY

This study utilized a qualitative research paradigm and followed an interactive interpretivist research approach (see Maxwell, 2005). Based on this, it operated within a descriptive and interpretive case study design. This type of research design enables a researcher to analyze and interpret data with a view to theorizing it inductively against the backcloth of a given theoretical framework (see Griffee, 2012; Zacharias, 2012). In the current study, the data collected consisted of chunks of messages written through the researcher's and participants' mobile phones. This data was analyzed in relation to an ecological framework delineated earlier on. Participants together with Twitter and Facebook, then, represented a case studied in this instance.

Statement of the Problem

Both Twitter and Facebook rank among the most highly used social media applications, making them some of the most preferred social networking tools by, especially, young adults. The same applies to South Africa where these two social media applications are used by, among others, young adults for chatting and social networking, and for social relationship purposes (see Chaka, 2013b; Vosloo, 2009; World Wide Worx &Fuseware, 2012). Mostly, these young adults use their personal mobile phones as Internet devices to access these two social media tools and other related online mobile applications. Likewise, participants in this study accessed Twitter and Facebook from their personal mobile phones. Much as Twitter and Facebook are preferred social networking tools by young adults in South Africa - including those who participated in this study - they are, nonetheless, not often embraced as tools for educational purposes by most HEIs. This partly has to with the view that these two social media tools are implicated in retarding and corrupting users' English grammar - and language use in general – due to the texting or messaging (Chaka, 2012; Vosloo, 2009) in which users engage every time they leverage them. Again, this also partly has to do with the fact that most HE faculty members are reluctant to use and averse to embracing students' own personal mobile devices – which resonate with the BYOD approach – for educa-

tional purposes, save for announcements, alerts and emergency purposes. The third reason has to with the informal writing that social media tools such as Twitter and Facebook facilitate.

Despite the concerns cited above about the use of social networking tools, this study set out to employ Twitter and Facebook for educational cloud computing purposes. In so doing, it sought to discover some of the personal mobile cloud computing affordances these two social networking tools have for educational purposes.

Research Questions

In the light of the above, this study sought to answer the following questions:

- What types of personal mobile educational cloud computing affordances can Twitter and Facebook offer to designated groups of undergraduate students?
- Is it possible to facilitate formal writing for a designated group of undergraduate students using Facebook as a mobile cloud computing social networking tool?

Participants and Sampling

This study consisted of two projects: the Twitter and the Facebook projects. It sought participants' consent to take part in the two projects. The Twitter project involved 50 undergraduate students (out of a population of 200 students) enrolled in a first-year bi-semester English Academic Purposes (EAP) course in 2011 at a rural university in South Africa. Of these students, 28 were females and 22 were males, and their average age was 21 years (SD=0.87). All of the students used English as a second language and spoke one of South African indigenous languages as their mother tongue. The Facebook project had 30 students (out of a population of 100 students), who had enrolled in a first year intensive English writing course in 2012 at the self-same university, as its participants. Of these students, 18 were females and 12 were males whose average age was 22 years (SD=0.75). These students, too, spoke English as a second language and used one of South African indigenous languages as their mother tongue. Two sampling techniques, opportunistic and quota sampling techniques, were used (Teddlie & Yu, 2007; cf. Green, 2007; Yount, 2006; Zacharias, 2012). In the first instance, participants were chosen over a period of three weeks in August 2011 (for the first course) and in March 2012 (for the second course) after the researcher realized that they had their own mobile devices (mobile phones) that they used for accessing Twitter and Facebook. In the second instance, participants (in both groups) who showed to be persistent users of Twitter and Facebook were selected.

Twitter Project: Instruments, Materials, and Procedures

Participants' personal mobile phones were the main instruments through which the Twitter data was obtained and through which participants accessed mobile cloud computing. These participants were 50 students who had enrolled in the first-year bi-semester English Academic Purposes (EAP Economic Science) course in 2011 at a specified South African university. The course focused mainly on academic writing and communication skills as they related to the business and management context. So, in the second semester of 2011 academic year, participants were informed that for the next three months (from August to October) the course information and some of the content of the course would be made available to them via the instructor's Twitter account. Then, in the first week of August, those participants who did not have Twitter accounts were requested to sign up for such accounts and follow the instructor on his Twitter account. Once the participants

had signed up for Twitter accounts, requests (see *Exemplar 1*), reminders, announcements and alerts, snippets of the course content definitions or explanations, some practice course activities and a course assignment were tweeted and displayed on the instructor's Twitter's timeline.

Exemplar 1. A sample of a screenshot of one of the tweets sent to participants

18 Aug.

So, let's all together make Twitter an interactive learning platform and not just a 'follow me' medium or a 'personality' following medium.

Facebook Project: Instruments, Materials, and Procedures

Similarly, in respect of this project, participants' personal mobile phones served as both instruments to obtain the Facebook data and mobile devices for accessing cloud computing. The participants here were 30 students who had enrolled in a first year intensive English writing course in 2012 at a university mentioned above. The intensive English writing course in question – whose major focus was descriptive writing - was one of the English course offerings that participants had to do in the first semester as part of their Bachelor of Education in Humanities degree program. Even though it was a first year course, participants could only enroll in it when they were in their second year level of their degree program. At the beginning of March 2012, participants were informed that certain course activities would be provided to them on a Facebook group page. Subsequently, a class Facebook group page was created for participants which they were requested to join. Those who did not have Facebook accounts, were advised to sign up for them with a view to joining the class Facebook group page. Writing activities were then posted on the group page and participants had, in turn, to do them by posting their responses to the self-same group page. Comments about the course were also posted on the group page's wall by both the instructor and participants. In addition, feedback to participants' responses and comments was sent to individual participants using the Facebook group page facility. Moreover, at times, the instructor communicated with participants through a Facebook group's chat feature. The agreement between participants and their instructor was that all Facebook activities and their feedback to them, would not be done in a physical face-to-face encounter in class. One Facebook writing activity, as depicted in *Figure 2*, is the focus of this project:

FINDINGS AND DISCUSSION

Data Analysis

A composite analytic approach incorporating conversational and discourse analysis was used for analyzing the data for this study. The former - conversational analysis – analyses human conversation and focuses on, among other things, elements like talk, conversation structure, adjacency pairs and turn-taking (see Sacks, 1994; Sacks, Schegloff & Jefferson, 1974; Wooffitt, 2005). For its part, discourse analysis deals with features of discourse or language such as sentences, discourse markers, discourse patterns within given texts (Burman & Parker, 1993; Jones, 2012; Norris, 2004; Römer & Schulze, 2010; Wooffitt, 2005). Pertaining to the Twitter and Facebook projects, in particular, conversation and discourse were typified by tweets and posts either from participants or from their instructor, or from both parties. These tweets and posts constituted the data types for this study and were, accordingly, subjected to conversational and discourse analysis. Above all, the findings related to the Twitter project are discussed in response to and on the basis of the first research question, while those pertaining to the Facebook project are discussed in response to both research questions. These findings are, therefore, contextual as environments for Twitter and Facebook as instances of personal mobile educational cloud computing deployed on participants' mobile devices – especially their mobile phones – vary according to contexts of use and application.

Twitter and Mobile Cloud Computing-Based Teaching and Learning

The findings presented and discussed in this subsection are informed by the instructor's tweets to EAP Economic Science students as displayed on his timeline. Therefore, the discussion of these findings is in response to the following research question:

- What types of personal mobile educational computing affordances can Twitter offer to a designated group of undergraduate students?

As pointed out earlier on, after the participants had signed up for their respective Twitter accounts and had been requested to follow their instructor on his Twitter account, requests, reminders, announcements and alerts, snippets of the course content definitions or explanations, some practice course activities and a course assignment were tweeted and displayed on the instructor's Twitter's timeline. Two instances of requests are depicted in *Figure 3*.

In the same breath, the following instance exemplifies two reminders that were tweeted to the instructor's timeline for participants to note as represented in *Figure 4*.

As the use of Twitter gathered traction, tweets expressing gratitude to participants were also tweeted to the instructor's timeline as depicted in *Figure 5*.

In the midst of all this, announcements were tweeted for participants to view in the course of this

Figure 2. A sample of a Facebook writing activity given to participants

on Wednesday, May 9, 2012 at 9:56am

Question 1 (25 marks)
Using sensory, colour and relational descriptions, write a four-paragraph objective descriptive essay on the following topic:
Mthatha and East London are completely different from each other in all respects
NB: Making sure that your essay has the following elements:

- Proper parallel structures
- Appropriate linking words/Transitional expressions, and
- At least one compound-complex sentence

Due Date: 10 May 2012

Like · Comment

Twitter project. *Figure 6* provides four examples of such announcements.

Moreover, snippets of the course content were tweeted and posted on the instructor's Twitter timeline. These snippets were mainly intended to provide definitions or explanations of the designated aspects of the course content that were sometimes accompanied by relevant short questions. The snippets themselves were tweeted at different times throughout the duration of the Twitter project. Samples of such tweets are illustrated by *Figure 7*.

Finally, some tweets were meant for asking short questions related to the course content while others were intended for course content assignment purposes. Two such tweets exemplifying these two aspects of the course content are featured in *Figure 8*.

The uses that Twitter was put to as outlined in the preceding figures are a proof positive of some of the personal mobile educational cloud computing affordances this social networking tool could offer users. Firstly, it was deployed as a cloud based virtual platform for posting requests, reminders and announcements to participants about both micro- and macro-aspects of their course. In this sense, it served as a virtual notice board and a digital communication medium interfacing both participants and their instructor concerning the course information. Since both parties accessed Twitter from their personal mobile phones, the leveraging of Twitter for this particular educational cloud affordance occurred within the overall BYOD ecosystem. Secondly, Twitter was exploited as a cloud based virtual blackboard onto which snippets of the course content in the form of definitions and explanations and course related questions – including a course assignment question - were tweeted for participants to view and follow from their mobile phones anytime, wherever they were. This means that it served as a digital mobile cloud environment in which bite-sized teaching and learning occurred. This type of micro-teaching and micro-learning took place synchronously and asynchronously. Additionally, it was timeless (had no time constraints),

Figure 3. Two screenshots of two requests tweeted for participants

13 Sep

Pls hang on to your assignments till we're able to receive them. For now circumstances are still not favourable! Cheers, missing u all!

Details   Reply | Retweet | Favorite

14 Sep

[1/2] Can I request each one of u to ask any Econ Sci students you know to join me on Twitter & they too to ask others to do likewise? ...

Details   Reply | Retweet | Favorite

Figure 4. Two screenshots of two requests tweeted for participants

8 Sep

[2/2] you sign submission registers! NB: Don't put your assignment copies under your tutors' office doors - they won't be marked!

Details   7 : 15

8 Sep

[1/2] Reminder to all EAP Econ Scie: Today's the Due Date for your Assignments! Submit your work in person to your tutors & see to it that

Details   7 : 10

14 Sep

Even though we're not able to meet now, remember what I said in the lecture: most test & exam questions will come from posted tweets! Bye!

Details   16 : 52

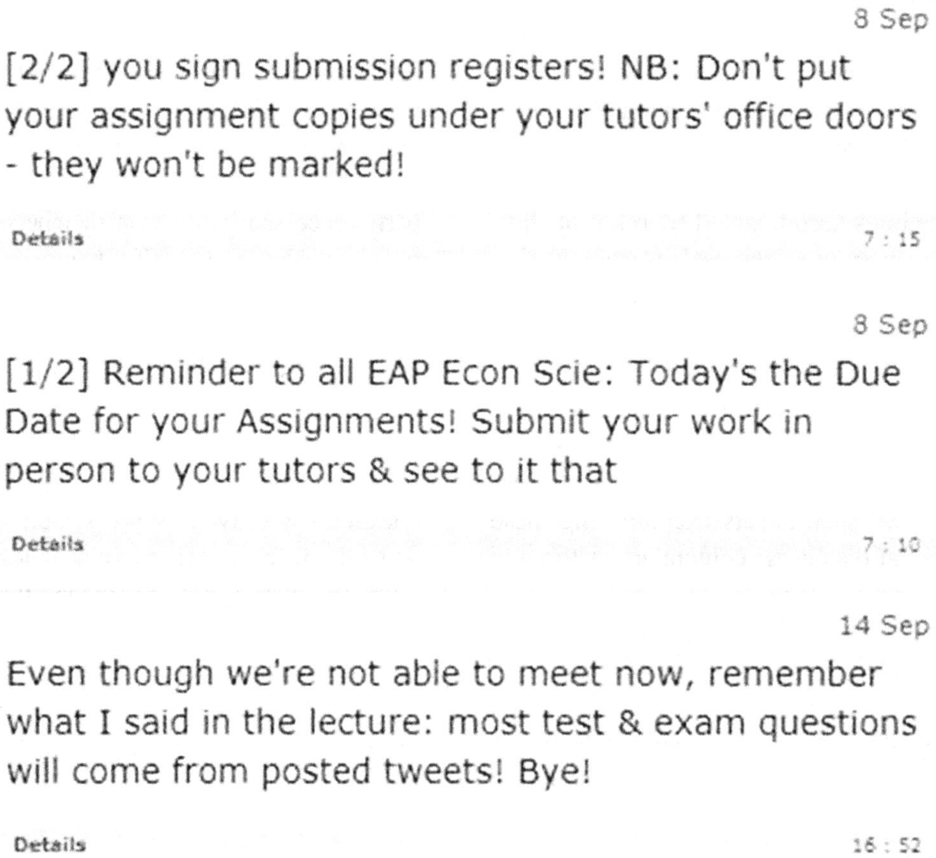

Figure 5. A screenshot of a gratitude-expressing tweet

18 Aug

Halo my EAP Econ Scie Grp 5! Thanks so much for agreeing to use Twitter for teaching & learning! Doing that is a giant step!

Details   17 : 34

Figure 6. Four screenshots of four announcement tweets

18 Aug

EAP Econ Scie Grp 5! Things to note: Tweets about parts of my lecture will be posted for you to follow or to respond to. See next tweet ...

Details   17 : 46

14 Sep

From Friday, short snippets & nuggets of my remaining section - the part I wasn't able to teach - (plus questions) will be posted on Twitter

Details   17 : 06

21 Sep

[1/2]Econ Sci Grps: Events always overtake us! Now with   closed, we can only have snippets of my lecture anytime anywhere once there ...

Details   8 : 33

10 Aug

ELS 1205: Please note that the final exam for this module for 2011 (2nd Sem) is as follows: Date: 04 November 211; Time: 09h00; Day: Friday

Details   17 : 59

Figure 7. Three screenshots of the snippets of the course content definitions/explanations some of which were accompanied by short course content questions

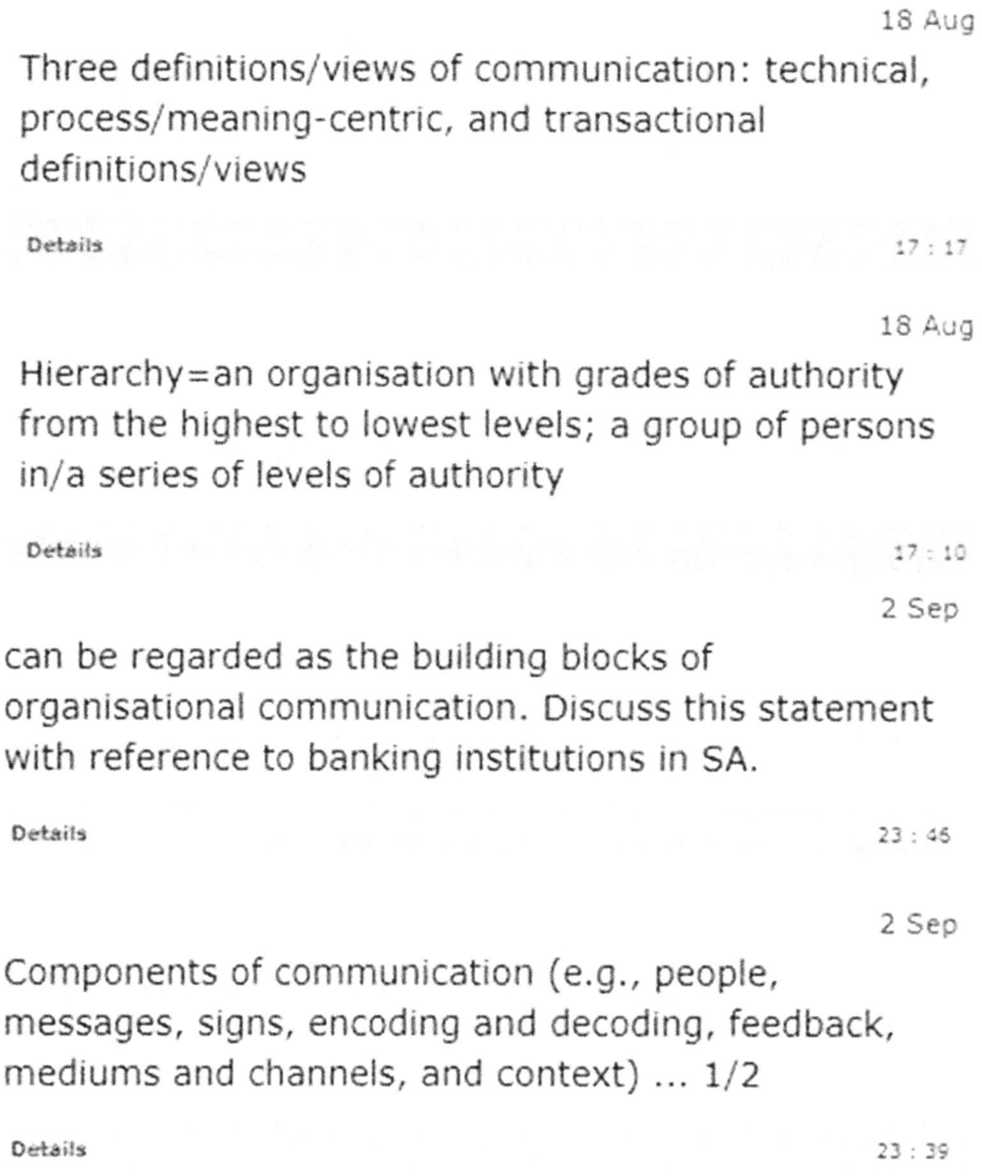

18 Aug

Three definitions/views of communication: technical, process/meaning-centric, and transactional definitions/views

Details   17 : 17

18 Aug

Hierarchy=an organisation with grades of authority from the highest to lowest levels; a group of persons in/a series of levels of authority

Details   17 : 10

2 Sep

can be regarded as the building blocks of organisational communication. Discuss this statement with reference to banking institutions in SA.

Details   23 : 46

2 Sep

Components of communication (e.g., people, messages, signs, encoding and decoding, feedback, mediums and channels, and context) ... 1/2

Details   23 : 39

borderless (had no geographic boundaries), and virtual. And above all, it was BYOD-driven, and device-agnostic. Most importantly, it required no further mobile infrastructure than participants' own mobile devices.

Facebook and Mobile Cloud Computing-Based Writing

As is the case with the previous sub-section, the findings presented and discussed in this sub-section are based on the responses and comments made by the intensive English writing course par-

Figure 8. Two screenshots, one for a short course content question and the other for a course content assignment

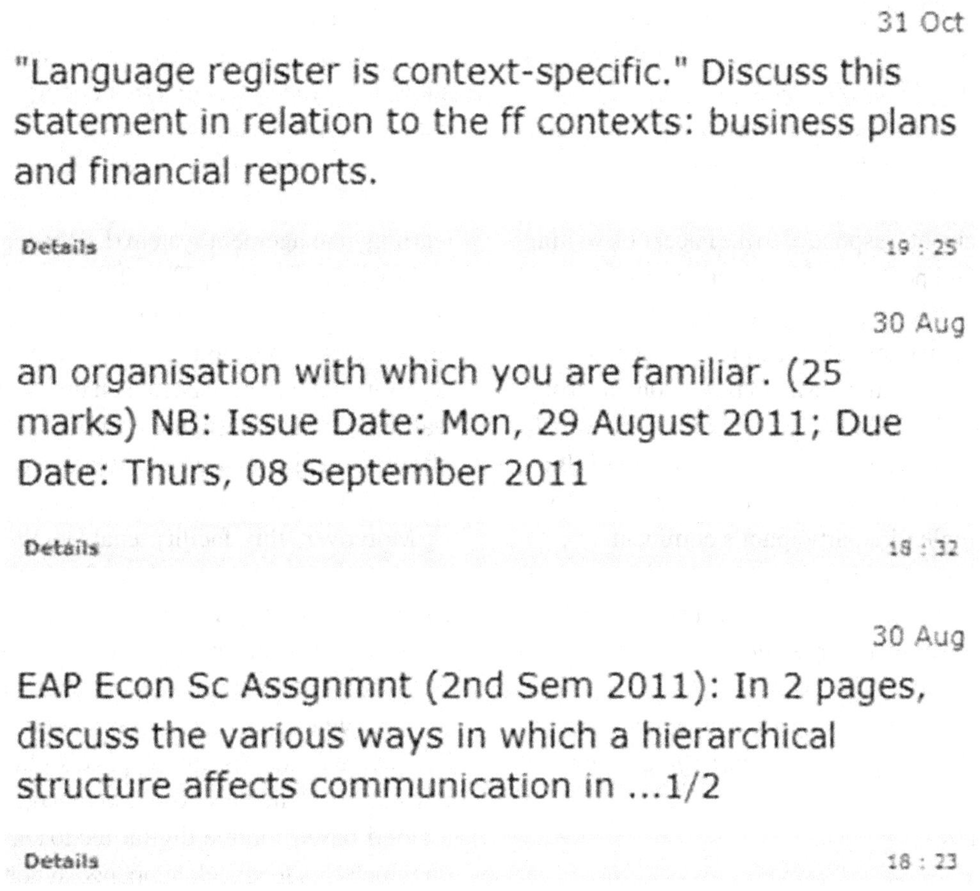

31 Oct

"Language register is context-specific." Discuss this statement in relation to the ff contexts: business plans and financial reports.

Details   19 : 25

30 Aug

an organisation with which you are familiar. (25 marks) NB: Issue Date: Mon, 29 August 2011; Due Date: Thurs, 08 September 2011

Details   18 : 32

30 Aug

EAP Econ Sc Assgnmnt (2nd Sem 2011): In 2 pages, discuss the various ways in which a hierarchical structure affects communication in ...1/2

Details   18 : 23

ticipants concerning a Facebook writing activity posted on the class Facebook group page. They also incorporate some of the instructor's feedback to participants' responses and comments. So, therefore, it is in response to the following two research questions:

- What types of personal mobile educational cloud computing affordances can Facebook offer to a designated group of undergraduate students?
- Is it possible to facilitate formal writing for this group of undergraduate students using

Facebook as a mobile cloud computing social networking tool?

As mentioned earlier on, after all participants in this project had been requested to sign up for Facebook accounts, they were subsequently asked to join a class Facebook group page facility. Thereafter, writing activities were posted on the Facebook group page that participants were required to do using the self-same group page. Additionally, comments about the course were also posted on the group page's wall by both the instructor and participants. Moreover, feedback to participants' responses and comments was sent to individual participants as messages using the Facebook group page facility. One instance of a participant' response to the Facebook writing activity mentioned earlier on in *Figure 2*, is displayed in *Figure 9*.

Another instance of a participant's response to this Facebook writing activity is represented in *Figure 10*.

Participants responded to the Facebook writing activity and posted their respective responses on their class Facebook group page facility. In turn, the instructor responded and provided feedback to participants' written tasks as posted on the group page. But, in addition, participants posted their comments as well. In this regard, *Figure 11* illustrates two instances of the instructor's feedback and a sample of a participant's comment.

Moreover, notification and gratitude messages to participants were posted on the Facebook group page as exemplified by *Exemplar 2*.

Exemplar 2: A notification and gratitude message posted to participants on a group page's wall

June 2, 2012

Hi everybody! I've now wrapped up all FB submissions and I'll pass on your marks to Mr M ....! Thanx and God Bless each one of you! It has been nice interacting with all of you on FB!!! Cheerio!!!

As illustrated in the preceding figures, with reference to the first question of the Facebook project, the class Facebook group page facility served as a cloud based mobile computing environment in which a course-specific writing activity (see *Figure 3*) was posted to which participants had to respond by leveraging the self-same group page facility. In this instance, this environment managed to mediate and facilitate a writing process between the instructor and participants in the same way as a real-life physical environment exploiting paper or a chalkboard would do. Therefore, it

digitally and virtually simulated a real-life student writing environment. Since the writing activity and participants' written responses to it occurred digitally and virtually, the Facebook group page facility acted as a digital and virtual blackboard. In addition, as the instructor at times communicated with participants via a Facebook group page's chat feature, this enabled the Facebook group page to function in the same as way as a conventional learning management system (LSM) deployed on mainstream university ITs. This is more so when considering that a Facebook group page allows messages or comments to be emailed and SMSed in addition to their being posted on the group page's wall. In this case, then, the Facebook group page offered both the instructor and participants some of the affordances provided by conventional LMSs.

Moreover, this facility enabled the instructor and participants to engage in asynchronous communication and writing (when messages or comments were posted on the group page's wall) and in synchronous communication and writing (when messages or comments were sent live via a Facebook group page's chat feature. Furthermore, the Facebook group page served as a cloud based mobile digital feedback platform on which this feedback happened synchronously and asynchronously (Chaka, 2014a, 2014b; Chaka & Ngesi, 2010; see Kabilan, Ahmad & Abidin, 2010; Lam, 2012). As this feedback was sent to individual participants, it means, thus, that it was also personalized in the same way as paper-based written student feedback becomes personalized when it is given to individual students in a real-life university situation. Since all the Facebook group page affordances in this project occurred on the instructor's and participants' own mobile devices (and especially on mobile phones) for university's enterprise/educational purposes, so, the leveraging of Facebook here had elements of consumerization and BYOD as mentioned earlier on. These affordances all together provided participants with a mobile cloud computing-based writing.

Figure 9. A participant's response to the Facebook writing activity

Most heroes came from the villages surrounding this city to mention the few Doctor Nelson Mandela the first Black and democratic president, Walter Sisulu, Stive Biko, Govern Mbeki and others. This city is rich with history as it was the capital city at former Transkei. It has tallest sky scripts buildings with bright orange and cream white colour reminding us with ancient struggles and political conflicts. These buildings were the head offices of the Transkei demarcation that was why all the movements and premier attracts took place in this city during that time. Even these honoured sky scripts buildings are named with the ancient heroes. The tallest was named as Bota Sigwcawu building and the second KD Mathanzima building. These buildings are closer to one another but were the head offices for the Lion and the Buck. Those were the Kings leading the people in Transkei demarcation and they were also enemies.

East London is on the former Ciskei demarcation boarder. This city is just near the sea, beautiful with its green vegetation and coolest fresh air from the ocean. This is the biggest city compared to Umtata but just medium size city against the metropolitan cities as it is the metropolitan city. There are bigger roads compared to the roads at Umtata city.

Figure 10. Another participant's response to the Facebook writing activity

Mtata and East london are completely differnt from each other in all respect.Mtata and east london are the major tonwns of eastern cape,both of them are situated in a southern part of hemespher geographicaly,but they are differen from each other interms of population,civilization,anfrustructure and enviroment.Mtata town is happily and comfidently with political structures which also affect university of mtata(NMD).Mtata is well known with political leaders such as Dr Rolihlahla mandela,this town is olso atractive to tourism while there is a bad infrastructure.East london is neatly and politetly enviroment,East london town is well known as a good town in eastern cape as whole.this town also situated near occeans,and East london beaches are scatterd with shells.in East london there so many different kinds of people whites,blacks,indians and chines it is clear that East london is a beautiful town,when you look at their new system of doing things,mtata is very old fashioned by contrast,where-as East london is a bill gates.

Figure 11. Two instances of the instructor's feedback and a sample of a participant's comment

Hi M   ! I've read your essay and thanks for your wonderful effort! Even though your essay has some misspellings and a few other mechanical errors, it nonetheless makes a fascinating read! I'm particularly impressed by your use of comparative and colour descriptions. But since there is some penalty attached to your essay submission, your final mark is

I've read through your Descriptive Writing essay. It's a well balanced comparative essay on the two cities. I'm aware that you've used comparative, relational, colour and visual descriptions. But remember that as a punitive measure, you can't get more than   . So, your mark is   .

Z   M   Thank you Doc. This will really equip us to be a better writing teachers. We looking forward to see result hoping that we did well.

June 2, 2012 at 4:02pm · Like

With respect to the second question, participants produced different pieces of writing. Some of these pieces of writing reflected the following features: well structured paragraphs; acceptable English grammar and language use; fewer spelling errors; proper use of punctuation marks (see Aziz, Shamim, Aziz & Avais, 2013; DuBay, 2004). Others displayed forms that deviated from these features in varying degrees (see *Figure 8* and *9*). So, overall, the different pieces of writing that participants produced as part of their responses to the writing activity given to them on the Facebook group page depicted varying degrees of formal writing (Aziz et al., 2013; DuBay, 2004). All of these pieces of writing did not have textisms characteristic of instant messaging or SMS language.

LIMITATIONS AND FUTURE RESEARCH DIRECTIONS

As stated earlier on, this study employed an interactive interpretivist research approach and a descriptive and interpretive case study design. In its case design, it had 50 and 30 participants in its Twitter and Facebook projects, respectively. So, in all, in both cases its total sample was small. One of the reasons for the small sample was to make it possible for the researcher to pay attention to all participants in each project with a view to giving each of them personalized responses, comments and feedback. This was necessary as in a teaching and learning environment provided by the two social networking sites (SNSs), participants who felt neglected or perceived not to be attended to, were likely to discontinue partaking in a project of which they were part. This potential drawback was more likely in the case of the Facebook project than in the Twitter project which allowed course announcements, requests, reminders and questions to be posted en mass to participants on the instructor's Twitter timeline. Of course, pertaining to Twitter, in particular, its major inherent downside is the 140-character quota per tweet.

In addition, a cloud based educational environment offered by these two SNSs only allowed that student written work be assessed and graded by a human instructor and not by an intelligent or a virtual tutor. However, though, the forms of writing that participants were required to produce could not be assessed and graded by such intelligent or virtual tutors, even if they had been embedded into these SNSs. Again, once participants had posted their responses on the Facebook group page for submission purposes, especially, they could not edit or revise them without having to delete them altogether. Even then, they would have needed to get the instructor's permission as he was the sole administrator of the class Facebook group page. Yet, the kind of writing in which participants engaged, required some editing and revising before and, at times, after submitting. Most importantly, the findings of this study are more valuable for their transferability and replicability than for their generalizablity as is the case with most studies grounded on case study designs (see, for example, Griffee, 2012; Maxwell, 2005; Zacharias, 2012).

Furthermore, the present study explored the use of Twitter and Facebook for sharing course content with participants and for engaging participants in the writing process, respectively, over a limited period of time. Even, then, the two projects were one-off efforts. As a result, it is necessary that future research employing these two SNSs for educational purposes in the HE sector, do so over a sustained period of time. Such research will need to have integrated and corresponding follow-up projects. Additionally, in this study, both Twitter and Facebook were employed separately for each project. It is, therefore, advisable that future research intending leveraging these two SNSs synergize them within each project with a

view to harnessing their optimal mobile educational cloud computing affordances (cf.. George & Dellasega, 2011).

CONCLUSION

The present study investigated the use of Twitter and Facebook for sharing course content with participants and for engaging participants in the writing process, respectively. Each of these two SNSs constituted a project on its own, making the study a dual project study, each with its own group of participants. The two groups of participants were enrolled in two different undergraduate courses at a rural university in South Africa and spoke English as a second language. With respect to the Twitter project, some of the mobile educational cloud affordances it could offer were tapped. Firstly, it was deployed as a cloud based virtual platform for posting requests, reminders and announcements to participants about both the micro- and macro-aspects of their course. Secondly, it was exploited as a cloud based virtual blackboard for snippets of the course content, thereby facilitating anytime, anywhere bite-sized or micro-teaching and micro-learning.

The Facebook project, offered some of the mobile educational cloud affordances that participants harnessed. First, a class Facebook group page facility served as a cloud based mobile computing environment in which a course-specific writing process was mounted by both the instructor and participants. Second, this group page facility lent itself well as a mobile cloud and digital platform for feedback for both the instructor and participants. Third, participants exploited a Facebook group page to produce varying degrees of formal writing. Fourth and last, the use of both Twitter and Facebook as deployed especially from the instructor's and from participants' own mobile devices, embodied elements of both consumcrization and BYOD approaches to teaching and learning. Finally, these two SNSs provided participants with mobile cloud computing-based learning affordances.

REFERENCES

Alberta Education. (2012). *Bring your own device: A guide for schools*. Retrieved April 2, 2014, from https://education.alberta.ca/media/6749210/byod%20guide%20revised%202012-09-05.pdf

Aziz, S., Shamim, M., Aziz, M. F., & Avais, P. (2013). The impact of texting/SMS language on academic writing of students - What do we need to panic about? *Elixir Linguistics and Translation, 55*, 12884–12890.

Behrend, T. S., Wiebe, E. N., London, J. E., & Johnson, E. C. (2010). Cloud computing adoption and usage in community colleges. *Behaviour & Information Technology, 30*(2), 231–240. doi:10.1080/0144929X.2010.489118

Boylan, M. (2004). *Questioning (in) school mathematics: Lifeworlds and ecologies of practice* (Unpublished doctoral dissertation). Sheffield Hallam University, Sheffield.

Brooke, C. (2009). *Lingua fracta: Towards a rhetoric of new media*. Cresskill, NJ: Hampton Press.

Buck, A. (2012). Examining digital literacy practices on social network sites. *Research in the Teaching of English, 47*(1), 9–38. http://www.ncte.org/library/NCTEFiles/Resources/Journals/RTE/0471-aug2012/RTE0471Examining.pdf Retrieved April 2, 2014

Burman, E., & Parker, I. (1993). Introduction - discourse analysis: The turn to the text. In E. Burman & I. Parker (Eds.), *Discourse analytic research: Repertoires and readings of texts in action* (pp. 1–13). London: Routledge.

Burmeister, B. (2014, February 27). Benefits (and risks) of the mobile organisation. *Finweek, 3*, 7.

Castro, C. M. C., & Chala, P. A. (2013). Undertaking the act of writing as a situated social practice: Going beyond the linguistic and the textual. *Colombian Applied Linguistics Journal, 15*(1), 25–42. doi:10.14483/udistrital.jour.calj.2013.1.a02

Chaka, C. (2012). Mobiles for sustainable learning environments: Mobile phones and MXit with a South African school context. *Journal for Community Communication and Information Impact, 17*, 161–182.

Chaka, C. (2013a). Virtualization and cloud computing: Business models in the virtual cloud. In A. W. Loo (Ed.), *Distributed computing innovations for business, engineering, and science* (pp. 176–190). Hershey, PA: IGI Global. doi:10.4018/978-1-4666-2533-4.ch009

Chaka, C. (2013b). Digitization and consumerization of identity, culture, and power among Gen Mobinets in South Africa. In R. Luppicini (Ed.), *Handbook of research on technoself: Identity in a technological society* (pp. 77–96). Hershey, PA: IGI Global. doi:10.4018/978-1-4666-2211-1.ch022

Chaka, C. (2014a). Facebook's cloud value chain for higher education. *Infosys Labs Briefings, 11*(4), 84–89.

Chaka, C. (2014b). Social media as technologies for asynchronous formal writing and synchronous paragraph writing in the South African higher education context. In V. Benson & S. Morgan (Eds.), *Cutting-edge technologies and social media use in higher education* (pp. 213–241). Hershey, PA: IGI Global. doi:10.4018/978-1-4666-5174-6.ch009

Chaka, C., & Ngesi, N. (2010). Mobile writing: Using SMSes to write short paragraphs in English. In R. Guy (Ed.), *Mobile learning: Pilot projects and initiatives* (pp. 185–233). Santa Rosa, California: Informing Science Press.

Cheston, R. W. (2012). *BYOD & consumerization: Why the cloud is key to a viable implementation.* Retrieved May 10, 2014, from https://kapost-files-prod.s3.amazonaws.com/uploads/direct/20130709-2006-19803-4221/BYOD-Consumerization-White-Paper-Rich-Cheston-Aug-2012.pdf

Dell Inc. (2012). *University enhances education through the cloud.* Retrieved May 10, 2014, from http://i.dell.com/sites/doccontent/corporate/case-studies/en/Documents/2012-europea-madrid-10011452.pdf

DuBay, W. H. (2004). *The principles of readability.* Retrieved April 10, 2014, from http://en.copian.ca/library/research/readab/readab.pdf

George, D. R., & Dellasega, C. (2011). Use of social media in graduate-level medical humanities education: Two pilot studies from Penn State College of Medicine. *Medical Teacher, 33*(8), e429–e434. doi:10.3109/0142159X.2011.586749 PMID:21774639

Green, J. (2007). *A guide to using qualitative research methodology.* Retrieved May 30, 2014, from http://fieldresearch.msf.org/msf/bitstream/10144/84230/1/Qualitative%20research%20methodology.pdf

Griffee, D. T. (2012). *An introduction to second language research methods: Design and data.* Retrieved June 24, 2014, from http://www.tesl-ej.org/pdf/ej60/sl_research_methods.pdf

Hershock, C., & LaVaque-Manty, M. (2012). *Teaching in the cloud: Leveraging online collaboration tools to enhance student engagement.* Retrieved June 24, 2014, from http://www.crlt.umich.edu/sites/default/files/resource_files/CRLT_no31.pdf

Hodgson, A., & Spours, K. (2009). *Collaborative local learning ecologies: Reflections on the governance of lifelong learning in England.* Retrieved June 24, 2014, http://www.niace.org.uk/lifelong-learninginquiry/docs/IFLL-Sector-Paper6.pdf

IBM. (2010). *Ozyegin University: Cloud computing with IBM.* Retrieved May 4, 2014, from http://www.ibm.com/ibm/files/W771375B62431S24/Ozyegin_EDB03009-USEN-00.pdf

Jones, R. H. (2012). *Discourse analysis: A resource book for students.* London: Routledge.

Kabilan, M. K., Ahmad, N., & Abidin, M. J. Z. (2010). Facebook: An online environment for learning of English in institutions of higher education? *The Internet and Higher Education, 3*(4), 179–187. doi:10.1016/j.iheduc.2010.07.003

Katz, R., Goldstein, P., & Yanosky, R. (2010). *Cloud computing in higher education.* Retrieved May 4, 2014, from http://net.educause.edu/section_params/conf/ccw10/highered.pdf

Kraan, W., & Yuan, L. (2009). *Cloud computing in institutions: A briefing paper.* Retrieved June 24, 2014, from http://wiki.cetis.ac.uk/images/1/11/Cloud_computing_web.pdf

Lam, L. (2012). An innovative research on the usage of Facebook in the higher education context of Hong Kong. *The Electronic Journal of e-Learning, 10*(4), 377-386.

Lin, Y.-T., Wen, M.-L., Jou, M., & Wu, D.-W. (2013). A cloud-based learning environment for developing student reflection abilities. *Computers in Human Behavior, 32,* 244–252. doi:10.1016/j.chb.2013.12.014

Maxwell, J. A. (2005). *Qualitative research design: An interactive approach.* Thousand Oaks, CA: Sage.

McDonald, D., MacDonald, A., & Breslin, C. (2010). *Final report from the JISC review of the environmental and organisational implications of cloud computing in higher and further education.* Retrieved April 2, 2014, from http://www.jisc.ac.uk/media/documents/programmes/greeningict/cloudstudyreport.pdf

Mircea, M., & Andreescu, A. I. (2011). Using cloud computing in higher education: A strategy to improve agility in the current financial crisis. *Communications of the IBIMA*, 1-15. doi:10.5171/2011.875547

Mitrano, T. (2009). *Outsourcing and cloud computing for higher education.* Retrieved April 2, 2014, from http://www.it.cornell.edu/cms/policies/publications/upload/Memo-on-Outsourcing-and-Cloud-Computing.pdf

Norris, S. (2004). *Analyzing multimodal interaction: A methodological framework.* London: Routledge.

Plummer, D. C., Bittman, T. J., Austin, T., Cearley, D. W., & Smith, D. M. (2008). *Cloud computing: Defining and describing an emerging phenomenon.* Retrieved from June 24, 2014, http://www.emory.edu/BUSINESS/readings/CloudComputing/Gartner_cloud_computing_defining.pdf

Römer, U., & Schulze, R. (Eds.). (2010). Patterns, meaningful units and specialized discourses. Philadephia. John Benjamins. doi:10.1075/bct.22

Sacks, H. (1994). *Lectures on conversation.* Oxford: Blackwell.

Sacks, H., Schegloff, E., & Jefferson, G. A. (1974). A simplest systematics for the organization of turn-taking for conversation. *Language*, *50*(4), 696–735. doi:10.1353/lan.1974.0010

Sarga, L. (2012). Cloud computing: An overview. *Journal of Systems Integration*, *4*, 1–12.

Teddlie, C., & Yu, F. (2007). Mixed methods sampling: A typology with examples. *Journal of Mixed Methods Research*, *1*(1), 77–100. doi:10.1177/2345678906292430

Thomas, P. Y. (2009). *Cloud Computing: A potential paradigm for practising the scholarship of teaching and learning.* Retrieved May 4, 2014, from http://www.ais.up.ac.za/digi/docs/thomas_paper.pdf

Vosloo, S. (2009). *The effects of texting on literacy: Modern scourge or opportunity?* Retrieved March 15, 2010, from http://vosloo.net/wp-content/uploads/pubs/texting_and_literacy_apr09_sv.pdf

Wakefield, J. S., Warren, S. J., & Alsobrook, M. (2011). Learning and teaching as communicative actions: A mixed-methods twitter study. *Knowledge Management & E-Learning: An International Journal*, *3*(4), 563–584.

Wang, M., Chen, Y., & Khan, M. J. (2014). Mobile cloud learning for higher education: A case study of Moodle in the cloud. *International Review of Research in Open and Distance Learning*, *15*(2), 254–267.

Wooffitt, R. (2005). *Conversation analysis and discourse analysis: A comparative and critical introduction.* London: Sage.

World Wide Worx & Fuseware. (2012). *South African social media landscape 2012 – Executive summary.* Retrieved April 21, 2013, from http://www.worldwideworx.com/wp-content/uploads/2012/10/Exec-Summary-Social-Media-20121.pdf

Yount, W. R. (2006). *Research design and statistical analysis for Christian ministry.* Louisville: NAPCE.

Zacharias, N. T. (2012). *Qualitative research methods for second language education: A coursebook.* Newcastle upon Tyne: Cambridge Scholars Publishing.

KEY TERMS AND DEFINITIONS

BYOD (Bring Your Own Device): An approach or strategy adopted within an information technology framework according to which users or employees bring and use their own convenient devices – in lieu of company's infrastructure and tools - at their respective workplaces.

Cloud Computing Ecosystem: A network of different permutations of cloud computing in relation to one another and in respect to how they operate and exist in a computing ecosystem. Some of the examples of consumer cloud computing services are Google Apps, Dropbox, iCloud and SkyDrive.

Consumerization: In the information technology (IT) field, consumerization refers to the adoption and use of consumer-grade mobile devices, applications, and platforms by employees to enhance their workplace productivity.

Facebook: A social networking site (started at Harvard University by Mark Zuckenberg) enabling users to create networks of friends, and share personal profiles, blogs, music, photos, and video clips.

Higher Education: This refers to tertiary education, and includes institutions such as colleges, institutes of technology, and universities.

Post-PC Trends: These are computing trends that relate mainly to non-PC devices such as laptops, tablets, smartphones, gaming consoles, and other related mobile devices.

Twitter: A messaging site (also an application or a platform) allowing users to post messages that do not exceed a 140 character limit per post, and to post and share pictures, music, and video clips.

Chapter 5
Applying Kolb Learning Experiential Theory with Cloud Computing in Higher Education Institutions:
Tanzania

Camilius Sanga
Sokoine University of Agriculture, Tanzania

George Kibirige
Sokoine University of Agriculture, Tanzania

ABSTRACT

The maturity of free and open source movement has brought a number of ICT tools. It has affected the way courses are delivered, the way contents are developed, the way data are interoperable, the way learning and teaching materials are shared, the way learners access classes and the way library resources are shared. In developing countries, several libraries are migrating into digital libraries using low cost technologies readily available due to open access, free and open source technology and e-publishing tools. Recent development of cloud computing technology provides state of art tools for libraries. It provides a common platform for easy information storage and sharing. Thus, there is lowering of the cost required to procure and manage library ICT infrastructure due to the capability of that cloud computing which allows the storage to be on a single, efficient system that saves cost and time. In developing countries where most libraries suffer from limited budgets for ICT services, it is anticipated that the future of digital libraries is on cloud libraries.

1. INTRODUCTION

The advent of Information and Communication Technology (ICT) has changed the landscape of libraries in the world. The libraries in developed and developing countries no longer depend only from print materials for its customers (Wiederhold, 1995). Thus, with the advancement of ICT even the conventional definition of library need to be revisited so that it includes aspects of electronic resources:

DOI: 10.4018/978-1-4666-8339-6.ch005

A place in which literary and artistic materials, such as books, periodicals, newspapers, pamphlets, prints, records, and tapes, are kept for reading, reference, or lending. (Hartman, 2007; Plutchak, 2012)

Libraries are incorporating traditional methods of keeping, referencing and lending literary materials with new methods using ICT. This is what is referred as "digital library" (Lyons, 2007). Examples of ICT applications which use digital libraries include: television and radio; Compact Discs (CDs) and Digital Versatile Discs (DVDs); video conferencing; mobile technologies; web-based library management technologies; and electronic learning platforms. Challenges facing libraries in developing countries to adopt digital library are inherent contributed by challenges affecting Higher Education Institutions (HEIs) in adopting new ICTs tools as mentioned by Sife et al. (2007) in paper titled "New technologies for teaching and learning: Challenges for higher education institutions in developing countries". The challenges are namely: lack of systemic approach for ICT implementation, awareness and attitude towards ICTs, administrative support, technical support, staff development, lack of ownership and inadequate funds (Sife, Lwoga, & Sanga., 2007). Other challenges include: cost of acquiring, managing, and maintaining ICT infrastructure, high cost of bandwidth, inadequate competent technical staff and lack of cloud and digital library policies (Fox, 2009). Nonetheless, the advancement of ICT in cloud computing and Free and Open Source Software (FOSS) provide an opportunity for libraries in developing countries to address some of these challenges by effectively utilizing the potential of cloud services.

By definition, cloud computing from the National Institute of Standards and Technology (NIST) is defined as follows:

Cloud computing is a model for enabling convenient, on-demand network access to a shared pool of configurable computing resources (e.g., networks, servers, storage, applications, and services) that can be rapidly provisioned and released with minimal management effort or service provider interaction. (Mell &Grance, 2011).

The cloud computing is characterized by communication, information sharing, collaboration, interoperability and user-centered design. Inherently these characteristics of cloud computing are well embedded in FOSS (Yuan *et al.*, 2008).

FOSS has brought new movement in education. These include open acess, open educational resources, open courseware etc. The advocacy of open education argues that knowledge can be shared using different ICT tools. This knowledge sharing can be in different forms, for example, (i) sharing in scholarly research (open access) (ii) sharing in teaching and learning materials (open educational resources) (iii) sharing in computer code (open source) (iv) sharing in research data in a machine readable format (open data) (v) sharing in how you work/learn (open practice) (vi) sharing in courses to classes (either open courses or massive open online course) (Yuan, MacNeill, & Kraan 2008). These characteristics provide basis for implementing cloud library (Xinping, 2010). Mavodza (2013) argues that cloud library is going to shift the problems of HEI from hardware and software demands for storing and organizing data, to information access concerns. The reason behind this is because there is exponential growth of information sources and it is associated with its complexities that limit capacity of libraries in developing countries to host their own electronic information resources in its entirety. Thus, this necessitates opting for alternatives solutions using cloud computing (Mavodza, 2013). Libraries in developing countries are migrating from conventional library to digital library and cloud library which is for virtual library (Lwoga, 2012). This migration to virtual library is supported by tools from cloud computing (CC, 2014). Cloud computing refers as a model of network computing where

Figure 1. Software paradigm (adapted from Mei and Liu, 2011)

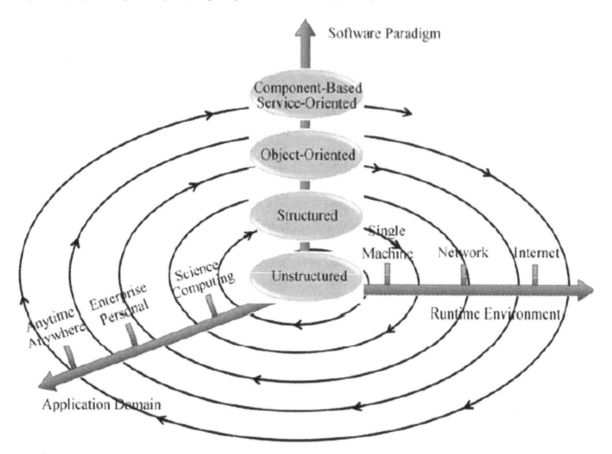

a program or application runs on a connected server or servers rather than on a local computing device such as a PC, tablet or Smartphone. Thus, cloud computing utilizes the concept of virtualization where one or more physical servers can be configured and partitioned into multiple independent "virtual" servers, all functioning independently and appearing to the user to be a single physical device.

Cloud computing has changed even the software development paradigms (Figure 1) from unstructured paradigm to structured paradigm, and to object oriented paradigm and component based paradigm to component based service oriented (Mei & Liu, 2011). In a library which has adopted cloud computing, cloud users access library services either as free "subscription-based"

or by paying "pay-per-use service in real time over the Internet" (Scale, 2010). Thus, using cloud computing different cloud library stakeholders can access library services anywhere anytime (24 hours, 7days, 365days).

The emerging of cloud computing has started revolutionizing services offered from conventional library to digital library (Rasmussen & Jochumsen, 2009) and cloud library. In cloud library, services of libraries and its ICT infrastructure, library software and applications can be hosted into cloud servers and its digital services accessed via Internet with some predefined permission to different type of stakeholders. Thus, adoption of cloud library has the potential to lower the cost. With cloud library, the cost associated with managing digital ICT application for library, paying licenses fees for software, procuring the hardware and salaries for ICT staff can be minimized. These are some of the benefits which can be obtained from adoption of cloud library because of the seamless integration of computing devices, human society and physical objects (Mei & Liu, 2011). Other benefits of cloud computing to digital library are similar to those for blended learning in HEIs, namely: reduction of ICT investment, support for maintenance is guaranteed, the accessibility and reliability of cloud services is higher, reduction of cost since the cloud services are paid as per use model, increased storage space which can be personalized into quota for each user of library, improve efficiency and effectiveness of library from the access of high performance computing (HPC) facilities and easy to scale up the access of high performance cloud service (Harris, 2012; Mtebe, 2013; Shimba, 2010; Shimba *et al.*, 2014). In addition, other benefits are: risk mitigation (i.e. services host far away from library and incase of catastrophic event the services are still uptime), speed of delivery of services, no need of new staff when scaling up services, improved services and universities are left with their core functions rather than technical issues of cloud library.

In summary, the advantages of cloud computing as identified by He *et al.* (2011) include:

1. **Less Maintenance:** Hardware, applications and bandwidth are managed by the provider.
2. **Continuous Availability:** Public cloud services are available wherever you are located.
3. **Scalability:** Pay only for the applications and data storage you need.
4. **Elasticity:** Private clouds can be scaled to meet your changing IT system demands.
5. **Expert Service:** Expedient's cloud computing services are continuously monitored and maintained by onsite staff of expert data center technicians.
6. **Automatic Software Integration:** In the cloud, software integration is usually something that occurs automatically. This means

that no need to take additional efforts to customize and integrate applications as per users' preferences. Cloud computing allows users' to customize their options with great ease. Hence, users' can handpick just those services and software applications that you think will best suit their particular enterprise.

7. **Backup and Recovery:** Since all your data is stored in the cloud, backing it up and restoring the same is relatively much easier than storing the same on a physical device. Furthermore, most cloud service providers are usually competent enough to handle recovery of information. Hence, this makes the entire process of backup and recovery much simpler than other traditional methods of data storage.

From the literature review, the critical analysis of benefits which can be obtained by HEIs in developing countries after adopting cloud computing services into their digital library is presented. It is anticipated that some of the challenges which libraries in developing countries are now experiencing can be addressed by adopting cloud computing services. This book chapter presents different aspects of the application of cloud computing in libraries, different platforms available, how to create cloud libraries, challenges and opportunities, and the role of cloud librarians along with situation analysis from selected Tanzania's HEIs libraries. The literature review identified that previous studies did not apply any theory to guide their researches (Harris, 2012; Mtebe, 2013; Shimba, 2010; Shimba *et al.*, 2014). This is one of the major weaknesses of the previous researches done in cloud computing. Thus, this study differs from earlier studies by applying Kolb Experiential Learning theory (Kolb, Boyatzis, & Mainemelis,, 2001). Kolb experiential learning theory is built on six propositions namely: (i) Learning is best conceived as a process, not in terms of outcomes. (ii) All learning is re-learning. (iii) Learning requires the resolution of conflicts between dialectically opposed modes of adaptation to the world. (iv) Learning is a holistic process of adaptation to the world. (v) Learning results from synergetic transactions between the person and the environment (vi) Learning is the process of creating knowledge (Kolb, & Kolb 2005). Also, Kolb experiential learning theory is a recursive process which involves experiencing, reflecting, thinking, and acting (Kolb, & Kolb, 2005), The fundamental aspect of Kolb experiential learning theory is experience. Kolb experiential learning theory differs from behavioral and cognitive learning theories which are rational learning theory based on empirical epistemology (Kolb, 1984). Epistemology deals with theory of knowledge under which the research is seeking to contribute (Crotty, 1998). Epistemology stances for Kolb experiential learning theory combine theories from other school of thoughts that is why Kolb (1984) argues that Kolb experiential learning theory is holistic integrative approach which combines experience, perception, cognition and behavior. Thus, learning is defined as the process of creating new knowledge or skills through experience transformation. The experience transformations are done in objective or subjective forms to the learner. This forms the basis for choosing the theoretical perspective of the research which is to be undertaken (Crotty, 1998). HEIs need to change their setting so as to create a conducive environment for problem solvers by adopting different forms of Kolb experiential learning theory. Kolb and Kolb(2005) suggested that HEIs must have enabling environment for promoting lifelong learning through (i) evaluation of educational structures and processes against promotion of learning criteria. (ii) longitudinal outcome studies to determine learning value added. (iii) becoming a learner-centered institution. (iv) continuous research and inquiry about the learning process. (v) becoming a learning organization by having regular stakeholder conversation. The aim of these criteria for promoting lifelong learning at HEIs is towards developing open system for a university.

The university with open system is one which has adopted either open courseware or open data or open source software or open educational resources or massive open online course.

Scale (2010) assessment of the impact of cloud computing on library services can be taken as supporting evidence which shows that libraries of different organizations are striving to make their libraries as open system rather than close systems. The basis for this argument is that for a library in this digital era to be competitive and remain relevant to different users who are mobile and using Web 2.0 tools, there is a need of adopting cloud computing which facilitates open systems development. Scale (2010) proposed that if libraries are to adopt cloud computing, the concept of physical libraries will have different implications if compared to cloud library in provisions of libraries services. Hence, there is no way for convetional library to escape adopting cloud library since the stakeholders of most e-government services, which include library services from conventional library, are nomad (Ochara-Muganda & Van Belle, 2010). Nomadicity for stakeholders of library is driven by technologies such as portable computers, laptops, notebooks, Personal Digital Assistants (PDA), Smart Card devices (e.g. IPAD), mobiles (mobile phones) and now cloud computing services. This is one of the feature of nomadicity when combined with portability increases the probability of having a good results from the implementation of cloud library in developing countries where the conventional libraries are not adequate. It is from this analysis that the application of cloud computing in library is an emerging area of concern for library in developing countries. Also, cloud computing for library is among the development informatics research agenda in area of ICT for Development (Heeks, 2014). Thus, this book chapter contributes toward filling this research gap in knowledge by adding more critical analysis literature in area of cloud computing for digital library. The concept 'cloud computing' for digital library was conceptualized using Kolb experiential learning theory. Kolb experiential learning theory was chosen since it works better in analyzing the dynamics of exploitation and exploration in intra- and inter-organizational learning processes (Holmqvist, 2004). This differentiated this study from other previous researchers (He et al., 2011;Scale, 2010) who were not guided by theoretical stance in their studies that is why there results are not grounded in particular theory and thus, difficult to understand their claim in knowledge contribution. Heeks (2014) argues that any study which is not supported by a good philosophical stance, theoretical knowledge, research methodology and research method its results / findings are as good as fallacy.

Therefore, the research design for this study was formulated by choosing a combination of techniques: namely; philosophical stance, theoretical knowledge, research methodology and research method. The research approach was designed based on techniques suggested by Crotty (1998). According to Crotty (1998) four questions are considered when designing a research:

1. **What Epistemology?:** This deals with theory of knowledge embedded in the theoretical perspectives which informs the research (e.g. objectivism, subjectivism, etc.).
2. **What Theoretical Perspectives?:** This deals with philosophical stance which lies behind the chosen research methodology in your research (e.g. positivism, post-positivism, interpretivism, critical theory, etc.)
3. **What Methodology?:** This deals with strategy or plan of action that links research methods to outcomes. Outcome governs the researcher choice and use of research methods (e.g. experimental research, survey research, ethnography, etc.)
4. **What Methods?:** This deals with techniques and procedures proposed by research to use in data collection and data analysis (e.g. questionnaire, interview, focus groups, etc.)

These four questions (Figure 2) are usually missing in many previous researches done in area of ICT for development (ICT4D) (Heeks, 2014).

In order to fill the identified research gap in cloud library literature and to better help different library stakeholders' understand and adopt cloud computing (Heeks, 2014), this book chapter provides some insights for developing cloud computing strategies for libraries in developing countries, based on the literature review and on the authors' years of practical experience in ICT4D projects. These insights are intended to assist different library stakeholders in developing countries when they are integrating cloud computing in their either digital library or conventional library as part of their ICT strategy planning (Kamel, 2010).

Furthermore, this book chapter contributes by adding literature from both the industry and the academia as cloud library is still not comprehensive and mature field of study. This is the research gap which was identified by (Shimba, 2010).

This book chapter is organized as follows: section one presents the introduction, literature review in cloud library and Kolb experiential learning theory. Also, section one describes benefits that cloud computing brings to conventional library. Section two describes the research methodology. The remaining sections present the cloud computing architecture, including its delivery models and deployment methods. Also, the sub – section of section two presents the challenges of cloud computing in library. Furthermore, it offers insights for different stakeholders of library who are interested in adopting and implementing cloud computing in their digital library or conventional library. Finally, conclusions and suggestions for future research areas are presented.

2. RESEARCH METHODOLOGY

This research was conducted in Tanzania. The research methodology which was adopted in this study was desk research. It included meta - analysis

Figure 2. Four elements of the research process

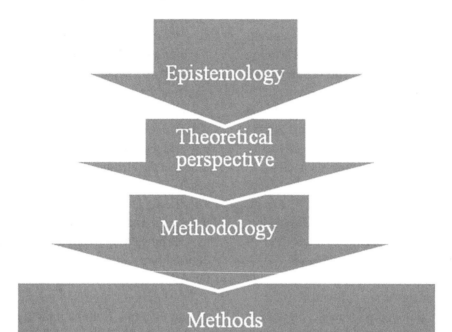

approach mixed with Kolb Experiential Learning Model (Kolb et al., 2001).

The study employed a meta-analysis approach where several studies on cloud computing in developing countries were analyzed (Harris, 2012; Mtebe, 2013; Shimba, 2010; Shimba et al., 2014). Meta -analysis approach was selected because several studies on cloud services have been conducted, however; each study has limited itself to some general aspects of cloud computing services. This study was conducted to address specific issues related to cloud library.

The Kolb Experiential Learning Model enabled the author to start by being observant and critically reflective on cloud computing and then, they develop some abstract concepts on cloud library (that can be generalized) and thereafter, we designed new ideas and experiment on them and finally, we end up with concrete experience and this provided avenue for repeating the cycle in future study (Kolb *et al.*, 2001). Previous stud-

ies which presented on this theory started with concrete experience but in this book chapter, we started with the observation and critical reflection because the researchers wanted to avoid biasness (Figure 3). The biasness can be attributed by the researcher after having concrete experience of the matter which s/he wants to research.

The studies selected in Meta – analysis were conducted in between 2012 and 2013; choice of this time interval was due to the fact that huge investments in the information sector have taken place over the recent years. For example, the recent rollout of SEACOM, EASSy and TEAMs marine cables increased internet speed up to 155Mbps as well reducing telecommunication costs by 95% (Swarts & Wachira, 2010). This is one of the factors which creates enabling environment for cloud library.

Since the theory chosen for this study need both qualitative and quantitative research methods thus, the mixed research methods (i.e. triangulation)

Figure 3. The Kolb experiential learning cycle (Adapted from Kolb et al., 2001)

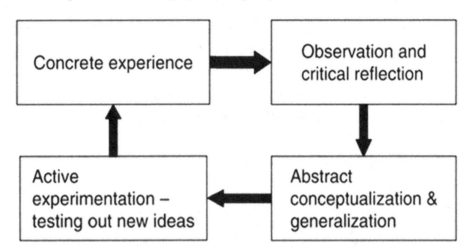

were adopted. The aim of triangulation is to have counter effect between qualitative and quantitative research methods where by the advantages of qualitative research methods will address the weakness of quantitative research method and vice versa (Sanga, 2010).

The outline of the research for this research (using Crotty's model) is represented in Figure 2 and Figure 4.

Case study was chosen as research method in order to explore in depth how libraries in HEIs of Tanzania have adopted digital library supported by cloud computing services. Using different cases of computerization of library, the researchers collected detailed information using a variety of data over a specified period of time. Then evaluation was done to do the comparison. Thereafter, the experiment was set to know the level of digital library and cloud computing adoption in 5 HEIs out of 48 HEIs found in Tanzania. This was the sample size used in this research.

Since time and finance was limited, thus desk research was adopted as research methodology. It fits well with this kind of researches which aimed at looking into what others have done in the area of cloud library and also, doing comparison studies.

Without specifying theoretical perspective and epistemology in the research design there is a great chance of obtaining results which are not filtered in proper scientific lenses. Thus it was unavoidable to follow this principle. Theoretical perspective which was used in this research was Kolb experiential learning theory. The reason for choosing this theory is as discussed earlier.

Finally, post-positivist was chosen as philosophical stance. Before starting the research, the authors selected some knowledge claims so that they can be guided well while looking for new knowledge. As Crotty (1994) argues that "knowledge that develops through a post-positivist lens is based on careful observation and measurement of the objective reality that exists "out here" in the world". It is from this premise that post – positivist was chosen.

3. RESULTS AND DISCUSSION

The Kolb Experiential Learning Cycle (KELC) guided the study and resulted into the following outcomes which is presented in the below section.

Observation and critical reflection: under this initial phase of KELC different literature were searched on cloud computing and Meta – analysis was done. The outcome of the literature search enabled the authors to confirm that there is a need

Figure 4. The four elements of research as was used in this research

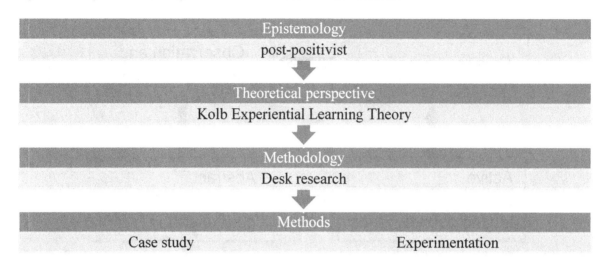

of integration of cloud computing and not any other computing systems such as cluster and grid computing systems (Buyya, Ranjan, & Calheiros N., 2009). The comparisons of these different computing systems are as shown in Table 1.

From Table 1, the characteristics of cloud computing systems outperform those of grid and cluster computing systems. This is the reason why cloud systems in library was preferred than grid library or cluster library (Figure 5).

1. Different, new, aspects of the application of cloud computing in libraries:
    a. The literature search about cloud library delivery model showed that there are four categories for delivery, namely:
        i. **Consumption:** How users of digital library consume the applications and business processes
        ii. **Creation:** What's required to build applications and business processes
        iii. **Orchestration:** How parts are integrated or pulled from an applications server

    iv. **Infrastructure:** Where the core guts such as servers, storage, and networks reside
2. Different cloud platforms presently available are namely:
    a. **Business Services and Software-as-a-Service (SaaS): The** traditional applications layer in the cloud includes software as service apps, business services, and business processes on the server side (Figure 6).
        i. **Development-as-a-Service (DaaS):** Development tools take shape in the cloud as shared community tools, web based dev tools, and mashup based services (Figure 6). This category is not in the Figure 6 but it has been list in the classification by Sodhi and Prabhakar (2011).
    b. **Platform-as-a-Service (PaaS):** Middleware manifests in the cloud with app platforms, database, integration, and process orchestration (Figure 6).

Table 1. Characteristics of cluster, grid and cloud computing systems (Adapted from Buyya et al., 2009)

Characteristics	Systems		
	Clusters	**Grids**	**Clouds**
Population	Commodity computers	High-end computers (servers, clusters)	Commodity computers and high-end servers and network attached storage
Size/scalability	100s	1000s	100s to 1000s
Node Operating System (OS)	One of the standard OSs (Linux, Windows)	Any standard OS (dominated by Unix)	A hypervisor (VM) on which multiple OSs run
Ownership	Single	Multiple	Single
Interconnection network‖speed	Dedicated, high-end with low latency and high bandwidth	Mostly Internet with high latency and low bandwidth	Dedicated, high-end with low latency and high bandwidth
Security/privacy	Traditional login/ password-based. Medium level of privacy–depends on user privileges.	Public/private key pair based authentication and mapping a user to an account. Limited support for privacy.	Each user/application is provided with a virtual machine. High security/privacy is guaranteed. Support for setting per-file access control list (ACL).
Discovery	Membership services	Centralised indexing and decentralised info services	Membership services
Service negotiation	Limited	Yes, SLA based	Yes, SLA based
User management	Centralised	Decentralised and also virtual organization (VO)-based	Centralised or can be delegated to third party
Resource management	Centralized	Distributed	Centralized/Distributed
Allocation/scheduling	Centralised	Decentralised	Both centralised/decentralized
Standards/inter-operability	Virtual Interface Architecture (VIA)-based	Some Open Grid Forum standards	Web Services (SOAP and REST)
Single system image	Yes	No	Yes, but optional
Capacity	Stable and guaranteed	Varies, but high	Provisioned on demand
Failure management (Self-healing)	Limited (often failed tasks/applications are restarted).	Limited (often failed tasks/applications are restarted).	Strong support for failover and content replication. VMs can be easily migrated from one node to other.
Pricing of services	Limited, not open market	Dominated by public good or privately assigned	Utility pricing, discounted for larger customers
Internetworking	Multi-clustering within an Organization	Limited adoption, but being explored through research efforts such as Gridbus InterGrid	High potential, third party solution providers can loosely tie together services of different Clouds
Application drivers	Science, business, enterprise computing, data centers	Collaborative scientific and high throughput computing applications	Dynamically provisioned legacy and web applications, Content delivery
Potential for building 3rd party or value-added solutions	Limited due to rigid architecture	Limited due to strong orientation for scientific computing	High potential — can create new services by dynamically provisioning of compute, storage, and application services and offer as their own isolated or composite Cloud services to users

Figure 5. Cloud Systems (Adapted from Jeffrey and Neidecker-Lutz, 2010)

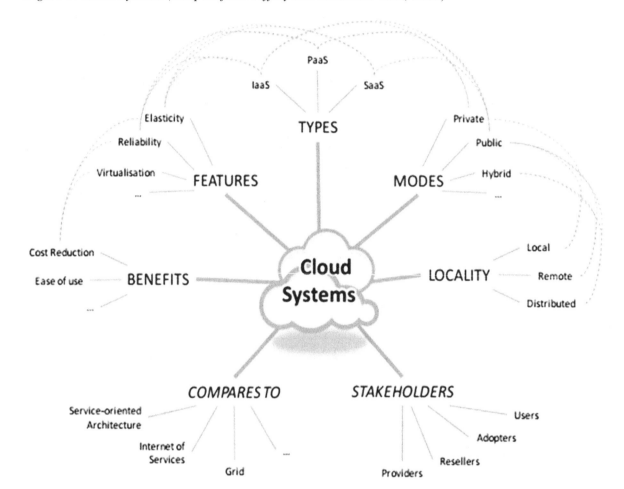

c. **Infrastructure-as-a-Service (IaaS):** The physical world goes virtual with servers, networks, storage, and systems management in the cloud (Figure 6).

3. How to create cloud libraries, challenges and opportunities:

a. **SaaS:** With SaaS, there is no control of underlying infrastructure network, servers, operating systems, storage, or individual application capabilities which are needed from the IT department of any HEI which need to adopt cloud library (Figure 10). The IT department can have a control of a limited set of user-specific application

configuration settings which require no programming. The greatest concern for SaaS is the issue of privacy in the user generated data since they are controlled by cloud provider (Figure 7).

b. **PaaS:** PaaS is characterized by allowing only HEI to support data and application. The cloud provider has control of underlying infrastructure network, servers, operating systems, or storage (Figure 10). Thus, PaaS provides limited flexibility to the end user who in this case is any HEI which has transformed its library into cloud library (Figure 8).

c. **IaaS:** IaaS is characterized by providing back-bones computing infrastructure storage, computer networking. This is often done using virtual machine (VM) where cloud user is given responsible to install and manage all software on VM (Figure 10). Also, cloud user is allowed to monitor resource utilization and reacting to events in different user applications. Furthermore, the cloud user is given limited control on networking components (e.g. host firewalls). In comparison to IaaS and PaaS, IaaS is the most flexible cloud variant user can configure and control the VM and software stack. On other hand, this means the cloud user is needed to be competent to configure, install, operate and maintain IaaS (Figure 9).

Abstract conceptualization and generalization: After the critical reflection has been done then conceptual framework for the cloud library were identified as per KELC framework. The framework is generic and thus, it caters for any service to be offered under cloud computing.

In summary, Figure 10 depicts how the integrated architecture will look like.

After the description of each cloud platform then there is a need to find out how they can be integrated. The following proposed architecture (Figure 11) shows integration of IaaS, PaaS and SaaS which can be adopted for cloud library.

One peculiar feature for the integrated architecture is that the weaknesses of each constitute architecture is strengthened by the advantages of other combined architecture.

There is justification why there is a need for such integration of different platforms for cloud computing in digital library. The reasons for this are:

1. Advancement of ICT with resulted into lowering cost for computing devices
2. Plenty of ICT tools are available either as free and open source library software or as proprietary library software
3. The computer methods, techniques and algorithms for developing interactivity on tools for digital library have increased substantially
4. In near future, the price for procuring bandwidth will be reduced due to landing of fiber optical cable (e.g. SEACOM, EASSy and TEAMs) in Tanzania.

The logical view of the proposed integration of architecture which favors the enabling environment due to above factors is as depicted below (Figure 10) wheel for the integration of cloud categories:

Applications for each category (i.e. SaaS, PaaS, IaaS) shown in Figure 12 are depicted and briefly explained in Figure 13 below:

Under the proposed integrated architecture, there is need of multi-stakeholders to work as cloud providers, cloud consumers, cloud infrastructural providers, virtulization software providers as well as IaaS, PaaS and SaaS providers (or vendor) (Figure 14).

The Table 2 shows some example of the cloud service providers (Figure 14) which can also be for cloud library service providers.

Table 2 fits well with the cloud computing landscape which is shown in the Figure 15 below.

The advantage of this architecture is that the disadvantages of each model complement to each other. Also, it has additional model for dSaaS which is an extension of SaaS.

Active Experimentation of Ideas

The aim of this phase of KELC is to come up with an empirical experiment which can validate some concepts in cloud library. There is a good

Figure 6. Cloud computing categories (adapted from Mtebe, 2013)

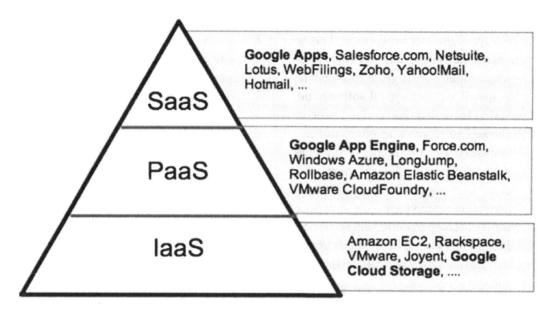

Figure 7. SaaS architecture (Adapted from Sodhi and Prabhakar, 2011)

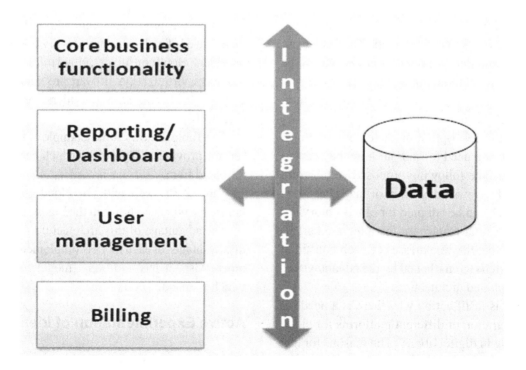

Figure 8. PaaS architecture for cloud library (Adapted from Sodhi and Prabhakar, 2011)

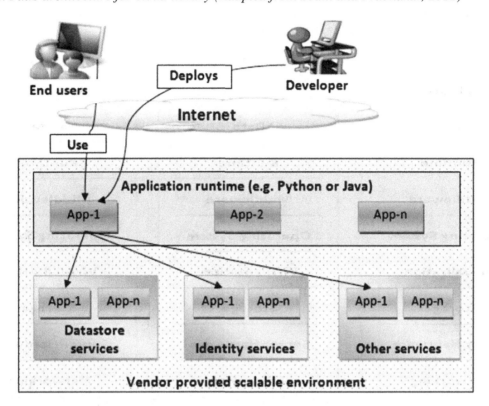

Figure 9. IaaS architecture for cloud library (Adapted from Sodhi and Prabhakar, 2011)

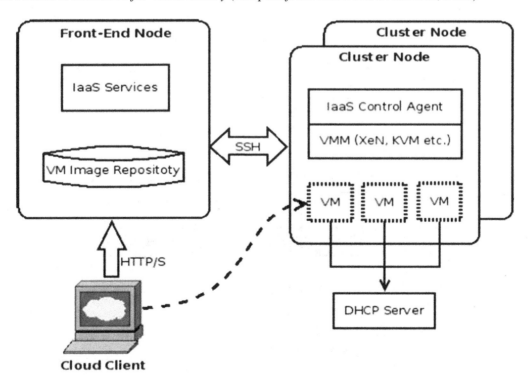

Figure 10. Combined figure showing what cloud user and cloud vendor manage (Adapted from Sodhi & Prabhakar, 2011)

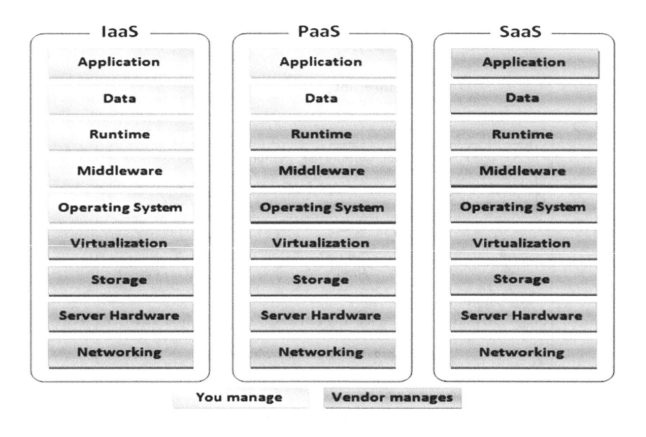

Figure 11. Proposed integrated Iaas, PaaS and SaaS (Adapted from Sodhi and Prabhakar, 2011)

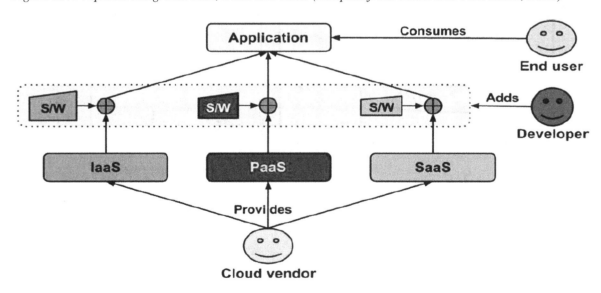

Figure 12. Logical view of integrated IaaS, PaaS and SaaS (MOOC, 2013)

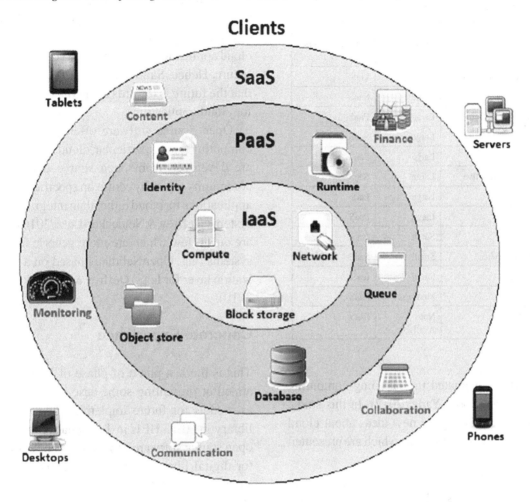

Figure 13. Applications belonging to each category of cloud computing (MOOC, 2013)

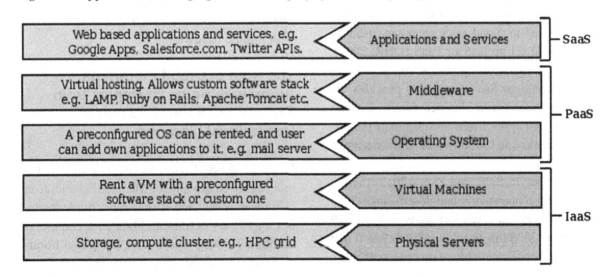

Table 2. Example of cloud service providers (MOOC, 2013)

Service Provider	Company Size	Platform Type
Microsoft SQL Azure	Large	IaaS
Google Docs	Large	SaaS
Google Apps Engine	Large	PaaS
Amazon	Large	SaaS
Salesforce.com	Large	SaaS
Microsoft office live	Large	SaaS
Oracle	Large	IaaS
Accenture	Large	PaaS
Rackspace	Small	IaaS
Cloud9Analytics	Small	SaaS
Cloudworks	Small	IaaS
Gogrid	Medium	PaaS
CloudAppy	Not Available	PaaS

study which evaluated the clouding computing (Buyya et al., 2009; Yang, 2012). In this study, the results of testing out new ideas about cloud library provided the findings which are presented in Table 3.

Examples of Open Source Application in Cloud Computing

There is a lot of open source applications software that are used in cloud as SaaS others used by industries to set up IaaS or PaaS (OHR, 2014). Many of the current Open Source Software is now available on SaaS basis, this provides the benefit to customer to obtained quality services with low-cost applications and eliminate the difficult of deploying software on their own servers (OSS, 2014)

According to Salih and Zang (2012) the the comparison of open source and closed source cloud applications are as shown in Figure 18, Figure 19 and Figure 20. Salih and Zang (2012) found that most cloud application based on open source are

for IaaS followed by PaaS and very few are from SaaS. The closed source applications for cloud are costly compared to those from open source but cloud applications based on open source are more secure. Hence, Salih and Zang (2012) concluded that the future is towards using open source tools for cloud applications.

Open Source software offer tools for cloud computing (and in particular, cloud library) which are developed from open source development community typically centre on specific computer applications for cloud rather than integrated cloud systems (Jeffrey & Neidecker-Lutz, 2010). There are only a few which are more generic for cloud systems (e.g. OpenNebula is based on a virtualization layer for IaaS) (Jeffrey & Neidecker-Lutz, 2010).

Concrete Experience

This is the last phase of phase of KELC which aimed at presenting some case studies to work as models for future implementations of cloud library in HEIs. HEIs in Tanzania are using both open source software and closed source software for digital library computer systems. Staff and students in East African HEIs are using Google Apps such as Gmail, Google Calendar, Google Talk, and Google Docs and Spreadsheets in a daily basis (GCP, 2014; Wanjiku, 2009;). These cloud services are best suited for HEIs in East Africa with limited bandwidth.

The Role of Cloud Librarians Along with Some Examples from Tanzania's Higher Education Institutions' Libraries

From the above discussions the role of cloud library has been explained. After this, libraries from HEIs were evaluated if they have implemented library 2.0. By definition, library 2.0 consists of traditional library which have integrated library systems (digital library) which embedded web

Figure 14. Multiple Stakeholders in proposed integrated cloud architecture (MOOC, 2013)

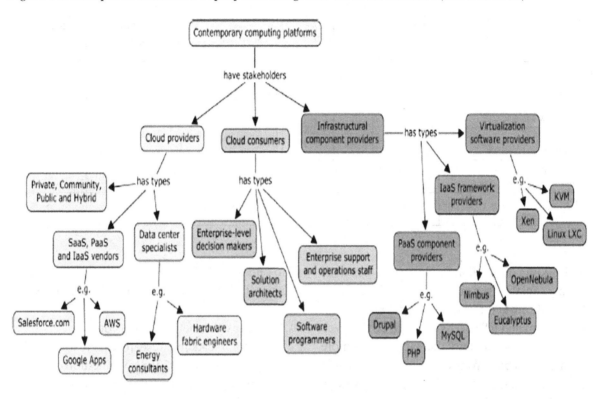

Figure 15. Integrated SaaS, PaaS, IaaS, and dSaaS

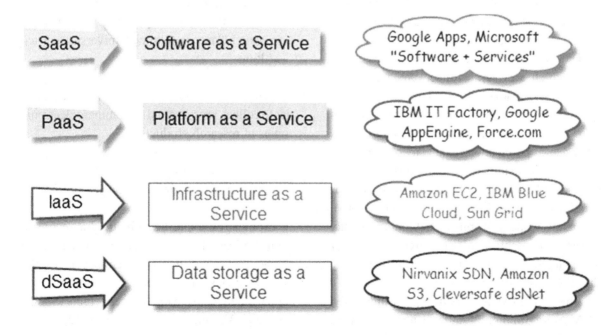

Table 3. Evaluation of the integration of web 2.0 to libraries of universities in Tanzania

	Delicious	Blog	RSS feeds	Social Networks (facebook)	Wiki	Institutional repository	Online public catalogue
MUHAS http://www.muhas.ac.tz	√	√	√	√	√	√	√
UDSM http://www.udsm.ac.tz	×	√	×	√	√	×	√
SUA http://www.suanet.ac.tz	×	√	√	√	√	√	√
MZUMBE http://www.mzumbe.ac.tz	×	×	×	√	×	×	√
OUT http://www.out.ac.tz/	×	×	√	√	√	√	×

2.0. Building digital library with web 2.0 consist of using social bookmark, social media platform, blogs, wiki instant messaging (e.g. twitter), tagging system and RSS feeds (Lwoga, 2012). Web 2.0 is a set of technology that facilitates a more socially connected Web where everyone is able to add and edit the information space (Anderson, 2007). These include blogs, wikis, and multimedia sharing services, content syndication, podcasting and content tagging services. Integration of web 2.0 and library is called library 2.0. It is arises from the theory that knowledge is socially constructed (i.e. constructivism theory).

The universities selected for evaluation are those which are public funded and with good ranking in Tanzania (UR, 2014).

Also, the libraries of these four universities were evaluated if they are using online tools for research publication management (Table 3). These tools help university to improve its visibility. Examples of such tools are Google Scholar Citations (http://scholar.google.com/citations), Microsoft Academic Publication (http://academic. research.microsoft.com/), researchgate (http://researchgate.net/), academic.edu and mendeley (http://mendeley.com/).

Among the five universities under this study, SUA has good number of staff who have subscribed to online tools for research publication management. The following are some of the links for SUA:

1. https://suanet.academia.edu/
2. http://academic.research.microsoft.com/Organization/15768/sokoine-university-of-agriculture?query=sokoine%20university%20of%20agriculture
3. http://scholar.google.com/citations?hl=en&view_op=search_authors&mauthors=suanet.ac.tz
4. http://www.mendeley.com/research-papers/search/?query=sokoine+university+agriculture

SUA and MUHAS have institutional repositories to collect, preserve and disseminate electronic copies of research products.

- http://ir.muhas.ac.tz:8080/jspui/
- http://www.taccire.suanet.ac.tz/xmlui/

In order to mitigate the problem which can arise from intellectual property right of materials to be uploaded in cloud library system it is better the free and open source software are used. Also the contents need to have open access rights (Sanga, Lwoga, & Venter, 2006; Suleman, 2012).

Another problem hindering electronic users of digital library is the use of multiple credentials required in order to use some online databases and e-resources subscribed by certain university. This problem at SUA and MUHAS has been resolved through the use of single interface for all e-resources found in each library. The service is accessible within and outside the Local area Network of SUA and when the user is accessing outside the network of SUA, she / he must supply other credentials for authentication. This service is found at the below link:

- http://libhub.kiox.org/ or http://www.sua-sis.suanet.ac.tz/authentication?url=   or http://libhub.kiox.org.proxy.suanet.ac.tz/

There is an initiative to host journal on web server of SUA. Currently, testing is being done to evaluate if the local journal in the Faculty of Agriculture can be hosted locally (Appendix A: Figure 17).

As Mavodza (2013) summarized that when discussing cloud computing in a library context, it is important to evaluate the models of clouds used in terms of the types of services involved, the infrastructure used, the platform on which applications are built and the associated applications. For example, the use of a Platform as a Service (PaaS) refers to a situation where software already exists, such as when the library uses an Integrated Library System whether it is open source such as Koha or Greenstone or ABCD, or proprietary such as Millennium Innovative Interfaces or SirsiDynix, library catalogues, subject catalogues, OverDrive, Googledocs, and WorldCat. SUA uses ABCD as library catalogue and loan system which is accessible at http://snal.suanet.ac.tz/cgi-bin/wxis.exe/iah/scripts/ (Emmanuel & Sife, 2008).

On the other hand, Software as a Service (SaaS) can be viewed in the use of LibGuides, the library catalogue, WorldCat, OverDrive, aggregated subject gateways that support systematic unified web-scale resource discovery such as SUMMON

(a ProQuest business), Ebsco Discovery Service, Primo Central (Ex Libris), Free and Open Source Software (FOSS), FOSS library management system, Citation Management software. From these examples which already they are in wide use in libraries of HEIs in Tanzania, the demarcation between PaaS and SaaS is very difficult since library systems use both platforms and software,. Services that are referred to as cloud-based services also include the provision of actual resources, for example, OverDrive e-books, research guides and online reference services that are ready for use. The examples of cloud applications is shown by Google Docs or library e-book readers such as for elibrary books or Safari books that are normally accessed with a web browser. At SUA, the free e-reources are found at http://www.lib.suanet.ac.tz/index.php?option=com_content&view=article&id=86:environmental-management-index-&catid=69:free-electronic-resources-&Itemid=49

Also, in HEIs' libraries online database are accessed as cloud applications. Cloud Infrastructure (IaaS) refers mostly to the space/time that users can buy to use external servers for electronic storage as in institutional digital repositories or institutional archives. On this aspect, for example there is digital repository for climate change research output at SUA which is shared among HEIs in Tanzania. It is also the infrastructure that enables open-source software for running repositories, for example, D-Space, FEDORA, Eprints, or hosted software packages such as Digital Commons, and SimpleDL. At SUA, DSpace is a platform used of an institutional repository. It is found at http://www.taccire.suanet.ac.tz/xmlui/

From this book chapter, one can deduce that librarians in HEIs in Tanzania are using cloud tools which are found on Internet. Even though the implementation of cloud library is at infancy stage but this necessitate the change of functions of librarians. This is the reason Scale (2010) argues that "cloud computing is an unresolved area of concern and debatable among the library profession". According to Scale (2010), cloud computing is enabling librarians to shift from the paradigm of ownership and maintenance of resources towards the provision of access to information maintained and controlled by others libraries. This is already happening in Tanzania for example journals subscribes by libraries of HEIs in Tanzania provide more opportunities for librarians not to be tasked for its daily maintenance of the servers hosting those journals from abroad libraries.

When cloud computing services will be fully implemented in libraries of HEIs of Tanzania then the roles of librarians will need to be revised so that it includes not only provision of access to resources but also collection, preservation, and ownership of information resources (materials). Some fields such as information resource management and information security need to be included in the training of librarians. Other aspects which must be included in the curriculum of librarians are as shown in Figure 16.

From this analysis, it is found that HEIs in Tanzania have not migrated fully to digital library and thus, they are good candidate to be involved in migration into cloud library to minimize the problems which traditional libraries are facing. The mentioned ICT tools which are used in HEIs of Tanzania are part of the tools needed to be integrated to form cloud library (Chen, Zhang, Li, Li, & Gao, Y., 2011; Buyya et al., 2009; Fox, 2009). It is proposed that the modified framework for adoption of cloud computing suggested by Shimba could be used in adopting cloud library for HEIs in Tanzania (Shimba, 2010).

The proposed framework (Figure 16) differ from those proposed by different researchers in previous studies (Galvin & Sun, 2012; Mitchell, 2010; Nuernberg, Leggett, & McFarland,, 2012) since it is grounded on philosophical stance, theory of knowledge, research methodology and research method. Also, it is guided by principles underlying developing a good framework

(Ochara-Muganda & Van Belle, 2010). According to Ochara-Muganda and Van Belle (2010) a framework for any e-government project (which include cloud library) need to incorporate the key technological drivers that underlie the development of computing technology which are mobility, digital convergence and mass scale. Thus, there is adequacy of mobility due to physical, digital, social and human resources for cloud library (Ochara, 2008). In cloud library there is digital convergence since it favors integration of different architectures, platforms, vendors, networks and operating systems as depicted in Figure 6 up to Figure 15 due to interoperability. Also, in digital library there is mass scale of utilization of cloud library services since it advocates open data and open access. This characteristic allows many stakeholders to have free access of the cloud library services. This confirms that the proposed framework for adopting cloud library is good since it has all required attributes (i.e. mobility, digital convergence and mass scale).

One good example for cloud library which was found through literature search is that reported by Ruz (2014). It reports how cloud computing has started improving the literacy of people in rural areas of Africa.

The end product of using the Kolb Experiential Learning Cycle is presenting concrete experience gained after experimentation of ideas. The example given of cloud library serves this purpose (Kolb et al., 2001). Also, for this purpose there are well documented cloud library called CALIS (Buyya et al., 2009; Chen et al., 2011; Fox, 2009; Yang, 2012) which are already in use in developed countries which can be adopted in developing countries.

Using the proposed framework for adopting cloud library (Figure 16), one need to make sure that the disadvantages of cloud computing are minimized. According to He et al. (2011), some of the disadvantages of cloud computing includes:

Figure 16. Adoption framework for cloud computing (modified from Shimba, 2010)

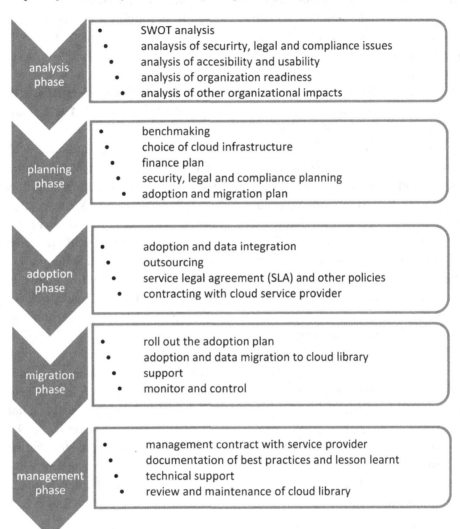

- **More Elasticity Means Less Control:** While public clouds for library are great for quickly scaling up and down your resources, companies that require complete and total control over their data and applications will need to avoid the public cloud library. Alternative solutions for cloud library include hybrid clouds, private clouds, and co-location (Buyya et al., 2009; Chen et al., 2011; Fox, 2009).
- **Not Everything Fits into the Cloud Library:** Depending on the cloud library provider, you may face restrictions on available applications, operating systems, and infrastructure options. Complicating matters more is the simple fact that not all platforms can live in the cloud library. To combat this, it is important to ensure that the cloud library provider you choose also offers physical co-location services. Then if your platform in the cloud needs to speak to applications on other platforms, this flexibility of physical co-location will work to ensure successful interoperation (Buyya et al., 2009; Chen et al., 2011;; Fox, 2009).

- **Technical Issues:** Though it is true that information and data on the cloud library can be accessed anytime and from anywhere at all, there are times when this system can have some serious dysfunction. You should be aware of the fact that this technology is always prone to outages and other technical issues. Even the best cloud service providers run into this kind of trouble, in spite of keeping up high standards of maintenance. Besides, you will need a very good Internet connection to be logged onto the server at all times otherwise one will invariably be stuck in case of network, bandwidth shortage and connectivity problems (Buyya et al., 2009; Chen et al., 2011;; Fox, 2009). This is very problematic for HEIs in developing countries.
- **Security in the Cloud:** The other major issue while in the cloud library is that of security issues. Before adopting this technology, you should know that you will be surrendering all your organization's sensitive information to a third-party cloud service provider. This could potentially put your organization to great risk. Hence, you need to make absolutely sure that you choose the most reliable service provider of the cloud library, who will keep your information totally secure (Buyya et al., 2009; Chen et al., 2011;; Fox, 2009).
- **Prone to Attack:** Storing information in the cloud library could make your organization vulnerable to external hack attacks and threats. This is due to the fact that nothing on the Internet is completely secure and hence, there is always the possibility of losing sensitive data (Buyya et al., 2009; Chen et al., 2011;; Fox, 2009)● Phobia from the librarians and other stakeholders to adopt cloud library: even though there are promising potential benefits of cloud library but the resistance might arise from different stakeholders of library since

there is a need of changing their mindset from comfort zones which they are familiar or used to (Buyya et al., 2009; Chen et al., 2011;; Fox, 2009).

Proposing Cloud Computing Security Approach for Cloud Library

Cloud computing security concerns all the aspects of making cloud computing secure. Nowadays with increase of technology and attack tools, data are vulnerable to attack irrespectively where it is stored, for example, the recent breach in eBay security. In everyday life different security mechanism are created to achieve the goal of information security which are: Confidentiality, Integrity, and Availability (CIA). Cloud computing security encompasses all the topics of computing security, including the design of security architectures, minimization of attack surfaces, protection from malware, and enforcement of access control. But there are some aspects of cloud computing security that appear to be specific to that domain (Chen et al., 2010; Christodorescu et al., 2009; CSA, 2010).

Below are the challenges that need security mechanism to prevent or minimize its effects (Carlin & Curran, 2011; Hamlen, Kantarcioglu, Khan & Thuraisingham, 2010; Tilley & Parveen, 2013).

1. Cloud-based data is usually intentionally widely accessible by potentially insecure protocols and APIs across public networks.
2. Data in the cloud is vulnerable to being lost (e.g., accidentally deleted) or incorrectly modified by the cloud provider.
3. Data in the cloud can be accessed by the cloud provider, its subcontractors and employees.

The currently solutions which can be used to solve challenges (*a* and *b*) mentioned above include: authentication protocols, authorization frameworks, and encryption. Loss of data is addressed by careful backup policies (Ryan, 2012). The other security challenge is based on cloud provider and his /her relationship with customer. For example, if the task of the provide is to store data on behalf of customer then security implementation will be encrypting the data with the customer hold the key.

In other situation like those listed below, different security technology need to be adopted (Ryan, 2012).

- The data may be financial data, payroll data, human resource data, banking data, etc., and the computation is usual business processing.
- The data is documents and photographs, and the cloud is expected to enforce access rules that depend on the content.
- The data may be scientific data obtained by experiment and observation, and the computation may be to find patterns, or organize the data according to rules. Other examples in this category include data-intensive financial modelling or network traffic modelling.
- The data is an email archive, and the cloud is expected to handle email in a way that depends on its content (e.g., spam filtering, topic classification, compliance with corporate disclosure policies).
- The data may be documents to review (job applications, research papers, business tenders) and the computation may be to support the review process (sending to reviewers, collating reviews, etc.).

Based on the functionality of cloud provider in cloud library it's better to use the security approach called CryptDB (a weaker attacker model). CryptDB is a framework that allows query processing over an encrypted database. The database is stored and managed by the cloud provider, but data items are encrypted with keys that are not under the cloud provider's control. It works by executing SQL queries over the encrypted database using a collection of efficient SQL-aware encryp-

tion schemes. To achieve database operations such as equality checks and order comparisons, CryptDB uses encryption schemes that allow such comparisons to be made on ciphertexts. CryptDB supports a wider set of applications, although it is still restricted to database searches (Ryan, 2012).

For any organization looking to implement cloud library the underlying principle is that it must review its ICT policy so that aspects of cloud computing are included. Jaeger et al. (2008) argue that

Cloud computing is likely to present policy questions and raise many issues as it becomes more commonplace.

Jaeger et al. (2008) identified the following questions which need some guidelines from the ICT policy of any organization adopting cloud computing. The questions are:

1. What expectations for privacy, security, reliability, and anonymity do users of cloud computing have?
2. Are there variations in these expectations among individuals, corporate users, academic users, and governmental users?
3. Would greater degrees of privacy, security, reliability, and anonymity influence users' decisions about which cloud providers to use?
4. Have users even considered issues like privacy, security, reliability, and anonymity?
5. Do users have any concerns about protection of their intellectual property in the cloud?
6. Do users have any concerns about the monitoring of their activities in the cloud by providers or by the government?
7. Do users only trust cloud computing for certain types of functions?
8. Can information policies for print-based environments intelligibly translate to cloud computing? If so, how?

9. What issues of cloud computing are completely unaddressed in the current policy environment?

The above mentioned questions need some security measures which must be implemented in cloud library so that the potential benefits of cloud library are realized. According to Goldner (2010) and Rosenthal et al. (2010), the fundamental benefits of cloud library over the traditional library are:

1. Take advantage of current and rapidly emerging technology to fully participate in the Web's information landscape
2. Increased visibility and accessibility of library digital collections
3. Reduced duplication of effort from networked technical services and collection management
4. Streamlined workflows, optimized to fully benefit from network participation
5. Cooperative intelligence and improved service levels enabled by the large-scale aggregation of usage data
6. Make libraries greener by sharing computing power thus reducing carbon footprints

4. CONCLUSION AND RECOMMENDATIONS

The concept of cloud computing in relation to library has been introduced in this book chapter using Kolb Experiential Learning Model. Different cloud architectures have also been discussed from literature with their characteristics and advantages. The proposed integrated architecture for cloud computing in library has been presented. Thereafter, the situation analysis of digital libraries in HEIs of Tanzania has been given out. In order for Tanzania's HEIs to adopt cloud library there is need of framework for cloud computing adoption which has been given out as generic model. Currently, applications from cloud computing which are being used by different stakeholders of libraries in Tanzania's HEIs are at infancy stage. A framework has been modified to be used as guideline for HEIs which are adopting cloud library. Thus, the given framework will help to fill gap which exists in knowledge. Currently, there are frameworks proposed which are not well researched. In order to test the validity of the proposed framework in this book chapter, there is need of future study to explore its usefulness in specific environment of Tanzania's HEI. Students in HEIs are using cloud based resources such as Google Docs, Facebook and Youtube for accessing and uploading learning materials. This has changed the paradigm from teacher centred learning and teaching to student centred learning and teaching. The students are no longer consumers of learning materials but they are becoming both consumers and producers (Mtega *et al.*, 2012).

The recommendation from this book chapter is that for cloud library to be fully implemented in HEIs of Tanzania the Government and HEIs should revise their library, research and ICT policies so that they state categorically how cloud user, cloud provider, cloud vendor, cloud consumer, cloud broker and cloud service management (cloud carrier or cloud grid management) will work together in the business of cloud library which is already happening in developed HEIs. The expected outcomes for the implementation of cloud library depend on the chosen framework (Harris, 2012). This process need to be guided by a good evaluation algorithm since there are multi-criteria attributes to be considered during the migration from conventional library or digital library by HEI. For successful implementation of cloud library, stakeholders' involvement must be participatory in all the phases of the implementation as shown in Figure 16. This must be guided by the proposed framework embedded in the KELC.

ACKNOWLEDGMENT

The author would like to thank the instructors who taught a Massive Open Online Course for Development titled Mobiles for Development. Its Open Educational Resources are available at: http://m4d.colfinder.org/node/2372

REFERENCES

Buyya, R., Ranjan, R., & Calheiros, R. N. (2009). Modeling and simulation of scalable Cloud computing environments and the CloudSim toolkit: Challenges and opportunities. In *High Performance Computing & Simulation, June 2009. HPCS'09. International Conference on* (pp. 1-11). IEEE.

Buyya, R., Yeo, C. S., Venugopal, S., Broberg, J., & Brandic, I. (2009). Cloud computing and emerging IT platforms: Vision, hype, and reality for delivering computing as the 5th utility. *Future Generation Computer Systems*, *25*(6), 599–616. doi:10.1016/j.future.2008.12.001

Carlin, S., & Curran, K. (2011). Cloud computing security. *International Journal of Ambient Computing and Intelligence*, *3*(1), 14–19. doi:10.4018/jaci.2011010102

Chen, Y., Paxson, V., & Katz, R. H. (2010). *What's new about cloud computing security?* Technical Report UCB/EECS-2010-5, Electrical Engineering and Computer Sciences, University of California at Berkeley.

Chen, Y., Zhang, R., Li, H., Li, R., & Gao, Y. (2011). CALIS-based cloud library services platform model. *AISS: Advances in Information Sciences and Service Sciences*, *3*(6), 204–212. doi:10.4156/aiss.vol3.issue6.25

Christodorescu, M., Sailer, R., Schales, D. L., Sgandurra, D., & Zamboni, D. (2009). Cloud security is not (just) virtualization security: a short paper. In *Proceedings of the 2009 ACM Workshop on Cloud Computing Security* (pp. 97–102). doi:10.1145/1655008.1655022

Cloud Security Alliance (CSA). (2010). *Top threats to cloud computing v1.0*. Retrieved on 3th June 2014, from https://cloudsecurityalliance.org/topthreats/csathreats.v1.0.pdf

Crotty, M. (1998). The foundations of social research: Meaning and perspective in the research process. *Sage (Atlanta, Ga.)*.

Emmanuel, G., & Sife, A. (2008). Challenges of managing information and communication technologies for education: Experiences from Sokoine National Agricultural Library. *International Journal of Education and Development using ICT*, *4*(3).

Fox, R. (2009). Library in the clouds. *OCLC Systems & Services*, *25*(3), 156–161. doi:10.1108/10650750910982539

Galvin, D., & Sun, M. (2012). Avoiding the death zone: Choosing and running a library project in the cloud. *Library Hi Tech*, *30*(3), 418–427. doi:10.1108/07378831211266564

Google Cloud Platform (GCP). (2014). Retrieved from https://cloud.google.com/

Goldner, M. R. (2010). Winds of change: Libraries and cloud computing. *BIBLIOTHEK Forschung und Praxis*, *34*(3), 270–275. doi:10.1515/bfup.2010.042

Hamlen, K., Kantarcioglu, M., Khan, L., & Thuraisingham, B. (2010). Security issues for cloud computing. *International Journal of Information Security and Privacy*, *4*(2), 36–48. doi:10.4018/jisp.2010040103

Harris, A. (2012). *The Legal Standing of Data in a Cloud Computing Environment* (Doctoral dissertation, Dublin Institute of Technology).

Hartman, T. (2007). The changing definition of US libraries. *Libri, 57*(1), 1–8. doi:10.1515/LIBR.2007.1

He, W., Cernusca, D., & Abdous, M. H. (2011). Exploring cloud computing for distance learning. *Online Journal of Distance Learning Administration, 14*(3).

Heeks, R. (2014). *Future Priorities for Development Informatics Research from the Post-2015 Development Agenda.* Working Paper Series, paper no. 57, Centre for Development Informatics - IDPM, University of Manchester, UK. Retrieved from http://www.seed.manchester.ac.uk/medialibrary/IDPM/working_papers/di/di_wp57.pdf

Holmqvist, M. (2004). Experiential Learning Processes of Exploitation and Exploration Within and Between Organizations: An Empirical Study of Product Development. *Organization Science, 15*(1), 70–81.

Jaeger, P. T., Lin, J., & Grimes, J. M. (2008). Cloud computing and information policy: Computing in a policy cloud? *Journal of Information Technology & Politics, 5*(3), 269–283. doi:10.1080/19331680802425479

Jeffrey, K. and Neidecker-Lutz, B. (2010). *The Future of Cloud Computing: Opportunities for European Cloud Computing Beyond 2010: Expert Group Report. European Commission, Information Society and Media.*

Kamel, S. (2010). *E-strategies for Technological Diffusion and Adoption: National ICT Approaches for Socioeconomic Development. Information Science Reference.* IGI Global USA. doi:10.4018/978-1-60566-388-3

Kolb, A. Y., & Kolb, D. A. (2005). Learning styles and learning spaces: Enhancing experiential learning in higher education. *Academy of Management Learning & Education, 4*(2), 193–212. doi:10.5465/AMLE.2005.17268566

Kolb, D. A. (1984). *Experiential learning: Experience as the source of learning and development* (Vol. 1). Englewood Cliffs, NJ: Prentice-Hall.

Kolb, D. A., Boyatzis, R. E., and Mainemelis, C. (2001). Experiential learning theory: Previous research and new directions. *Perspectives on thinking, learning, and cognitive styles, 1*, 227-247.

Lwoga, E. T. (2012). *Building a virtual academic library with Web 2.0 technologies in Tanzania, IST-Africa 2012 Conference, Dar es salaam.* Retrieved on 9-11 May 2012, from: http://hdl.handle.net/123456789/17

Lyons, C. (2007). The library: A distinct local voice? *First Monday, 12*(3). doi:10.5210/fm.v12i3.1629

Mei, H., & Liu, X. Z. (2011). Internetware: An emerging software paradigm for Internet computing. *Journal of Computer Science and Technology, 26*(4), 588–599. doi:10.1007/s11390-011-1159-y

Mell, P. and Grance, T. (2011). *The NIST Definition of Cloud Computing.* Recommendations of the National Institute of Standards and Technology, Special Publication 800-145, September 2011

Mitchell, E. (2010). Using cloud services for library IT infrastructure. *code4lib Journal, 9.*

MOOC. (2013). *Mobiles for Development: A Massive Open Online Course for Development.* Open Educational Resources. Retrieved on 01 January 2014, from http://m4d.colfinder.org/node/2372

Mtebe, J. S. (2013). Exploring the Potential of Clouds to Facilitate the Adoption of Blended Learning in Tanzania. *International Journal of Education and Research, 1*(8).

Mtega, W. P., Bernard, R., Msungu, A. C., & Sanare, R. (2012). Using mobile phones for teaching and learning purposes in higher learning institutions: The case of Sokoine University of Agriculture in Tanzania. In *Proceedings and report of the 15th UbuntuNet alliance Annual Conference*.

Nuernberg, P., Leggett, J., & McFarland, M. (2012). Cloud as infrastructure at the Texas Digital Library. *Journal of Digital Information, 13*(1).

Ochara, N. M. (2008). Emergence of the e-Government artifact in an environment of social exclusion in Kenya. *The African Journal of Information Systems, 1*(1), 3.

Ochara-Muganda, N., & Van Belle, J. (2010). A proposed framework for E-Government knowledge infrastructures for Africa's transition economies. Journal of e-Government Studies and Best Practices, *2010*, 1–9.

Open Hybrid Resources (OHR). (2014). Retrieved on, from http://www.redhat.com/solutions/open-hybrid-cloud/cloud-resources/

OSS. (2014). Plutchak, T. S. (2012). Breaking the barriers of time and space: The dawning of the great age of librarians. *Journal of the Medical Library Association: JMLA, 100*(1), 10. http://www.datamation.com/open-source/60-open-source-apps-you-can-use-in-the-cloud-1.html Retrieved on 3th June 2014

Popa, R. A., Redfield, C. M. S., Zeldovich, N., & Balakrishnan, H. (2012). CryptDB: Processing queries on an encrypted database. *Communications of the ACM, 55*(9), 103–111. doi:10.1145/2330667.2330691

Rasmussen, C. H., & Jochumsen, H. (2009). The fall and rise of the physical library. In *The 17th BOBCATSSS Symposium*. Retrieved on 01 January 2014, from http://pure.iva.dk/files/30767688/The_Fall_and_Rise_-_Bobcatsss_2009.pdf

Rosenthal, A., Mork, P., Li, M. H., Stanford, J., Koester, D., & Reynolds, P. (2010). Cloud computing: A new business paradigm for biomedical information sharing. *Journal of Biomedical Informatics, 43*(2), 342–353.

Ruz, C. (2014). Cloud computing key to improving literacy in Africa. Retrieved from http://www.isgtw.org/feature/cloud-computing-key-improving-literacy-africa

Ryan, M. D. (2013). Cloud computing security: The scientific challenge, and a survey of solutions. *Journal of Systems and Software, 86*(9), 2263–2268. doi:10.1016/j.jss.2012.12.025

Sanga, C. (2010). *A technique for the evaluation of free and open source e-learning systems*. Doctoral dissertation, University of the Western Cape.

Sanga, C., Lwoga, E. T., & Venter, I. M. (2006). Open Courseware as a Tool for Teaching and Learning in Africa, *Fourth IEEE International Workshop on Technology for Education in Developing Countries*, 2006 (pp. 55-56).

Salih, N. K., & Zang, T. (2012). Survey and comparison for Open and closed sources in cloud computing. *arXiv preprint arXiv:1207.5480*.

Scale, M.-S. E. (2010). Assessing the Impact of Cloud Computing and Web Collaboration on the Work of Distance Library Services. *Journal of Library Administration, 50*(7-8), 7–8, 933–950. doi:10.1080/01930826.2010.488995

Shimba, F. (2010). *Cloud Computing: Strategies for Cloud Computing Adoption*. Retrieved on 08 August 2013, from http://arrow.dit.ie/cgi/viewcontent.cgi?article=1028&context=scschcomdis

Shimba, F. J., Koloseni, D., & Nungu, A. (2014). Challenges and Implications of adoption of cloud services in healthcare in developing countries. In A. Moumtzoglou (Ed.), *Cloud Computing Applications for Quality Health Care Delivery*. Hershey, PA: IGI Global Publishers.

Sife, A., Lwoga, E., & Sanga, C. (2007). New technologies for teaching and learning: Challenges for higher learning institutions in developing countries. *International Journal of Education and Development using ICT, 3*(2). Retrieved from http://ijedict.dec.uwi.edu/viewarticle.php?id=246

Sodhi, B., & Prabhakar, T. V. (2011). Application architecture considerations for cloud platforms, *Communication Systems and Networks (COMSNETS), 2011 Third International Conference on*, 1-4, 4-8 Jan. 2011 doi:10.1109/COMSNETS.2011.5716417

Suleman, H. (2012). *Why should African academics care about Open Access?* Retrieved from http://repository.up.ac.za/handle/2263/18808

Swarts, P., & Wachira, E. (2010). ICT in Education Situational Analysis. Tanzania: Global e-Schools and Communities Initiative. Retrieved from http://www.gesci.org/assets/files/Knowledge Centre/Situational Analysis_Tanzania.pdf

Tilley, S. R., & Parveen, T. (2013). *Software Testing in the Cloud: Perspectives on an Emerging Discipline*. Information Science Reference. doi:10.4018/978-1-4666-2536-5

University Ranking (UR). (2014). Retrieved from http://www.webometrics.info/en/Ranking_africa/Sub_saharan_Africa

Xinping, H. (2010). The Concept of Cloud Library. *Information Studies: Theory & Application, 6*, 009.

Yang, S. Q. (2012). Move into the Cloud, shall we? *Library Hi Tech News, 29*(1), 4–7. doi:10.1108/07419051211223417

Yuan, L., MacNeill, S., & Kraan, W. (2008). Open educational resources—Opportunities and challenges for higher education. Retrieved from http://learn.creativecommons.org/wp-content/uploads/2008/09/oer_briefing_paper.pdf

Wanjiku, R. (2009). East African universities take advantage of Google cloud. *Info World*. Retrieved from http://news.idg.no/cw/art.cfm?id=D3ED873F-1A64-6A71-CE-3B759E5A305061

Wiederhold, G. (1995). Digital libraries, value, and productivity. *Communications of the ACM, 38*(4), 85–96.

ADDITIONAL READING

Al-Zoube, M., Abou El-Seoud, S., & Wyne, M. F. (2010). Cloud computing based e-learning system. *International Journal of Distance Education Technologies, 8*(2), 58–71. doi:10.4018/jdet.2010040105

Buyya, R., Ranjan, R., & Calheiros, R. N. (2009, June). Modeling and simulation of scalable Cloud computing environments and the CloudSim toolkit: Challenges and opportunities. In *High Performance Computing & Simulation, 2009. HPCS'09. International Conference on* (pp. 1-11). IEEE.

Carlin, S., & Curran, K. (2011). Cloud computing security. [IJACI]. *International Journal of Ambient Computing and Intelligence, 3*(1), 14–19. doi:10.4018/jaci.2011010102

Chen, Y., Zhang, R., Li, H., Li, R., & Gao, Y. (2011). CALIS-based cloud library services platform model. *AISS: Advances in Information Sciences and Service Sciences, 3*(6), 204–212. doi:10.4156/aiss.vol3.issue6.25

Fox, R. (2009). Library in the clouds. *OCLC Systems & Services, 25*(3), 156–161. doi:10.1108/10650750910982539

Galvin, D., & Sun, M. (2012). Avoiding the death zone: Choosing and running a library project in the cloud. *Library Hi Tech, 30*(3), 418–427. doi:10.1108/07378831211266564

Hamlen, K., Kantarcioglu, M., Khan, L., & Thuraisingham, B. (2010). Security issues for cloud computing. *International Journal of Information Security and Privacy*, *4*(2), 36–48. doi:10.4018/jisp.2010040103

Lei, M., Lu, G., Guo, Y., and Wang, A. (2011). Cloud-Computing Based Solution for Campus Computer Laboratory Administration. *Computer*, *18*, 024.

Li, Y. X., Luan, X. L., & Li, S. S. (2009). On the Application of Cloud Computing Technology in Library. *The Journal of the Library Science in Jiangxi*, *1*, 67–71.

Mavodza, J. (2013). The impact of cloud computing on the future of academic library practices and services. *New Library World*, *114*(3/4), 132–141. doi:10.1108/03074801311304041

Mitchell, E. (2010). Using cloud services for library IT infrastructure. *code4lib Journal*, *9*.

Nuernberg, P., Leggett, J., & McFarland, M. (2012). Cloud as infrastructure at the Texas Digital Library. *Journal of Digital Information*, *13*(1).

Peng, X. (2009). The Dual Impact of Cloud Computing on the Library Career. *Researches in Library Science*, *8*, 012.

Sclater, N. (2010). eLearning in the Cloud. [IJVPLE]. *International Journal of Virtual and Personal Learning Environments*, *1*(1), 10–19. doi:10.4018/jvple.2010091702

Tilley, S. R., & Parveen, T. (2013). *Software Testing in the Cloud: Perspectives on an Emerging Discipline*. Hershey, PA: IGI Global.

KEY TERMS AND DEFINITIONS

Cloud Computing: Is a term used to refer to a model of network computing where a program or application runs on a connected server or servers rather than on a local computing device such as a personal computer, tablet or smartphone (http://en.wikipedia.org/wiki/Cloud_computing).

Library: Is an organized collection of sources of information and similar resources which are made accessible to a defined community for reference or borrowing. The material can be physical or digital confined in either a physical building or room, or a virtual space, or both (http://en.wikipedia.org/wiki/Library).

Electronic Library: (Digital library or digital repository) is a collection of digital objects that can include text, visual material, audio material, video material, stored as electronic media formats. Also, it involves the means of organizing, storing, and retrieving the files and media contained in the library digital collection. This normally is opposed to print, micro form, or other media (http://en.wikipedia.org/wiki/Digital_library).

Information and Communications Technology (ICT): Refers to all types of technology used to handle telecommunications, broadcast media, intelligent building management systems, audio-visual processing and transmission systems, and network-based control and monitoring functions (http://en.wikipedia.org/wiki/Information_and_communications_technology).

"Stakeholder" or "User" or "Actor": Refers generically to organizations or or community or individuals who use or exploit cloud library. While these types of users / stakeholders may have some different interests and perhaps different concerns based on scale of data involved, generally a corporate / organization and an individual user are going to have different expectations and concerns related to cloud library.

APPENDIX

Snapshot of the Journal Hosted at SUA Web Server

Figure 17. Webpage of TAJAS

Figure 18. Comparison of open and closed source in SaaS (adapted from Salih & Zang, 2012)

	Autonomy Interwoven Teamsite CMS	AxCMS.net	Contegro	amilia CMS	Liferay Community Edition	AdaptCMS Lite	mojoPortal	Bricolage
Platform	Perl, Java	ASP.NET	ASP.NET	PHP	Java	PHP	ASP.NET	Perl on mod_perl
Supported	Oracle, SQL Server, DB2	SQL Server	SQL Server	MySQL	HSQLDB, MySQL, Oracle, SQL Server, DB2, Apache Derby, Informix, InterBase, JDataStore	MySQL	SQL Server, MySQL, PostgreSQL, SQLite, Firebird, SQLCE	MySQL, PostgreSQL
Web management	Yes	Yes	Yes	Yes	yes	yes	yes	yes
Software provider	Interwoven TeamSite	Axinom	Kiwi CMS	Amilia Corporation Inc	Liferay .com	Charlie Page's	Packt	Salon.com,
Software type	Closed	Closed	Closed	Closed	Open	Open	Open	Open

Figure 19. Comparison of open and closed source in PaaS (adapted from Salih & Zang, 2012)

	Windows Azure	Google App Engine	Force.com	Manjrasoft Aneka	Red Hat OpenShift	VMware	TioLive	WSO2 Stratos
Service type	Web and none web application	Web app	Web services	Compute/data ,Web and non-web apps	Web app	Simplified infrastructures	Web app	SOA middleware services
OS support	Windows	Windows or Linux	Apex	Linux, Windows	Linux	Linux, Windows	GNU/Linux	Linux, Window
Deployment language	Visual Studio, and .Net C#, C++,	Python, java	Apex	Java	java EE	PHP,java	java	PHP,java
User access interface	Microsoft windows azure portal	Web-based administration console	Adobe's Flex	Workbench, web-based portal	Command line. GUI.	vSphere Web	ERP5	Command line. GUI
Compatibility	with the Microsoft app	Amazon's EC2, S3	Amazon's EC2	Amazon's EC2, Xen	Amazon EC2	Eucalyptus, Amazon's EC2	Amazon EC2, Gpars	Amazon's EC2, Eucalyptus, Ubuntu Enterprise Cloud
Source type	closed	Closed	Closed	Closed	Open	Open	Open	Open
Owner	Microsoft	Google	salesforce.com	Manjrasoft	Red Hat	VMware Inc	Nexedi	WSO2

Figure 20. Comparison of open and closed source in IaaS (adapted from Salih & Zang, 2012)

	Agathon Group	Amazon EC2	Cisco	IBM	Eucalyptus	OpenNebula	Reservoir	Nimbus
Provider	Agathon Group	Amazon EC2	Cisco	IBM	Eucalyptus	OpenNebula	Reservoir	Melia Technologies
OS	Gentoo,Linux,Windows server 2008	Gentoo,Linux,Windows	CentOS, ,Linux, Windows server 2008	Red Hat Enterprise Linux SUSE Linux	Cent OS	Linux,Open solaris,open SUSE	Linux	Microsoft Windows XP/Vista
Language Supported	PHP, XMLmosaic	Java,php,python,ruby, WinDev	-	all the programming languages	Java	Java, Perl, PHP,	Java, Perl, PHP,SAS,SQL	HTML
Monitoring	No	Yes free	Yes free	Yes	Yes, Free	Yes, Free	Yes, Free	yes
Web Service	Yes, Free	No	Yes, Free	Yes	No	No	Yes, Free	yes
Control Interface	API (Application Programming Interface)	API (Application Programming Interface),command line	Web Based Application/ Control Panel	Web Based Application/Control Panel,API	Web Based Application/ Control Panel	Web Based Application/ Control Panel	API (Application Programming Interface)	Web Services based
Source type	Closed	Closed	Closed	Closed	Open	Open	Open	Open

Section 3
Business Models in Cloud Computing Environment

Chapter 6
Big Data in Cloud Computing Environment for Market Trends

K. Hariharanath
SSN School of Management & Computer Applications, India

ABSTRACT

The Industrial and Business landscape is changing because of the convergence of information technology and communication technologies. This convergence is creating new types of companies competing with each other. It is not about east or west, or developed markets versus developing markets; It is all about how soon a business enterprise understands the emerging technology and adapts it into its business. It is not enough that a business enterprise understands the technology but one has to be good at thinking about the applications of the technology. Now it has become a necessity for business enterprises to manage complex and interdisciplinary requirements in their organization. This chapter explores a business model developed by a textile mill to remain competitive in global market that uses the concepts of big data, cloud computing, virtual reality, and data warehousing.

INTRODUCTION

Globalization which was initially viewed with fear and distrust has opened up huge new markets for many business enterprises across the globe. This has been focusing on the need for an innovative approach in conducting business by enterprises. It is apt to recall the observation of Peter Ducker on innovation. "A Business enterprise has to and only two basic functions, marketing and innovation. Marketing and innovation produce results. All the rest are cost". The dividing factors in the market are niche markets and unique products or services. Innovative approach is needed to achieve the above factors in the present competitive market. Strategic thinking is required for any innovative approach. Strategic thinking decisions are based on the following

1. An understanding of the current and emerging needs,
2. An understanding of the organizations current and anticipated future core competences such as special skills or knowledge resources and culture and,
3. A future view of the industry sector and market place.

DOI: 10.4018/978-1-4666-8339-6.ch006

Even the most stable industries and the strongest brands can be blown to bits by the emerging concepts in information and communication technologies. Technology is forcing to rethink its business models and organizational designs as it contributes to the rebalancing of power in the market place. It is no longer guaranteed to those organizations that have financial resources and size on their side. Smaller organizations that are fast and flexible can now outmaneuver the traditional large enterprises by employing new technology that enables them to deliver goods and services to their customers at a faster pace and lower cost (Kumar & Kumar, 2013).

NEED FOR A BUSINESS MODEL

The problem arises when the organizations are spending too much time tinkering with the existing business models of their organizations instead of re allying their teams around the potential to do something extraordinary in the market place. Tinkering is like painting a Car when the engine is weak. The challenge today is to develop sustainable business that is compatible with the current economic reality. In the present global market scenario an enterprise remaining competitive in the market depends on its ability to focus on core business and adapting to changes quickly. Now it has become imperative for every business enterprise to innovate a process that will help them to remain competitive in the market. Innovative process is nothing but identifying what is relevant to the emerging technologies and develop a business model suitable to their business enterprise.

DESIGNING A BUSINESS MODEL

One of the most interesting opportunities in the present scenario is the dynamic nature of the information and communication technology capabilities available in almost every sector that one could imagine. Business enterprises need to know how to make use of the capabilities of information and communication technology and their relevance and context to their business requirements. Business process, technological applications, practices, past business performances, market potential and target market are the factors to be considered for designing a business model. A case study of a textile mill in India is discussed in this chapter and how they developed a business model on the basis of the above factors transforming their business process and market share.

CASE ILLUSTRATION

3G Textile Mill is one of leading textile mills in India. This Textile mill has been in the business over five decades. The unique aspect of this mill is that it is managed by a management team consisting of a President, Senior Vice President and Vice President who belong to three different generations. Their approach and decisions are based on their experiences, business insight and education.

3G Textile Mill products range from western and Indian cloth materials for ladies, suiting and shirting materials and readymade garments for ladies and gents. Each management team member has taken the responsibility to be in charge of one of their products range. Their responsibility covers all the activities related from production to marketing of the product. The major financial activities such as purchase of capital items and investment activities will be the responsibility of the Management Team. The product design, production schedule, purchase of raw materials and other materials will be purchased by the concerned team member of the product he is associated with. The cost of common support services such as finance, human resource and administrative are borne by the product divisions. Activity based costing method is followed in allocating the cost of common support services.

Selection of cotton and mix of various varieties of cotton for the production of different "count of yarn" is the main activity in any textile mill in India It is interesting to note the method followed for the selection of cotton and mix of cotton varies among the management team.

The President of 3G Textile Mill who is looking after the activity related to the production of ladies cloth materials and ladies garments has three decades of rich experience in all the aspects related to the textile field. Though he has no formal education, he updates himself in information technology, textile technology and marketing aspects of textile products. Further he is aware of Indian and Global economy. The method he follows is the method of testing the strength of the cotton manually. He interacts with the vendors who bring the cotton sample. In his interaction with them, he gets the information such as the year of crop, place and country of origin of cotton. He mentally calculates the costing for the mix of two varieties of cotton. He also recalls the economic conditions, weather conditions, currency exchange rates and other relevant information pertaining to the year of crop and preceding years on the basis of these factors. He fixes the purchase price for imported cotton and the cotton produced in India. He also further visualizes the design of the end market for a particular market segment.

The senior vice president who is looking after the activities related to "shirting" material has a degree in textile technology and fifteen years of experience in the Textile Industry. He has formal business interaction with the cotton vendors. Then he selects few samples of cotton and sends them to quality department for testing and analysis of the cotton. He works out the costing for the mix of cotton for the production of yarn on the basis of the report given by the quality department. He uses the calculator to arrive at the cost of "Mix of Cotton". He negotiates with vendors for the purchase price.

The Vice President who is in charge of the activities related to "Pant Material" has a master degree in textile technology and a Masters Degree in Business Management from a world renowned University. He never meets any cotton vendor. Vendors are expected to handover the samples of cotton to the group of purchase executives identified for this type of assignment. It is the responsibility of this group to send the samples to the quality department for testing. They arrive at the costing of the cotton mix on the basis of the report given by the quality department. Costing for the different mix of cotton is arrived at by using a software developed for this purpose. The report generated from the computer system is sent along with the report given by the quality department to the Vice President. He decides the purchase of the cotton on the basis of the reports received by him.

The 3G textiles mills have been making profits even though the three management team members follow their own methods. They also never claim that their methods are best. Every team member has his own information system for his product related activities such as production, design, purchases and marketing. The information pertaining to finance is only integrated for all the activities related to all the products manufactured by 3G textiles, 3G textile mill has been in the market over a period of three decades. Their business models worked well. Their products are well received in the market. Their market has been encouraging. Though the overall profit and the market share of the company is fluctuating, overall performance of 3G textiles is not affected. It is because one product's dip in profit is offset by the other products profits of the company. The management team has felt this trend is not encouraging a healthy sign. The President of the company has analyzed the situation and came to the conclusion that the linear process in their business models that is research through design, development and marketing is not conductive to the present globalization scenario. It is also due to global market being open to many players across the globe.

SERVICES OF A CONSULTANCY FIRM

3G Textile Mills hired the services of a consultancy firm who have experience in textile domain, information and communication technology and global market scenario. The assignment given to them is to study the present working of the mills. On the basis of their study they are expected to suggest a business process. New business process needs to be discussed with the management before developing a business model.

The study conducted by the Consultant indicated that 3G Textile Mills has cost advantage over the competitors in the areas of process technology and size of business enterprise. They do not have an edge over the competitors in the areas of distribution networking, product technology and brands in the global market. The company has barriers to entry due to brands and retaliatory capability. But the company has vertical bargaining power due to sound financial resources. Information systems in the company are isolated and not integrated. Further the company has not made use of the emerging concepts in the areas of information and communication technologies.

BUSINESS MODEL FOR 3G TEXTILE MILLS

The consultants have designed a business model for 3G Textile Mills with cloud computing as a base component with the concepts of virtual reality, data warehouse and big data (Jorgensen, Rowland, Welch, Clark, Price, & Mitchell, 2014).

The information pertaining to all the products produced by the three divisions is to be integrated and stored in a centralized system. Purchase of cotton for the production of cloth material is to be centralized. Marketing information and its activities are to be centralized. Domain experts with rich experience across the globe in the area of textile sector need to be hired. The domain experts

can operate with their team members from their respective countries. Their role is to design the textile material (cloth) and readymade garments for men and women. Domain experts are expected to design as per the tastes of the people of their country. Domain experts would guide the technical personnel of the 3G Textile Mills in India for implementing the design developed by them. Types of cotton and mix of cotton information will be provided for their design. The color of dyes and combination and the required quantities are to be provided by the domain experts. Vendors who will supply cotton, dyes and other materials as per the ISO standards, they will be given access to the bills of material module in the system for knowing the quantity of cotton and dyes, date of supply. The domain experts are expected to suggest marketing strategies that would work in their countries. The approach suggested by the domain experts is based on virtual organizations.

CLOUD COMPUTING FOR VIRTUAL ORGANIZATION

The essence of Virtual Organization is a collaboration of participants who are both geographically and organizationally distributed. Cloud Computing helps to implement virtualization in information and communication technologies. Advancements in internet has facilitated that there is no need to limit group collaboration to a single enterprises network environment. Use from multiple locations within their and other organizations can have access to the systems through internet. Cloud computing helps the users to create a centralized pool of virtual servers, storage and networking equipment (Mather, Kumaraswamy, & Latif, 2010)

Applications virtualization allows for an application to run from a remote server rather than on the user's system. Each application is bundled with its own configuration set and the user can execute it on demand.

VIRTUAL REALITY

Virtual reality refers to the presentation of computer generated data made available in such a way that those who use it can perceive the information at their disposal. The ability to get real world perception inter activity through computers explain interest associated with 3-D Graphics Virtual Reality. One can master the concept of virtual reality through simulation. The way business model is being developed provides scope for the study of complex real world situations. It also helps to develop steps for simulation and studying complex business concepts.

DATA MANAGEMENT

Data formats are most important aspect in any integrated database. The data may be put into the particular resource and the results from the resource on the execution of a specific task if the database is not designed properly. The data movement in geographically distributed systems can cause scalability problems. Data movement in any cloud computing environment requires absolutely secure data transfers both to and from the respective resources.

MOBILE COMPUTING

The concept of mobile computing is to facilitate end users to have access to data, Information or logical objects through a device in any network while one is on the move. It also enables the users to perform a task from anywhere using a computer device which has features or mobile computing. Generally mobile computing is used in different contexts with different names. The most common names are 1. Mobile computing, 2 Any where any time information, 3. Virtual home environment, 4 Normadic Computing, 5 Pervasive Computing, 6 Ubiquitous Computing, 7 Global service portability, and 8 Wearable Computers.

DEVICES

The convergence of information and communication technology is responsible for the production of new generation devices working on wireless technology. These devices can make concept of cloud computing a workable solution in virtual organization scenario. Even though many mobile and wireless devices are available there will be many more in the future. There is no precise classification of such devices by size, shape, weight or computing power. Currently the mobile device range is sensors, mobile phones, pocket computer, note book, laptop, tablet and I pads.

BIG DATA

The term "Big Data" it suggests "Bigness" in data (Franks, 2014). It indicates volume of data is only the major factor. In industry analyst firm Gartner defines it as: Big data is high volume, high velocity and high variety information assets that demand cost-effective, innovative forms information processing for enhanced insight and decision making.

A major driving force behind this big data growth is ubiquitous connectivity through rapidly growing mobile devices constantly connected to the networks (Schmarzo, 2014). It is remarkable to note that only a small portion of the digital universe is visible, in the form of videos, pictures, documents and tweets. A vast of data is being created about humans by the digital universe. Data will be analyzed by the enterprise such as internet service providers and Cloud Service providers of different varieties of services. They are infrastructure-as-a-service, platform-as-a-service and software-as-a-service.

Social data, websites, machine generated data and traditional enterprise data are the main elements for big data. Social data in social media sites cover face book, twitter and LinkedIn. Sensor reading and satellite communication form a part of machine generated data. Data in websites, blogs and portals provide specific information. Traditional enterprise data is confined to products, purchase, sales, customer and finance information. Figure 1 shows the elements in big data.

PROCESSING OF DATA IN BIG DATA

Technology provides access to a vast amount of usable information in big data. The users in enterprises need to master integrating that information and those technology capabilities to create relevant context. The relevance and content would come out of what would actually help in transforming their business.

The following steps are required to be considered while making use of big data.

Figure 1. The elements of big data

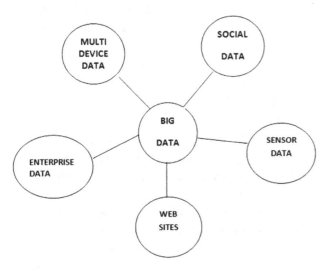

1. **Search Engines:** Search engines are available to analyze large unstructured data.
2. **Business Intelligence Tools:** Analytics tools are used to get new and create visualizations to intuitively depict the meaning of data.
3. **Storage of Data:** Private and public cloud are made use of the required infrastructure to store the big data.
4. **Cloud Computing:** Software-as-a–service in cloud environment will be useful to run the required software for processing the big data.
5. **Predictive Analytics:** This will be more effective for analyzing data from multiple dimesions.

Enterprises in the present business scenario need more data for analysis. Till recently it was possible only to store selected important data in the systems of business enterprises. This was due to cost effective way of storing data for business decision. Business analysts feel for the need of huge volume of data for analysis and designing of business models. Mathematical and statistic tools are required to be used for designing these business models. These models facilitate to solve complex business problems. In the present business context big data is considered to be a better solution for storing data for business analysis. Velocity, variety and volume are the three main elements in big data. Generally it is known as 3rd of big data.

The term "BIG DATA" can be pretty nebulous in the same way that the term "CLOUD" covers diverse technologies. Input data to big data systems could be from social networks, web server logs, traffic flow sensors, satellite imagery, broad cast audio systems, and content of web pages, GPS trails and market data. This list indicates the basis for 3 elements in big data. The three elements volume, velocity and variety can be referred as lens to view and understand the data and the software platforms for making use of them. Volume refers to the said of data in terms of petabytes or xetabytes. Velocity talks about the rate at which the data is growing. Variety indicates structured, semi structured and unstructured another three features which play an important role in creating a database, they are consistency, availability and platform tolerance. Consistency means even if current updates are happening, users will get updated data irrespective of the place from where they are accessing the data, available to the users 24 x 7 irrespective of the load on the server. Platform tolerance means even in the case of partial failures the system should be functional.

WHY BIG DATA?

Big data is considered for exceeding the processing capacity of conventional data base systems. Big data is required wherever the data is too big and does not fit the structures of the conventional data base architectures. Big data is an alternative way to process the data. It facilitates to gain value from this data. Big data has become viable as cost effective approach. Earlier information was hidden because of the amount of work required to extract them.

The value of big data to an enterprise falls into two categories. One is for analytical use and another is for enabling new products. Big data analytics can reveal insights hidden previously by data too costly to process (Minelli, Chambers, & Dhiraj, 2014). Big data helps to reveal peer influence among customers by analyzing shoppers' transactions, social and geographical data. It enables to process every item of data in reasonable time. It removes the need for sampling and promotes an investigative approach to data. It facilitates to avoid static nature of generating predetermined reports. The past decades successful web startups are important examples of big data used as an enabler for introducing new products and services.

Face book has been to make use of highly personalized user experience and create a new kind of advertising business. It is no coincidence that the major shares of ideas and tools in big data have emerged from Google, Yahoo, Amazon and Face book. The emergence of big data in the business enterprises has made the experiment and explore for the business purposes. The business purposes can be for the creation of new products or looking for ways to gain competitive advantage.

VOLUME, VELOCITY, AND VARIETY

Many business innovators are excited about the potential use in creating new design and developing a wide of range of new products and services based on big data concept. Volume, Velocity and Variety need to be understood clearly by them.

Volume

The benefit gained from the ability to process large amounts of data is the main attraction for big data analytics. More data for analysis helps to create better models. Any complex mathematics formulas will appear more simple and effective in big data as many factors as 500 factors can be considered for forecasting to know demand pattern. This volume presents a challenge to conventional information technology structures. Then it calls for scalable storage and a distributed approach to querying. Many companies have large amounts of achieved data. They may not have required capacity to process it.

Data warehouse needs predetermined schemas suiting a regular dataset. Apache hadoop on the other hand places no conditions on the structure of the data it can process. Hadoop is a platform for distributing computing problems across a number of servers. First developed and released as an open source by Yahoo. It implements the map reduce approach pioneered by Google in compiling its search indexes. Hadoop's map reduce involves distributing data set among multiple servers and operating on the data at map stage. The partial results are then recombined at the reduce stage.

To store data Hadoop utilized its own distributed file systems. HEFS makes data available to multiple computing nodes. A typical hadoop usage pattern involves three stages. They are (1) Loading data into HDFS (2) Map reduce operation and (3) Retrieving results from HDFS. This process is by nature a batch operation suited for analytical purpose or non interactive computing tasks. It can be considered as an adjunct to a data base.

Velocity

Increasing rate at which data flows into an enterprise is on increase. Data's velocity problems similar to volume previously restricted to certain segments of industry are now presenting themselves in a much broader setting. The internet and mobile era is making velocity more complex. On line retailers are able to compile large histories of customers every click and interaction not just the final sales. Retailers will gain a competitive advantage by making use of the information for recommending additional purchase. The Smart Phone era is also increasing the rate of data inflow. Consumers who carry these devices will have a stream source of Geo Located Imagery and audio data.

Streaming data or complex event processing are the terms used in enterprises. The term complex event processing was used more in product categories before the term streaming processing data gained more widespread relevance. There are two main reasons to consider streaming processing. The first is when the input data are too fast to store in their entirety. In order to keep storage requirements practical, some level of analysis must occur as the data streams in. The second reason is where the application requires immediate response to the data.

Variety

A common theme in big data systems that source data is diverse and does not fall into neat rational structure. Data can be from social networks, image data, and data from sensor source. None of this comes ready for integration in to application. A common use of big data processing is to take unstructured data and convert it into meaningful data or structured input for an application.

CLOUD SERVICES FOR BIG DATA

The majority if big data solutions are now provided in three methods. They are (1) Software only (2) An Application and (3) Cloud –Based. Selection of a method depends on many factors. Some of the factors are location of Data, Privacy, Regulations, Human Resources and Project Requirements. Generally Enterprises prefer hybrid computing. They make use of the resources of private cloud along with public cloud. Cloud environment is preferred for processing because the nature of data being big (Reese, 2010). Another aspect is required to be considers besides information technology infrastructure cleaning the data. It is apt to recall Pete wardens observation in his big data glossary. "I probably spend more time turning messy source data into some timing usable than I do on the rest of the data analysis process combined".

DATA SCIENCE

Data science is a discipline that combines Mathematics, Statistics and software programming. Big data has also similar features of Data science. Business analytics that make use of big data concepts need to have the qualities such as experience, curiosity, storytelling and innovation.

EXPERTISE

Expertise is required in one of the areas such as mathematics or statistics or software programming with good knowledge of either mathematics or statistics.

CURIOSITY

A desire is required to go deep into the data for analysis and creating a set of hypotheses for testing.

STORY TELLING

One should have the ability to use data to tell a story.

INNOVATION

Ability is needed to look at a problem differently and suggest an innovative solution.

ETHICS OF BIG DATA

Big Data is persistent. It is persistent in a way that business and society have never experienced before persistence of data influences the very important concepts such as privacy, ownership and identity for both individuals and enterprises, as information is aggregated and correlated by not only the originating entity, but also by those who may seek to further innovate products and services using the original information. It is very difficult to have a control over the information used once it is out of one's hands (Davis, & Patterson, 2012).

Big data is mostly about people and their characteristics, and behavior. The potential use of this acquired data extends in a great many directions. The concerns about the consequences of having personal data captured, aggregated and linked to other data are slowly realized now. These risks are not just limited to individuals. It is equally applicable to enterprises. Enterprises are not in the business of misusing the information of their customers. Hospitals generally do not disclose the patient's confidentiality. Yet there is a risk of using big data technology.

Organizations must explicitly and transparently evaluate the ethical impacts of the data they collect from their customers. Ethical evaluation must indicate the utilization of the customers data. It must clearly describe the historical actions, characteristics, data handed practices and the value system followed by the organization, organizations work more effectively once their value is shared across their organization.

PRIVACY

Digital data can be used by any one. It does not differentiate the users. It is inevitable that Governments change, laws change, social mores change, but data once collected and placed on a global distributed net work, such as the internet, is for all practical purposes permanent. The laws are required to regulate the usage of data collected. If the regulations are strict in saying that no data should be collected without user consent, then only there will be hope for privacy in data (Craig, & Ludloff, 2013).

SOFTWARE TOOLS

There has been an innovative approach in the development of data /software tools. The innovative approach has become possible due to the trends in information and communication technology discipline. These trends can be classified under three areas (1) Techniques originally developed by website for scaling issues are being extended to other domains. (2) Google has proven that research techniques from computer science can be effective at solving problems and creating value in many real world situations. (3) Presently the machines with a decent amount of processing power can be hired for large scale date processing tasks. Open source has become an alternative for high priced data software.

These trends have led to explosion of new software tools, and systems for big data. They cover data bases, storage systems, and servers, processing tools, machine learning systems, acquisition tools, data visualization tools and serialization (Singh, & Kumar, 2014).

DATA MANAGEMENT IN CLOUD ENVIRONMENT

Data movement is an important factor especially in the development of a hybrid solution. Generally the requirement is moving data to and from the cloud environment. An effective software tool is needed to move data to either populate a solution in the cloud with the data or to bring the data from the cloud to the enterprise computing environment. It would be better to integrate big data solution to the analytics and business intelligence infrastructure of the enterprises. This will facilitate many executives in the enterprise to gain insights in the solutions (Warden, 2012).

EVALUATION OF BIG DATA STRATEGY

The following points need to be considered for evolving a big data strategy for an enterprise.

BUSINESS UNITS INVOLVEMENT

It must be remembered that big data is not an isolated activity. Enterprises can leverage huge volumes of data to learn more about customers, process and events with big data. Proper implementation of big data strategy can have a broad impact on the effectiveness of business strategy.

CLOUD COMPUTING FOR DATA

Big data has petabytes of data. Cloud computing environment infrastructure has the facility to store and manage petabytes of data.

BIG DATA AND DATA WARE HOUSE

It is a common opinion among the many enterprises that traditional data ware house is no longer required. It is because of big data analytics are providing the required results for them. This is not correct. Enterprises have to make use of the results of big data analytics in conjunction with their data ware house. The data ware house. The data ware house includes the information about the enterprise operate. It is advisable to compare the big data results against the bench marks of the core data for decision making.

CONSISTENT META DATA

Enterprises have to be careful while taking data from customer service sites and social media environment. Generally the data from these sources is not cleansed. Enterprises have to make sure that they are dealing with a consistent set of mata data for analysis.

HANDLING DATA

A Proper tool has to be selected for managing volume, velocity and variety of data.

BIG DATA ANALYTICS

A lot of important technologies are available for big data analysis. They are text analytics, predictive analytics, streaming data environments and spatial data analysis. Evaluation of each technology is required for the job to be accomplished.

SUGGESTION

It is advisable that enterprises start with pilot projects to gain experience. Enterprises need to take experts advice to avoid, mistakes in inference and decision making.

INTEGRATION OF DATA

Many good technologies in the market are focused on making it easier to integrate the results of big data analytics with other data sources.

MANAGEMENT OF DATA

Big data demonstrates that enterprises can make use of more data than before at a faster rate of speed than before. Enterprises are benefited by this capability. If the data is not managed in an effective way, it will create problems for the enterprises. Enterprises need a road map for managing data under big data (Bhandarkard, 2013).

SECURITY

Security is a part of big data life cycle. Enterprises should be aware of the third party data licenses and government regulations.

BIG DATA IN THE MARKETING PERSPECTIVE

Traditionally the major source of data has been from expanding CRM application. In the present business scenario the complexity of data sources is on increase. The data sources which contribute to the complexity are (1) Primary Research, (2) Secondary Research, (3) Internet data (4) Device Data, (5) Image Data, and (6) Supply Chain Data.

(1).Primary Research provides data related to surveys, experiments, and observations. (2). Secondary Data is based on business data, industries reports, market place and competitive date (3). The source for internet data is click stream, social media, and social networking (4). The data from the devices such as mobile phones, sensors, RF devices and telemetry add to the complexity of data. (5). Image data plays an important role in Big Data and (6). Vendor data and pricing from supply chain data are considered as another important source. The data from the above sources become the part of volume, velocity and variety in the data storage of big data (Hurwitz, Nugent, Halper, & Kaufman, 2014).

NEW SCHOOL OF MARKETING UNDER BIG DATA

It is apt to quote the observation of DAN SPRINGER CEO of responses on new school of marketing "To days consumers have changed. They have put down the news paper, they fast forward through TV commercials, and they junk unsolicited email. Why? They have new options that better fit their digital life style. They can choose which marketing messages they receive, when, where, and from whom. They prefer marketers who talk with them, not at them. New school marketers deliver what today's consumers want: relevant interactive communication across the digital power channels: email, mobile, social, display and the web".

Cross channel life cycle marketing approach is gaining importance. This approach only talks about conversation, stickiness, win back and permission.

CLOUD AND BIG DATA

Most of the data in big data is unstructured. Cloud is an ideal computing environment to store big data sets. Big data is known in its volume, variety and velocity. These 3 V's can be managed without much difficulty in the cloud computing environment. Market economics are forcing enterprises to consider new business models (Miller, 2009).

BUSINESS ANALYTICS

Analytics is generally defined as the scientific approach of transforming data into insight for making better decisions. Business analytical professionals require special skills, and they are to be familiar with technologies, business applications and practices for continuous interactive exploration and analyzing of past business performance to gain insight and prepare business planning.

BIG DATA ANALYTICS

Big data analytics need new skills such as fairly good knowledge in mathematics and information technology. They should be adept at visualizing large data and discerning between signal and noise. They need to be in position to weave together data that has traditionally not been woven together. The skill required in this product or organization on is the face book with the contents made recently about the product or organization on Twitter. Once all data is woven together, the quality of the prediction gets better and better

PRIVATE CLOUD ENVIRONMENT

Infrastructure in private cloud environment is owned or leased by a single enterprise and is operated solely for that organization. The advantage being in private cloud environment is highly secure, flexible, visible, traceable and manageable (Miller, 2009).

CONCEPTS AND PRACTICES

Concepts and practice are generally divergent. Challenge of developing an effective business model by a global virtual team is substantially greater than identifying relevant concepts in management and information and communication technology. The consultants have indicated that in order to grow in global market, it is not just enough to be competitive. The products produced by 3G Textile Mills should be acceptable in global market, so also domain experts in the areas of design, production and marketing of the products manufactured by the 3G Textile Mills. The Domain experts are based in Paris (Europe), Sydney (Australia), Singapore and HongKong. The global virtual team is familiar with the global development team frame. They are also aware that 3G Textile Mills business has become highly competitive and dominated by a set off aggressive global players.

Figure 2 gives an overview of the concepts made use of in the business models developed by the domain experts in the respective countries.

Business model for 3G Textile Mills focuses on the three main areas.

1. Designing cloth materials and Readymade garments
2. Materials required for manufacturing products of the above in bill of materials module and

Figure 2. Business model for 3G textile mills

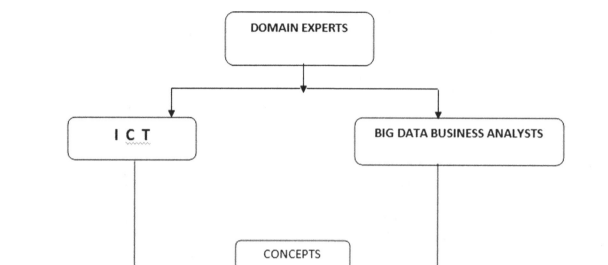

3. Analyzing the global market scenario with company's performance.

MACRO LEVEL DESIGN

The Figure 3 indicates the use of resources such as hardware and software made by the domain experts from their respective countries.

CLOTH MATERIAL

Cloth material is designed by the domain experts from their experience based on the needs of the consumer requirements. Color combination of dyes with the cotton mix will be suggested by them. Virtual reality concept is made use of in designing the cloth material.

READYMADE GARMENTS

The domain experts design and create readymade garments on the basis of real world requirements. Simulated version of readymade garments are carried out in computer systems in the cloud computing environment. The concept of virtual reality helped them to look from the real world situation. Resources in cloud computing has made it possible for the domain experts to make use of virtual reality concepts.

3G TEXTILE MILLS IN INDIA

The management team along with their technical executives of 3G Textile Mills in India is able to view the designs of cloth and design of readymade garments. On their system from India they can also suggest changes if required.

Figure 3. Big data in cloud

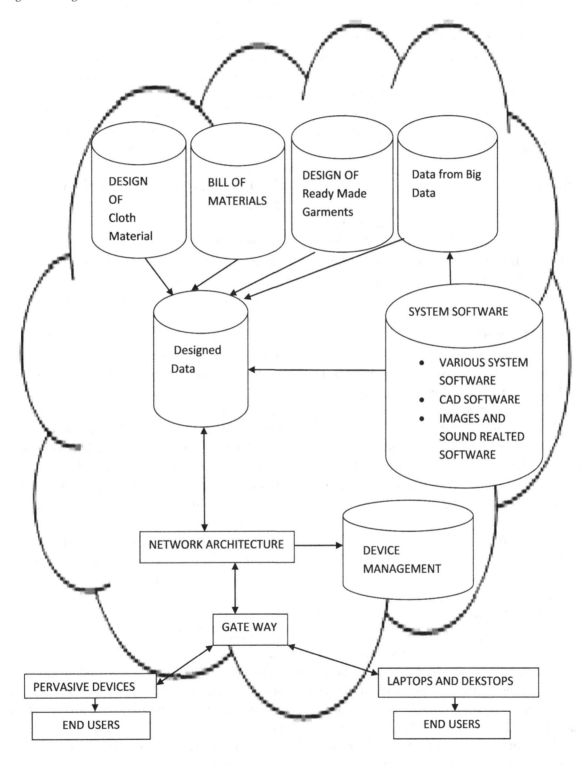

Marketing Wing

The proposed design of readymade garments are uploaded in company's portal and face book by the marketing executives for feed back from their prospective customers. After evaluating the feed back from the prospective customers, production and marketing plan will be prepared for different country's requirements.

Vendors

Vendors of 3G Textile Mills are given an access to the information needed for the supply of materials by them. Bill of materials will provide details of the quality, variety of cotton, dyes and other material to the Vendors.

Device Management

The need for device management is required in cloud computing environment. Heterogeneous devices, applications and users needed to be managed. The core functionality of a private device is to perform task with high speed. The main requirement of device management is to take care of operating system, structure, memory protection, security and multi-tasking.

Development of a New Product in 3G Textile Mills

The domain experts have proved that a new product can be jointly designed by the experts in a global virtual team through a process of continuous exchange of ideas between members dispersed across the globe. This process helps in generating alternative ideas by taking inputs from different sources and structuring through virtual reality application. This models provides an idea for the creation of global innovation model. Further it helps to structure the work flow by visualizing the various phases of the development of a product. Customers' tastes are becoming more

homogeneous around the globe. Consequently, 3G Textile Mills can provide a good product through the economies of scale with common design. 3G Textile Mills model can increase the chances of successfully defusing knowledge, technology and process. Advanced tele-communication technologies have drastically changed the business operation providing new services and creating an inter-connected world-wide community.

Summary of the Development of 3G Textile Mills

Till recently the standard model of innovation has been a linear process from research through design, development and then manufacturing. In the case of 3G Textile Mills model many of these processes are carried out concurrently and collaborating through the concepts of information technology in private cloud deployment model. In the management team of 3G Textile Mills could hire the services of the domain experts from the respective countries. The employees of 3G Textile Mills and Domain experts with their team members have formed virtual team to develop 3G Textile Mills model. It is because of cloud computing, they could develop 3G Textile Mills models by making use of the virtual reality concept and the features in Big Data. At the same time the bill of materials required for readymade garments and designing of cloth material to be produced is made available in 3G Textile Mills model.

CONCLUSION

In today's knowledge rich environment, enterprises can no longer afford to rely entirely on their ideas to advance their business nor can they restrict their innovation to a single path market (O'Reilly Media Inc, 2013). As a result, the traditional model for innovation which has been largely internally focused or a "closed one" has become obsolete. Emerging in its place is a new paradigm "open innovation". This strategically leverages internal and external sources of ideas and takes them to market through multiple paths. Global enterprises can take advantage of unique knowledge and resource wherever they are located. Information and communication technology has increased virtualization in business activities and ways of working. The term "virtual" is now appearing in many forms. 3G Textile Mills models explains how to adopt innovative approach in invoking global enterprises by applying the concept of "mind invoking".

It may be observed that 3G Textile Mills has made use of the services of the domain experts from the respective countries. The concept of virtual reality and multimedia are made use of in their development process of designing readymade garments and cloth material for global market. At the same time, Vendors are able to get the required information for the supply of their materials.

Cloud computing concept facilitated innovation at 3G Textile Mills. 3G Textile Mills has found that private cloud is a better solution for their organization in leveraging the benefits of cloud computing within their firewall. 3G Textile Mills has proved that the concept of virtual organization is the key to cloud computing.

REFERENCES

Bhandarkar, M. (2013, April). Big Data Systems: Past, Present & (Possibly) Future. *CSI Communications Journal*, *37*(1), 7–16.

Craig, T., & Ludlof, M. E. (2013). *Privacy and Big Data*. Mumbai: Shroff Publishers & Distributors Private Limited.

Davis, K., & Patterson, D. (2012). *Ethics of Big Data*. Mumbai: Shroff Publishers & Distributors Private Limited.

Franks, B. (2014). *Taming the Big Data Tidal Wave*. New Delhi: Wiley India Private Limited.

Hurwitz, J., Nugent, A., Halper, F., & Kaufman, M. (2014). *Big Data for Dummies*. New Delhi: Wiley India Private Limited.

Jorgensen, A., Rowland-Jones, J., Welch, J., Clark, D., Price, C., & Brain, M. (2014). *Microsoft Big Data Solutions*. New Delhi: Wiley India Private Limited.

Kumar, S., & Kumar, S. (2013, April). Big Data: A Big game changer. *CSI Communications Journal*, *37*(1), 9–10.

Mather, T., Kumaraswamy, S., & Latif, S. (2010). *Cloud Security and Privacy*. Mumbai: Shroff Publishers & Distributors Private Limited.

Miller, M. (2009). *Cloud Computing; New Delhi: Dorling Kindersley*, India: Private Limited.

Minelli, M., Chambers, M., & Dhiraj, A. (2014). *Big Data Analytics*. New Delhi: Wiley India Private Limited.

O'Reilly Media Inc. (2013). *Big Data Now Current Perspectives from O'Reilly Media*. Mumbai: Shroff Publishers & Distributors Private Limited.

Reese, G. (2010). *Cloud Application Architecture*. Mumbai: Shorff Publishers & Distributors Private Limited.

Schmarzo, B. (2014). *Big Data Understanding How Data Powers Big Business*. New Delhi: Wiley India Private Limited.

Singh, R., & Kumar, S. (2014, November). Big Data Visualization using Cassandra and R; Mumbai. *CSI Communications Journal*, *38*(8), 15–21.

Warden, P. (2012). *Big Data Glossary*. Mumbai: Shroff Publishers & Distributors Private Limited.

KEY TERMS AND DEFINITIONS

Big Data: The capability to manage a huge volume of disparate data, at the right speed and within the right time frame, to allow real time analysis and reaction.

Cloud Computing: A computing Model that makes information technology resources such as servers, middleware, and applications available over the internet as services to business organizations in a self-service manner.

Data Cleansing: Software used to identify potential data quality problems.

Data Ware House: A large data store containing the organization's historical data, which is used primarily for data analysis and data mining.

Predictive Analytics: A statistical or data mining solution consisting of algorithms and techniques that can be used on both structured and unstructured data to determine future outcomes.

Private Cloud: A private cloud is a set of computing resources within the organization that serves only the organization.

Streaming Data: An analytic computing platform that is used on speed.

Unstructured Data: Data that does not follow a specific data format.

Chapter 7
Cloud Computing:
An Enabler in Managing Natural Resources in a Country

N. Raghavendra Rao
FINAIT Consultancy Services, India

ABSTRACT

The growth of the Internet has provided scope for multiple applications. Governments in both developed and developing nations have started making use of the Internet in their functioning. The idea behind these governments moving from manual work to IT enabled systems through the Internet is to improve governance. Framing policies pertaining to natural resources and managing them will not be with one department under any government. E-governance, consisting of multidisciplinary experts, is required to develop a model for natural resources management in a country. The electronic governance will help the members of the e-governance and the various departments in the government to facilitate in managing their natural resources. E-governance in the area of natural resources management in any country will be successful only when there is coordination among the various government departments. Cloud computing is economically viable for implementation of e-governance projects. This chapter suggests a conceptual model for managing natural resources and natural disaster management for a country under cloud computing environment.

INTRODUCTION

Economic development has helped to raise the standard of living and has also led to mismanagement of natural resources. This has resulted in environmental issues. Wisdom is used in maintaining a balance between the needs of human beings and supplies from natural resources so that the delicate ecological balance is not disturbed. Governments in many countries in their zeal to go ahead with ambitious plans of development, integration of knowledge relating to environmental sciences, economics, space technology and information and communication technologies has escaped the attention of the governments.

DOI: 10.4018/978-1-4666-8339-6.ch007

The advancements in information and communication technologies have resulted in new concepts being developed in this discipline. Cloud computing is one among the number of other concepts. Cloud computing is a concept generally defined as the clusters of scalable and virtualized resources such as distributed computers, storage, system software and application software which make use of internet to provide on-demand services to the user.

This chapter explains the components of natural resources and the human activities on natural resources. Further it recommends a model for making use of space technology and Cloud computing to create knowledge based system for natural resources. This model will mainly be useful to the various government departments which are involved in the management of natural resources and environmental issues. Further it also suggests a model for handling the damage caused by natural disasters.

GOVERNMENT AND GOVERNANCE

Governments in both developed and developing countries aim at protecting the interests of their people and preserving the resources of their Country. They pass laws to implement their plans. In this process they also recommend new policies and propose changes as needed in the existing policies and programs.

One needs to be clear about the distinction between government and governance. A quotation going back to 1656 is relevant in understanding the distinction. "Wise princes ought not to be admired for their Government, but governance". The distinction that is drawn at present briefly runs as follows: While Government refers to actions carried out within a formal legal setting, governance involves all activities of government along with

informal activities, even outside a formal government setting that are meant to achieve goals.

COORDINATION FOR E-GOVERNANCE

UNESCO defines E-Governance as: "Governance refers to the exercise of political, economic and administrative authority in the management of Country's affairs, including citizen's articulation of their interests and exercise of their legal rights and obligations. E-governance may be understood as the performance of this governance via the disseminating information to the public, and other agencies, and for performing government administrative activities.

UNESCO definition indicates the importance of coordination among the Government departments to provide and improve the Government services, transactions with citizens, business, and other departments of government. E-Governance in the area of natural resource management in any country will be successful only when there is coordination among the various government departments.

Framing policies pertaining to natural resource and managing them will not be with one department under any government. An e-governance consisting of a multidisciplinary expert is required to develop a model for resources management in a country (Kaushik, & Kaushik, 2006). Electronic governance will help the members of the core team and the various departments in the government to facilitate in managing their resources. When they work as a team, they need to have centralized data pertaining to geographical information both quantitative and textual content. Then only it will be possible to develop a knowledge based system for natural resources management. Further the knowledge based system will be useful for environmental management and natural disaster management. Cloud computing is more useful for data-intensive application such as knowledge based system for natural resources management. This application has to manage data replication for facilitating data recovery and responding dynamically to changes in the volume of data in databases. Cloud computing supports the above requirements (Buyya,& Sukumar, 2011).

CLOUD COMPUTING FOR E-GOVERNANCE

Cloud computing has a real advantage over other conventional systems. Technological benefits and cost advantage together makes it a viable Technology. Cloud computing has inbuilt features like scalability, virtualization, rapid elasticity, pay as per usages, on demand access to software, storage, network and other platform services. Many governments across the world have realized the importance of Cloud computing in e-governance. The analyst firm Gartner has predicted that Cloud Computing will be the top most technology area in information technology.

Japanese Government has undertaken a major initiative to bring all the Government ministries under Cloud Computing, known as "KASUMI-GASEKI CLOUD" and is likely to be completed by 2015. Accordingly to Japan's ministry of internal affairs and communication it will have benefits like integrated and consolidated hardware, shared platform services and security. It will greatly reduce the Government's efforts in terms of electronic governance related to development and operating cost.

The United Kingdom Government has accepted the proposal of creation of "G-CLOUD" for Government wide Cloud Computing as a strategic priority. The Digital Britain report prepared by the department of business innovation and skills and the department of culture, media, sports outlined the benefits of Cloud and supported this national initiative. According to UK Government, they have identified the initiatives under this plan such as standardization and simplification of the desktop, standardization of networking, realization of data centre estate, making use of open source, open standards and reuse strategy, green IT, information security and assurance.

United States Government has also started efforts for shifting information systems to the Cloud across the US Federal Government. It may be noted that the efforts in this direction have already been started by general services administration, national aeronautics and space administration, department of health and human services, census bureau and White House.

ECONOMIC DEVELOPMENT

Generally economic development and natural resources management; are considered mutually antagonistic. Promotion of one would inevitably mean damage to the other. In the present globalization scenario it has become a necessity for integrating natural resources concerns into economic development activities. If the agenda of any government is to concentrate only on urban development, there will be a risk of losing natural resources. This is because the former will take over the latter. The stress on the earth's surface requires careful assessment. A new natural resources management agenda is needed for reducing the stress on natural management. The type of information required for the purpose of analysis and framing policies for natural resources management varies from country to country. It also depends on the resources available and their usage in the respective areas in a country.

ADVANTAGES OF CLOUD COMPUTING FOR GOVERNMENT

Cloud computing based systems are better alternative systems to high capacity and high computing power hardware at each department in the government. There would be reduction in investments and in operating cost in Cloud computing environment. Every department in the government can make use of the services such as storage, platform, and software as per its needs. Infrastructure at a remote centre will help the government to minimize the investment on software and its licenses. Further, it helps to reduce the power consumption. DARREL M. WEST – Vice President and Director of Governance Studies at Brookings has reported Cost Savings Estimates from various sources. The Cost Saving Analysis based on its reports says a minimum of 40% cost reduction in almost all the cases.

SCALABILITY

Changing needs in the conventional architecture, scaling requires procurement, deployment and configuration of hardware and software. Generally there will be delays in the procurement process in the government. To avoid delays in the procurement process, each department procures the information Technology infrastructure, more than its needs within the Budget sanctioned limit. In most of the cases there will be under utilization of its resources.

The Cloud computing architecture is designed in such a way that additional requirement can be provided to each department at any time. The size of Cloud architecture can be scaled up or down effectively. Internally, the resources can be shared by the different government departments. Distribution of resources can be determined on the basis of each department's needs. This provides elasticity within the systems wherein each department get s its requirement fulfilled.

USEFULNESS TO GOVERNMENT

Generally the data is largely unutilized by the government except for preparation of few departmental reports under the conventional E-Governance procedure. Cloud based e-governance model facilitates to monitor the centrally managed data centre of the government, stores the vital information pertaining to the various departments. This will have the real time as well as the historic data. Software tools can be used for analyzing the data at the centralized government data centre for framing policies and planning strategies (Levin, 2013).

DISASTER MANAGEMENT

Disaster is inevitable and unpredictable. It can be either natural disaster or human error. Any disaster leads to loss of lives, property or data security and safety of electronic data is vital in e-governance. Disaster management is an integral part of Cloud based architecture which provides data protection and fault tolerance to the client as a part of its service. Internal Cloud service providers replicate their data at multiple locations so loss of one data centre's data due to any disaster does not lead to loss of information for its clients. Similarly the government in a Country can have their data centers at different locations in their Country.

IMPLEMENTATION

It is easier to implement e-governance application at one location under Cloud computing based architecture compared to a similar application being implemented at multiple locations. The latter approach requires a uniform infrastructure at all locations which can be expensive and may not be available in certain situations. Even if it is available it may lead to inconsistency due to variations in versions of Software.

MIGRATION TO NEW TECHNOLOGY

Generally the government polices of various ministries change from time to time requiring appropriate changes in e-governance applications. Many times it may need to migrate to new technology. Migration is a challenging task in the distributed computing environment. Comparatively migration to new technology is relatively easier and faster in the Cloud based architecture. This is because changes at one location alone ensure migration to new application by the concerned department (Majumdar, 2011).

GREEN COMPUTING

Traditional infrastructure requires personal computers, number of servers, printers and other related devices in every government department. Maintaining environmental condition will be required at least in Server Rooms. It is not considered to be a healthy practice for the environment to have more systems in the various departments in government. It also accumulates large stock of obsolete hardware waste that need to be destroyed properly over the years. The Cloud computing architecture optimizes utilization of resources cleverly ensuring lower consumption of electricity, less emission of harmful gases and lower stock pile of obsolete hardware.

EXISTING E-GOVERNANCE PRACTICE

E-governance adopted by many government departments is in isolation and scattered pattern. This procedure lacks an integrated approach towards e-governance. Information available with one department is not easily accessible by the other departments. This is due to lack of standardization and uniformity in platform, data and software

instead of sharing the data, departments go for creation of their own data.

CASE ILLUSTRATION

Managing natural resources and economic development in a country are considered mutually antagonistic, because promoting one would result in damaging the other and economic development is given more importance to remain competitive in the globalization scenario. It is important that a Government in a Country should realize the necessity for integrating natural resources concerns into economic development activity. Careful assessment is required to assess the stress on the earth's surface. A good natural resources management agenda is needed especially in the developing countries. The agenda should concentrate to reduce the stress on natural resources and to manage environmental issues in urban areas. The type of data and information for the purpose of analysis and framing policies for natural resources management varies from country to country. It also depends on the availability of natural resources and its uses in the respective areas in a country. A well-structured database and information systems are required by the authorities who are involved in planning and framing the policies for managing the natural resources under their control. Developing countries need a model that helps them to manage their country's resources judiciously (Henry, & Heinke, 2004). It is a general practice in many countries that the government assigns the responsibility to one department or two or more departments for managing the components of natural resources. In most of the cases there will not be co-ordination among departments for handling the issues related to natural resources management. So a core team consisting of multi-disciplinary experts to develop a model for managing natural resources is needed. The concept of cloud computing and other collaborative technologies will be the backbone for this model (Tiwari, 2010).

COMPONENTS OF NATURAL RESOURCES

It is needless to say that nature belongs to all of us. It is important that the authorities who are involved in managing the natural resources are expected to be aware of the structural composition and functions of natural resources. These components play an important role as life supporting systems. The structural components of life systems are land, mines, water resources and forest resources. These components are otherwise known as natural resources. It is to be remembered that natural eco system operates themselves under natural conditions without any interference by human beings (Sharada, 2006). Misuse of natural resources will affect the human beings on the planet earth.

E-GOVERNANCE

Natural resource management is inter-disciplinary where co-ordination is required among the various government departments. It is advisable to form a core team consisting of the representatives of the various departments along with environmental and bio-technology experts, professionals in the areas of space, information and communication technologies will provide their expertise to the e-governance for creation of knowledge based model for natural resources. Members of the core team can analyze and draw conclusion from the knowledge based model. This model will help them framing policies pertaining to usage of natural resources.

KNOWLEDGE BASED MODEL

This Model can be created with five sub modules. They are 1) Geographical data for a Country 2) Quantitative and textual contents of geographical data 3) Data for environmental management

4) Knowledge base for natural resources and 5) Disaster Management Data

1. **Geographical Data for a Country:** GIS Software is required for creating geographical data of a Country.
2. **Quantitative and Textual Contents of Geographical Data:** Geographical data is the base for converting into quantitative and textual data. This data will be useful for analysis and framing policies and issues related to natural resources.
3. **Data for Environmental Management:** The type of data required for Analysis for environmental issues related to urban areas can be stored under this module.
4. **Knowledge Base for Natural Resources:** The data related to analysis done under the sub mode 1 and 2 can be stored in this sub module.
5. **Disaster Management Data:** Places prone to natural disaster can be identified from this sub Module 4. The information in this sub module will be useful for handling the natural disasters.

CLOUD DEPLOYMENT FOR E-GOVERNANCE

Cloud Computing can be classified and deployed under four ways. They are 1) Private Cloud 2) Public Cloud 3) Community Cloud and 4) Hybrid Cloud

1. **Private Cloud:** The Cloud infrastructure is owned or leased by single enterprise. It is operated solely for that organization.
2. **Public Cloud:** The Cloud infrastructure is owned by an organization which provides the Cloud services for a fee. Generally these services are made use by the general public and business enterprises.

3. **Community Cloud:** The Cloud infrastructure is shared by several organizations and supports a specific community.

4. **Hybrid Cloud:** The Cloud infrastructure is composition of two or more Clouds such as private, community or public that remains unique entities. They are bound together by standardized or proprietary technology that enables data and application portability.

DATA INTENSIVE APPLICATIONS

Cloud Computing is more useful for data intensive application. Data for natural resource management falls under this category. The core team members require the data for sharing and analyzing data across a Country. Data related to land, mines, forest and rivers need to be maintained in the database consisting Region wise and country wide data replication of the above components is required to be maintained in the system. Further it will have the facility of data recovery and responding dynamically to changes in the volume of data in databases (Krutz & Vines, 2010).

PRIVATE CLOUD

Data related to natural resources is considered to be sensitive data for any Country. A Government in a Country should have its own data center. Private Cloud is the best solution for a Government data center. High volume and sensitive data of a government can be maintained in the private cloud.

With the growing use of internet there is no need to limit group collaboration to a single department's network environment. Users from multiple locations within the government and multiple governments can collaborate on data and information related to natural resources stored in private cloud environment with ease. Many leading manufacturers in the area of infrastructure are offering to build cloud network.

Similarly the software companies are offering the cloud based software applications. Essence of cloud computing concepts is to facilitate users of any device which has an internet feature such as mainly mobile phones and laptops. It is clear from the above that cloud computing concept make e-governance reasonably simple (Sahoo, Mehfuza, & Rai, 2013).

GEOGRAPHICAL INFORMATION SYSTEM

Geographical Information System is associated with basic terms such as geography and information system. The literal interpretation of geography is "Writing about the Earth". Geography is the base for identifying the relationship of land with human beings (Quazi, 2009) and (Kraak & Ormelling, 2004).

Geographical information system is a tool for handling geographic (Spatial and Descriptive) data. It is an organized collection of computer hardware, software with geographic data. This is designed efficiently to capture, store, retrieve, update and manipulate data. This data can be used for analysis and displaying all forms of geographically referenced information as per the user defined specifications. One can visualize the real world consisting of much geography such as topography, land use, coverage of land, soil, crops, forests, water bodies, districts, and towns (Chandra, & Ghosh, 2006).

GEOGRAPHICAL DATA FOR A COUNTRY

The details of natural resources, population, and location of industries, educational institutions, town and cities are available in the various departments in a government. Most of the above information is not available in the integrated system. Many Governments do not have integrated system due to heavy investment on infrastructure. Many governments across the world find it very difficult to frame policies in respect of management of natural resources in their countries.

Geographical Information System (GIS) facilitates to know the inventory of natural resources and exact location of the resources. Once the data obtained by GIS System is stored in the database under the cloud computing environment, then it can be accessible by many government departments across the country.

COMPONENTS OF NATURAL RESOURCES

The components of natural resources can be classified as renewable resources and non-renewable resources. Renewable resources have the inherent ability to repair or replenish themselves by recycling, reproduction or replacement. These renewable resources are water, plants, animals, soil and living organisms. Non-renewable resources are the earth's geologic environment such as minerals and fossil fuels. These resources are available in the fixed quantity in the environment. It is required that every member of the core team needs to be aware of this.

QUANTITATIVE AND TEXTUAL CONTENTS IN THE SUB MODEL

A quantitative and textual data in reference to geographical data can be classified and stored in the sub modules. They are the following

- **Forests:** Data related to different types of forests such as moist topical forests, dry topical forests, mountain sub tropical forests, mountain temporal forests, sub alpine forests and alpine scrubs. Classification of forest varies from country to country.
- **Water Resources:** Data related to fresh water, lakes, rivers, ground water and oceans falls under this category.
- **Minerals:** Data related to metallic and non metallic are stored under this category.
- **Agricultural Land:** Data related to cultivable and non cultivable land will be stored under this category.
- **Industrial Areas:** This will contain data pertaining to various industries such as automobile, textiles, pharmaceuticals, consumer durables and consumer related products. This is not an exhaustive list.
- **Urban Areas:** Data related to residential, roads, transport, infrastructure and utility falls under this category.
- **Rural Areas:** Data related to the areas which do not fall under the category of urban areas can be Considered under this category.
- **Service Units:** Data related to educational institutions, healthcare units and other related units fall under this category.
- **Business Units:** Data related to trading organizations, financial institutions, hospitality units and other similar units fall under this category.

The above category of data in the sub modules of the database in the cloud computing will be useful for framing policies to manage resources of a Country.

NATURAL RESOURCES AND ENVIRONMENTAL MANAGEMENT

Industrialization and urbanization has become a worldwide phenomenon. Industrialization and urbanization raise many environmental issues. It is because of the requirements of people living in urban and industrial areas are increasing. Managing their requirements need to be accessed properly.

The relationship between the availability of natural resources and its consumption can be established from the quantitative and textual data in any particular area. Further it helps to address the environmental issues (Thakur, 2006). This also helps the policy makers to understand minimizing environmental hazards and avoiding the depletion of resources. The details pertaining to water usage, solid waste products, disposition of package materials and other related information can be made available from this model. This will be more useful for environmental management. The type of data required for analyzing environmental issues are 1) Underground composition of urban areas 2) Water usage 3) Disposition of wastage and 4) Air pollutants

1. **Underground Composition of Urban Areas:** Earth is being dug up in the developing countries very frequently for the purpose of laying lines for communication, electricity, water mains, sanitary and sewage lines. Generally it is not well planned activity especially in the developing countries. The details of the information pertaining to every area in cities and sub-urban parts are required for analysis and developing urban areas. The data in the module in Cloud computing environment will help the town planners for action.

2. **Water Usage:** The data related to water consumption by residents and industrial, service and business sectors can be ascertained and stored in this module. This will be useful in accessing the requirements of consumption of water by these sectors. The contingency plan at the time of shortage of water can be prepared on the basis of information in this module.

3. **Disposition of Wastage:** The advancement in the package industry has created a good scope of marketing of the products manufactures across the globe. Demand for packed products is on the rise in the developing countries. Disposal of every kind of packaging materials at the end are to be carried out by the civic authorities. Statistics of discarded packaging material is required for allocation of places in cities and suburban areas. This module will provide the required information.

4. **Air Pollutants:** Oxygen and nitrogen are the major constituents of the atmosphere. Coal, fuel oil and gasoline used by us emit carbon monoxide. This human activity is contributing to changes in the atmosphere. The largest single source of this emission from automobile pollution in air is from the above factors. The health of human beings is affected by this pollution. The data in this Model will help the policy makers to think of workable solutions.

REMOTE SENSING FOR EARTH RESOURCES MANAGEMENT

Remote sensing data and image have been used to derive thematic information on various natural resources and environment. The type and level of information extracted depends on the expertise of the analyst's requirements. The utilization of remote sensing data can be broadly classified into three categories 1) To identify the category to which the earth surface express belongs 2) To infer a particular parameter or phenomenon using the part of data for suitable modeling 3) under the third category, surface expressions are the indicators of certain resources, which are not directly observable by remote sensing.

DATA FOR NATURAL DISASTER MANAGEMENT

It is said that global warming causes climatic changes and natural disasters. Unprecedented rains, floods, earthquakes, tsunami, severely dry and wet weather are considered as natural disasters. It is the responsibility of governments in a country to have a proper "Disaster Management" plan. It is required under this plan to provide services to the victims of natural disasters whenever they acquire.

The stress caused on planet earth needs a careful assessment of the use of natural resources. Satellite systems facilitate to observe atmospheric changes and disturbances (Rao, 2005). High resolution remote sensing satellites integrated GPS system provides the inputs at the various phases of natural disasters for preparedness, prevention, mitigation and disaster management.

Any disaster management needs data. The past data can be used as guidance for preparedness to handle disasters. Same approach is needed for managing natural disasters. Disaster prevention measures can be improved in three ways. They are 1) Mapping the disaster prone areas 2) Forecasting impending areas and 3) Disaster affected areas.

Geostationary satellite data is capable of providing information every half an hour and is useful in monitoring short term disaster by cyclones and tornadoes. It is felt that the combination of high spatial, temporal and spectral resolution data would certainly be beneficial in disaster management.

DISASTER MANAGEMENT

It is said that natural disasters are likely to occur more often due to global warming. Information pertaining to the type of help and services rendered is to be stored in the information system. This will be more useful for taking action in an emergency. The kinds of services needed are medical services, transporting people from the affected areas to safe places and organizing food and provisions to the people in distress. The macro level data and information in the disaster management system are given below:

The experiences of the people who have been directly involved in providing services to the victims of disaster will be the inputs for creating this database.

Resource Allocation Module

This Module will have the list of basic supplies such as food items, clothes, rain coats and umbrellas required to help the victims of natural disasters. Addresses of voluntary rescue team, medical doctors and paramedical professionals are to be stored in this module.

Transport Module

The details of heavy transport vehicles that can wade through water, boats and aerial survey aircrafts should be available in this module.

Evacuation Module

Vulnerable areas and safe regions' exact locations are to be stored in this module by using GIS application.

Shelter Module

This module will contain the details of resources of various shelter locations.

Deprivation Module

This module will contain the details of short supply of food items in the earlier disaster affected areas and statistics of number of people infected with diseases. This information will be useful for avoiding such type of situations.

Disaster Module

This module will contain the details of handling the various situations at various disaster management operations. Success and failure of the rescue operations can be derived from information from this Module. It will be useful for the future operations.

CLOUD BASED NATURAL RESOURCES DATA MODEL

Experts in the areas of information technology, space technology, domain and functional experts and executives in the government departments are the backbone of the e-governance. The role of the e-governance is to design cloud based natural resources data module. This model will take care of the basic data of the natural resources of a Country. The e-governance's analysis and solutions can be stored in this model. Data and information in this model can be made available to the executive of the various governments who are associated with the natural resources management, environmental issues and natural disaster management systems. Access to this module by them will be through e-governance.

Remote sensing systems and geographical systems are used for acquiring data of natural resources in a Country. Private Cloud can be made use of storing and organizing data. The type of and level of information required depends on the expertise of analysts. Data pertaining to geographical, quantitative and textual in respect of natural resources will be the base for graphical, data ware house and text database in this model. This model will have the data at a Country, state, region, city, town and village levels. This will provide a good scope for analyzing the various aspects of natural resources.

Software tools such as GIS analysis, data mining and text mining can be made use of analysis (Pujari, 2010). The data analyzed by the specialists identified by the E-Governance will be available in this Model. The analyzed data will help the policy makers to frame policies for their Country. This model stresses the importance of systematic approach in the creation of this Model. The exponential increase in computing power under the cloud environment and advancements in space technology have led to design this conceptual model.

Data in this Model will also be useful for managing environmental issues and managing natural disasters. Figure 1 gives an idea of a model at macro level. Figure 2 talks about the macro level contents for analyzing for environmental issues. Figure 3 explains the macro level data and information needed in the disaster management system.

FUTURE TRENDS

The policy of many countries is to encourage adapting Cloud computing concepts in the information technology infrastructure programs. The advancements in space technology and geographical information system will be collaborative technology to develop modules under cloud computing environment. It is because of the above policy followed by many countries, there is scope in making use of expertise of multi-disciplinary professionals to develop modules under cloud computing environment.

CONCLUSION

The major problem in the developing countries is in identification of the effects of mismanagement of natural resources. Assessment of mismanagement of natural resources can be carried out only when the core team is aware of the functionality of each component of natural resources.

Figure 1. Classification of data of a country

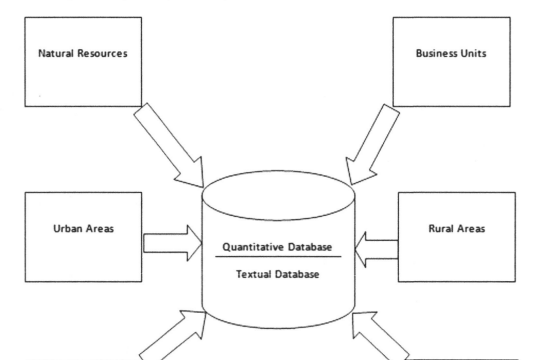

A government in a country uses the resources of nature such as forests, water resources, mines and land to create economic activities such as industrialization, globalization and technology. These activities result in green house change such as carbon dioxide, methane, nitrous oxide, ozone and carbons. These results will have an effect on changing environment. Changes in the environment will lead to unprecedented rains, floods, earthquakes, tsunami and dry and wet weather conditions.

Managing resources of nature are diverse and approaches toward their solution to mitigation depend on the information, monitoring and pressure for action which is acute. Cloud based natural resources data model will help the government in a country to change their practices for using the natural resources. Further it will also help addressing the problems of depletion of non renewable resources. This Model facilitates to handle environmental issues and to manage natural disaster. Involvement of the executives of the various government departments is possible under cloud computing environment with e-governance.

Figure 2. Environmental data

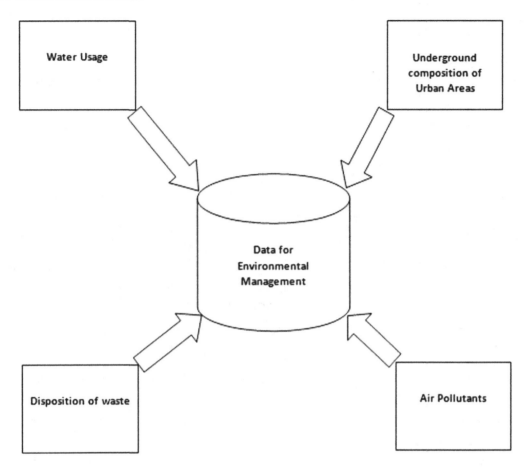

Figure 3. Modules in disaster management systems

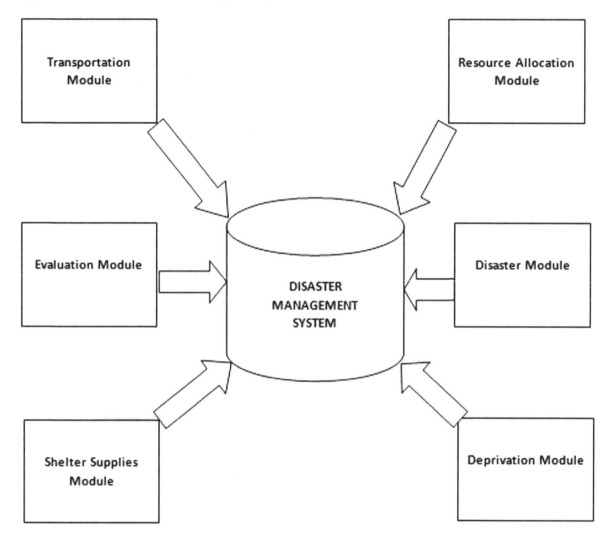

REFERENCES

Chandra, A. H., & Ghosh, S. K. (2006). *Image Interpretation, Remote sensing and Geographical Information System*. New Delhi: Narosa Publishing House.

Henry Glynn, J., & Heinke Gary, W. (2004). *Environmental Science and Engineering; New Delhi: Pearson Education*. Singapore: Private Limited.

Kaushik, A., & Kaushik, C. P. (2006). *Environmental Studies-A Multidisciplinary Subject: Perspectives in Environmental Studies*. New Delhi: New Age International Publishers.

Krutz, R. L., & Dean, V. R. (2010). *Cloud Security*. New Delhi: Wiley India Private Limited.

Kumar, B. R., & Karthik, S. (2011, May). Platforms for Building and Developing Applications for Cloud Computing. *CSI Communications Journal, 35*(2), 6–11.

Levin, S. (2013). Cooperation and Sustainability. In G. Madhavan, B. Oakley, D. Green, D. Koon, & P. Low (Eds.), *Practicing Sustainability* (pp. 39–41). New York: Springer.

Menno-Jan, K., & Ferjan, O. (2004). *Cartography Visualization of Geospatial Data; New Delhi: Pearson Education*. Singapore: Private Limited.

Pujari Arun, K. (2004). *Data mining Techniques; New Delhi: Universities Press*. India: Private Limited.

Quazi, S. A. (2009). *Principles of Physical Geography*. New Delhi: APH Publishing Corporation.

Rao Raja, K. N. (2005). *An Overview of Space and Satellite: Fundamental of Satellite Communication*. New Delhi: Prentice Hall of India.

Sahoo, G., Shabana, M., & Rashmi, R. (2013, November). Applications of Cloud Computing for Agriculture Sector. *CSI Communications Journal, 37*(8), 10–17.

Sharada, V. N. (2006). *Environment & Agriculture*. New Delhi: Malhotra Publishing House.

Shikharesh, M. (2011, May). Resource Management on Clouds: Handling Uncertainties in Parameters and Polices. *CSI Communications Journal, 35*(2), 16–17.

Thakur, I. S. (2006). *Introduction Environmental Biotechnology*. New Delhi: IK International.

Tiwari, A. K. (2010). *Infrastructure for Sustainable Rural Development*. New Delhi: Regal Publications.

KEY TERMS AND DEFINITIONS

Cloud Computing: A computing model that makes information technology resources such as servers, middleware, and applications available over the internet as services to business organizations in self service manner.

Data Ware House: A large data store containing the organization's historical data, which is used primarily for data analysis and data mining.

Ecosystem: A biological community and its physical environment exchanging matter and energy.

Elasticity: The ability to expand or shrink a computing resource in real time, based on need.

Natural Disasters: Hazards that destroy or damage wild life habitats, damages property and human settlements.

Scalability: Regarding hard ware, the ability to go from small to large amounts of processing power with the same architecture.

Urbanization: Increasing concentration of people in cities.

Section 4
Supply Chain in Cloud Computing Environment

Chapter 8

IPCRESS:
Tracking Intellectual Property through Supply Chains in Clouds

Lee Gillam
University of Surrey, UK

Simon Broome
Jaguar Land Rover, UK

Scott Notley
University of Surrey, UK

Debbie Garside
GeoLang, UK

ABSTRACT

This paper provides an overview of the dual challenges involved in protecting intellectual property while distributing business information that will need to be readable/viewable at some point such that it can be acted upon by parties external to the organization. We describe the principles involved with developing such a system as a means to engender trust in such situations – as a deperimeterized supply chain likely acting through the Cloud – discuss the requirements for such a system, and demonstrate that such a system is feasible for written text by formulating the problem as one related to plagiarism detection. The core of the approach, developed previously, has been shown to be effective in finding similar content (precision: 0.88), and has some robustness to obfuscation, without needing to reveal the content being sought.

INTRODUCTION

Document archives and systems of any organization, coherently managed or not, can contain a variety of high-value information relating to collaborating and competing businesses, business transactions, research and development plans, market analysis and strategy, and so on. Large organisations may have many such documents spread very widely across devices used by numerous siloed business units, with highly evolved but disparate systems, approaches, and practices. Careful curation across such a variety can be costly and difficult to implement, and enforced changes to practices which are geared towards making the business as productive as possible may be poorly received. Custodians may wish to impose constraints on the use of such systems for very sound

DOI: 10.4018/978-1-4666-8339-6.ch008

business reasons, but where these actively impede everyday activities the organization will risk users exploring unconstrained workarounds, and so such impositions will encourage the emergence of new problems. Free-flowing communication, sometimes across geographical and legislative borders through a wide variety of mechanisms including email, also presents a risk to such businesses. Whilst free-flowing communication is essential when organizations are not self-sufficient – i.e. when they act in supply chains – communication, deliberate and accidental, can readily flow bi-directionally. Recipient recommendation, with a simple auto-completion mechanism when an email address begins to be typed, without checking on the suitability of the recommendation, is but one way in which accidents can happen (Carvalho and Cohen, 2007). Such accidents can also be quite difficult to recover from subsequently.

Of interest for this paper is that deperimeterization, the lack of a readily definable organizational boundary, is inherent in Supply Chains, in which companies must trust aspects of their work to others, and becomes amplified when Supply Chains act through the Cloud, and often through the most prevalent cloud service model of Software as a Service (SaaS) (Mell and Grance, 2011). This deperimeterization presents risks, and of key importance for us is the risk presented to high value Intellectual Property, by which we mean the expression of some novel aspect of a particular product. Costs of Intellectual Property risks have been reported, albeit with subsequent controversy regarding the difficulty in justifying such a figure, at £9.2bn annually for the UK with the notion that insider assistance is typical (OCSIA/Detica, 2011). A figure as high as $300bn annually has been mooted for the US with issues identified with protection when dealing with specific nations who "literally copy patents from any country and have them filed and granted", but with similar difficulty in justifying any such value (The National Bureau of Asian Research, 2013).

In a collaborative research and development project between Jaguar Land Rover, University of Surrey, and GeoLang Ltd, and with funding from the UK government-backed Technology Strategy Board for 18 months, we are constructing the Intellectual Property Protecting Cloud Services in Supply Chains (IPCRESS) system to address just such a predicament in respect to Supply Chains and barriers to Cloud adoption. The focus for IPCRESS is this difficulty of entrusting valuable Intellectual Property (IP) to third parties, through the Cloud, as is necessary to allow for the construction of components in the supply chain: such information needs to be readily readable and usable by suppliers so that they can see what to build and understand vital properties of the things being built, and so encryption-based approaches may become, at best, inconvenient; at worst, they will encourage removal of protection through transformations of the received information into forms that avoid such inconvenience. IPCRESS is developing a capability for being able to track IP through supply chains without unnecessarily exposing or otherwise revealing the IP in the tracking process. IPRCESS is built around Surrey's approach to privacy-preserving plagiarism detection - which might be considered also as a kind of private search capability – that has been formulated for this very purpose (US patent filed November 2011; PCT filed November 2012). This kind of tracking is well-suited to the tasks of (i) preventing IP leakage; (ii) detecting IP leakage or theft; and (iii) identifying retention beyond allowed review periods. Discussions around such a system and its uses have been presented previously (Cooke & Gillam, 2011). In this paper, we offer an overview of the overall context (Section II), expected formulation of the system (Section III), and information regarding the operation of the approach (Section IV) and its evaluation (Section V). We conclude by speculating on the potential business value of adopting such a system.

BACKGROUND

Organisations of various kinds have become very familiar with the risks of information that is in their possession leaking out to undesirable and/or unexpected parties. Where this concerns the data collected about people covered under data protection legislation, the need in various jurisdictions to disclose, and potentially be fined for, 'allowing' such problems to exist at least leads to a better understanding of the extent of this problem – in the UK, for example, the National Health Service, which should be safeguarding sensitive personal/medical information, appears to suffer the most from data leakage, although an alternative explanation is that they are simply the most open and transparent about the existence of such issues and a large majority elsewhere remain unreported. For the purposes of this paper, however, we are not focused on protection of data about individuals, nor in respect to companies whose business model involves trade in personal data. Our concern is with the need to protect valuable corporate information – the Intellectual Property, and by extension Trade Secrets, which would be related to competitive advantage in products and services. This covers information prior to public disclosure, for example ahead of a patent becoming published for inspection, embargoed marketing materials and press releases, business strategies, information as may relate to initial public offerings (IPOs) and so on. According to the FBI's pages on Corporate Espionage, "methods of targeting or acquiring trade secrets", which would also cover IP, include:

- "Steal, conceal, or carry away by fraud, artifice, or deception;
- Copy, duplicate, sketch, draw, photograph, download, upload, alter, destroy, photocopy, replicate, transmit, deliver, send, mail, communicate, or convey; and,
- Receive, buy, or possess a trade secret, knowing the same to have been stolen or

appropriated, obtained, or converted without authorization."

With these methods in mind, there are two main risks to such information: systems and people (although people are also responsible for the former), with weakly secured systems offering an inbound route to such information, and weakly secure people creating an outbound route. The latter is our concern, with the focus on the insider assistance referred to previously (OCSIA/Detica, 2011). However, the true extent of this problem is quite unclear - here we will draw for the first of several times, on the UK's Home Office report on "Cyber crime: a review of the evidence" which addresses the robustness of such figures (McGuire and Dowling 2003):

As outlined by the Home Affairs Select Committee report on e-crime (Home Affairs Select Committee, 2013), the precision of Detica's (2011) £27 billion estimate has been questioned due to the lack of robust and transparent data upon which their estimates were based. [..]The UK cyber security strategy (Cabinet Office, 2011) recognised the challenges in this area and noted "a truly robust estimate will probably never be established, but it is clear the costs are high and rising. [Emphasis added]

the issue of finding reliable data from which to extrapolate:

'Insider-threats' are a prominent issue reported in business surveys. However, the limited evidence available is mixed on whether they are a bigger problem than outsider attacks. [..] The majority (86%) of recent online crime incidents reported by businesses in the CVS (Home Office, 2013b) were thought to be external attacks from outside the organisation, with just 2 per cent thought to be internal (for the remaining 12% of cases, respondents did not know if they were internal or external). However, it is not possible to verify

the accuracy of these reports. Another survey of 1,007 businesses in 2008 reported that over half of the most serious incidents (57%) were believed to have an internal cause, whereas 38 per cent had an external cause (BERR, 2008). However, this difference may simply reflect the different scope of the two surveys, making direct comparisons problematic.

and qualifies the difference between the deliberate and the accidental:

'Insider threats' from members of staff may be malicious and targeted activity, for example, someone seeking revenge if they know they are about to be fired. However, they may also be accidental or generally negligent, for example, emailing data to the incorrect person, or losing a memory stick (and recorded as data loss rather than theft).

We further consider that those with deliberate intent are likely to have formulated strategies to achieve their goal whilst avoiding detection, which likely involves trying to avoid using systems which may be monitored, and that those with deliberate intent are also in a minority. And the nature of subsequent actions would also differ, ranging from expensive legal actions, such as when designs are imitated[1], or when deliberate acts of espionage are alleged[2]. On the other hand, accidents will tend to occur in close proximity to the existing systems, which could be monitored for this with prevention a possibility if only the capability were available.

However, the notion of 'insider' itself demands challenge, especially within the framing of the so-called *extended enterprise*, which seems to be the fashionable way to cover the notion of the Supply Chain. We will refer to the Supply Chain in this paper, as we feel this best expresses the interaction of one corporate entity with other parties that are entirely separated from the corporate entity. The creation of a wide variety of products now relies on the interactions between a number

of different organizations with aligned interests – typically monetary – in such supply chains. And, in certain industries, supply chains have a very extensive influence on the final product: figures of 65-70% of components being built in the the automotive supply chain are typical. In such large, and complex, supply chains, the very definition of an insider becomes rather more complex. If we consider an insider as somebody with sufficient access to information that would allow for deliberate or accidental propagation of this information to a party whom, in normal business operations, would not be expected to be a recipient of this information, individuals within the organization with the requirement are prime, and this naturally extends to individuals within those suppliers with whom information is shared directly. But this must also be extended at each point where the information of interest is then shared onwards in order to supply those suppliers, and so on.

Adding Cloud into this mix means that those involved with hosting the means of sharing the information should also be considered as insiders, although Cloud providers themselves would likely want to be considered as excluded from this. Large corporations with large supply chains operating through the Cloud would seem to have a very large set of insiders, employed directly in various ways and through their supply chain and systems (Cloud) providers, and without a means of command and control must work on effective means to police such a setup. But even this consideration is limited. The very large set of insiders must also include those within companies who have tendered, unsuccessfully, for work in the process of which they have been made privy to information about nature of the work to be done, perhaps for a fixed period of time, and may have learnt from the information provided in this manner to it in order to offer to supply similar to others. This offers potential for less scrupulous suppliers to win business with others and deliberately or inadvertently to end up supplying a very similar item. Aside from the kinds of self-destructing documents as provided for by digital rights management systems, checks that such suppliers have destroyed all forms of related correspondence when unsuccessful are difficult to make. Indeed, the need for convenience, for example, to pass on to the suppliers to the supplier, may have led the supplier to reproduce this information in a manner now unprotected. The problem is now one of detection of such unprotected information in the document collections of the entire supply chain, or in the worst case, on the web. Put another way, there is a need to find (or not find) existence of a whole document, or parts thereof, in the archives of a multiplicity of other organizations, some of whom will be directly engaged and some of whom may not. Put more simply, such a question could be formulated as: "Can we search all your documents to see if you've got any of ours?". And an approach to find reproduction on the web might involve a question of: "Shall we put all the paragraphs into the Google, Bing, etc., search engine and see if we get any hits?". This latter, of course, is already exposing the information to the search engine. Clearly, there is a need but the means to achieve must multilaterally prevent exposure of such information. Worse still, though out of scope of our present concerns, is that if detecting retention or leakage is quite a challenge; acting on such information requires yet wider consideration.

Such supply chains, then, present the need for management of at least two key elements: the components which must be formed into the product; and the information which is required in order for those components to be constructed. The information necessarily travels, to a certain point, opposite to the components. But at some point, the need for propagating information regarding what is being built any further will cease, and may even become negotiated. For example, in manufacturing, the size, length and number of bolts and screws would no longer necessarily impart information about their specific use in respect to a particular part or set of parts, so those needing them to secure parts may avoid propagating the information about the parts being secured; those providing the natural resources from which the screws and bolts are forged also have no need for further information – indeed, here the information about details such as size, length, and forging process may be propagated in either direction as a requirement or an availability of supply. This is not to suggest, however, that this is the limit of information provision.

By way of example, we can consider specific information regarding the launch of a new car, and assume that the manufacturer wishes to keep its design and composition entirely secret until its launch event. A variety of information, including but not limited to sketches of the concept, complex 3D computer aided designs, moulds, repair manuals, and photographs, videos and other materials as required for product marketing, will all be needed at various stages of the process. A near-production version of the vehicle may need to be moved to various sites, not least for road tests. And a variety of supply chain members must be engaged with at various stages with various quantities of this information in order to bring it all together. The appetite for information about such a car means that certain measures can be taken to try to prevent disclosure, including the addition of camouflaging panels to hide various aspects of the final body shape. But information can still get out somehow, as a Google search for *Jaguar F-type leaked* [or *Lamborghini leaked*, *Ferrari leaked*, and so on would] quickly reveal the level of interest on the web for such items[3], with even a "Fiat Punto facelift – new images leaked" creating interest. Clearly this is somewhat preferable to the kinds of vehicles for which leaks are more directly related to fuel, water and oil which indicates an issue of maintenance (and quality), and the depth to which one has to explore in search results for the Jaguar, Lamborghini, Ferrari and Fiat Punto to identify any such issue may be interesting for some – perhaps in contrast to a similar search for a less desirable vehicle. And it would also be naïve to underestimate the potential for any apparently standard/familiar processes such as translation to be considered immune from the possibility of becoming a leak point when even the scripts for a popular television programme can end up online "after being sent to the BBC's new Latin American headquarters for translation"[4].

THE IPCRESS CONTEXT

Protection of IP rights (IPR) is critical to the presence and growth of business activities in ensuring that those investing in research and development have a means by which to recoup such costs, and to protect against being undercut on price by those who have not had to take the exposure to such investment – and associated risk (Choate, 2005). This creates an awkward tension: price-sensitive consumers want cheap goods, and businesses who can create similar goods more cheaply have a market niche here – and consumers are perhaps unsympathetic to the claims of revenues harmed and jobs being lost in large corporations because they view corporate wealth as residing in a few very rich hands, rather than considering the plight of the newly jobless. Nations in Western Europe, the US, Japan and Singapore have well-established regulations with stringent and enforceable rules for IP protection. Many emerging economies recognize that this is vital to attract and maintain foreign investment, so Malaysia, Hungary, India, and China also begin to craft legislation to improve IP protection standards. And yet even with these stringent and enforceable rules large-scale markets exist in counterfeits. This is brought into sharp relief when counterfeits include medicines and aircraft parts: Choate cites the FAA's report that counterfeit parts were involved with some 174 aircraft crashes in the US between 1973 and 1996, suggests that most of the world's 2,000 to 5,000 aircraft parts dealers (in the supply chains) are unregulated, and that 2% of aircraft parts may be counterfeit, stolen, too old, or improperly re-

conditioned. Laws exist, but require enforcement. And for IP, this largely also comes at a cost.

Even the tracking of IP across companies in these nations where each has different considerations for IP remains a significant problem. In IP-heavy industries, an innovative IP tracking system to monitor data across multiple silos without incurring high costs of manual curation or risking loss of IP in the process is appealing. Again we consider the automotive industry, with its 65-70% reliance on the supply chain. An exemplar in this industry is Jaguar Land Rover, which has several UK sites and several off-shore sites to actively take production to emerging markets. Although the focus on IP generation is in the UK, it must be trusted first amongst these sites and from there to suppliers for various of these sites. Locations of suppliers, then, becomes important, as do the required information security approaches. Technological 'solutions' typically take the view of securing organisational borders against outside threats, which are less relevant here, and then the network - reinforcing a view of a safe perimeter. Such a view helps to retain the illusion that it is possible to control all technologies, and indeed people, at all points of the supply chain. All of this can be somewhat at odds with business needs as R&D strategies demand more connectivity outside the enterprise. However, distrust and perimeterisation will tend to become the norm across industries that suffer most from IP theft. Our aim, then, is to offer a means of safer deperimeterisation whilst fostering recognition of IP value across the supply chain. Such an environment could facilitate new and lucrative manufacturing and development partnerships and consequently enable confident utilisation of cloud technologies.

A system such as that proposed in IPCRESS should help to encourage similar levels of respect for IP even where local legal systems for IP are poor or under-enforced, or cultural importance is lacking. Clearly elaborated operational protocols are required which, allied to software-based tracking methods, act to deter opportunistic industrial theft and become off-putting to an 'insider', who we might want now to be defined as: "individuals that are trusted, and have (some) authorized access over the organization's assets" (Franqueira et al, 2010), which would seem to offer greater embodiment of the supply chain (or extended enterprise).

IPCRESS, as a project, is developing a capability for tracking IP through supply chains, offering Cloud services to (i) prevent IP leakage; (ii) detect IP leakage, or theft; and (iii) identify information retention beyond allowed periods. The approach to be trialled within Jaguar Land Rover is based on a computationally efficient method for finding IP without exposing IP, referred to as private search, but with an additional novelty (patents filed by the University of Surrey) of avoiding costs of encryption.

To act effectively, the system needs to account for the following requirements:

1. **Scale to the Entire (Potentially Deep) Web:** Information as leaked straight out 'to public' would need to be traced. This requires a system that can process such information efficiently.

2. **Be Used Against (Private) Corporate Resources:** Information within a corporate must first be indexed. Care must, of course, be taken with such an index since it also, in theory at least, contains a trace of the valuable information and, indeed, likely of rather more valuable information, in pulling together all such information of value, than would ever be shared in any individual interaction.

3. **Be Used Across (Private) Corporates:** The key challenge, since it requires corporates to be willing to share their indexes, which, from 2 above, may include trace of all their valuable information, whilst still unwilling to share actual content. This places a specific on the index not being a route to revealing the content – this is the key novelty of the

approach being embedded into IPCRESS, and which helps to satisfy 1 and 2 here.

4. **Be Built In and For 'The Cloud':** If we have achieved, in particular, 3, the entire system and all of the produced corporate indexes could be deployed in 'the Cloud' to allow for scalable processing.

The system needs to be responsive – ideally, operating for queries at the speed of search (1) – and should be usable directly within an organization (2) for 'private search' – for us, the ability to find information without exposing the queries being used, and hence not leaking information through any other exposure (3).

The approach shares some similarities with a Federated Search capability across different instances of the same Enterprise Content Management (ECM) system (for example, Shokouhi & Si, 2011). In a Federated Search approach, the same query – likely a few keywords - is presented to each individual instance of the system, and results are presented in a single page but partitioned according to instances searched. A user at any of the locations can search for content in any of the instances exposed this way. Each instance maintains its own search index across the underlying server farm that hosts the documents, generally to support querying, and the Federated Search consolidates efforts that would be needed to separately search each instance. However, this is a product-specific approach – most likely locked-in to a single vendor - for a distributed large enterprise, where full access is likely to be granted to content across the Federation and where the cost of maintenance of multiple geographically distributed instances is easier to justify than attempting to produce a single monolithic system with concomitant difficulties associated to latency and bandwidth. Relevance ranking is provided with respect to the query issued for each separate instance rather than a consolidated ranking being offered. In IPCRESS, we consider the Federation as being across enterprises, and the query comprises the patterns generated from entire documents. With this external-first view, the approach should also be readily suited to search within an organisation. And so, for a given document, all documents containing matching segments from both inside and outside the organisation should be identifiable. Companies can then manage and protect such materials internally, using this as a means to bootstrap such provision and assist in confidentiality marking of documents.

ADDRESSING THE IPCRESS REQUIREMENTS

We consider the implications around the first 3 of the 4 requirements of the IPCRESS system, discussed briefly in the previous section, and the relationship this has to common systems for plagiarism detection, in the remainder of this section.

Private Search in Public (Req.1)

Public content, here web texts, need to be composable into an index produced in a manner consistent with the approach for internal resources. Matches are made against patterns, with ranking by largest extent of match. This can offer a similar capability to a search engine, but one in which complete (but private) documents are the query, rather than a few clear text keywords. The actual content of the private documents never leaves the organisation in this process, having only been involved in pattern production; moreover, the matching system need retain no trace of patterns matched against. Consider, for example, a user with a document open in a common Word Processing application on a laptop. They have available to them a menu bar offering one initial button – 'Private Search'. On pressing this button, the pattern production process takes place on this laptop (within the Word Processing application). The patterns produced, and only the patterns, are exchanged with

the server. The server finds all instances of these patterns in its index and collects associated document identifiers. Results are ranked by frequency of occurrence of the document identifiers. The Word Processing application retrieves the list of matches (alarms) which can be explored adjacent to the existing document. Documents of interest to the user would then, and only then, be retrieved, with matching segments in documents aligned for inspection post-retrieval. A simple alarm, for one document, could carry the following initial information:

1. An identifier for the source document;
2. Web address (URL) of matching document – to allow retrieval;
3. Extent of match by proportion;
4. Title, description, and other useful metadata of the matching document

For inspection, following retrieval, the following are also needed:

5. List of fragments of document involved in match – to able to view sections involved with the match without yet needing to retrieve the matching document - including, for each match fragment:

   a. Start and end location of fragment in source document;
   b. Start and end location of fragment in matching document

Private Search Internally (Req.2)

Full archive match would operate similarly, but in relation to full indexes –potentially one per business unit - already produced, likely as background processing. The approach is inherently similar, but without the involvement of Word Processor software - more likely, with index generation operating in close technical proximity to the Enterprise Content Management system.

Subsequent investigation of matches of significant concern – document segments in business units that might not be expected, for example the very latest and most technical innovations being near to 'press releases'. Internal private search helps to demonstrate external operation, and enables tracking of the IP through the organisation. This may also imply indexing and matching within the email system and any other collaborative platform.

Private Search Across Privates (Req.3)

As above, matches are made against indexes, with ranking by largest extent of match. Again, the capability is similar to a search engine, with full (but private) documents as the query. Here, the actual content of the private documents being matched never leaves any of the organisations and again the matching system need retain no trace of patterns matched against.

Most importantly, when a match in private content is detected an alarm is generated multilaterally to inform all parties to which it is relevant of a potential concern. But the matching content is not revealed at this stage. The information identified as being carried with an alarm varies as follows:

1. Instead of URL, a supply chain member identifier and document id is provided – to assist in investigations;
2. Title, description, and other useful metadata of the matching document is not made available to either party – indeed, each organisation's metadata may need authorised access before they can even see which files are implicated on their own side.

Having received such an alarm, investigation is now required by all implicated parties. This necessitates the description of a protocol for investigation. Such a protocol could involve, for example, a mediation process, or the exposure of smaller fragments implicated in the match that still do not reveal the critical content – for example, by redaction and selective revealing.

Though a potentially very effective technical approach, it cannot be adopted readily without cross-organisational agreement and buy-in, and so the protocol for investigation will become a key dependency as the project progresses.

OPERATION OF THE IPCRESS APPROACH

The need to search for sections of documents as are re-used would immediately suggest the use of existing approaches for copy detection (which some may equate narrowly to plagiarism detection systems). These perform reasonably, reliant on the extent of coverage of their indexes, across documents of which all the content is readily readable – i.e. when the queries and texts can be exposed in entirety.

For efficiency reasons, the index is likely formed of n-grams, hashes, or encrypted data – n-grams mean the documents could be reconstituted if document id and n-gram position are known; hashing and encryption both add processing costs, but consistency requires the hash or encrypted value to be reasonably unique – and particularly for hashing, data similarity does not mean hash similarity: a one character difference will change the hash value quite significantly. Relative uniqueness, and access to keys, as well as access to the same hashing approach, means that such techniques, whilst offering potential look-up efficiency in an index, are unlikely to be worth the processing cost. Indeed, typical techniques for plagiarism detection will readily fail the first three of our requirements. Homomorphic encryption such as that proposed by Gentry (2009) promises to offer a processable trace of the encrypted data, and researchers including Wang et al (2010) are generating encrypted search indices to support search in private, yet costs of processing may be prohibitive.

Addressing the requirements means that it must not be readily possible to reverse-engineer the document, or to be able to achieve this by knowing the approach and the simple expedient of brute force. Such a system will work well if it is possible to generate many possible inputs for a single pattern – typically, hashing should be collision-avoiding; here, we are collision-embracing, and hash proximity/similarity and data similarity have a much clearer relationship – in particular, the extent of change in the hash is a direct reflection on the extent of change in the data. In addition, reasonable detection performance must be assured at speed, and so linguistic processing (part of speech tagging) approaches are also mitigated against. The patented approach does, we believe, meet such requirements. For a set of documents, we are able to convert the plain text of each document to a set of (statistically almost irreversible) patterns, and insert these patterns into an index (pattern as key, value as document and pattern start position. Such an index can readily be sharded by key to allow for scaling. Consider a simplified example source index where a key is assigned to a specific text pattern (it would be repeated if the pattern is found in other documents). The index would be of the form [key, document, position]:

001, 1, 75

002, 1, 84

003, 1, 99

004, 2, 2574

005, 2, 2599

The approach to detection is similar. For a document of interest [d], another index is produced, although for a single document we need not be concerned about its id. Matches in the indexes are generated from the same key production process. Each detection returns only the pair of document id and position, so sorting on document and then position, and subsequently identifying the document with the most detections and addressing the nature of the overlapping positions, helps to compose the results.

So, if d returned all the examples above, documents 1 and 2 are of interest with matching segments spanning 75, 84, 99 and 2574, 2599. Segment sizes depend on the length of encoded data, so if we assumed a 14-gram (14 word segment), for document 1 we have a continuous segment from words 75-113. For document 2, however, there is a gap between the 2 segments. However, here we can apply a notion of a stitch distance, allied to a confidence value relative to the length of the stitch, such that we retain just one continuous segment from 2574-2613, but with a slightly lowered match confidence [here, 10 words are missing, so we could say 30 plus 10 x 4/14 to account for the stitchable distance] of (about) 33 vs 39. So, documents would remain ordered 1, 2. The combination of an ambiguous pattern production approach, and a confidence weighting for missing detections, helps to overcome some obfuscation.

One key generation approach for plagiarism detection is to use MD5hash. Suppose that we break each document into 5-grams that overlap by 2 words, and produce a hash value for each (Table 1).

These positions would be '1', '4', '7'. Key length is '5', so if the second pattern went undetected (somebody changes 'over' to 'across' in their document, which results in an entirely

Table 1. Overlapping 5-grams and their corresponding MD5 hash values

Text	MD5 Hash
the quick brown fox jumped	e0c19dedd2e35a44b70ca531144ac953
fox jumped over the lazy	842ff3fabd7032a95c5cd5cc919a7e6b
the lazy dog and cat	2b4032a8f7fa15aa933dd916e93cf8d2

different hash value), a stitch distance of 1 would allow for a continuous segment to be reported albeit with a slightly lower confidence. It should be apparent how brittle such a hash-based approach is. Somebody wishing to avoid detection would need change only 2 words (e.g. 'jumped', 'lazy' to 'jumps', 'tired') and none of the resulting hashes would be matchable. To see the effect of this, consider switching dog to dogs in the third 5-gram. This results in a hash of f15f022792d-b93722733b4b5b2b6f548. Our approach does not suffer this (see Figure 1).

Furthermore, with common n-gram patterns available from Google and Microsoft for research purposes, such approaches have even greater brute-forceability. Imagine, now, that many n-grams produce the same (ambiguous) hash, and the value of the approach should be clearer.

EVALUATION OF THE IPCRESS APPROACH: PAN

The Uncovering Plagiarism, Authorship, and Social Software Misuse (PAN) activity first appeared in 2007. The external detection part of the plagiarism detection task, where external refers to matching to source texts that are also available, changed markedly in 2012 from a prior moderate-sized index comparison to two tasks: i) a retrieval of documents from a search engine as might be useful in match; ii) a matching between given pairs of documents. Offering a search engine for the first of these avoids the need for those who have struggled to construct an efficient index with a few gigabytes of text to struggle further with terabytes. However, common search engines work best for plagiarism detection with long quoted phrases, although the offered search system does not. Further, this means presenting segments of the text in-clear to the search system, which doesn't readily fit with our context. We focus here on results obtained for ii) in 2012 and 2013, with a brief view of results in 2011 and the very latest available for 2014 by way of contrast.

In Cooke et al (2011) we described various aspects of our system as used for the external plagiarism detection task, which could process the entire PAN11 collection within relatively short timescales without requiring a specialized computer cluster, and which was still able to produce a reasonable degree of matching performance (4th place, with PlagDet=0.2467329, Recall=0.1500480, Precision=0.7106536, Granularity=1.0058894). In 2012, we again showed good granularity (at or near 1, meaning that the same passage is not indicated multiple times) with high recall and precision for non-obfuscated text. A beneficial side-effect is that some obfuscation is handled by the same approach, but additional efforts need to be focused on obfuscation to offer a truly robust system (Table 2).

In 2013, apart from for non-obfuscated data, descriptions of the nature of data used seem also

Figure 1. Fragment of a matching suspicious document (above) and source (below) from PAN (see next section), showing robustness to variations in both lexical selection and spelling

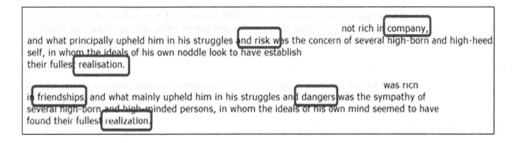

Table 2. Surrey's results in PAN for four parts of the text alignment task in 2012

Test	Plagdet Score	Recall	Precision	Granularity
02_no_obfuscation	0.85884	0.83788	0.88088	**1.0**
03_random_obfuscation	0.04191	0.02142	**0.95968**	**1.0**
04_translation_obfuscation	0.01224	0.00616	**0.97273**	**1.0**
05_summary_obfuscation	0.00218	0.00109	**0.99591**	**1.0**

to have shifted from the previous year. Our precision and granularity figures remain high (Table 3), but it is difficult to conclude anything with regard to performance comparison for the other tasks – and prior examples of random obfuscation (see examples in Potthast et al, 2010) suggest that this is not a realistic problem worth focusing on.

PAN 2014 test results, only available as a broad characterization for two test corpora at the time of writing, evidence expected values for granularity and precision (Table 4), which is reassuring given the re-engineering of our approach between 2013 and 2014, but offers a surprising difference between values for recall. Subsequent investigations discovered a bug in detecting UTF-8 codes having a significant impact here.

The best performing approaches, for three different years Grman and Ravas (2011), Kong et al (2012) and Torrejon and Ramos (2013) all involve the creation of indexes containing clear text (strings that comprise the texts). No other approach has yet been seen which attempts the same as has been described here.

In addition, we have been exploring ways to handle the kinds of obfuscation inherent in the competition data. We have initially considered two approaches based on transformations of a single query into closely related queries. Since the hash-like codes mentioned above are formulated such that code similarity can be indicative of data similarity, the 'closeness' of any two queries becomes meaningful, which means that a value for similarity can be determined on the basis of (binary) distance approaches such as Hamming and Levenshtein. Results from initial evaluations

against PAN 2012 (Table 5) and 2013 (Table 6) data demonstrate improvements in recall without loss of precision, although much more rigorous evaluation will be required to determine the fullest extent of impact achievable by these, and other related, approaches on the hash-like codes.

EVALUATION OF THE IPCRESS APPROACH: LAND ROVER MANUALS

Suppose that a new vehicle is in production, for which a repair manual is being produced. A manual with 'similar' content for a different vehicle appears elsewhere on the web, with the suggestion that the costs of preparation of such a manual might have been avoided either by a less scrupulous manufacturer, or this might have occurred through some supply chain member who acts on behalf of both manufacturers. Or perhaps this is a large chunk of the original document that simply should not be propagated by email. The need in every instance is to be able to find such an occurrence but in the process of detection the original content should not be exposed generally to the web, to the website, nor to the email. The irreversible IPCRESS patterns, which do not expose content, are the limit of what is needed to effect the detection, ahead of any subsequent need for evaluation of similarity.

As a small scale test of such a scenario, we obtained the Land Rover Defender 1999 and 2002 MY Workshop Manual Supplement and Body Repair Manual, and the Land Rover Discovery

Table 3. Surrey's results in PAN for four parts of the text aligment task in 2013

Test	Plagdet Score	Recall	Precision	Granularity
02_no_obfuscation	**0.92530**	**0.90449**	**0.94709**	**1.0**
03_artificial_low	0.09837	0.05374	**0.93852**	**1.04688**
04_artificial_high	0.01508	0.00867	**0.96822**	**1.20313**
06_simulated_paraphrase	0.11229	0.05956	**0.97960**	**1.0**

Table 4. Surrey's results in PAN 2014 for two test corpora

Test Data	Plagdet	Precision	Recall	Granularity	*Runtime*
Corpus 2	0.28302	0.88630	*0.16840*	1.00000	*00:00:55*
Corpus 3	0.44076	0.85744	0.29661	1.00000	*00:00:56*

Table 5. Testing obfuscation handling approaches against PAN 2012 data

IPCRESS Raw – PAN 2012 Data				
Test	Plagdet Score	Recall	Precision	Granularity
02_no_obfuscation	0.9437	0.9045	0.9877	1.0008
03_artificial_low	0.0956	0.0525	0.9942	1.0608
04_artificial_high	0.0200	0.0118	0.9852	1.2459
06_simulated_paraphrase	0.0992	0.0522	0.9922	1.0000
Obfuscation Handler #1 (Hamming)				
02_no_obfuscation	0.9358	0.9048	0.9703	1.0008
03_artificial_low	0.1970	0.1110	0.9853	1.0178
04_artificial_high	0.0373	0.0201	0.9577	1.0759
06_simulated_paraphrase	0.1512	0.0825	0.9038	1.0000
Obfuscation Handler #2 (Levenshtein)				
02_no_obfuscation	0.9236	0.9057	0.9423	1.0000
03_artificial_low	0.1888	0.1066	0.9820	1.0266
04_artificial_high	0.0682	0.0368	0.9489	1.0535
06_simulated_paraphrase	0.1345	0.0723	0.9572	1.0000

1995 MY Body Repair Manual (see Figure 2) in PDF from online sources and converted these to plain text. We assume, for the sake of this paper, that the Discovery manual is derived from the Defender manual (the reverse, indeed, of the likely scenario but we operate this way around to reduce the expectation bias). On conversion, the Defender manual has over 107,000 words, and the Discovery manual over 35,000. No checks are made on the quality of the conversion.

A comparison between the two using the IP-CRESS approach involves creating an index of

Table 6. Testing obfuscation handling approaches against PAN 2013 data

IPCRESS Raw – PAN 2013 Data				
Test	**Plagdet Score**	**Recall**	**Precision**	**Granularity**
02_no_obfuscation	**0.9253**	**0.9273**	**0.9233**	**1.0000**
03_random_obfuscation	0.1356	0.0729	**0.9675**	**1.0000**
04_translation_obfuscation	0.0243	0.0123	**0.9865**	**1.0000**
05_summary_obfuscation	0.0022	0.0011	**0.9959**	**1.0000**
Obfuscation Handler #1 (Hamming)				
02_no_obfuscation	**0.9029**	**0.9289**	**0.8783**	**1.0000**
03_random_obfuscation	0.1297	0.1297	**0.9120**	**1.0000**
04_translation_obfuscation	0.0244	0.0244	**0.8953**	**1.0000**
05_summary_obfuscation	0.0035	0.0017	**0.9807**	**1.0000**
Obfuscation Handler #2 (Levenshtein)				
02_no_obfuscation	**0.9058**	**0.9274**	**0.8853**	**1.0000**
03_random_obfuscation	0.2151	0.1224	**0.8936**	**1.0000**
04_translation_obfuscation	0.0743	0.0386	**0.9533**	**1.0000**
05_summary_obfuscation	0.0035	0.0017	**0.9920**	**1.0000**

the Defender manual (Source), and then querying this index with patterns derived from Discovery (Suspicious). It is useful to note, at this point, that using the Discovery document against the PAN 2012 collection produces no false positives, and the same would be expected against all PAN collections.

Where keys relate to overlapping data by start position and key length, these are merged into fewer larger segments (now of varying size) as shown below in Table 7, ordered by match length, for the first 23 matches - each are of over 100 words and account for a span of some 4380 words. The remaining 38 matches of 49 words or more account cover a further span of 2578 words.

A merging ('stitching') strategy is demonstrated below in Table 8: the distance between segments (Suspicious Start plus Match Length) for the fragments shown is: 6, 0, 14, **15992,** 73. Stitching takes place when the fragment distance is less than 900, and since the first 4 fragments satisfy this condition they are merged into a single

result. The remaining 2 fragments represent the start of the next result.

Using this strategy, the 61 segments found offer suitable proximity to allow stitching into 4 major chunks covering some 10895 words (in decreasing size order, chunks of 4807, 4684, 944, and 460 words).

Figure 3, above, shows a matching fragment that has been detected between the two documents using the IPCRESS patterns, prior to stitching. There are several important factors to note here. First and foremost, it is important to clarify the nature of precision scores in PAN. These relate to the number of *characters* which are considered involved with the match – the proportion of those which should be reported versus those which should not be. The text in Figure 3which is shown darker is that which is implicated in the detection by the IPCRESS patterns. This is also what we report for the purposes of the PAN evaluation, so that results offer a very clear sense of the match efficacy of the patterns against unseen text. From this, it should be quite apparent that

Figure 2. Covers of the online repair manuals for Land Rover's Defender and Discovery (PDF)

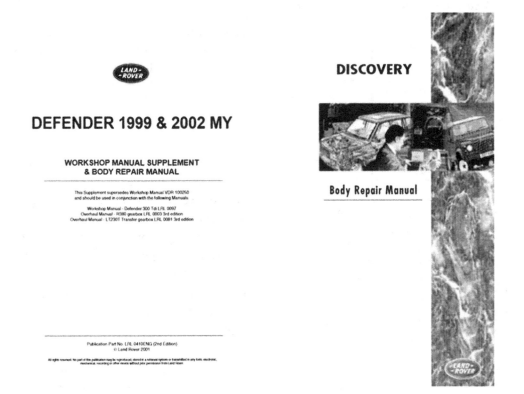

this will result in a lower precision score in PAN that would be possible if considering this from the perspective of content that is *available* for inspection. It should also be quite readily apparent that this kind of match indication can be quite readily refined towards higher precision score at the point at which access can be provided to the content of *both* of the texts for the purposes of making such an alignment. Figure 3 also shows that there is a near perfect match of over 50 words after this 8 word mismatch, starting with "Where possible, the original production...." through to "spot welds" and passing over a variation in expression of the imperial measurement. In the Defender content, we then see a further 11 words highlighted which are not shared between these two. Subsequent to this, we also see a segment which again appears in both. At this stage of the process, this would be treated as a separate fragment. The 'stitching' would then be expected to step over those 11

words to produce a coherent segment that covers at least these two.

The challenge of scaling such an approach relates to remaining able to discover such a match across two or more very large document archives. Suppose company A and company B each have 100,000 documents. Company A is interested in whether any of B's 100,000 documents contains content from them. The same may also be true in reverse. This comparison will require an index to be generated on both sides for all of the documents. And once such an index has been built, to address similar questions in future it would make sense to retain this index. In particular, this supports a similar interaction in respect to companies C, D, and so on, who are also within the supply chain. Company A may only be interested in the results for a specific subset of their 100,000 documents, but that certainly does not mean that they should only create an index of only these documents for

Table 7. Merged overlapping results from the indexed Defender document, queries using the Discovery document

Match Length (words)	Suspicious Start	Source Start
552	23250	78933
338	549	774
307	22869	78552
299	4613	75040
237	23799	79490
210	26857	84780
209	25751	81023
182	260	449
174	26273	84271
171	22383	78062
158	25310	80814
156	105	295
154	22720	78400
147	24385	77461
144	25057	80267
133	25525	81230
125	6124	76910
124	3008	2870
121	24261	77248
111	1148	74782
110	23158	78841
110	24682	77771
108	929	74528

Table 8. Strategy for merging ('stitching') non-contiguous segments

Match Length (words)	Suspicious Start	Source Start
84	6034	76821
125	6124	76910
75	6249	77035
53	6338	77129
171	22383	78062
85	22627	78277

B, or C, or D, to check against. As such, every company would be required to produce an index against which other parties can check their own documents. IPCRESS supports this kind of cross-index comparison capability.

CONCLUSION

Widespread adoption of a system such as IPCRESS could engender a culture of IP protection irrespective of the sharpness of the legal teeth in any particular jurisdiction, and offer an ability to address an apparent security risk (one of the four categories of supply chain risks for Manuj and Mentzer (2008)): supply, demand, operational and security) through information sharing of an over-eager or careless nature. It is likely in the interests of companies to adopt such a system, but assurances are vital in order to engender trust in its operation. And, in fact, the reputation of members of supply chains could be enhanced by a trustmark allied to a relative lack of identified IP issues, or be drawn substantially into question where unresolved issues have leave to remain. The means by which such issues are identified, and the process towards resolution is another important aspect of the processes and procedures for IPCRESS, but is still to be defined. IPCRESS must be acceptable to adopt, and enforceable by contract within the supply chain in order to be successful. Of course, if such a system can be adopted in one supply chain, it is more likely to be adopted across all supply chains that involve each party. The view of supply chains as of sequences of producer/consumer relationships, akin to food chains, does not account for the complex reality of many supply chains. These can be variously interconnected with the same organisation acting many times on both sides of the supposed divide, and with larger organisations readily acting as suppliers to smaller ones. Larger companies in

Figure 3. A matching fragment detected using IPCRESS patterns, prior to stitching

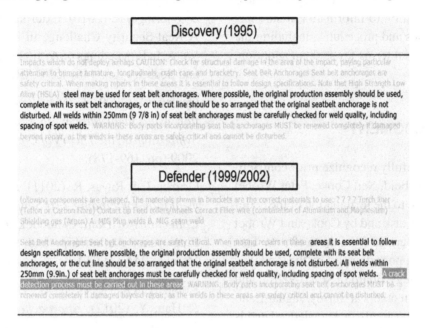

these supply chains would be readily positioned for such a scale of adoption.

The results shown against document sets use in a plagiarism detection competition (PAN) are certainly not going to be suitably near to the best that is achievable when it is possible to evaluate similarity between texts based on the content being fully exposed. However, that is not our challenge, and it is important to note again that we are attempting to undertake plagiarism detection in such a way as would be impervious to a range of attempts to discover the content being matched against – a kind of privacy-preserving plagiarism detection that can be used against documents whose content should be kept from plain sight. To understand the effectiveness of the approach, it is also important to understand how such evaluation figures are generated in PAN, and to see that good quality matches are indeed produced – since the alarms that would be generated by systems should be based on such good quality matches and this has to be possible absent the original document. Although the present approach works well, better treatment of obfuscation is likely an essential

additional ingredient for adoption. The open publication of data, as here, regarding evaluations can only be helpful in trying to achieve this, and the strength/lossy nature of pattern production is readily demonstrable by Gedankenexperiment to private audiences, and is fully described in the patent filing. Where organisations were to agree on such an undertaking, exposure of the organisational archives to the pattern production process is the vital step, which presents a new but minor risk to information security: the pattern production process is one-way, but as with any such processing requires, temporarily, full access to unencrypted (clear text) document content. Such processing should ideally be undertaken in a network-isolated or security assertion enforcing system so as to assure the organisations that their document content cannot be leaked during such processing. The resulting index can also be visually inspected prior to release to increase the degree of assurance, and the mechanism for release should be relatively constrained also. Indeed, a vital effort in IPCRESS is to craft the set of acceptable processes and procedures for deploying IPCRESS and identifying associated risk levels in relation to information assurance. Related processes and procedures, including the drafting contractual terms for such an adoption, are also required.

ACKNOWLEDGMENT

The authors gratefully recognize prior contributions of Neil Newbold, Neil Cooke, Peter Wrobel and Henry Cooke to the formulation of the codebase used for this task and by Cooke and Wrobel to the patents generated from these efforts. This work has been supported in part by the the UK's Technology Strategy Board (TSB, 169201), and contributions from others at Surrey, Jaguar Land Rover and GeoLang are also acknowledged in this respect, and by EPSRC and JISC (EP/I034408/1). We recognize also the efforts of the PAN13 organizers in system evaluation (Section V).

REFERENCES

Carvalho, V. R., & Cohen, W. W. (2007) *Preventing Information Leaks in Email. Proceedings of the SIAM International Conference on Data Mining*, Minneapolis.

Choate, P. (2005). *Hot Property: The Stealing of Ideas in an Age of Globalization*. New York: Alfred A. Knopf.

Cooke, N., & Gillam, L. (2011). Clowns, Crowds and Clouds: A Cross-Enterprise Approach to Detecting Information Leakage without Leaking Information. In Z. Mahmood & R. Hill (Eds.), *Cloud Computing for Enterprise Architectures*. London: Springer. doi:10.1007/978-1-4471-2236-4_16

Franqueira, V. N. L., van Cleeff, A., van Eck, P., & Wieringa, R. (2010). External Insider Threat: A Real Security Challenge in Enterprise Value Webs. In Proceedings of Availability, Reliability, and Security (pp. 446–453). ARES.

Gentry, C. (2009) *Fully homomorphic encryption using ideal lattices*. In *Proceedings of the Symposium on the Theory of Computing (STOC)*, 2009 (pp. 169-178).

Grman, J. & Ravas, R. (2011). *Improved Implementation for Finding Text Similarities in Large Collections of Data*. Notebook for Uncovering Plagiarism, Authorship, and Social Software Misuse (PAN) at CLEF.

Kong, L., Qi, H., Wang, S., Du, C., Wang, S. & Han, Y. (2012). *Approaches for Candidate Document Retrieval and Detailed Comparison of Plagiarism Detection*. Notebook for Uncovering Plagiarism, Authorship, and Social Software Misuse (PAN) at CLEF.

Manuj, I., & Mentzer, J. T. (2008). Global supply chain risk management strategies. *International Journal of Physical Distribution & Logistics Management*, *38*(3), 192–223. doi:10.1108/09600030810866986

McGuire, M., & Dowling, S. (2003). *Cyber crime: a review of the evidence*. Home Office. Retrieved 9 July, 2014, from https://www.gov.uk/government/publications/cyber-crime-a-review-of-the-evidence

Mell, P., & Grance, T. (2011). *The NIST Definition of Cloud Computing* (pp. 800–145). Gaithersburg, MD: NIST Special Publication.

National Bureau of Asian Research. (2013). The IP Commission Report: The report on the theft of American Intellectual Propery. Retrieved 18 March, 2014, from http://www.ipcommission.org/report/IP_Commission_Report_052213.pdf

OCSIA/Detica. (2011). *The cost of cyber crime. A Detica report in partnership with the Office of Cyber Security and Information Assurance in the Cabinet Office.* Retrieved 18 March, 2014, from https://www.baesystemsdetica.com/uploads/press_releases/THE_COST_OF_CYBER_CRIME_SUMMARY_FINAL_14_February_2011.pdf

Potthast, M., Barrón-Cedeño, A., Stein, B., & Rosso, P. (2010). *An Evaluation Framework for Plagiarism Detection. Proceedings of the 23rd International Conference on Computational Linguistics (COLING)* 2010, August 23-27, Beijing, China.

Shokouhi, M., & Si, L. (2011). Federated Search. *Foundations and Trends in Information Retrieval, 5*(1), 1–102. doi:10.1561/1500000010

Torrejón, D.A.R. & Ramos, J.M.M. (2013). *Text Alignment Module in CoReMo 2.1 Plagiarism Detector.* Notebook for Uncovering Plagiarism, Authorship, and Social Software Misuse (PAN) at CLEF.

Wang, C., Cao, N., Li, J., Ren, K., & Lou, W. (2010) *Secure Ranked Keyword Search over Encrypted Cloud Data. Proceedings of the 30th International Conference on Distributed Computing Systems (ICDCS'10),* Genoa, Italy, June 21-25, 2010. doi:10.1109/ICDCS.2010.34

ADDITIONAL READING

Antonopoulos, N., & Gillam, L. (Eds.). (2010). *Cloud Computing: Principles, Systems and Applications.* London: Springer-Verlag. doi:10.1007/978-1-84996-241-4

Berger, S., Cáceres, R., Goldman, K., Pendarakis, D., Perez, R., Rao, J. R., & Valdez, E. et al. (2009). Security for the cloud infrastructure: Trusted virtual data center implementation. *IBM Journal of Research and Development,* 560–571.

Bull, J., Collins, C., Coughlin, C., & Sharp, D. (2000). *Technical Review of Free Text Plagiarism Detection Software.* JISC.

Cao, N., Wang, C., Li, M., Ren, K., & Lou, W. (2011). *Privacy-preserving multi-keyword ranked search over encrypted cloud data.* In *Proceedings of IEEE INFOCOM, IEEE Shanghai, China* (pp. 829–837). doi:10.1109/INFCOM.2011.5935306

Cooke, N., & Gillam, L. (2011). Clowns, Crowds and Clouds: A Cross-Enterprise Approach to Detecting Information Leakage without Leaking Information. In Z. Mahmood & R. Hill (Eds.), *Cloud Computing for Enterprise Architectures.* London: Springer. doi:10.1007/978-1-4471-2236-4_16

Cooke, N., Gillam, L., Wrobel, P., Cooke, H., & Al-Obaidli, F. (2011). *A high performance plagiarism detection system. Proceedings of the 3rd PAN workshop.*

Culwin, F. (2009). *The Efficacy of Turnitin and Google. Proceedings of the 9th HEA-ICS Conference,* Kent, U.K.

Denz, R., & Taylor, S. (2013). *A survey on securing the virtual cloud.* Journal of Cloud Computing: Advances. *Systems and Applications, 2*(17). doi:10.1186/2192-113X-2-17

Doran, D. (2004). Rethinking the supply chain: An automotive perspective. *Supply Chain Management: An International Journal, 9*(1), 102–109. doi:10.1108/13598540410517610

Dubin, D. (2004). The most influential paper Gerard Salton never wrote. *Library Trends*, *52*(4), 748–764.

Gillam, L. (2013). *Guess again and see if they line up: Surrey's runs at plagiarism detection. Proceedings of the 5th PAN workshop.*

Gillam, L., Broome, S., & Garside, G. (2013) *On Supply Chains, Deperimeterization and the IPCRESS Solution. Fifth International Conference on Internet Technologies and Applications (ITA)*, 10-13 September 2013, Wrexham, UK

Gillam, L., Newbold, N., & Cooke, N. (2012). *Educated guesses and equality judgements: using search engines and pairwise match for external plagiarism detection. Proceedings of the 4th PAN workshop.*

Grolinger, K., Higashino, W. A., Tiwari, A., & Capretz, M. A. M. (2013). *Data management in cloud environments: NoSQL and NewSQL data stores.* Journal of Cloud Computing: Advances. *Systems and Applications*, *2*(22). doi:10.1186/2192-113X-2-22

Hamming, R. W. (1950). Error detecting and error correcting codes. *The Bell System Technical Journal*, *29*(2), 147–160. doi:10.1002/j.1538-7305.1950.tb00463.x

Lancaster, S., & Clarke, R. (2009). *Automated Essay Spinning. Proceedings of the 9th HEA-ICS Conference*, Kent, U.K.

Levenshtein, V. I. (1966). Binary codes capable of correcting deletions, insertions, and reversals. *Soviet Physics, Doklady*, *10*(8), 707–710.

Luhn, H. P. (1957). A statistical approach to mechanized encoding and searching of literary information. *IBM Journal of Research and Development*, *1*(4), 309–317. doi:10.1147/rd.14.0309

Miemczyk, J., & Howard, M. (2008). Supply strategies for build-to-order: Managing global auto operations. *Supply Chain Management: An International Journal*, *13*(1), 3–8. doi:10.1108/13598540810850265

Morris, D., Donnelly, T., & Donnelly, T. (2004). Supplier parks in the automotive industry. *Supply Chain Management: An International Journal*, *9*(2), 129–133. doi:10.1108/13598540410527024

Rabin, M. O. (1981). *Finger printing by random polynomials*. Center for Research in Computing Technology Harvard University Report TR-15-81.

Stefanov, E., Papamanthou, C., & Shi, E. (2014). Practical Dynamic Searchable Encryption with Small Leakage. *Proceedings of NDSS '14*, San Diego, CA, USA. doi:10.14722/ndss.2014.23298

Sun, X., Zhu, Y., Xia, Z., & Chen, L. (2014). *Secure ranked semantic keyword search over encrypted cloud data*. Journal of Cloud Computing: Advances. *Systems and Applications*, *3*, 8.

Teufel, S., & Moens, M. (2000). *What's yours and what's mine: Determining Intellectual Attribution in Scientific Text. Proceedings of the Joint SIGDAT Conference on Empirical Methods in Natural Language Processing and Very Large Corpora*, Hong Kong. doi:10.3115/1117794.1117796

Wang, C., Cao, N., Ren, K., & Lou, W. (2012). Enabling secure and efficient ranked keyword search over outsourced cloud data. *IEEE Transactions on Parallel and Distributed Systems*, *23*(8), 1467–1479. doi:10.1109/TPDS.2011.282

Wang, Z., & Gemmell, J. (2006). *Clean Living: Eliminating Near-Duplicates in Lifetime Personal Storage*. Microsoft Research Redmond.

Wiengarten, F., Fynes, B., Humphreys, P., Chavez, R. C., & McKittrick, A. (2011). Assessing the value creation process of e-business along the supply chain. *Supply Chain Management: An International Journal, 16*(4), 207–219. doi:10.1108/13598541111139035

Wiengarten, F., Humphreys, P., Cao, G., Fynes, B., & McKittrick, A. (2010). Collaborative supply chain practices and performance: Exploring the key role of information quality. *Supply Chain Management: An International Journal Volume, 15*(6), 463–473. doi:10.1108/13598541011080446

Yang, C., Zhang, W., Xu, J., Xu, J., & Yu, N. (2012). *A Fast Privacy-Preserving Multi-keyword Search Scheme on Cloud Data. Proceedings of International Conference on Cloud and Service Computing (CSC)*. IEEE, Shanghai, China, pp 104–110 doi:10.1109/CSC.2012.23

KEY TERMS AND DEFINITIONS

Cloud Computing: The flexible and on-demand provision of specific computational capabilities by identifiable parties external to a given company and whose business relationship with the company is specific to this provision such that the company does not provide the computational capability to itself.

Data Leak: An event in which data is made available to parties to whom it should not have been by some deliberate, accidental, or negligent means.

Insiders: Individuals that are trusted, and have (some) authorized access over the organization's assets (Franqueira et al, 2010).

Intellectual Property: Creations of the mind, such as inventions; literary and artistic works; designs; and symbols, names and images used in commerce (source: WIPO).

Plagiarism Detection: The ability to find passages that have been copied from one source to another, where such copying is disallowed and the intention of the copying party is to gain advantage either by recognition or by reducing their own efforts.

Stitching: The joining together, given a certain threshold of distance, of fragments of copied text that would otherwise be considered separated.

Supply Chain / Extended Enterprise: The set of actors – sole traders, and small and large companies - involved in the creation, production, distribution, sales, and related activities, for a given good, service, or commodity, with an identifiable brand.

ENDNOTES

[1] http://www.telegraph.co.uk/finance/yourbusiness/8936685/Sir-James-Dyson-attacks-China-over-designs-theft.html

[2] http://www.theguardian.com/business/2012/oct/24/dyson-accuses-bosch-paying-research-spy

[3] For just one example, Jaguar F-Type Project 7 leaks in production trim ahead of Goodwood debut: http://www.autoblog.com/2014/06/24/jaguar-f-type-project-7-production-leaked/

[4] http://www.theguardian.com/technology/2014/jul/08/new-doctor-who-scripts-leak-deep-breath

Chapter 9
The Role of Cloud Computing in Global Supply Chain

Kijpokin Kasemsap
Suan Sunandha Rajabhat University, Thailand

ABSTRACT

This chapter reviews the role of cloud computing in global supply chain, thus describing the theoretical and practical concepts of cloud computing and supply chain management (SCM); the significance of cloud computing in global supply chain; the overview of electronic supply chain management (e-SCM); and the organizational information processing theory within global supply chain. The utilization of cloud computing is necessary for modern organizations that seek to serve suppliers and customers, increase business performance, strengthen competitiveness, and achieve continuous success in global business. Therefore, it is essential for modern organizations to examine their cloud computing applications, develop a strategic plan to regularly check their practical advancements, and immediately respond to the cloud computing needs of customers in global supply chain. Applying cloud computing in global supply chain will extremely improve organizational performance and reach business goals in the digital age.

INTRODUCTION

For modern organizations competing in the greatly potential markets, the search for new sources of competitive advantage is necessary in order to sustain in the social media age (Kasemsap, 2015). In the globalized world with its ever-changing economic conditions, enterprises are urged to react on threats and opportunities in an adjustable manner (Krumeich, Weis, Werth, & Loos, 2014). The use of cloud computing technology is increasing among customers and information management development focuses on the increased cost and time efficiencies derived from using innovative services (Ratten, 2014). Supply chain management (SCM) is a highly integrative discipline, which is jointly connected with key management functions such as strategic management, marketing, and finance (Kaufmann & Saw, 2014). Stable supply chain processes in a dynamic environment support enterprise competitiveness (Ivanov & Sokolov, 2012). Supply chain practically shapes competitive management prospect (Christopher, 2012).

Cloud computing has become a rising paradigm in the information and communication technology (ICT) industry (Hung, Bui, Morales, Nguyen,

DOI: 10.4018/978-1-4666-8339-6.ch009

& Huh, 2014), with wide benefits extending to diverse areas including cost cutting, better management of business (Sagar, Bora, Gangwal, Gupta, Kumar, & Agarwal, 2013). Cloud computing has been envisioned as key technology to achieve economy of scale in the deployment and operation of information technology (IT) solutions (Chen, Wu, & Vasilakos, 2014). Cloud computing is an ascending technology that has introduced a new paradigm by making a computational model possible (Durao, Carvalho, Fonseka, & Garcia, 2014). Cloud computing is the new era of information processing and has proved its benefits in high scalability and functional diversity (Shon, Cho, Han, & Choi, 2014). Cloud computing has emerged as the latest development in IT (Yoo, 2011) that embodies economic advantages in terms of the increased efficiency in modern organizations (Gottschalk & Kirn, 2013).

Cloud computing is the modern computing paradigm that transparently distributes ICT resources (Ranjan, Buyya, Leitner, Haller, & Tai, 2014). Cloud computing is functionally utilized by a large number of innovative organizations (Rajaraman, 2014). Cloud computing produces the high quality, on-demand services with service-oriented architecture (Wang, Liu, Sun, Zou, & Yang, 2014). Cloud computing services have become more cost effective and technically flexible than traditional solutions (Stieninger & Nedbal, 2014). Cloud computing has the potential to reshape the landscape of the IT industry (Yu, Sheng, & Han, 2013). The dimension of IT relates to a high dependency of modern organizations regarding information system infrastructure (Bajgoric, 2014). The Internet has been employed in multidimensional ways in various supply chains (Durowoju, Chan, & Wang, 2011). Cloud computing for customers is an increasing subject of discussion in business world because of its rapid emergence as an innovative marketing technology (Stein, Ware, Laboy, & Schaffer, 2013). There is a global increase in the utilization of cloud computing services as more people use the Internet to access, transfer, and store electronic information (Leymann, Fehling, Mietzner, Nowak, & Dustdar, 2011).

SCM as philosophy has both theoretical and managerial implications, and is positively related to organization's orientation, recognizing the way that the organization integrates supply chain implications throughout decisions that the organization makes (Ellram & Cooper, 2014). As the industrial environment becomes more competitive, SCM has attained growing attention from practical and academic societies as an essential discipline (Shafieezadeh & Sadegheih, 2014). Organizations adopt cloud computing technologies that align with their SCM strategy and enable them to generate organizational capabilities effectively utilized to facilitate business performance (Wu, Cegielski, Hazen, & Hall, 2013). As organizations look for ways to enhance competitive advantage by leveraging their supply chains (Barney, 2012; Hunt & Davis, 2012; Priem & Swink, 2012), many IT solutions have been realized to improve management effectiveness and supply chain process performance (Fawcett, Wallin, Allred, Fawcett, & Magnan, 2011). Cloud computing helps organizations to maintain the alignment between supply chain initiatives and IT, thus promoting organizational agility (Vickery, Droge, Setia, & Sambamurthy, 2010).

The strength of this chapter is on the thorough literature consolidation of cloud computing in global supply chain. The extant literature of cloud computing in global supply chain provides a contribution to practitioners and researchers by describing a comprehensive view of the functional applications of cloud computing in global supply chain to appeal to different segments of cloud computing in global supply chain in order to maximize the business impact of cloud computing in global supply chain.

BACKGROUND

Cloud Computing application comes about in order to potentially arrange and use massive amount of data with the development of the Internet (Kang, Barolli, Park, & Jeong, 2014). Cloud computing is a model for enabling convenient, on-demand network access to a shared pool of configurable computing resources (Chun & Choi, 2014). As a technological innovation, cloud computing is adopted into regular usage by customers as it continues to develop because of its dynamic cloud computing nature (Ratten, 2014).

Cloud computing services reduce the upfront costs from technological innovations by delivering the functionality of existing IT services (Marston, Li, Bandyopadhyay, Zhang, & Ghalsasi, 2011). Cloud computing frameworks such as Amazon Web Services, Google AppEngine and Windows Azure are popular among IT organizations and developers (Rahimi, Ren, Liu, Vasilakos, & Venkatasubramanian, 2014). As cloud computing is expanding and adopted in numerous business domains, it starts drawing attention of supply chain practitioners (Truong, 2014). Organizations choose cloud computing to be their primary ways of sourcing applications. Cloud computing is new to modern organizations in supply chains (Truong, 2014).

Cloud computing can provide on-demand computing services with high reliability, scalability and availability in a distributed environment (Xun, 2012). Developing scalability to build, access, manage, deploy, and maintain cloud computing applications has become critical (Ranjan, Buyya, & Benatallah, 2012). Cloud computing is a valuable resource that helps organizations to create sustainable competitive advantage (Truong, 2010). Cloud computing technologies are useful for managing supply chain (Cegielski, Jones-Farmer, Wu, & Hazen, 2012). Cloud computing introduces the new delivery models and supply chains that

will mature over time in modern organizations (Lindner, Galan, Chapman, Clayman, Henriksson, & Elmroth, 2010). Business enterprises and their supply chains focus on economic activities (Jakhar, 2014). Organizations must rely on many inter-organizational relationships to ensure efficient and effective movements within their supply chains (Kotzab, Grant, Teller, & Halldorsson, 2009).

Since its introduction as a concept in the 1980s, SCM has undergone significant modification and expansion (Stock, Boyer, & Harmon, 2010). Business processes integration provides an efficient way for the flow of information to improve the flow of work and material (Faisal, Azher, Ramzan, & Malik, 2011). Current trends in IT progress for networked systems include the development of cyber-physical networks, cloud service environments, pervasive computing, and data mining (Jain, Wadhwa, & Deshmukh, 2009; Bardhan, Demirkan, Kannan, Kauffman, & Sougstad, 2010; Zhuge, 2011). Using cloud computing improves organizational innovation in global business (Willcocks, Venters, & Whitley, 2013). Organizational innovation is potentially correlated with organizational performance in the social media age (Kasemsap, 2013a, 2014a, 2014b). Organizations, which plan to utilize cloud computing, analyze costs to minimize risks concerning cost types (Walterbusch, Martens, & Teuteberg, 2013).

THE ROLE OF CLOUD COMPUTING IN GLOBAL SUPPLY CHAIN

This section reviews the theoretical and practical concepts of cloud computing and supply chain management (SCM); the significance of cloud computing in global supply chain; the overview of electronic supply chain management (e-SCM); and the organizational information processing theory within global supply chain.

Concept of Cloud Computing

Cloud computing is defined as a collection of disembodied services accessible from anywhere using any mobile device with an Internet-based connection (Misra & Mondal, 2010; Sultan, 2010). Cloud computing is defined as a type of parallel and distributed system consisting of a collection of interconnected and virtualized computers that are dynamically provisioned and presented as the unified computing resources based on service-level agreements established through negotiation between the service providers and consumers (Buyya, Chee Shin, & Venugopal, 2008). Cloud computing emerges as a paradigm of Internet computing in which dynamical, scalable and often virtualized resources are provided as services (Liu, Ma, Zhang, Li, & Chen, 2011).

The concept of cloud computing is based on utilizing the distributed resources for application and services that need massive amount of computing assets for a specific short period of time (Khasnabish, Huang, Bai, Bellavista, Martinez, & Antonopoulos, 2012). Cloud computing is one of the major topics in the distributed systems (Blair, Kon, Cirne, Milojicic, Ramakrishnan, Reed, & Silva, 2011). Cloud computing is one of the management methods for distributed data processing and storage (Dudin & Smetanin, 2011). Cloud computing is considered as the virtualized resources (i.e., software, infrastructure, and platforms) to support various degrees of organizational need for optimized system utilization (Vaquero, Rodero-Merino, Caceres, & Lindner, 2008), and provide customized computing environments for end-users (Wang, von Laszewski, Younge, He, Kunze, Tao, & Fu, 2011).

Cloud computing is a recent advancement wherein IT infrastructure and applications are provided as services to end-users under the usage-based payment model (Calheiros, Ranjan, Beloglazov, De Rose, & Buyya, 2011). Cloud computing resources are provided as services over the Internet and users can access resources based on their payments (Chen, Violetta, & Yang, 2013). Cloud computing is a model of service delivery and access where virtualized resources are provided as a service over the Internet (Rimal, Jukan, Katsaros, & Goeleven, 2011). The use of ICT can improve business competitiveness, and has provided genuine advantages for small and medium-sized enterprises (SMEs), enabling them to compete with large organizations (Bayo-Moriones & Lera-Lopez, 2007).

Cloud computing is a new way of delivering computing resources (Helmbrecht, 2010). Cloud computing is recognized as one of the modern innovative technologies (Arutyunov, 2012). Cloud computing is a management platform for entrepreneurship to drive corporate efficiency (Kushida, Murray, & Zysman, 2011). Cloud computing can arrange a high capacity for massive computing, storage as well as processing (Liang, Wang, & Zhang, 2011). Cloud computing offers the scalable on-demand services to customers with greater flexibility and lesser infrastructure investment (Modi, Patel, Borisaniya, Patel, & Rajarajan, 2012). Cloud-based end-user services, such as e-mail and office applications, are well-known in daily business practices, offering new opportunities and capabilities, but equally creating new challenges for stakeholders (Alshamaila, Papagiannidis, & Li, 2013).

Cloud computing systems are widely considered as a promising paradigm for an IT infrastructure capable of creating an added value for business, society, and administration (Aoyama & Sakai, 2011). Cloud computing uses the advances of technology communication such as grid computing for delivering a range of technology services delivered through the Internet and private or public networks (Chonka, Xiang, Zhou, & Bonti, 2011). These services are delivered to customers in a self-service fashion enabling resources to be shared and released with minimal service provider interaction from any device and location (Marston et al., 2011). Cloud computing has enabled more people to access and share information on cyberspace that can be seen by other users at the same time (Ratten, 2014). Public cloud providers are open to all individuals, companies, and organizations while private cloud providers are usually set up by one organization for a specific purpose with limited access (Vouk, 2008).

Leaders of global businesses should arrange training and contribute essential ICT skills for all employees to improve their knowledge to deal with the advanced technologies in the digital age (Kasemsap, 2014c). Some of the promised benefits from cloud computing can be very appealing for modern organizations, which need to maximize the return on their investment, and still remain competitive in an ever-demanding business environment. Saya, Pee, and Kankanhalli (2010) stated that while extant research has studied cloud computing architecture, potential applications (Liu & Orban, 2008), and benefits (Assuncao, Costanzo, & Buyya, 2009), the decision making on cloud computing adoption has not been empirically examined. Cloud computing involves a large number of computers connected through a communication network such as the Internet, similar to utility computing (Carroll, Kotze, & van der Merwe, 2010). Cloud computing reshapes the IT sector and the IT marketplace in modern business (Prasad, Gyani, & Murti, 2012).

Cloud computing deployments support the improved business intelligence (Gendron, 2014). Cloud computing has revolutionized availability and access to cloud computing and storage resources (Afgan, Chapman, Jadan, Franke, & Taylor, 2012). The emergence of cloud computing contributes to the integration of multiple services, in particular Voice over Internet Protocol (VoIP) services (Dabbebi, Badonnel, & Festor, 2014). Cloud computing environments have led to research in the areas of data processing, virtual environments, and access control (Lee, Cho, Seo, Shon, & Won, 2013). The infrastructure, platforms, and software applications are offered as services using cloud computing technologies (Perera, Zaslavsky, Cristen, & Georgakopoulos, 2014).

Concept of Supply Chain Management

SCM is quickly growing as both a strategic initiative and an academic discipline (Richey, Roath, Whipple, & Fawcett, 2010). Supply chain is a coordinated system in moving products or services from supplier to customer (Saberi, Nookabadi, & Hejazi, 2012). SCM is an ongoing process and needs continuous efforts to get the desired results (Siddiqui, Haleem, & Sharma, 2012). Supply chains and SCM are the significant areas of business practices that overlap with the discipline and practice of marketing and marketing management (Mentzer & Gundlach, 2010). One of the main research issues in SCM is to improve the global efficiency of supply chains (Ahn & Lee, 2004). SCM creates value from cost and working capital (Brandenburg & Seuring, 2011). Supply chain orientation is essential to accomplish customers' requirements (Min, Mentzer, & Ladd, 2007). Supply chains and modern industries are the examples of socio-economic systems affecting a country's economy (Shoushtari, 2013).

Recent trends toward outsourcing and global sourcing have created more complex supply chains (Mena, Humphries, & Choi, 2013). SCM improves competitiveness of the supply chain through a long-term commitment to supply chain relationships and a cooperative approach to business processes (Om, Lee, & Chang, 2007). Organizations launch strategic supply chain initiatives through project implementation (Mathieu & Pal, 2011). Organizations integrate sustainability in their SCM practices (Wolf, 2011). SMEs are facing customers in a global marketplace with increasing performance demands in terms of delivery consistency and reduction of lead times (Soderberg & Bengtsson, 2010). SCM must adopt different and more innovative strategies that support a better response to customer needs in an uncertain environment (Carvalho, Azevedo, & Cruz-Machado, 2012).

Effective SCM requires the integration of various business functions, organizational units, and channel partners such that each has a well-defined role in accomplishing SCM objectives (Manuj & Sahin, 2011). Supply chain integration is broadly conceptualized as an aggregation consisting of supplier integration, internal integration, and customer integration (Mackelprang, Robinson, Bernardes, & Webb, 2014). The practical integrations of business functions and SCM channels are important toward achieving overall SCM objectives (Sahin & Robinson, 2005). The dynamic nature of supply chains with their multiplicity of organizations, processes, and flows yield highly complex, multifaceted, and large-scale systems, referring to supply chain complexity (Choi & Hong, 2002). Manuj and Sahin (2011) stated that the degree of complexity is derived from the structural properties of system determined by a variety of elements defining the supply chains and their interactions (i.e., the number of participants, facilities, products, transportation links, and information flows).

Supply chains have to satisfy the demands and needs of their stakeholders (Pagell & Shevchenko, 2014). The functional roles within business organizations have changed as SCM has evolved in importance within modern organizations (Zacharia, Sanders, & Fugate, 2014). The highly complex supply chains, due to the vastness of data, decision variables, intricate interrelationships among variables and system constraints, and performance trade-offs present many challenges for management in arriving at effective business decisions (Manuj & Sahin, 2011). Supply chains are the adaptive systems (Choi, Dooley, & Rungtusanatham, 2001; Wycisk, McKelvey, & Hulsmann, 2008), and their efficient management poses many challenges for business professionals (Ellinger, Ellinger, & Keller, 2002). Supply chain complexity is widely recognized as a key issue confronting supply chain managers and executives (Choi & Krause, 2006). Supply chain complexity can weaken brand image, lower brand loyalty, stagnate category management, and disturb channel trade relations (Quelch & Kenny, 1994),

and reduce supply chain adaptability (Masson, Iosif, MacKerron, & Fernie, 2007). Knowledge management is a strategy for reducing supply chain decision-making complexity (Manuj & Sahin, 2011). Knowledge management leads to the increased job performance in global business (Kasemsap, 2013b).

SCM promises competitive advantages for industrial organizations (Arlbjørn, de Haas, & Munksgaard, 2013). SCM focuses on the management of exchange flows across the organizational members of supply chain (Esper, Defee, & Mentzer, 2010). Defee and Stank (2005) reviewed the supply chain structure literature and proposed five structural elements and five external contingency factors necessary to develop a complete supply chain strategy-structure-performance theoretical model. Structural dimensions include information integration, communications, standardization, decision-making authority, and rewards. Three of the structural elements in the proposed model are empirically tested and validated (Defee, Stank, Esper, & Mentzer, 2009). Structural elements developed by organizations are the results of organizational design activities. The structures developed by the supply chain-oriented organizations promote cross-functional thinking, communication, and information sharing (Esper et al., 2010). Eliminating non-value added steps in distribution channels simplifies supply chain processes, reduces costs, and diminishes managerial complexity (Manuj & Sahin, 2011).

SCM is a human-centric phenomenon (Myers, Griffith, Daugherty, & Lusch, 2004). Over 90 percent of logistics activities take place outside of direct supervision (Bowersox, Closs, & Stank, 2000), exhibiting the importance of effective people to supply chain excellence. Although financial, equipment, technological and market-based resources are necessary for effective SCM, the people that accomplish organizational tasks are critical for effective functioning and exploitation of each of these resource categories (Richey, Tokman, & Wheeler, 2006). Collaboration is considered as a driving force necessary for effective SCM (Horvath, 2001). Collaboration is an interdependent relationship, where parties closely work with each other to create beneficial outcomes (Sinkovics & Roath, 2004). Collaboration should be developed across functional areas inside the organizations, with the goal of creating the more integrated internal operations (Kahn & Mentzer, 1996). Effective intra-organizational collaboration is strongly associated with external collaboration (Gimenez & Ventura, 2003). Esper et al. (2010) suggested the development of learning capabilities and transformational leadership styles to facilitate the creation of supply chain ideas.

Performance of supply chain depends on the effectiveness of communication and coordination (Chen & Huang, 2007). Developing performance measurement model is a critical task for supply chain and its members in order to examine their current status and identify improvement opportunities for steering their future direction (Lin & Li, 2010). Performance evaluation is necessary for effective SCM (Yang, Wu, Liang, Bi, & Wu, 2011). Measuring supply chain performance is one of the main indicators of business success (Oztemel & Tekez, 2009). An important issue in measuring supply chain performance is the lack of holistic measures spanning all members (Holmberg, 2000; Lambert & Pohlen, 2001).

Brewer and Speh (2000) stated that the measures such as logistics service quality (Mentzer, Flint, & Kent, 1999), the perfect customer order (Novack & Thomas, 2004), and the balanced scorecard (BSC) practically exhibit supply chain performance from a customer's perspective. This is especially important considering the perceptual gaps that often exist between an organizational view of their performance and the perceptions of other supply chain entities (Forslund, 2006), the historical lack of emphasis on service elements of supply chain performance (Novack, Rinehart, & Langley, 1996), and the increased emphasis on the holistic supply chain (Mentzer, DeWitt, Min, Nix, Smith, & Zacharia, 2001). Organizations

place great emphasis on both supply chains and BSC to develop effective measures to evaluate organizational performance (Chang, Hung, Wong, & Lee, 2013). Supply chain measures facilitate operational integration and focus on monitoring supply chain performance (Esper et al., 2010).

The Supply Chain Operations Reference (SCOR) model, published in 1996 by Supply Chain Council (SCC), is based on the concepts of business process reengineering, benchmarking, and process measurement (Jalalvand, Teimoury, Makui, Aryanezhad, & Jolai, 2011). The SCOR model provides a process-oriented language, which helps supply chain partners to communicate with each other (Lockamy & McCormack, 2004). The SCOR model spans customer interactions, physical material transactions, and market interactions from supplier's supplier to customer's customer. The SCOR model is organized around the five processes (i.e., plan, source, make, deliver, and return). Five performance attributes of SCOR model (i.e., reliability, responsiveness, agility, cost, asset management) are the standard characteristics to describe supply chain, evaluated against other supply chains (Jalalvand et al., 2011).

Brewer and Speh (2000) indicated that the measures of supply chain favorably facilitate learning and innovation in modern business. Considering strategic emphasis on supporting supply chain operations for competitive advantage, learning and innovation are the key areas to measure in the supply chain-oriented organizations (Esper et al., 2010). Measures such as new product development cycle time and process improvement rates are important (Brewer & Speh, 2000). Lambert and Pohlen (2001) emphasized the importance of connecting supply chain initiatives to economic value and profit and loss statements. Lambert and Pohlen (2001) facilitated the use of non-financial measures to align the behavior of supply chain-related operational personnel with strategic goals.

From the global supply chain contexts, non-financial measures include a valuable focus on integration with suppliers and customers to support collaborative supply chain strategies and initiatives (Esper et al., 2010). In addition, non-financial measures such as the perfect customer order place emphasis on internal integration by adopting a measure of operational performance (Novack & Thomas, 2004). Enterprise value chains must develop and support a broader sustainability perspective to ensure that its customer, business, supply chain, community, and environmental relationships remain viable (Closs, Speier, & Meacham, 2011).

Significance of Cloud Computing in Global Supply Chain

Cloud computing promises a radical shift in the facility of computing resources within enterprises (Khajeh-Hosseini, Greenwood, Smith, & Sommerville, 2012). Cloud computing is attractive to business owners as it eliminates the requirement for users to plan ahead for provisioning when there is an increase in service demand (Zhang, Cheng, & Boutaba, 2010). A marketplace for cloud computing represents a promising alternative for obtaining standardized IT resources in a highly flexible manner (Hauff, Huntgeburth, & Veit, 2014). Business agility involves the utilization of computing services through the reduction of initial costs in enterprise information systems (Ratten, 2014). Technological advancements in information systems over the past few decades have enabled the organizations to work with major suppliers and customers in their supply chains in order to improve the performance of entire channels (Drake & Schlachter, 2008). By the use of strategic supply chain networks, the essential improvement of supply chain flexibility can be achieved in global business (Winkler, 2009).

Holtgrewe (2014) exhibited the convergence of telecommunications and related developments of ubiquitous computing concerning ICT working

environments and ICT value chains. Individuals can collect data about their habits, routines, and environments using ubiquitous computing technologies (Shilton, 2012). The increase in cloud computing services has been in conjunction with the emerging trends in IT toward the improved organizational efficiency and business agility (Hameed, Counsell, & Swift, 2012). Efficiency of hardware and software resources encourages the use of interactive applications that respond to users' requirements, thus incorporating resource efficiency in which computers are located in geographic areas with cheap electricity (Marston et al., 2011). The creation of strategic agility within enterprise information systems is an important way for organizations to increase innovative adoption rates (Doz & Kosonen, 2010). This can be done through aligning business agility from technology innovations (Tallon & Pinsonneault, 2011). Both efficiency and business agility have enabled the flexible deployment of consumers' business applications (Ratten, 2014).

Concerning cloud computing, IT is described as a critical prerequisite ability for organizations attempting to use their logistics capabilities to create competitive advantage (Bowersox & Daugherty, 1995; Closs, Goldsby, & Clinton, 1997). IT serves as a coordinating mechanism providing connection across departments across organizations in global supply chain (Simchi-Levi, Kaminski, & Simchi-Levi, 2008). Logistics IT can be separated into internal and external components (Closs & Savitskie, 2003; Savitskie, 2007). Internal IT facilitates tighter internal integration (Brah & Lim, 2006) and internal collaboration in logistics and supply chain organizations (Sanders & Premus, 2005). It is the presence of effective IT-enabled internal coordination (Lewis & Talalayevsky, 1997) that allows the organization to expand collaborative efforts outside its own boundaries to include other organizations across supply chain (Sanders & Premus, 2002). IT is broadly recognized as a critical tool for effective logistics and supply chain organizations for over 20 years (Closs et al., 1997; Forman & Lippert, 2005). The perspective of IT relates to increased emphasis on the integration and collaboration of supply chain (Esper et al., 2010).

IT is considered as a critical enabler of SCM processes (Mabert & Venkataramanan, 1998; Auramo, Kauremaa, & Tanskanen, 2005). The organizational goals for IT in the SCM context include ensuring information availability at a single point of data access, creating visibility to upstream and downstream changes in demand or supply, and enabling effective decision-making based on the wide information of supply chain (Simchi-Levi et al., 2008). IT is needed to improve operational quality and organizational performance by reducing lead time, improving efficiency, and eliminating errors in global business (Brah & Lim, 2006). The availability of supply chain information allows the supply chain organization to mitigate its risks (Christopher & Lee, 2004). The difficulties of connecting multiple disparate systems (Narasimhan & Kim, 2001) lead to a shift from the functionally-centered applications to the process-oriented applications across organizations (Edwards, Peters, & Sharman, 2001). The ability of IT to make information available potentially facilitates the implementation of integrated logistics processes (Gustin, Daugherty, & Stank, 1995).

Regarding global supply chain, customers have been affected by cloud computing services (Marston et al., 2011). This is due to cloud computing incorporating a comprehensive computing platform that can be configured on demand. This allows the digital ecosystem of information to be constantly generated, converged, and expanded (Karakas & Manisaligil, 2012). It also encourages the cloud computing infrastructure to be effectively utilized (Vouk, 2008). Some of the most important

determinants of adoption behavior of technology are perceived ease of use and perceived usefulness from the technology acceptance model, which focus on consumers' attitudes of usage (Gao, Rohm, Sultan, & Huang, 2012).

Concerning cloud-based supply chain, the technology acceptance model is the most common theory that investigates user's acceptance of new IT (Chen & Chang, 2013). The technology acceptance model is a widely used perspective to understand consumer's adoption of technological innovations (Gao et al., 2012). The technology acceptance model focuses on how perceived ease of use and perceived usefulness predict technology adoption (Davis, Bagozzi, & Warshaw, 1989). The technology acceptance model is one of the first theories specifically developed for the IT context (Venkatesh & Davis, 2000). The technology acceptance model is a simplistic model frequently used in technology innovation studies to understand, explain, and predict human behavior (Bagozzi, 2007). While the technology acceptance model is first introduced to study information systems, it has been extended to other types of technology products and services including mobile services (Revels, Tojib, & Tsarenko, 2010) and Internet banking (Yousafzai, Foxall, & Pallister, 2010). The technology acceptance model has been enlarged to the unified theory of acceptance and use of technology (Venkatesh, Morris, Davis, & Davis, 2003). This has meant that the technology acceptance model has been applied to more complex services that have resulted in technology innovations (Wang & Lin, 2012).

Lindner et al. (2010) defined a cloud-based supply chain as two or more parties connected by the provisions of cloud computing services, related information, and funds. Cloud-based supply chain represents a network of interconnected organizations in the cloud computing area involved in the provision of products and services required by customers. In cloud-based supply chain, logistics process is handled using cloud computing services in which shipping schedule, shipping notice, receiving notice, and payment information are stored and shared through cloud computing applications. While the promising benefits of cloud computing lead to the likelihood of adopting cloud-based solutions in supply chain, organizations need to be fully aware of risks associated with new cloud computing technology.

Most studies either focus on defining cloud supply chain (Lindner et al., 2010), proposing lists of benefits and challenges for organizations considering cloud supply chain solutions (Demirkan, Cheng, & Bandyopadhyay, 2010; Durowoju et al., 2011; Li, Zhang, & Chen, 2012), cloud supply chain adoption model (Casey, Cegielski, Jones-Farmer, Wu, & Hazen, 2012; Wu et al., 2013), and exploring architectures and applications of cloud computing environment (Bu & Wang, 2011; Ferguson & Hadar, 2011). Organizations that adopt cloud supply chain solutions need to ensure the efficiency of cloud supply chain operations given their current resources.

Cloud computing enables customers convenient access to the cloud computing resources by delivering information on a mobile technology format, which is created from cloud computing environment using information accessed in any geographic and time location (Wang & Lin, 2012). SCM can benefit from using cloud computing since it promises to enable a wide range of capabilities in SCM about reducing startup costs, increasing supply chain visibility, reducing lead time, enhancing inter-organizational collaboration and supply chain integration, and reducing response time to customers (Shacklett, 2010; Marston et al., 2011; Schramm, Nogueira, & Jones, 2011). While cloud-based supply chain solutions help reduce startup costs, they usually increase recurring costs (Truong, 2014). Standardization, integration, visibility,

and control of processes, enabled by enterprise systems, potentially help the organizations in improving their ability to form customers' needs and build business agility into their decision-making processes (Seethamraju, 2014).

Organizations may be interested in cloud-based supply chain solutions regarding their potential benefits but they may not be fully aware of challenges and difficulties in using cloud computing. Integrating cloud-based supply chain solutions to in-house systems and applications can be challenging and requires strategic decisions (Truong, 2010). Since organizations in global supply chain share important information about products, orders, inventory, shipment, payment, and customer profile through cloud computing systems and applications, they need to be ensured that there is no data leakage or any potential privacy and legal issues (Truong, 2014). Since operations are the cloud-based supply chains, a cloud service outage situation will have dramatic effect on supply chain performance. Thus, it is important for global supply chain executives to assess and control risks associated with the use of cloud computing in global supply chain.

Overview of Electronic Supply Chain Management

A new era for development is needed and business needs to play an important role in the social media age (Lenssen & Van Wassenhove, 2012). Evolutions rooted in technology in market arena, business, and demands practically reforms in global supply chain (Aliei, Sazvar, & Ashrafi, 2012). Cloud computing is a suitable artifact through organizational information processing capability. The cloud-based infrastructure supports individual artifacts for e-SCM utilized in communication, collaboration, and coordination (Cegielski et al., 2012). The e-SCM includes the concepts of electronic business and SCM and depicts how trade channel members are working together to optimize resources and opportunities.

The e-SCM is considered as a potential remedy for operational issues that construct supply chain effectiveness and efficiency (Boyer & Hult, 2005; Rai, Patnayakuni, & Seth, 2006). Internet-enabled e-SCM facilitates the development of effective supply chain (Olson & Boyer, 2005; Wang, Tai, & Wei, 2006). Cloud computing technology supports some of traditional advantages of e-SCM (Cegielski et al., 2012). The e-SCM is the operational and strategic enhancement in communication, coordination, and collaboration across organizations (Autry, Grawe, Daugherty, & Richey, 2010; Liu, Ke, Wei, Gu, & Chen, 2010). Many organizations that participate in supply chain recognize e-SCM as an essential component of their supply chain strategy (Boyer & Hult, 2005; Liu et al., 2010).

Within the technological aspect of Internet-enabled e-SCM, the advances in cloud computing technology offer organizations opportunity to improve the flexibility of their technology infrastructure while reducing total cost of ownership for systems (IBM, 2009). Organizations can support cloud-based IT services from providers such as Google and IBM to rapidly scale systems to meet their organizational needs for capacity, collaboration, and coordination in modern business (Lohr, 2007). Many researchers have examined the e-SCM in a number of different theoretical and empirical contexts (Ke, Liu, Wei, Gu, & Chen, 2009; Autry et al., 2010; Liu et al., 2010).

Organizational Information Processing Theory within Global Supply Chain

The organizational information processing theory characterizes organizations as systems that possess both requirement and ability to prepare information as a method to reduce uncertainty in organizations (Galbraith, 1974). The organizational informa-

tion processing theory indicates three important concepts: information processing requirements, information processing capability, and the fit between the two to obtain optimal performance in modern business.

1. Information Processing Requirements

The information processing requirements of organization are defined as the disconnection between necessary information and general information for decision-making process (Premkumar, Ramamurthy, & Saunders, 2005). SCM is often defined by the levels of uncertainty, and there exists a large body of research devoted to examining and reducing uncertainties (Van der Vorst & Beulens, 2002; Sanchez-Rodrigues, Potter, & Naim, 2010). With the assumption that organizations are open systems, the organizational information processing theory categorizes the three sources of uncertainty: environmental uncertainty, task uncertainty, and inter-organizational uncertainty, to which organizations must respond (Tushman & Nadler, 1978). Regarding global supply chain, the sources of uncertainty increase decision making complexity and affect organizational requirement for information (Premkumar et al., 2005).

Regarding environmental uncertainty, each participant is exposed to environmental uncertainty (Peck & Juttner, 2000; Peck, 2005). Organizational members in supply chain organizations must be responsive to the environmental uncertainty created through interfaces with external environment. Organizations require information to reduce environmental uncertainty that they face while attempting to make decisions (Christopher & Lee, 2004; Christopher, Lowson, & Peck, 2004). For instance, a transportation provider must positively account for environmental uncertainty related to fluctuations in the availability of commodity. The perspective of environmental uncertainties contributes to the availability of environmental resources (Cegielski et al., 2012). The patterns of environmental uncertainty enhance levels of risk and impact organizations (Juttner, Peck, & Christopher, 2003; Juttner, 2005).

Task uncertainty is universal among organizations (Premkumar et al., 2005). Organizations seek to reduce task uncertainty through the application of information to their decision-making processes. For instance, manufacturing organizations utilize information to support quality improvement initiatives of improving their manufacturing processes and eliminating waste regarding product defects (Cegielski et al., 2012). Inter-organizational uncertainty is obtained from the nature of relationship among units, responsibilities of each unit, and leadership of each unit (Melville & Ramirez, 2008). To make appropriate decisions, organizational members of supply chain should use information to reduce uncertainty associated with complicated interactions (Christopher & Peck, 2004).

2. Information Processing Capability

Tushman and Nadler (1978) considered information processing capability as an organization's capacity to utilize information in a meaningful procedure that supports decision-making process. IT is a key aspect of an organization's information processing capability (Premkumar et al., 2005; Melville & Ramirez, 2008). Tushman and Nadler (1978) stated that formalized information system is the highest capacity to facilitate organizational information processing. Many researchers have proposed various IT artifacts as the delegates to measure an organization's information processing capability (Premkumar et al., 2005; Melville & Ramirez, 2008). Communication, collaboration, and coordination technologies such as electronic data interchange, e-SCM, and IT-based production controls have been utilized as proxies for an organization's information processing capability (Premkumar et al., 2005; Melville & Ramirez, 2008).

3. The Fit between Information Processing Requirements and Information Processing Capability

Organizations have two strategies to cope with uncertainty and information needs: develop buffers to reduce the effect of uncertainty; and implement structural mechanisms and information processing capability to enhance information flow and reduce uncertainty. A basic example of the first strategy is building inventory buffers to reduce the effect of uncertainty in demand or supply. An example of the second strategy is the redesign of business processes in modern organizations and implementation of integrated information system in order to improve information flow and reduce uncertainty in modern business. A business strategy creates better information flow between organizations to exhibit uncertainties in global supply chain (Premkumar et al., 2005).

FUTURE RESEARCH DIRECTIONS

The strength of this chapter is on the thorough literature consolidation of cloud computing in global supply chain. The extant literature of cloud computing in global supply chain provides a contribution to practitioners and researchers by describing a comprehensive view of the functional applications of cloud computing in global supply chain to appeal to different segments of cloud computing in global supply chain in order to maximize the business impact of cloud computing in global supply chain. The classification of the prevailing literature in the domain of cloud computing in global supply chain will provide the potential opportunities for future research. Future research direction should broaden the perspectives in the implementation of cloud computing in the knowledge-based supply chain organizations.

Practitioners and researchers should identify the applicability of a more multidisciplinary approach toward research activities in implementing cloud computing in global supply chain with knowledge management-related variables (i.e., knowledge-sharing behavior, knowledge creation, organizational learning, learning orientation, and motivation to learn). It will be useful to bring additional disciplines together (i.e., strategic management, marketing, finance, and human resources) to support a more holistic examination of cloud computing in global supply chain in order to combine or transfer existing theories and approaches to inquiry in this area. Although cloud computing itself has many open problems, researchers in the field have already made the leap to realize inter-cloud computing (Grozev & Buyya, 2014). Inter-cloud research is still in its infancy, and the body of knowledge in the area of inter-cloud computing has not been well defined yet (Grozev & Buyya, 2014). An examination of linkages between inter-cloud computing in global supply chain and business management would seem to be viable for future research efforts.

CONCLUSION

This chapter reviewed the role of cloud computing in global supply chain, thus describing the theoretical and practical concepts of cloud computing and supply chain management (SCM); the significance of cloud computing in global supply chain; the overview of electronic supply chain management (e-SCM); and the organizational information processing theory within global supply chain. This chapter examined the extent to which environmental uncertainty, task uncertainty, and inter-organizational uncertainty affect intention to adopt cloud computing technology in the supply chain. As an emerging technology, cloud computing changes the form and function of IT infrastructures in global supply chain. From a broader literature review, given the prevalence of the adoption of Internet-enabled technologies

like cloud computing in global supply chain environment, researchers and practitioners would expect the importance of cloud computing to gain sustainable competitive advantage in the social media age. Applying cloud computing in global supply chain will greatly increase business performance and gain competitive advantage in modern organizations.

REFERENCES

Afgan, E., Chapman, B., Jadan, M., Franke, V., & Taylor, J. (2012). Using cloud computing infrastructure with CloudBioLinux, CloudMan, and Galaxy. *Current Protocols in Bioinformatics, 38,* 11.9.1-11.9.20.

Ahn, H. J., & Lee, H. (2004). An agent-based dynamic information network for supply chain management. *BT Technology Journal, 22*(2), 18–27. doi:10.1023/B:BTTJ.0000033467.83300.c0

Aliei, M., Sazvar, A., & Ashrafi, B. (2012). Assessment of information technology effects on management of supply chain based on fuzzy logic in Iran tail industries. *International Journal of Advanced Manufacturing Technology, 63*(1-4), 215–223. doi:10.1007/s00170-012-3900-2

Alshamaila, Y., Papagiannidis, S., & Li, F. (2013). Cloud computing adoption by SMEs in the north east of England: A multi-perspective framework. *Journal of Enterprise Information Management, 26*(3), 250–275. doi:10.1108/17410391311325225

Aoyama, T., & Sakai, H. (2011). Inter-cloud computing. *Business & Information Systems Engineering, 3*(3), 173–177. doi:10.1007/s12599-011-0158-4

Arlbjørn, J. S., de Haas, H., & Munksgaard, K. B. (2013). Exploring supply chain innovation. *Logistics Research, 3*(1), 3–18. doi:10.1007/s12159-010-0044-3

Arutyunov, V. V. (2012). Cloud computing: Its history of development, modern state, and future considerations. *Scientific and Technical Information Processing, 39*(3), 173–178. doi:10.3103/S0147688212030082

Assuncao, M., Costanzo, A., & Buyya, R. (2009). *Evaluating the cost-benefit of using cloud computing to extend the capacity of clusters.* Paper presented at the 18th ACM International Symposium on High Performance Distributed Computing, Garching, Germany.

Auramo, J., Kauremaa, J., & Tanskanen, K. (2005). Benefits of it in supply chain management: An explorative study of progressive companies. *International Journal of Physical Distribution & Logistics Management, 35*(2), 82–100. doi:10.1108/09600030510590282

Autry, C. W., Grawe, S. J., Daugherty, P., & Richey, R. G. (2010). The effects of technological turbulence and breadth on supply chain technology acceptance and adoption. *Journal of Operations Management, 28*(6), 522–536. doi:10.1016/j.jom.2010.03.001

Bagozzi, R. P. (2007). The legacy of the technology acceptance model and a proposal for a paradigm shift. *Journal of the Association for Information Systems, 8*(4), 244–254.

Bajgoric, N. (2014). Business continuity management: A systemic framework for implementation. *Kybernetes, 43*(2), 156–177. doi:10.1108/K-11-2013-0252

Bardhan, I. R., Demirkan, H., Kannan, P. K., Kauffman, R., & Sougstad, R. (2010). An interdisciplinary perspective on IT services management and service science. *Journal of Management Information Systems, 26*(4), 13–64. doi:10.2753/MIS0742-1222260402

Barney, J. B. (2012). Purchasing, supply chain management and sustained competitive advantage: The relevance of resource-based theory. *Journal of Supply Chain Management, 18*(2), 3–6. doi:10.1111/j.1745-493X.2012.03265.x

Bayo-Moriones, A., & Lera-Lopez, F. (2007). A firm-level analysis of determinants of ICT adoption in Spain. *Technovation, 27*(6-7), 352–366. doi:10.1016/j.technovation.2007.01.003

Blair, G., Kon, F., Cirne, W., Milojicic, D., Ramakrishnan, R., Reed, D., & Silva, D. (2011). Perspectives on cloud computing: Interviews with five leading scientists from the cloud community. *Journal of Internet Services and Applications, 2*(1), 3–9. doi:10.1007/s13174-011-0023-1

Bowersox, D. J., Closs, D. J., & Stank, T. P. (2000). Ten mega-trends that will revolutionize supply chain logistics. *Journal of Business Logistics, 21*(2), 1–15.

Bowersox, D. J., & Daugherty, P. J. (1995). Logistics paradigms: The impact of information technology. *Journal of Business Logistics, 16*(1), 65–80.

Boyer, K. K., & Hult, G. T. M. (2005). Extending the supply chain: Integrating operations and marketing in the online grocery industry. *Journal of Operations Management, 23*(6), 642–661. doi:10.1016/j.jom.2005.01.003

Brah, S. A., & Lim, H. Y. (2006). The effects of technology and TQM on the performance of logistics companies. *International Journal of Physical Distribution & Logistics Management, 36*(3), 192–209. doi:10.1108/09600030610661796

Brandenburg, M., & Seuring, S. (2011). Impacts of supply chain management on company value: Benchmarking companies from the fast moving consumer goods industry. *Logistics Research, 3*(4), 233–248. doi:10.1007/s12159-011-0056-7

Brewer, P. C., & Speh, T. W. (2000). Using the balanced scorecard to measure supply chain performance. *Journal of Business Logistics*, *21*(1), 75–95.

Bu, Y., & Wang, L. (2011). *Leveraging cloud computing to enhance supply chain management in automobile industry*. Paper presented at the 2011 International Conference on Business Computing and Global Informatization (BCGIn 2011), Shanghai, China.

Buyya, R., Chee Shin, Y., & Venugopal, S. (2008). *High performance computing and communications*. Paper presented at the 10th IEEE International Conference, Dalian, China.

Calheiros, R. N., Ranjan, R., Beloglazov, A., De Rose, C. A. F., & Buyya, R. (2011). CloudSim: A toolkit for modeling and simulation of cloud computing environments and evaluation of resource provisioning algorithms. *Software, Practice & Experience*, *41*(1), 23–50. doi:10.1002/spe.995

Carroll, M., Kotze, P., & van der Merwe, A. (2010). Securing virtual and cloud environments. In I. Ivanov, M. van Sinderen, & B. Shishkov (Eds.), *Cloud computing and services science* (pp. 73–90). Berlin, Germany: Springer-Verlag.

Carvalho, H., Azevedo, S., & Cruz-Machado, V. (2012). Agile and resilient approaches to supply chain management: Influence on performance and competitiveness. *Logistics Research*, *4*(1-2), 49–62. doi:10.1007/s12159-012-0064-2

Casey, G., Cegielski, L., Jones-Farmer, A., Wu, Y., & Hazen, B. T. (2012). Adoption of cloud computing technologies in supply chains. *International Journal of Logistics Management*, *23*(2), 184–211. doi:10.1108/09574091211265350

Cegielski, C. G., Jones-Farmer, L. A., Wu, Y., & Hazen, B. T. (2012). Adoption of cloud computing technologies in supply chains: An organizational information processing theory approach. *International Journal of Logistics Management*, *23*(2), 184–211. doi:10.1108/09574091211265350

Chang, H. H., Hung, C. J., Wong, K. H., & Lee, C. H. (2013). Using the balanced scorecard on supply chain integration performance: A case study of service businesses. *Service Business*, *7*(4), 539–561. doi:10.1007/s11628-012-0175-5

Chen, H. C., Violetta, M. A., & Yang, C. Y. (2013). Contract RBAC in cloud computing. *The Journal of Supercomputing*, *66*(2), 1111–1131. doi:10.1007/s11227-013-1017-5

Chen, K. Y., & Chang, M. L. (2013). User acceptance of "near field communication" mobile phone service: An investigation based on the unified theory of acceptance and use of technology model. *Service Industries Journal*, *33*(6), 609–623. doi:10.1080/02642069.2011.622369

Chen, M., Wu, Y., & Vasilakos, A. V. (2014). Advances in mobile cloud computing. *Mobile Networks and Applications*, *19*(2), 131–132. doi:10.1007/s11036-014-0503-1

Chen, S. J., & Huang, E. (2007). A systematic approach for supply chain improvement using design structure matrix. *Journal of Intelligent Manufacturing*, *18*(2), 285–299. doi:10.1007/s10845-007-0022-z

Choi, T. Y., Dooley, K. J., & Rungtusanatham, M. (2001). Supply networks and complex adaptive systems: Control versus emergence. *Journal of Operations Management*, *19*(3), 351–366. doi:10.1016/S0272-6963(00)00068-1

Choi, T. Y., & Hong, Y. (2002). Unveiling the structure of supply networks: Case studies in Honda, Acura, and DaimlerChrysler. *Journal of Operations Management, 20*(5), 469–493. doi:10.1016/S0272-6963(02)00025-6

Choi, T. Y., & Krause, D. R. (2006). The supply base and its complexity: Implications for transaction costs, risks, responsiveness, and innovation. *Journal of Operations Management, 24*(5), 637–652. doi:10.1016/j.jom.2005.07.002

Chonka, A., Xiang, Y., Zhou, W., & Bonti, A. (2011). Cloud security defence to protect cloud computing against HTTP-DOS and XML-DOS attacks. *Journal of Network and Computer Applications, 34*(4), 1097–1107. doi:10.1016/j.jnca.2010.06.004

Christopher, M. (2012). *Logistics and supply chain management: Creating value-adding networks.* Dorchester, UK: Financial Times Prentice-Hall.

Christopher, M., & Lee, H. (2004). Mitigating supply chain risk through improved confidence. *International Journal of Physical Distribution & Logistics Management, 34*(5), 388–396. doi:10.1108/09600030410545436

Christopher, M., Lowson, R., & Peck, H. (2004). Creating agile supply chains in the fashion industry. *International Journal of Retail & Distribution Management, 32*(8), 367–376. doi:10.1108/09590550410546188

Christopher, M., & Peck, H. (2004). Building the resilient supply chain. *International Journal of Logistics Management, 15*(2), 1–13. doi:10.1108/09574090410700275

Chun, S. H., & Choi, B. S. (2014). Service models and pricing schemes for cloud computing. *Cluster Computing, 17*(2), 529–535. doi:10.1007/s10586-013-0296-1

Closs, D. J., Goldsby, T. J., & Clinton, S. R. (1997). Information technology influences on world class logistics capability. *International Journal of Physical Distribution & Logistics Management, 27*(1), 4–17. doi:10.1108/09600039710162259

Closs, D. J., & Savitskie, K. (2003). Internal and external logistic information technology integration. *International Journal of Logistics Management, 14*(1), 63–76. doi:10.1108/09574090310806549

Closs, D. J., Speier, C., & Meacham, N. (2011). Sustainability to support end-to-end value chains: The role of supply chain management. *Journal of the Academy of Marketing Science, 39*(1), 101–116. doi:10.1007/s11747-010-0207-4

Dabbebi, O., Badonnel, R., & Festor, O. (2014). Leveraging countermeasures as a service for VoIP security in the cloud. *International Journal of Network Management, 24*(1), 70–84. doi:10.1002/nem.1853

Davis, F. D., Bagozzi, R. P., & Warshaw, P. R. (1989). User acceptance of computer technology: A comparison of two theoretical models. *Management Science, 35*(8), 982–1003. doi:10.1287/mnsc.35.8.982

Defee, C. C., & Stank, T. P. (2005). Applying the strategy-structure-performance paradigm to the supply chain environment. *International Journal of Logistics Management, 16*(1), 28–50. doi:10.1108/09574090510617349

Defee, C. C., Stank, T. P., Esper, T. L., & Mentzer, J. T. (2009). The role of followers in supply chains. *Journal of Business Logistics, 30*(2), 65–84. doi:10.1002/j.2158-1592.2009.tb00112.x

Demirkan, H., Cheng, H. K., & Bandyopadhyay, S. (2010). Coordination strategies in an SaaS supply chain. *Journal of Management Information Systems, 26*(4), 119–143. doi:10.2753/MIS0742-1222260405

Drake, M. J., & Schlachter, J. T. (2008). A virtue-ethics analysis of supply chain collaboration. *Journal of Business Ethics*, *82*(4), 851–864. doi:10.1007/s10551-007-9597-8

Dudin, E. B., & Smetanin, Y. G. (2011). A review of cloud computing. *Scientific and Technical Information Processing*, *38*(4), 280–284. doi:10.3103/S0147688211040083

Durao, F., Carvalho, J. F. S., Fonseka, A., & Garcia, V. C. (2014). A systematic review on cloud computing. *The Journal of Supercomputing*, *68*(3), 1321–1346. doi:10.1007/s11227-014-1089-x

Durowoju, O. A., Chan, H. K., & Wang, X. (2011). The impact of security and scalability of cloud service on supply chain performance. *Journal of Electronic Commerce Research*, *12*(4), 243–256.

Edwards, P., Peters, M., & Sharman, G. (2001). The effectiveness of information systems in supporting the extended supply chain. *Journal of Business Logistics*, *22*(1), 1–27. doi:10.1002/j.2158-1592.2001.tb00157.x

Ellinger, A. E., Ellinger, A. D., & Keller, S. B. (2002). Logistics managers' learning environments and firm performance. *Journal of Business Logistics*, *23*(1), 19–37. doi:10.1002/j.2158-1592.2002.tb00014.x

Ellram, L. M., & Cooper, M. C. (2014). Supply chain management: It's all about the journey, not the destination. *Journal of Supply Chain Management*, *50*(1), 8–20. doi:10.1111/jscm.12043

Esper, T. L., Defee, C. C., & Mentzer, J. T. (2010). A framework of supply chain orientation. *International Journal of Logistics Management*, *21*(2), 161–179. doi:10.1108/09574091011071906

Faisal, C. M. M., Azher, E. M. K., Ramzan, E. B., & Malik, M. S. A. (2011). Cloud computing: SMEs issues and UGI based integrated collaborative information system to support Pakistani textile SMEs. *Interdisciplinary Journal of Contemporary Research in Business*, *3*(1), 564–573.

Fawcett, S., Wallin, C., Allred, C., Fawcett, A. M., & Magnan, G. M. (2011). Information technology as an enabler of supply chain collaboration: A dynamic-capabilities perspective. *Journal of Supply Chain Management*, *47*(1), 38–59. doi:10.1111/j.1745-493X.2010.03213.x

Ferguson, D. F., & Hadar, E. (2011). Optimizing the IT business supply chain utilizing cloud computing. In *Paper presented at the 8th International Conference & Expo on Emerging Technologies for a Smarter World* (CEWIT 2011), Hauppauge, NY.

Forman, H., & Lippert, S. K. (2005). Toward the development of an integrated model of technology internalization within the supply chain context. *International Journal of Logistics Management*, *16*(1), 4–27. doi:10.1108/09574090510617330

Forslund, H. (2006). Performance gaps in the dyadic order fulfillment process. *International Journal of Physical Distribution & Logistics Management*, *36*(8), 580–595. doi:10.1108/09600030610702871

Galbraith, J. R. (1974). Organization design: An information processing view. *Interfaces*, *4*(3), 28–36. doi:10.1287/inte.4.3.28

Gao, T., Rohm, A. J., Sultan, F., & Huang, S. (2012). Antecedents of consumer attitudes toward mobile marketing: A comparative study of youth markets in the United States and China. *Thunderbird International Business Review*, *54*(2), 211–225. doi:10.1002/tie.21452

Gendron, M. S. (2014). *Business intelligence and the cloud*. Hoboken, NJ: John Wiley & Sons. doi:10.1002/9781118915240

Gimenez, C., & Ventura, E. (2003). Supply chain management as a competitive advance in the Spanish grocery sector. *International Journal of Logistics Management, 14*(1), 77–88. doi:10.1108/09574090310806558

Gottschalk, I., & Kirn, S. (2013). Cloud computing as a tool for enhancing ecological goals? *Business & Information Systems Engineering, 5*(5), 299–313. doi:10.1007/s12599-013-0284-2

Grozev, N., & Buyya, R. (2014). Inter-Cloud architectures and application brokering: Taxonomy and survey. *Software, Practice & Experience, 44*(3), 369–390. doi:10.1002/spe.2168

Gustin, C. M., Daugherty, P. J., & Stank, T. P. (1995). The effects of information availability on logistics integration. *Journal of Business Logistics, 16*(1), 1–21.

Hameed, M. A., Counsell, S., & Swift, S. (2012). A conceptual model for the process of IT innovation adoption in organizations. *Journal of Engineering and Technology Management, 29*(3), 358–390. doi:10.1016/j.jengtecman.2012.03.007

Hauff, S., Huntgeburth, J., & Veit, D. (2014). Exploring uncertainties in a marketplace for cloud computing: A revelatory case study. *Journal of Business Economics, 84*(3), 441–468. doi:10.1007/s11573-014-0719-3

Helmbrecht, U. (2010). Data protection and legal compliance in cloud computing. *Datenschutz und Datensicherheit, 34*(8), 554-556.

Holmberg, S. (2000). A systems perspective on supply chain measurements. *International Journal of Physical Distribution & Logistics Management, 30*(10), 847–868. doi:10.1108/09600030010351246

Holtgrewe, U. (2014). New new technologies: The future and the present of work in information and communication technology. *New Technology, Work and Employment, 29*(1), 9–24. doi:10.1111/ntwe.12025

Horvath, L. (2001). Collaboration: The key to value creation in supply chain management. *Supply Chain Management: An International Journal, 6*(5), 205–207. doi:10.1108/EUM0000000006039

Hung, P. P., Bui, T. A., Morales, M. A. G., Nguyen, M. V., & Huh, E. N. (2014). Optimal collaboration of thin–thick clients and resource allocation in cloud computing. *Personal and Ubiquitous Computing, 18*(3), 563–572. doi:10.1007/s00779-013-0673-z

Hunt, S. D., & Davis, D. F. (2012). Grounding supply chain management in resource-advantage theory: In defense of a resource-based view of the firm. *Journal of Supply Chain Management, 48*(2), 14–20. doi:10.1111/j.1745-493X.2012.03266.x

IBM. (2009). *The benefits of cloud computing*. Retrieved September 6, 2014, from http://public.dhe.ibm.com/common/ssi/ecm/en/diw03004u-sen/DIW03004USEN.PDF

Ivanov, D., & Sokolov, B. (2012). The interdisciplinary modeling of supply chains in the context of collaborative multi-structural cyber-physical networks. *Journal of Manufacturing Technology Management, 23*(8), 976–997. doi:10.1108/17410381211276835

Jain, V., Wadhwa, S., & Deshmukh, S. G. (2009). Revisiting information systems to support a dynamic supply chain: Issues and perspectives. *Production Planning and Control, 20*(1), 17–29. doi:10.1080/09537280802608019

Jakhar, S. K. (2014). Designing the green supply chain performance optimisation model. *Global Journal of Flexible Systems Management, 15*(3), 235–259. doi:10.1007/s40171-014-0069-6

Jalalvand, F., Teimoury, E., Makui, A., Aryane-zhad, M. B., & Jolai, F. (2011). A method to compare supply chains of an industry. *Supply Chain Management: An International Journal*, *16*(2), 82–97. doi:10.1108/13598541111115347

Juttner, U. (2005). Supply chain risk management: Understanding the business requirements from a practitioner perspective. *International Journal of Logistics Management*, *16*(1), 120–141. doi:10.1108/09574090510617385

Juttner, U., Peck, H., & Christopher, M. (2003). Supply chain risk management: Outlining an agenda for future research. *International Journal of Logistics Research and Applications*, *6*(4), 197–210. doi:10.1080/13675560310001627016

Kahn, K. B., & Mentzer, J. T. (1996). Logistics and interdepartmental integration. *International Journal of Physical Distribution & Logistics Management*, *26*(8), 6–14. doi:10.1108/09600039610182753

Kang, A. N., Barolli, L., Park, J. H., & Jeong, Y. S. (2014). A strengthening plan for enterprise information security based on cloud computing. *Cluster Computing*, *17*(3), 703–710. doi:10.1007/s10586-013-0327-y

Karakas, F., & Manisaligil, A. (2012). Reorienting self-directed learning for the creative digital era. *European Journal of Training and Development*, *36*(7), 712–731. doi:10.1108/03090591211255557

Kasemsap, K. (2013a). Unified framework: Constructing a causal model of Six Sigma, organizational learning, organizational innovation, and organizational performance. *The Journal of Interdisciplinary Networks*, *2*(1), 268–273.

Kasemsap, K. (2013b). Innovative framework: Formation of causal model of organizational culture, organizational climate, knowledge management, and job performance. *Journal of International Business Management & Research*, *4*(12), 21–32.

Kasemsap, K. (2014a). Strategic innovation management: An integrative framework and causal model of knowledge management, strategic orientation, organizational innovation, and organizational performance. In P. Ordóñez de Pablos & R. D. Tennyson (Eds.), *Strategic approaches for human capital management and development in a turbulent economy* (pp. 102–116). Hershey, PA: IGI Global. doi:10.4018/978-1-4666-4530-1.ch007

Kasemsap, K. (2014b). The role of knowledge sharing on organisational innovation: An integrated framework. In L. Al-Hakim & C. Jin (Eds.), *Quality innovation: Knowledge, theory, and practices* (pp. 247–271). Hershey, PA: IGI Global. doi:10.4018/978-1-4666-4769-5.ch012

Kasemsap, K. (2014c). The role of social networking in global business environments. In P. A. C. Smith & T. Cockburn (Eds.), *Impact of emerging digital technologies on leadership in global business* (pp. 183–201). Hershey, PA: IGI Global. doi:10.4018/978-1-4666-6134-9.ch010

Kasemsap, K. (2015). Implementing enterprise resource planning. In M. Khosrow-Pour (Ed.), *Encyclopedia of information science and technology* (3rd ed., pp. 798–807). Hershey, PA: IGI Global; doi:10.4018/978-1-4666-5888-2.ch076

Kaufmann, L., & Saw, A. A. (2014). Using a multiple-informant approach in SCM research. *International Journal of Physical Distribution & Logistics Management*, *44*(6), 511–527. doi:10.1108/IJPDLM-05-2013-0099

Ke, W., Liu, H., Wei, K. K., Gu, J., & Chen, H. (2009). How do mediated and non-mediated power affect electronic supply chain management system adoption? The mediation effects of trust and institutional pressures. *Decision Support Systems*, *46*(4), 839–851. doi:10.1016/j.dss.2008.11.008

Khajeh-Hosseini, A., Greenwood, D., Smith, J. W., & Sommerville, I. (2012). The cloud adoption toolkit: Supporting cloud adoption decisions in the enterprise. *Software, Practice & Experience, 42*(4), 447–465. doi:10.1002/spe.1072

Khasnabish, B., Huang, D., Bai, X., Bellavista, P., Martinez, G., & Antonopoulos, N. (2012). Cloud computing, networking, and services. *Journal of Network and Systems Management, 20*(4), 463–467. doi:10.1007/s10922-012-9254-0

Kotzab, H., Grant, D. B., Teller, C., & Halldorsson, A. (2009). Supply chain management and hypercompetition. *Logistics Research, 1*(1), 5–13. doi:10.1007/s12159-008-0002-5

Krumeich, J., Weis, B., Werth, D., & Loos, P. (2014). Event-driven business process management: Where are we now? A comprehensive synthesis and analysis of literature. *Business Process Management Journal, 20*(4), 615–633. doi:10.1108/BPMJ-07-2013-0092

Kushida, K. E., Murray, J., & Zysman, J. (2011). Diffusing the cloud: Cloud computing and implications for public policy. *Journal of Industry, Competition and Trade, 11*(3), 209–237. doi:10.1007/s10842-011-0106-5

Lambert, D. M., & Pohlen, T. L. (2001). Supply chain metrics. *International Journal of Logistics Management, 12*(1), 1–19. doi:10.1108/09574090110806190

Lee, J., Cho, J., Seo, J., Shon, T., & Won, D. (2013). A novel approach to analyzing for detecting malicious network activity using a cloud computing testbed. *Mobile Networks and Applications, 18*(1), 122–128. doi:10.1007/s11036-012-0375-1

Lenssen, J. J., & Van Wassenhove, L. N. (2012). A new era of development: The changing role and responsibility of business in developing countries. *Corporate Governance, 12*(4), 403–413. doi:10.1108/14720701211267766

Lewis, I., & Talalayevsky, A. (1997). Logistics and information technology: A coordination perspective. *Journal of Business Logistics, 18*(1), 141–157.

Leymann, F., Fehling, C., Mietzner, R., Nowak, A., & Dustdar, S. (2011). Moving applications to the cloud: An approach based on application model enrichment. *International Journal of Cooperative Information Systems, 20*(3), 307–356. doi:10.1142/S0218843011002250

Li, Q., Zhang, X., & Chen, M. (2012). *Design on enterprise knowledge supply chain based on cloud computing.* Paper presented at the 2012 Fifth International Conference on Business Intelligence and Financial Engineering (BIFE 2012), Gansu, China. doi:10.1109/BIFE.2012.28

Liang, Q., Wang, Y. Z., & Zhang, Y. H. (2011). Resource virtualization model using hybrid-graph representation and converging algorithm for cloud computing. *International Journal of Automation and Computing, 10*(6), 597–606. doi:10.1007/s11633-013-0758-1

Lin, L. C., & Li, T. S. (2010). An integrated framework for supply chain performance measurement using six-sigma metrics. *Software Quality Journal, 18*(3), 387–406. doi:10.1007/s11219-010-9099-2

Lindner, M., Galan, F., Chapman, C., Clayman, S., Henriksson, D., & Elmroth, E. (2010). *The cloud supply chain: A framework for information, monitoring, accounting and billing.* Retrieved September 6, 2014, from https://www.ee.ucl.ac.uk/,sclayman/docs/CloudComp2010.pdf

Liu, H., Ke, W., Wei, K. K., Gu, J., & Chen, H. (2010). The role of institutional pressures and organizational culture in the firm's intention to adopt Internet-enabled supply chain management systems. *Journal of Operations Management, 28*(5), 372–384. doi:10.1016/j.jom.2009.11.010

Liu, H., & Orban, D. (2008). *Gridbatch: Cloud computing for large-scale data-intensive batch applications.* Paper presented at the 8th IEEE International Symposium on Cluster Computing and the Grid, Lyon, France. doi:10.1109/CCGRID.2008.30

Liu, Y. C., Ma, Y. T., Zhang, H. S., Li, D. Y., & Chen, G. S. (2011). A method for trust management in cloud computing: Data coloring by cloud watermarking. *International Journal of Automation and Computing, 8*(3), 280–285. doi:10.1007/s11633-011-0583-3

Lohr, S. (2007). *Google and I.B.M. Join in "cloud computing" research.* New York Times. Retrieved September 6, 2014, from http://www.csun.edu/pubrels/clips/Oct07/10-08-07E.pdf

Mabert, V. A., & Venkataramanan, M. A. (1998). Special research focus on supply chain linkages: Challenges for design and management in the 21st century. *Decision Sciences, 29*(3), 537–552. doi:10.1111/j.1540-5915.1998.tb01353.x

Mackelprang, A. W., Robinson, J. L., Bernardes, E., & Webb, G. S. (2014). The relationship between strategic supply chain integration and performance: A meta-analytic evaluation and implications for supply chain management research. *Journal of Business Logistics, 35*(1), 71–96. doi:10.1111/jbl.12023

Manuj, I., & Sahin, F. (2011). A model of supply chain and supply chain decision-making complexity. *International Journal of Physical Distribution & Logistics Management, 41*(5), 511–549. doi:10.1108/09600031111138844

Marston, S., Li, Z., Bandyopadhyay, S., Zhang, J., & Ghalsasi, A. (2011). Cloud computing: The business perspective. *Decision Support Systems, 51*(1), 176–189. doi:10.1016/j.dss.2010.12.006

Masson, R., Iosif, L., MacKerron, G., & Fernie, J. (2007). Managing complexity in agile global fashion industry supply chains. *International Journal of Logistics Management, 18*(2), 238–254. doi:10.1108/09574090710816959

Mathieu, R. G., & Pal, R. (2011). The selection of supply chain management projects: A case study approach. *Operations Management Research, 4*(3-4), 164–181. doi:10.1007/s12063-011-0058-2

Melville, N., & Ramirez, R. (2008). Information technology innovation diffusion: An information requirements paradigm. *Information Systems Journal, 18*(3), 247–273. doi:10.1111/j.1365-2575.2007.00260.x

Mena, C., Humphries, A., & Choi, T. Y. (2013). Toward a theory of multi-tier supply chain management. *Journal of Supply Chain Management, 49*(2), 58–77. doi:10.1111/jscm.12003

Mentzer, J. T., DeWitt, W., Min, S., Nix, N. W., Smith, C. D., & Zacharia, Z. G. (2001). Defining supply chain management. *Journal of Business Logistics, 22*(2), 1–25. doi:10.1002/j.2158-1592.2001.tb00001.x

Mentzer, J. T., Flint, D. J., & Kent, J. L. (1999). Developing a logistics service quality scale. *Journal of Business Logistics, 20*(1), 9–32.

Mentzer, J. T., & Gundlach, G. (2010). Exploring the relationship between marketing and supply chain management: Introduction to the special issue. *Journal of the Academy of Marketing Science, 38*(1), 1–4. doi:10.1007/s11747-009-0150-4

Min, S., Mentzer, J. T., & Ladd, R. T. (2007). A market orientation in supply chain management. *Journal of the Academy of Marketing Science, 35*(4), 507–522. doi:10.1007/s11747-007-0020-x

Misra, S. C., & Mondal, A. (2010). Identification of a company's suitability for the adoption of cloud computing and modelling its corresponding return on investment. *Mathematical and Computer Modelling*, *53*(3-4), 504–521. doi:10.1016/j.mcm.2010.03.037

Modi, C., Patel, D., Borisaniya, B., Patel, A., & Rajarajan, M. (2012). A survey on security issues and solutions at different layers of Cloud computing. *The Journal of Supercomputing*, *63*(2), 561–592. doi:10.1007/s11227-012-0831-5

Myers, M. B., Griffith, D. A., Daugherty, P. J., & Lusch, R. F. (2004). Maximizing the human capital equation in logistics: Education, experience, and skills. *Journal of Business Logistics*, *25*(1), 211–232. doi:10.1002/j.2158-1592.2004.tb00175.x

Narasimhan, R., & Kim, S. W. (2001). Information system utilization strategy for supply chain integration. *Journal of Business Logistics*, *22*(2), 51–75. doi:10.1002/j.2158-1592.2001.tb00003.x

Novack, R. A., Rinehart, L. M., & Langley, C. J. (1996). A comparative assessment of senior and logistics executives' perceptions of logistics value. *Journal of Business Logistics*, *17*(1), 135–178.

Novack, R. A., & Thomas, D. J. (2004). The challenges of implementing the perfect order concept. *Transportation Journal*, *43*(1), 5–17.

Olson, J. R., & Boyer, K. K. (2005). Internet ticketing in a not-for-profit, service organization: Building customer loyalty. *International Journal of Operations & Production Management*, *25*(1), 74–92. doi:10.1108/01443570510572259

Om, K., Lee, J., & Chang, J. (2007). Using supply chain management to enhance industry-university collaborations in IT higher education in Korea. *Scientometrics*, *71*(3), 455–471. doi:10.1007/s11192-007-1690-3

Oztemel, E., & Tekez, E. K. (2009). Interactions of agents in performance based supply chain management. *Journal of Intelligent Manufacturing*, *20*(2), 159–167. doi:10.1007/s10845-008-0229-7

Pagell, M., & Shevchenko, A. (2014). Why research in sustainable supply chain management should have no future. *Journal of Supply Chain Management*, *50*(1), 44–55. doi:10.1111/jscm.12037

Peck, H. (2005). Drivers of supply chain vulnerability: An integrated framework. *International Journal of Physical Distribution & Logistics Management*, *35*(4), 210–232. doi:10.1108/09600030510599904

Peck, H., & Juttner, U. (2000). Strategy and relationships: Defining the interface in supply chain contexts. *International Journal of Logistics Management*, *11*(2), 33–44. doi:10.1108/09574090010806146

Perera, C., Zaslavsky, A., Cristen, P., & Georgakopoulos, D. (2014). Sensing as a service model for smart cities supported by Internet of Things. *Transactions on Emerging Telecommunications Technologies*, *25*(1), 81–93. doi:10.1002/ett.2704

Prasad, M. R., Gyani, J., & Murti, P. R. K. (2012). Mobile cloud computing: Implications and challenges. *Journal of Information Engineering and Applications*, *2*(7), 7–16.

Premkumar, G., Ramamurthy, K., & Saunders, C. S. (2005). Information processing view of organizations: An exploratory examination of fit in the context of interorganizational relationships. *Journal of Management Information Systems*, *22*(1), 257–294.

Quelch, J. A., & Kenny, D. (1994). Extend profits, not product lines. *Harvard Business Review*, *72*(5), 153–160.

Rahimi, M. R., Ren, J., Liu, C. H., Vasilakos, A. V., & Venkatasubramanian, N. (2014). Mobile cloud computing: A survey, state of art and future directions. *Mobile Networks and Applications*, *19*(2), 133–143. doi:10.1007/s11036-013-0477-4

Rai, A., Patnayakuni, R., & Seth, N. (2006). Firm performance impacts of digitally enabled supply chain integration capabilities. *Management Information Systems Quarterly*, *30*(2), 225–246.

Rajaraman, V. (2014). Cloud computing. *Resonance*, *19*(3), 242–258. doi:10.1007/s12045-014-0030-1

Ranjan, R., Buyya, R., & Benatallah, B. (2012). Special section: Software architectures and application development environments for Cloud computing. *Software, Practice & Experience*, *42*(4), 391–394. doi:10.1002/spe.1144

Ranjan, R., Buyya, R., Leitner, P., Haller, A., & Tai, S. (2014). A note on software tools and techniques for monitoring and prediction of cloud services. *Software, Practice & Experience*, *44*(7), 771–775. doi:10.1002/spe.2266

Ratten, V. (2014). A US-China comparative study of cloud computing adoption behavior: The role of consumer innovativeness, performance expectations and social influence. *Journal of Entrepreneurship in Emerging Economies*, *6*(1), 53–71. doi:10.1108/JEEE-07-2013-0019

Revels, J., Tojib, D., & Tsarenko, Y. (2010). Understanding consumer intention to use mobile services. *Australasian Marketing Journal*, *18*(2), 74–80. doi:10.1016/j.ausmj.2010.02.002

Richey, R. G. Jr, Roath, A. S., Whipple, J. M., & Fawcett, S. E. (2010). Exploring a governance theory of supply chain management: Barriers and facilitators to integration. *Journal of Business Logistics*, *31*(1), 237–256. doi:10.1002/j.2158-1592.2010.tb00137.x

Richey, R. G., Tokman, M., & Wheeler, A. R. (2006). A supply chain manager selection methodology: Empirical test and suggested application. *Journal of Business Logistics*, *27*(2), 163–190. doi:10.1002/j.2158-1592.2006.tb00221.x

Rimal, B. P., Jukan, A., Katsaros, D., & Goeleven, Y. (2011). Architectural requirements for cloud computing systems: An enterprise cloud approach. *Journal of Grid Computing*, *9*(1), 3–26. doi:10.1007/s10723-010-9171-y

Saberi, S., Nookabadi, A. S., & Hejazi, S. R. (2012). Applying agent-based system and negotiation mechanism in improvement of inventory management and customer order fulfillment in multi echelon supply chain. *Arabian Journal for Science and Engineering*, *37*(3), 851–861. doi:10.1007/s13369-012-0197-2

Sagar, M., Bora, S., Gangwal, A., Gupta, P., Kumar, A., & Agarwal, A. (2013). Factors affecting customer loyalty in cloud computing: A customer defection-centric view to develop a void-in-customer loyalty amplification model. *Global Journal of Flexible Systems Management*, *14*(3), 143–156. doi:10.1007/s40171-013-0035-8

Sahin, F., & Robinson, E. P. Jr. (2005). Information sharing and coordination in make-to-order supply chains. *Journal of Operations Management*, *23*(6), 579–598. doi:10.1016/j.jom.2004.08.007

Sanchez-Rodrigues, V., Potter, A., & Naim, M. M. (2010). The impact of logistics uncertainty on sustainable transport operations. *International Journal of Physical Distribution & Logistics Management*, *40*(1-2), 61–83.

Sanders, N. R., & Premus, R. (2005). Modeling the relationship between firm it capability, collaboration, and performance. *Journal of Business Logistics*, *26*(1), 1–23. doi:10.1002/j.2158-1592.2005.tb00192.x

Savitskie, K. (2007). Internal and external logistics information technologies: The performance impact in an international setting. *International Journal of Physical Distribution & Logistics Management, 37*(6), 454–468. doi:10.1108/09600030710763378

Saya, S., Pee, L., & Kankanhalli, A. (2010). *The impact of institutional influences on perceived technological characteristics and real options in cloud computing adoption.* Paper presented at the 31st International Conference on Information Systems (ICIS 2010), St. Louis, Missouri.

Schramm, T., Nogueira, S., & Jones, D. (2011). Cloud computing and supply chain: A natural fit for the future. Retrieved September 6, 2014, from: http://www.aberdeen.com/aberdeen-library/7470/RA-software-service-cloud.aspx

Seethamraju, R. (2014). Enterprise systems and demand chain management: A cross-sectional field study. *Information Technology Management, 15*(3), 151–161. doi:10.1007/s10799-014-0178-0

Shacklett, M. (2010). Is supply chain management emerging from the clouds? The short answer is "yes," and now's the time to take a more serious look. *World Trade, 23*(4), 34–37.

Shafieezadeh, M., & Sadegheih, A. (2014). Developing an integrated inventory management model for multi-item multi-echelon supply chain. *International Journal of Advanced Manufacturing Technology, 72*(5-8), 1099–1119. doi:10.1007/s00170-014-5684-z

Shilton, K. (2012). Participatory personal data: An emerging research challenge for the information sciences. *Journal of the American Society for Information Science and Technology, 63*(10), 1905–1915. doi:10.1002/asi.22655

Shon, T., Cho, J., Han, K., & Choi, H. (2014). Toward advanced mobile cloud computing for the Internet of Things: Current issues and future direction. *Mobile Networks and Applications, 19*(3), 404–413. doi:10.1007/s11036-014-0509-8

Shoushtari, K. D. (2013). Redesigning a large supply chain management system to reduce the government administration: A socio-functional systems approach. *Systemic Practice and Action Research, 26*(2), 195–216. doi:10.1007/s11213-012-9244-x

Siddiqui, F., Haleem, A., & Sharma, C. (2012). The impact of supply chain management practices in total quality management practices and flexible system practices context: An empirical study in oil and gas industry. *Global Journal of Flexible Systems Management, 13*(1), 11–23. doi:10.1007/s40171-012-0002-9

Simchi-Levi, D., Kaminski, P., & Simchi-Levi, E. (2008). *Designing and managing the supply chain: Concepts, strategies, and case studies.* New York, NY: McGraw-Hill/Irwin.

Sinkovics, R. R., & Roath, A. S. (2004). Strategic orientation, capabilities, and performance in manufacturer - 3PL relationships. *Journal of Business Logistics, 25*(2), 43–64. doi:10.1002/j.2158-1592.2004.tb00181.x

Soderberg, L., & Bengtsson, L. (2010). Supply chain management maturity and performance in SMEs. *Operations Management Research, 3*(1), 90–97. doi:10.1007/s12063-010-0030-6

Stein, S., Ware, J., Laboy, J., & Schaffer, H. E. (2013). Improving K-12 pedagogy via a cloud designed for education. *International Journal of Information Management, 33*(1), 235–241. doi:10.1016/j.ijinfomgt.2012.07.009

Stieninger, M., & Nedbal, D. (2014). Characteristics of cloud computing in the business context: A systematic literature review. *Global Journal of Flexible Systems Management*, *15*(1), 59–68. doi:10.1007/s40171-013-0055-4

Stock, J. R., Boyer, S. L., & Harmon, T. (2010). Research opportunities in supply chain management. *Journal of the Academy of Marketing Science*, *38*(1), 32–41. doi:10.1007/s11747-009-0136-2

Sultan, N. (2010). Cloud computing for education: A new dawn? *International Journal of Information Management*, *30*(2), 109–116. doi:10.1016/j.ijinfomgt.2009.09.004

Truong, D. (2010). How cloud computing enhances competitive advantages: A research model for small businesses. *The Business Review, Cambridge*, *15*(1), 59–65.

Truong, D. (2014). *Cloud-based solutions for supply chain management: A post-adoption study*. Paper presented at the ASBBS 21st Annual Conference, Las Vegas, CA.

Tushman, M. L., & Nadler, D. A. (1978). Information processing as an integrating concept in organizational design. *Academy of Management Review*, *3*(3), 613–624.

Van der Vorst, J. G. A. J., & Beulens, A. J. M. (2002). Identifying sources of uncertainty to generate supply chain redesign strategies. *International Journal of Physical Distribution & Logistics Management*, *32*(6), 409–430. doi:10.1108/09600030210437951

Vaquero, L. M., Rodero-Merino, L., Caceres, J., & Lindner, M. (2008). A break in the clouds: Towards a cloud definition. *Computer Communication Review*, *39*(1), 50–55. doi:10.1145/1496091.1496100

Venkatesh, V., & Davis, F. D. (2000). A theoretical extension of the technology acceptance model: Four longitudinal field studies. *Management Science*, *46*(2), 186–204. doi:10.1287/mnsc.46.2.186.11926

Venkatesh, V., Morris, M. G., Davis, G. B., & Davis, F. D. (2003). User acceptance of information technology: Toward a unified view. *Management Information Systems Quarterly*, *27*(3), 425–478.

Vickery, S. K., Droge, C., Setia, P., & Sambamurthy, V. (2010). Supply chain information technologies and organizational initiatives: Complementary versus independent effects on agility and firm performance. *International Journal of Production Research*, *48*(23), 7025–7042. doi:10.1080/00207540903348353

Vouk, M. A. (2008). Cloud computing: Issues, research and implementations. *Journal of Computing and Information Technology*, *16*(4), 235–246.

Walterbusch, M., Martens, B., & Teuteberg, F. (2013). Evaluating cloud computing services from a total cost of ownership perspective. *Management Research Review*, *36*(6), 613–638. doi:10.1108/01409171311325769

Wang, E. T. G., Tai, J. C. F., & Wei, H. L. (2006). A virtual integration theory of improved supply-chain performance. *Journal of Management Information Systems*, *23*(2), 41–64. doi:10.2753/MIS0742-1222230203

Wang, K., & Lin, C. L. (2012). The adoption of mobile value-added services: Investigating the influence of IS quality and perceived playfulness. *Managing Service Quality*, *22*(2), 184–208. doi:10.1108/09604521211219007

Wang, L., von Laszewski, G., Younge, A., He, X., Kunze, M., Tao, J., & Fu, C. (2011). Cloud computing: A perspective study. *New Generation Computing*, *28*(2), 137–146. doi:10.1007/s00354-008-0081-5

Wang, S., Liu, Z., Sun, Q., Zou, H., & Yang, F. (2014). Towards an accurate evaluation of quality of cloud service in service-oriented cloud computing. *Journal of Intelligent Manufacturing*, *25*(2), 283–291. doi:10.1007/s10845-012-0661-6

Willcocks, L. P., Venters, W., & Whitley, E. A. (2013). Cloud sourcing and innovation: Slow train coming? A composite research study. *Strategic Outsourcing: An International Journal*, *6*(2), 184–202. doi:10.1108/SO-04-2013-0004

Winkler, H. (2009). How to improve supply chain flexibility using strategic supply chain networks. *Logistics Research*, *1*(1), 15–25. doi:10.1007/s12159-008-0001-6

Wolf, J. (2011). Sustainable supply chain management integration: A qualitative analysis of the German manufacturing industry. *Journal of Business Ethics*, *102*(2), 221–235. doi:10.1007/s10551-011-0806-0

Wu, Y., Cegielski, C. G., Hazen, B. T., & Hall, D. J. (2013). Cloud computing in support of supply chain information system infrastructure: Understanding when to go to the cloud. *Journal of Supply Chain Management*, *49*(3), 25–41. doi:10.1111/j.1745-493x.2012.03287.x

Wycisk, C., McKelvey, B., & Hulsmann, M. (2008). Smart parts, supply networks as complex adaptive systems: Analysis and implications. *International Journal of Physical Distribution & Logistics Management*, *38*(2), 108–125. doi:10.1108/09600030810861198

Xun, X. (2012). From cloud computing to cloud manufacturing. *Robotics and Computer-integrated Manufacturing*, *28*(1), 75–86. doi:10.1016/j.rcim.2011.07.002

Yang, F., Wu, D., Liang, L., Bi, G., & Wu, D. D. (2011). Supply chain DEA: Production possibility set and performance evaluation model. *Annals of Operations Research*, *185*(1), 195–211. doi:10.1007/s10479-008-0511-2

Yoo, C. S. (2011). Cloud computing: Architectural and policy implications. *Review of Industrial Organization*, *38*(4), 405–421. doi:10.1007/s11151-011-9295-7

Yousafzai, S. Y., Foxall, G. R., & Pallister, J. G. (2010). Explaining internet banking behavior: Theory of reasoned action, theory of planned behavior, or technology acceptance model? *Journal of Applied Social Psychology*, *40*(5), 1172–1202. doi:10.1111/j.1559-1816.2010.00615.x

Yu, J., Sheng, Q. Z., & Han, Y. (2013). Introduction to special issue on cloud and service computing. *Service Oriented Computing and Applications*, *7*(2), 75–76. doi:10.1007/s11761-013-0132-8

Zacharia, Z. G., Sanders, N. R., & Fugate, B. S. (2014). Evolving functional perspectives within supply chain management. *Journal of Supply Chain Management*, *50*(1), 73–88. doi:10.1111/jscm.12022

Zhang, Q., Cheng, L., & Boutaba, R. (2010). Cloud computing: State-of-the-art and research challenges. *Journal of Internet Services and Applications*, *1*(1), 7–18. doi:10.1007/s13174-010-0007-6

Zhuge, H. (2011). Semantic linking through spaces for cyber-physical-socio intelligence: A methodology. *Artificial Intelligence*, *175*(5-6), 988–1019. doi:10.1016/j.artint.2010.09.009

ADDITIONAL READING

Amies, A., Sluiman, H., Tong, Q. G., & Liu, G. N. (2012). *Developing and hosting applications on the cloud*. Indianapolis, IN: IBM Press.

Berman, S. J., Kesterson-Townes, L., Marshall, A., & Srivathsa, R. (2012). How cloud computing enables process and business model innovation. *Strategy and Leadership*, *40*(4), 27–35. doi:10.1108/10878571211242920

Breeding, M. (2012). *Cloud computing for libraries*. Chicago, IL: American Library Association.

Carlo, J. L., Lyytinen, K., & Rose, G. M. (2011). Internet computing as a disruptive technology: The role of strong order effects. *Information Systems Journal*, *21*(1), 91–122. doi:10.1111/j.1365-2575.2009.00345.x

Chaisiri, S., Lee, B. S., & Niyato, D. (2012). Optimization of resource provisioning cost in cloud computing. *Computer*, *5*(2), 1–32.

Chang, V., Li, C. S., De Roure, D., Wills, G., Walters, R., & Chee, C. (2011). The financial clouds review. *International Journal of Cloud Applications and Computing*, *1*(2), 41–63. doi:10.4018/ijcac.2011040104

Chang, V., Walters, R., & Wills, G. (2012). Business Integration as a Service. *International Journal of Cloud Applications and Computing*, *2*(1), 16–40. doi:10.4018/ijcac.2012010102

Chang, V., Walters, R. J., & Wills, G. (2013). The development that leads to the Cloud Computing Business Framework. *International Journal of Information Management*, *33*(3), 524–538. doi:10.1016/j.ijinfomgt.2013.01.005

Ghezzi, A. (2012). Emerging business models and strategies for mobile platforms providers: A reference framework. *Info*, *14*(5), 36–56. doi:10.1108/14636691211256296

Ghezzi, A., Cortimiglia, M., & Balocco, R. (2012). Mobile content and service delivery platforms: A technology classification model. *Info*, *14*(2), 72–88. doi:10.1108/14636691211204879

Goldner, M. (2011). Winds of change: Libraries and cloud computing. *Multimedia Information & Technology*, *37*(3), 24–28.

Goldner, M., & Birch, K. (2012). Resource sharing in a cloud computing age. *Interlending & Document Supply*, *40*(1), 4–11. doi:10.1108/02641611211214224

Hall, D. J., Huscroft, J. R., Hazen, B. T., & Hanna, J. B. (2013). Reverse logistics goals, metrics, and challenges: Perspectives from industry. *International Journal of Physical Distribution & Logistics Management*, *43*(9), 768–785. doi:10.1108/IJPDLM-02-2012-0052

Han, Y. (2013). IaaS cloud computing services for libraries: Cloud storage and virtual machines. *OCLC Systems & Services: International digital library. Perspectives*, *29*(2), 87–100.

Harmon, R. R., Demirkan, H., & Raffo, D. (2012). Roadmapping the next wave of sustainable IT. *Foresight*, *14*(2), 121–138. doi:10.1108/14636681211222401

Hazen, B. T., & Byrd, T. A. (2012). Toward creating competitive advantage with logistics information technology. *International Journal of Physical Distribution & Logistics Management*, *42*(1), 8–35. doi:10.1108/09600031211202454

Hazen, B. T., Hall, D. J., & Hanna, J. B. (2012). Reverse logistics disposition decision-making: Developing a decision framework via content analysis. *International Journal of Physical Distribution & Logistics Management*, *42*(3), 244–274. doi:10.1108/09600031211225954

Ivanov, D., Sokolov, B., & Kaschel, J. (2011). Integrated supply chain planning based on a combined application of operations research and optimal control. *Central European Journal of Operations Research*, *19*(3), 219–317. doi:10.1007/s10100-010-0185-0

Krikos, A. (2011). Cloud computing as a disruptive technology. *Cloudbook Journal*, *2*(2), 13–18.

Mavodza, J. (2013). The impact of cloud computing on the future of academic library practices and services. *New Library World*, *114*(3-4), 132–141. doi:10.1108/03074801311304041

Neirotti, P., Paolucci, E., & Raguseo, E. (2013). Is it all about size? Comparing organizational and environmental antecedents of IT assimilation in small and medium-sized enterprises. *International Journal of Technology Management*, *61*(1), 82–108. doi:10.1504/IJTM.2013.050245

Ross, P. K. (2011). How to keep your head above the clouds: Changing ICT worker skill sets in a cloud computing environment. *The Employment Relations Record*, *11*(1), 62–74.

Sanders, N. R., & Wagner, S. M. (2011). Multidisciplinary and multimethod research for addressing contemporary supply chain challenges. *Journal of Business Logistics*, *32*(4), 317–323. doi:10.1111/j.0000-0000.2011.01027.x

Sutherland, E. (2013). The enterprise and the digital single market: Business telecommunications. *Info*, *15*(2), 62–72. doi:10.1108/14636691311305425

Tangpong, C. (2011). Content analytic approach to measuring constructs in operations and supply chain management. *Journal of Operations Management*, *29*(6), 627–638. doi:10.1016/j.jom.2010.08.001

Tokar, T., Aloysius, J. A., Waller, M. A., & Williams, B. D. (2011). Retail promotions and information sharing in the supply chain: A controlled experiment. *International Journal of Logistics Management*, *22*(1), 5–25. doi:10.1108/09574091111127534

Truong, H. L., & Dustdar, S. (2012). A survey on cloud-based sustainability governance systems. *International Journal of Web Information Systems*, *8*(3), 278–295. doi:10.1108/17440081211258178

Wu, W. W., Lan, L. W., & Lee, Y. T. (2013). Factors hindering acceptance of using cloud services in university: A case study. *The Electronic Library*, *31*(1), 84–98. doi:10.1108/02640471311299155

KEY TERMS AND DEFINITIONS

Application Software: The complete, self-contained computer program that performs a specific useful task.

Cloud Computing: The process where a task is solved by using a wide variety of technologies, including computers, networks, servers, and the Internet.

Information Processing: The interpretation of the incoming information to make a response suitable within the context of an objective, problem, or situation.

Information Technology: A set of tools, processes, and associated equipment employed to collect, process, and present information.

Internet: A means of connecting a computer to any other computer anywhere in the world via routers and servers.

Network: The operating system that enables users of data communications lines to exchange information over long distances by connecting with each other through a system of routers, servers, switches, and the like.

Operating System: The master control program that automatically runs first when a computer is switched on, and remains in the background until the computer is turned off.

Supply Chain: The entire network of entities, directly or indirectly interlinked and interdependent in serving the same customer.

Supply Chain Management: The management of material and information flow in a supply chain to provide the highest degree of customer satisfaction at the lowest possible cost.

Section 5
Cloud Computing in Health Sector

Chapter 10

Establishing Synergy between Cloud Computing and Colloborative Technology in Medical Informatics

N. Raghavendra Rao
FINAIT Consultancy Services, India

ABSTRACT

The Health care sector needs information driven service. Information is a major resource which is important to health of individual patient and the success of hospitals. The understanding between medical professionals and software professionals can be a main force behind the design, management and use of health care data and information. Health care information systems need to move from traditional integrated database to knowledge based database. Generally, data in health care sector is available as disperse elements; when it is compiled into a meaningful pattern, then it becomes information. And as information is converted into valid basis for action, then it becomes knowledge. This chapter explains making use of the concepts such as cloud computing, pervasive computing, virtual reality along with the other collaborative technology which will facilitate to create knowledge based health care system.

INTRODUCTION

Health has been a concern of major importance across the world. The kind and amount of resources available now are increasing day by day. Technology has been the most important new resource in the present century. Emergence of new tools and devices has been helping the medical profession. Further it is enhancing the medical professionals to offer better service to their patients. Advancements in information and communication technology have been making medicine and medical information systems integrated (Sunitha, & Preethi, 2013). Electronic health or e-health is the result of the above integration. Most of the hospitals in the world have reasonably good information systems to manage the internal administrative and clinical processes for their patients (Vijayrani,

DOI: 10.4018/978-1-4666-8339-6.ch010

2013). Exchange of information in the above infrastructure is mostly confined to their hospital and the hospitals attached to them.

Now it has become a necessity to integrate geographically distributed and organizationally independent organizations for medical information system. This integration gives a scope for designing a knowledge based system for health care sector. The present information and communication technology provides several concepts that enable to develop a health care information system more effectively.

Cloud Computing, Pervasive computing, Virtual Reality and other collaborative technologies are among a number of other concepts provided by information and communication technology. There are two types of approaches prevalent in health care sector. They are 'Conservative approach' and 'Adaptive Change Approach'. The elements in the latter approach are reasoning knowledge based understanding and enlightened creative wisdom blended with professional values. Implementation of emerging concepts in information and communication technology is possible under the latter approach.

NEED FOR KNOWLEDGE BASED SYSTEM

Due to the change in the life style of the people across the Globe, the nuclear family has become the order of the day. There used to be a doctor for each family when the joint family was prevalent. Most of these doctors knew the entire medical history of all the members of the family. These doctors used to organize all the medical services through their professional contacts whenever the family needed their services. The family doctor was considered as a part of the family, philosopher, and guide. The concept of 'Family Doctor" has disappeared today. In the present scenario hospitals are the most important element in health care delivery system. Every time a patient or patient's

relative approaches a hospital, he or she comes with an expectation. What happens next will form an experience. A good experience may increase one's confidence in the hospital and he/she recommends the same hospital to friends and relatives. But a bad experience may dissuade probable patients not to make use of the services provided by a hospital. Health problems and needs are increasing and becoming more complex. The demands and pressures on the hospitals are also increasing. Providing timely service and care is the primary responsibility of all the hospital authorities. The ability to recognize this process and to actively manage it, forms the basis for "Knowledge Based Health Care System".

Health care organizations have a large volume of data which is generated by the number of transactions that take place during the services rendered to patients. One of the greatest difficulties in health care organizations is not so much in gathering data but deciding what needs to be gathered to provide the necessary information and making sure that it is distributed to the right people at the right time and in the right form. "Knowledge Based Health Care System" will be useful in taking care of the above requirements.

Innovative Approach

Globalization has been forcing health care sector to focus on the need for innovative approach in designing and developing knowledge based health care system. The World is poised to take a huge leap at the rate innovation is gaining importance. This is the result of use of enhanced sharing of information and collaborative possibilities provided by cloud computing. Cloud computing (Buyya, Vecchiola, & Selvi, 2013) provides infrastructure for creation of virtual hospitals with knowledge based health care system. The following case illustration gives an idea of developing knowledge based health care information system by a hospital in India.

CASE ILLUSTRATION 1

A team of four medical doctors started a medical consulting center a decade ago at Chennai in India. They have taken a small area in a big building on rent. The area taken on rent could accommodate two doctors and twenty patients at any point of time in a day. These doctors would provide their services in their areas of specialization. It was because of the constraint in the space they have agreed among themselves to the specific time allotted to each doctor for their consultancy. They had a tie up with the selected clinical laboratories and investigating medical equipments Centers. These doctors would refer their patients to these centers for tests and investigations. Medical consulting center had a standalone system with readymade application software for health care information system. This readymade application software would support some basic functions required by the doctors. Over a period of time much advancement has taken place in the area of information and communication technology. To take advantage of these advancements, they have changed to an integrated health care information system in a relation database under client server technology. The new system has been more useful to the doctors in their professional work.

"Diagnosis" is the essence of patient's health management. The doctors at the medical consulting center have proved themselves to be good at correct diagnosis and appropriate treatment. India has been becoming more popular as one of the good health care service providers in the globalization scenario. Consequent to this many patients across the globe started preferring India for their health care destination. Some of the patients have been keen to visit medical consulting center at Chennai.

This has led the doctors at the center to start a separate fully fledged hospital with the advanced infrastructure. Care plus Cure hospital limited has been established by them. Many more specialists have joined the hospital to serve. The hospital has acquired the latest medical equipments for investigations. The hospital has set up its own clinical laboratories for testing. The hospital has been particular to concentrate on the following areas besides providing the regular health care services. The areas are 1) Medical Research 2) Medical education to patients 3) Developing formulas for medicines with the collaboration with the reputed pharmaceutical companies 4) Information for acquiring medical equipments 5) Sharing medical knowledge with the students of medicine 6) Providing hospital management systems to the hospitals who want to make use of this service.

Core teams in the hospital consisting of medical doctors who have knowledge in information and communication technology and software professionals have designed, developed and have been managing the system.

Many young medical doctors in India are evincing interest to start medical centers in the rural areas. They are looking for medical information system to support in their ventures. Care plus Cure hospital limited has been extending its service to the young medical doctors in their venture. It is interesting to note that cloud computing and the collaborative technologies are the main components for the creation of "Care plus Cure" integrated health care system. Figure-1 illustrates the integrated hospital management system at Care plus Cure Hospital Limited.

GOALS OF CARE PLUS CURE HOSPITAL LIMITED

Every enterprise has mission and vision goal for its enterprise. Care plus Cure hospital Limited has realized the need for an integrated health care system under cloud computing environment. Their health care system is designed to support the following.

Figure 1. Integrated hospital management system

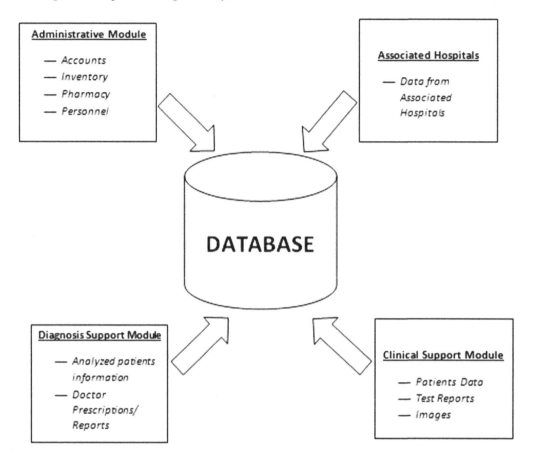

1. **Mission:** To provide health care and health care related services to their hospital and the needs of the other hospitals.
2. **Strategy:** Designing integrating information health care system to support their mission.
3. **Health Care Process Models:** Developing medical information process models to accomplish their strategy.
4. **Hospital Functions:** To define the technology infrastructure needed for supporting the data and application in the health care system.
5. **Standards:** To document the required standards for hospitals.

CLOUD COMPUTING IN HEALTH CARE SECTOR

Making use of cloud capabilities is more than the latest technology. It is moving from traditional model to knowledge based model. Medical doctors, medical students, patients, and research scholars are the main participants in the latter model. It is much more important for the health care sector to understand the changing trends in the information and communication technology. The changing trends help health care sector also define the best strategy to leverage cloud computing. Basically cloud computing can divide the data center into application cloud, hardware cloud, and computing cloud. Adoption of the cloud idea itself emphasizes that it is a mixture of centralized and distributed architecture.

CLOUD COMPUTING PROVIDES THE FOLLOWING ADVANTAGES

1. **Investment on infrastructure**: Capital Investment optimizes the reduction of costs of hardware and software. This investment helps hospitals to make use of economies of scale and operational costs in information and communication technology.
2. **Innovative Approach**: Developing models under cloud computing environment facilitate to adopt innovative approach in health care information system.
3. **Electronic Devices:** Most of the electronic devices are connected to the internet. Internet is the main access in the cloud computing environment. Electronic Devices are more useful in a health care system.

PRIVATE CLOUD ENVIRONMENT IN CAR PLUS CURE HOSPITAL LIMITED

There are four different models under cloud computing concept with different characteristics. Care plus Cure hospital limited has chosen private cloud for their information system. Private cloud (Chorafas, 2011) is considered to be suitable for maintaining sensitive data in health care systems. Private cloud can be said to be a private data center and residing within the organization. This data center is exclusive for the use of their organization. This is shared and multi user environment built on highly efficient, automated and virtualized infrastructure. The advantage of Private cloud is setting up and managing the cloud services under the control of the enterprise who owns it. The

enterprise can take a better control of security and regulatory compliance issues. Private cloud is a better solution for health care organizations in leveraging the benefits of cloud computing within their firewall.

VIRTUAL ENVIRONMENT

One of the big changes that is emerging in the present globalization scenario is virtual environment. This has given a scope for virtual medical conferences, virtual consultations and even virtual hospitals. The professional isolation that is experienced by so many professionals working away from distant places has become largely a thing of the past. Now they can take part in interactive exchanges and have access to online knowledge bases and expertise as anyone and anywhere in the World. The idea behind choosing private cloud by care plus cure hospital limited is to provide health care services under virtual environment.

VIRTUAL REALITY IN VIRTUAL ENVIRONMENT

Virtual reality is a way of creating a three dimensional image of an object or scene. It is possible for the user to move through or around the image. Virtual reality imitates the way the real object or scene looks and changes. Information system helps to use information in databases to stimulate. The line dividing simulated tasks and their real world counter parts is very thin. Virtual reality systems are designed to produce in the participant the cognitive effects of feeling immersed in the environment created by computer system. The computer system uses sensory inputs such as vision, hearing, feeling and sensation of motion. The concept of multimedia is required in virtual reality process. The components of multimedia are tactile (Touch), Visual (Image) and auditory (Sound).

The concept of virtual reality is more useful for showing the advancements taking place in the health care sector especially in the area of surgery. Medical students will be benefited by upgrading their knowledge. Simulated tasks replicate the real medical tasks. Care plus Cure hospital Limited wants to make use of this concept in explaining the latest developments in surgery to medical students.

RESEARCH ACTIVITIES IN HEALTH CARE SECTOR

Certain diseases are peculiar to certain countries (Auewarkul, 2008). An independent research center or a center for a group of hospitals can be established to analyze the disease and its causes. Many samples of information are required for analysis. Generally database in any hospital has the current information only to optimize the use of database. The data from the database are transferred to historical database as backup.

Four types of hospital enterprises provide medical services in India (Govil, & Purohit, 2011). They are 1) Corporate Hospitals 2) Government Hospitals 3) Hospitals managed by a group of trustees and 4) Nursing homes. Care plus Cure Hospitals limited along with some of the above mentioned hospitals have agreed to have a joint research center. Care plus Cure Hospitals limited is ready to store their data along with the data of other hospitals in their private cloud. It is mutually agreed that the data is to be used for research purpose only. Historical data and spatial data collected from several databases from different hospitals are stored in one database under private cloud at Care plus Cure hospitals limited. Private cloud provides an extremely useful activity in the medical field for research. Figure-2 gives an overview of medical research base at Care plus Cure Hospital Limited.

Data ware house concept is used by the above hospitals for their research work. Data ware house is a central store of data that is extracted either from

Figure 2. Medical research base

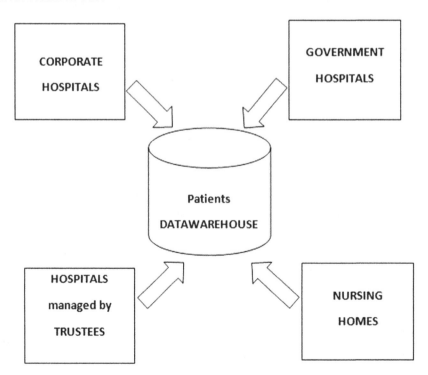

operational data base or from historical data base. The data in data ware house is subject oriented, non-volatile and of a historical nature. So data ware house tends to contain extremely large data sets. It can be inferred that the purpose of data ware house is 1) To slice and dice through data 2) To ensure that past data is stored accurately 3) To provide one version of data 4) To operate for analytical process and 5) To support the decision process.

Data Mining (Pujari K, 2003) is a concept used in Data ware house. Data Mining deals with discovering hidden data and unexpected patterns and rules in large data base. The terms "Data Mining" and KDD (Knowledge Discovery in Databases) are considered as synonyms. At the first international conference on KDD in Montreal in the year 1995, it was proposed that the term "KDD" be employed to describe the whole process of extraction of knowledge from data. In this context knowledge means relationships and patterns between data and elements. It was proposed that the term "Data Mining" (Adriaans, & Zantinge, 1999) should be used exclusively for the discovery stage of the KDD process. It is clear that KDD is not an activity that stands on its own. A good foundation in terms of data ware house is a necessary condition for effective implementation. Four types of knowledge can be identified in Data Mining. They are 1) Shallow Knowledge 2) Multi-Dimensional Knowledge 3) Hidden Knowledge 4) Deep Knowledge

SHALLOW KNOWLEDGE

Information can be easily retrieved from databases using a query tool such as structured query language (SQL)

MULTI-DIMENSIONAL KNOWLEDGE

Information can be analyzed using online analytical processing tools.

HIDDEN KNOWLEDGE

Data can be found relatively easily by using pattern recognition or machine learning algorithms.

DEEP KNOWLEDGE

Information that is stored in the database can be located if one has a clue that tells the user where to look.

INFORMATION AT A HOSPITAL LEVEL

The primary entity for a hospital is the patient. The information pertaining to patients such as activities, habits, health problems, treatment and reactions to medicines may be available at a particular hospital where all the services needed are provided to patients. The information pertaining to the services rendered may be available in a same database or different databases and at different locations.

The required information transferred to data ware house in the private cloud at Care plus Cure Hospitals is limited for research. Combinations of data ware house and data mining indicates an innovative approach to information management. Private cloud environment at Care plus Cure hospital limited has given a strategic source of opportunity to the doctors attached to the various hospitals to be a part of research group for making use of their medical knowledge and experience in the area of research.

CASE ILLUSTRATION 2

The doctors have been highlighting some of the side effects of the drugs prescribed by them to their patients at the various medical conferences being held in India. It has been the practice among some of the pharmaceutical companies to send their executives in their R and D Departments to attend these conferences. On Call pharma Limited which has a base in India has felt it would be better to associate with a hospital to analyze the medical cases for improving and discovering a drug. On the basis of the proposal submitted by the above pharmaceutical company, Care plus Cure Hospitals Limited has accepted their proposal and is ready to share the data with them for discovering a drug. It has been mutually agreed that discovering a drug (Bandopadhyay, 2013) should be on a rational approach. Further it has been agreed to create a core team consisting of medical doctors, paramedical professionals, research executives and information technology professionals for this project. Members of the core team are from On Call Pharma Limited, Care plus Cure Hospital Limited and the professionals from the hospitals associated with Care plus Cure hospitals limited. The data in the private cloud at Care plus Cure hospital limited will be the base for research purpose.

DISCOVERY OF A DRUG

A Drug is a molecule that interacts with target biological molecule in the body and through such interaction triggers a physiological effect. The target molecules are usually proteins. Drugs can be beneficial or harmful depending on their effect. The aim of discovering a drug is with specific beneficial effects to treat diseases in human beings.

Discovering a drug can be arrived by two methods (Ignacimuthu, 2005). The methods are empirical and rational. Empirical method is a blind or loose method. It is also called black box method. Thousands of chemical compounds are tested on the disease without even knowing the target on which the drug acts and the mechanism of action. Rational method starts from the clear knowledge of the target as well as the mechanism by which it is to be attacked. Drugs act either to stimulate or block the activity of the target protein.

ROLE OF BIO-INFORMATICS IN DRUG DISCOVERY

Bio Informatics is the storage, manipulation, and analysis of biological information by making use of information technology. Bio Informatics is an essential infrastructure under pinning biological research (Bergeron, 2003). Adoption of bioinformatics based approach to drug discovery provides an important advantage in rational approach.

BIOLOGICAL DATA

The properties that characterize a living organism (Species) are based on its fundamental set of genetics information. It is important to understand the fundamental aspects of terms such as DNA, RNA, Protein and their information in relation to Genome.

Different sequences of bases in DNA specify different sequences of bases in RNA. The sequence of bases in RNA specifies the sequences of amino acids in proteins. The central dogma states that DNA is transcribed into RNA which is then translated later into protein (Teresa, & David, 2005).

The main advantage in Bioinformatics discipline is biological data are available on the various web sites (Krane, & Raymer, 2005). The databases in these websites can be classified into two types such as generalized and specialized databases. The generalized databases contain information related to DNA, Protein or similar types. The generalized databases can again be further split into sequence databases and structured databases. Sequence databases hold the individual sequence records of either nucleotides or amino acids or proteins. Structured databases contain the individual sequence records of bio-chemically solved structures of macro-molecules.

Specialized databases are 1) EST (Expressed Sequence Tags) 2) GSS (Genome Survey Sequences) 3) SNP (Single Nucleotide Polymorphism) 4) STS (Sequence Tag Sites) 5) KABAT for Immunology Proteins and LIGAND for enzymes reaction legends. These databases can be further split into three types based on the complexity of the data stored.

1. **Primary Databases:** These databases contain data in its original form from the sequences.
2. **Secondary Databases:** These databases have value added data and derived information from the primary databases.
3. **Composite Databases:** Composite databases amalgamate a variety of different primary databases structured into one. There are various software tools available to facilitate search in the above databases.

Developing or designing a drug is possible by making use of the information in the diverse chemical libraries along with the information pertaining to biological functions stored in the above databases before starting laboratory based experiment. It is always possible to generate as much information as possible about potential drug and target interaction from the above databases and chemical libraries.

ENVIRONMENTAL DATA IN HEALTH CARE MANAGEMENT

Care plus Cure Hospital limited plans to emulate the UK experience in the environmental data in health care management. It is interesting to note a database containing environmental conditions and diagnosis at a patient's surroundings can be made use of in health care system. This will facilitate in diagnosing and providing treatment for an individual patient. This was a pioneer health care system for diagnosing and monitoring asthma patients via internet. This was introduced before Cloud computing came into existence.

Care plus Cure Hospitals limited wants to collate data from different parts in India and monitor the patients, since they have the patient's data in the private cloud environment (Kumar, & Joy, 2013).

Middle Sex University has created a central disease management system. Asthma patients and those with a chronic obstructive pulmonary disease would use a portable monitoring device to record breathing patterns up to four times a day in the comfort of their homes. The data was sent via modem and telephone lines to central disease management system. It was processed and results were sent to the patient's doctor using the cable and wireless secure internet way. This system would record the date and time, temperature and humidity measures critical for analyzing the health of asthma patient's surroundings such as air pollution and quality which would assist in providing the correct treatment and diagnosis for individual patients. More over patients would record their symptoms and use of medication as well as their lung functions data in central disease management which would contain two parts of data in respect of asthma patients. One part of data would be in respect of patient's data pertaining to date and time, temperature and humidity measure. The second part of data would relate to environmental condition, air pollution and quality.

NEED FOR SELF LEARNING AMONG MEDICAL STUDENTS

Learning any subject and in depth understanding of it requires that learners actively construct their own personal meanings of the things they learn and integrate with their prior knowledge and skills. Medical students once they qualify themselves as professionals bear the responsibility for translating their in depth knowledge into practice. As their skills grow learners can work towards enhancing themselves and improving both competence and confidence.

The knowledge based system developed at Care plus Cure Hospitals limited provides the mechanism of interaction with their system. Patient Data Ware House in their system is useful for evidence based information resource. A medical student or a doctor makes use of the knowledge based system to get answers for the questions formulated on the basis of "Background" of a particular disorder/disease and "Fore Ground" of treatment of the patients concerned.

CASE ILLUSTRATION 3

Mr. X is an accounts executive in a private firm in India. He is 52 years old moderately obese with type 2 diabetes, diagnosed 11 years ago. He has been trying to quit his smoking habit of 25 years. No diabetic complications have been detected so far. His blood sugar is well controlled. But his blood pressure has been mildly elevated averaging 158/94 mm HG during the past three visits to the hospital. He has been unable to reduce his weight during the past two years despite his doctor's suggestion. He is also not keen to further medicate himself preferring "Natural Remedies". However he is open to taking medicines if their efficacy proved in lowering his blood pressure and blood sugar. As an accounts executive, he wants to quantify the result of additional medication prescribed. The data related to the above patient

is available in the patient data ware house, at Care plus Cure Hospitals limited in the private cloud environment. Each patient's information is stored under three groups. They are 1) History of the patient 2) History of the treatment prescribed, and 3) Summary of treatment given to the patients of similar complaints.

1. History of a patient consists of diagnosis, habits, tests conducted, test results, treatments, allergies, and reactions.
2. History of the treatment prescribed covers drugs prescribed, composition of drugs, dosage, precautions, and likely reactions.
3. The data related to the patients of similar complaints is available under the separate head in the patient's data ware house.

A medical student or a doctor has to search from the basis of diseases and the treatments prescribed to similar patients. They can review the information downloaded from the patient data ware house and can prepare an abstract. They can compare with the treatment perceived by the medical student or a doctor. This helps them to assess their knowledge in a particular case.

ANALYSIS OF THE APPROACH OF CARE PLUS CURE HOSPITAL LTD

Care plus Cure Hospital limited has created a knowledge based health care system. The idea behind creation of medical informatics system under the cloud computing environment is for easy accessibility by them and other hospitals associated with them. One more salient feature of the cloud computing is it enables delivery of business models for IT services over the internet. Further most of the electronic devices are connected to the Internet. Care plus Cure Hospital Limited has felt that it is an advantage to make use of private cloud computing for their requirements. Core team at Care plus Cure Hospital limited has made use of the collaborative technology in the private cloud computing environment to create a virtual hospital enterprise. Virtual hospital enterprise approach is to extend its services to the hospitals attached to them. Following paragraphs indicate the benefits derived by this approach.

HOSPITALS IN RURAL AREAS

Medical fraternity who started the hospitals in the rural areas in India has taken advantage of the integrated hospital management system at Care+Cure hospital limited. More over medical doctors are the part of the core team for designing and developing the system. The integrated hospital management system provides the benefits such as 1) Validation of data across the system 2) Parameterization in application software 3) Multilevel security 4) Multilevel authorization 5) Reduction in patients' waiting time 6) Elimination of wastage of stationery 7) Accuracy of Data 8) Educating Patients 9) Analysis of the reactions of medicines, and 10) Better co-ordination among different departments. Further their data is stored in the above system and is available to the broad group of users at different locations.

DRUG DESIGN

The purpose behind Care plus Cure Hospital Limited and hospitals associated with them is designing a drug with On Call Pharma limited. They have actual data of medicines prescribed and the reactions on their patients. This data is most important for research in designing a drug. Private cloud provides the required space for storing and analysis. Rational method in designing a drug needs data from genial and the specialized databases in bio informatics.

The research team could make use of data related to the components of drugs prescribed and the relations on the patients for guidance for their

research. This approach emphasizes the need for integrating health service research and designing research to reduce reactions on the patients. It is expected this approach will be better before laboratory tests take place in respect of new drugs produced. Figure 3 illustrates rational approach for discovery and development of drugs.

MEDICAL RESEARCH ACTIVITIES

Any Research needs a large volume of data for research. There is not dearth of medical data in India. It is general practice in many hospitals in India for the sake of optimizing the use of database; their databases contain one year data only. The earlier years' data either is transferred to another system as back up or deleted. The historical data is never made use of for any research purpose. Care plus Cure Hospital limited has initiated the process of the historical data of the patients of the hospitals associated with them for research. They could persuade corporate hospitals, Government hospitals, hospitals managed by trustees, and nursing homes to transfer the historical data of their patients to the patient data ware house in their private cloud environment. Medical doctors who have research bent of mind working in the above hospitals are associated with the research. The doctors at these hospitals need not move out of their hospitals for their research work. This has become possible because of private cloud environment and access through internet. They can conduct research with ease from their work place by making use of data mining tool in the patient data ware house in the system.

VIRTUAL REALITY CONCEPT UNDER PRIVATE CLOUD ENVIRONMENT

The inputs provided by the medical doctor who performed surgical operations by them is the lat-

Figure 3. Rational base approach for discovery and development of drugs

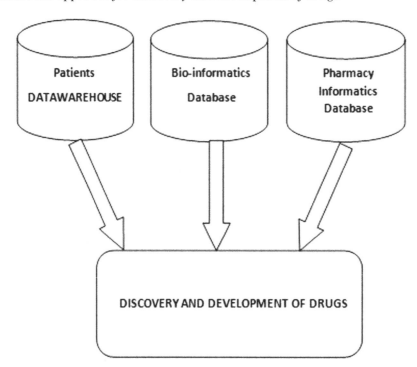

est methodology, core team will develop a model. This model will consider the real medical world requirements. Parameters will be created on the basis of the requirements. Simulated version of human body is designed and operation is carried out in the computer systems in the private cloud environment. Medical doctors in the core team have immersed themselves in every aspect of the design and testing. They have worked in front of a large screen of a computer, which has given a sense of surgical operation is taking place in the real medical world situation. The concept of virtual has helped them to look from the real medical world situation. Private cloud environment has facilitated the above process with virtual reality.

Medical doctors working at Care plus Cure Hospital Limited, the hospitals associated with them and medical students can take advantage of updating themselves the advancements made in the surgical operations. It is said visualization is more effective than giving a detailed description of an event (Epstetin, & Macvoy, 2011).

EMULATING AN INNOVATIVE APPROACH

Some years ago a telemedicine project was implemented in the United Kingdom. The participants of this project were telecommunication firm, Consortium of Industrial Academia, Clinical Partners across Europe including university college, London, Middle Sex University, A German medical diagnostic Business, The Whittington Hospital National Health Service Trust (North London) and Spains Hospital General.

The main essence of this project was the use of portable monitoring device to record breathing patterns in the comfort of the patient's home. Modem and telephone lines were made use of sending data to central disease management system where it would be processed and results sent directly to the patient's consultant using the cable and wireless secure internet gateway.

The Core team at the Care plus Cure Hospital Limited has taken a lead from the above project.

The team is evaluating the various portable medical devices on the similar type of project. Cloud computing has all the required features to support this type of project. In order to provide good health care to their patients in India and foreign Countries, the core team is working on this project. Once this model is developed and tested, there will be advantages to the patients. This model aims to save patient patient's time and travel expenses. Further it reduces stress as they no longer have to visit the hospitals so frequently and do not have to keep paper records to monitor health. The core team wants to make use of their private cloud computing environment for developing this model with the various portable medical devices.

EVIDENCE BASED LEARNING

Patient Data Ware House at Care plus Cure Hospital Limited is useful for evidenced based learning. A medical student can make use of this data ware house to get answers for the questions formulated on the basis of "Background" of a particular disorder/disease and 'for ground' of treatment concerned. Patient data ware house contains the case history of the patients treated at various hospitals for learning purposes.

Three Dimensional Visualization has the great potential in medical education and training. By making use of virtual reality concepts doctors and medical students can practice the surgical procedures. Pilots have been training on flight simulators for decades. The simulators are realistic that the trainee pilots before their first real flight can perform thousands of perfect take off and landing. Same way the medical students can learn the surgical skills before operating on the first patient. Figure 4 provides an idea of evidenced based learning.

MEDICAL INFORMATION TO PATIENTS

Increasing number of people seeking information pertaining to disease/symptoms/drugs/reactions is on the increase. One cannot be sure of the authenticity of the information available on the net.

Care plus Cure Hospital Limited has created an exclusive database in their system for their patients. This database provides the required information to dispel doubts arising in the minds of their patients. Access to this database is possible by their patients through internet to private cloud environment.

DEVICE MANAGEMENT

The need for device management is obvious in cloud computing environment. Heterogeneous devices, applications, and users needs are to be administered. The important functionality of a pervasive device is to perform a task with high speed. For each application and type of device it has to support different kinds of user interfaces. The main requirement of device management is to take care of operating system, structure, memory protection, security and multi tasking.

HEALTH CARE SYSTEM UNDER CLOUD COMPUTING

Knowledge based health care system developed by Care plus Cure Hospital Limited proves that a useful system can be developed for medical fraternity. Main significance in the system is making use of private cloud along with the collaborative technology. This system can increase the chances of successfully diffusing knowledge, technology and process. Advanced concepts in information

Figure 4. Evidence based learning

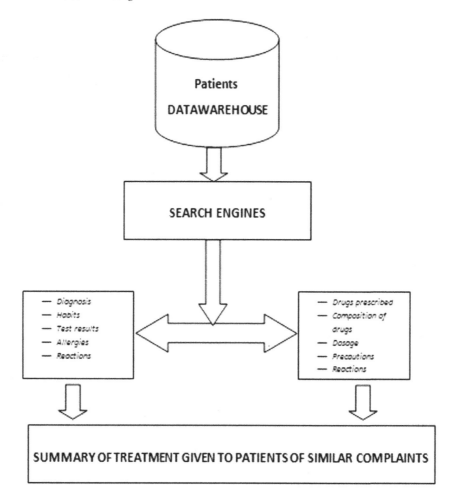

and communication technology have drastically changed the medical informatics, providing new services and creating an inter connected medical fraternity.

FUTURE TRENDS

Many more requirements in the area of medical informatics will be needed. There will be increased use of cloud computing concepts with collaborative technologies. In the era of globalization, cloud computing will provide a lot of scope for developing knowledge based health care models. There is a good scope for research scholars to develop innovative models in health care sector.

CONCLUSION

In today's knowledge rich environment, information and communication technology has increased virtualization in the activities of health care sector and ways of working. The term "Virtual" is now appearing in many forms. Knowledge based health care system at Care plus Cure Hospital Limited explains the need for adopting innovative approach in involving medical fraternity by applying the concept of "Mind invoking".

It may be observed that Care+ plus Cure Hospital Limited has made use of the services of the core team in designing and developing a system for health care sector.

Hospitals will find that private cloud is better solution for them in leveraging the benefits of cloud computing within their firewall. Care plus Cure Hospital Limited has proved the concept of virtual hospital which is the key to cloud computing. It will be beneficial for virtual hospitals sharing the common resources for computing power and accessing data across the globe.

REFERENCES

Adrains, P., & Zantinge, D. (1999). *Data Mining*. England: Addison Wesley Longman.

Attwood, T. K., & Parry, S. D. J. (2005). *Introduction to Bioinformatics; New Delhi: Pearson Education*. Singapore: Private Limited.

Auewarkul, P. (2008). The Past and Present Threat of Avian Influenza in Thailand. In E. M. Yichenlu & B. Roberts (Eds.), *Emerging Infections in Asia* (pp. 31–34). New York, NY: Springer. doi:10.1007/978-0-387-75722-3_2

Bandopadhyay, D. (2013, December). A Technology Lead Business Model for Pharma: Collaborative Patient Care. *CSI Communications Journal, 37*(9), 12–26.

Bergeron, B. (2003). *Bioinformatics Computing; New Delhi: Pearson Education*. Singapore: Private Limited.

Buyya, R., Vecchiola, C., & Selvi, T. S. (2013). *Mastering Cloud Computing. New Delhi: McGraw Hill Education*. India: Private Limited.

Chorafas, D. N. (2011). *Cloud Computing Strategies*. Boca Raton: CRC Press Taylor & Francis Group.

Epstein, R. A., & Macvoy, S. P. (2011). Making A Scene in the Brain. In L. R. Harris & M. R. M. Jenkin (Eds.), *Vision in 3D Environments* (pp. 270–273). Cambridge: Cambridge University Press. doi:10.1017/CBO9780511736261.012

Govil, D., & Prohit, N. (2011). Health Care Systems in India. In H. S. Rout (Ed.), *Health Care Systems – A Global Survey* (pp. 576–612). New Delhi: New Century Publications.

Ignacimuthu, S. (2005). *Basic Informatics*. New Delhi: Narosa Publishing House.

Krane, D. E., & Raymer, M. L. (2005). *Fundamental Concepts of Bioinformatics; New Delhi: Pearson Education*. Singapore: Private Limited.

Kumar, K. L., & Joy, J. (2013, December). Application of Zigbee Wireless Frequency for Patient Monitoring System; Mumbai. *CSI Communications Journal, 37*(9), 17–18.

Pujari, A. K. (2003). *Data Mining Techniques; Hyderabad: Universities Press*. India: Private Limited.

Sunitha, C., Kokilam, V. K., & Preethi, M. B. (2013, December). Medical Informatics-Perk up Health Care through Information; Mumbai. *CSI Communications Journal, 37*(9), 7–8.

Vijayrani, S. (2013, December). Economic Health Records: An Overview. Mumbai. *CSI Communications Journal, 37*(9), 9–11.

KEY TERMS AND DEFINITIONS

Collaborative Technology: Various concepts in information and communication technology facilitate to work jointly in developing an application software.

Core Team: A team consisting of domain experts to perform a multi disciplinary activities.

Globalization: The process by which business starts operating on a global scale.

Knowledge Based System: Information system containing information and skills gained through experience of education.

Pervasive Device: A piece of equipment made for a particular purpose. User will be able to use both local and remote services.

Software Tool: A readymade software is developed to perform a particular task in a computer system.

Virtual Reality: A system in which images that look like real, three dimensional objects are created by a computer system.

Pervasive Computing: This is a new dimension of personal computing that integrates mobile communication, ubiquitous embedded computer system, and consumer electronics with the power of internet.

Mind Invoking: Making an earnest effort in an innovative approach.

Data Ware House: A subject-Oriented, integrated, time variant, non volatile collection of data in support of management's decision making process.

Data Mining: The process of analyzing large data sets in a data ware house to find number of obvious patterns.

Private Cloud: A Cloud computing like environment within the boundaries of an organization and typically for its exclusive use, typically hosted on an enterprises private network.

Section 6
Technical Issues in Cloud Computing

Chapter 11
Heuristic Task Consolidation Techniques for Energy Efficient Cloud Computing

Dilip Kumar
National Institute of Technology, India

Bibhudatta Sahoo
National Institute of Technology, India

Tarni Mandal
National Institute of Technology, India

ABSTRACT

The energy consumption in the cloud is proportional to the resource utilization and data centers are almost the world's highest consumers of electricity. The complexity of the resource allocation problem increases with the size of cloud infrastructure and becomes difficult to solve effectively. The exponential solution space for the resource allocation problem can be searched using heuristic techniques to obtain a sub-optimal solution at the acceptable time. This chapter presents the resource allocation problem in cloud computing as a linear programming problem, with the objective to minimize energy consumed in computation. This resource allocation problem has been treated using heuristic approaches. In particular, we have used two phase selection algorithm 'FcfsRand', 'FcfsRr', 'FcfsMin', 'FcfsMax', 'MinMin', 'MedianMin', 'MaxMin', 'MinMax', 'MedianMax', and 'MaxMax'. The simulation results indicate in the favor of MaxMax.

1. INTRODUCTION

Cloud computing infrastructures are designed to support the accessibility and deployment of various service oriented applications by the users (Hwang, Fox, & Dongarra, 2012; Mell & Grance, 2011). Cloud computing services are made available through the server firms or data centers. The concept of cloud computing has been emerging from the concept of heterogeneous distributed computing, grid computing, utility computing and autonomic computing (Buyya, Broberg,

DOI: 10.4018/978-1-4666-8339-6.ch011

& Goscinski, 2010b; Mezmaz et al., 2011). A cloud computing is the convergence of 3 major trends, these trends are Virtualization, Utility components, and Software as a service. To meet the growing demand for computations and large volume of data, the cloud computing environment provides high performance servers and high speed mass storage devices (Beloglazov, Abawajy, & Buyya, 2012). These resources are the major source of the power consumption in data centers along with air conditioning and cooling equipment (Rodero et al., 2010). Moreover the energy consumption in the cloud is proportional to the resource utilization and data centers are almost the world's highest consumers of electricity (Buyya, Beloglazov, & Abawajy, 2010a). Due to the high energy consumption by data centers, it requires efficient technology to design green data center (Liu et al., 2009). Cloud data center, on the other hand, can reduce the energy consumed through server consolidation, whereby different workloads can share the same server or physical host using virtualization and hence un-used servers or physical host can be switched off.

Power management represents a collection of IT processes and supporting technologies geared toward optimizing data center performance against cost and structural constraints. This includes increasing the deploy-able number of servers per rack, when the racks are subject to power or thermal limitations, and making power consumption more predictable and easier to plan for. Power manager comes in two categories: static and dynamic. Static power management deals with fixed power caps to manage aggregate power, while the policies under dynamic power management take advantage of additional degrees of freedom inherent through virtualization, as well as the dynamic behaviors supported by advanced platform power management technologies (ITU, 2012).

Generally, clouds are deployed to customers giving them three levels of access: Software-as-a-Service (SaaS), Platform-as-a-Service (PaaS), and Infrastructure-as-a-Service (IaaS). Clouds use virtualization technology in distributed data centers to allocate resources to customers as they need them. The task originated by the customer can differ greatly from customer to the customer. Entities in the Cloud are autonomous and self-interested; however, they are willing to share their resources and services to achieve their individual and collective goals. In such an open environment, the scheduling decision is a challenge given the decentralized nature of the environment. Each entity has specific requirements and objectives that need to achieve. Server consolidation is allowing the multiple servers running on a single physical server simultaneously to minimize the energy consumed in a data center (Ye, Huang, Jiang, Chen, & Wu, 2010). Running the multiple servers on a single physical server are realized through virtual machine concept. The task consolidation is also known as server/workload consolidation problem (Lee & Zomaya, 2012). Resource allocation problem discussed in this chapter is the task consolidation problem on cloud data center. Task consolidation problem addressed in this chapter is to assign n task to a set of r resources in a cloud computing environment. This energy efficient load management maintains the utilization of all computing nodes and distributes virtual machines in a way that is energy efficient. The goal of this algorithm is to maintain availability to compute nodes while reducing the total power consumed by the cloud.

Cloud computing resources are managed through the centralized resource manager. The centralized resource manager assigned the tasks to the appropriate VMs. The resources of cloud data center are available to the users/applications through Virtual Machines (VMs). Virtual Machines are used to meet the resource requirement and run time support for the applications. In particular executing an application for required resource can be made available through two steps: creating an instance of the virtual machine as required by the application (VMs provisioning) and scheduling the request to the physical resources otherwise known as resource provisioning (Rodero et al., 2010). The Virtual Machine (VM) here is to describe the operating system concept: a software abstraction with the looks of a computer system's hardware (real machine) (Rosenblum, 2004). A virtual machine is sufficiently similar to the underlying physical machine running existing software unmodified. The VM technology has become popular in recent years in data centers and cloud computing environments because it has a number of benefits including server consolidation, live migration, and security isolation. Cloud computing is based on the concept of virtualization that encapsulates various services that can meet the user requirement in a cloud computing environment (Jing,, Ali, She, & Zhong, 2013). Virtual machines (VMs) are designed to run on a server to provide a multiple OS environment with the support of various applications. One or more VM(s) can be placed or deployed on a physical machine that meet the requirement for the VM. The task can be scheduled dynamic to have the load balanced among the hosts in cloud computing environments. Task consolidation is an aim to maximize utilization of cloud computing resources. Maximizing resource utilization provides various benefits such as the rationalization of maintenance, IT service customization, QoS and reliable services, etc.

The energy efficiency of clouds has become one of most crucial research issues (Lee & Zomaya, 2012). Advancements in hardware technologies (Venkatachalam & Franz, 2005), such as low power CPUs, solid state drives, and energy efficient computer monitors have helped relieve this energy issue to a certain degree. In the meantime, there also have been a considerable amount of research conducted using software approaches, such as scheduling, server consolidation (Lee & Zomaya, 2012) and task consolidation (Srikantaiah, Kansal, & Zhao, 2008).

Task scheduling problems are related to the efficiency of all cloud computing facilities and are of paramount importance. Scheduling algorithms in distributed systems usually have the goal of spreading the load on the processors and maximizing their utilization while minimizing the total task execution time (zomaya & Yee, 2011). Task scheduling, one of the best known combinatorial optimization problems, plays a key role in improving flexible and reliable distributed systems. Its main purpose is to schedule tasks over resources dynamically, taking into account the resources available for execution, which involves the discovery of a suitable sequence in which tasks can be executed under transaction logic constraints (Zhao & Zhang, 2001). The task consolidation problem in a cloud computing environment has been shown, in general, to be NP-complete, requiring the development of heuristic techniques. The complexity of the resource allocation problem increases with the size of cloud infrastructure and becomes difficult to solve effectively. The exponential solution space for the resource allocation problem can search using heuristic techniques to obtain a suboptimal solution at the acceptable time. This chapter formulated the resource allocation problem in cloud computing as a linear programming problem, with the objective to minimize energy consumed in computation. A set of ten greedy heuristics for task consolidation algorithms have been used to solve task consolidation problem. All these heuristics from the literature have been selected: adapted, implemented, and analyzed under one set of common assumptions considering ETC task model. These heuristic algorithms are greedy algorithm and operate in two phases, selection of task from the task pool, followed by selection of cloud resource. The greedy paradigm provides a framework to design an algorithm that works in stages, considering one input at a time. At each stage a particular input is selected through a selection procedure. Then a decision is made regarding the selected input, whether to include it into the partially constructed optimal solution. The selection procedure can be realized using a 2-phase heuristic. In particular, we have used 'FcfsRand', 'FcfsRr', 'FcfsMin', 'FcfsMax',

'MinMin', 'MedianMin', 'MaxMin', 'MinMax', 'MedianMax', and 'MaxMax'. The simulation results indicate in favor of MaxMax. In MaxMax the first Max indicates the task has to be selected which required the Maximum resource utilization and the second Max indicate that the resource are allocated for that task, which is maximum utilized and also it can compute the selected task without exceeding the peak load. The performance of these algorithms has been analyzed with in house simulator designed using Matlab. This discrete event simulation uses the task set represented as ETC matrix.

The remainder of this chapter is organized as follows. Section 2, discusses related research work on energy aware scheduling and resource allocation for cloud computing systems. Section 3 presents the model of cloud computing system, task model and energy consumption of the system. Based upon this system model, we have defined the Linear Programming Problem to minimize the energy in a cloud computing environment in Section 4. In Section 5 discusses the different heuristic allocation algorithms to allocate tasks to VMs. Section 6 discusses our simulation setup and analyses the obtained simulation results. Finally, conclusions and directions for future research are discussed in Section 7.

2. BACKGROUND

Current research in the area of cloud computing load balancing focuses on the availability of resources. The specific load balancing approach depends on the type of resource offered. In a cloud environment, the number of individual tasks, as well as the number of available resources, can change very quickly, especially when virtual resources are allocated. Calculating all possible tasks-resource mappings in a cloud environment and selecting the optimal mapping is not feasible, since the complexity grows exponentially with the number of tasks and resources (Juhnke, Dornemann, Bock, & Freisleben, 2011). The use of a heuristic algorithm ensures an acceptable runtime of the scheduling algorithm because it significantly reduces the complexity of the search space. This provides a compromise between the scheduling tasks to processors at runtime and the optimality of the assignment (Juhnke, Dornemann, Bock, & Freisleben, 2011). As the initiator of dynamic collaboration, the Task Manager needs an efficient local task selection and allocation algorithm to partition all the tasks and allocate those tasks that are to be executed locally. Galloway, Smith, and Vrbsky (2011) has proposed a load balancing algorithm for infrastructure as a service (IaaS) for cloud infrastructure implemented on the cluster. There are many proposed systems utilizing market-based resource management for various computing areas (Yeo & Buyya, 2006; Buyy, Beloglazov & Abawajy 2010a; Kusic, Kephart, Hanson, Kandasamy, & Jiang, 2009) have stated the problem of continuous consolidation as a sequential optimization and addressed it using Limited Look ahead Control (LLC). The proposed model requires simulation-based learning for the application specific adjustments. Due to the complexity of the model the optimization controller execution time reaches 30 minutes, even for a small number of nodes (e.g. 15), that is not suitable for large-scale real-world systems. Srikantaiah, Kansal, and Zhao (2008) have studied the problem of requests, scheduling for multi-tiered web-applications in virtualized heterogeneous systems in order to minimize energy consumption, while meeting performance requirements. To handle the optimization over multiple resources, the authors have proposed a heuristic for the multidimensional bin packing problem as an algorithm for workload consolidation. Song, Wang, Li, Feng, and Sun, (2009) have proposed resource allocation to applications according to their priorities in a multi-application virtualized cluster. The approach requires machine-learning to obtain utility functions for the applications and defined application priorities. Cardosa, Korupolu, and Singh (2009) have explored the problem of power efficient allocation of VMs in virtualized heterogeneous computing environments. They have leveraged min, max and shares parameters of VMM that represent minimum, maximum and proportion of CPU allocated to VMs sharing the same resource. The approach suits only enterprise environments or private Clouds. Verma, Ahuja, and Neogi (2008) have formulated the problem of dynamic placement of applications in virtually heterogeneous systems as continuous optimization: at each time frame the placement of VMs is optimized to minimize power consumption and maximize performance. The authors have applied a heuristic for the bin packing problem with variable bin sizes and costs. The authors have introduced the notion of cost of VM live migration, but the information about the cost calculation is not provided. Calheiros, Buyya, and Rose (2009) have investigated the problem of mapping VMs on physical nodes optimizing network communication between VMs, however, the problem has not been explored in the context of energy consumption minimization. The studies show that software-driven thermal management and temperature aware workload placement bring additional energy savings.

The placement problems can be classified into static and dynamic. In the static allocation problem, the VM requirement and PM capacities are known as priori and do not change, and the object is to find out a placement in which they turned on PMs consume less energy than other placements. In static allocation problem, the algorithm can be run offline, allowing it to use a rather long time. Besides the static consolidation, the live VM migration technique has also been applied to further reduce energy consumption by migrating VMs to fewer physical nodes when

fewer VMs are running, and doing the opposite when the number of running VM is larger. In the dynamic problem, although the size VMs and PMs are assumed known, the existing VMs may be decommissioned and new VMs can be created. The PM number can also change due to old PMs exiting and new ones joining, when some PMs need to maintain or are out of order, or when additional PMs are required. As a result, both the numbers and sizes of the VMs and PMs change with time, making the variation hard to predict; therefore the allocation of the VMs cannot be arranged beforehand. The placement can only be adjusted online, according to the current VM requirement and the provision of PMs. Because of the 'online' nature of the problem, the algorithm must be able to give results in the expected time frame, so that the rearrangement can still be valid to accommodate the changing demands of the VMs. Dynamic reallocation to another physical server is assumed to be done by performing live VM migration. A greedy algorithm solving the problem by making the locally optimal choice at each with the hope of finding a global optimum stage (Black, 2005). In many problems, a greedy strategy does not in general produce an optimal solution, but nonetheless a greedy heuristic may yield locally optimal solutions that approximate a global optimal solution in a reasonable time. Song, Hassan, and Huh (2010) proposed a general task selection and allocation framework to apply directly in a dynamic collaboration environment and improve resource utilization for PCP. To achieve better results in task scheduling, Li et al. (2012) have taken the resource allocation pattern into account and proposed a task and resource optimization mechanism. Their approach contains two online dynamic task scheduling algorithms: dynamic cloud list scheduling and dynamic cloud min–min scheduling. These algorithms have been designed to schedule tasks for an IaaS with pre-emptable tasks and task priorities. The authors considered task maps, and task types such as

Advance Reservation or Benefit Effort (Li et al, 2012), to determine tasks priorities. Their algorithms dynamically adjust the resource allocation based on updated actual task execution, which can be calculated by applying the information about the resource status. Li et al. (2011) applied another heuristic optimization approach to propose an algorithm called Normal Best-Oriented Ant Colony Optimization (NBOACO). Taheri, Lee, Zomaya, and Siegel (2013) proposed a Job Data Scheduling algorithm using Bee Colony (JDS-BC). JDS-BC includes two collaborating mechanisms to schedule jobs onto computational nodes and replicate datafiles on storage nodes in a system. In their proposed method, they simultaneously minimized makespan and total datafile transfer time that are two independent, and in many cases conflicting objectives of such heterogeneous systems. Kolodziej and Xhafa (2011) presented two general non-cooperative game approaches, namely, the symmetric non-zero sum game and the asymmetric Stackelberg game for modeling grid user behavior defined as user requirements to effectively express the hierarchical nature of computational grids in the task and resource allocation optimization model in grid scheduling problems. They designed and implemented Genetic Algorithm (GA) based hybrid schedulers to approximate the equilibrium points for both games. Zomaya, and The (2001) ; Zhao (2009) applied GA to develop a load balancing algorithm whereby optimal or near optimal task allocation evolves during the operation of the parallel computing system. Juhnke, Dornemann, Bock, and Freisleben (2011) proposed a multiobjective scheduling algorithm for cloud-based workflow applications by applying the Pareto Archived Evolution Strategy (PAES), which is a type of GA that is capable of dealing with multi-objective optimization problems. Although GA has provided an optimal solution for task scheduling in previous works, it may not be the best method; as illustrated by Zhang, Chen, Sun, Jing, and Yang (2008), It takes more time to compute the optimal solution.

3. CLOUD COMPUTING SYSTEM MODEL

The cloud computing system consists of fully interconnected set of m resources denoted as R. These computing resources are the physical machine in the cloud data center and referred as host computing system or host in this chapter. These resources are to be allocated on demand to run applications time to time. Figure 1 depicts the system model of cloud computing system, that has been referred in this Chapter. We have assumed the centralized cloud is hosted in a data center that is composed of a large number of heterogeneous servers. Each of server may be assigned to perform different or similar functions.

The virtualization technologies allow the creation of multiple virtual machine on any of the available physical host. There for a task can be flexibly assigned to any server. Servers can be modeled as a system that consumes energy in an idle state to perform maintenance functions and to have all the subsystems ready while it waits for task to arrive. On arrival of task, a VM processes the task and host may spend an additional amount of energy, which depends on the number of resources demanded by the task, it is represented as resource utilization in the work load model.

Although a cloud can span across multiple geographical locations (i.e., distributed), the cloud model in our study is assumed to be confined to a particular physical location. We assume that resources are homogeneous in terms of their computing capability and capacity; this can be justified by using virtualization technologies (Lee & Zomaya, 2012). It is also assumed that a message can be transmitted from one resource to another while a task is being executed on the recipient resource, which is possible in many systems (Lee & Zomaya, 2012). The maximum and minimum energy consumption of the server in a cloud computing system are denoted as pick load state and idle state.

Figure 1. Cloud computing architecture

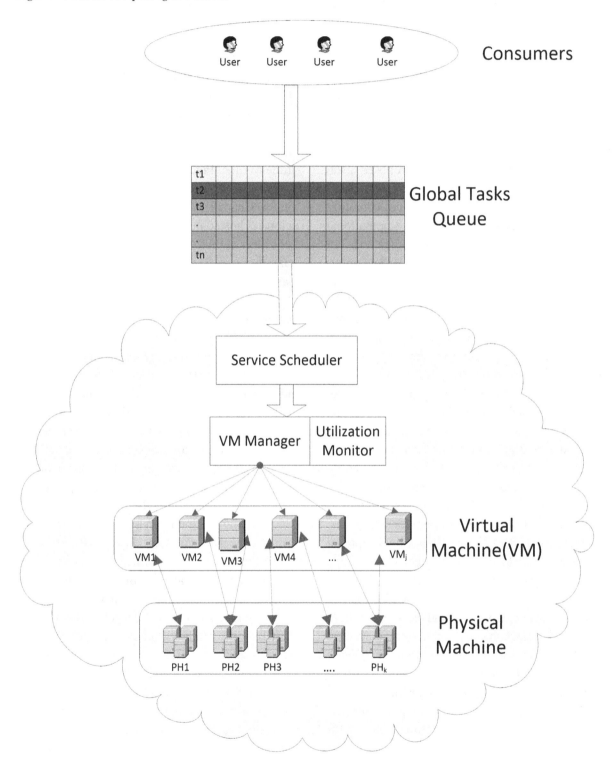

3.1 Energy Consumption in Cloud

The CPU is the main hardware of a physical machine and its consumed up to 35% of the total energy usages. (Chedid, Yu, & Lee, 2005) surveyed a variety of energy models at different levels. So, the computational energy models help to understand the energy consumption in cloud computing and to develop suitable strategies to improve energy efficiency in the cloud computing system.

As formulated in (Chedid, Yu, & Lee, 2005), energy consumption is defined as E and characterised for digital static CMOS circuits can be given by

$$E \propto C_{eff} V^2 f_{clk}$$

where C_{eff} is the effective switching capacitance of the operation, V is the supply voltage, and f_{clk} is the clock frequency. Furthermore, f_{clk} is relevant to supply voltage as in the equation:

$$f_{clk} = \frac{\left(V - V_k \right)^\alpha}{V}$$

where v is the supply voltage, v_k is the empirical voltage for dynamic power consumption of leakage power dissipation and α is the activity factor which depends on workload.

Equation 1 and 2 represents the relationships among the energy, voltage and frequency lead to a way of dynamically adjusting voltage and frequency according to the current workloads to conserve energy. However, how much energy can be saved depends largely on the hardware design. Unfortunately, many types of server CPU do not have as many levels of voltage and frequency as CPUs for embedded devices, and therefore the power saving acquired by adjusting frequency and voltage vary significantly from one CPU type to another. As the CPU is responsible for approximately only one third of the total energy of a typical server, the method of adjusting frequency and voltage only is not enough to solve the power conservation problem.

It is generally believed that the energy consumed by a Physical Machine should be proportional to workloads running on it. However, this is far from true in reality. According to the measurement results by (SPECpower, 2013), even with a nearly zero percentage of CPU utilization, a server can cost up to 50% - 60% of the maximum power consumption (VMware, 2012; Packard, 2011; Gray, Kumar, & Li, 2008).

This means that it is better to push up the CPU utilization rate to achieve better energy efficiency. However, the system performance may degrade significantly if 100% of CPU or memory utilization is sustained. Instead of 100% resource usage, most servers can handle 70 - 80% CPU workloads or memory without performance degradation, and high end servers can push the value up to approximately 90% (SPECpower, 2013). Energy consumption by host varying with CPU workloads For the whole machine, the power consumption, which varies with CPU utilization, can be formulated as the Equation 3 (Verma, Ahuja, & Neogi, 2008; Minas & Ellison, 2009; Lee & Zomaya, 2012):

$$E \left(u \right) = \left(P_{max} - P_{min} \right) * \frac{u}{100} + P_{min}$$

In the equation, u is the percent value of the processor utilization, E(u) is the Energy consumed by CPU at the utilization u%, and P_{max} and P_{min} are the power consumption in watt at maximum performance and at idle respectively.

4. PROBLEM MODEL FOR ENERGY EFFICIENT RESOURCE ALLOCATION

Total Energy E consumed by CPU utilization in time τ by the cloud computing infrastructure by an efficient allocation of resources to the set of tasks. The resource allocation problem with cloud computing are based on the following assumptions.

- Virtualization technologies allow the creation of multiple virtual machines on any of the available host.
- Each host may be assigned to perform different or similar services.
- Hosts consumes energy in an idle state to perform maintenance functions and denoted as P_{min}.
- Hosts consumes more energy as per utilization of the CPU by the tasks.
- Hosts consumes maximum energy at the pick level and denoted as P_{max}.
- Hosts put the task in waiting queue, if its CPU utilization is at pick level.

The work load submitted to the cloud is assumed to be in the form of tasks. These tasks are submitted service scheduler. The service scheduler allocates the tasks to VMs on different computing hosts. We have assumed the task as the computational unit to execute on the allocated VM. The task model refered in this chapter are with following assumption.

- A task represents a user's computing or service request.
- A task is an independent scheduling entity and its execution cannot be preempted.
- The tasks can be executed on any node.
- Arriving task t_j is associated with a task ID, arrival time, CPU utilization, and expected time to compute as shown in Table 1 for example.

- Tasks arrival rate is Poisson.
- Resource utilization by task is normal distribution between 10% and 100%.
- The resource allocated to a particular task must sufficiently provide the resource usage for that task. If resources are not sufficient, providing the resource usage for a particular task, then task putted in waiting queue.

As shown in Table 1 one row of the task arrival list contains the task id, task arrival time, resource utilization by task and estimated execution times for a given task on each machine.

The ETC(t_j, 1) indicates the task id, ETC(t_j, 2) indicates the task arrival time which is poisson, ETC(t_j, 3) indicates the resource utilization by the task t_j and ETC(t_j, 4) indicates the estimated execution times on VM_1, and so on.

Energy efficient resource allocation for cloud computing can be represented as a linear programming problem to minimize the total energy consumed E, and represented as Equation 4.

$$\text{Minimize } E = \sum_{\tau=1}^{\tau}\sum_{i=1}^{m} E_i\left(\tau\right)$$

Subjected to:

$$E_i\left(\tau\right) = \left(P_{max} - P_{min}\right) * \frac{u\left(i, \tau\right)}{100} + P_{min}$$

$$U_i(\tau) = \sum_{i=1}^{n} u(i, j) \leq peakload \; at \; \tau,$$
$$\forall \; R_i \in R \; and \; \forall \; t_j \in T$$

$$u\left(i, j\right) = 0;$$
when the task j is not assigned to node R_i.

Table 1. Example of arrival tasks list

Task ID	Task	Resource	Task Execution Time on VM									
	Arrival time	Utilization (%)	M1	M2	M3	M4	M5	M6	M7	M8	M9	M10
1	1	54	12	12	12	12	12	12	12	12	12	12
2	1	62	5	5	5	5	5	5	5	5	5	5
3	1	31	7	7	7	7	7	7	7	7	7	7
4	1	51	12	12	12	12	12	12	12	12	12	12
5	1	97	9	9	9	9	9	9	9	9	9	9
6	2	59	8	8	8	8	8	8	8	8	8	8
7	2	57	11	11	11	11	11	11	11	11	11	11
8	2	31	8	8	8	8	8	8	8	8	8	8
9	2	54	10	10	10	10	10	10	10	10	10	10
10	2	66	10	10	10	10	10	10	10	10	10	10
11	2	71	17	17	17	17	17	17	17	17	17	17
12	3	45	17	17	17	17	17	17	17	17	17	17
13	3	43	13	13	13	13	13	13	13	13	13	13
14	3	99	9	9	9	9	9	9	9	9	9	9
15	3	13	7	7	7	7	7	7	7	7	7	7
16	3	90	12	12	12	12	12	12	12	12	12	12
17	4	93	12	12	12	12	12	12	12	12	12	12
18	4	82	11	11	11	11	11	11	11	11	11	11
19	4	18	6	6	6	6	6	6	6	6	6	6
20	4	33	14	14	14	14	14	14	14	14	14	14

$$u(i, j) = u_{ij};$$

when the task j is assigned to node R_i.

The above Equation 4 show that the minimization of energy is subjected to the utilization of resources by the task for the time τ.

5. HEURISTIC TASK CONSOLIDATION ALGORITHMS

Heuristic and meta-heuristic algorithms are the most effective technology for resource allocation problem due to their ability to deliver high quality solutions in reasonable time. The selection procedure can be realized using a 2-phase heuristic. In this section, we present the greedy heuristic algorithms for task allocation in a data center. The general form of task allocation algorithms for the resource utilization of cloud server resources is presented in Algorithm-4.

This algorithm allocates tasks to the physical resource and maintain the utilization matrix. The Algorithm-4 operates by finding the task which uses mthe task queueource from the currently available task in task queue.

The function TaskChoosingPolicy() returns the task from the task queue tempQ and the function

ResourceChoosingPolicy() returns the resource for the task t_j for which maximum threshold value less then or equal to 100%. If no such fit found, it returns null. If resource R_i is found such that utilization is maximum for task t_j and utilization is not exceeding 100%. After allocating task j to resource R_i, the task is removed from the task queue mainQ and temporary queue tempQ. If no suitable fit is found, then the task j is removed from the temporary queue, but not from main queue, this process proceeds to a new iteration. These heuristic algorithms are simple to realize with very little computational cost in comparison to the effort by resource allocation algorithm (See Algorithm 1).

5.1 FCFS to Random Utilized (FcfsRand)

The FsfsRand heuristic is the first two-phase heuristic algorithms in our scenario, this algorithm select task in first phase in First Come First Serve (FCFS) basis of the global task waiting queue. This selection method is very simple and has lowest time complexity to choose the items from the queue.

In Second phase the resource is selected for appropriate tasks. The selection methods for resource in our algorithm is random (using uniform distribution) among the available VMs. The selected resource is allocated to the task only if

Algorithm 1. General task allocation algorithm

```
Input: Task Matrix
Output: Utilization Matrix
1: Initialize τ
2: Initialize Utilization Matrix, U*← ∅
3: R* ← ∅
4: while mainQ ≠ ∅ do
5:    tempQ ← All jobs from main queue, mainQ, where arrival time ≤ τ.
6:              while tempQ ≠ ∅ do
7:                      j ← TaskChoosingPolicy()
8:                      i ← ResourceChoosingPolicy ()
9:                  if i ≠ Null then
10:                         Assign task t_j to R_i
11:                         Update Utilization Matrix U( τ, i).
12:                         Remove task t_j from mainQ and tempQ.
13:                  else
14:                         Remove task t_j from tempQ.
15:                  end if
16:              end while
17:       Increment τ.
18: end while
19: return U.
20: end algorithm.
```

the resource utilization, including selected task in phase-1 is not exceeded threshold value. The threshold value in our case is 100%. i.e. The task is assigned to the Virtual Machine R_i, if and only if R_i utilization is not exceeding the threshold value 100% including the currently selected task. Iteration continues till all tasks are allocated to VMs.

5.2 FCFS to Round-Robin Utilized (FcfsRr)

The FcfsRr heuristic algorithm works similarly in phase-1 as FcfsRand, it selects the task in FCFS basis from the global waiting task queue and in phase-2 the resource is allocated to the task using Round Robin(RR) basis among the available VMs. The selected resource is allocated to the task only if the resource utilization, including selected task in phase-1 is not exceeded threshold value. The threshold value in our case is 100%. i.e. The task is assigned to the Virtual Machine R_i, if and only if R_i utilization is not exceeding the threshold value 100% including the currently selected task. Iteration continues till all tasks are allocated to VMs.

5.3 FCFS to Minimum Utilized (FcfsMin)

In the FcfsMin heuristic algorithm, the task selection process also follows FCFS principle in phase-1. In phase-2, the resource is allocated to the selected task. The appropriate resource is selected by finding the current minimum utilized resource among the available active resources. The VM with minimum utilization is selected among the available VMs. The utilization of selected resource is computed by adding the resource utilization by task. The selected resource is allocated to the task only if the resource utilization, including selected task in phase-1 is not exceeded threshold value. If the selected resource has not enough room for the task, then the next task is processed with the selected resource. The threshold value in our case is 100%. i.e The task is assigned to the Virtual

Machine R_i, if and only if R_i utilization is not exceeding the threshold value 100% including the currently selected task. Iteration continues till all tasks are allocated to VMs.

5.4 FCFS to Maximum Utilized (FcfsMax)

In the FcfsMax heuristic algorithm, the task selection process also follows FCFS principle in phase-1. In phase-2, the resource is allocated to the selected task. The appropriate resource is selected by finding the current maximum utilized resource among the available active resources. The VM with maximum utilization is selected among the available VMs. The utilization of selected resource is computed by adding the resource utilization by task. The selected resource is allocated to the task only if the resource utilization, including selected task in phase-1 is not exceeded threshold value. If the selected resource has not enough room for the task, then the next maximum utilized resource is selected. The threshold value in our case is 100%. i.e The task is assigned to the Virtual Machine R_i, if and only if R_i utilization is not exceeding the threshold value 100% including the currently selected task. Iteration continues till all tasks are allocated to VMs.

5.5 Minimum to Minimum Utilized (MinMin)

Above four heuristic algorithms uses the same techniques, FCFS, in phase-1 for selecting the task. This MinMin heuristic algorithm finds the task in phase-1, which required the minimum resource utilization. In phase-2, to the current minimum utilizing resources is chosen. The appropriate resource is selected by finding the current minimum utilized resource among the available active resources. The VM with minimum utilization is selected among the available VMs. The utilization of selected resource is computed by adding the resource utilization by task. The selected resource is allocated to the task only if the resource utilization, including selected task in phase- 1 is not exceeded threshold value. If the selected resource has not enough room for the task, then the system will wait for one or more pre allocated task to be finished. The threshold value in our case is 100%. i.e The task is assigned to the Virtual Machine R_i, if and only if R_i utilization is not exceeding the threshold value 100% including the currently selected task. Iteration continues till all tasks are allocated to VMs.

5.6 Median to Minimum Utilized (MedianMin)

The MedianMin heuristic algorithm finds the task in phase- 1, which required the median resource utilization among the tasks. In phase- 2, to the current minimum utilizing resources is chosen. The appropriate resource is selected by finding the current minimum utilized resource among the available active resources. The VM with minimum utilization is selected among the available VMs. The utilization of selected resource is computed by adding the resource utilization by task. The selected resource is allocated to the task only if the resource utilization, including selected task in phase- 1 is not exceeded threshold value. If the selected resource has not enough room for the task, then the next near to median task is selected which required less utilization of resource. The threshold value in our case is 100%. i.e The task is assigned to the Virtual Machine R_i, if and only if R_i utilization is not exceeding the threshold value 100% including the currently selected task. Iteration continues till all tasks are allocated to VMs.

5.7 Maximum to Minimum Utilized (MaxMin)

The MaxMin heuristic algorithm finds the task in phase- 1, which required the maximum resource utilization among the tasks. In phase- 2, to the

current minimum utilizing resources is chosen. The appropriate resource is selected by finding the current minimum utilized resource among the available active resources. The VM with minimum utilization is selected among the available VMs. The utilization of selected resource is computed by adding the resource utilization by task. The selected resource is allocated to the task only if the resource utilization, including selected task in phase- 1 is not exceeded threshold value. If the selected resource has not enough room for the task, then the next task is selected which required next maximum utilization of resource. The threshold value in our case is 100%. I.e the task is assigned to the Virtual Machine R_i, if and only if R_i utilization is not exceeding the threshold value 100% including the currently selected task. Iteration continues till all tasks are allocated to VMs.

5.8 Minimum to Maximum Utilized (MinMax)

The MinMax heuristic algorithm finds the task in pahse- 1, which required the minimum resource utilization among the tasks. In phase- 2, to the current maximum utilizing resources is chosen. The appropriate resource is selected by finding the current maximum utilized resource among the available active resources. The VM with maximum utilization is selected among the available VMs. The utilization of selected resource is computed by adding the resource utilization by task. The selected resource is allocated to the task only if the resource utilization, including selected task in phase- 1 is not exceeded threshold value. If the selected resource has not enough room for the task, then the next maximum utilizing resource is selected. The threshold value in our case is 100%. i.e The task is assigned to the Virtual Machine R_i, if and only if R_i utilization is not exceeding the threshold value 100% including the currently selected task. Iteration continues till all tasks are allocated to VMs.

5.9 Median to Maximum Utilized (MedianMax)

The MedianMax heuristic algorithm finds the task in phase- 1, which required the median resource utilization among the sorted tasks (ordered by resource utilization). In phase- 2, to the current minimum utilizing resources is chosen. The appropriate resource is selected by finding the current maximum utilized resource among the available active resources. The VM with maximum utilization is selected among the available VMs. The utilization of selected resource is computed by adding the resource utilization by task. The selected resource is allocated to the task only if the resource utilization, including selected task in phase- 1 is not exceeded threshold value. If the selected resource has not enough room for the task, then the next near to median task is selected which required less utilization of resource. The threshold value in our case is 100%. i.e The task is assigned to the Virtual Machine R_i, if and only if R_i utilization is not exceeding the threshold value 100% including the currently selected task. Iteration continues till all tasks are allocated to VMs.

5.10 Maximum to Maximum Utilized (MaxMax)

This MaxMax heuristic algorithm finds the task in phase- 1, which required the maximum resource utilization. In phase- 2, to the current maximum utilizing resources is chosen if it has enough room for the task. The appropriate resource is selected by finding the current maximum utilized resource among the available active resources. The VM with maximum utilization is selected among the available VMs. The utilization of selected resource is computed by adding the resource utilization by task. The selected resource is allocated to the task only if the resource utilization, including selected task in phase- 1 is not exceeded threshold value. If the selected resource has not enough room for

the task, then the next maximum utilized resource is selected. If no resource has enough room for the task, then the next maximum required task is selected for processing. Otherwise the cloud infrastructure will wait for one or more pre allocated task to be finished. The threshold value in our case is 100%. i.e The task is assigned to the Virtual Machine R_i, if and only if R_i utilization is not exceeding the threshold value 100% including the currently selected task. Iteration continues till all tasks are allocated to VMs.

The pseudo-code for the 2-phase proposed MaxMax algorithm for the task required maximum utilization of the maximum utilized resource is allocated in cloud computing infrastructure is presented in Algorithm-4.10. This algorithm allocates tasks (which required the maximum resource utilization) to the current maximum utilizing resources. First the algorithm operated on task queue, which is the resulted on arrival of task till the time of selection. The task is selected from the task queue having maximum resource utilization. The Algorithm 3 MaxResourceUtilizingTask (temQ) return the maximum resource utilizing task from the task queue tempQ and the Algorithm 4 MaxUtilizedResource (U, τ, j) return the resource which has maximum utilization of resources for task t_j, but less then or equal to maximum threshold value 100% if no such fit found it return 0 value. If resource R_i is found such that utilization is maximum for task t_j and utilization is not exceeding 100%. After allocating task j to resource R_i, the task is removed from the main queue mainQ and temporary queue tempQ. If no suitable fit is found then the task j will be removed from temporary queue but not from main queue, the iterative process continue till the successful allocation of all tasks to VMs.

Allocation list in Table 2 is obtained by using Algorithm 4 on allocating 20 tasks on 10 VMs in cloud. Table 2 shows the allocation of 20 tasks to 10 VMs. The corresponding utilization at a time for 10 VMs is shown in Table 3.

Algorithm 2. MaxMax task allocation algorithm

```
Input: Task Matrix
Output: Utilization Matrix
1: Initialize τ
2: Initialize Utilization Matrix, U*← Ø
3: R* ← Ø
4: while mainQ ≠ Ø do
5:        tempQ ← All jobs from mainQ where arrival time ≤ τ.
6:              while tempQ ≠ Ø do
7:                      j ← MaxResourceUtilizingTask(temQ)
8:                      i ← MaxUtilizedResource(U, τ, j)
9:                      if i ≠ Null then
10:                             Assign task tⱼ to Rᵢ
11:                             Update Utilization Matrix U( τ, i).
12:                             Remove task tⱼ from mainQ and tempQ.
13:                      else
14:                             Remove task tⱼ from tempQ.
15:                      end if
16:              end while
17:        Increment τ.
18: end while
19: return U.
20: end Algorithm
```

Algorithm 3. MaxResourceUtilizingTask algorithm

```
Input: Task Queue, Tq
Output: Task id
1: Sort Task queue(Tq) by utilization in descending order,T
2: retrun (Task id of T(1))
3: end Algorithm
```

Example of Maximum to Maximum Utilized allocations and utilization are shown in Table 2 and 3 for allocation of 20 tasks to 10VMs.

6. EXPERIMENTAL EVALUATION AND RESULT

We have simulated the discrete event simulator for performance analysis of ten task consolidation greedy heuristic with 5000 tasks. The tasks are generated for different set of VMs using an inconsistent ETC generation algorithm suggested by Ali, Siegel, Maheswaran, and Hensgen (2000).

The experiment has been conducted using in house simulator designed using Matlab for 5000 task on two- phases resource allocations. The tasks are arriving with a rate λ to the central server queue having an infinite queue length. We have considered task arrival interval is 1 unit of time and arrival rate to be 60 for our experiments. We observed the following experiments:

Algorithm 4. MaxUtilizedResource Algorithm

```
Input: Utilization Matrix, U; τ ; and Task id, j.
Output: Resource id, if fit found otherwise return 0.
1: Temp Utilization Matrix, TempU = ∅
2: pt = expected time to execute on each machine for task j.
3: for i = 1 to n do
4:          for k = 1 to pt(I) do
5:              update utilization matrix, tempU(k) = U(τ + k) + utilization(j)
6:          end for
7: end for
8: Remove the resource id, if utilization is more then peakload from tempU.
9: find best fit resource id with maximum utilization, [ c, i ] = max (sum
(tempU))
10: return, i
11: end Algorithm
```

Table 2. Example of maximum required to maximum utilized, tasks allocation table for 20 tasks on 10 VMs

Time/VM	M1	M2	M3	M4	M5	M6	M7	M8	M9	M10
1	[5]	[2]	[1, 3]	[4]	-	-	-	-	-	-
2	[5]	[2]	[1, 3]	[4]	[11]	[10, 8]	[6]	[7]	[9]	-
3	[5]	[2]	[1, 3, 15]	[4, 12]	[11]	[10, 8]	[6]	[7, 13]	[9]	[14]
4	[5]	[2]	[1, 3, 15]	[4, 12]	[11, 19]	[10, 8]	[6]	[7, 13]	[9, 20]	[14]
5	[5]	[2]	[1, 3, 15]	[4, 12]	[11, 19]	[10, 8]	[6]	[7, 13]	[9, 20]	[14]
6	[5]	[17]	[1, 3, 15]	[4, 12]	[11, 19]	[10, 8]	[6]	[7, 13]	[9, 20]	[14]
7	[5]	[17]	[1, 3, 15]	[4, 12]	[11, 19]	[10, 8]	[6]	[7, 13]	[9, 20]	[14]
8	[5]	[17]	[1, 15]	[4, 12]	[11, 19]	[10, 8]	[6]	[7, 13]	[9, 20]	[14]
9	[5]	[17]	[1, 15]	[4, 12]	[11, 19]	[10, 8]	[6]	[7, 13]	[9, 20]	[14]
10	[16]	[17]	[1]	[4, 12]	[11]	[10]	[18]	[7, 13]	[9, 20]	[14]
11	[16]	[17]	[1]	[4, 12]	[11]	[10]	[18]	[7, 13]	[9, 20]	[14]
12	[16]	[17]	[1]	[4, 12]	[11]	-	[18]	[7, 13]	[20]	-
13	[16]	[17]	-	[12]	[11]	-	[18]	[13]	[20]	-
14	[16]	[17]	-	[12]	[11]	-	[18]	[13]	[20]	-
15	[16]	[17]	-	[12]	[11]	-	[18]	[13]	[20]	-
16	[16]	[17]	-	[12]	[11]	-	[18]	-	[20]	-
17	[16]	[17]	-	[12]	[11]	-	[18]	-	[20]	-
18	[16]	-	-	[12]	[11]	-	[18]	-	-	-
19	[16]	-	-	[12]	-	-	[18]	-	-	-
20	[16]	-	-	-	-	-	[18]	-	-	-
21	[16]	-	-	-	-	-	-	-	-	-

Table 3. Example of maximum to maximum resources utilized, resource allocation table for 20 tasks on 10 VMs

Time/VM	M1	M2	M3	M4	M5	M6	M7	M8	M9	M10
1	97	62	85	51	0	0	0	0	0	0
2	97	62	85	51	71	97	59	57	54	0
3	97	62	98	96	71	97	59	100	54	99
4	97	62	98	96	89	97	59	100	87	99
5	97	62	98	96	89	97	59	100	87	99
6	97	93	98	96	89	97	59	100	87	99
7	97	93	98	96	89	97	59	100	87	99
8	97	93	67	96	89	97	59	100	87	99
9	97	93	67	96	89	97	59	100	87	99
10	90	93	54	96	71	66	82	100	87	99
11	90	93	54	96	71	66	82	100	87	99
12	90	93	54	96	71	0	82	100	33	0
13	90	93	0	45	71	0	82	43	33	0
14	90	93	0	45	71	0	82	43	33	0
15	90	93	0	45	71	0	82	43	33	0
16	90	93	0	45	71	0	82	0	33	0
17	90	93	0	45	71	0	82	0	33	0
18	90	0	0	45	71	0	82	0	0	0
19	90	0	0	45	0	0	82	0	0	0
20	90	0	0	0	0	0	82	0	0	0
21	90	0	0	0	0	0	0	0	0	0

- Resource utilization with ten different heuristic algorithms on 128 VMs, arrival interval 1 and arrival rate 60 with 5000 tasks are observed.
- Energy consumption with ten different heuristic algorithms on 128 VMs, arrival interval 1 and arrival rate 60 with 5000 tasks are observed.
- Energy saving with ten different heuristic algorithms on 128 VMs, arrival interval 1 and arrival rate 60 with 5000 tasks are observed.

The name of ten greedy heuristic algorithms used in this chapter are listed in Table 4.

Table 4. 10 greedy heuristic algorithms

Stage 1 Task Selection	Stage 2 Resource Selection	Algorithm Name
FCFS	Random	FcfsRand
FCFS	Round Robin	FcfsRr
FCFS	MIN	FcfsMin
FCFS	MAX	FcfsMax
MIN	MIN	MinMin
Median	MIN	MedianMin
MAX	MIN	MaxMin
MIN	MAX	MinMax
Median	MAX	MedianMax
MAX	MAX	MaxMax

The resource utilization graph of our simulation using the in-house simulator for 5000 tasks on 128 VMs are presented in Figure 2. The comparative analysis of resource utilization by the ten different algorithms has been presented for 5000 tasks. The simulation process terminates after the successful execution of 5000 allocated tasks. The maximum resource utilization is due to MaxMax and completed in minimum time compared to others 2-phase greedy heuristic algorithms.

The simulation results for energy consumption for 5000 tasks on 128 VMs are presented in

Figure 2. Resource utilization by 5000 tasks on 128 VMs

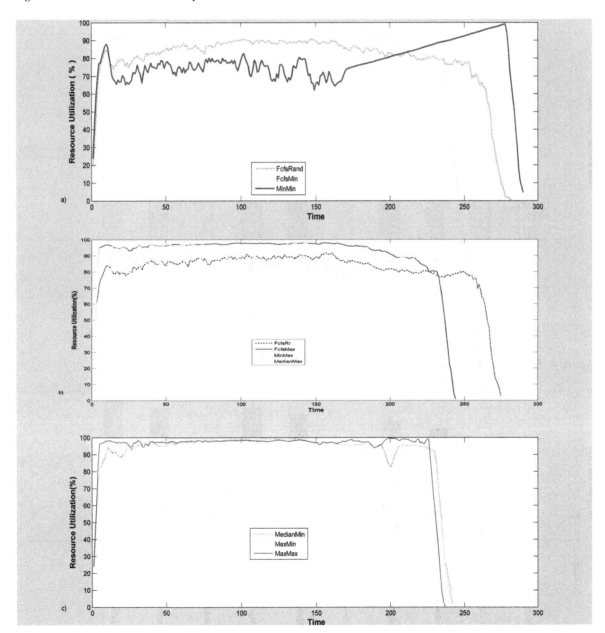

Figure 3. The comparative analysis of total energy consumption of the ten different algorithms has been presented for 5000 tasks indicates the least energy consumed by MaxMax.

The simulation results for energy consumption for 5000 tasks on 128 VMs are presented in Figure 3. The comparative analysis of total energy consumption of the ten different algorithms has been presented for 5000 tasks indicates the least energy consumed by MaxMax. In Figure 4 percentage of energy saving has been shown for different heuristic algorithms. The maximum energy saved is 11.5% by MaxMax compared to FcfsRand.

Figure 3. Energy consumption by 5000 tasks on 128 VMs

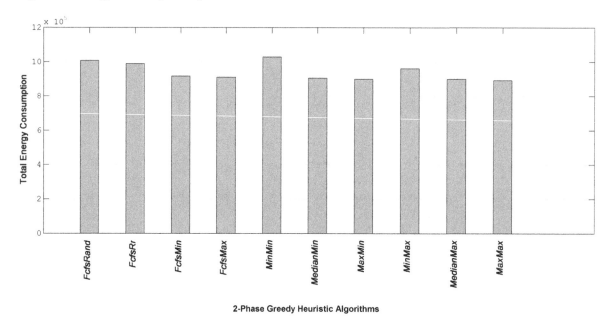

Figure 4. Energy saving comparison

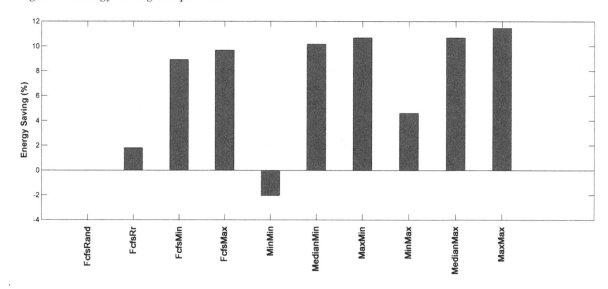

7. CONCLUSION AND FUTURE WORKS

This chapter introduced the basic concepts of the task consolidation problem in the cloud computing system. Task consolidation problem allocates the VMs to the tasks. This problem on cloud computing environments is represented as a linear programming problem, with the objective to minimize the total energy consumed. Model for energy consumed in a cloud computing environment has been presented as the sum of the energy consumed by the hosts. A 2-phase greedy heuristic algorithm framework has been presented. The experimental evaluation of ten different heuristic is also presented to study the performance of different task consolidation algorithms.

In future work, the scope of designing task consolidation algorithm using evolutionary algorithms like Genetic algorithm (GA), Particle swarm optimization (PSO), Ant colony optimization (ACO), Simulated annealing (SA) etc.

The task consolidation problem in cloud computing may also be represented in more general form with multiobjective like memory, network, and storage.

REFERENCES

Ali, S., Siegel, H. J., Maheswaran, M., & Hensgen, D. (2000). *Task execution time modeling for heterogeneous computing systems*. In Heterogeneous Computing Workshop, 2000. (HCW 2000) Proceedings. 9th, (pp. 185-199). IEEE. doi:10.1109/HCW.2000.843743

Beloglazov, A., Abawajy, J., & Buyya, R. (2012). Energy-aware resource allocation heuristics for efficient management of data centers for cloud computing. *Future Generation Computer Systems*, *28*(5), 755–768. doi:10.1016/j.future.2011.04.017

Black, P. E. (2005). Greedy algorithm. *Dictionary of Algorithms and Data Structures*.

Buyya, R., Beloglazov, A., & Abawajy, J. (2010a). *Energy-efficient management of data center resources for cloud computing: A vision, architectural elements, and open challenges*. arXiv preprint arXiv: 1006.0308.

Buyya, R., Broberg, J., & Goscinski, A. M. (2010b). *Cloud computing: Principles and paradigms* (volume 87).

Calheiros, R. N., Buyya, R., & De Rose, C. A. (2009). A heuristic for mapping virtual machines and links in emulation testbeds. In International Conference on Parallel Processing, 2009 (pp. 518-525). ICPP'09. IEEE. doi:10.1109/ICPP.2009.7

Cardosa, M., Korupolu, M. R., & Singh, A. (2009). Shares and utilities based power consolidation in virtualized server environments. In IFIP/IEEE International Symposium on Integrated Network Management, 2009 (pp. 327-334). IM' 09. IEEE. doi:10.1109/INM.2009.5188832

Chedid, W., Yu, C., & Lee, B. (2005). Power analysis and optimization techniques for energy efficient computer systems. *Advances in Computers*, *63*, 129–164. doi:10.1016/S0065-2458(04)63004-X

Eberhart, R. C., & Kennedy, J. (1995, October). A new optimizer using particle swarm theory. In *Proceedings of the sixth international symposium on micro machine and human science* (Vol. 1, pp. 39-43). doi:10.1109/MHS.1995.494215

Galloway, J. M., Smith, K. L., & Vrbsky, S. S. (2011). Power aware load balancing for cloud computing. In *Proceedings of the World Congress on Engineering and Computer Science*, *1* (pp. 19–21).

Gray, L., Kumar, A., & Li, H. (2008). Characterization of specpower_ssj2008 benchmark. In *SPEC Benchmark Workshop*.

Guo, L., Zhao, S., Shen, S., & Jiang, C. (2012). Task scheduling optimization in cloud computing based on heuristic algorithm. *Journal of Networks*, *7*(3), 547–553. doi:10.4304/jnw.7.3.547 553

Hwang, K., Fox, G., & Dongarra, J. (2012). *Distributed and Cloud Computing: From Parallel Processing to the Internet of Things*. Morgan Kaufmann.

ITU. F. (2012). Fg cloud technical report v1.0. International Telecommunication Union.

Jing, S.-Y., Ali, S., She, K., & Zhong, Y. (2013). State-of-the-art research study for green cloud computing. *The Journal of Supercomputing*, 1–24.

Juhnke, E., Dornemann, T., Bock, D., & Freisleben, B. (2011, July). *Multi-objective scheduling of BPEL workflows in geographically distributed clouds*. In Cloud Computing (CLOUD), 2011 IEEE International Conference on (pp. 412-419). IEEE.

Kołodziej, J., & Xhafa, F. (2011). Modern approaches to modeling user requirements on resource and task allocation in hierarchical computational grids. *International Journal of Applied Mathematics and Computer Science*, *21*(2), 243–257. doi:10.2478/v10006-011-0018-x

Kusic, D., Kephart, J. O., Hanson, J. E., Kandasamy, N., & Jiang, G. (2009). Power and performance management of virtualized computing environments via lookahead control. *Cluster Computing*, *12*(1), 1–15. doi:10.1007/s10586-008-0070-y

Lee, Y. C., & Zomaya, A. Y. (2012). Energy efficient utilization of resources in cloud computing systems. *The Journal of Supercomputing*, *60*(2), 268–280. doi:10.1007/s11227-010-0421-3

Li, J., Qiu, M., Ming, Z., Quan, G., Qin, X., & Gu, Z. (2012). Online optimization for scheduling preemptable tasks on IaaS cloud systems. *Journal of Parallel and Distributed Computing*, *72*(5), 666–677. doi:10.1016/j.jpdc.2012.02.002

Li, J. F., Peng, J., Cao, X., & Li, H. Y. (2011). A task scheduling algorithm based on improved ant colony optimization in cloud computing environment. *Energy Procedia*, *13*, 6833–6840.

Liu, H., Abraham, A., Snášel, V., & McLoone, S. (2012). Swarm scheduling approaches for work-flow applications with security constraints in distributed data-intensive computing environments. *Information Sciences*, *192*, 228–243. doi:10.1016/j.ins.2011.12.032

Liu, L., Wang, H., Liu, X., Jin, X., He, W. B., Wang, Q. B., & Chen, Y. (2009). Greencloud: a new architecture for green data center. In *Proceedings of the 6th international conference industry session on Autonomic computing and communications industry session*, (pp. 29–38). ACM. doi:10.1145/1555312.1555319

Mell, P. & Grance, T. (2011). *The NIST definition of cloud computing* (draft). NIST special publication, 800(145):7.

Mezmaz, M., Melab, N., Kessaci, Y., Lee, Y. C., Talbi, E.-G., Zomaya, A. Y., & Tuyttens, D. (2011). A parallel bi-objective hybrid metaheuristic for energy-aware scheduling for cloud computing systems. *Journal of Parallel and Distributed Computing*, *71*(11), 1497–1508. doi:10.1016/j.jpdc.2011.04.007

Minas, L. & Ellison, B. (2009). *The problem of power consumption in servers*. Intel Corporation. Dr. Dobb's.

Packard, H. (2011). *Power regulator for proliant servers*.

Ramezani, F., Lu, J., & Hussain, F. K. (2014). Task-Based System Load Balancing in Cloud Computing Using Particle Swarm Optimization. *International Journal of Parallel Programming*, *42*(5), 739–754. doi:10.1007/s10766-013-0275-4

Rodero, I., Jaramillo, J., Quiroz, A., Parashar, M., Guim, F., & Poole, S. (2010). Energy-efficient application-aware online provisioning for virtualized clouds and data centers. In 2010 International Green Computing Conference (pp. 31–45). IEEE. doi:10.1109/GREENCOMP.2010.5598283

Rosenblum, M. (2004). The reincarnation of virtual machines. *Queue*, *2*(5), 34. doi:10.1145/1016998.1017000

Song, B., Hassan, M. M., & Huh, E. N. (2010, November). *A novel heuristic-based task selection and allocation framework in dynamic collaborative cloud service platform*. In Cloud Computing Technology and Science (CloudCom), 2010 IEEE Second International Conference on (pp. 360-367). IEEE.

Song, Y., Wang, H., Li, Y., Feng, B., & Sun, Y. (2009). Multi-tiered on-demand resource scheduling for vm-based data center. In *Proceedings of the 2009 9th IEEE/ACM International Symposium on Cluster Computing and the Grid*, (pp. 148–155). IEEE Computer Society. doi:10.1109/CCGRID.2009.11

SPECpower (2013). Benchmark results summary of hitachi model no: Ha8000/ss10 (dl2).

Srikantaiah, S., Kansal, A., & Zhao, F. (2008). Energy aware consolidation for cloud computing. In *Proceedings of the 2008 conference on Power aware computing and systems*, 10. USENIX Association.

Taheri, J., Choon Lee, Y., Zomaya, A. Y., & Siegel, H. J. (2013). A Bee Colony based optimization approach for simultaneous job scheduling and data replication in grid environments. *Computers & Operations Research*, *40*(6), 1564–1578. doi:10.1016/j.cor.2011.11.012

Venkatachalam, V., & Franz, M. (2005). Power reduction techniques for microprocessor systems. *ACM Computing Surveys*, *37*(3), 195–237. doi:10.1145/1108956.1108957

Verma, A., Ahuja, P., & Neogi, A. (2008). pmapper: power and migration cost aware application placement in virtualized systems. In Middleware 2008 (pp. 243–264). Springer.

VmWare (2012). Vmware.

Ye, K., Huang, D., Jiang, X., Chen, H., & Wu, S. (2010). Virtual machine based energy-efficient data center architecture for cloud computing: a performance perspective. In *Proceedings of the 2010 IEEE/ACM Int'l Conference on Green Computing and Communications & Int'l Conference on Cyber, Physical and Social Computing* (pp. 171–178). IEEE Computer Society. doi:10.1109/GreenCom-CPSCom.2010.108

Yeo, C. S., & Buyya, R. (2006). A taxonomy of market-based resource management systems for utility-driven cluster computing. *Software, Practice & Experience*, *36*(13), 1381–1419. doi:10.1002/spe.725

Zhang, L., Chen, Y., Sun, R., Jing, S., & Yang, B. (2008). A task scheduling algorithm based on PSO for grid computing. *International Journal of Computational Intelligence Research*, *4*(1), 37–43. doi:10.5019/j.ijcir.2008.123

Zhao, C., Zhang, S., Liu, Q., Xie, J., & Hu, J. (2009, September). *Independent tasks scheduling based on genetic algorithm in cloud computing*. In Wireless Communications, Networking and Mobile Computing, 2009. WiCom'09. 5th International Conference on (pp. 1-4). IEEE.

Zomaya, A. Y., & Teh, Y. H. (2001). Observations on using genetic algorithms for dynamic load-balancing. Parallel and Distributed Systems. *IEEE Transactions on*, *12*(9), 899–911.

KEY TERMS AND DEFINITIONS

Cloud Computing: Cloud computing infrastructures are designed to support the accessibility and deployment of various service oriented applications by the users. The concept of cloud computing has been emerging from the concept of heterogeneous distributed computing, grid computing, utility computing and autonomic computing. To meet the growing demand for computations and large volume of data, the cloud computing environment provides high performance servers and high speed mass storage devices.

Energy Efficient: It is a way to managing energy consumption in the organization. If the systems deliver more services for the same energy input, the system is more energy efficient.

Greedy Algorithm: A greedy algorithm follows heuristic techniques to making the locally optimal choice at each stage with the hope of finding a global optimum.

Green Computing: In Green Computing, organizations adopt such policy for the setup and operations to produce the minimal carbon footprint. Green computing, also called green technology, is the environmentally responsible use of computers and related resources.

Heuristics: A heuristic is a technique for getting a approximate solution more quickly than solving with classic methods. Heuristic and meta-heuristic algorithms are the most effective technology for resource allocation problem due to their ability to deliver high quality solutions in reasonable time.

Server Consolidation: Server consolidation is mainly used to reduce the number of servers required in computations in an organization.

Task Consolidation: Task consolidation is a way of maximizing cloud computing resources.

Chapter 12
Virtual Machine Placement Strategy for Cloud Data Center

Sourav Kanti Addya
National Institute of Technology, India

Bibhudutta Sahoo
National Institute of Technology, India

Ashok Kumar Turuk
National Institute of Technology, India

ABSTRACT

The data center is the physical infrastructure layer in cloud architecture. To run a large data center requires a huge amount of power. A proper strategy can minimize the number of servers used. Minimization of active servers caused minimization of power consumption. But the maximum number of virtual machine placement will be a monetary benefit for cloud service providers. To earn maximum revenue, the CSP is to maximize resource utilization. VM placement is one of the major issues to achieve minimum power consumption as well as to earn maximum revenue by CSP. In this research chapter, we have formulated an optimization problem for initial VM placement in the data center. An iterative heuristic using simulated annealing has been used for VM placement problem. The proposed heuristic has been analysis to be scalable and the coding scheme shows that the proposed technique is outperforming traditional FFD on bin packing technique.

1. INTRODUCTION

Cloud computing is an emerging computing technology that uses the Internet and central remote servers to maintain data and applications. This technology is expected to be much more efficient computing than the presently available technology by centralizing the storage, memory, processing and bandwidth. It allows consumers and businesses to use applications without installation and access their personal files on any computer with the help of Internet. A list of a few organizations and their contribution in the field of cloud computing is shown in Table 1 (Marston et al., 2011). Some of the dominant cloud computing products are Amazon EC2, Microsoft Window

DOI: 10.4018/978-1-4666-8339-6.ch012

Table 1. Contribution of Different organization in cloud computing

Organization Name	Cloud Name	Remarks
IBM	Blue Cloud	By using this cloud they access those tools that allow all to manage large scale of application and database. The organization spends $400 million and try to expand the number of researchers in the area of cloud computing
Google	App Engine	This cloud mainly offers client organizations access to company's platform by which they can build and host web applications.
Microsoft	Windows Azure	It is a cloud operating system mainly build on the concept of PaaS to appear in early 2010. Addition with this the organization creating a windows azure operating system to provide different client access several Microsoft product like .NET, SQL, LIVE etc.
AT & T	Synaptic Hosting Synaptic storage	By this all clients will be able to store Windows server and Linux client server applications. Along with they also able to store various we applications. IT is enabling clients to store their data on AT&T's cloud.

Azure platform, Google App engine, etc. Over the past few years IBM, Google, Amazon and Microsoft are able to provide powerful, efficient and reliable cloud computing infrastructures. The major benefits that are achieved from the cloud computing infrastructures are *No up-front investment, Lowering operating cost, Highly scalable, easy access, Improved automation and Sustainability* (Zhang et al., 2010).

Some renowned organization, such that The National Institute of Standards and Technology (NIST) (NIST, n.d), Cisco (Bakshi, 2009) made standard definition for cloud computing.

- **NIST Definition:** Cloud computing is a model for enabling convenient, on-demand network access to a shared pool of configurable computing resources (e.g., networks, servers, storage, applications and services) that can be rapidly provisioned and released with minimal management effort of service provider interaction.
- **Cisco Definition:** IT resources and services that are abstracted from the underlying infrastructure and provide "on-demand" and "at scale" in a multitenant environment.

Setting up and maintaining the IT infrastructure for any small or large scale organization to meet their IT need is a difficult task, especially for non IT organization. The up-front, operational and maintenance cost is higher which may not be actually need for the organization. Cloud computing offers the solutions for these types of problem as well as maintain the client data and information secure. Public cloud offers on-demand storage and virtual host (VM) to the client at a low rate. Beside these, the few other cloud environment offers the development environment without complete purchase of the application.

Two main important characteristic to implement a large scale cloud data centers are a great deal of flexibility and agility. In the real time scenario, the needs of *computer resources* to be available in a short time period for the dynamic scaling and shrinking requirement. At the time of overloaded condition of hardware resources, the dynamic transfer is required for some load to another system with a minimum downtime for the users' service. *Virtualization technology* can provide this kind of flexibility.

Characteristics

The cloud computing, grid computing, high performance computing (HPC) / supercomputing, and data center computing all belongs to the family of parallel computing. HPC focuses on scientific computing, which is computationally intensive and delay sensitive. Grid computing is based on HPC center in which many HPC centers form a large grid, which owns a powerful underlying *service oriented architectures (SOA)* concept. Some other creative and impressive concepts like utility computing and autonomic computing do not come into reality. The cloud computing, which is based on data center is more widely accepted than grid computing. Data centers, which only pursue powerful processing performance and low delay is more balanced than HPC center. The comparable characteristics of cloud computing and grid computing are listed in Table - 2. The *Half* in the Table - 2 means not owning the whole characteristic to a certain extent. This paper doesn't pay much attention on the similarities and difference between them and focuses on the essential characteristics of cloud computing. For detailed comparisons on grid and cloud computing, refer (Gonzalez et al., 2009).

Some of the advantages of cloud computing are: (*i*) Increased Storage: Organization can store more data than on their private computer systems, (*ii*) Reduced Cost: Cloud technology is paid incrementally (you pay only for what you need), saving organizations money which can be used for other important resources, (*iii*) More Mobility: Employees can access information wherever they are, rather than having to remain at their desks, (*iv*) Highly Automated: IT personnel need not keep their software up-to-date as the maintenance is left to the cloud the service provider, and (*v*) Allows IT to Shift Focus: No longer having to worry about constant server updates and other computing issues, government organizations will be free to concentrate on innovations.

Few of the demerits of cloud computing are: (*i*) Security: There is no security standard, (*ii*) Cost of transition: This is the cost associated with moving from the existing architecture to the cloud architecture, (*iii*) Reliance on 3rd Party: Control over own data is lost in the hands of a "difficult-to-rust" provider, and (*iv*) Uncertainty of benefits: The question of any long term benefits.

The benefits of cloud computing include:

1. In a cloud computing environment the client would able to access their data and applications at any time and from anywhere using just any computer with an Internet connection.
2. As the data is being stored in the server there is no need of installing any substantial amount of memory on the client system. This will effectively reduce expenditure.
3. There is no need to purchase software or software licenses for every employee. Consumption is usually billed on a utility (resources consumed, like electricity) or subscription (time-based, like a newspaper) basis with little or no upfront cost.

Table 2. Characteristics: cloud computing vs. grid computing

Characteristic	Cloud Computing	Grid Computing
Server Oriented	Yes	Yes
Loose Coupling	Yes	Half
Strong Fault Tolerant	Yes	Half
Business Model	Yes	No
Ease Use	Yes	Half
TCP/IP based	Yes	Half
High Security	Half	Half
Virtualization	Yes	Half

Cloud Architecture

Cloud architecture is yet to be standardized. Every enterprise is using a different architecture for their development and research. Current trends in cloud computing architecture are shown in Figure 1. Cloud architecture, mainly consists of two layers: Resource Layer and Service Layer. Resource Layer contains all physical resources and consists of two sub-layers: Virtual Resource Layer and Physical Resource Layer. All hardware components are included in the resource layer. Service Layer is mainly used to provide specific services to the users. Service layer can be split into three sub-layers, each providing specific service to the users. A brief description about service layers are given below:

1. **Infrastructure as a Service (IaaS):** This sub-layer support computing resources and storage resources for the users. In the case of a particular service constrains, IaaS provides an intermediate platform to run arbitrary operating systems and software.
2. **Platform as a Service (PaaS):** This sub-layer provides a a more personalized hardware and software services, and a lot of infrastructure module, such as a remote call module, distributed data module, building module, etc.
3. **Software as a Service (SaaS):** This sub-layer provides application, which is closest to the user service and allows deploying the software in the network environment. It allows software to run under the multi-user platform.

Classification of Cloud Computing

Cloud computing is broadly classified into three types: Public, Private and Hybrid Cloud. A brief description about these classifications is explained below:

1. **Public Cloud:** A public cloud is a model which allows users' access to the cloud via interfaces using mainstream web browsers. It is typically based on a pay-per-use model, similar to a prepaid electricity metering system which is flexible enough to cater for spikes in demand for cloud optimization. This helps cloud clients to better match their

Figure 1. Layred architecture

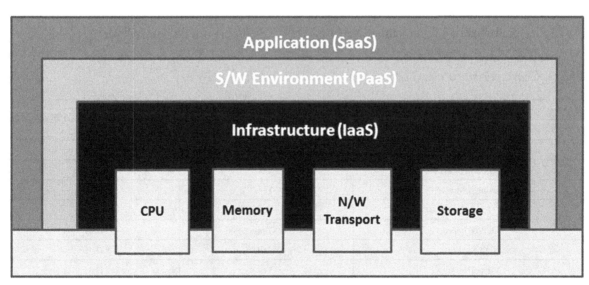

IT expenditure at an operational level by decreasing their capital expenditure on IT infrastructure (March, 2010). Public clouds are less secure than the other cloud models because it places an additional burden of ensuring all applications and data accessed on the public cloud are not subjected to malicious attacks. Therefore trust and privacy concerns are rife when dealing with public clouds with the cloud service layer architecture (SLA) at its core. A key management consideration, which needs to be answered within the SLA deals with ensuring that ample security controls are put in place. One option for both the cloud vendor and client is to mutually agree in sharing joint responsibility in enforcing cloud checks and validation are performed across their own systems. The alternative option will be for each party to set out individual roles and responsibilities in dealing with cloud computing security within their utilization boundaries.

2. **Private Cloud:** A private cloud is set up within an organization's internal enterprise data center. It is easier to align with security, compliance, and regulatory requirements, and provides more enterprise control over deployment and use. In a private cloud, scalable resources and virtual applications provided by the cloud vendor are pooled together and available for cloud users to share and use. It differs from the public cloud in that all the cloud resources and applications are managed by the organization itself, similar to Internet functionality. Utilization on the private cloud can be much more secure than in the public cloud because of its specified internal exposure. Only the organization and designated stakeholders may have access to operate on a specific private cloud (Dooley, 2010).

3. **Hybrid Cloud:** A hybrid cloud is a private cloud linked to one or more external cloud services, centrally managed, provisioned as a single unit, and circumscribed by a secure network (Ramgovind, 2010). It provides virtual IT solutions through a mix of both public and private clouds. Hybrid clouds provide a more secure control of data and applications, and allows various parties to access information over the Internet. It also has an open architecture that allows interfacing with other management systems. On cloud deployment model- networking platform, storage, and software infrastructure are provided as services that scales up or down depending on the demand (Lofstrand, 2009). In deciding which type of cloud to deploy, business managers need to holistically assess the security considerations from an enterprise architectural point of view, taking into account the information security differences of each cloud deployment model mentioned above.

This chapter illustrates Virtual Machine Placement Strategy in the public Cloud Data Center.

Background Technologies: Virtualization

Virtualization is the most important technology among the technologies such as virtualization, cyber-infrastructure, and service orient infrastructure that made cloud computing feasible (Vouk, 2008). It provides a promising approach through which resources can be partitioned into multiple execution environments. Virtualization partitions the resources of one or more machines into multiple execution environments, each of which act as a complete system. Each of these logical isolated platforms is called a virtual machine (VM). It enhances system impregnability, software interoperability and platform versatility. Virtualization enables dynamic sharing of physical resources in cloud environments. Through virtualization, physical resources such as CPU, memory, disk space are made available to applications on demand (Kusic et al., 2009). It also enables a cloud service provider (CSP) can ensure the quality-of-service (QoS) delivered to the users while achieving a high server utilization and energy efficiency. The idea is to maintain a separation between hardware and software for better system level efficiency. For example, by the concept of virtual memory, a user gained access to much enlarged memory space. Similarly, this virtualization can be used to enhance the use of computing resources.

Virtual Machine: In modern virtualization technology not only applied to subsystem like, disk, but it can be applied to an entire machine. To support the desired architecture, the VM developers add a new layer to a real machine. This entire new model is implemented as a virtual machine and it can circumvent hardware resource constraints and real machine compatibility. The term virtual machine was originated in early 1970s (Creasy, 1981) during the development of system VMs. The requirement for development of these VMs to share very large and expensive mainframe hardware among the numbers of users, who can install different operating systems.

Though the term "virtual" is associated with the name of the VM, but there is no significant difference with it and computer architecture. By understanding the meaning of "machine" from both a system and process, prospective, it can be easily described what a VM is.

A system VM is a complete, persistent system environment that supports an operating system along with its application processes. It provides the guest OS with access to virtual hardware resources, I/O network, etc. In contrast, a process VM is a virtual platform that helps to execute an individual process. This process VM is created and terminated with process creation a termination.

The underlying platform that supports the VM is the host, while the system or process that runs on VM is the guest. The software which is responsible for virtualizing a process or system VM are

typically called" runtime software" and "virtual machine monitor" respectively. In this chapter, we mainly deal with system VM and VMM.

System Virtual Machine: Like a complete physical system, a system also provides a complete environment where an operating system, application software etc. is available. Multiple system VMs can be hosted on the single host hardware platform. An isolated guest operating system can be created by installing a different operating system in different VMs. Figure 2 shows the with and without VM in any physical host. The left side picture shows a normal physical machine where a general operating system is running on the top of hardware resources. All application software is expected on operating system. The right side picture shows two numbers of VMs are placed on a hypervisor (VMM) which is basically an inter mediator between VMs and hardware resources. Different operating system can install on different VMs when utilizing same hardware resources. Applications can be run on these operating systems and those are independent for different VMs.

In the modern age of computer, the system VMs are required to share the server or server farms among many users or groups access from geographically different location. System VMs provides the isolation between multiple systems executing concurrently on the same hardware environment. Another important characteristic of it is security. If any guest OS is compromised or any system failure occurs, but the application software running in other guest operating system will run smoothly.

The process of mapping virtual machines to physical machines (PM) is called Virtual machine placement. VM placement is an important approach for improving power efficiency and resource utilization of cloud infrastructures. Properly placed VM onto the cloud infrastructure can decrease the energy consumption of data centers and increase the revenue earned by the cloud service provider. The importance of placing VMs

Figure 2. With and without VM

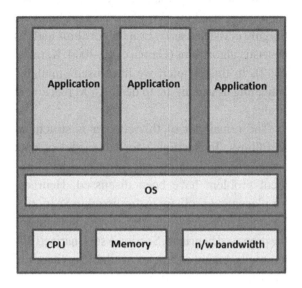
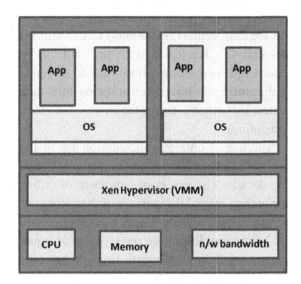

appropriately in a data center has been addressed by several researches (Cardosa et al., 2009; Gao et al., 2013).

There are some well-known global industries who introduced their won virtual machine placement tool. Few of them are IBM WebSphere CloudBurst (WebSphere, n.d), VMware Capacity Planner (VMware, n.d), Novell PlateSpin Recon (Novell, n.d). These tools automatically distribute the virtual machines in data center based on the requirements of the CPU, physical memory, etc. These tools partially consider the security requirement of users and SLA for cloud service providers as well as they do not consider the demands of application awareness. The Less secure VM can motivate the user to opt a new service provider and other hand partial SLA can caused for CSP in less profit.

Data center management is a big issue in Cloud Computing. It is reported that about 75% of the operational cost of a data center is spent to meet the energy bill where 25% is spent on the IT infrastructure. The high energy consumption is attributed not only to the power consumed by the IT resources and the cooling system, but also due to the inefficient usages of IT resources. In 2006,

data centers in the US consumed more than 1.5% of the total energy generated in that year, and the percentage is projected to grow 18% annually. An average data center consumes as much energy as 5,000 households, hence; infrastructure providers are under enormous pressure to reduce energy consumption. Thus, more recently researchers have focused on reducing power consumption in the data center. Efficient power management technique can reduce power consumption of IT resources. The cloud data center runs numerous servers to provide different business oriented services to the users. Many techniques are proposed in the literature to reduce the power consumption. One way to reduce power consumption in a data center is to consolidate the active servers. That is, to minimize the number of active servers, without violating the service level agreement between the user and the cloud service provider (CSP). There exist a few techniques for server consolidation. Proper and efficient resource (virtual machine) distribution among data centers is one of them. It is reported that although servers are usually not idle, utilization rarely approaches 100%, and most of the time servers operate at 10 to 50% of their full capacity. Therefore, optimized distribution of virtual machines among data centers causes minimization of power consumption. In order to run the data centers, more energy is consumed and more CO_2 is released to the environment. To reduce the energy cost, efforts should be made to minimize the power consumption in a data center. This effort is also in the direction of green computing.

The use of online application or use of the Internet has been incremented massively in last one decade. The access of increment of online application caused the increase of the number of servers in data centers, energy consumption and CO2 emission. Recent survey says that an equal amount of energy consumes from the average data center than 25,000 households and data center CO2 emissions is predicted to be double by next six to seven years (Buyya & Abawajy, 2010). It is possible to reduce an organization's and overall carbon footprint by using green IT technology. A recent study on energy use of data center (Thibodeau, 2011) shows it is 2% of total US energy consumption. Among the total power consumption, almost half of it consumes by active servers in data centers and the rest half consume by data center cooling systems, n/w communication etc.

This chapter presents an optimization problem model for initial VM placements in a data center have been formulated. The objective of the model to minimize the total energy consumption on a cloud data center in a particular time frame. The VM placement problem has been reduced to a multi-dimensional bin packing problem, which is a well-known combinatorial NP-Hard problem (Yao, 1980; Feller et al., 2011; Bksi et al., 2000). The problem is therefore intractable with number VMs or computing machines exceeds a few units. Then the *n* number VMs can be mapped to *m* number of servers at most with *$m.2^n$* trials. The VM placement problem has been evenly treated, in both the fields of computer science and theory of optimization/ operational research. The algorithm approaches used for VM placement problem are roughly classified as (i) exact algorithms and (ii) heuristic algorithms (Gamal et al., 2004; Karatza, 2002). In this chapter, we have used simulated annealing as a heuristic to design VM placement strategy.

The remainder of this chapter is structured as follows. In Section 2 formal model of data center and application and formalize the placement problem have been discussed. Heuristic for placement problem is discussed in Section 3. Section 4 provides simulation results and analysis the proposed heuristic. Section 5 summarized different placement strategies available in literature and final conclusion in Section 6.

2. PLACEMENT MODEL

This section presents a model for optimal placement of VMs in a data center, in order to achieve energy efficiency and cost effectiveness. Cloud data center architecture for the proposed VM placement heuristics is shown in Figure 3. Here the proposed cloud model is partitioned by three main layers. All organizations or individual users belong to uppermost layers. Requests for VM placement are generated from this layer and passes to next bottom layer. All entities of this layer are true cloud service seekers. The next layer is an intermediate layer, which seeking services from cloud infrastructure unit called "data center" and provide service to upper user layer. The actors of this intermediate layer are two types, (i) Global Resource manager or cloud broker and (ii) Cloud Service provider (CSP). A Cloud broker manages the SLA with end users according to user's demand and service available from different CSP. After fixing up the SLA, cloud broker passes all requests to respective CSP for further process.

Figure 3. Proposed cloud datacenter architecture

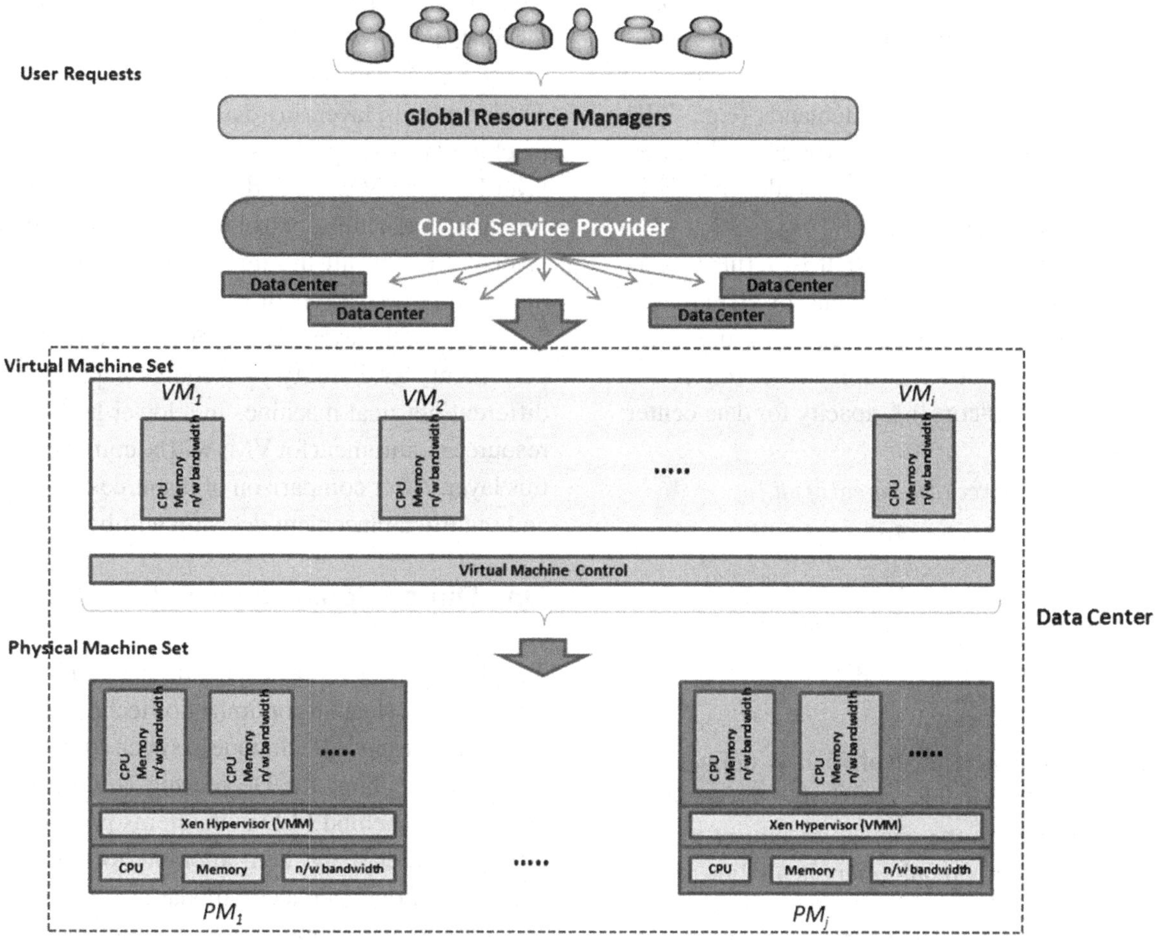

Server capacity constraints and user requirement constraint as well as SLA between the CSP and user in the process have been considered. The formulations are introduced firstly, and then modeling works will be detailed in the following subsections.

Placement Problem

To run a large data center needs huge amount of power. The cooling systems and huge number of servers consume most of the power in data centers (Tang et al., 2008). Power consumes by cooling systems is hard to minimize but a proper strategy with appropriate techniques can minimize the number of servers used in a particular time frame. Minimization of active servers caused minimization of power consumption. The total revenue earned by cloud service providers (CSP) mainly depends on the number of VMs request placed in different servers. To maximize the revenue, the goal of CSP is to map maximum VM requests onto a server, at the same time turn off the idle servers.

VM placement is categorized into two types: (i) initial placement and (ii) migration. In this work we have considered only the initial placement. The following three structural constraints are considered for initial placement:

1. **Assignment Constraint:** For placement the assignment constraint is the lower bound of resource allocation for each VM where SLA required to meet for service of each of it. A set of resource demands (e.g., CPU, memory, #cores) is given by each VM where the requested demands should provide by the placement plan.

2. **Capacity Constraint:** It is defined as the total resource requirements by all requested VMs will less than or equal to total available resources in all dimensions (e.g., CPU, memory, #cores). Capacity for data center:

$$\sum \begin{array}{l} Total\ resource\ requirment\ of\ all \\ requested\ VMs\ for\ all\ dimensions \end{array}$$
$$\leq$$
$$\sum \begin{array}{l} Total\ available\ resource\ capacity \\ of\ active\ servers\ for\ all\ dimensions \end{array}$$

3. **Placement Constraint:** It is defined that one VM can only be assigned and should be assigned to the one server subject to meet the capacity requirement in all dimensions.

Placement Scenario Description

In this proposed model we introduced different layers in a cloud data center. Fig 2 show details layered architecture of the proposed cloud model. Organizations or individual users may opt for multiple VMs with associated different constraints in demand. A user's request for VMs will distributed in different data centers, located in various places in the Globe. In any data center, total number of VMs to be placed, will generate in the VM set from the user's request passing through CSP layer. Before final deployment of VMs in physical servers, will pass different layers in the proposed cloud model. VM set indicates total number of VM to be placed and their individual requirements for placement in a particular time frame. Here,

total number of VMs in VM set will be more or equal to the total number of the user's request for VM. Because it is considered that one user or organization may request for one or more VM. The lower most layers in a data center are physical machine layer where VMs are to be placed. The layer between VM set and physical machine set is a virtual machine control layer. The job of this layer is to keep all the information about both upper and lower layers of it.

Mainly, this layer plays a major role for VM placement. Availability of resource capacity of different physical machines in a lower layer and resource requirement for VMs will be compared in this layer. After comparison of resource capacity and require a placement decision will be made.

One Dimensional Approach

To solve the objective a heuristic algorithm 1 over traditional Bin Packing optimization technique has been used. Proposed technique has been compared with existing First Fit Decreasing (FFD). The general idea behind FFD is the items process in arbitrary order. Each item attempts to place in the first bin that can accommodate it. If the bin is not found, then it moves to a new bin and puts the selected item within the new bin.

Three sets of data are used for this proposed one-dimensional experiment where average resource requirement vs. number of servers has been plotted for a fixed number of VMs 5, 10, 20 respectively in Figures 4, 5,6. In this proposed algorithm all VMs and servers are one dimensional in nature. But in real scenario all VMs and Servers in data centers are multi-dimensional, i.e. CPU, i/o etc. A multi-dimensional optimization problem has been considered in subsection 2.4.

For one dimensional approach simulation has been performed with 5, 10 and 20 number of VMs respectively. It is clearly shown that the proposed algorithm is performing better than the existing FFD.

Algorithm 1. Algorithm for VM placement

```
Input: Vm number, resource requirement, server number, server capacity
Result: Vm placement
1  s=0;
2  t=0;
3  Sort VM set with resource requirement;
4  while s < total servers do
5          while t < total VMs do
6                      if Server capacity >= VM requirement then
7                              Server ← VM;
8                              Server capacity = Server capacity - VM requirement;
9                              save the configuration;
10                      else
11                              break;
12                      end
13                      t=t+1;
14          end
15          s=s+1;
16 end
```

Figure 4. Average resource requirement vs. number of servers used when number of VMs=5

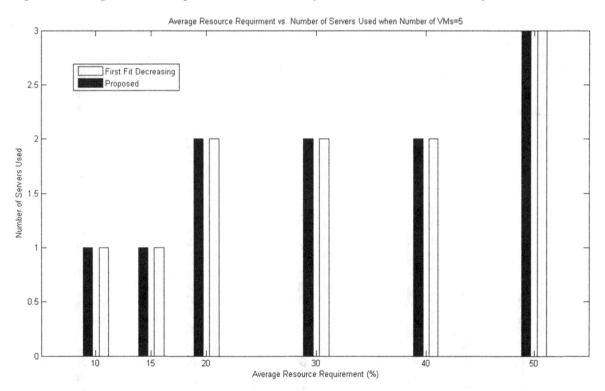

271

Figure 5. Average resource requirement vs. number of servers used when number of VMs=10

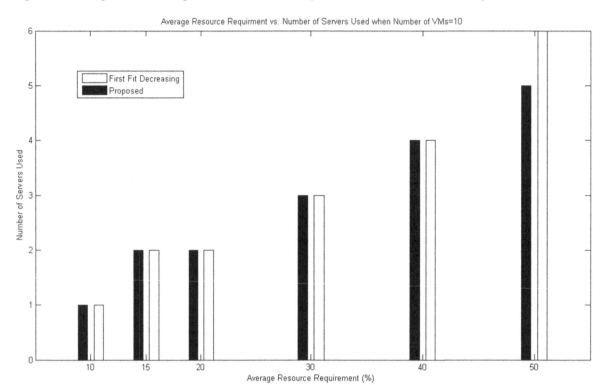

Figure 6. Average resource requirement vs. number of servers used when number of VMs=20

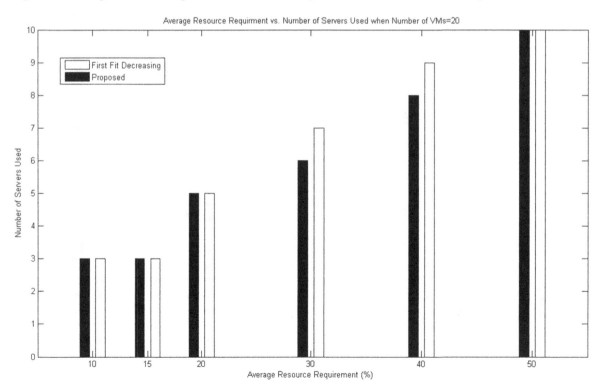

Multidimensional Approach

In multi-dimensional approach VMs capacity requirement and server's capacity available are in multi dimension such as CPU, memory, n/w bandwidth, etc. Few important notations of our proposed model are described in table 3.

There are two decision variables $B_{ij}^{\bar{v}}$ and $D^{\bar{v}}$. $B_{ij}^{\bar{v}} = 1$ if $\bar{v}_i$ is placed in S_j, otherwise the value is zero and if the request $\bar{v}_i$ Included into placement, then value of another decision variable $D^{\bar{v}} = 1$ or zero otherwise. A set VM will generate where any VM $\bar{v}_i \in VM$, $1 \le i \le n$ and $\bar{v} = \{C\bar{v}\}$ where a vector $C\bar{v}$ Is capacity require-

ments of the virtual machine $\bar{v}$. A capacity requirement is a property in multiple dimension (d) for any $\bar{v}$ where r can be cpu core, cpu speed, memory etc. and is $C\bar{v}_d(d)$ returns the required values of each dimension (e.g. 2 core, 2.1 GHz, 4 GB). A physical server S_j exists only at the lower layer physical machine set (S) of a data center with a capacity vector $CS_r(j)$. Capacity vector denotes the available capacity of server j with r dimensions. A capacity is a property in multiple dimension (r) of a physical server S_j, where r can be cpu core, cpu speed, memory etc. and $CS_r(j)$ returns the available value of each dimension (e.g. 12 core, 2.1 GHz, 32 GB).

Table 3. Important notations

Notation	Description and Condition
S	Set of physical server in a data center
$S_j \in S$	Any server in set S, where $1 \le j \le m$
VM	Set of virtual machine
$\bar{v}_i \in VM$	Any vm in set VM, where $1 \le i \le n$
$\bar{v} = \{C\bar{v}\}$	Information carried by any virtual machine
$C\bar{v}$	Capacity requirements by virtual machine $\bar{v}$
$C\bar{v}_d(i)$	Capacity requirement by of vmi with d dimensions
$CS_r(j)$	Available capacity of server j with r dimensions
$u_r(j)$	Percentage of utilization by r dimensions in S_j
e_j	Total energy consumption by server S_j
$e_{max}(j)$	Total energy consumption by server S_j when $u_r(j) = 100\%$
$e_{idle}(j)$	Total energy consumption by server S_j when $u_r(j) = 0\%$

Calculation of Utilization and Energy Consumption

Utilization of *cpu* for any server Sj can be calculated by

$$u_{cpu}(j) = \frac{\sum_{i=1}^{n} C\bar{v}_{cpu}(i) \times B_{ij}^{\bar{v}}}{CS_{cpu}(j)} \quad (1)$$

Energy consumption e_j by any server S_j can be calculated (Kusic et al., 2009) by:

$$e_j = \left(e_{max}(j) - e_{idle}(j)\right) \times U_{cpu}(j) + e_{idle} \quad (2)$$

ILP Formulation

$$Minimize \sum_{j=1}^{m} e_j \quad (3)$$

The objective of the above algorithm is total energy consumption by active servers in the data center will be minimized.

$$\sum_{j=1}^{m} B_{ij}^{\bar{v}} = 1 \quad ; \quad \forall i \in \{1,...,n\} \quad (4)$$

If it is considered that all requested VMs in VM set will be placed in physical servers, then equation 4 will be 1 and one VM will be placed in one server only.

$$\sum_{i=1}^{n} C\bar{v}_d(i).B_{ij}^{\bar{v}} \leq CS_r(j) \; ; \forall j; \forall d; \forall r \quad (5)$$

Equation 5 describes the capacity requirement in all dimensions (e.g., CPU, #cores, memory) for all placed VMs will be less or equal to the capacity available in all dimensions for all active servers.

$$D^{\bar{v}} \in \{0,1\}; q \in \{1,...,R\};$$
$$t \in \{1,...,w\}; \; q_t \in \{1,...,n\}; \quad (6)$$

The virtual machine placement problem, as stated earlier, is an NP-Hard problem. To find an optimal solution is infeasible to such a problem because as the problem size will increase the solution space will also increase exponentially. Randomized algorithm is one way to address this problem. Simulated annealing, one of the popular randomized algorithm. Discussion about SA is in following section.

3. ALGORITHM FORMULATIONS FOR MULTI-DIMENSIONAL APPROACH

We solve our bi-objective problem using the Simulated Annealing optimization technique. The motivation behind using simulated annealing is, an exceptionally simple evolution technique which is significantly more robust and faster in numerical optimization and more likely to find a function's for true global optimum. It is a heuristic method that has been implemented to obtain good solutions for an objective function. The simulated annealing method mimics the physical process of heating a material and then slowly lowering the temperature (cooling) to decrease defects so as to minimize the system energy. There are mainly four steps for SA. We mapped those steps with our proposed model and describe accordingly in following subsections.

Initial Configuration

The first step is to generate an initial configuration of VM placement which may not be an optimal placement, but satisfying all mentioned constrained and it must provide objective value.

All virtual machines in set VM have to place in server set S. It is assumed that one VM can place in one server only. To represent the placement scenario a linear array is used. Equation 7 shows general structure of the VM linear array and Figure 7 describe how linear array is constructed. In this example, there are 15 VM will be placed in four servers, which are numbered from 1 to 4. After placement the of the array represents the VM number and the value of indexed represented as server number where that particular VM has been placed.

$$VM = \left\{ \bar{v_1}, \bar{v_2}, ..., \bar{v_i}, ..., \bar{v_n} \right\} \qquad (7)$$

The index of the linear array is the VM number and the value indexed by the VM number in the array is the server number to which the VM is placed. For example, we have 15 VMs indexed from 1 to 15 and 4 servers numbered from 1 to 4. In S1 virtual machine v1, v3, v6, got placed. The length of the array is the maximum number of tasks in the window, also termed as *WinSize*. This will denote the number of VM to place in one allocation step from n number of virtual machine set VM. It is assumed that number of task n is an integer multiple of *WinSize*. Linear array helps the

index to be used as a VM number in the window so that a one dimensional list representation is possible for the solution. Simulated annealing based dynamic placement in Algorithm 5 operates in batch mode and selects a batch of VM B[i] in every iteration. Algorithm 6 is executed to produce an optimal schedule for the selected batch of VM B [I] in a fixed number of iterations.

New Neighboring Configuration

After generation of initial configuration the next step for SA is generation of new neighboring configuration. The objective of a new configuration is to achieve a better placement solution. To accept the new solution after initial solution, there are certain acceptance criteria discussed in the next subsection. For a generation of next new configuration of initial configuration we define a new neighborhood state as the new VM placement array generated by randomly picking three algorithms namely, (i) inversion, (ii) translation and (iii) switching. These algorithms are used to produce new configuration VM' on each iteration from the neighborhood of current solutions VM.

1. **Inversion:** The inversion process applied to a VM placement array to create a new

Figure 7. VM array representation

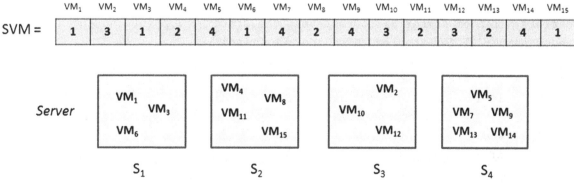

placement array by swapping few positions. Here, we selected four randomly chosen consecutive positions and replace them in reverse order of the pattern. The inversion process describes in Algorithm 2.

2. **Translation:** To generate new configuration VM', translation process removes two or more consecutive nodes from the VM placement array and place those nodes in between any two randomly selected consecutive nodes. This process performed by Algorithm 3.

3. **Switching:** New configuration VM' can be constructed using switching technique as describe in algorithm 4. It is randomly selected two nodes and switches them in an array.

Acceptance Criteria

After generation of new configuration the criteria will decide which configuration will become the next new state. In this proposed model a new configuration is feasible and accepted as new states, if it fulfills all constraints defined by equation 4, 5, 6, and the value of the objective function

will be min than the previous state. The simulated annealing framework in Algorithm 6 uses a fixed number of iteration max. The VMP (VM) is the objective function that computes a fitness value for the initial solution VM. Starting from the initial solution, the algorithm computes a new solution VM' on each iteration from the neighborhood of the current solution VM. The value of the objective function of the two solutions is compared to select the solution to be used for the next iteration. If the current computed solution is worse than the previous solution, it can be accepted with a certain probability with reference to current temperature value. The cooling schedule starts with initial temperature T0, and decrease by a factor $' \in (0,1]$ and takes a constant value for the fixed number of iterations. The cooling process of temperature is realized with $T_k \leftarrow T_0 \delta^k$. The cooling process continues *for k = 1, 2, 3, ...,max* to meet the termination condition.

Temperature Scheduling

In the simulated annealing methodology, one of the very important aspects is temperature sched-

Algorithm 2. Inversion (VM, WinSize)

```
Input: VM = (vm₁, vm₂, vm₃, ..., vm₁₀): VM placement array, WinSize= Size of the
VM
Result: VM₊ = (vm₁, vm₂, vm₃, ..., vm₁₀): new VM placement array
generate a random number S1 to represent the starting 1 point and another
random number L1 for the length of the substring;
2 let SS = StringReverse(SubString VM, S1,L1);
3 for i = 1 to WinSize do
4         if i < S1 or (i > S1 and i _ S1 + L1) then
5                 S = concat(S,VM(i)) ;
6         end
7         if i == S1 then
8                 S = concat(S,SS);
9         end
10 end
11 return(VM);
```

Algorithm 3. Translation (VM, WinSize)

```
Input: VM = (vm₁, vm₂, vm₃, ..., vm₁₀): VM placement array, WinSize= Size of the
VM
Result: VM* = (vm₁, vm₂, vm₃, ..., vm₁₀): new VM placement array
generate a random number S1 to represent the starting 1 point and another
random number L1 for the length of the substring;
2 generate a random number I1 for the insertion point;
3 let SS = StringReverse(SubString(VM, S1,L1);
4 for i = 1 to WinSize do
5          if (i < I1) or (i > S1 and i _ S1 + L1) then
6                    S = concat(S,VM(i));
7          end
8          if i == S1 then
9                    S = concat(VM,SS);
10         end
11         if (i > I1) or (i < S1 and i _ S1 + L1) then
12                    S = concat(S,VM(i));
13         end
14 end
15 return(VM);
```

Algorithm 4. Switching (VM, WinSize)

```
Input: VM = (vm₁, vm₂, vm₃, ..., vm₁₀): VM placement array,
          WinSize = Size of the VM
Result: VM* = (vm₁, vm₂, vm₃, ..., vm₁₀): new VM placement array
1 generate a random number i to represent the VM 1 and another random
   number j to represent VM 2;
2 swap(VM(i),VM(j));
3 return(VM);
```

uling. The result will be far from optimal one because of quick quenching [[Kirkpatrick et al. 1983]. Temperature is used as a control parameter in SA and decreases gradually with each iteration. This decides the probability of accepting a worse solution at any step and commonly used as a *stopping criterion*. The initial temperature used is an integer value and decreased by a rate called annealing schedule. For this experiment the upper bound of temperature sets at 1000 degrees and it reduces towards lower bound at 0 degrees by each time 5 degree.

4. EVALUATION AND ANALYSIS

All mentioned algorithm has been implemented by in house simulation using JAVA on a workstation computer with Intel (R) core (TM) 2 Duo CPU of 3.00 GHz and 4.00 GB memory. The test data used

Algorithm 5. VM Schedular

```
Input: n: number of VM, m: number of server, batch size: WinSize
Result: L: placement
1 L_j ←  0 for all servers;
2 for i = 1 to n/WinSize do
3          select a batch of VM B[i];
4          call Algorithm 6: VMP(B[i],WinSize);
5          assign VM in B[i] to servers as per VM;
6          update information of the assigned server;
7          update placement time for each server;
8 end
9 L  ← max_j L_j return placement: L
```

for this simulation study uses eleven set of virtual machines on a fixed number of servers equal to 30. In order to check the scalability of the proposed set of algorithms using simulated annealing, a plot of the execution time curve for the situation when the number of virtual machines in VM sets increased from 10 to 150 with an incremental of 10 whereas the number of servers was fixed in 30. Figure 8 shows the observation inform of a line graph, showing the execution time of the proposed algorithms increases very close to linearly when the number of VMs increases and the number of servers is fixed. Thus, it can be concluded that the proposed set of algorithm is scalable with respect to the number of virtual machines.

The experiment result of a number of virtual machine vs. energy cost has been plotted in Figure 9. A comparison has given to the FFD algorithm with the same set of test data as mentioned in Table 4. From graph 7 it is clearly shown that the proposed placement model significantly outperforms than exiting FFD algorithm.

The reason behind this is, in the FFD, beams are placed onto the first server, where they first fit. This placement is non-optimal though it allows for faster placement. FFD placement is a deterministic one, it does not attempt to minimize the number of servers used. The proposed model, attempts to minimize the number of servers used by looking all possible solutions.

5. BACKGROUND

Provide broad definitions and discussions of the topic and incorporate views of others (literature review) into the discussion to support, refute or demonstrate your position on the topic.[1]

In this section, we made an investigation of different VM placement strategies in data centers. There are two types of VM-placement decisions are made in a cloud data center. They are:(i) initial placement of vms (Cardosa et al., 2011; Meng et al., 2010; Xu & Fortes, 2010; Bellur & Rao, 2010; Sindelar et al., 2011; Mark et al., 2011; Kantarci et al., 2012; Chaisiri et al., 2009; Speitkamp & Bichler, 2010) and (ii) migration (and/or resizing) of VMs over time (Wood et al., 2007; Shrivastava et al., 2011; Zhang et al., 2012; Clark et al., 2005; Zhao & Figueiredo, 2007; Wood et al., 2009). As the availability of physical machine (PM) changes over time, necessitates the consolidation of VMs to conserve power, as well as to meet the required service level agreement (SLA). We describe below the schemes reported in the literatures for initial VM placement.

Algorithm 6. Virtual machine placement

Input: VM number, capacity requirement, Server capacity, Initial
         temperature, temperature cooling schedule
Result: Placement of Virtual Machine, Energy saved, Revenue earned
         randomly generate initial solution 1 VM for a batch of VM B[i];
2 initialize T_0, max;
3 k $\leftarrow$ 0;
4 **while** T_0 > 0 **do**
5   set i=0;
6   **for** i = 1, 2, ...,max **do**
7   generate a random integer m from the set 1,2,3;
8   **if** *m = 1* **then**
9   VM' $\leftarrow$ INV ERSION(VM,WinSize);
10   **end**
11   **if** *m = 2* **then**
12   VM' $\leftarrow$ TRANSLAT ION(VM,WinSize);
13   **end**
14   **if** *m = 3* **then**
15   VM' $\leftarrow$ SWITCHING(VM,WinSize);
16   **end**
17   **if** (VMP(VM') - VMP(VM) < 0) **then**
18   set VM $\leftarrow$ VM' ;
19   Save the placement if it is least objectives so
far;
20   **else**
21   generate random x uniformly in the range [0,1];
22                $T_k \leftarrow T_0 \delta^k$;

If   x < $\exp \dfrac{VMP(VM') - VMP(VM)}{T_k}$ **then**

24   set S $\leftarrow$ S' ;
25   **end**
26   **end**
27   **end**
28 decrement T_0 ;
29 k $\leftarrow$ k + 1;
30 **end**
31 return VM and VMP(VM);

Figure 8. VM vs. Time when server = 30

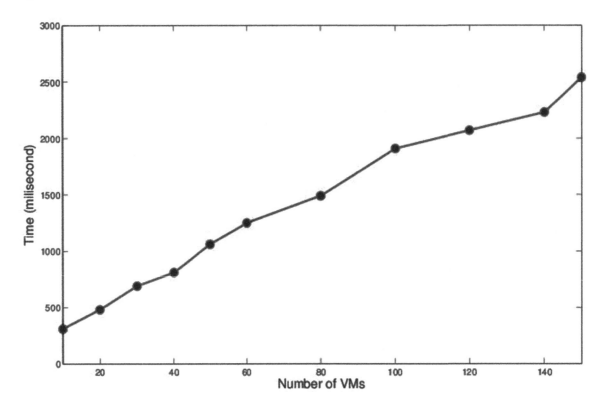

Figure 9. Number of Vm vs. energy cost when server = 30

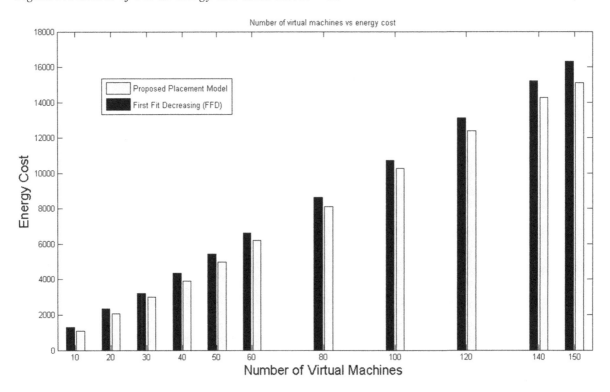

Table 4. Test data

SL. NO.	VM	SERVER
1	10	30
2	20	30
3	30	30
4	40	30
5	50	30
6	60	30
7	80	30
8	100	30
9	120	30
10	140	30
11	150	30

Initial VM Placement

A number of heuristics have been proposed in the literature for initial VM placement of VMs in a cloud data center. A few of them are described below. The bin packing problem is the very well-known technique to solve optimization problems. It has been used several times for VM placement with different heuristics. First Fit Decreasing (FFD) is among popular algorithm for it (Yao, 1980; Feller et al., 2011; Bksi et al., 2000). However, FFD has its some limitations. In FFD all bins are in one dimension, where all servers in data centers are multi-dimensional.

Genetic Algorithm has been used for solving VM placement optimization problem (Xu & Fortes, 2010; Mi et al., 2010). Fewest GA approaches give good result of energy efficient VM placement. A modified genetic algorithm with fuzzy multi-objective evaluation was proposed for efficiently searching the large solution space and conveniently combining possibly conflicting objectives (Xu & Fortes, 2010).

Liner Programming is another analytical approach for VM placement (Kantarci et al., 2012; Chaisiri et al., 2009; Speitkamp & Bichler, 2010). The authors described linear programming formulations of server consolidation problems. They

considered the existence of both reservation and on-demand payment plans for hosting the virtual machines. Given that only the probability distribution of the future demand and resource pricing is known, the algorithm stochastically finds the optimal allocation that minimizes the costs spent using these plans.

Constraint programming methods have also been applied for VM placement in various environments (Van et al., 2010; Hermenier et al., 2009). The Authors expressed VM provisioning and placement problems as two constraint satisfaction problem. They proposed Entropy resource manager, which performs dynamic consolidation based on constraint programming and takes into account both the problems of allocating the VMs to the available nodes and the problem of how to migrate the VMs to these nodes.

These previous works achieved many issues in different point of view and motivates us to handle the virtual machine problem using optimization theory.

6. CONCLUSION AND FUTURE DIRECTIONS

The cloud service providers are trying to maximize the resource available with their data centers by meeting the users' requirements with the minimum use physical resources which leads to the minimization of the energy consumed by these resources. The ongoing research on data center management in cloud computing emphasizes the use of online resources has been increased gradually in last one decade. It ceased to increase the number of servers in data centers.

To run this huge number of servers needs huge power consumption. Virtualization provides the proper resource utilization. Optimally placed VMs on the server can minimize the power consumption in the data center. The simulated annealing optimization technique has been implemented in this proposed model. The motivation behind using simulated annealing is, an exceptionally simple evolution technique which is significantly more robust and faster in numerical optimization and more likely to find a function's for true global optimum. The proposed model of this research document for VM placement gives a significantly better performance than existing FFD technique.

The idea of virtual machine contract may introduce as future work in order to enhance the overall data center management for virtual machine placement. A virtual machine contract (VMC) is a platform independent way of automating the communication and management of users' resource requirements. Basically, VMC is adding management metadata to the package in which VMs are stored and communicated (Matthews et al., 2009).

Another important research area in this direction is the service level agreement (SLA) based virtual machine management. Today, all data centers run various types of applications on different VMs without a prior knowledge of differential SLA requirements, which leads to SLA violation and mismanagement between different cloud service providers. A proper strategy for efficient resource management scheme for avoiding such type of problem.

7. MORE THEORY: SIMULATED ANNEALING

The simulated annealing method resembles the cooling process of molten metals through annealing. At high temperature, the atoms in the molten metal can move freely with respect to each other, but as the temperature is reduced, the movement of the atoms gets restricted. The atoms start to get ordered and final form crystals having the minimum possible energy. However, the formulation of the crystal, mostly depends on the cooling rate. If the temperature is reduced at a very fast rate, the crystalline state may not be achieved at all; instead, the system may end up in a polycrystalline state, which may have a higher energy state than the crystalline state. Therefore, in order to achieve the absolute minimum energy state, the temperature needs to be reduced at a slow rate. The process of slow cooling is known as *annealing* in metallurgical parlance.

The simulated annealing procedure simulates this process of slow cooling molten metal to achieve the minimum function value in a minimization problem. The cooling phenomenon is simulated by controlling a temperature like parameter introduced to the concept of the Boltzmann probability distribution. According to the Boltzmann probability distribution, a system in thermal equilibrium at a temperature T has its energy distributed probabilistically according to $P(E) = \exp(-E/kT)$, when k is the Boltzmann constant. This expression suggests that a system at a high temperature has an almost uniform probability of being in any energy state, but at a low temperature it has a small probability of being in a high energy state. Therefore, by controlling the temperature T and assuming that the search process follows the Boltzmann probability distribution, the convergence of an algorithm can be controlled.

Simulated annealing is a point-by-point method. The algorithm begins with an initial point and a high temperature T. A second point is created at random in the vicinity of the initial point and the difference in the function values (ΔE) at these two points is calculated. If the second point has a smaller functional value, the point is accepted; otherwise the point is accepted with a probability $\exp(-\Delta E/T)$. This completes one iteration of the simulated annealing procedure. In the next generation, another point is created at random in the neighborhood of the current point and the Metropolis algorithm is used to accept or

Algorithm 7. Simulated annealing template

```
Step 1 Choose an initial point x⁽⁰⁾, a termination criterion  ∈. Set T a suffi-
ciently high value, number of
           iteration to be performed at a particular temperature n, and set t
= 0.;
Step 2 Calculate a neighboring point xᵗ⁺¹ = N(xᵗ⁾). Usually, a random point in
the neighborhood is
           created.;
Step 3 If Δ = E(xᵗ⁺¹) - E(xᵗ⁾) < 0, set t = t + 1;
           Else create a random number (r) in the range (0, 1). If r ≤ exp(-
Δ /T)
           set t = t + 1;
           Else go to Step 2.
Step 4 If |xᵗ⁺¹⁾ - xᵗ⁾ | < ∈.  and T is small, Terminate ;
           Else if (t mod n) = 0 then lower T according to a cooling schedule.
Go to Step 2;
           Else go to Step 2.
```

reject the point. In order to simulate the thermal equilibrium at every temperature, a number of points (n) are usually tested at a particular temperature, before reducing the temperature. The algorithm is terminated when a sufficient small temperature is obtained or a small enough change in function values is found.

REFERENCES

A Platform Computing Whitepaper (March 2010);

Bakshi, K. (2009). *Cisco Cloud Computing: Data Center Strategy, Architecture, and Solutions* (1st edition, pp. 1-16). white paper for U.S public sector, Cisco System, Inc.

Bksi, J., Galambos, G., & Kellerer, H. (2000). A 5/4 linear time bin packing algorithm. *Journal of Computer and System Sciences*, 60(1), 145–160. doi:10.1006/jcss.1999.1667

Buyya, R., & Abawajy, A. B. (2010). Energy efficient management of data center resources for cloud computing: A vision, architectural elements, and open challenges. *In 2010 International Conference on Parallel and Distributed Processing Techniques and Applications. PDPTA.*

Cardosa, M., Korupolu, M. R., & Singh, A. (2009), Shares and utilities based power consolidation in virtualized server environments, *In Proceedings of the 11th IFIP/IEEE International Conference on Symposium on Integrated Network Management, IM'09* (pp. 327–334), *Piscataway, NJ, USA. IEEE Press.* doi:10.1109/INM.2009.5188832

Cardosa, M., Singh, A., Pucha, H., & Chandra, A. (2011), Exploiting spatiotemporal tradeoffs for energy-aware mapreduce in the cloud. *In Proceedings of the 2011 IEEE 4th International Conference on Cloud Computing, CLOUD '11* (pages 251–258). *Washington, DC, USA. IEEE Computer Society.* doi:10.1109/CLOUD.2011.68

Chaisiri, S., Lee, B.-S., & Niyato, D. (2009), Optimal virtual machine placement across multiple cloud providers, *In Services Computing Conference, 2009. APSCC 2009. IEEE Asia Pacific,* (pp. 103–110).

Clark, C., Fraser, K., Hand, S., Hansen, J. G., Jul, E., Limpach, C., ... Warfield, A. (2005). Live migration of virtual machines. *In Proceedings of the 2nd Conference on Symposium on Networked Systems Design & Implementation - Volume 2, NSDI'05,* (pp. 273–286). *Berkeley, CA, USA. USENIX Association.*

Creasy, R. (1981, September). The origin of the vm/370 timesharing system. *IBM Journal of Research and Development, 25*(5), 483–490. doi:10.1147/rd.255.0483

Dooley, B., (2010), Architectural Requirements Of The Hybrid Cloud, *Information Management Online; 10.*

Enterprise Cloud Computing:Transforming IT; 13; 6.

Feller, E., Rilling, L., & Morin, C. (2011), Energy-aware ant colony based workload placement in clouds. In *12th IEEE/ACM International Conference on Grid Computing (GRID), 2011,* (pp. 26–33).

Gamal, A., & Yskandar, H. (2004). Two phase algorithm for load balancing in heterogeneous distributed systems. In *Proceedings of the 12th Euromicro Conference on Parallel, Distributed and Network-Based Processing,* 2004, (pp. 434-439). IEEE.

Gao, Y., Guan, H., Qi, Z., Hou, Y., & Liu, L. (2013). A multi-objective ant colony system algorithm for virtual machine placement in cloud computing. *Journal of Computer and System Sciences, 79*(8), 1230–1242. doi:10.1016/j.jcss.2013.02.004

Gonzalez, L. M. V., Rodero-Merino, L., Caceres, J., & Lindner, M. A. (2009). A break in the clouds: Towards a cloud definition. *Computer Communication Review, 39*(1), 50–55.

Helen, D., & Karatza, R., & Hilzer., C. (2002). Load Sharing in Heterogeneous Distributed Systems. In *Proceeding of the winter simulation conference* (pp. 489-496).

Hermenier, F., Lorca, X., Menaud, J.-M., Muller, G., & Lawall, J. (2009). Entropy: A consolidation manager for clusters. In *Proceedings of the 2009 ACM SIGPLAN/SIGOPS International Conference on Virtual Execution Environments, VEE '09* (pp. 41–50). *New York, NY, USA. ACM.* doi:10.1145/1508293.1508300

Kantarci, B., Foschini, L., Corradi, A., & Mouftah, H. (2012). Inter-and-intra data center vm-placement for energy-efficient large scale cloud systems. In Globecom Workshops (GC Wkshps), 2012, (pp. 708–713). IEEE.

Kirkpatrick, S., Gelatt, C. D., & Vecchi, M. P. (1983). Optimization by simulated annealing. *Science, 220*(4598), 671–680. doi:10.1126/science.220.4598.671 PMID:17813860

Kusic, D., Kephart, J. O., Hanson, J. E., Kandasamy, N., & Jiang, G. (2009). Power and performance management of virtualized computing environments via lookahead control. *Cluster Computing, 12*(1), 1–15. doi:10.1007/s10586-008-0070-y

Lee, Y. C., & Zomaya, A. Y. (2012). Energy efficient utilization of resources in cloud computing systems. *The Journal of Supercomputing, 60*(2), 268–280. doi:10.1007/s11227-010-0421-3

Lofstrand M. (2009) The VeriScale Architecture: Elasticity and Efficiency for Private Clouds"; *Sun BluePrint; Sun Microsystems; Online, Revision 1.1, Part No 821-0248-11.*

Mark, C., Niyato, D., & Chen-Khong, T. (2011). Evolutionary optimal virtual machine placement and demand forecaster for cloud computing. *In Advanced Information Networking and Applications (AINA), 2011 IEEE International Conference on, pages 348–355.*

Marston, S., Li, Z., Bandyopadhyay, S., & Ghalsasi, A. (2011). Cloud computing the business perspective. In *HICSS* (pp. 1–11). IEEE Computer Society.

Matthews, J., Garfinkel, T., Hoff, C., & Wheeler, J. Virtual Machine Contracts for Data Center and Cloud Computing Environments. *In Proceedings of the 1st Workshop on Automated Control for Datacenters and Clouds. New York, NY, USA. ACM. pages* 25-30. 2009

Meng, X., Pappas, V., & Zhang, L. (2010). Improving the scalability of data center networks with traffic-aware virtual machine placement. *In INFOCOM, Proceedings IEEE, pages* 1–9.

Mi, H., Wang, H., Yin, G., Zhou, Y., Shi, D., & Yuan, L. (2010). Online self-reconfiguration with performance guarantee for energy efficient large-scale cloud computing data centers. *In Services Computing (SCC), 2010 IEEE International Conference on, pages 514–521.*

NIST. (n.d) Definition of Cloud Computing v 15, csrc.nist.gov/groups/SNS/cloud-computing/cloud-def-v 15.doc

Novell (1983). Platespin recon. http://www.novell.com/products/recon/

Ramgovind, S., Eloff, M. M., & Smith, E. The Management of Security in Cloud Computing"; Information Security for South Africa (ISSA); IEEE; 1-7. 2010

Shrivastava, V., Zerfos, P., Lee, K.-W., Jamjoom, H., Liu, Y.-H., & Banerjee, S. (2011). Application-aware virtual machine migration in data centers. *In INFOCOM, 2011 Proceedings IEEE, pages 66–70.*

Sindelar, M., Sitaraman, R. K., & Shenoy, P. (2011). Sharing-aware algorithms for virtual machine colocation. *In Proceedings of the 23rd ACM Symposium on Parallelism in Algorithms and Architectures, SPAA '11, pages 367–378, New York, NY, USA. ACM.*

Speitkamp, B., & Bichler, M. (2010). A mathematical programming approach for server consolidation problems in virtualized data centers. *Services Computing. IEEE Transactions on, 3*(4), 266–278.

Tang, Q., Gupta, S. K. S., & Varsamopoulos, G. (2008). Energy-efficient thermal aware task scheduling for homogeneous high performance computing data centers: A cyber-physical approach. *IEEE Transactions on Parallel and Distributed Systems, 19*(11), 1458–1472.

Thibodeau, P. (August 03, 2011). Data centers use 2% of u.s. energy, below forecast. *Computerworld.*

Umesh, B. & S, R. C. (2010). Optimal placement algorithms for virtual machines. *arXiv preprint arXiv:1011.5064.*

Van, H. N., Tran, F., & Menaud, J.-M. (2010). Performance and power management for cloud infrastructures. *In Cloud Computing (CLOUD), 2010 IEEE 3rd International Conference on, pages 329–336.*

VMware. (1983). Capacity planner. http://www.vmware.com/products/capacityplanner/

Vouk, M. A. (2008). Virtualization of information technology resources. In *Electronic Commerce: A Managerial Perspective 2008* (5th ed.). Prentice-Hall Business Publishing.

WebSphere. I. (1983). Cloudburst. http://www-01. ibm.com/software/webservers/cloudburst/

Wood, T., Shenoy, P. J., Venkataramani, A., & Yousif, M. S. (2007). Black-box and gray-box strategies for virtual machine migration. In NSDI, volume 7, pages 229–242.

Wood, T., Tarasuk-Levin, G., Shenoy, P., Desnoyers, P., Cecchet, E., & Corner, M. D. (2009). Memory buddies: Exploiting page shar- ing for smart colocation in virtualized data centers. *In Proceedings of the 2009 ACM SIGPLAN/SIGOPS International Conference on Virtual Execution Environments, VEE '09, pages* 31–40, *New York, NY, USA. ACM.*

Xu, J., & Fortes, J. A. B. (2010). Multi-objective virtual machine placement in virtualized data center environments. *In Proceedings of the 2010 IEEE/ACM Int'L Conference on Green Computing and Communications & Int'L Conference on Cyber, Physical and Social Computing, GREENCOM-CPSCOM '10, pages* 179–188, *Washington, DC, USA. IEEE Computer Society.*

Yao, A. C.-C. (1980). New algorithms for bin packing. *Journal of the ACM, 27(2),* 207–227.

York, NY, USA. ACM.

Zhang, X., Shae, Z.-Y., Zheng, S., & Jamjoom, H. (2012). Virtual machine migration in an over-committed cloud. In *Network Operations and Management Symposium (NOMS),* 2012 *IEEE, pages* 196–203.

Zhang Qi, Cheng Lu & Boutaba Raouf (2010). Cloud computing: state-of-the-art and research challenges. *Journal of Internet Services and Applications. Springer-Verlag. 1(1), pages 7-18.*

Zhao, M., & Figueiredo, R. J. (2007). Experimental study of virtual machine migration in support of reservation of cluster resources. *In Proceedings of the 2Nd International Workshop on Virtualization Technology in Distributed Computing, VTDC '07, pages 5:1–5:8, New*

KEY TERMS AND DEFINITIONS

Cloud Computing: Cloud computing is a model for enabling ubiquitous, convenient, on-demand network access to a shared pool of configurable computing resources (e.g., networks, servers, storage, applications, and services) that can be rapidly provisioned and released with minimal management effort or service provider interaction.

Data Center: A data center is a centralized repository, either physical or virtual, for the storage, management, and dissemination of data and information organized around a particular body of knowledge or pertaining to a particular business.

Hypervisor: It is also known as a Virtual Machine Monitor (VMM), which is basically an intermediate layer between VMs and hardware resources. It manages all VMs, depending upon hardware resource availability.

Simulated Annealing: Simulated annealing is a method of finding optimal values numerically. Simulated annealing is a search method as opposed to a gradient based algorithm. It chooses a new point, and (for optimization) all uphill points are accepted while some downhill points are accepted depending on a probabilistic criteria.

Virtual Machine (VM): A virtual machine is a software computer that, like a physical computer, runs an operating system and applications. The virtual machine is comprised of a set of specification and configuration files and is backed by the physical resources of a host. Every virtual machine has virtual devices that provide the same functionality as physical hardware and have additional benefits in terms of portability, manageability, and security.

Virtualization: Virtualization is the concept that hides the physical behavior of a computational platform from the end user mainly, instead presenting an abstract and emulated computational platform.

VM Placement: The process of mapping VMs to Physical Machines (PM) is called Virtual machine placement. One hypervisor layer is exists between VMs and physical resources, such that cpu, memory, storage etc. VM placement is an important approach for improving power efficiency and resource utilization of cloud Data center.

Related References

To continue our tradition of advancing information science and technology research, we have compiled a list of recommended IGI Global readings. These references will provide additional information and guidance to further enrich your knowledge and assist you with your own research and future publications.

Aalmink, J., von der Dovenmühle, T., & Gómez, J. M. (2013). Enterprise tomography: Maintenance and root-cause-analysis of federated erp in enterprise clouds. In P. Ordóñez de Pablos, H. Nigro, R. Tennyson, S. Gonzalez Cisaro, & W. Karwowski (Eds.), *Advancing information management through semantic web concepts and ontologies* (pp. 133–153). Hershey, PA: Information Science Reference. doi:10.4018/978-1-4666-2494-8.ch007

Abu, S. T., & Tsuji, M. (2011). The development of ICT for envisioning cloud computing and innovation in South Asia. *International Journal of Innovation in the Digital Economy*, 2(1), 61–72. doi:10.4018/jide.2011010105

Abu, S. T., & Tsuji, M. (2012). The development of ICT for envisioning cloud computing and innovation in South Asia. In *Grid and cloud computing: Concepts, methodologies, tools and applications* (pp. 453–465). Hershey, PA: Information Science Reference. doi:10.4018/978-1-4666-0879-5.ch207

Abu, S. T., & Tsuji, M. (2013). The development of ICT for envisioning cloud computing and innovation in South Asia. In I. Oncioiu (Ed.), *Business innovation, development, and advancement in the digital economy* (pp. 35–47). Hershey, PA: Business Science Reference. doi:10.4018/978-1-4666-2934-9.ch003

Adams, R. (2013). The emergence of cloud storage and the need for a new digital forensic process model. In K. Ruan (Ed.), *Cybercrime and cloud forensics: Applications for investigation processes* (pp. 79–104). Hershey, PA: Information Science Reference. doi:10.4018/978-1-4666-2662-1.ch004

Adeyeye, M. (2013). Provisioning converged applications and services via the cloud. In D. Kanellopoulos (Ed.), *Intelligent multimedia technologies for networking applications: Techniques and tools* (pp. 248–269). Hershey, PA: Information Science Reference. doi:10.4018/978-1-4666-2833-5.ch010

Aggarwal, A. (2013). A systems approach to cloud computing services. In A. Bento & A. Aggarwal (Eds.), *Cloud computing service and deployment models: Layers and management* (pp. 124–136). Hershey, PA: Business Science Reference. doi:10.4018/978-1-4666-2187-9.ch006

Ahmed, K., Hussain, A., & Gregory, M. A. (2013). An efficient, robust, and secure SSO architecture for cloud computing implemented in a service oriented architecture. In X. Yang & L. Liu (Eds.), *Principles, methodologies, and service-oriented approaches for cloud computing* (pp. 259–282). Hershey, PA: Business Science Reference. doi:10.4018/978-1-4666-2854-0.ch011

Ahuja, S. P., & Mani, S. (2013). Empirical performance analysis of HPC benchmarks across variations in cloud computing. *International Journal of Cloud Applications and Computing, 3*(1), 13–26. doi:10.4018/ijcac.2013010102

Ahuja, S. P., & Rolli, A. C. (2011). Survey of the state-of-the-art of cloud computing. *International Journal of Cloud Applications and Computing, 1*(4), 34–43. doi:10.4018/ijcac.2011100103

Ahuja, S. P., & Rolli, A. C. (2013). Survey of the state-of-the-art of cloud computing. In S. Aljawarneh (Ed.), *Cloud computing advancements in design, implementation, and technologies* (pp. 252–262). Hershey, PA: Information Science Reference. doi:10.4018/978-1-4666-1879-4.ch018

Ahuja, S. P., & Sridharan, S. (2012). Performance evaluation of hypervisors for cloud computing. *International Journal of Cloud Applications and Computing, 2*(3), 26–67. doi:10.4018/ijcac.2012070102

Akyuz, G. A., & Rehan, M. (2013). A generic, cloud-based representation for supply chains (SC's). *International Journal of Cloud Applications and Computing, 3*(2), 12–20. doi:10.4018/ijcac.2013040102

Al-Aqrabi, H., & Liu, L. (2013). IT security and governance compliant service oriented computing in cloud computing environments. In X. Yang & L. Liu (Eds.), *Principles, methodologies, and service-oriented approaches for cloud computing* (pp. 143–163). Hershey, PA: Business Science Reference. doi:10.4018/978-1-4666-2854-0.ch006

Al-Zoube, M., & Wyne, M. F. (2012). Building integrated e-learning environment using cloud services and social networking sites. In Q. Jin (Ed.), *Intelligent learning systems and advancements in computer-aided instruction: Emerging studies* (pp. 214–233). Hershey, PA: Information Science Reference. doi:10.4018/978-1-61350-483-3.ch013

Alam, N., & Karmakar, R. (2014). Cloud computing and its application to information centre. In S. Dhamdhere (Ed.), *Cloud computing and virtualization technologies in libraries* (pp. 63–76). Hershey, PA: Information Science Reference. doi:10.4018/978-1-4666-4631-5.ch004

Alhaj, A., Aljawarneh, S., Masadeh, S., & Abu-Taieh, E. (2013). A secure data transmission mechanism for cloud outsourced data. *International Journal of Cloud Applications and Computing, 3*(1), 34–43. doi:10.4018/ijcac.2013010104

Alharbi, S. T. (2012). Users' acceptance of cloud computing in Saudi Arabia: An extension of technology acceptance model. *International Journal of Cloud Applications and Computing, 2*(2), 1–11. doi:10.4018/ijcac.2012040101

Ali, S. S., & Khan, M. N. (2013). ICT infrastructure framework for microfinance institutions and banks in Pakistan: An optimized approach. *International Journal of Online Marketing, 3*(2), 75–86. doi:10.4018/ijom.2013040105

Aljawarneh, S. (2011). Cloud security engineering: Avoiding security threats the right way. *International Journal of Cloud Applications and Computing, 1*(2), 64–70. doi:10.4018/ijcac.2011040105

Aljawarneh, S. (2013). Cloud security engineering: Avoiding security threats the right way. In S. Aljawarneh (Ed.), *Cloud computing advancements in design, implementation, and technologies* (pp. 147–153). Hershey, PA: Information Science Reference. doi:10.4018/978-1-4666-1879-4.ch010

Alshattnawi, S. (2013). Utilizing cloud computing in developing a mobile location-aware tourist guide system. *International Journal of Advanced Pervasive and Ubiquitous Computing, 5*(2), 9–18. doi::10.4018/japuc.2013040102

Alsmadi, I. (2013). Software development methodologies for cloud computing. In K. Buragga & N. Zaman (Eds.), *Software development techniques for constructive information systems design* (pp. 110–117). Hershey, PA: Information Science Reference. doi:10.4018/978-1-4666-3679-8.ch006

Anand, V. (2013). Survivable mapping of virtual networks onto a shared substrate network. In X. Yang & L. Liu (Eds.), *Principles, methodologies, and service-oriented approaches for cloud computing* (pp. 325–343). Hershey, PA: Business Science Reference. doi:10.4018/978-1-4666-2854-0.ch014

Antonova, A. (2013). Green, sustainable, or clean: What type of IT/IS technologies will we need in the future? In P. Ordóñez de Pablos (Ed.), *Green technologies and business practices: An IT approach* (pp. 151–162). Hershey, PA: Information Science Reference. doi:10.4018/978-1-4666-1972-2.ch008

Ardissono, L., Bosio, G., Goy, A., Petrone, G., Segnan, M., & Torretta, F. (2011). Collaboration support for activity management in a personal cloud environment. *International Journal of Distributed Systems and Technologies*, 2(4), 30–43. doi:10.4018/jdst.2011100103

Ardissono, L., Bosio, G., Goy, A., Petrone, G., Segnan, M., & Torretta, F. (2013). Collaboration support for activity management in a personal cloud environment. In N. Bessis (Ed.), *Development of distributed systems from design to application and maintenance* (pp. 199–212). Hershey, PA: Information Science Reference. doi:10.4018/978-1-4666-2647-8.ch012

Argiolas, M., Atzori, M., Dessì, N., & Pes, B. (2012). Dataspaces enhancing decision support systems in clouds. *International Journal of Web Portals*, 4(2), 35–55. doi:10.4018/jwp.2012040103

Arinze, B., & Anandarajan, M. (2012). Factors that determine the adoption of cloud computing: A global perspective. In M. Tavana (Ed.), *Enterprise Information Systems and Advancing Business Solutions: Emerging Models* (pp. 210–223). Hershey, PA: Business Science Reference. doi:10.4018/978-1-4666-1761-2.ch012

Arinze, B., & Sylla, C. (2012). Conducting research in the cloud. In L. Chao (Ed.), *Cloud computing for teaching and learning: Strategies for design and implementation* (pp. 50–63). Hershey, PA: Information Science Reference. doi:10.4018/978-1-4666-0957-0.ch004

Arshad, J., Townend, P., & Xu, J. (2011). An abstract model for integrated intrusion detection and severity analysis for clouds. *International Journal of Cloud Applications and Computing*, 1(1), 1–16. doi:10.4018/ijcac.2011010101

Arshad, J., Townend, P., & Xu, J. (2013). An abstract model for integrated intrusion detection and severity analysis for clouds. In S. Aljawarneh (Ed.), *Cloud computing advancements in design, implementation, and technologies* (pp. 1–17). Hershey, PA: Information Science Reference. doi:10.4018/978-1-4666-1879-4.ch001

Arshad, J., Townend, P., Xu, J., & Jie, W. (2012). Cloud computing security: Opportunities and pitfalls. *International Journal of Grid and High Performance Computing*, 4(1), 52–66. doi:10.4018/jghpc.2012010104

Baars, T., & Spruit, M. (2012). Designing a secure cloud architecture: The SeCA model. *International Journal of Information Security and Privacy*, 6(1), 14–32. doi:10.4018/jisp.2012010102

Bai, X., Gao, J. Z., & Tsai, W. (2013). Cloud scalability measurement and testing. In S. Tilley & T. Parveen (Eds.), *Software testing in the cloud: Perspectives on an emerging discipline* (pp. 356–381). Hershey, PA: Information Science Reference. doi:10.4018/978-1-4666-2536-5.ch017

Baldini, G., & Stirparo, P. (2014). A cognitive access framework for security and privacy protection in mobile cloud computing. In J. Rodrigues, K. Lin, & J. Lloret (Eds.), *Mobile networks and cloud computing convergence for progressive services and applications* (pp. 92–117). Hershey, PA: Information Science Reference. doi:10.4018/978-1-4666-4781-7.ch006

Balduf, S., Balke, T., & Eymann, T. (2012). Cultural differences in managing cloud computing service level agreements. In *Grid and cloud computing: Concepts, methodologies, tools and applications* (pp. 1237–1263). Hershey, PA: Information Science Reference. doi:10.4018/978-1-4666-0879-5.ch512

Banerjee, S., Sing, T. Y., Chowdhury, A. R., & Anwar, H. (2013). Motivations to adopt green ICT: A tale of two organizations. *International Journal of Green Computing*, *4*(2), 1–11. doi:10.4018/jgc.2013070101

Barreto, J., Di Sanzo, P., Palmieri, R., & Romano, P. (2013). Cloud-TM: An elastic, self-tuning transactional store for the cloud. In D. Kyriazis, A. Voulodimos, S. Gogouvitis, & T. Varvarigou (Eds.), *Data intensive storage services for cloud environments* (pp. 192–224). Hershey, PA: Business Science Reference. doi:10.4018/978-1-4666-3934-8.ch013

Belalem, G., & Limam, S. (2011). Fault tolerant architecture to cloud computing using adaptive checkpoint. *International Journal of Cloud Applications and Computing*, *1*(4), 60–69. doi:10.4018/ijcac.2011100105

Belalem, G., & Limam, S. (2013). Fault tolerant architecture to cloud computing using adaptive checkpoint. In S. Aljawarneh (Ed.), *Cloud computing advancements in design, implementation, and technologies* (pp. 280–289). Hershey, PA: Information Science Reference. doi:10.4018/978-1-4666-1879-4.ch020

Ben Belgacem, M., Abdennadher, N., & Niinimaki, M. (2012). Virtual EZ grid: A volunteer computing infrastructure for scientific medical applications. *International Journal of Handheld Computing Research*, *3*(1), 74–85. doi:10.4018/jhcr.2012010105

Bhatt, S., Chaudhary, S., & Bhise, M. (2013). Migration of data between cloud and non-cloud datastores. In A. Ionita, M. Litoiu, & G. Lewis (Eds.), *Migrating legacy applications: Challenges in service oriented architecture and cloud computing environments* (pp. 206–225). Hershey, PA: Information Science Reference. doi:10.4018/978-1-4666-2488-7.ch009

Biancofiore, G., & Leone, S. (2014). Google apps as a cloud computing solution in Italian municipalities: Technological features and implications. In S. Leone (Ed.), *Synergic integration of formal and informal e-learning environments for adult lifelong learners* (pp. 244–274). Hershey, PA: Information Science Reference. doi:10.4018/978-1-4666-4655-1.ch012

Bibi, S., Katsaros, D., & Bozanis, P. (2012). How to choose the right cloud. In *Grid and cloud computing: Concepts, methodologies, tools and applications* (pp. 1530–1552). Hershey, PA: Information Science Reference. doi:10.4018/978-1-4666-0879-5.ch701

Bibi, S., Katsaros, D., & Bozanis, P. (2012). How to choose the right cloud. In X. Liu & Y. Li (Eds.), *Advanced design approaches to emerging software systems: Principles, methodologies and tools* (pp. 219–240). Hershey, PA: Information Science Reference. doi:10.4018/978-1-60960-735-7.ch010

Bitam, S., Batouche, M., & Talbi, E. (2012). A bees life algorithm for cloud computing services selection. In S. Ali, N. Abbadeni, & M. Batouche (Eds.), *Multidisciplinary computational intelligence techniques: Applications in business, engineering, and medicine* (pp. 31–46). Hershey, PA: Information Science Reference. doi:10.4018/978-1-4666-1830-5.ch003

Bittencourt, L. F., Madeira, E. R., & da Fonseca, N. L. (2014). Communication aspects of resource management in hybrid clouds. In H. Mouftah & B. Kantarci (Eds.), *Communication infrastructures for cloud computing* (pp. 409–433). Hershey, PA: Information Science Reference. doi:10.4018/978-1-4666-4522-6.ch018

Bonelli, L., Giudicianni, L., Immediata, A., & Luzzi, A. (2013). Compliance in the cloud. In D. Kyriazis, A. Voulodimos, S. Gogouvitis, & T. Varvarigou (Eds.), *Data intensive storage services for cloud environments* (pp. 109–131). Hershey, PA: Business Science Reference. doi:10.4018/978-1-4666-3934-8.ch008

Boniface, M., Nasser, B., Surridge, M., & Oliveros, E. (2012). Securing real-time interactive applications in federated clouds. In *Grid and cloud computing: Concepts, methodologies, tools and applications* (pp. 1822–1835). Hershey, PA: Information Science Reference. doi:10.4018/978-1-4666-0879-5.ch806

Boukhobza, J. (2013). Flashing in the cloud: Shedding some light on NAND flash memory storage systems. In D. Kyriazis, A. Voulodimos, S. Gogouvitis, & T. Varvarigou (Eds.), *Data intensive storage services for cloud environments* (pp. 241–266). Hershey, PA: Business Science Reference. doi:10.4018/978-1-4666-3934-8.ch015

Bracci, F., Corradi, A., & Foschini, L. (2014). Cloud standards: Security and interoperability issues. In H. Mouftah & B. Kantarci (Eds.), *Communication infrastructures for cloud computing* (pp. 465–495). Hershey, PA: Information Science Reference. doi:10.4018/978-1-4666-4522-6.ch020

Brown, A. W. (2013). Experiences with cloud technology to realize software testing factories. In S. Tilley & T. Parveen (Eds.), *Software testing in the cloud: Perspectives on an emerging discipline* (pp. 1–27). Hershey, PA: Information Science Reference. doi:10.4018/978-1-4666-2536-5.ch001

Calcavecchia, N. M., Celesti, A., & Di Nitto, E. (2012). Understanding decentralized and dynamic brokerage in federated cloud environments. In M. Villari, I. Brandic, & F. Tusa (Eds.), *Achieving federated and self-manageable cloud infrastructures: Theory and practice* (pp. 36–56). Hershey, PA: Business Science Reference. doi:10.4018/978-1-4666-1631-8.ch003

Calero, J. M., König, B., & Kirschnick, J. (2012). Cross-layer monitoring in cloud computing. In H. Rashvand & Y. Kavian (Eds.), *Using cross-layer techniques for communication systems* (pp. 328–348). Hershey, PA: Information Science Reference. doi:10.4018/978-1-4666-0960-0.ch014

Cardellini, V., Casalicchio, E., & Silvestri, L. (2012). Service level provisioning for cloud-based applications service level provisioning for cloud-based applications. In A. Pathan, M. Pathan, & H. Lee (Eds.), *Advancements in distributed computing and internet technologies: Trends and issues* (pp. 363–385). Hershey, PA: Information Science Publishing: doi:10.4018/978-1-61350-110-8.ch017

Cardellini, V., Casalicchio, E., & Silvestri, L. (2012). Service level provisioning for cloud-based applications service level provisioning for cloud-based applications. In *Grid and cloud computing: Concepts, methodologies, tools and applications* (pp. 1479–1500). Hershey, PA: Information Science Reference. doi:10.4018/978-1-4666-0879-5. ch611

Carlin, S., & Curran, K. (2013). Cloud computing security. In K. Curran (Ed.), *Pervasive and ubiquitous technology innovations for ambient intelligence environments* (pp. 12–17). Hershey, PA: Information Science Reference. doi:10.4018/978-1-4666-2041-4.ch002

Carlton, G. H., & Zhou, H. (2011). A survey of cloud computing challenges from a digital forensics perspective. *International Journal of Interdisciplinary Telecommunications and Networking, 3*(4), 1–16. doi:10.4018/jitn.2011100101

Carlton, G. H., & Zhou, H. (2012). A survey of cloud computing challenges from a digital forensics perspective. In *Grid and cloud computing: Concepts, methodologies, tools and applications* (pp. 1221–1236). Hershey, PA: Information Science Reference. doi:10.4018/978-1-4666-0879-5. ch511

Carlton, G. H., & Zhou, H. (2013). A survey of cloud computing challenges from a digital forensics perspective. In M. Bartolacci & S. Powell (Eds.), *Advancements and innovations in wireless communications and network technologies* (pp. 213–228). Hershey, PA: Information Science Reference. doi:10.4018/978-1-4666-2154-1.ch016

Carpen-Amarie, A., Costan, A., Leordeanu, C., Basescu, C., & Antoniu, G. (2012). Towards a generic security framework for cloud data management environments. *International Journal of Distributed Systems and Technologies, 3*(1), 17–34. doi:10.4018/jdst.2012010102

Casola, V., Cuomo, A., Villano, U., & Rak, M. (2012). Access control in federated clouds: The cloudgrid case study. In M. Villari, I. Brandic, & F. Tusa (Eds.), *Achieving Federated and Self-Manageable Cloud Infrastructures: Theory and Practice* (pp. 395–417). Hershey, PA: Business Science Reference. doi:10.4018/978-1-4666-1631-8.ch020

Casola, V., Cuomo, A., Villano, U., & Rak, M. (2013). Access control in federated clouds: The cloudgrid case study. In *IT policy and ethics: Concepts, methodologies, tools, and applications* (pp. 148–169). Hershey, PA: Information Science Reference. doi:10.4018/978-1-4666-2919-6.ch008

Celesti, A., Tusa, F., & Villari, M. (2012). Toward cloud federation: Concepts and challenges. In M. Villari, I. Brandic, & F. Tusa (Eds.), *Achieving federated and self-manageable cloud infrastructures: Theory and practice* (pp. 1–17). Hershey, PA: Business Science Reference. doi:10.4018/978-1-4666-1631-8.ch001

Chaka, C. (2013). Virtualization and cloud computing: Business models in the virtual cloud. In A. Loo (Ed.), *Distributed computing innovations for business, engineering, and science* (pp. 176–190). Hershey, PA: Information Science Reference. doi:10.4018/978-1-4666-2533-4.ch009

Chang, J. (2011). A framework for analysing the impact of cloud computing on local government in the UK. *International Journal of Cloud Applications and Computing, 1*(4), 25–33. doi:10.4018/ijcac.2011100102

Chang, J. (2013). A framework for analysing the impact of cloud computing on local government in the UK. In S. Aljawarneh (Ed.), *Cloud computing advancements in design, implementation, and technologies* (pp. 243–251). Hershey, PA: Information Science Reference. doi:10.4018/978-1-4666-1879-4.ch017

Chang, J., & Johnston, M. (2012). Cloud computing in local government: From the perspective of four London borough councils. *International Journal of Cloud Applications and Computing*, 2(4), 1–15. doi:10.4018/ijcac.2012100101

Chang, K., & Wang, K. (2012). Efficient support of streaming videos through patching proxies in the cloud. *International Journal of Grid and High Performance Computing*, 4(4), 22–36. doi:10.4018/jghpc.2012100102

Chang, R., Liao, C., & Liu, C. (2013). Choosing clouds for an enterprise: Modeling and evaluation. *International Journal of E-Entrepreneurship and Innovation*, 4(2), 38–53. doi:10.4018/ijeei.2013040103

Chang, V., De Roure, D., Wills, G., & Walters, R. J. (2011). Case studies and organisational sustainability modelling presented by cloud computing business framework. *International Journal of Web Services Research*, 8(3), 26–53. doi:10.4018/JWSR.2011070102

Chang, V., Li, C., De Roure, D., Wills, G., Walters, R. J., & Chee, C. (2011). The financial clouds review. *International Journal of Cloud Applications and Computing*, 1(2), 41–63. doi:10.4018/ijcac.2011040104

Chang, V., Li, C., De Roure, D., Wills, G., Walters, R. J., & Chee, C. (2013). The financial clouds review. In S. Aljawarneh (Ed.), *Cloud computing advancements in design, implementation, and technologies* (pp. 125–146). Hershey, PA: Information Science Reference. doi:10.4018/978-1-4666-1879-4.ch009

Chang, V., Walters, R. J., & Wills, G. (2012). Business integration as a service. *International Journal of Cloud Applications and Computing*, 2(1), 16–40. doi:10.4018/ijcac.2012010102

Chang, V., & Wills, G. (2013). A University of Greenwich case study of cloud computing: Education as a service. In D. Graham, I. Manikas, & D. Folinas (Eds.), *E-logistics and e-supply chain management: Applications for evolving business* (pp. 232–253). Hershey, PA: Business Science Reference. doi:10.4018/978-1-4666-3914-0.ch013

Chang, V., Wills, G., Walters, R. J., & Currie, W. (2012). Towards a structured cloud ROI: The University of Southampton cost-saving and user satisfaction case studies. In W. Hu & N. Kaabouch (Eds.), *Sustainable ICTs and management systems for green computing* (pp. 179–200). Hershey, PA: Information Science Reference. doi:10.4018/978-1-4666-1839-8.ch008

Chang, Y., Lee, Y., Juang, T., & Yen, J. (2013). Cost evaluation on building and operating cloud platform. *International Journal of Grid and High Performance Computing*, 5(2), 43–53. doi:10.4018/jghpc.2013040103

Chao, L. (2012). Cloud computing solution for internet based teaching and learning. In L. Chao (Ed.), *Cloud computing for teaching and learning: Strategies for design and implementation* (pp. 210–235). Hershey, PA: Information Science Reference. doi:10.4018/978-1-4666-0957-0.ch015

Chao, L. (2012). Overview of cloud computing and its application in e-learning. In L. Chao (Ed.), *Cloud computing for teaching and learning: Strategies for design and implementation* (pp. 1–16). Hershey, PA: Information Science Reference. doi:10.4018/978-1-4666-0957-0.ch001

Chauhan, S., Raman, A., & Singh, N. (2013). A comparative cost analysis of on premises IT infrastructure and cloud-based email services in an Indian business school. *International Journal of Cloud Applications and Computing*, 3(2), 21–34. doi:10.4018/ijcac.2013040103

Chen, C., Chao, H., Wu, T., Fan, C., Chen, J., Chen, Y., & Hsu, J. (2011). IoT-IMS communication platform for future internet. *International Journal of Adaptive, Resilient and Autonomic Systems*, 2(4), 74–94. doi:10.4018/jaras.2011100105

Chen, C., Chao, H., Wu, T., Fan, C., Chen, J., Chen, Y., & Hsu, J. (2013). IoT-IMS communication platform for future internet. In V. De Florio (Ed.), *Innovations and approaches for resilient and adaptive systems* (pp. 68–86). Hershey, PA: Information Science Reference. doi:10.4018/978-1-4666-2056-8.ch004

Chen, C. C. (2013). Cloud computing in case-based pedagogy: An information systems success perspective. *International Journal of Dependable and Trustworthy Information Systems*, 2(3), 1–16. doi:10.4018/jdtis.2011070101

Cheney, A. W., Riedl, R. E., Sanders, R., & Tashner, J. H. (2012). The new company water cooler: Use of 3D virtual immersive worlds to promote networking and professional learning in organizations. In Organizational learning and knowledge: Concepts, methodologies, tools and applications (pp. 2848-2861). Hershey, PA: Business Science Reference. doi::10.4018/978-1-60960-783-8.ch801

Chiang, C., & Yu, S. (2013). Cloud-enabled software testing based on program understanding. In S. Tilley & T. Parveen (Eds.), *Software testing in the cloud: Perspectives on an emerging discipline* (pp. 54–67). Hershey, PA: Information Science Reference. doi:10.4018/978-1-4666-2536-5.ch003

Chou, Y., & Oetting, J. (2011). Risk assessment for cloud-based IT systems. [IJGHPC]. *International Journal of Grid and High Performance Computing*, 3(2), 1–13. doi:10.4018/jghpc.2011040101

Chou, Y., & Oetting, J. (2012). Risk assessment for cloud-based IT systems. In *Grid and cloud computing: Concepts, methodologies, tools and applications* (pp. 272–285). Hershey, PA: Information Science Reference. doi:10.4018/978-1-4666-0879-5.ch113

Chou, Y., & Oetting, J. (2013). Risk assessment for cloud-based IT systems. In E. Udoh (Ed.), *Applications and developments in grid, cloud, and high performance computing* (pp. 1–14). Hershey, PA: Information Science Reference. doi:10.4018/978-1-4666-2065-0.ch001

Cohen, F. (2013). Challenges to digital forensic evidence in the cloud. In K. Ruan (Ed.), *Cybercrime and cloud forensics: Applications for investigation processes* (pp. 59–78). Hershey, PA: Information Science Reference. doi:10.4018/978-1-4666-2662-1.ch003

Cossu, R., Di Giulio, C., Brito, F., & Petcu, D. (2013). Cloud computing for earth observation. In D. Kyriazis, A. Voulodimos, S. Gogouvitis, & T. Varvarigou (Eds.), *Data intensive storage services for cloud environments* (pp. 166–191). Hershey, PA: Business Science Reference. doi:10.4018/978-1-4666-3934-8.ch012

Costa, J. E., & Rodrigues, J. J. (2014). Mobile cloud computing: Technologies, services, and applications. In J. Rodrigues, K. Lin, & J. Lloret (Eds.), *Mobile networks and cloud computing convergence for progressive services and applications* (pp. 1–17). Hershey, PA: Information Science Reference. doi:10.4018/978-1-4666-4781-7.ch001

Creaner, G., & Pahl, C. (2013). Flexible coordination techniques for dynamic cloud service collaboration. In G. Ortiz & J. Cubo (Eds.), *Adaptive web services for modular and reusable software development: Tactics and solutions* (pp. 239–252). Hershey, PA: Information Science Reference. doi:10.4018/978-1-4666-2089-6.ch009

Crosbie, M. (2013). Hack the cloud: Ethical hacking and cloud forensics. In K. Ruan (Ed.), *Cybercrime and cloud forensics: Applications for investigation processes* (pp. 42–58). Hershey, PA: Information Science Reference. doi:10.4018/978-1-4666-2662-1.ch002

Curran, K., Carlin, S., & Adams, M. (2012). Security issues in cloud computing. In L. Chao (Ed.), *Cloud computing for teaching and learning: Strategies for design and implementation* (pp. 200–208). Hershey, PA: Information Science Reference. doi:10.4018/978-1-4666-0957-0.ch014

Dahbur, K., & Mohammad, B. (2011). Toward understanding the challenges and countermeasures in computer anti-forensics. *International Journal of Cloud Applications and Computing*, *1*(3), 22–35. doi:10.4018/ijcac.2011070103

Dahbur, K., Mohammad, B., & Tarakji, A. B. (2011). Security issues in cloud computing: A survey of risks, threats and vulnerabilities. *International Journal of Cloud Applications and Computing*, *1*(3), 1–11. doi:10.4018/ijcac.2011070101

Dahbur, K., Mohammad, B., & Tarakji, A. B. (2012). Security issues in cloud computing: A survey of risks, threats and vulnerabilities. In *Grid and cloud computing: Concepts, methodologies, tools and applications* (pp. 1644–1655). Hershey, PA: Information Science Reference. doi:10.4018/978-1-4666-0879-5.ch707

Dahbur, K., Mohammad, B., & Tarakji, A. B. (2013). Security issues in cloud computing: A survey of risks, threats and vulnerabilities. In S. Aljawarneh (Ed.), *Cloud computing advancements in design, implementation, and technologies* (pp. 154–165). Hershey, PA: Information Science Reference. doi:10.4018/978-1-4666-1879-4.ch011

Daim, T., Britton, M., Subramanian, G., Brenden, R., & Intarode, N. (2012). Adopting and integrating cloud computing. In E. Eyob & E. Tetteh (Eds.), *Customer-oriented global supply chains: Concepts for effective management* (pp. 175–197). Hershey, PA: Information Science Reference. doi:10.4018/978-1-4666-0246-5.ch011

Davis, M., & Sedsman, A. (2012). Grey areas: The legal dimensions of cloud computing. In C. Li & A. Ho (Eds.), *Crime prevention technologies and applications for advancing criminal investigation* (pp. 263–273). Hershey, PA: Information Science Reference. doi:10.4018/978-1-4666-1758-2.ch017

De Coster, R., & Albesher, A. (2013). The development of mobile service applications for consumers and intelligent networks. In I. Lee (Ed.), *Mobile services industries, technologies, and applications in the global economy* (pp. 273–289). Hershey, PA: Information Science Reference. doi:10.4018/978-1-4666-1981-4.ch017

De Filippi, P. (2014). Ubiquitous computing in the cloud: User empowerment vs. user obsequity. In J. Pelet & P. Papadopoulou (Eds.), *User behavior in ubiquitous online environments* (pp. 44–63). Hershey, PA: Information Science Reference. doi:10.4018/978-1-4666-4566-0.ch003

De Silva, S. (2013). Key legal issues with cloud computing: A UK law perspective. In A. Bento & A. Aggarwal (Eds.), *Cloud computing service and deployment models: Layers and management* (pp. 242–256). Hershey, PA: Business Science Reference. doi:10.4018/978-1-4666-2187-9.ch013

Deed, C., & Cragg, P. (2013). Business impacts of cloud computing. In A. Bento & A. Aggarwal (Eds.), *Cloud computing service and deployment models: Layers and management* (pp. 274–288). Hershey, PA: Business Science Reference. doi:10.4018/978-1-4666-2187-9.ch015

Deng, M., Petkovic, M., Nalin, M., & Baroni, I. (2013). Home healthcare in cloud computing. In M. Cruz-Cunha, I. Miranda, & P. Gonçalves (Eds.), *Handbook of research on ICTs and management systems for improving efficiency in healthcare and social care* (pp. 614–634). Hershey, PA: Medical Information Science Reference. doi:10.4018/978-1-4666-3990-4.ch032

Desai, A. M., & Mock, K. (2013). Security in cloud computing. In A. Bento & A. Aggarwal (Eds.), *Cloud computing service and deployment models: Layers and management* (pp. 208–221). Hershey, PA: Business Science Reference. doi:10.4018/978-1-4666-2187-9.ch011

Deshpande, R. M., Patle, B. V., & Bhoskar, R. D. (2014). Planning and implementation of cloud computing in NIT's in India: Special reference to VNIT. In S. Dhamdhere (Ed.), *Cloud computing and virtualization technologies in libraries* (pp. 90–106). Hershey, PA: Information Science Reference. doi:10.4018/978-1-4666-4631-5.ch006

Dhamdhere, S. N., & Lihitkar, R. (2014). The university cloud library model and the role of the cloud librarian. In S. Dhamdhere (Ed.), *Cloud computing and virtualization technologies in libraries* (pp. 150–161). Hershey, PA: Information Science Reference. doi:10.4018/978-1-4666-4631-5.ch009

Di Martino, S., Ferrucci, F., Maggio, V., & Sarro, F. (2013). Towards migrating genetic algorithms for test data generation to the cloud. In S. Tilley & T. Parveen (Eds.), *Software testing in the cloud: Perspectives on an emerging discipline* (pp. 113–135). Hershey, PA: Information Science Reference. doi:10.4018/978-1-4666-2536-5.ch006

Di Sano, M., Di Stefano, A., Morana, G., & Zito, D. (2013). FSaaS: Configuring policies for managing shared files among cooperating, distributed applications. *International Journal of Web Portals*, 5(1), 1–14. doi:10.4018/jwp.2013010101

Dippl, S., Jaeger, M. C., Luhn, A., Shulman-Peleg, A., & Vernik, G. (2013). Towards federation and interoperability of cloud storage systems. In D. Kyriazis, A. Voulodimos, S. Gogouvitis, & T. Varvarigou (Eds.), *Data intensive storage services for cloud environments* (pp. 60–71). Hershey, PA: Business Science Reference. doi:10.4018/978-1-4666-3934-8.ch005

Distefano, S., & Puliafito, A. (2012). The cloud@ home volunteer and interoperable cloud through the future internet. In M. Villari, I. Brandic, & F. Tusa (Eds.), *Achieving federated and self-manageable cloud infrastructures: Theory and practice* (pp. 79–96). Hershey, PA: Business Science Reference. doi:10.4018/978-1-4666-1631-8.ch005

Djoleto, W. (2013). Cloud computing and ecommerce or ebusiness: "The now it way" – An overview. In *Electronic commerce and organizational leadership: perspectives and methodologies* (pp. 239–254). Hershey, PA: Business Science Reference. doi:10.4018/978-1-4666-2982-0.ch010

Dollmann, T. J., Loos, P., Fellmann, M., Thomas, O., Hoheisel, A., Katranuschkov, P., & Scherer, R. (2011). Design and usage of a process-centric collaboration methodology for virtual organizations in hybrid environments. *International Journal of Intelligent Information Technologies*, 7(1), 45–64. doi:10.4018/jiit.2011010104

Dollmann, T. J., Loos, P., Fellmann, M., Thomas, O., Hoheisel, A., Katranuschkov, P., & Scherer, R. (2013). Design and usage of a process-centric collaboration methodology for virtual organizations in hybrid environments. In V. Sugumaran (Ed.), *Organizational efficiency through intelligent information technologies* (pp. 45–64). Hershey, PA: Information Science Reference. doi:10.4018/978-1-4666-2047-6.ch004

Dreher, P., & Vouk, M. (2012). Utilizing open source cloud computing environments to provide cost effective support for university education and research. In L. Chao (Ed.), *Cloud computing for teaching and learning: Strategies for design and implementation* (pp. 32–49). Hershey, PA: Information Science Reference. doi:10.4018/978-1-4666-0957-0.ch003

Drum, D., Becker, D., & Fish, M. (2013). Technology adoption in troubled times: A cloud computing case study. *Journal of Cases on Information Technology*, *15*(2), 57–71. doi:10.4018/jcit.2013040104

Dunaway, D. M. (2013). Creating virtual collaborative learning experiences for aspiring teachers. In R. Hartshorne, T. Heafner, & T. Petty (Eds.), *Teacher education programs and online learning tools: Innovations in teacher preparation* (pp. 167–180). Hershey, PA: Information Science Reference. doi:10.4018/978-1-4666-1906-7.ch009

Dykstra, J. (2013). Seizing electronic evidence from cloud computing environments. In K. Ruan (Ed.), *Cybercrime and cloud forensics: Applications for investigation processes* (pp. 156–185). Hershey, PA: Information Science Reference. doi:10.4018/978-1-4666-2662-1.ch007

El-Refaey, M., & Rimal, B. P. (2012). Grid, SOA and cloud computing: On-demand computing models. In *Grid and cloud computing: Concepts, methodologies, tools and applications* (pp. 12–51). Hershey, PA: Information Science Reference. doi:10.4018/978-1-4666-0879-5.ch102

El-Refaey, M., & Rimal, B. P. (2012). Grid, SOA and cloud computing: On-demand computing models. In N. Preve (Ed.), *Computational and data grids: Principles, applications and design* (pp. 45–85). Hershey, PA: Information Science Reference. doi:10.4018/978-1-61350-113-9.ch003

Elnaffar, S., Maamar, Z., & Sheng, Q. Z. (2013). When clouds start socializing: The sky model. *International Journal of E-Business Research*, *9*(2), 1–7. doi:10.4018/jebr.2013040101

Elwood, S., & Keengwe, J. (2012). Microbursts: A design format for mobile cloud computing. *International Journal of Information and Communication Technology Education*, *8*(2), 102–110. doi:10.4018/jicte.2012040109

Emeakaroha, V. C., Netto, M. A., Calheiros, R. N., & De Rose, C. A. (2012). Achieving flexible SLA and resource management in clouds. In M. Villari, I. Brandic, & F. Tusa (Eds.), *Achieving federated and self-manageable cloud infrastructures: Theory and practice* (pp. 266–287). Hershey, PA: Business Science Reference. doi:10.4018/978-1-4666-1631-8.ch014

Etro, F. (2013). The economics of cloud computing. In A. Bento & A. Aggarwal (Eds.), *Cloud computing service and deployment models: Layers and management* (pp. 296–309). Hershey, PA: Business Science Reference. doi:10.4018/978-1-4666-2187-9.ch017

Ezugwu, A. E., Buhari, S. M., & Junaidu, S. B. (2013). Virtual machine allocation in cloud computing environment. *International Journal of Cloud Applications and Computing*, *3*(2), 47–60. doi:10.4018/ijcac.2013040105

Fauzi, A. H., & Taylor, H. (2013). Secure community trust stores for peer-to-peer e-commerce applications using cloud services. *International Journal of E-Entrepreneurship and Innovation*, *4*(1), 1–15. doi:10.4018/jeei.2013010101

Ferguson-Boucher, K., & Endicott-Popovsky, B. (2013). Forensic readiness in the cloud (FRC): Integrating records management and digital forensics. In K. Ruan (Ed.), *Cybercrime and cloud forensics: Applications for investigation processes* (pp. 105–128). Hershey, PA: Information Science Reference. doi:10.4018/978-1-4666-2662-1. ch005

Ferraro de Souza, R., Westphall, C. B., dos Santos, D. R., & Westphall, C. M. (2013). A review of PACS on cloud for archiving secure medical images. *International Journal of Privacy and Health Information Management*, 1(1), 53–62. doi:10.4018/ijphim.2013010104

Firdhous, M., Hassan, S., & Ghazali, O. (2013). Statistically enhanced multi-dimensional trust computing mechanism for cloud computing. *International Journal of Mobile Computing and Multimedia Communications*, 5(2), 1–17. doi:10.4018/jmcmc.2013040101

Formisano, C., Bonelli, L., Balraj, K. R., & Shulman-Peleg, A. (2013). Cloud access control mechanisms. In D. Kyriazis, A. Voulodimos, S. Gogouvitis, & T. Varvarigou (Eds.), *Data intensive storage services for cloud environments* (pp. 94–108). Hershey, PA: Business Science Reference. doi:10.4018/978-1-4666-3934-8.ch007

Frank, H., & Mesentean, S. (2012). Efficient communication interfaces for distributed energy resources. In E. Udoh (Ed.), *Evolving developments in grid and cloud computing: Advancing research* (pp. 185–196). Hershey, PA: Information Science Reference. doi:10.4018/978-1-4666-0056-0.ch013

Gallina, B., & Guelfi, N. (2012). Reusing transaction models for dependable cloud computing. In H. Yang & X. Liu (Eds.), *Software reuse in the emerging cloud computing era* (pp. 248–277). Hershey, PA: Information Science Reference. doi:10.4018/978-1-4666-0897-9.ch011

Garofalo, D. A. (2013). Empires of the future: Libraries, technology, and the academic environment. In E. Iglesias (Ed.), *Robots in academic libraries: Advancements in library automation* (pp. 180–206). Hershey, PA: Information Science Reference. doi:10.4018/978-1-4666-3938-6. ch010

Gebremeskel, G. B., He, Z., & Jing, X. (2013). Semantic integrating for intelligent cloud data mining platform and cloud based business intelligence for optimization of mobile social networks. In V. Bhatnagar (Ed.), *Data mining in dynamic social networks and fuzzy systems* (pp. 173–211). Hershey, PA: Information Science Reference. doi:10.4018/978-1-4666-4213-3.ch009

Gentleman, W. M. (2013). Using the cloud for testing NOT adjunct to development. In S. Tilley & T. Parveen (Eds.), *Software testing in the cloud: Perspectives on an emerging discipline* (pp. 216–230). Hershey, PA: Information Science Reference. doi:10.4018/978-1-4666-2536-5.ch010

Ghafoor, K. Z., Mohammed, M. A., Abu Bakar, K., Sadiq, A. S., & Lloret, J. (2014). Vehicular cloud computing: Trends and challenges. In J. Rodrigues, K. Lin, & J. Lloret (Eds.), *Mobile networks and cloud computing convergence for progressive services and applications* (pp. 262–274). Hershey, PA: Information Science Reference. doi:10.4018/978-1-4666-4781-7.ch014

Giannakaki, M. (2012). The "right to be forgotten" in the era of social media and cloud computing. In C. Akrivopoulou & N. Garipidis (Eds.), *Human rights and risks in the digital era: Globalization and the effects of information technologies* (pp. 10–24). Hershey, PA: Information Science Reference. doi:10.4018/978-1-4666-0891-7.ch002

Gillam, L., Li, B., & O'Loughlin, J. (2012). Teaching clouds: Lessons taught and lessons learnt. In L. Chao (Ed.), *Cloud computing for teaching and learning: Strategies for design and implementation* (pp. 82–94). Hershey, PA: Information Science Reference. doi:10.4018/978-1-4666-0957-0.ch006

Gonsowski, D. (2013). Compliance in the cloud and the implications on electronic discovery. In K. Ruan (Ed.), *Cybercrime and cloud forensics: Applications for investigation processes* (pp. 230–250). Hershey, PA: Information Science Reference. doi:10.4018/978-1-4666-2662-1.ch009

Gonzalez-Sanchez, J., Conley, Q., Chavez-Echeagaray, M., & Atkinson, R. K. (2012). Supporting the assembly process by leveraging augmented reality, cloud computing, and mobile devices. *International Journal of Cyber Behavior, Psychology and Learning*, 2(3), 86–102. doi:10.4018/ijcbpl.2012070107

Gopinath, R., & Geetha, B. (2013). An e-learning system based on secure data storage services in cloud computing. *International Journal of Information Technology and Web Engineering*, 8(2), 1–17. doi:10.4018/jitwe.2013040101

Gossin, P. C., & LaBrie, R. C. (2013). Data center waste management. In P. Ordóñez de Pablos (Ed.), *Green technologies and business practices: An IT approach* (pp. 226–235). Hershey, PA: Information Science Reference. doi:10.4018/978-1-4666-1972-2.ch014

Goswami, V., Patra, S. S., & Mund, G. B. (2012). Performance analysis of cloud computing centers for bulk services. *International Journal of Cloud Applications and Computing*, 2(4), 53–65. doi:10.4018/ijcac.2012100104

Goswami, V., & Sahoo, C. N. (2013). Optimal resource usage in multi-cloud computing environment. *International Journal of Cloud Applications and Computing*, 3(1), 44–57. doi:10.4018/ijcac.2013010105

Gräuler, M., Teuteberg, F., Mahmoud, T., & Gómez, J. M. (2013). Requirements prioritization and design considerations for the next generation of corporate environmental management information systems: A foundation for innovation. *International Journal of Information Technologies and Systems Approach*, 6(1), 98–116. doi:10.4018/jitsa.2013010106

Grieve, G. P., & Heston, K. (2012). Finding liquid salvation: Using the cardean ethnographic method to document second life residents and religious cloud communities. In N. Zagalo, L. Morgado, & A. Boa-Ventura (Eds.), *Virtual worlds and metaverse platforms: New communication and identity paradigms* (pp. 288–305). Hershey, PA: Information Science Reference. doi:10.4018/978-1-60960-854-5.ch019

Grispos, G., Storer, T., & Glisson, W. B. (2012). Calm before the storm: The challenges of cloud computing in digital forensics. *International Journal of Digital Crime and Forensics*, 4(2), 28–48. doi:10.4018/jdcf.2012040103

Grispos, G., Storer, T., & Glisson, W. B. (2013). Calm before the storm: The challenges of cloud computing in digital forensics. In C. Li (Ed.), *Emerging digital forensics applications for crime detection, prevention, and security* (pp. 211–233). Hershey, PA: Information Science Reference. doi:10.4018/978-1-4666-4006-1.ch015

Guster, D., & Lee, O. F. (2011). Enhancing the disaster recovery plan through virtualization. *Journal of Information Technology Research*, 4(4), 18–40. doi:10.4018/jitr.2011100102

Hanawa, T., & Sato, M. (2013). D-Cloud: Software testing environment for dependable distributed systems using cloud computing technology. In S. Tilley & T. Parveen (Eds.), *Software testing in the cloud: Perspectives on an emerging discipline* (pp. 340–355). Hershey, PA: Information Science Reference. doi:10.4018/978-1-4666-2536-5.ch016

Hardy, J., Liu, L., Lei, C., & Li, J. (2013). Internet-based virtual computing infrastructure for cloud computing. In X. Yang & L. Liu (Eds.), *Principles, methodologies, and service-oriented approaches for cloud computing* (pp. 371–389). Hershey, PA: Business Science Reference. doi:10.4018/978-1-4666-2854-0.ch016

Hashizume, K., Yoshioka, N., & Fernandez, E. B. (2013). Three misuse patterns for cloud computing. In D. Rosado, D. Mellado, E. Fernandez-Medina, & M. Piattini (Eds.), *Security engineering for cloud computing: Approaches and tools* (pp. 36–53). Hershey, PA: Information Science Reference. doi:10.4018/978-1-4666-2125-1.ch003

Hassan, Q. F., Riad, A. M., & Hassan, A. E. (2012). Understanding cloud computing. In H. Yang & X. Liu (Eds.), *Software reuse in the emerging cloud computing era* (pp. 204–227). Hershey, PA: Information Science Reference. doi:10.4018/978-1-4666-0897-9.ch009

Hasselmeyer, P., Katsaros, G., Koller, B., & Wieder, P. (2012). Cloud monitoring. In M. Villari, I. Brandic, & F. Tusa (Eds.), *Achieving federated and self-manageable cloud infrastructures: Theory and practice* (pp. 97–116). Hershey, PA: Business Science Reference. doi:10.4018/978-1-4666-1631-8.ch006

Hertzler, B. T., Frost, E., Bressler, G. H., & Goehring, C. (2011). Experience report: Using a cloud computing environment during Haiti and Exercise24. *International Journal of Information Systems for Crisis Response and Management*, *3*(1), 50–64. doi:10.4018/jiscrm.2011010104

Hertzler, B. T., Frost, E., Bressler, G. H., & Goehring, C. (2013). Experience report: Using a cloud computing environment during Haiti and Exercise24. In M. Jennex (Ed.), *Using social and information technologies for disaster and crisis management* (pp. 52–66). Hershey, PA: Information Science Reference. doi:10.4018/978-1-4666-2788-8.ch004

Ho, R. (2013). Cloud computing and enterprise migration strategies. In A. Loo (Ed.), *Distributed computing innovations for business, engineering, and science* (pp. 156–175). Hershey, PA: Information Science Reference. doi:10.4018/978-1-4666-2533-4.ch008

Hobona, G., Jackson, M., & Anand, S. (2012). Implementing geospatial web services for cloud computing. In *Grid and cloud computing: Concepts, methodologies, tools and applications* (pp. 615–636). Hershey, PA: Information Science Reference. doi:10.4018/978-1-4666-0879-5.ch305

Hochstein, L., Schott, B., & Graybill, R. B. (2011). Computational engineering in the cloud: Benefits and challenges. *Journal of Organizational and End User Computing*, *23*(4), 31–50. doi:10.4018/joeuc.2011100103

Hochstein, L., Schott, B., & Graybill, R. B. (2013). Computational engineering in the cloud: Benefits and challenges. In A. Dwivedi & S. Clarke (Eds.), *Innovative strategies and approaches for end-user computing advancements* (pp. 314–332). Hershey, PA: Information Science Reference. doi:10.4018/978-1-4666-2059-9.ch017

Honarvar, A. R. (2013). Developing an elastic cloud computing application through multi-agent systems. *International Journal of Cloud Applications and Computing*, *3*(1), 58–64. doi:10.4018/ijcac.2013010106

Hossain, S. (2013). Cloud computing terms, definitions, and taxonomy. In A. Bento & A. Aggarwal (Eds.), *Cloud computing service and deployment models: Layers and management* (pp. 1–25). Hershey, PA: Business Science Reference. doi:10.4018/978-1-4666-2187-9.ch001

Hudzia, B., Sinclair, J., & Lindner, M. (2013). Deploying and running enterprise grade applications in a federated cloud. In *Supply chain management: Concepts, methodologies, tools, and applications* (pp. 1350–1370). Hershey, PA: Business Science Reference. doi:10.4018/978-1-4666-2625-6.ch080

Hung, S., Shieh, J., & Lee, C. (2011). Migrating android applications to the cloud. *International Journal of Grid and High Performance Computing, 3*(2), 14–28. doi:10.4018/jghpc.2011040102

Hung, S., Shieh, J., & Lee, C. (2013). Migrating android applications to the cloud. In E. Udoh (Ed.), *Applications and developments in grid, cloud, and high performance computing* (pp. 307–322). Hershey, PA: Information Science Reference. doi:10.4018/978-1-4666-2065-0.ch020

Islam, S., Mouratidis, H., & Weippl, E. R. (2013). A goal-driven risk management approach to support security and privacy analysis of cloud-based system. In D. Rosado, D. Mellado, E. Fernandez-Medina, & M. Piattini (Eds.), *Security engineering for cloud computing: Approaches and tools* (pp. 97–122). Hershey, PA: Information Science Reference. doi:10.4018/978-1-4666-2125-1.ch006

Itani, W., Kayssi, A., & Chehab, A. (2013). Hardware-based security for ensuring data privacy in the cloud. In D. Rosado, D. Mellado, E. Fernandez-Medina, & M. Piattini (Eds.), *Security engineering for cloud computing: Approaches and tools* (pp. 147–170). Hershey, PA: Information Science Reference. doi:10.4018/978-1-4666-2125-1.ch008

Jackson, A., & Weiland, M. (2013). Cloud computing for scientific simulation and high performance computing. In X. Yang & L. Liu (Eds.), *Principles, methodologies, and service-oriented approaches for cloud computing* (pp. 51–70). Hershey, PA: Business Science Reference. doi:10.4018/978-1-4666-2854-0.ch003

Jaeger, M. C., & Hohenstein, U. (2013). Content centric storage and current storage systems. In D. Kyriazis, A. Voulodimos, S. Gogouvitis, & T. Varvarigou (Eds.), *Data intensive storage services for cloud environments* (pp. 27–46). Hershey, PA: Business Science Reference. doi:10.4018/978-1-4666-3934-8.ch003

James, J. I., Shosha, A. F., & Gladyshev, P. (2013). Digital forensic investigation and cloud computing. In K. Ruan (Ed.), *Cybercrime and cloud forensics: Applications for investigation processes* (pp. 1–41). Hershey, PA: Information Science Reference. doi:10.4018/978-1-4666-2662-1.ch001

Jena, R. K. (2013). Green computing to green business. In P. Ordóñez de Pablos (Ed.), *Green technologies and business practices: An IT approach* (pp. 138–150). Hershey, PA: Information Science Reference. doi:10.4018/978-1-4666-1972-2.ch007

Jeyarani, R., & Nagaveni, N. (2012). A heuristic meta scheduler for optimal resource utilization and improved QoS in cloud computing environment. *International Journal of Cloud Applications and Computing, 2*(1), 41–52. doi:10.4018/ijcac.2012010103

Jeyarani, R., Nagaveni, N., & Ram, R. V. (2011). Self adaptive particle swarm optimization for efficient virtual machine provisioning in cloud. *International Journal of Intelligent Information Technologies, 7*(2), 25–44. doi:10.4018/jiit.2011040102

Jeyarani, R., Nagaveni, N., & Ram, R. V. (2013). Self adaptive particle swarm optimization for efficient virtual machine provisioning in cloud. In V. Sugumaran (Ed.), *Organizational efficiency through intelligent information technologies* (pp. 88–107). Hershey, PA: Information Science Reference. doi:10.4018/978-1-4666-2047-6.ch006

Jeyarani, R., Nagaveni, N., Sadasivam, S. K., & Rajarathinam, V. R. (2011). Power aware meta scheduler for adaptive VM provisioning in IaaS cloud. *International Journal of Cloud Applications and Computing, 1*(3), 36–51. doi:10.4018/ijcac.2011070104

Jeyarani, R., Nagaveni, N., Sadasivam, S. K., & Rajarathinam, V. R. (2013). Power aware meta scheduler for adaptive VM provisioning in IaaS cloud. In S. Aljawarneh (Ed.), *Cloud computing advancements in design, implementation, and technologies* (pp. 190–204). Hershey, PA: Information Science Reference. doi:10.4018/978-1-4666-1879-4.ch014

Jiang, J., Huang, X., Wu, Y., & Yang, G. (2013). Campus cloud storage and preservation: From distributed file system to data sharing service. In X. Yang & L. Liu (Eds.), *Principles, methodologies, and service-oriented approaches for cloud computing* (pp. 284–301). Hershey, PA: Business Science Reference. doi:10.4018/978-1-4666-2854-0.ch012

Jing, S. (2012). The application exploration of cloud computing in information technology teaching. *International Journal of Advanced Pervasive and Ubiquitous Computing, 4*(4), 23–27. doi:10.4018/japuc.2012100104

Johansson, D., & Wiberg, M. (2012). Conceptually advancing "application mobility" towards design: Applying a concept-driven approach to the design of mobile IT for home care service groups. *International Journal of Ambient Computing and Intelligence, 4*(3), 20–32. doi:10.4018/jaci.2012070102

Jorda, J., & M'zoughi, A. (2013). Securing cloud storage. In D. Rosado, D. Mellado, E. Fernandez-Medina, & M. Piattini (Eds.), *Security engineering for cloud computing: Approaches and tools* (pp. 171–190). Hershey, PA: Information Science Reference. doi:10.4018/978-1-4666-2125-1.ch009

Juiz, C., & Alexander de Pous, V. (2014). Cloud computing: IT governance, legal, and public policy aspects. In I. Portela & F. Almeida (Eds.), *Organizational, legal, and technological dimensions of information system administration* (pp. 139–166). Hershey, PA: Information Science Reference. doi:10.4018/978-1-4666-4526-4.ch009

Kaisler, S. H., Money, W., & Cohen, S. J. (2013). Cloud computing: A decision framework for small businesses. In A. Bento & A. Aggarwal (Eds.), *Cloud computing service and deployment models: Layers and management* (pp. 151–172). Hershey, PA: Business Science Reference. doi:10.4018/978-1-4666-2187-9.ch008

Kanamori, Y., & Yen, M. Y. (2013). Cloud computing security and risk management. In A. Bento & A. Aggarwal (Eds.), *Cloud computing service and deployment models: Layers and management* (pp. 222–240). Hershey, PA: Business Science Reference. doi:10.4018/978-1-4666-2187-9.ch012

Karadsheh, L., & Alhawari, S. (2011). Applying security policies in small business utilizing cloud computing technologies. *International Journal of Cloud Applications and Computing, 1*(2), 29–40. doi:10.4018/ijcac.2011040103

Karadsheh, L., & Alhawari, S. (2013). Applying security policies in small business utilizing cloud computing technologies. In S. Aljawarneh (Ed.), *Cloud computing advancements in design, implementation, and technologies* (pp. 112–124). Hershey, PA: Information Science Reference. doi:10.4018/978-1-4666-1879-4.ch008

Kaupins, G. (2012). Laws associated with mobile computing in the cloud. [IJWNBT]. *International Journal of Wireless Networks and Broadband Technologies, 2*(3), 1–9. doi:10.4018/ijwnbt.2012070101

Kemp, M. L., Robb, S., & Deans, P. C. (2013). The legal implications of cloud computing. In A. Bento & A. Aggarwal (Eds.), *Cloud computing service and deployment models: Layers and management* (pp. 257–272). Hershey, PA: Business Science Reference. doi:10.4018/978-1-4666-2187-9.ch014

Khan, N., Ahmad, N., Herawan, T., & Inayat, Z. (2012). Cloud computing: Locally sub-clouds instead of globally one cloud. *International Journal of Cloud Applications and Computing*, 2(3), 68–85. doi::10.4018/ijcac.2012070103

Khan, N., Noraziah, A., Ismail, E. I., Deris, M. M., & Herawan, T. (2012). Cloud computing: Analysis of various platforms. *International Journal of E-Entrepreneurship and Innovation*, 3(2), 51–59. doi:10.4018/jeei.2012040104

Khansa, L., Forcade, J., Nambari, G., Parasuraman, S., & Cox, P. (2012). Proposing an intelligent cloud-based electronic health record system. *International Journal of Business Data Communications and Networking*, 8(3), 57–71. doi:10.4018/jbdcn.2012070104

Kierkegaard, S. (2012). Not every cloud brings rain: Legal risks on the horizon. In M. Gupta, J. Walp, & R. Sharman (Eds.), *Strategic and practical approaches for information security governance: Technologies and applied solutions* (pp. 181–194). Hershey, PA: Information Science Reference. doi:10.4018/978-1-4666-0197-0.ch011

Kifayat, K., Shamsa, T. B., Mackay, M., Merabti, M., & Shi, Q. (2013). Real time risk management in cloud computation. In D. Rosado, D. Mellado, E. Fernandez-Medina, & M. Piattini (Eds.), *Security engineering for cloud computing: Approaches and tools* (pp. 123–145). Hershey, PA: Information Science Reference. doi:10.4018/978-1-4666-2125-1.ch007

King, T. M., Ganti, A. S., & Froslie, D. (2013). Towards improving the testability of cloud application services. In S. Tilley & T. Parveen (Eds.), *Software testing in the cloud: Perspectives on an emerging discipline* (pp. 322–339). Hershey, PA: Information Science Reference. doi:10.4018/978-1-4666-2536-5.ch015

Kipp, A., Schneider, R., & Schubert, L. (2013). Encapsulation of complex HPC services. In C. Rückemann (Ed.), *Integrated information and computing systems for natural, spatial, and social sciences* (pp. 153–176). Hershey, PA: Information Science Reference. doi:10.4018/978-1-4666-2190-9.ch008

Kldiashvili, E. (2012). The cloud computing as the tool for implementation of virtual organization technology for ehealth. *Journal of Information Technology Research*, 5(1), 18–34. doi:10.4018/jitr.2012010102

Kldiashvili, E. (2013). Implementation of telecytology in georgia for quality assurance programs. *Journal of Information Technology Research*, 6(2), 24–45. doi:10.4018/jitr.2013040102

Kosmatov, N. (2013). Concolic test generation and the cloud: deployment and verification perspectives. In S. Tilley & T. Parveen (Eds.), *Software testing in the cloud: Perspectives on an emerging discipline* (pp. 231–251). Hershey, PA: Information Science Reference. doi:10.4018/978-1-4666-2536-5.ch011

Kotamarti, R. M., Thornton, M. A., & Dunham, M. H. (2012). Quantum computing approach for alignment-free sequence search and classification. In S. Ali, N. Abbadeni, & M. Batouche (Eds.), *Multidisciplinary computational intelligence techniques: Applications in business, engineering, and medicine* (pp. 279–300). Hershey, PA: Information Science Reference. doi:10.4018/978-1-4666-1830-5.ch017

Kremmydas, D., Petsakos, A., & Rozakis, S. (2012). Parametric optimization of linear and non-linear models via parallel computing to enhance web-spatial DSS interactivity. *International Journal of Decision Support System Technology, 4*(1), 14–29. doi:10.4018/jdsst.2012010102

Krishnadas, N., & Pillai, R. R. (2013). Cloud computing diagnosis: A comprehensive study. In X. Yang & L. Liu (Eds.), *Principles, methodologies, and service-oriented approaches for cloud computing* (pp. 1–18). Hershey, PA: Business Science Reference. doi:10.4018/978-1-4666-2854-0.ch001

Kübert, R., & Katsaros, G. (2011). Using free software for elastic web hosting on a private cloud. *International Journal of Cloud Applications and Computing, 1*(2), 14–28. doi:10.4018/ijcac.2011040102

Kübert, R., & Katsaros, G. (2013). Using free software for elastic web hosting on a private cloud. In S. Aljawarneh (Ed.), *Cloud computing advancements in design, implementation, and technologies* (pp. 97–111). Hershey, PA: Information Science Reference. doi:10.4018/978-1-4666-1879-4.ch007

Kumar, P. S., Ashok, M. S., & Subramanian, R. (2012). A publicly verifiable dynamic secret sharing protocol for secure and dependable data storage in cloud computing. *International Journal of Cloud Applications and Computing, 2*(3), 1–25. doi:10.4018/ijcac.2012070101

Lasluisa, S., Rodero, I., & Parashar, M. (2013). Software design for passing sarbanes-oxley in cloud computing. In C. Rückemann (Ed.), *Integrated information and computing systems for natural, spatial, and social sciences* (pp. 27–42). Hershey, PA: Information Science Reference. doi:10.4018/978-1-4666-2190-9.ch002

Lasluisa, S., Rodero, I., & Parashar, M. (2014). Software design for passing sarbanes-oxley in cloud computing. In *Software design and development: Concepts, methodologies, tools, and applications* (pp. 1659–1674). Hershey, PA: Information Science Reference. doi:10.4018/978-1-4666-4301-7.ch080

Lee, W. N. (2013). An economic analysis of cloud: "Software as a service" (saas) computing and "virtual desktop infrastructure" (VDI) models. In A. Bento & A. Aggarwal (Eds.), *Cloud computing service and deployment models: Layers and management* (pp. 289–295). Hershey, PA: Business Science Reference. doi:10.4018/978-1-4666-2187-9.ch016

Levine, K., & White, B. A. (2011). A crisis at hafford furniture: Cloud computing case study. *Journal of Cases on Information Technology, 13*(1), 57–71. doi:10.4018/jcit.2011010104

Levine, K., & White, B. A. (2013). A crisis at Hafford furniture: Cloud computing case study. In M. Khosrow-Pour (Ed.), *Cases on emerging information technology research and applications* (pp. 70–87). Hershey, PA: Information Science Reference. doi:10.4018/978-1-4666-3619-4.ch004

Li, J., Meng, L., Zhu, Z., Li, X., Huai, J., & Liu, L. (2013). CloudRank: A cloud service ranking method based on both user feedback and service testing. In X. Yang & L. Liu (Eds.), *Principles, methodologies, and service-oriented approaches for cloud computing* (pp. 230–258). Hershey, PA: Business Science Reference. doi:10.4018/978-1-4666-2854-0.ch010

Liang, T., Lu, F., & Chiu, J. (2012). A hybrid resource reservation method for workflows in clouds. *International Journal of Grid and High Performance Computing, 4*(4), 1–21. doi:10.4018/jghpc.2012100101

Lorenz, M., Rath-Wiggins, L., Runde, W., Messina, A., Sunna, P., Dimino, G., & Borgotallo, R. et al. (2013). Media convergence and cloud technologies: Smart storage, better workflows. In D. Kyriazis, A. Vouolodimos, S. Gogouvitis, & T. Varvarigou (Eds.), *Data intensive storage services for cloud environments* (pp. 132–144). Hershey, PA: Business Science Reference. doi:10.4018/978-1-4666-3934-8.ch009

M., S. G., & G., S. K. (2012). An enterprise mashup integration service framework for clouds. *International Journal of Cloud Applications and Computing, 2*(2), 31-40. doi:10.4018/ijcac.2012040103

Maharana, S. K., Mali, P. B., Prabhakar, G. J. S., & Kumar, V. (2011). Cloud computing applied for numerical study of thermal characteristics of SIP. *International Journal of Cloud Applications and Computing, 1*(3), 12–21. doi:10.4018/ijcac.2011070102

Maharana, S. K., Mali, P. B., Prabhakar, G. J. S., & Kumar, V. (2013). Cloud computing applied for numerical study of thermal characteristics of SIP. In S. Aljawarneh (Ed.), *Cloud computing advancements in design, implementation, and technologies* (pp. 166–175). Hershey, PA: Information Science Reference. doi:10.4018/978-1-4666-1879-4.ch012

Maharana, S. K., P, G. P., & Bhati, A. (2012). A study of cloud computing for retinal image processing through MATLAB. *International Journal of Cloud Applications and Computing, 2*(2), 59–69. doi:10.4018/ijcac.2012040106

Maharana, S. K., Prabhakar, P. G., & Bhati, A. (2013). A study of cloud computing for retinal image processing through MATLAB. In *Image processing: Concepts, methodologies, tools, and applications* (pp. 101–111). Hershey, PA: Information Science Reference. doi:10.4018/978-1-4666-3994-2.ch006

Mahesh, S., Landry, B. J., Sridhar, T., & Walsh, K. R. (2011). A decision table for the cloud computing decision in small business. *Information Resources Management Journal, 24*(3), 9–25. doi:10.4018/irmj.2011070102

Mahesh, S., Landry, B. J., Sridhar, T., & Walsh, K. R. (2013). A decision table for the cloud computing decision in small business. In M. Khosrow-Pour (Ed.), *Managing information resources and technology: Emerging Applications and theories* (pp. 159–176). Hershey, PA: Information Science Reference. doi:10.4018/978-1-4666-3616-3.ch012

Marquezan, C. C., Metzger, A., Pohl, K., Engen, V., Boniface, M., Phillips, S. C., & Zlatev, Z. (2013). Adaptive future internet applications: Opportunities and challenges for adaptive web services technology. In G. Ortiz & J. Cubo (Eds.), *Adaptive web services for modular and reusable software development: Tactics and solutions* (pp. 333–353). Hershey, PA: Information Science Reference. doi:10.4018/978-1-4666-2089-6.ch014

Marshall, P. J. (2012). Cloud computing: Next generation education. In L. Chao (Ed.), *Cloud computing for teaching and learning: Strategies for design and implementation* (pp. 180–185). Hershey, PA: Information Science Reference. doi:10.4018/978-1-4666-0957-0.ch012

Martinez-Ortiz, A. (2012). Open cloud technologies. In L. Vaquero, J. Cáceres, & J. Hierro (Eds.), *Open source cloud computing systems: Practices and paradigms* (pp. 1–17). Hershey, PA: Information Science Reference. doi:10.4018/978-1-4666-0098-0.ch001

Massonet, P., Michot, A., Naqvi, S., Villari, M., & Latanicki, J. (2013). Securing the external interfaces of a federated infrastructure cloud. In *IT policy and ethics: Concepts, methodologies, tools, and applications* (pp. 1876–1903). Hershey, PA: Information Science Reference. doi:10.4018/978-1-4666-2919-6.ch082

Mavrogeorgi, N., Gogouvitis, S. V., Voulodimos, A., & Alexandrou, V. (2013). SLA management in storage clouds. In D. Kyriazis, A. Voulodimos, S. Gogouvitis, & T. Varvarigou (Eds.), *Data intensive storage services for cloud environments* (pp. 72–93). Hershey, PA: Business Science Reference. doi:10.4018/978-1-4666-3934-8.ch006

Mehta, H. K. (2013). Cloud selection for e-business a parameter based solution. In K. Tarnay, S. Imre, & L. Xu (Eds.), *Research and development in e-business through service-oriented solutions* (pp. 199–207). Hershey, PA: Business Science Reference. doi:10.4018/978-1-4666-4181-5.ch009

Mehta, H. K., & Gupta, E. (2013). Economy based resource allocation in IaaS cloud. *International Journal of Cloud Applications and Computing*, 3(2), 1–11. doi:10.4018/ijcac.2013040101

Miah, S. J. (2012). Cloud-based intelligent DSS design for emergency professionals. In S. Ali, N. Abbadeni, & M. Batouche (Eds.), *Multidisciplinary computational intelligence techniques: Applications in business, engineering, and medicine* (pp. 47–60). Hershey, PA: Information Science Reference. doi:10.4018/978-1-4666-1830-5.ch004

Miah, S. J. (2013). Cloud-based intelligent DSS design for emergency professionals. In *Data mining: Concepts, methodologies, tools, and applications* (pp. 991–1003). Hershey, PA: Information Science Reference. doi:10.4018/978-1-4666-2455-9.ch050

Mikkilineni, R. (2012). Architectural resiliency in distributed computing. *International Journal of Grid and High Performance Computing*, 4(4), 37–51. doi:10.4018/jghpc.2012100103

Millham, R. (2012). Software asset re-use: Migration of data-intensive legacy system to the cloud computing paradigm. In H. Yang & X. Liu (Eds.), *Software reuse in the emerging cloud computing era* (pp. 1–27). Hershey, PA: Information Science Reference. doi:10.4018/978-1-4666-0897-9.ch001

Mircea, M. (2011). Building the agile enterprise with service-oriented architecture, business process management and decision management. *International Journal of E-Entrepreneurship and Innovation*, 2(4), 32–48. doi:10.4018/jeei.2011100103

Modares, H., Lloret, J., Moravejosharieh, A., & Salleh, R. (2014). Security in mobile cloud computing. In J. Rodrigues, K. Lin, & J. Lloret (Eds.), *Mobile networks and cloud computing convergence for progressive services and applications* (pp. 79–91). Hershey, PA: Information Science Reference. doi:10.4018/978-1-4666-4781-7.ch005

Moedjiono, S., & Mas'at, A. (2012). Cloud computing implementation strategy for information dissemination on meteorology, climatology, air quality, and geophysics (MKKuG). *Journal of Information Technology Research*, 5(3), 71–84. doi:10.4018/jitr.2012070104

Moiny, J. (2012). Cloud based social network sites: Under whose control? In A. Dudley, J. Braman, & G. Vincenti (Eds.), *Investigating cyber law and cyber ethics: Issues, impacts and practices* (pp. 147–219). Hershey, PA: Information Science Reference. doi:10.4018/978-1-61350-132-0.ch009

Moreno, I. S., & Xu, J. (2011). Energy-efficiency in cloud computing environments: Towards energy savings without performance degradation. *International Journal of Cloud Applications and Computing*, *1*(1), 17–33. doi:10.4018/ijcac.2011010102

Moreno, I. S., & Xu, J. (2013). Energy-efficiency in cloud computing environments: Towards energy savings without performance degradation. In S. Aljawarneh (Ed.), *Cloud computing advancements in design, implementation, and technologies* (pp. 18–36). Hershey, PA: Information Science Reference. doi:10.4018/978-1-4666-1879-4.ch002

Muñoz, A., Maña, A., & González, J. (2013). Dynamic security properties monitoring architecture for cloud computing. In D. Rosado, D. Mellado, E. Fernandez-Medina, & M. Piattini (Eds.), *Security engineering for cloud computing: Approaches and tools* (pp. 1–18). Hershey, PA: Information Science Reference. doi:10.4018/978-1-4666-2125-1.ch001

Mvelase, P., Dlodlo, N., Williams, Q., & Adigun, M. O. (2011). Custom-made cloud enterprise architecture for small medium and micro enterprises. *International Journal of Cloud Applications and Computing*, *1*(3), 52–63. doi:10.4018/ijcac.2011070105

Mvelase, P., Dlodlo, N., Williams, Q., & Adigun, M. O. (2012). Custom-made cloud enterprise architecture for small medium and micro enterprises. In *Grid and cloud computing: Concepts, methodologies, tools and applications* (pp. 589–601). Hershey, PA: Information Science Reference. doi:10.4018/978-1-4666-0879-5.ch303

Mvelase, P., Dlodlo, N., Williams, Q., & Adigun, M. O. (2013). Custom-made cloud enterprise architecture for small medium and micro enterprises. In S. Aljawarneh (Ed.), *Cloud computing advancements in design, implementation, and technologies* (pp. 205–217). Hershey, PA: Information Science Reference. doi:10.4018/978-1-4666-1879-4.ch015

Naeem, M. A., Dobbie, G., & Weber, G. (2014). Big data management in the context of real-time data warehousing. In W. Hu & N. Kaabouch (Eds.), *Big data management, technologies, and applications* (pp. 150–176). Hershey, PA: Information Science Reference. doi:10.4018/978-1-4666-4699-5.ch007

Ofosu, W. K., & Saliah-Hassane, H. (2013). Cloud computing in the education environment for developing nations. *International Journal of Interdisciplinary Telecommunications and Networking*, *5*(3), 54–62. doi:10.4018/jitn.2013070106

Oliveros, E., Cucinotta, T., Phillips, S. C., Yang, X., Middleton, S., & Voith, T. (2012). Monitoring and metering in the cloud. In D. Kyriazis, T. Varvarigou, & K. Konstanteli (Eds.), *Achieving real-time in distributed computing: From grids to clouds* (pp. 94–114). Hershey, PA: Information Science Reference. doi:10.4018/978-1-60960-827-9.ch006

Orton, I., Alva, A., & Endicott-Popovsky, B. (2013). Legal process and requirements for cloud forensic investigations. In K. Ruan (Ed.), *Cybercrime and cloud forensics: Applications for investigation processes* (pp. 186–229). Hershey, PA: Information Science Reference. doi:10.4018/978-1-4666-2662-1.ch008

Pakhira, A., & Andras, P. (2013). Leveraging the cloud for large-scale software testing – A case study: Google Chrome on Amazon. In S. Tilley & T. Parveen (Eds.), *Software testing in the cloud: Perspectives on an emerging discipline* (pp. 252–279). Hershey, PA: Information Science Reference. doi:10.4018/978-1-4666-2536-5.ch012

Pal, K., & Karakostas, B. (2013). The use of cloud computing in shipping logistics. In D. Graham, I. Manikas, & D. Folinas (Eds.), *E-logistics and e-supply chain management: Applications for evolving business* (pp. 104–124). Hershey, PA: Business Science Reference. doi:10.4018/978-1-4666-3914-0.ch006

Pal, S. (2013). Cloud computing: Security concerns and issues. In A. Bento & A. Aggarwal (Eds.), *Cloud computing service and deployment models: Layers and management* (pp. 191–207). Hershey, PA: Business Science Reference. doi:10.4018/978-1-4666-2187-9.ch010

Pal, S. (2013). Storage security and technical challenges of cloud computing. In D. Kyriazis, A. Voulodimos, S. Gogouvitis, & T. Varvarigou (Eds.), *Data intensive storage services for cloud environments* (pp. 225–240). Hershey, PA: Business Science Reference. doi:10.4018/978-1-4666-3934-8.ch014

Palanivel, K., & Kuppuswami, S. (2014). A cloud-oriented reference architecture to digital library systems. In S. Dhamdhere (Ed.), *Cloud computing and virtualization technologies in libraries* (pp. 230–254). Hershey, PA: Information Science Reference. doi:10.4018/978-1-4666-4631-5.ch014

Paletta, M. (2012). Intelligent clouds: By means of using multi-agent systems environments. In L. Chao (Ed.), *Cloud computing for teaching and learning: Strategies for design and implementation* (pp. 254–279). Hershey, PA: Information Science Reference. doi:10.4018/978-1-4666-0957-0.ch017

Pallot, M., Le Marc, C., Richir, S., Schmidt, C., & Mathieu, J. (2012). Innovation gaming: An immersive experience environment enabling co-creation. In M. Cruz-Cunha (Ed.), *Handbook of research on serious games as educational, business and research tools* (pp. 1–24). Hershey, PA: Information Science Reference. doi:10.4018/978-1-4666-0149-9.ch001

Pankowska, M. (2011). Information technology resources virtualization for sustainable development. *International Journal of Applied Logistics*, *2*(2), 35–48. doi:10.4018/jal.2011040103

Pankowska, M. (2013). Information technology resources virtualization for sustainable development. In Z. Luo (Ed.), *Technological solutions for modern logistics and supply chain management* (pp. 248–262). Hershey, PA: Business Science Reference. doi:10.4018/978-1-4666-2773-4.ch016

Parappallil, J. J., Zarvic, N., & Thomas, O. (2012). A context and content reflection on business-IT alignment research. *International Journal of IT/ Business Alignment and Governance*, *3*(2), 21–37. doi:10.4018/jitbag.2012070102

Parashar, V., Vishwakarma, M. L., & Parashar, R. (2014). A new framework for building academic library through cloud computing. In S. Dhamdhere (Ed.), *Cloud computing and virtualization technologies in libraries* (pp. 107–123). Hershey, PA: Information Science Reference. doi:10.4018/978-1-4666-4631-5.ch007

Pendyala, V. S., & Holliday, J. (2012). Cloud as a computer. In X. Liu & Y. Li (Eds.), *Advanced design approaches to emerging software systems: Principles, methodologies and tools* (pp. 241–249). Hershey, PA: Information Science Reference. doi:10.4018/978-1-60960-735-7.ch011

Petruch, K., Tamm, G., & Stantchev, V. (2012). Deriving in-depth knowledge from IT-performance data simulations. *International Journal of Knowledge Society Research*, *3*(2), 13–29. doi:10.4018/jksr.2012040102

Philipson, G. (2011). A framework for green computing. *International Journal of Green Computing*, *2*(1), 12–26. doi:10.4018/jgc.2011010102

Philipson, G. (2013). A framework for green computing. In K. Ganesh & S. Anbuudayasankar (Eds.), *International and interdisciplinary studies in green computing* (pp. 12–26). Hershey, PA: Information Science Reference. doi:10.4018/978-1-4666-2646-1.ch002

Phythian, M. (2013). The 'cloud' of unknowing – What a government cloud may and may not offer: A practitioner perspective. *International Journal of Technoethics*, *4*(1), 1–10. doi:10.4018/jte.2013010101

Pym, D., & Sadler, M. (2012). Information stewardship in cloud computing. In *Grid and cloud computing: Concepts, methodologies, tools and applications* (pp. 185–202). Hershey, PA: Information Science Reference. doi:10.4018/978-1-4666-0879-5.ch109

Pym, D., & Sadler, M. (2012). Information stewardship in cloud computing. In S. Galup (Ed.), *Technological applications and advancements in service science, management, and engineering* (pp. 52–69). Hershey, PA: Business Science Reference. doi:10.4018/978-1-4666-1583-0.ch004

Qiu, J., Ekanayake, J., Gunarathne, T., Choi, J. Y., Bae, S., & Ruan, Y. … Tang, H. (2013). Data intensive computing for bioinformatics. In *Bioinformatics: Concepts, methodologies, tools, and applications* (pp. 287-321). Hershey, PA: Medical Information Science Reference. doi::10.4018/978-1-4666-3604-0.ch016

Rabaey, M. (2012). A public economics approach to enabling enterprise architecture with the government cloud in Belgium. In P. Saha (Ed.), *Enterprise architecture for connected e-government: Practices and innovations* (pp. 467–493). Hershey, PA: Information Science Reference. doi:10.4018/978-1-4666-1824-4.ch020

Rabaey, M. (2013). A complex adaptive system thinking approach of government e-procurement in a cloud computing environment. In P. Ordóñez de Pablos, J. Lovelle, J. Gayo, & R. Tennyson (Eds.), *E-procurement management for successful electronic government systems* (pp. 193–219). Hershey, PA: Information Science Reference. doi:10.4018/978-1-4666-2119-0.ch013

Rabaey, M. (2013). Holistic investment framework for cloud computing: A management-philosophical approach based on complex adaptive systems. In A. Bento & A. Aggarwal (Eds.), *Cloud computing service and deployment models: Layers and management* (pp. 94–122). Hershey, PA: Business Science Reference. doi:10.4018/978-1-4666-2187-9.ch005

Rak, M., Ficco, M., Luna, J., Ghani, H., Suri, N., Panica, S., & Petcu, D. (2012). Security issues in cloud federations. In M. Villari, I. Brandic, & F. Tusa (Eds.), *Achieving federated and self-manageable cloud infrastructures: Theory and practice* (pp. 176–194). Hershey, PA: Business Science Reference. doi:10.4018/978-1-4666-1631-8.ch010

Ramanathan, R. (2013). Extending service-driven architectural approaches to the cloud. In R. Ramanathan & K. Raja (Eds.), *Service-driven approaches to architecture and enterprise integration* (pp. 334–359). Hershey, PA: Information Science Reference. doi:10.4018/978-1-4666-4193-8.ch013

Ramírez, M., Gutiérrez, A., Monguet, J. M., & Muñoz, C. (2012). An internet cost model, assignment of costs based on actual network use. *International Journal of Web Portals*, *4*(4), 19–34. doi:10.4018/jwp.2012100102

Rashid, A., Wang, W. Y., & Tan, F. B. (2013). Value co-creation in cloud services. In A. Lin, J. Foster, & P. Scifleet (Eds.), *Consumer information systems and relationship management: Design, implementation, and use* (pp. 74–91). Hershey, PA: Business Science Reference. doi:10.4018/978-1-4666-4082-5.ch005

Ratten, V. (2012). Cloud computing services: Theoretical foundations of ethical and entrepreneurial adoption behaviour. *International Journal of Cloud Applications and Computing, 2*(2), 48–58. doi:10.4018/ijcac.2012040105

Ratten, V. (2013). Exploring behaviors and perceptions affecting the adoption of cloud computing. *International Journal of Innovation in the Digital Economy, 4*(3), 51–68. doi:10.4018/jide.2013070104

Ravi, V. (2012). Cloud computing paradigm for Indian education sector. *International Journal of Cloud Applications and Computing, 2*(2), 41–47. doi:10.4018/ijcac.2012040104

Rawat, A., Kapoor, P., & Sushil, R. (2014). Application of cloud computing in library information service sector. In S. Dhamdhere (Ed.), *Cloud computing and virtualization technologies in libraries* (pp. 77–89). Hershey, PA: Information Science Reference. doi:10.4018/978-1-4666-4631-5.ch005

Reich, C., Hübner, S., & Kuijs, H. (2012). Cloud computing for on-demand virtual desktops and labs. In L. Chao (Ed.), *Cloud computing for teaching and learning: strategies for design and implementation* (pp. 111–125). Hershey, PA: Information Science Reference. doi:10.4018/978-1-4666-0957-0.ch008

Rice, R. W. (2013). Testing in the cloud: Balancing the value and risks of cloud computing. In S. Tilley & T. Parveen (Eds.), *Software testing in the cloud: Perspectives on an emerging discipline* (pp. 404–416). Hershey, PA: Information Science Reference. doi:10.4018/978-1-4666-2536-5.ch019

Ruan, K. (2013). Designing a forensic-enabling cloud ecosystem. In K. Ruan (Ed.), *Cybercrime and cloud forensics: Applications for investigation processes* (pp. 331–344). Hershey, PA: Information Science Reference. doi:10.4018/978-1-4666-2662-1.ch014

Sabetzadeh, F., & Tsui, E. (2011). Delivering knowledge services in the cloud. *International Journal of Knowledge and Systems Science, 2*(4), 14–20. doi:10.4018/jkss.2011100102

Sabetzadeh, F., & Tsui, E. (2013). Delivering knowledge services in the cloud. In G. Yang (Ed.), *Multidisciplinary studies in knowledge and systems science* (pp. 247–254). Hershey, PA: Information Science Reference. doi:10.4018/978-1-4666-3998-0.ch017

Saedi, A., & Iahad, N. A. (2013). Future research on cloud computing adoption by small and medium-sized enterprises: A critical analysis of relevant theories. *International Journal of Actor-Network Theory and Technological Innovation, 5*(2), 1–16. doi:10.4018/jantti.2013040101

Saha, D., & Sridhar, V. (2011). Emerging areas of research in business data communications. *International Journal of Business Data Communications and Networking, 7*(4), 52–59. doi:10.4018/IJBDCN.2011100104

Saha, D., & Sridhar, V. (2013). Platform on platform (PoP) model for meta-networking: A new paradigm for networks of the future. *International Journal of Business Data Communications and Networking, 9*(1), 1–10. doi:10.4018/jbdcn.2013010101

Sahlin, J. P. (2013). Cloud computing: Past, present, and future. In X. Yang & L. Liu (Eds.), *Principles, methodologies, and service-oriented approaches for cloud computing* (pp. 19–50). Hershey, PA: Business Science Reference. doi:10.4018/978-1-4666-2854-0.ch002

Salama, M., & Shawish, A. (2012). Libraries: From the classical to cloud-based era. *International Journal of Digital Library Systems, 3*(3), 14–32. doi::10.4018/jdls.2012070102

Sánchez, C. M., Molina, D., Vozmediano, R. M., Montero, R. S., & Llorente, I. M. (2012). On the use of the hybrid cloud computing paradigm. In M. Villari, I. Brandic, & F. Tusa (Eds.), *Achieving federated and self-manageable cloud infrastructures: Theory and practice* (pp. 196–218). Hershey, PA: Business Science Reference. doi:10.4018/978-1-4666-1631-8.ch011

Sasikala, P. (2011). Architectural strategies for green cloud computing: Environments, infrastructure and resources. *International Journal of Cloud Applications and Computing, 1*(4), 1–24. doi:10.4018/ijcac.2011100101

Sasikala, P. (2011). Cloud computing in higher education: Opportunities and issues. *International Journal of Cloud Applications and Computing, 1*(2), 1–13. doi:10.4018/ijcac.2011040101

Sasikala, P. (2011). Cloud computing towards technological convergence. *International Journal of Cloud Applications and Computing, 1*(4), 44–59. doi:10.4018/ijcac.2011100104

Sasikala, P. (2012). Cloud computing and e-governance: Advances, opportunities and challenges. *International Journal of Cloud Applications and Computing, 2*(4), 32–52. doi:10.4018/ijcac.2012100103

Sasikala, P. (2012). Cloud computing in higher education: Opportunities and issues. In *Grid and cloud computing: Concepts, methodologies, tools and applications* (pp. 1672–1685). Hershey, PA: Information Science Reference. doi:10.4018/978-1-4666-0879-5.ch709

Sasikala, P. (2012). Cloud computing towards technological convergence. In *Grid and cloud computing: Concepts, methodologies, tools and applications* (pp. 1576–1592). Hershey, PA: Information Science Reference. doi:10.4018/978-1-4666-0879-5.ch703

Sasikala, P. (2013). Architectural strategies for green cloud computing: Environments, infrastructure and resources. In S. Aljawarneh (Ed.), *Cloud computing advancements in design, implementation, and technologies* (pp. 218–242). Hershey, PA: Information Science Reference. doi:10.4018/978-1-4666-1879-4.ch016

Sasikala, P. (2013). Cloud computing in higher education: Opportunities and issues. In S. Aljawarneh (Ed.), *Cloud computing advancements in design, implementation, and technologies* (pp. 83–96). Hershey, PA: Information Science Reference. doi:10.4018/978-1-4666-1879-4.ch006

Sasikala, P. (2013). Cloud computing towards technological convergence. In S. Aljawarneh (Ed.), *Cloud computing advancements in design, implementation, and technologies* (pp. 263–279). Hershey, PA: Information Science Reference. doi:10.4018/978-1-4666-1879-4.ch019

Sasikala, P. (2013). New media cloud computing: Opportunities and challenges. *International Journal of Cloud Applications and Computing, 3*(2), 61–72. doi:10.4018/ijcac.2013040106

Schrödl, H., & Wind, S. (2013). Requirements engineering for cloud application development. In A. Bento & A. Aggarwal (Eds.), *Cloud computing service and deployment models: Layers and management* (pp. 137–150). Hershey, PA: Business Science Reference. doi:10.4018/978-1-4666-2187-9.ch007

Sclater, N. (2012). Legal and contractual issues of cloud computing for educational institutions. In L. Chao (Ed.), *Cloud computing for teaching and learning: Strategies for design and implementation* (pp. 186–199). Hershey, PA: Information Science Reference. doi:10.4018/978-1-4666-0957-0.ch013

Sen, J. (2014). Security and privacy issues in cloud computing. In A. Ruiz-Martinez, R. Marin-Lopez, & F. Pereniguez-Garcia (Eds.), *Architectures and protocols for secure information technology infrastructures* (pp. 1–45). Hershey, PA: Information Science Reference. doi:10.4018/978-1-4666-4514-1.ch001

Shah, B. (2013). Cloud environment controls assessment framework. In *IT policy and ethics: Concepts, methodologies, tools, and applications* (pp. 1822–1847). Hershey, PA: Information Science Reference. doi:10.4018/978-1-4666-2919-6.ch080

Shah, B. (2013). Cloud environment controls assessment framework. In S. Tilley & T. Parveen (Eds.), *Software testing in the cloud: Perspectives on an emerging discipline* (pp. 28–53). Hershey, PA: Information Science Reference. doi:10.4018/978-1-4666-2536-5.ch002

Shang, X., Zhang, R., & Chen, Y. (2012). Internet of things (IoT) service architecture and its application in e-commerce. *Journal of Electronic Commerce in Organizations*, *10*(3), 44–55. doi:10.4018/jeco.2012070104

Shankararaman, V., & Kit, L. E. (2013). Integrating the cloud scenarios and solutions. In A. Bento & A. Aggarwal (Eds.), *Cloud computing service and deployment models: Layers and management* (pp. 173–189). Hershey, PA: Business Science Reference. doi:10.4018/978-1-4666-2187-9.ch009

Sharma, A., & Maurer, F. (2013). A roadmap for software engineering for the cloud: Results of a systematic review. In X. Wang, N. Ali, I. Ramos, & R. Vidgen (Eds.), *Agile and lean service-oriented development: Foundations, theory, and practice* (pp. 48–63). Hershey, PA: Information Science Reference. doi:10.4018/978-1-4666-2503-7.ch003

Sharma, A., & Maurer, F. (2014). A roadmap for software engineering for the cloud: Results of a systematic review. In *Software design and development: Concepts, methodologies, tools, and applications* (pp. 1–16). Hershey, PA: Information Science Reference. doi:10.4018/978-1-4666-4301-7.ch001

Sharma, S. C., & Bagoria, H. (2014). Libraries and cloud computing models: A changing paradigm. In S. Dhamdhere (Ed.), *Cloud computing and virtualization technologies in libraries* (pp. 124–149). Hershey, PA: Information Science Reference. doi:10.4018/978-1-4666-4631-5.ch008

Shawish, A., & Salama, M. (2013). Cloud computing in academia, governments, and industry. In X. Yang & L. Liu (Eds.), *Principles, methodologies, and service-oriented approaches for cloud computing* (pp. 71–114). Hershey, PA: Business Science Reference. doi:10.4018/978-1-4666-2854-0.ch004

Shebanow, A., Perez, R., & Howard, C. (2012). The effect of firewall testing types on cloud security policies. *International Journal of Strategic Information Technology and Applications*, *3*(3), 60–68. doi:10.4018/jsita.2012070105

Sheikhalishahi, M., Devare, M., Grandinetti, L., & Incutti, M. C. (2012). A complementary approach to grid and cloud distributed computing paradigms. In *Grid and cloud computing: Concepts, methodologies, tools and applications* (pp. 1929–1942). Hershey, PA: Information Science Reference. doi:10.4018/978-1-4666-0879-5.ch811

Sheikhalishahi, M., Devare, M., Grandinetti, L., & Incutti, M. C. (2012). A complementary approach to grid and cloud distributed computing paradigms. In N. Preve (Ed.), *Computational and data grids: Principles, applications and design* (pp. 31–44). Hershey, PA: Information Science Reference. doi:10.4018/978-1-61350-113-9.ch002

Shen, Y., Li, Y., Wu, L., Liu, S., & Wen, Q. (2014). Cloud computing overview. In Y. Shen, Y. Li, L. Wu, S. Liu, & Q. Wen (Eds.), *Enabling the new era of cloud computing: Data security, transfer, and management* (pp. 1–24). Hershey, PA: Information Science Reference. doi:10.4018/978-1-4666-4801-2.ch001

Shen, Y., Li, Y., Wu, L., Liu, S., & Wen, Q. (2014). Main components of cloud computing. In Y. Shen, Y. Li, L. Wu, S. Liu, & Q. Wen (Eds.), *Enabling the new era of cloud computing: Data security, transfer, and management* (pp. 25–50). Hershey, PA: Information Science Reference. doi:10.4018/978-1-4666-4801-2.ch002

Shen, Y., Yang, J., & Keskin, T. (2014). Impact of cultural differences on the cloud computing ecosystems in the USA and China. In Y. Shen, Y. Li, L. Wu, S. Liu, & Q. Wen (Eds.), *Enabling the new era of cloud computing: Data security, transfer, and management* (pp. 269–283). Hershey, PA: Information Science Reference. doi:10.4018/978-1-4666-4801-2.ch014

Shetty, S., & Rawat, D. B. (2013). Cloud computing based cognitive radio networking. In N. Meghanathan & Y. Reddy (Eds.), *Cognitive radio technology applications for wireless and mobile ad hoc networks* (pp. 153–164). Hershey, PA: Information Science Reference. doi:10.4018/978-1-4666-4221-8.ch008

Shi, Z., & Beard, C. (2014). QoS in the mobile cloud computing environment. In J. Rodrigues, K. Lin, & J. Lloret (Eds.), *Mobile networks and cloud computing convergence for progressive services and applications* (pp. 200–217). Hershey, PA: Information Science Reference. doi:10.4018/978-1-4666-4781-7.ch011

Shuster, L. (2013). Enterprise integration: Challenges and solution architecture. In R. Ramanathan & K. Raja (Eds.), *Service-driven approaches to architecture and enterprise integration* (pp. 43–66). Hershey, PA: Information Science Reference. doi:10.4018/978-1-4666-4193-8.ch002

Siahos, Y., Papanagiotou, I., Georgopoulos, A., Tsamis, F., & Papaioannou, I. (2012). An architecture paradigm for providing cloud services in school labs based on open source software to enhance ICT in education. *International Journal of Cyber Ethics in Education*, 2(1), 44–57. doi:10.4018/ijcee.2012010105

Simon, E., & Estublier, J. (2013). Model driven integration of heterogeneous software artifacts in service oriented computing. In A. Ionita, M. Litoiu, & G. Lewis (Eds.), *Migrating legacy applications: Challenges in service oriented architecture and cloud computing environments* (pp. 332–360). Hershey, PA: Information Science Reference. doi:10.4018/978-1-4666-2488-7.ch014

Singh, J., & Kumar, V. (2013). Compliance and regulatory standards for cloud computing. In R. Khurana & R. Aggarwal (Eds.), *Interdisciplinary perspectives on business convergence, computing, and legality* (pp. 54–64). Hershey, PA: Business Science Reference. doi:10.4018/978-1-4666-4209-6.ch006

Singh, V. V. (2012). Software development using service syndication based on API handshake approach between cloud-based and SOA-based reusable services. In H. Yang & X. Liu (Eds.), *Software reuse in the emerging cloud computing era* (pp. 136–157). Hershey, PA: Information Science Reference. doi:10.4018/978-1-4666-0897-9.ch006

Smeitink, M., & Spruit, M. (2013). Maturity for sustainability in IT: Introducing the MITS. *International Journal of Information Technologies and Systems Approach*, 6(1), 39–56. doi:10.4018/jitsa.2013010103

Smith, P. A., & Cockburn, T. (2013). Socio-digital technologies. In *Dynamic leadership models for global business: Enhancing digitally connected environments* (pp. 142–168). Hershey, PA: Business Science Reference. doi:10.4018/978-1-4666-2836-6.ch006

Sneed, H. M. (2013). Testing web services in the cloud. In S. Tilley & T. Parveen (Eds.), *Software testing in the cloud: Perspectives on an emerging discipline* (pp. 136–173). Hershey, PA: Information Science Reference. doi:10.4018/978-1-4666-2536-5.ch007

Solomon, B., Ionescu, D., Gadea, C., & Litoiu, M. (2013). Geographically distributed cloud-based collaborative application. In A. Ionita, M. Litoiu, & G. Lewis (Eds.), *Migrating legacy applications: Challenges in service oriented architecture and cloud computing environments* (pp. 248–274). Hershey, PA: Information Science Reference. doi:10.4018/978-1-4666-2488-7.ch011

Song, W., & Xiao, Z. (2013). An infrastructure-as-a-service cloud: On-demand resource provisioning. In X. Yang & L. Liu (Eds.), *Principles, methodologies, and service-oriented approaches for cloud computing* (pp. 302–324). Hershey, PA: Business Science Reference. doi:10.4018/978-1-4666-2854-0.ch013

Sood, S. K. (2013). A value based dynamic resource provisioning model in cloud. *International Journal of Cloud Applications and Computing*, 3(1), 1–12. doi:10.4018/ijcac.2013010101

Sotiriadis, S., Bessis, N., & Antonopoulos, N. (2012). Exploring inter-cloud load balancing by utilizing historical service submission records. *International Journal of Distributed Systems and Technologies*, 3(3), 72–81. doi:10.4018/jdst.2012070106

Soyata, T., Ba, H., Heinzelman, W., Kwon, M., & Shi, J. (2014). Accelerating mobile-cloud computing: A survey. In H. Mouftah & B. Kantarci (Eds.), *Communication infrastructures for cloud computing* (pp. 175–197). Hershey, PA: Information Science Reference. doi:10.4018/978-1-4666-4522-6.ch008

Spyridopoulos, T., & Katos, V. (2011). Requirements for a forensically ready cloud storage service. *International Journal of Digital Crime and Forensics*, 3(3), 19–36. doi:10.4018/jdcf.2011070102

Spyridopoulos, T., & Katos, V. (2013). Data recovery strategies for cloud environments. In K. Ruan (Ed.), *Cybercrime and cloud forensics: Applications for investigation processes* (pp. 251–265). Hershey, PA: Information Science Reference. doi:10.4018/978-1-4666-2662-1.ch010

Srinivasa, K. G., S, H. R. C., H, M. K. S., & Venkatesh, N. (2012). MeghaOS: A framework for scalable, interoperable cloud based operating system. *International Journal of Cloud Applications and Computing*, 2(1), 53–70. doi:10.4018/ijcac.2012010104

Stantchev, V., & Stantcheva, L. (2012). Extending traditional IT-governance knowledge towards SOA and cloud governance. *International Journal of Knowledge Society Research*, 3(2), 30–43. doi:10.4018/jksr.2012040103

Stantchev, V., & Tamm, G. (2012). Reducing information asymmetry in cloud marketplaces. *International Journal of Human Capital and Information Technology Professionals*, *3*(4), 1–10. doi:10.4018/jhcitp.2012100101

Steinbuß, S., & Weißenberg, N. (2013). Service design and process design for the logistics mall cloud. In X. Yang & L. Liu (Eds.), *Principles, methodologies, and service-oriented approaches for cloud computing* (pp. 186–206). Hershey, PA: Business Science Reference. doi:10.4018/978-1-4666-2854-0.ch008

Stender, J., Berlin, M., & Reinefeld, A. (2013). XtreemFS: A file system for the cloud. In D. Kyriazis, A. Voulodimos, S. Gogouvitis, & T. Varvarigou (Eds.), *Data intensive storage services for cloud environments* (pp. 267–285). Hershey, PA: Business Science Reference. doi:10.4018/978-1-4666-3934-8.ch016

Sticklen, D. J., & Issa, T. (2011). An initial examination of free and proprietary software-selection in organizations. *International Journal of Web Portals*, *3*(4), 27–43. doi:10.4018/jwp.2011100103

Sun, Y., White, J., Gray, J., & Gokhale, A. (2012). Model-driven automated error recovery in cloud computing. In *Grid and cloud computing: Concepts, methodologies, tools and applications* (pp. 680–700). Hershey, PA: Information Science Reference. doi:10.4018/978-1-4666-0879-5.ch308

Sun, Z., Yang, Y., Zhou, Y., & Cruickshank, H. (2014). Agent-based resource management for mobile cloud. In J. Rodrigues, K. Lin, & J. Lloret (Eds.), *Mobile networks and cloud computing convergence for progressive services and applications* (pp. 118–134). Hershey, PA: Information Science Reference. doi:10.4018/978-1-4666-4781-7.ch007

Sutherland, S. (2013). Convergence of interoperability of cloud computing, service oriented architecture and enterprise architecture. *International Journal of E-Entrepreneurship and Innovation*, *4*(1), 43–51. doi:10.4018/jeei.2013010104

Takabi, H., & Joshi, J. B. (2013). Policy management in cloud: Challenges and approaches. In D. Rosado, D. Mellado, E. Fernandez-Medina, & M. Piattini (Eds.), *Security engineering for cloud computing: Approaches and tools* (pp. 191–211). Hershey, PA: Information Science Reference. doi:10.4018/978-1-4666-2125-1.ch010

Takabi, H., & Joshi, J. B. (2013). Policy management in cloud: Challenges and approaches. In *IT policy and ethics: Concepts, methodologies, tools, and applications* (pp. 814–834). Hershey, PA: Information Science Reference. doi:10.4018/978-1-4666-2919-6.ch037

Takabi, H., Joshi, J. B., & Ahn, G. (2013). Security and privacy in cloud computing: Towards a comprehensive framework. In X. Yang & L. Liu (Eds.), *Principles, methodologies, and service-oriented approaches for cloud computing* (pp. 164–184). Hershey, PA: Business Science Reference. doi:10.4018/978-1-4666-2854-0.ch007

Takabi, H., Zargar, S. T., & Joshi, J. B. (2014). Mobile cloud computing and its security and privacy challenges. In D. Rawat, B. Bista, & G. Yan (Eds.), *Security, privacy, trust, and resource management in mobile and wireless communications* (pp. 384–407). Hershey, PA: Information Science Reference. doi:10.4018/978-1-4666-4691-9.ch016

Teixeira, C., Pinto, J. S., Ferreira, F., Oliveira, A., Teixeira, A., & Pereira, C. (2013). Cloud computing enhanced service development architecture for the living usability lab. In R. Martinho, R. Rijo, M. Cruz-Cunha, & J. Varajão (Eds.), *Information systems and technologies for enhancing health and social care* (pp. 33–53). Hershey, PA: Medical Information Science Reference. doi:10.4018/978-1-4666-3667-5.ch003

Thimm, H. (2012). Cloud-based collaborative decision making: Design considerations and architecture of the GRUPO-MOD system. *International Journal of Decision Support System Technology*, 4(4), 39–59. doi:10.4018/jdsst.2012100103

Thomas, P. (2012). Harnessing the potential of cloud computing to transform higher education. In L. Chao (Ed.), *Cloud computing for teaching and learning: Strategies for design and implementation* (pp. 147–158). Hershey, PA: Information Science Reference. doi:10.4018/978-1-4666-0957-0.ch010

T.M. K., & Gopalakrishnan, S. (2014). Green economic and secure libraries on cloud. In S. Dhamdhere (Ed.), Cloud computing and virtualization technologies in libraries (pp. 297-315). Hershey, PA: Information Science Reference. doi::10.4018/978-1-4666-4631-5.ch017

Toka, A., Aivazidou, E., Antoniou, A., & Arvanitopoulos-Darginis, K. (2013). Cloud computing in supply chain management: An overview. In D. Graham, I. Manikas, & D. Folinas (Eds.), *E-logistics and e-supply chain management: Applications for evolving business* (pp. 218–231). Hershey, PA: Business Science Reference. doi:10.4018/978-1-4666-3914-0.ch012

Torrealba, S. M., Morales, P. M., Campos, J. M., & Meza, S. M. (2013). A software tool to support risks analysis about what should or should not go to the cloud. In D. Rosado, D. Mellado, E. Fernandez-Medina, & M. Piattini (Eds.), *Security engineering for cloud computing: Approaches and tools* (pp. 72–96). Hershey, PA: Information Science Reference. doi:10.4018/978-1-4666-2125-1.ch005

Trivedi, M., & Suthar, V. (2013). Cloud computing: A feasible platform for ICT enabled health science libraries in India. *International Journal of User-Driven Healthcare*, 3(2), 69–77. doi:10.4018/ijudh.2013040108

Truong, H., Pham, T., Thoai, N., & Dustdar, S. (2012). Cloud computing for education and research in developing countries. In L. Chao (Ed.), *Cloud computing for teaching and learning: Strategies for design and implementation* (pp. 64–80). Hershey, PA: Information Science Reference. doi:10.4018/978-1-4666-0957-0.ch005

Tsirmpas, C., Giokas, K., Iliopoulou, D., & Koutsouris, D. (2012). Magnetic resonance imaging and magnetic resonance spectroscopy cloud computing framework. *International Journal of Reliable and Quality E-Healthcare*, 1(4), 1–12. doi:10.4018/ijrqeh.2012100101

Turner, H., White, J., Reed, J., Galindo, J., Porter, A., Marathe, M., & Gokhale, A. et al. (2013). Building a cloud-based mobile application testbed. In *IT policy and ethics: Concepts, methodologies, tools, and applications* (pp. 879–899). Hershey, PA: Information Science Reference. doi:10.4018/978-1-4666-2919-6.ch040

Turner, H., White, J., Reed, J., Galindo, J., Porter, A., Marathe, M., & Gokhale, A. et al. (2013). Building a cloud-based mobile application testbed. In S. Tilley & T. Parveen (Eds.), *Software testing in the cloud: Perspectives on an emerging discipline* (pp. 382–403). Hershey, PA: Information Science Reference. doi:10.4018/978-1-4666-2536-5.ch018

Tusa, F., Paone, M., & Villari, M. (2012). CLEVER: A cloud middleware beyond the federation. In M. Villari, I. Brandic, & F. Tusa (Eds.), *Achieving federated and self-manageable cloud infrastructures: Theory and practice* (pp. 219–241). Hershey, PA: Business Science Reference. doi:10.4018/978-1-4666-1631-8.ch012

Udoh, E. (2012). Technology acceptance model applied to the adoption of grid and cloud technology. *International Journal of Grid and High Performance Computing*, 4(1), 1–20. doi:10.4018/jghpc.2012010101

Vannoy, S. A. (2011). A structured content analytic assessment of business services advertisements in the cloud-based web services marketplace. *International Journal of Dependable and Trustworthy Information Systems*, 2(1), 18–49. doi:10.4018/jdtis.2011010102

Vaquero, L. M., Cáceres, J., & Morán, D. (2011). The challenge of service level scalability for the cloud. *International Journal of Cloud Applications and Computing*, 1(1), 34–44. doi:10.4018/ijcac.2011010103

Vaquero, L. M., Cáceres, J., & Morán, D. (2013). The challenge of service level scalability for the cloud. In S. Aljawarneh (Ed.), *Cloud computing advancements in design, implementation, and technologies* (pp. 37–48). Hershey, PA: Information Science Reference. doi:10.4018/978-1-4666-1879-4.ch003

Venkatraman, R., Venkatraman, S., & Asaithambi, S. P. (2013). A practical cloud services implementation framework for e-businesses. In K. Tarnay, S. Imre, & L. Xu (Eds.), *Research and development in e-business through service-oriented solutions* (pp. 167–198). Hershey, PA: Business Science Reference. doi:10.4018/978-1-4666-4181-5.ch008

Venkatraman, S. (2013). Software engineering research gaps in the cloud. *Journal of Information Technology Research*, 6(1), 1–19. doi:10.4018/jitr.2013010101

Vijaykumar, S., Rajkarthick, K. S., & Priya, J. (2012). Innovative business opportunities and smart business management techniques from green cloud TPS. *International Journal of Asian Business and Information Management*, 3(4), 62–72. doi:10.4018/jabim.2012100107

Wang, C., Lam, K. T., & Kui Ma, R. K. (2012). A computation migration approach to elasticity of cloud computing. In J. Abawajy, M. Pathan, M. Rahman, A. Pathan, & M. Deris (Eds.), *Network and traffic engineering in emerging distributed computing applications* (pp. 145–178). Hershey, PA: Information Science Reference. doi:10.4018/978-1-4666-1888-6.ch007

Wang, D., & Wu, J. (2014). Carrier-grade distributed cloud computing: Demands, challenges, designs, and future perspectives. In H. Mouftah & B. Kantarci (Eds.), *Communication infrastructures for cloud computing* (pp. 264–281). Hershey, PA: Information Science Reference. doi:10.4018/978-1-4666-4522-6.ch012

Wang, H., & Philips, D. (2012). Implement virtual programming lab with cloud computing for web-based distance education. In L. Chao (Ed.), *Cloud computing for teaching and learning: Strategies for design and implementation* (pp. 95–110). Hershey, PA: Information Science Reference. doi:10.4018/978-1-4666-0957-0.ch007

Warneke, D. (2013). Ad-hoc parallel data processing on pay-as-you-go clouds with nephele. In A. Loo (Ed.), *Distributed computing innovations for business, engineering, and science* (pp. 191–218). Hershey, PA: Information Science Reference. doi:10.4018/978-1-4666-2533-4.ch010

Wei, Y., & Blake, M. B. (2013). Adaptive web services monitoring in cloud environments. *International Journal of Web Portals*, *5*(1), 15–27. doi:10.4018/jwp.2013010102

White, S. C., Sedigh, S., & Hurson, A. R. (2013). Security concepts for cloud computing. In X. Yang & L. Liu (Eds.), *Principles, methodologies, and service-oriented approaches for cloud computing* (pp. 116–142). Hershey, PA: Business Science Reference. doi:10.4018/978-1-4666-2854-0.ch005

Williams, A. J. (2013). The role of emerging technologies in developing and sustaining diverse suppliers in competitive markets. In *Enterprise resource planning: Concepts, methodologies, tools, and applications* (pp. 1550–1560). Hershey, PA: Business Science Reference. doi:10.4018/978-1-4666-4153-2.ch082

Williams, A. J. (2013). The role of emerging technologies in developing and sustaining diverse suppliers in competitive markets. In J. Lewis, A. Green, & D. Surry (Eds.), *Technology as a tool for diversity leadership: Implementation and future implications* (pp. 95–105). Hershey, PA: Information Science Reference. doi:10.4018/978-1-4666-2668-3.ch007

Wilson, L., Goh, T. T., & Wang, W. Y. (2012). Big data management challenges in a meteorological organisation. *International Journal of E-Adoption*, *4*(2), 1–14. doi:10.4018/jea.2012040101

Wu, R., Ahn, G., & Hu, H. (2012). Towards HIPAA-compliant healthcare systems in cloud computing. *International Journal of Computational Models and Algorithms in Medicine*, *3*(2), 1–22. doi:10.4018/jcmam.2012040101

Xiao, J., Wang, M., Wang, L., & Zhu, X. (2013). Design and implementation of C-iLearning: A cloud-based intelligent learning system. *International Journal of Distance Education Technologies*, *11*(3), 79–97. doi:10.4018/jdet.2013070106

Xing, R., Wang, Z., & Peterson, R. L. (2011). Redefining the information technology in the 21st century. *International Journal of Strategic Information Technology and Applications*, *2*(1), 1–10. doi:10.4018/jsita.2011010101

Xu, L., Huang, D., Tsai, W., & Atkinson, R. K. (2012). V-lab: A mobile, cloud-based virtual laboratory platform for hands-on networking courses. *International Journal of Cyber Behavior, Psychology and Learning*, *2*(3), 73–85. doi:10.4018/ijcbpl.2012070106

Xu, Y., & Mao, S. (2014). Mobile cloud media: State of the art and outlook. In J. Rodrigues, K. Lin, & J. Lloret (Eds.), *Mobile networks and cloud computing convergence for progressive services and applications* (pp. 18–38). Hershey, PA: Information Science Reference. doi:10.4018/978-1-4666-4781-7.ch002

Xu, Z., Yan, B., & Zou, Y. (2013). Beyond hadoop: Recent directions in data computing for internet services. In S. Aljawarneh (Ed.), *Cloud computing advancements in design, implementation, and technologies* (pp. 49–66). Hershey, PA: Information Science Reference. doi:10.4018/978-1-4666-1879-4.ch004

Yan, Z. (2014). Trust management in mobile cloud computing. In *Trust management in mobile environments: Autonomic and usable models* (pp. 54–93). Hershey, PA: Information Science Reference. doi:10.4018/978-1-4666-4765-7.ch004

Yang, D. X. (2012). QoS-oriented service computing: Bringing SOA into cloud environment. In X. Liu & Y. Li (Eds.), *Advanced design approaches to emerging software systems: Principles, methodologies and tools* (pp. 274–296). Hershey, PA: Information Science Reference. doi:10.4018/978-1-60960-735-7.ch013

Yang, H., Huff, S. L., & Tate, M. (2013). Managing the cloud for information systems agility. In A. Bento & A. Aggarwal (Eds.), *Cloud computing service and deployment models: Layers and management* (pp. 70–93). Hershey, PA: Business Science Reference. doi:10.4018/978-1-4666-2187-9.ch004

Yang, M., Kuo, C., & Yeh, Y. (2011). Dynamic rightsizing with quality-controlled algorithms in virtualization environments. *International Journal of Grid and High Performance Computing*, 3(2), 29–43. doi:10.4018/jghpc.2011040103

Yang, X. (2012). QoS-oriented service computing: Bringing SOA into cloud environment. In *Grid and cloud computing: Concepts, methodologies, tools and applications* (pp. 1621–1643). Hershey, PA: Information Science Reference. doi:10.4018/978-1-4666-0879-5.ch706

Yang, Y., Chen, J., & Hu, H. (2012). The convergence between cloud computing and cable TV. *International Journal of Technology Diffusion*, 3(2), 1–11. doi:10.4018/jtd.2012040101

Yassein, M. O., Khamayseh, Y. M., & Hatamleh, A. M. (2013). Intelligent randomize round robin for cloud computing. *International Journal of Cloud Applications and Computing*, 3(1), 27–33. doi:10.4018/ijcac.2013010103

Yau, S. S., An, H. G., & Buduru, A. B. (2012). An approach to data confidentiality protection in cloud environments. *International Journal of Web Services Research*, 9(3), 67–83. doi:10.4018/jwsr.2012070104

Yu, W. D., Adiga, A. S., Rao, S., & Panakkel, M. J. (2012). A SOA based system development methodology for cloud computing environment: Using uhealthcare as practice. *International Journal of E-Health and Medical Communications*, 3(4), 42–63. doi:10.4018/jehmc.2012100104

Yu, W. D., & Bhagwat, R. (2011). Modeling emergency and telemedicine heath support system: A service oriented architecture approach using cloud computing. *International Journal of E-Health and Medical Communications*, 2(3), 63–88. doi::10.4018/jehmc.2011070104

Yu, W. D., & Bhagwat, R. (2013). Modeling emergency and telemedicine health support system: A service oriented architecture approach using cloud computing. In J. Rodrigues (Ed.), *Digital advances in medicine, e-health, and communication technologies* (pp. 187–213). Hershey, PA: Medical Information Science Reference. doi:10.4018/978-1-4666-2794-9.ch011

Yuan, D., Lewandowski, C., & Zhong, J. (2012). Developing a private cloud based IP telephony laboratory and curriculum. In L. Chao (Ed.), *Cloud computing for teaching and learning: Strategies for design and implementation* (pp. 126–145). Hershey, PA: Information Science Reference. doi:10.4018/978-1-4666-0957-0.ch009

Yuvaraj, M. (2014). Cloud libraries: Issues and challenges. In S. Dhamdhere (Ed.), *Cloud computing and virtualization technologies in libraries* (pp. 316–338). Hershey, PA: Information Science Reference. doi:10.4018/978-1-4666-4631-5.ch018

Zaman, M., Simmers, C. A., & Anandarajan, M. (2013). Using an ethical framework to examine linkages between "going green" in research practices and information and communication technologies. In B. Medlin (Ed.), *Integrations of technology utilization and social dynamics in organizations* (pp. 243–262). Hershey, PA: Information Science Reference. doi:10.4018/978-1-4666-1948-7.ch015

Zapata, B. C., & Alemán, J. L. (2013). Security risks in cloud computing: An analysis of the main vulnerabilities. In D. Rosado, D. Mellado, E. Fernandez-Medina, & M. Piattini (Eds.), *Security engineering for cloud computing: Approaches and tools* (pp. 55–71). Hershey, PA: Information Science Reference. doi:10.4018/978-1-4666-2125-1.ch004

Zapata, B. C., & Alemán, J. L. (2014). Security risks in cloud computing: An analysis of the main vulnerabilities. In *Software design and development: Concepts, methodologies, tools, and applications* (pp. 936–952). Hershey, PA: Information Science Reference. doi:10.4018/978-1-4666-4301-7.ch045

Zardari, S., Faniyi, F., & Bahsoon, R. (2013). Using obstacles for systematically modeling, analysing, and mitigating risks in cloud adoption. In I. Mistrik, A. Tang, R. Bahsoon, & J. Stafford (Eds.), *Aligning enterprise, system, and software architectures* (pp. 275–296). Hershey, PA: Business Science Reference. doi:10.4018/978-1-4666-2199-2.ch014

Zech, P., Kalb, P., Felderer, M., & Breu, R. (2013). Threatening the cloud: Securing services and data by continuous, model-driven negative security testing. In S. Tilley & T. Parveen (Eds.), *Software testing in the cloud: Perspectives on an emerging discipline* (pp. 280–304). Hershey, PA: Information Science Reference. doi:10.4018/978-1-4666-2536-5.ch013

Zhang, F., Cao, J., Cai, H., & Wu, C. (2011). Provisioning virtual resources adaptively in elastic compute cloud platforms. *International Journal of Web Services Research, 8*(3), 54–69. doi:10.4018/jwsr.2011070103

Zhang, G., Li, C., Xue, S., Liu, Y., Zhang, Y., & Xing, C. (2012). A new electronic commerce architecture in the cloud. *Journal of Electronic Commerce in Organizations, 10*(4), 42–56. doi:10.4018/jeco.2012100104

Zhang, J., Yao, J., Chen, S., & Levy, D. (2011). Facilitating biodefense research with mobile-cloud computing. *International Journal of Systems and Service-Oriented Engineering, 2*(3), 18–31. doi:10.4018/jssoe.2011070102

Zhang, J., Yao, J., Chen, S., & Levy, D. (2013). Facilitating biodefense research with mobile-cloud computing. In D. Chiu (Ed.), *Mobile and web innovations in systems and service-oriented engineering* (pp. 318–332). Hershey, PA: Information Science Reference. doi:10.4018/978-1-4666-2470-2.ch017

Zheng, S., Chen, F., Yang, H., & Li, J. (2013). An approach to evolving legacy software system into cloud computing environment. In X. Yang & L. Liu (Eds.), *Principles, methodologies, and service-oriented approaches for cloud computing* (pp. 207–229). Hershey, PA: Business Science Reference. doi:10.4018/978-1-4666-2854-0.ch009

Zhou, J., Athukorala, K., Gilman, E., Riekki, J., & Ylianttila, M. (2012). Cloud architecture for dynamic service composition. *International Journal of Grid and High Performance Computing, 4*(2), 17–31. doi:10.4018/jghpc.2012040102

Compilation of References

Römer, U., & Schulze, R. (Eds.). (2010). Patterns, meaningful units and specialized discourses. Philadephia. John Benjamins. doi:10.1075/bct.22

A Platform Computing Whitepaper (March 2010) ;

Adrains, P., & Zantinge, D. (1999). *Data Mining*. England: Addison Wesley Longman.

Adriansyah, A., van Dongen, B., & van der Aalst, W. (2010). Towards robust conformance checking. In M. Muehlen & J. Su (Eds.), *Business Process Management Workshops* (pp. 122–133). Berlin, Germany: Springer.

Afgan, E., Chapman, B., Jadan, M., Franke, V., & Taylor, J. (2012). Using cloud computing infrastructure with CloudBioLinux, CloudMan, and Galaxy. *Current Protocols in Bioinformatics, 38*, 11.9.1-11.9.20.

Aggarwal, C., & Han, J. (2013). A Survey of RFID Data Processing. In C. Aggarwal (Ed.), *Managing and Mining Sensor Data* (pp. 349–382). New York, NY: Springer US. doi:10.1007/978-1-4614-6309-2_11

Agostinho, C., Jardim-Goncalves, R., & Steiger-Garcao, A. (2011). Using neighboring domains towards setting the foundations for Enterprise Interoperability science. In Callaos, N. et al. (Eds.) *International Symposium on Collaborative Enterprises in the Context of the 15th World-Multi-Conference on Systemic, Cybernetics and Informatics* (pp. 258-264, vol. II). Winter Garden, FL: International Institute of Informatics and Systemics.

Ahn, H. J., & Lee, H. (2004). An agent-based dynamic information network for supply chain management. *BT Technology Journal, 22*(2), 18–27. doi:10.1023/B:BTTJ.0000033467.83300.c0

Alberta Education. (2012). *Bring your own device: A guide for schools*. Retrieved April 2, 2014, from https://education.alberta.ca/media/6749210/byod%20guide%20revised%202012-09-05.pdf

Ali, S., Siegel, H. J., Maheswaran, M., & Hensgen, D. (2000). *Task execution time modeling for heterogeneous computing systems*. In Heterogeneous Computing Workshop, 2000. (HCW 2000) Proceedings. 9th, (pp. 185-199). IEEE. doi:10.1109/HCW.2000.843743

Aliei, M., Sazvar, A., & Ashrafi, B. (2012). Assessment of information technology effects on management of supply chain based on fuzzy logic in Iran tail industries. *International Journal of Advanced Manufacturing Technology, 63*(1-4), 215–223. doi:10.1007/s00170-012-3900-2

Allen, J. H. Barnum, S. Ellison, S. R. et al., (2008). *Software Security Engineering: A Guide for Project Managers*. Addison Wesley Professional.

Alshamaila, Y., Papagiannidis, S., & Li, F. (2013). Cloud computing adoption by SMEs in the north east of England: A multi-perspective framework. *Journal of Enterprise Information Management, 26*(3), 250–275. doi:10.1108/17410391311325225

Anderson, E., ... (2014, May 13). *Forecast Analysis: Public Cloud Services, Worldwide, 1Q14 Update. Document ref. G00261940*. Stamford, CT: Gartner. Retrieved May 31, 2014 from https://www.gartner.com/doc/2738817/forecast-analysis-public-cloud-services

Andres, C. (1999). *Great Web Architecture*. Foster City, CA: IDG Books World Wide.

Anschuetz, L., Keirnan, T., & Rosenbaum, S. (2002). Combining Usability Research with Documentation Development for Improved User Support. In *Proceedings of the SIGDOC*. Toronto, Canada: The Association of Computing Machinery.

Aoyama, T., & Sakai, H. (2011). Inter-cloud computing. *Business & Information Systems Engineering*, 3(3), 173–177. doi:10.1007/s12599-011-0158-4

Arlbjørn, J. S., de Haas, H., & Munksgaard, K. B. (2013). Exploring supply chain innovation. *Logistics Research*, 3(1), 3–18. doi:10.1007/s12159-010-0044-3

Armbrust, M., Stoica, I., Zaharia, M., Fox, A., Griffith, R., Joseph, A. D., & Rabkin, A. et al. (2010). A View of Cloud Computing. *Communications of the ACM*, 53(4), 50–58. doi:10.1145/1721654.1721672

Arutyunov, V. V. (2012). Cloud computing: Its history of development, modern state, and future considerations. *Scientific and Technical Information Processing*, 39(3), 173–178. doi:10.3103/S0147688212030082

Assuncao, M., Costanzo, A., & Buyya, R. (2009). *Evaluating the cost-benefit of using cloud computing to extend the capacity of clusters*. Paper presented at the 18th ACM International Symposium on High Performance Distributed Computing, Garching, Germany.

Athanasopoulos, G., Tsalgatidou, A., & Pantazoglou, M. (2006). Interoperability among Heterogeneous Services, in *International Conference on Services Computing* (pp. 174-181). Piscataway, NJ: IEEE Computer Society Press.

Attwood, T. K., & Parry, S. D. J. (2005). *Introduction to Bioinformatics; New Delhi: Pearson Education*. Singapore: Private Limited.

Auewarkul, P. (2008). The Past and Present Threat of Avian Influenza in Thailand. In E. M. Yichenlu & B. Roberts (Eds.), *Emerging Infections in Asia* (pp. 31–34). New York, NY: Springer. doi:10.1007/978-0-387-75722-3_2

Auramo, J., Kauremaa, J., & Tanskanen, K. (2005). Benefits of it in supply chain management: An explorative study of progressive companies. *International Journal of Physical Distribution & Logistics Management*, 35(2), 82–100. doi:10.1108/09600030510590282

Autry, C. W., Grawe, S. J., Daugherty, P., & Richey, R. G. (2010). The effects of technological turbulence and breadth on supply chain technology acceptance and adoption. *Journal of Operations Management*, 28(6), 522–536. doi:10.1016/j.jom.2010.03.001

Aziz, S., Shamim, M., Aziz, M. F., & Avais, P. (2013). The impact of texting/SMS language on academic writing of students - What do we need to panic about? *Elixir Linguistics and Translation*, 55, 12884–12890.

Babat, M., & Chauhan, M. (2011). A Tale of Migration to Cloud Computing for Sharing Experiences and Observations. *Workshop on Software Engineering for Cloud Computing*. Honolulu, HI: IEEE.

Bagozzi, R. P. (2007). The legacy of the technology acceptance model and a proposal for a paradigm shift. *Journal of the Association for Information Systems*, 8(4), 244–254.

Bajgoric, N. (2014). Business continuity management: A systemic framework for implementation. *Kybernetes*, 43(2), 156–177. doi:10.1108/K-11-2013-0252

Bakshi, K. (2009). *Cisco Cloud Computing: Data Center Strategy, Architecture, and Solutions* (1st edition, pp. 1-16). white paper for U.S public sector, Cisco System, Inc.

Bandopadhyay, D. (2013, December). A Technology Lead Business Model for Pharma: Collaborative Patient Care. *CSI Communications Journal*, 37(9), 12–26.

Bardhan, I. R., Demirkan, H., Kannan, P. K., Kauffman, R., & Sougstad, R. (2010). An interdisciplinary perspective on IT services management and service science. *Journal of Management Information Systems*, 26(4), 13–64. doi:10.2753/MIS0742-1222260402

Barham, P. T., Dragovic, B., Fraser, K., Hand, S., Harris, T. L., Ho, A., . . . Warfield, A. (2003). Xen and the art of virtualization. In *Symposium on Operating System Principles (SOSP)*. 19, 20, 28

Barney, J. B. (2012). Purchasing, supply chain management and sustained competitive advantage: The relevance of resource-based theory. *Journal of Supply Chain Management*, 18(2), 3–6. doi:10.1111/j.1745-493X.2012.03265.x

Bayo-Moriones, A., & Lera-Lopez, F. (2007). A firm-level analysis of determinants of ICT adoption in Spain. *Technovation*, *27*(6-7), 352–366. doi:10.1016/j.technovation.2007.01.003

Becker, S., & Mottay, F. (2001, January). A global perspective on website usability. *IEEE Software*, *18*(1), 61–54. doi:10.1109/52.903167

Behrend, T. S., Wiebe, E. N., London, J. E., & Johnson, E. C. (2010). Cloud computing adoption and usage in community colleges. *Behaviour & Information Technology*, *30*(2), 231–240. doi:10.1080/0144929X.2010.489118

Beloglazov, A., Abawajy, J., & Buyya, R. (2012). Energy-aware resource allocation heuristics for efficient management of data centers for cloud computing. *Future Generation Computer Systems*, *28*(5), 755–768. doi:10.1016/j.future.2011.04.017

Ben Arfa Rabai, L., Jouini, M., Ben Aissa, A., & Mili, A. (2013). A cybersecurity model in cloud computing environments, *Journal of King Saud University: Computer and Information Sciences*.

Bergeron, B. (2003). *Bioinformatics Computing; New Delhi: Pearson Education*. Singapore: Private Limited.

Berre, A. et al.. (2007). The ATHENA Interoperability Framework. In R. Gonçalves, J. Müller, K. Mertins, & M. Zelm (Eds.), *Enterprise Interoperability II* (pp. 569–580). London, UK: Springer. doi:10.1007/978-1-84628-858-6_62

Bhandarkar, M. (2013, April). Big Data Systems: Past, Present & (Possibly) Future. *CSI Communications Journal*, *37*(1), 7–16.

Binz, T., Breiter, G., Leyman, F., & Spatzier, T. (2012). Portable cloud services using Tosca. *IEEE Internet Computing*, *16*(3), 80–85. doi:10.1109/MIC.2012.43

Bist, M., Wariya, M., & Agarwal, A. (2013). Comparing delta, open stack and Xen Cloud Platforms: A survey on open source IaaS. In KalraB.GargD.PrasadR.KumarS. (Eds.) *3rd International Advance Computing Conference* (pp. 96-100). Piscataway, NJ: IEEE Computer Society Press. doi:10.1109/IAdCC.2013.6514201

Bksi, J., Galambos, G., & Kellerer, H. (2000). A 5/4 linear time bin packing algorithm. *Journal of Computer and System Sciences*, *60*(1), 145–160. doi:10.1006/jcss.1999.1667

Black, P. E. (2005). Greedy algorithm. *Dictionary of Algorithms and Data Structures*.

Blair, G., Kon, F., Cirne, W., Milojicic, D., Ramakrishnan, R., Reed, D., & Silva, D. (2011). Perspectives on cloud computing: Interviews with five leading scientists from the cloud community. *Journal of Internet Services and Applications*, *2*(1), 3–9. doi:10.1007/s13174-011-0023-1

Boehm, B. Huang, L. Jain, A., & Madachy, R. (2004). *The Nature of Information System Dependability: A Stakeholder/Value Approach*. USC-CSSE Technical Report.

Bowersox, D. J., Closs, D. J., & Stank, T. P. (2000). Ten mega-trends that will revolutionize supply chain logistics. *Journal of Business Logistics*, *21*(2), 1–15.

Bowersox, D. J., & Daugherty, P. J. (1995). Logistics paradigms: The impact of information technology. *Journal of Business Logistics*, *16*(1), 65–80.

Boyer, K. K., & Hult, G. T. M. (2005). Extending the supply chain: Integrating operations and marketing in the online grocery industry. *Journal of Operations Management*, *23*(6), 642–661. doi:10.1016/j.jom.2005.01.003

Boylan, M. (2004). *Questioning (in) school mathematics: Lifeworlds and ecologies of practice* (Unpublished doctoral dissertation). Sheffield Hallam University, Sheffield.

Brah, S. A., & Lim, H. Y. (2006). The effects of technology and TQM on the performance of logistics companies. *International Journal of Physical Distribution & Logistics Management*, *36*(3), 192–209. doi:10.1108/09600030610661796

Brandenburg, M., & Seuring, S. (2011). Impacts of supply chain management on company value: Benchmarking companies from the fast moving consumer goods industry. *Logistics Research*, *3*(4), 233–248. doi:10.1007/s12159-011-0056-7

Brewer, P. C., & Speh, T. W. (2000). Using the balanced scorecard to measure supply chain performance. *Journal of Business Logistics*, *21*(1), 75–95.

Brooke, C. (2009). *Lingua fracta: Towards a rhetoric of new media*. Cresskill, NJ: Hampton Press.

Brynjolfsson, E., Hofmann, P., & Jordan, J. (2010). Cloud computing and electricity: Beyond the utility model. *Communications of the ACM, 53*(5), 32–34. doi:10.1145/1735223.1735234

Bu, Y., & Wang, L. (2011). *Leveraging cloud computing to enhance supply chain management in automobile industry*. Paper presented at the 2011 International Conference on Business Computing and Global Informatization (BCGIn 2011), Shanghai, China.

Buck, A. (2012). Examining digital literacy practices on social network sites. *Research in the Teaching of English, 47*(1), 9–38. http://www.ncte.org/library/NCTEFiles/Resources/Journals/RTE/0471-aug2012/RTE0471Examining.pdf Retrieved April 2, 2014

Buecker, A., Guézo, L., Lodewijkx, K., Moss, H., Skapinetz, K., & Waidner, M. (2009). *Cloud Computing: guide de la sécurité Recommandations d'IBM pour la sécurisation de l'informatique en nuage.*

Burkhardt, J., Henn, H., Hepper, S., Rintdorff, K., & Schack, T. (2005). *Pervasive Computing New Delhi: Pearson Education*. Singapore: Private Limited.

Burman, E., & Parker, I. (1993). Introduction - discourse analysis: The turn to the text. In E. Burman & I. Parker (Eds.), *Discourse analytic research: Repertoires and readings of texts in action* (pp. 1–13). London: Routledge.

Burmeister, B. (2014, February27). Benefits (and risks) of the mobile organisation. *Finweek, 3*, 7.

Butrico, M., Silva, D., & Youseff, L. (2008). Toward a unified ontology of cloud computing. *Grid Computing Environments Workshop*. Austin, TX: IEEE.

Buyya, R., & Abawajy, A. B. (2010). Energy efficient management of data center resources for cloud computing: A vision, architectural elements, and open challenges. *In 2010 International Conference on Parallel and Distributed Processing Techniques and Applications. PDPTA.*

Buyya, R., Beloglazov, A., & Abawajy, J. (2010). *Energy-efficient management of data center resources for cloud computing: A vision, architectural elements, and open challenges.* arXiv preprint arXiv: 1006.0308.

Buyya, R., Broberg, J., & Goscinski, A. M. (2010). *Cloud computing: Principles and paradigms* (volume 87).

Buyya, R., Chee Shin, Y., & Venugopal, S. (2008). *High performance computing and communications*. Paper presented at the 10th IEEE International Conference, Dalian, China.

Buyya, R., Ranjan, R., & Calheiros, R. N. (2009). Modeling and simulation of scalable Cloud computing environments and the CloudSim toolkit: Challenges and opportunities. In *High Performance Computing & Simulation, June 2009. HPCS'09. International Conference on* (pp. 1-11). IEEE.

Buyya, R., & Sukumar, K. (2011, May). Platforms for Building and Deploying Applications for Cloud Computing. *CSI Communications Journal, 35*(2), 6–11.

Buyya, R., Vecchiola, C., & Selvi, T. S. (2013). *Mastering Cloud Computing. New Delhi: McGraw Hill Education*. India: Private Limited.

Buyya, R., Yeo, C. S., Venugopal, S., Broberg, J., & Brandic, I. (2009). Cloud computing and emerging IT platforms: Vision, hype, and reality for delivering computing as the 5th utility. *Future Generation Computer Systems, 25*(6), 599–616. doi:10.1016/j.future.2008.12.001

Calheiros, R. N., Buyya, R., & De Rose, C. A. (2009). A heuristic for mapping virtual machines and links in emulation testbeds. In International Conference on Parallel Processing, 2009 (pp. 518-525). ICPP'09. IEEE. doi:10.1109/ICPP.2009.7

Calheiros, R. N., Ranjan, R., Beloglazov, A., De Rose, C. A. F., & Buyya, R. (2011). CloudSim: A toolkit for modeling and simulation of cloud computing environments and evaluation of resource provisioning algorithms. *Software, Practice & Experience, 41*(1), 23–50. doi:10.1002/spe.995

Camarinha-Matos, L., Afsarmanesh, H., Garita, C., & Lima, C. (1999). Hierarchical Coordination in Virtual Enterprise Infrastructures. *Journal of Intelligent & Robotic Systems, 26*(3/4), 267–287. doi:10.1023/A:1008137110347

Cardosa, M., Korupolu, M. R., & Singh, A. (2009). Shares and utilities based power consolidation in virtualized server environments. In IFIP/IEEE International Symposium on Integrated Network Management, 2009 (pp. 327-334). IM' 09. IEEE. doi:10.1109/INM.2009.5188832

Cardosa, M., Singh, A., Pucha, H., & Chandra, A. (2011), Exploiting spatiotemporal tradeoffs for energy-aware mapreduce in the cloud. *InProceedings of the 2011 IEEE 4th International Conference on Cloud Computing, CLOUD '11* (pages 251–258). *Washington, DC, USA. IEEE Computer Society.* doi:10.1109/CLOUD.2011.68

Carlin, S., & Curran, K. (2011). Cloud computing security. *International Journal of Ambient Computing and Intelligence, 3*(1), 14–19. doi:10.4018/jaci.2011010102

Carr, N. (2004). *Does IT matter?: information technology and the corrosion of competitive advantage.* Boston, MA: Harvard Business Press.

Carroll, M., Kotze, P., & van der Merwe, A. (2010). Securing virtual and cloud environments. In I. Ivanov, M. van Sinderen, & B. Shishkov (Eds.), *Cloud computing and services science* (pp. 73–90). Berlin, Germany: Springer-Verlag.

Carvalho, H., Azevedo, S., & Cruz-Machado, V. (2012). Agile and resilient approaches to supply chain management: Influence on performance and competitiveness. *Logistics Research, 4*(1-2), 49–62. doi:10.1007/s12159-012-0064-2

Carvalho, V. R., & Cohen, W. W. (2007) *Preventing Information Leaks in Email.Proceedings of the SIAM International Conference on Data Mining,* Minneapolis.

Casey, G., Cegielski, L., Jones-Farmer, A., Wu, Y., & Hazen, B. T. (2012). Adoption of cloud computing technologies in supply chains. *International Journal of Logistics Management, 23*(2), 184–211. doi:10.1108/09574091211265350

Castro, C. M. C., & Chala, P. A. (2013). Undertaking the act of writing as a situated social practice: Going beyond the linguistic and the textual. *Colombian Applied Linguistics Journal,15*(1), 25–42. doi:10.14483/udistrital.jour.calj.2013.1.a02

Chaisiri, S., Lee, B.-S., & Niyato, D. (2009), Optimal virtual machine placement across multiple cloud providers, *In Services Computing Conference, 2009. APSCC 2009. IEEE Asia Pacific,* (pp. 103–110).

Chaka, C. (2012). Mobiles for sustainable learning environments: Mobile phones and MXit with a South African school context. *Journal for Community Communication and Information Impact, 17,* 161–182.

Chaka, C. (2013). Virtualization and cloud computing: Business models in the virtual cloud. In A. W. Loo (Ed.), *Distributed computing innovations for business, engineering, and science* (pp. 176–190). Hershey, PA: IGI Global. doi:10.4018/978-1-4666-2533-4.ch009

Chaka, C. (2013). Digitization and consumerization of identity, culture, and power among Gen Mobinets in South Africa. In R. Luppicini (Ed.), *Handbook of research on technoself: Identity in a technological society* (pp. 77–96). Hershey, PA: IGI Global. doi:10.4018/978-1-4666-2211-1.ch022

Chaka, C. (2014). Facebook's cloud value chain for higher education. *Infosys Labs Briefings, 11*(4), 84–89.

Chaka, C. (2014). Social media as technologies for asynchronous formal writing and synchronous paragraph writing in the South African higher education context. In V. Benson & S. Morgan (Eds.), *Cutting-edge technologies and social media use in higher education* (pp. 213–241). Hershey, PA: IGI Global. doi:10.4018/978-1-4666-5174-6.ch009

Chaka, C., & Ngesi, N. (2010). Mobile writing: Using SMSes to write short paragraphs in English. In R. Guy (Ed.), *Mobile learning: Pilot projects and initiatives* (pp. 185–233). Santa Rosa, California: Informing Science Press.

Chandler, D. (2007). *Semiotics: the basics.* New York, NY: Routledge.

Chandra, A. H., & Ghosh, S. K. (2006). *Image Interpretation, Remote sensing and Geographical Information System.* New Delhi: Narosa Publishing House.

Chang, H. H., Hung, C. J., Wong, K. H., & Lee, C. H. (2013). Using the balanced scorecard on supply chain integration performance: A case study of service businesses. *Service Business, 7*(4), 539–561. doi:10.1007/s11628-012-0175-5

Chedid, W., Yu, C., & Lee, B. (2005). Power analysis and optimization techniques for energy efficient computer systems. *Advances in Computers, 63*, 129–164. doi:10.1016/S0065-2458(04)63004-X

Chen, Y., Paxson, V., & Katz, R. H. (2010). *What's new about cloud computing security?* Technical Report UCB/EECS-2010-5, Electrical Engineering and Computer Sciences, University of California at Berkeley.

Chen, D. (2006). Enterprise interoperability framework. In MissikoffM.De NicolaA.D'AntonioF. (Eds.) *Open Interop Workshop on Enterprise Modelling and Ontologies for Interoperability*. Berlin, Germany: Springer-Verlag.

Chen, D., Doumeingts, G., & Vernadat, F. (2008). Architectures for enterprise integration and interoperability: Past, present and future. *Computers in Industry, 59*(7), 647–659. doi:10.1016/j.compind.2007.12.016

Chen, H. C., Violetta, M. A., & Yang, C. Y. (2013). Contract RBAC in cloud computing. *The Journal of Supercomputing, 66*(2), 1111–1131. doi:10.1007/s11227-013-1017-5

Chen, H., & Li, S. (2010). SRC: A Service Registry on Cloud Providing Behavior-aware and QoS-aware Service Discovery. In *International Conference on Service-Oriented Computing and Applications*. Perth, Australia: IEEE. doi:10.1109/SOCA.2010.5707179

Chen, K. Y., & Chang, M. L. (2013). User acceptance of "near field communication" mobile phone service: An investigation based on the unified theory of acceptance and use of technology model. *Service Industries Journal, 33*(6), 609–623. doi:10.1080/02642069.2011.622369

Chen, M., Wu, Y., & Vasilakos, A. V. (2014). Advances in mobile cloud computing. *Mobile Networks and Applications, 19*(2), 131–132. doi:10.1007/s11036-014-0503-1

Chen, S. J., & Huang, E. (2007). A systematic approach for supply chain improvement using design structure matrix. *Journal of Intelligent Manufacturing, 18*(2), 285–299. doi:10.1007/s10845-007-0022-z

Chen, Y., Zhang, R., Li, H., Li, R., & Gao, Y. (2011). CALIS-based cloud library services platform model. *AISS: Advances in Information Sciences and Service Sciences, 3*(6), 204–212. doi:10.4156/aiss.vol3.issue6.25

Cheston, R. W. (2012). *BYOD & consumerization: Why the cloud is key to a viable implementation*. Retrieved May 10, 2014, from https://kapost-files-prod.s3.amazonaws.com/uploads/direct/20130709-2006-19803-4221/BYOD-Consumerization-White-Paper-Rich-Cheston-Aug-2012.pdf

Choate, P. (2005). *Hot Property: The Stealing of Ideas in an Age of Globalization*. New York: Alfred A. Knopf.

Choi, T. Y., Dooley, K. J., & Rungtusanatham, M. (2001). Supply networks and complex adaptive systems: Control versus emergence. *Journal of Operations Management, 19*(3), 351–366. doi:10.1016/S0272-6963(00)00068-1

Choi, T. Y., & Hong, Y. (2002). Unveiling the structure of supply networks: Case studies in Honda, Acura, and DaimlerChrysler. *Journal of Operations Management, 20*(5), 469–493. doi:10.1016/S0272-6963(02)00025-6

Choi, T. Y., & Krause, D. R. (2006). The supply base and its complexity: Implications for transaction costs, risks, responsiveness, and innovation. *Journal of Operations Management, 24*(5), 637–652. doi:10.1016/j.jom.2005.07.002

Chonka, A., Xiang, Y., Zhou, W., & Bonti, A. (2011). Cloud security defence to protect cloud computing against HTTP-DOS and XML-DOS attacks. *Journal of Network and Computer Applications, 34*(4), 1097–1107. doi:10.1016/j.jnca.2010.06.004

Chorafas, D. N. (2011). *Cloud Computing Strategies*. Boca Raton: CRC Press Taylor & Francis Group.

Christodorescu, M., Sailer, R., Schales, D. L., Sgandurra, D., & Zamboni, D. (2009). Cloud security is not (just) virtualization security: a short paper. In *Proceedings of the 2009 ACM Workshop on Cloud Computing Security* (pp. 97–102). doi:10.1145/1655008.1655022

Christopher, M. (2012). *Logistics and supply chain management: Creating value-adding networks*. Dorchester, UK: Financial Times Prentice-Hall.

Christopher, M., & Lee, H. (2004). Mitigating supply chain risk through improved confidence. *International Journal of Physical Distribution & Logistics Management, 34*(5), 388–396. doi:10.1108/09600030410545436

Christopher, M., Lowson, R., & Peck, H. (2004). Creating agile supply chains in the fashion industry. *International Journal of Retail & Distribution Management, 32*(8), 367–376. doi:10.1108/09590550410546188

Christopher, M., & Peck, H. (2004). Building the resilient supply chain. *International Journal of Logistics Management, 15*(2), 1–13. doi:10.1108/09574090410700275

Chun, S. H., & Choi, B. S. (2014). Service models and pricing schemes for cloud computing. *Cluster Computing, 17*(2), 529–535. doi:10.1007/s10586-013-0296-1

Clark, C., Fraser, K., Hand, S., Hansen, J. G., Jul, E., Limpach, C., ... Warfield, A. (2005). Live migration of virtual machines. *In Proceedings of the 2nd Conference on Symposium on Networked Systems Design & Implementation - Volume 2, NSDI'05,* (pp. 273–286). *Berkeley, CA, USA. USENIX Association.*

Closs, D. J., Goldsby, T. J., & Clinton, S. R. (1997). Information technology influences on world class logistics capability. *International Journal of Physical Distribution & Logistics Management, 27*(1), 4–17. doi:10.1108/09600039710162259

Closs, D. J., & Savitskie, K. (2003). Internal and external logistic information technology integration. *International Journal of Logistics Management, 14*(1), 63–76. doi:10.1108/09574090310806549

Closs, D. J., Speier, C., & Meacham, N. (2011). Sustainability to support end-to-end value chains: The role of supply chain management. *Journal of the Academy of Marketing Science, 39*(1), 101–116. doi:10.1007/s11747-010-0207-4

Cloud Security Alliance (CSA). (2010). *Top threats to cloud computing v1.0.* Retrieved on 3th June 2014, from https://cloudsecurityalliance.org/topthreats/csathreats.v1.0.pdf

Cloud Security Alliance. (2009). *Security Guidance for Critical Areas of Focus in Cloud Computing V2.1.*

Cloud Security Alliance. (2010). *Top Threats to Cloud Computing V 1.0.*

Cooke, N., & Gillam, L. (2011). Clowns, Crowds and Clouds: A Cross-Enterprise Approach to Detecting Information Leakage without Leaking Information. In Z. Mahmood & R. Hill (Eds.), *Cloud Computing for Enterprise Architectures.* London: Springer. doi:10.1007/978-1-4471-2236-4_16

Craig, T., & Ludlof, M. E. (2013). *Privacy and Big Data.* Mumbai: Shroff Publishers & Distributors Private Limited.

Creasy, R. (1981, September). The origin of the vm/370 timesharing system. *IBM Journal of Research and Development, 25*(5), 483–490. doi:10.1147/rd.255.0483

Crotty, M. (1998). The foundations of social research: Meaning and perspective in the research process. *Sage (Atlanta, Ga.).*

Dabbebi, O., Badonnel, R., & Festor, O. (2014). Leveraging countermeasures as a service for VoIP security in the cloud. *International Journal of Network Management, 24*(1), 70–84. doi:10.1002/nem.1853

Davis, F. D., Bagozzi, R. P., & Warshaw, P. R. (1989). User acceptance of computer technology: A comparison of two theoretical models. *Management Science, 35*(8), 982–1003. doi:10.1287/mnsc.35.8.982

Davis, K., & Patterson, D. (2012). *Ethics of Big Data.* Mumbai: Shroff Publishers & Distributors Private Limited.

Defee, C. C., & Stank, T. P. (2005). Applying the strategy-structure-performance paradigm to the supply chain environment. *International Journal of Logistics Management, 16*(1), 28–50. doi:10.1108/09574090510617349

Defee, C. C., Stank, T. P., Esper, T. L., & Mentzer, J. T. (2009). The role of followers in supply chains. *Journal of Business Logistics, 30*(2), 65–84. doi:10.1002/j.2158-1592.2009.tb00112.x

Dell Inc. (2012). *University enhances education through the cloud.* Retrieved May 10, 2014, from http://i.dell.com/sites/doccontent/corporate/case-studies/en/Documents/2012-europea-madrid-10011452.pdf

Demchenko, Y., Makkes, M., Strijkers, R., & de Laat, C. (2012). Intercloud Architecture for interoperability and integration. In *4th International Conference on Cloud Computing Technology and Science* (pp.666-674). Piscataway, NJ: IEEE Computer Society Press. doi:10.1109/CloudCom.2012.6427607

Demirkan, H., Cheng, H. K., & Bandyopadhyay, S. (2010). Coordination strategies in an SaaS supply chain. *Journal of Management Information Systems*, 26(4), 119–143. doi:10.2753/MIS0742-1222260405

Dooley, B., (2010), Architectural Requirements Of The Hybrid Cloud, *Information Management Online; 10.*

Dooley, J., Spanoudakis, G., & Zisman, A. (2008). Proactive Runtime Service Discovery. In *Proceedings of IEEE 2008 International Service Computing Conference.* Honolulu, HI: IEEE.

Drake, M. J., & Schlachter, J. T. (2008). A virtue-ethics analysis of supply chain collaboration. *Journal of Business Ethics*, 82(4), 851–864. doi:10.1007/s10551-007-9597-8

DTMF. (2012). *Open Virtualization Format Specification.* Document Number: DSP0243, version 2.0.0. Portland, OR: Distributed Management Task Force, Inc. Retrieved May 30, 2014 from http://www.dmtf.org/sites/default/files/standards/documents/DSP0243_2.0.0.pdf

DTMF. (2013). *Cloud Infrastructure Management Interface (CIMI) Model and REST Interface over HTTP Specification.* Document Number: DSP0263, version 1.1.0. Portland, OR: Distributed Management Task Force, Inc. Retrieved May 30, 2014 from http://www.dmtf.org/sites/default/files/standards/documents/DSP0263_1.1.0.pdf

DuBay, W. H. (2004). *The principles of readability.* Retrieved April 10, 2014, from http://en.copian.ca/library/research/readab/readab.pdf

Dudin, E. B., & Smetanin, Y. G. (2011). A review of cloud computing. *Scientific and Technical Information Processing*, 38(4), 280–284. doi:10.3103/S0147688211040083

Duranti, L. (2013). *Records in the Cloud (RiC) User Survey Report, Records in the Cloud (RiC).* Project University of British Columbia.

Durao, F., Carvalho, J. F. S., Fonseka, A., & Garcia, V. C. (2014). A systematic review on cloud computing. *The Journal of Supercomputing*, 68(3), 1321–1346. doi:10.1007/s11227-014-1089-x

Durowoju, O. A., Chan, H. K., & Wang, X. (2011). The impact of security and scalability of cloud service on supply chain performance. *Journal of Electronic Commerce Research*, 12(4), 243–256.

Dzida, W., Herda, S., & Itzfelt, W. (1978). User-perceived quality of interactive systems. *IEEE Transactions on Software Engineering*, SE-4(4), 270–276. doi:10.1109/TSE.1978.231511

Eberhart, R. C., & Kennedy, J. (1995, October). A new optimizer using particle swarm theory. In *Proceedings of the sixth international symposium on micro machine and human science* (Vol. 1, pp. 39-43). doi:10.1109/MHS.1995.494215

Edmonds, A., Metsch, T., & Papaspyrou, A. (2011). Open Cloud Computing Interface in Data Management-Related Setups. In S. Fiore & G. Aloisio (Eds.), *Grid and Cloud Database Management* (pp. 23–48). Berlin, Germany: Springer. doi:10.1007/978-3-642-20045-8_2

Edwards, P., Peters, M., & Sharman, G. (2001). The effectiveness of information systems in supporting the extended supply chain. *Journal of Business Logistics*, 22(1), 1–27. doi:10.1002/j.2158-1592.2001.tb00157.x

EIF. (2010). *European Interoperability Framework (EIF) for European Public Services, Annex 2 to the Communication from the Commission to the European Parliament, the Council, the European Economic and Social Committee and the Committee of Regions 'Towards interoperability for European public services.* Retrieved May 30, 2014 from http://ec.europa.eu/isa/documents/isa_annex_ii_eif_en.pdf

El Raheb, K. et al.. (2011). Paving the Way for Interoperability in Digital Libraries: The DL.org Project. In A. Katsirikou & C. Skiadas (Eds.), *New Trends in Qualitive and Quantitative Methods in Libraries* (pp. 345–352). Singapore: World Scientific Publishing Company.

Ellinger, A. E., Ellinger, A. D., & Keller, S. B. (2002). Logistics managers' learning environments and firm performance. *Journal of Business Logistics, 23*(1), 19–37. doi:10.1002/j.2158-1592.2002.tb00014.x

Ellram, L. M., & Cooper, M. C. (2014). Supply chain management: It's all about the journey, not the destination. *Journal of Supply Chain Management, 50*(1), 8–20. doi:10.1111/jscm.12043

Emmanuel, G., & Sife, A. (2008). Challenges of managing information and communication technologies for education: Experiences from Sokoine National Agricultural Library. *International Journal of Education and Development using ICT, 4*(3).

ENISA. (2010). *Cloud computing: Benefits, risks and recommendations for information security.* Retrieved from http://www.enisa.europa.eu/act/rm/files/deliverables/cloud-computingrisk-assessment

Enterprise Cloud Computing:Transforming IT; 13; 6.

Epstein, R. A., & Macvoy, S. P. (2011). Making A Scene in the Brain. In L. R. Harris & M. R. M. Jenkin (Eds.), *Vision in 3D Environments* (pp. 270–273). Cambridge: Cambridge University Press. doi:10.1017/CBO9780511736261.012

Erl, T. (2008). *SOA: Principles of Service Design.* Upper Saddle River, NJ: Prentice Hall PTR.

Esper, T. L., Defee, C. C., & Mentzer, J. T. (2010). A framework of supply chain orientation. *International Journal of Logistics Management, 21*(2), 161–179. doi:10.1108/09574091011071906

Esposito, E., & Evangelista, P. (2014). Investigating virtual enterprise models: Literature review and empirical findings. *International Journal of Production Economics, 148*, 145–157. doi:10.1016/j.ijpe.2013.10.003

Euzenat, J., & Shvaiko, P. (2007). *Ontology matching.* Berlin, Germany: Springer.

Fadel, A., & Fayoumi, A. (2013). Cloud Resource Provisioning and Bursting Approaches. In TakahashiS.LeeR. (Eds.) *14th ACIS International Conference on Software Engineering, Artificial Intelligence, Networking and Parallel/Distributed Computing* (pp. 59-64). Piscataway, NJ: IEEE Computer Society Press.

Faisal, C. M. M., Azher, E. M. K., Ramzan, E. B., & Malik, M. S. A. (2011). Cloud computing: SMEs issues and UGI based integrated collaborative information system to support Pakistani textile SMEs. *Interdisciplinary Journal of Contemporary Research in Business, 3*(1), 564–573.

Fawcett, S., Wallin, C., Allred, C., Fawcett, A. M., & Magnan, G. M. (2011). Information technology as an enabler of supply chain collaboration: A dynamic-capabilities perspective. *Journal of Supply Chain Management, 47*(1), 38–59. doi:10.1111/j.1745-493X.2010.03213.x

Feller, E., Rilling, L., & Morin, C. (2011), Energy-aware ant colony based workload placement in clouds. In *12th IEEE/ACM International Conference on Grid Computing (GRID), 2011,* (pp. 26–33).

Ferguson, D. F., & Hadar, E. (2011). Optimizing the IT business supply chain utilizing cloud computing. In *Paper presented at the 8th International Conference & Expo on Emerging Technologies for a Smarter World* (CEWIT 2011), Hauppauge, NY.

Fernando, N., Loke, S., & Rahayu, W. (2013). Mobile cloud computing: A survey. *Future Generation Computer Systems, 29*(1), 84–106. doi:10.1016/j.future.2012.05.023

Fielding, R. (2000). *Architectural Styles and the Design of Network-based Software Architectures.* Doctoral dissertation. University of California at Irvine, CA.

Firesmith, D. (2004). Specifying Reusable Security Requirements. *Journal of Object Technology, 3*(1), 61–75. doi:10.5381/jot.2004.3.1.c6

Forman, H., & Lippert, S. K. (2005). Toward the development of an integrated model of technology internalization within the supply chain context. *International Journal of Logistics Management, 16*(1), 4–27. doi:10.1108/09574090510617330

Forslund, H. (2006). Performance gaps in the dyadic order fulfillment process. *International Journal of Physical Distribution & Logistics Management, 36*(8), 580–595. doi:10.1108/09600030610702871

Foster, I., Zhao, Y., Raicu, I., & Lu, S. (2008). Cloud computing and grid computing 360 degree compared. *InProceedings grid computing environments workshop: GCE 2008*, 1-10. DOI doi:10.1109/GCE.2008.4738445

Fox, R. (2009). Library in the clouds. *OCLC Systems & Services*, *25*(3), 156–161. doi:10.1108/10650750910982539

Franks, B. (2014). *Taming the Big Data Tidal Wave*. New Delhi: Wiley India Private Limited.

Franqueira, V. N. L., van Cleeff, A., van Eck, P., & Wieringa, R. (2010). External Insider Threat: A Real Security Challenge in Enterprise Value Webs. In Proceedings of Availability, Reliability, and Security (pp. 446–453). ARES.

Furht, B., & Escalante, A. (2010). *Handbook of cloud computing*. New York: Springer. doi:10.1007/978-1-4419-6524-0

Galbraith, J. R. (1974). Organization design: An information processing view. *Interfaces*, *4*(3), 28–36. doi:10.1287/inte.4.3.28

Galloway, J. M., Smith, K. L., & Vrbsky, S. S. (2011). Power aware load balancing for cloud computing. In *Proceedings of the World Congress on Engineering and Computer Science*, 1 (pp. 19–21).

Galvin, D., & Sun, M. (2012). Avoiding the death zone: Choosing and running a library project in the cloud. *Library HiTech*, *30*(3), 418–427. doi:10.1108/07378831211266564

Gamal, A., & Yskandar, H. (2004). Two phase algorithm for load balancing in heterogeneous distributed systems. In *Proceedings of the 12th Euromicro Conference on Parallel, Distributed and Network-Based Processing*, 2004, (pp. 434-439). IEEE.

Ganguly, A., Nilchiani, R., & Farr, J. (2009). Evaluating agility in corporate enterprises. *International Journal of Production Economics*, *118*(2), 410–423. doi:10.1016/j.ijpe.2008.12.009

Gao, T., Rohm, A. J., Sultan, F., & Huang, S. (2012). Antecedents of consumer attitudes toward mobile marketing: A comparative study of youth markets in the United States and China. *Thunderbird International Business Review*, *54*(2), 211–225. doi:10.1002/tie.21452

Gao, Y., Guan, H., Qi, Z., Hou, Y., & Liu, L. (2013). A multi-objective ant colony system algorithm for virtual machine placement in cloud computing. *Journal of Computer and System Sciences*, *79*(8), 1230–1242. doi:10.1016/j.jcss.2013.02.004

Gartner. (2013). *Will Private Cloud Adoption Increase by 2015?* Gartner Research Note G00250893 (12 May 2013).

Géczy, P., Izumi, N., & Hasida, K. (2012). Cloudsourcing: Managing Cloud Adoption. *Global Journal of Business Research*, *6*(2), 57–70.

Gendron, M. S. (2014). *Business intelligence and the cloud*. Hoboken, NJ: John Wiley & Sons. doi:10.1002/9781118915240

Gentry, C. (2009) *Fully homomorphic encryption using ideal lattices*. In *Proceedings of the Symposium on the Theory of Computing (STOC)*, 2009 (pp. 169-178).

George, D. R., & Dellasega, C. (2011). Use of social media in graduate-level medical humanities education: Two pilot studies from Penn State College of Medicine. *Medical Teacher*, *33*(8), e429–e434. doi:10.3109/0142159X.2011.586749 PMID:21774639

Gimenez, C., & Ventura, E. (2003). Supply chain management as a competitive advance in the Spanish grocery sector. *International Journal of Logistics Management*, *14*(1), 77–88. doi:10.1108/09574090310806558

Golden, B. (June 2010). *How Cloud Computing Can Transform Business*. Boston, MA, USA: Harvard Business Review

Goldner, M. R. (2010). Winds of change: Libraries and cloud computing. *BIBLIOTHEK Forschung und Praxis*, *34*(3), 270–275. doi:10.1515/bfup.2010.042

Gonzalez, L. M. V., Rodero-Merino, L., Caceres, J., & Lindner, M. A. (2009). A break in the clouds: Towards a cloud definition. *Computer Communication Review*, *39*(1), 50–55.

Google Cloud Platform (GCP). (2014). Retrieved from https://cloud.google.com/

Gottschalk, I., & Kirn, S. (2013). Cloud computing as a tool for enhancing ecological goals? *Business & Information Systems Engineering*, *5*(5), 299–313. doi:10.1007/s12599-013-0284-2

Gottschalk, P., & Solli-Sæther, H. (2008). Stages of e-government interoperability. *Electronic Government*. *International Journal (Toronto, Ont.)*, *5*(3), 310–320.

Govil, D., & Prohit, N. (2011). Health Care Systems in India. In H. S. Rout (Ed.), *Health Care Systems – A Global Survey* (pp. 576–612). New Delhi: New Century Publications.

Gray, L., Kumar, A., & Li, H. (2008). Characterization of specpower_ssj2008 benchmark. In *SPEC Benchmark Workshop*.

Green, J. (2007). *A guide to using qualitative research methodology*. Retrieved May 30, 2014, from http://fieldresearch.msf.org/msf/bitstream/10144/84230/1/Qualitative%20research%20methodology.pdf

Grefen, P., Mehandjiev, N., Kouvas, G., Weichhart, G., & Eshuis, R. (2009). Dynamic business network process management in instant virtual enterprises. *Computers in Industry*, *60*(2), 86–103. doi:10.1016/j.compind.2008.06.006

Griffee, D. T. (2012). *An introduction to second language research methods: Design and data*. Retrieved June 24, 2014, from http://www.tesl-ej.org/pdf/ej60/sl_research_methods.pdf

Grigoriu, A. (2009). *The Cloud Enterprise*. Wokingham: BP Trends Publications United Kingdom.

Grman, J. & Ravas, R. (2011). *Improved Implementation for Finding Text Similarities in Large Collections of Data*. Notebook for Uncovering Plagiarism, Authorship, and Social Software Misuse (PAN) at CLEF.

Grobauer, B., Walloschek, T., & Stocker, E. (2011). *Understanding Cloud Computing Vulnerabilities Security & Privacy, IEEE*, *9*(2), 50–57. doi:10.1109/MSP.2010.115

Grozev, N., & Buyya, R. (2014). Inter-Cloud architectures and application brokering: Taxonomy and survey. *Software, Practice & Experience*, *44*(3), 369–390. doi:10.1002/spe.2168

Guo, L., Zhao, S., Shen, S., & Jiang, C. (2012). Task scheduling optimization in cloud computing based on heuristic algorithm. *Journal of Networks*, *7*(3), 547–553. doi:10.4304/jnw.7.3.547-553

Gustin, C. M., Daugherty, P. J., & Stank, T. P. (1995). The effects of information availability on logistics integration. *Journal of Business Logistics*, *16*(1), 1–21.

Hagel, J., & Brown, J. S. (2010). *Cloud Computing's Stormy Future*. Boston: Harvard Business Review M A USA.

Hameed, M. A., Counsell, S., & Swift, S. (2012). A conceptual model for the process of IT innovation adoption in organizations. *Journal of Engineering and Technology Management*, *29*(3), 358–390. doi:10.1016/j.jengtecman.2012.03.007

Hamlen, K., Kantarcioglu, M., Khan, L., & Thuraisingham, B. (2010). Security issues for cloud computing. *International Journal of Information Security and Privacy*, *4*(2), 36–48. doi:10.4018/jisp.2010040103

Han, L. (2009). *Market Acceptance of Cloud Computing: An Analysis of Market Structure, Price models and systems management*. Retrieved from http://opus4.kobv.de/opus4-ubbayreuth/files/468/thesis_leihan.pdf

Hanna, S. (2009). *Cloud Computing: Finding the silver lining*.

Harris, A. (2012). *The Legal Standing of Data in a Cloud Computing Environment* (Doctoral dissertation, Dublin Institute of Technology).

Hartman, T. (2007). The changing definition of US libraries. *Libri*, *57*(1), 1–8. doi:10.1515/LIBR.2007.1

Hassan, M. Z. (2011, May). Cloud Networking. *CSI Communications Journal*, *35*(2), 20–21.

Hauff, S., Huntgeburth, J., & Veit, D. (2014). Exploring uncertainties in a marketplace for cloud computing: A revelatory case study. *Journal of Business Economics*, *84*(3), 441–468. doi:10.1007/s11573-014-0719-3

Heeks, R. (2014). *Future Priorities for Development Informatics Research from the Post-2015 Development Agenda*. Working Paper Series, paper no. 57, Centre for Development Informatics - IDPM, University of Manchester, UK. Retrieved from http://www.seed.manchester.ac.uk/medialibrary/IDPM/working_papers/di/di_wp57.pdf

Heiser, J., & Nicolett, M. (2008). *Assessing the Security Risks of Cloud Computing*. Gartner Research.

Helen, D., & Karatza, R., & Hilzer., C. (2002). Load Sharing in Heterogeneous Distributed Systems. In *Proceeding of the winter simulation conference* (pp. 489-496).

Helmbrecht, U. (2010). Data protection and legal compliance in cloud computing. *Datenschutz und Datensicherheit, 34*(8), 554-556.

Henry Glynn, J., & Heinke Gary, W. (2004). *Environmental Science and Engineering; New Delhi: Pearson Education.* Singapore: Private Limited.

Heraclitus., & Patrick, G. (Eds.). (2013) The Fragments of Heraclitus. New York, NY: Digireads.com Publishing.

Hermenier, F., Lorca, X., Menaud, J.-M., Muller, G., & Lawall, J. (2009). Entropy: A consolidation manager for clusters. In *Proceedings of the 2009 ACM SIGPLAN/SIGOPS International Conference on Virtual Execution Environments, VEE '09* (pp. 41–50). *New York, NY, USA. ACM.* doi:10.1145/1508293.1508300

Hershock, C., & LaVaque-Manty, M. (2012). *Teaching in the cloud: Leveraging online collaboration tools to enhance student engagement.* Retrieved June 24, 2014, from http://www.crlt.umich.edu/sites/default/files/resource_files/CRLT_no31.pdf

He, W., Cernusca, D., & Abdous, M. H. (2011). Exploring cloud computing for distance learning. *Online Journal of Distance Learning Administration, 14*(3).

Hodgson, A., & Spours, K. (2009). *Collaborative local learning ecologies: Reflections on the governance of lifelong learning in England.* Retrieved June 24, 2014, http://www.niace.org.uk/lifelonglearninginquiry/docs/IFLL-Sector-Paper6.pdf

Holmberg, S. (2000). A systems perspective on supply chain measurements. *International Journal of Physical Distribution & Logistics Management, 30*(10), 847–868. doi:10.1108/09600030010351246

Holmqvist, M. (2004). Experiential Learning Processes of Exploitation and Exploration Within and Between Organizations: An Empirical Study of Product Development. *Organization Science, 15*(1), 70–81.

Holtgrewe, U. (2014). New new technologies: The future and the present of work in information and communication technology. *New Technology, Work and Employment, 29*(1), 9–24. doi:10.1111/ntwe.12025

Horvath, L. (2001). Collaboration: The key to value creation in supply chain management. *Supply Chain Management: An International Journal, 6*(5), 205–207. doi:10.1108/EUM0000000006039

Hung, P. P., Bui, T. A., Morales, M. A. G., Nguyen, M. V., & Huh, E. N. (2014). Optimal collaboration of thin–thick clients and resource allocation in cloud computing. *Personal and Ubiquitous Computing, 18*(3), 563–572. doi:10.1007/s00779-013-0673-z

Hunt, S. D., & Davis, D. F. (2012). Grounding supply chain management in resource-advantage theory: In defense of a resource-based view of the firm. *Journal of Supply Chain Management, 48*(2), 14–20. doi:10.1111/j.1745-493X.2012.03266.x

Hurwitz J., Kaufman R., Bloor M, & Halper F. (2010). *Cloud Computing for Dummies.* New Delhi: Willey India Private Limited.

Hurwitz, J., Nugent, A., Halper, F., & Kaufman, M. (2014). *Big Data for Dummies.* New Delhi: Wiley India Private Limited.

Huth, A., & Cebula, J. (2011). *The Basics of Cloud Computing.*

Hwang, K., Fox, G., & Dongarra, J. (2012). *Distributed and Cloud Computing: From Parallel Processing to the Internet of Things.* Morgan Kaufmann.

IBM. (2009). *The benefits of cloud computing.* Retrieved September 6, 2014, from http://public.dhe.ibm.com/common/ssi/ecm/en/diw03004usen/DIW03004USEN.PDF

IBM. (2010). *Ozyegin University: Cloud computing with IBM.* Retrieved May 4, 2014, from http://www.ibm.com/ibm/files/W771375B62431S24/Ozyegin_EDB03009-USEN-00.pdf

Ibrahim, A. S., Hamlyn-Harris, J., & Grundy, J. (2010). *Emerging security challenges of cloud virtual infrastructure.* The Asia Pacific Software Engineering Conference 2010 Cloud Workshop.

Ignacimuthu, S. (2005). *Basic Informatics.* New Delhi: Narosa Publishing House.

Imache, R., Izza, S., & Ahmed-Nacer, M. (2012). An enterprise information system agility assessment model. *Computer science and information systems, 9*(1), 107-133.

ISO. (2011). *CEN EN/ISO 11354-1, Advanced Automation Technologies and their Applications, Part 1: Framework for Enterprise Interoperability*. Geneva, Switzerland: International Standards Office.

ISO/IEC. (1994). *ISO/IEC 7498-1, Information technology – Open Systems Interconnection – Basic Reference Model: The Basic Model, 2nd edition*. Geneva, Switzerland: International Standards Office. Retrieved May 31, 2014 from http://standards.iso.org/ittf/PubliclyAvailableStandards/index.html

ISO/IEC. (2012). *Information technology -- Cloud Data Management Interface (CDMI). ISO/IEC Standard 17826:2012*. Geneva, Switzerland: International Organization for Standardization.

ITU. F. (2012). Fg cloud technical report v1.0. International Telecommunication Union.

Ivanov, D., & Sokolov, B. (2012). The inter-disciplinary modeling of supply chains in the context of collaborative multi-structural cyber-physical networks. *Journal of Manufacturing Technology Management, 23*(8), 976–997. doi:10.1108/17410381211276835

Jackson, K. (2012). *OpenStack Cloud Computing Cookbook*. Birmingham, UK: Packt Publishing Ltd.

Jaeger, P. T., Lin, J., & Grimes, J. M. (2008). Cloud computing and information policy: Computing in a policy cloud? *Journal of Information Technology & Politics, 5*(3), 269–283. doi:10.1080/19331680802425479

Jain, V., Wadhwa, S., & Deshmukh, S. G. (2009). Revisiting information systems to support a dynamic supply chain: Issues and perspectives. *Production Planning and Control, 20*(1), 17–29. doi:10.1080/09537280802608019

Jakhar, S. K. (2014). Designing the green supply chain performance optimisation model. *Global Journal of Flexible Systems Management, 15*(3), 235–259. doi:10.1007/s40171-014-0069-6

Jalalvand, F., Teimoury, E., Makui, A., Aryanezhad, M. B., & Jolai, F. (2011). A method to compare supply chains of an industry. *Supply Chain Management: An International Journal, 16*(2), 82–97. doi:10.1108/13598541111115347

Janecek, P. (2007). Faceted classification in web information architecture: A framework for using semantic web tools. *The Electronic Library, 25*(2), 219–233. doi:10.1108/02640470710741340

Jangra, A., & Bala, R. (2011). Spectrum of Cloud Computing Architecture: Adoption and Avoidance Issues. *International Journal of Computing and Business Research, 2*(2).

Jardim-Goncalves, R., Agostinho, C., & Steiger-Garcao, A. (2012). A reference model for sustainable interoperability in networked enterprises: Towards the foundation of EI science base. *International Journal of Computer Integrated Manufacturing, 25*(10), 855–873. doi:10.1080/0951192X.2011.653831

Jardim-Goncalves, R., Grilo, A., Agostinho, C., Lampathaki, F., & Charalabidis, Y. (2013). Systematisation of interoperability body of knowledge: The foundation for enterprise interoperability as a science. *Enterprise Information Systems, 7*(1), 7–32. doi:10.1080/17517575.2012.684401

Jeffrey, K. and Neidecker-Lutz, B. (2010). *The Future of Cloud Computing: Opportunities for European Cloud Computing Beyond 2010: Expert Group Report*. European Commission, Information Society and Media.

Jeng, J. (2005). Usability assessment of academic digital libraries: Effectiveness, efficiency, satisfaction, and learnability. *Libri: International Journal of Libraries and Information Services, 55*(2/3), 96–121.

Jennings R. (2010). *Cloud Computing with the Windows Azure Platform*. New Delhi: Wiley India Private Limited.

Jeong, B., Lee, D., Cho, H., & Lee, J. (2008). A novel method for measuring semantic similarity for XML schema matching. *Expert Systems with Applications, 34*(3), 1651–1658. doi:10.1016/j.eswa.2007.01.025

Jing, S.-Y., Ali, S., She, K., & Zhong, Y. (2013). State-of-the-art research study for green cloud computing. *The Journal of Supercomputing*, 1–24.

Jones, R. H. (2012). *Discourse analysis: A resource book for students*. London: Routledge.

Jorgensen, A., Rowland-Jones, J., Welch, J., Clark, D., Price, C., & Brain, M. (2014). *Microsoft Big Data Solutions*. New Delhi: Wiley India Private Limited.

Joseph, J., & Fellenstein, F. (2004). *Grid Computing New Delhi: Pearson Education*. Singapore: Private Limited.

Jouini, M., Ben Arfa Rabai, L., Ben Aissa, A., & Mili, A. (2012). Towards quantitative measures of Information Security: A Cloud Computing case study. *International Journal of Cyber-Security and Digital Forensics*, *1*(3), 265–279.

Juhnke, E., Dornemann, T., Bock, D., & Freisleben, B. (2011, July). *Multi-objective scheduling of BPEL workflows in geographically distributed clouds*. In Cloud Computing (CLOUD), 2011 IEEE International Conference on (pp. 412-419). IEEE.

Juric, M., & Pant, K. (2008). *Business Process Driven SOA using BPMN and BPEL: From Business Process Modeling to Orchestration and Service Oriented Architecture*. Birmingham, UK: Packt Publishing.

Juttner, U. (2005). Supply chain risk management: Understanding the business requirements from a practitioner perspective. *International Journal of Logistics Management*, *16*(1), 120–141. doi:10.1108/09574090510617385

Juttner, U., Peck, H., & Christopher, M. (2003). Supply chain risk management: Outlining an agenda for future research. *International Journal of Logistics Research and Applications*, *6*(4), 197–210. doi:10.1080/1367556 0310001627016

Kabilan, M. K., Ahmad, N., & Abidin, M. J. Z. (2010). Facebook: An online environment for learning of English in institutions of higher education? *The Internet and Higher Education*, *3*(4), 179–187. doi:10.1016/j.iheduc.2010.07.003

Kahn, K. B., & Mentzer, J. T. (1996). Logistics and interdepartmental integration. *International Journal of Physical Distribution & Logistics Management*, *26*(8), 6–14. doi:10.1108/09600039610182753

Kamel, S. (2010). *E-strategies for Technological Diffusion and Adoption: National ICT Approaches for Socioeconomic Development. Information Science Reference*. IGI Global USA. doi:10.4018/978-1-60566-388-3

Kang, A. N., Barolli, L., Park, J. H., & Jeong, Y. S. (2014). A strengthening plan for enterprise information security based on cloud computing. *Cluster Computing*, *17*(3), 703–710. doi:10.1007/s10586-013-0327-y

Kantarci, B., Foschini, L., Corradi, A., & Mouftah, H. (2012). Inter-and-intra data center vm-placement for energy-efficient large scale cloud systems. In Globecom Workshops (GC Wkshps), 2012, (pp. 708–713). IEEE.

Karakas, F., & Manisaligil, A. (2012). Reorienting self-directed learning for the creative digital era. *European Journal of Training and Development*, *36*(7), 712–731. doi:10.1108/03090591211255557

Karat, J. (1997). User-centered software evaluation methodologies. In M. Helander, T. K. Landauer, & P. Prabhu (Eds.), *Handbook of Human-Computer Interaction* (pp. 689–704). New York: Elsevier Press.

Karvonen, K. (2000). The beauty of simplicity. In *Proceedings of the ACM Conference on Universal Usability*. Arlington, VA: The Association of Computing Machinery.

Kasemsap, K. (2013). Unified framework: Constructing a causal model of Six Sigma, organizational learning, organizational innovation, and organizational performance. *The Journal of Interdisciplinary Networks*, *2*(1), 268–273.

Kasemsap, K. (2013). Innovative framework: Formation of causal model of organizational culture, organizational climate, knowledge management, and job performance. *Journal of International Business Management & Research*, *4*(12), 21–32.

Kasemsap, K. (2014). Strategic innovation management: An integrative framework and causal model of knowledge management, strategic orientation, organizational innovation, and organizational performance. In P. Ordóñez de Pablos & R. D. Tennyson (Eds.), *Strategic approaches for human capital management and development in a turbulent economy* (pp. 102–116). Hershey, PA: IGI Global. doi:10.4018/978-1-4666-4530-1.ch007

Kasemsap, K. (2014). The role of knowledge sharing on organisational innovation: An integrated framework. In L. Al-Hakim & C. Jin (Eds.), *Quality innovation: Knowledge, theory, and practices* (pp. 247–271). Hershey, PA: IGI Global. doi:10.4018/978-1-4666-4769-5.ch012

Kasemsap, K. (2014). The role of social networking in global business environments. In P. A. C. Smith & T. Cockburn (Eds.), *Impact of emerging digital technologies on leadership in global business* (pp. 183–201). Hershey, PA: IGI Global. doi:10.4018/978-1-4666-6134-9.ch010

Kasemsap, K. (2015). Implementing enterprise resource planning. In M. Khosrow-Pour (Ed.), *Encyclopedia of information science and technology* (3rd ed., pp. 798–807). Hershey, PA: IGI Global; doi:10.4018/978-1-4666-5888-2.ch076

Katz, R., Goldstein, P., & Yanosky, R. (2010). *Cloud computing in higher education*. Retrieved May 4, 2014, from http://net.educause.edu/section_params/conf/ccw10/highered.pdf

Kaufmann, L., & Saw, A. A. (2014). Using a multiple-informant approach in SCM research. *International Journal of Physical Distribution & Logistics Management*, *44*(6), 511–527. doi:10.1108/IJPDLM-05-2013-0099

Kaushik, A., & Kaushik, C. P. (2006). *Environmental Studies-A Multidisciplinary Subject: Perspectives in Environmental Studies*. New Delhi: New Age International Publishers.

Kenneth Kofi, F. (2010). *Cloud security requirements analysis and security policy development using a high-order object-oriented modeling technique*. Thesis.

Ke, W., Liu, H., Wei, K. K., Gu, J., & Chen, H. (2009). How do mediated and non-mediated power affect electronic supply chain management system adoption? The mediation effects of trust and institutional pressures. *Decision Support Systems*, *46*(4), 839–851. doi:10.1016/j.dss.2008.11.008

Khadka, R., ... (2011). Model-Driven Development of Service Compositions for Enterprise Interoperability. In van Sinderen, M., & Johnson, P. (Eds.), Enterprise Interoperability (pp. 177-190). Berlin, Germany: Springer-Verlag. doi:10.1007/978-3-642-19680-5_15

Khajeh-Hosseini, A., Greenwood, D., Smith, J. W., & Sommerville, I. (2012). The cloud adoption toolkit: Supporting cloud adoption decisions in the enterprise. *Software, Practice & Experience*, *42*(4), 447–465. doi:10.1002/spe.1072

Khasnabish, B., Huang, D., Bai, X., Bellavista, P., Martinez, G., & Antonopoulos, N. (2012). Cloud computing, networking, and services. *Journal of Network and Systems Management*, *20*(4), 463–467. doi:10.1007/s10922-012-9254-0

Kim, D., & Shen, W. (2007). An Approach to Evaluating Structural Pattern Conformance of UML Models. In *ACM Symposium on Applied Computing* (pp. 1404-1408). New York, NY: ACM Press. doi:10.1145/1244002.1244305

Kirkpatrick, S., Gelatt, C. D., & Vecchi, M. P. (1983). Optimization by simulated annealing. *Science*, *220*(4598), 671–680. doi:10.1126/science.220.4598.671 PMID:17813860

Kokash, N., & Arbab, F. (2009). Formal Behavioral Modeling and Compliance Analysis for Service-Oriented Systems. In F. Boer, M. Bonsangue, & E. Madelaine (Eds.), *Formal Methods for Components and Objects* (pp. 21–41). Berlin, Germany: Springer-Verlag. doi:10.1007/978-3-642-04167-9_2

Kolb, D. A., Boyatzis, R. E., and Mainemelis, C. (2001). Experiential learning theory: Previous research and new directions. *Perspectives on thinking, learning, and cognitive styles*, *1*, 227-247.

Kolb, A. Y., & Kolb, D. A. (2005). Learning styles and learning spaces: Enhancing experiential learning in higher education. *Academy of Management Learning & Education*, *4*(2), 193–212. doi:10.5465/AMLE.2005.17268566

Kolb, D. A. (1984). *Experiential learning: Experience as the source of learning and development* (Vol. 1). Englewood Cliffs, NJ: Prentice-Hall.

Kołodziej, J., & Xhafa, F. (2011). Modern approaches to modeling user requirements on resource and task allocation in hierarchical computational grids. *International Journal of Applied Mathematics and Computer Science*, *21*(2), 243–257. doi:10.2478/v10006-011-0018-x

Kong, L., Qi, H., Wang, S., Du, C., Wang, S. & Han, Y. (2012). *Approaches for Candidate Document Retrieval and Detailed Comparison of Plagiarism Detection*. Notebook for Uncovering Plagiarism, Authorship, and Social Software Misuse (PAN) at CLEF.

Kotzab, H., Grant, D. B., Teller, C., & Halldorsson, A. (2009). Supply chain management and hypercompetition. *Logistics Research*, *1*(1), 5–13. doi:10.1007/s12159-008-0002-5

Kraan, W., & Yuan, L. (2009). *Cloud computing in institutions: A briefing paper*. Retrieved June 24, 2014, from http://wiki.cetis.ac.uk/images/1/11/Cloud_computing_web.pdf

Krane, D. E., & Raymer, M. L. (2005). *Fundamental Concepts of Bioinformatics; New Delhi: Pearson Education*. Singapore: Private Limited.

Krikos A (2010). *Disruptive Technology Business Models in Cloud Computing*. Cambridge: MIT USA.

Kruchten, P. (2004). *The rational unified process: an introduction*. Boston, MA: Pearson Education Inc.

Krug, S. (2000). *Don't Make Me Think*. Indianapolis, IN: New Riders Publishing.

Krumeich, J., Weis, B., Werth, D., & Loos, P. (2014). Event-driven business process management: Where are we now? A comprehensive synthesis and analysis of literature. *Business Process Management Journal, 20*(4), 615–633. doi:10.1108/BPMJ-07-2013-0092

Krutz R. L., & Vines R. D. (2010). *Cloud Security*. New Delhi: Willey India Private Limited.

Krutz, R. L., & Dean, V. R. (2010). *Cloud Security*. New Delhi: Wiley India Private Limited.

Krutz, R. L., & Vines, R. D. (2010). *Cloud security: A comprehensive guide to secure cloud computing*. John Wiley & Sons.

Kumar, B. R., & Karthik, S. (2011, May). Platforms for Building and Developing Applications for Cloud Computing. *CSI Communications Journal, 35*(2), 6–11.

Kumar, K. L., & Joy, J. (2013, December). Application of Zigbee Wireless Frequency for Patient Monitoring System; Mumbai. *CSI Communications Journal, 37*(9), 17–18.

Kumar, S., & Kumar, S. (2013, April). Big Data: A Big game changer. *CSI Communications Journal, 37*(1), 9–10.

Kushida, K. E., Murray, J., & Zysman, J. (2011). Diffusing the cloud: Cloud computing and implications for public policy. *Journal of Industry, Competition and Trade, 11*(3), 209–237. doi:10.1007/s10842-011-0106-5

Kusic, D., Kephart, J. O., Hanson, J. E., Kandasamy, N., & Jiang, G. (2009). Power and performance management of virtualized computing environments via lookahead control. *Cluster Computing, 12*(1), 1–15. doi:10.1007/s10586-008-0070-y

Lam, L. (2012). An innovative research on the usage of Facebook in the higher education context of Hong Kong. *The Electronic Journal of e-Learning, 10*(4), 377-386.

Lambert, D. M., & Pohlen, T. L. (2001). Supply chain metrics. *International Journal of Logistics Management, 12*(1), 1–19. doi:10.1108/09574090110806190

Lecerof, A., & Paterno, F. (1998). Automatic Support for Usability Evaluation. *IEEE Transactions on Software Engineering, 24*(10), 863–888. doi:10.1109/32.729686

Lee, J., Cho, J., Seo, J., Shon, T., & Won, D. (2013). A novel approach to analyzing for detecting malicious network activity using a cloud computing testbed. *Mobile Networks and Applications, 18*(1), 122–128. doi:10.1007/s11036-012-0375-1

Lee, Y. C., & Zomaya, A. Y. (2012). Energy efficient utilization of resources in cloud computing systems. *The Journal of Supercomputing, 60*(2), 268–280. doi:10.1007/s11227-010-0421-3

Lenssen, J. J., & Van Wassenhove, L. N. (2012). A new era of development: The changing role and responsibility of business in developing countries. *Corporate Governance, 12*(4), 403–413. doi:10.1108/14720701211267766

Levin, S. (2013). Cooperation and Sustainability. In G. Madhavan, B. Oakley, D. Green, D. Koon, & P. Low (Eds.), *Practicing Sustainability* (pp. 39–41). New York: Springer.

Lewis, G. (2012). The Role of Standards in Cloud-Computing Interoperability, *Software Engineering Institute*, Paper 682. Retrieved May 30, 2014 from http://repository.cmu.edu/sei/682

Lewis, G., Morris, E., Simanta, S., & Wrage, L. (2008). Why Standards Are Not Enough To Guarantee End-to-End Interoperability. In Ncube C. Carvallo J. (Eds.) *Seventh International Conference on Composition-Based Software Systems* (pp. 164-173). Piscataway, NJ: IEEE Computer Society Press. doi:10.1109/ICCBSS.2008.25

Lewis, I., & Talalayevsky, A. (1997). Logistics and information technology: A coordination perspective. *Journal of Business Logistics, 18*(1), 141–157.

Leymann, F., Fehling, C., Mietzner, R., Nowak, A., & Dustdar, S. (2011). Moving applications to the cloud: An approach based on application model enrichment. *International Journal of Cooperative Information Systems, 20*(3), 307–356. doi:10.1142/S0218843011002250

Li, Q., Zhang, X., & Chen, M. (2012). *Design on enterprise knowledge supply chain based on cloud computing*. Paper presented at the 2012 Fifth International Conference on Business Intelligence and Financial Engineering (BIFE 2012), Gansu, China. doi:10.1109/BIFE.2012.28

Liang, Q., Wang, Y. Z., & Zhang, Y. H. (2011). Resource virtualization model using hybrid-graph representation and converging algorithm for cloud computing. *International Journal of Automation and Computing, 10*(6), 597–606. doi:10.1007/s11633-013-0758-1

Li, J. F., Peng, J., Cao, X., & Li, H. Y. (2011). A task scheduling algorithm based on improved ant colony optimization in cloud computing environment. *Energy Procedia, 13*, 6833–6840.

Li, J., Qiu, M., Ming, Z., Quan, G., Qin, X., & Gu, Z. (2012). Online optimization for scheduling preemptable tasks on IaaS cloud systems. *Journal of Parallel and Distributed Computing, 72*(5), 666–677. doi:10.1016/j.jpdc.2012.02.002

Lindner, M., Galan, F., Chapman, C., Clayman, S., Henriksson, D., & Elmroth, E. (2010). *The cloud supply chain: A framework for information, monitoring, accounting and billing*. Retrieved September 6, 2014, from https://www.ee.ucl.ac.uk/,sclayman/docs/CloudComp2010.pdf

Lin, L. C., & Li, T. S. (2010). An integrated framework for supply chain performance measurement using six-sigma metrics. *Software Quality Journal, 18*(3), 387–406. doi:10.1007/s11219-010-9099-2

Linthicum, D. S. (2010). *Cloud Computing and SOA Convergence in your Enterprise New Delhi: Dorling Kindersley*. India: Private Limited.

Lin, Y.-T., Wen, M.-L., Jou, M., & Wu, D.-W. (2013). A cloud-based learning environment for developing student reflection abilities. *Computers in Human Behavior, 32*, 244–252. doi:10.1016/j.chb.2013.12.014

Liu, H., & Orban, D. (2008). *Gridbatch: Cloud computing for large-scale data-intensive batch applications*. Paper presented at the 8th IEEE International Symposium on Cluster Computing and the Grid, Lyon, France. doi:10.1109/CCGRID.2008.30

Liu, H., Abraham, A., Snášel, V., & McLoone, S. (2012). Swarm scheduling approaches for work-flow applications with security constraints in distributed data-intensive computing environments. *Information Sciences, 192*, 228–243. doi:10.1016/j.ins.2011.12.032

Liu, H., Ke, W., Wei, K. K., Gu, J., & Chen, H. (2010). The role of institutional pressures and organizational culture in the firm's intention to adopt Internet-enabled supply chain management systems. *Journal of Operations Management, 28*(5), 372–384. doi:10.1016/j.jom.2009.11.010

Liu, L., Wang, H., Liu, X., Jin, X., He, W. B., Wang, Q. B., & Chen, Y. (2009). Greencloud: a new architecture for green data center. In *Proceedings of the 6th international conference industry session on Autonomic computing and communications industry session*, (pp. 29–38). ACM. doi:10.1145/1555312.1555319

Liu, Q., Weng, C., Li, M., & Luo, Y. (2010). An In-VM measuring framework for increasing virtual machine security in clouds. *IEEE Security Privacy Journal, 8*(6), 56–62. doi:10.1109/MSP.2010.143

Liu, Y. C., Ma, Y. T., Zhang, H. S., Li, D. Y., & Chen, G. S. (2011). A method for trust management in cloud computing: Data coloring by cloud watermarking. *International Journal of Automation and Computing, 8*(3), 280–285. doi:10.1007/s11633-011-0583-3

Lofstrand M. (2009) The VeriScale Architecture: Elasticity and Efficiency for Private Clouds"; *Sun BluePrint; Sun Microsystems; Online, Revision 1.1, Part No 821-0248-11*.

Lohr, S. (2007). *Google and I.B.M. Join in "cloud computing" research*. New York Times. Retrieved September 6, 2014, from http://www.csun.edu/pubrels/clips/Oct07/10-08-07E.pdf

Loutas, N., Kamateri, E., Bosi, F., & Tarabanis, K. (2011). Cloud computing interoperability: the state of play. In LambrinoudakisC.RizomiliotisP.WlodarczykT. (Eds.) *International Conference on Cloud Computing Technology and Science* (pp. 752-757). Piscataway, NJ: IEEE Computer Society Press. doi:10.1109/CloudCom.2011.116

Loutas, N., Peristeras, V., & Tarabanis, K. (2011). Towards a reference service model for the Web of Services. *Data & Knowledge Engineering*, *70*(9), 753–774. doi:10.1016/j.datak.2011.05.001

Lwoga, E. T. (2012). *Building a virtual academic library with Web 2.0 technologies in Tanzania, IST-Africa 2012 Conference, Dar es salaam*. Retrieved on 9-11 May 2012, from: http://hdl.handle.net/123456789/17

Lyons, C. (2007). The library: A distinct local voice? *First Monday*, *12*(3). doi:10.5210/fm.v12i3.1629

Mabert, V. A., & Venkataramanan, M. A. (1998). Special research focus on supply chain linkages: Challenges for design and management in the 21st century. *Decision Sciences*, *29*(3), 537–552. doi:10.1111/j.1540-5915.1998.tb01353.x

Mackelprang, A. W., Robinson, J. L., Bernardes, E., & Webb, G. S. (2014). The relationship between strategic supply chain integration and performance: A meta-analytic evaluation and implications for supply chain management research. *Journal of Business Logistics*, *35*(1), 71–96. doi:10.1111/jbl.12023

Malik, N. (2009). Toward an Enterprise Business Motivation Model. *The Architecture Journal*, *19*, 10–16.

Manuj, I., & Mentzer, J. T. (2008). Global supply chain risk management strategies. *International Journal of Physical Distribution & Logistics Management*, *38*(3), 192–223. doi:10.1108/09600030810866986

Manuj, I., & Sahin, F. (2011). A model of supply chain and supply chain decision-making complexity. *International Journal of Physical Distribution & Logistics Management*, *41*(5), 511–549. doi:10.1108/09600031111138844

Mark, C., Niyato, D., & Chen-Khong, T. (2011). Evolutionary optimal virtual machine placement and demand forecaster for cloud computing. *In Advanced Information Networking and Applications (AINA), 2011 IEEE International Conference on, pages 348–355*.

Marston, S., Li, Z., Bandyopadhyay, S., & Ghalsasi, A. (2011). Cloud computing the business perspective. In *HICSS* (pp. 1–11). IEEE Computer Society.

Marston, S., Li, Z., Bandyopadhyay, S., Zhang, J., & Ghalsasi, A. (2011). Cloud computing: The business perspective. *Decision Support Systems*, *51*(1), 176–189. doi:10.1016/j.dss.2010.12.006

Masson, R., Iosif, L., MacKerron, G., & Fernie, J. (2007). Managing complexity in agile global fashion industry supply chains. *International Journal of Logistics Management*, *18*(2), 238–254. doi:10.1108/09574090710816959

Mather, T., Kumaraswamy, S., & Latif, S. (2010). *Cloud Security and Privacy*. Mumbai: Shroff Publishers & Distributors Private Limited.

Mathieu, R. G., & Pal, R. (2011). The selection of supply chain management projects: A case study approach. *Operations Management Research*, *4*(3-4), 164–181. doi:10.1007/s12063-011-0058-2

Matthews, J., Garfinkel, T., Hoff, C., & Wheeler, J. Virtual Machine Contracts for Data Center and Cloud Computing Environments. *In Proceedings of the 1st Workshop on Automated Control for Datacenters and Clouds. New York, NY, USA. ACM. pages25-30. 2009*

Maxwell, J. A. (2005). *Qualitative research design: An interactive approach*. Thousand Oaks, CA: Sage.

McCarthy, L. (2011). Adoption of Cloud Computing. Retrieved from http://askvisory.com/research/adoption-of-cloudcomputing/

McDonald, D., MacDonald, A., & Breslin, C. (2010). *Final report from the JISC review of the environmental and organisational implications of cloud computing in higher and further education*. Retrieved April 2, 2014, from http://www.jisc.ac.uk/media/documents/programmes/greeningict/cloudstudyreport.pdf

McGuire, M., & Dowling, S. (2003). *Cyber crime: a review of the evidence*. Home Office. Retrieved 9 July, 2014, from https://www.gov.uk/government/publications/cyber-crime-a-review-of-the-evidence

Mei, H., & Liu, X. Z. (2011). Internetware: An emerging software paradigm for Internet computing. *Journal of Computer Science and Technology, 26*(4), 588–599. doi:10.1007/s11390-011-1159-y

Meiko, J., Jorg, S., Nils, G., & Luigi, L. I. (2009). On Technical Security Issues in Cloud Computing.*IEEE International Conference on Cloud Computing*.

Mell, P., & Grance, T. (2011). The NIST definition of cloud computing. Special publication 800-145, *National Institute of Standards and Technology*. Retrieved May 30, 2014 from http://csrc.nist.gov/publications/nistpubs/800-145/SP800-145.pdf

Mell, P.and Grance, T. (2011). *The NIST Definition of Cloud Computing*. Recommendations of the National Institute of Standards and Technology, Special Publication 800-145, September 2011

Mell, P., & Grance, T. (2009). Effectively and Securely Using the Cloud Computing Paradigm.*ACM Cloud Computing Security Workshop*.

Mell, P., & Grance, T. (2011). *The NIST Definition of Cloud Computing* (pp. 800–145). Gaithersburg, MD: NIST Special Publication.

Melville, N., & Ramirez, R. (2008). Information technology innovation diffusion: An information requirements paradigm. *Information Systems Journal, 18*(3), 247–273. doi:10.1111/j.1365-2575.2007.00260.x

Mena, C., Humphries, A., & Choi, T. Y. (2013). Toward a theory of multi-tier supply chain management. *Journal of Supply Chain Management, 49*(2), 58–77. doi:10.1111/jscm.12003

Meng, X., Pappas, V., & Zhang, L. (2010). Improving the scalability of data center networks with traffic-aware virtual machine placement. *In INFOCOM, Proceedings IEEE, pages* 1–9.

Menken, I., & Blokdijk, G. (2009). *Cloud Computing Virtualization Specialist Complete Certification Kit - Study Guide Book and Online Course*. Emereo Pty Ltd.

Menno-Jan, K., & Ferjan, O. (2004). *Cartography Visualization of Geospatial Data; New Delhi: Pearson Education*. Singapore: Private Limited.

Mentzer, J. T., DeWitt, W., Min, S., Nix, N. W., Smith, C. D., & Zacharia, Z. G. (2001). Defining supply chain management. *Journal of Business Logistics, 22*(2), 1–25. doi:10.1002/j.2158-1592.2001.tb00001.x

Mentzer, J. T., Flint, D. J., & Kent, J. L. (1999). Developing a logistics service quality scale. *Journal of Business Logistics, 20*(1), 9–32.

Mentzer, J. T., & Gundlach, G. (2010). Exploring the relationship between marketing and supply chain management: Introduction to the special issue. *Journal of the Academy of Marketing Science, 38*(1), 1–4. doi:10.1007/s11747-009-0150-4

Mezmaz, M., Melab, N., Kessaci, Y., Lee, Y. C., Talbi, E.-G., Zomaya, A. Y., & Tuyttens, D. (2011). A parallel bi-objective hybrid metaheuristic for energy-aware scheduling for cloud computing systems. *Journal of Parallel and Distributed Computing, 71*(11), 1497–1508. doi:10.1016/j.jpdc.2011.04.007

Mi, H., Wang, H., Yin, G., Zhou, Y., Shi, D., & Yuan, L. (2010). Online self-reconfiguration with performance guarantee for energy efficient large-scale cloud computing data centers. *In Services Computing (SCC), 2010 IEEE International Conference on, pages 514–521*.

Miller, M. (2009). *Cloud Computing; New Delhi: Dorling Kindersley*. India: Private Limited.

Miller, M. (2009). *Under Standing Cloud Computing; Cloud Computing. New Delhi: Dorling Kindersley*. India: Private Limited.

Minas, L. & Ellison, B. (2009). *The problem of power consumption in servers*. Intel Corporation. Dr. Dobb's.

Minelli, M., Chambers, M., & Dhiraj, A. (2014). *Big Data Analytics*. New Delhi: Wiley India Private Limited.

Minhas, U. F. (2013). *Scalable and Highly Available Database Systems in the Cloud*. PhD thesis, University of Waterloo.

Min, S., Mentzer, J. T., & Ladd, R. T. (2007). A market orientation in supply chain management. *Journal of the Academy of Marketing Science, 35*(4), 507–522. doi:10.1007/s11747-007-0020-x

Mircea, M., & Andreescu, A. I. (2011). Using cloud computing in higher education: A strategy to improve agility in the current financial crisis. *Communications of the IBIMA*, 1-15. doi:10.5171/2011.875547

Misra, S. C., & Mondal, A. (2010). Identification of a company's suitability for the adoption of cloud computing and modelling its corresponding return on investment. *Mathematical and Computer Modelling*, *53*(3-4), 504–521. doi:10.1016/j.mcm.2010.03.037

Mitchell, E. (2010). Using cloud services for library IT infrastructure. *code4lib Journal, 9.*

Mitrano, T. (2009). *Outsourcing and cloud computing for higher education.* Retrieved April 2, 2014, from http://www.it.cornell.edu/cms/policies/publications/upload/Memo-on-Outsourcing-and-Cloud-Computing.pdf

Modi, C., Patel, D., Borisaniya, B., Patel, A., & Rajarajan, M. (2012). A survey on security issues and solutions at different layers of Cloud computing. *The Journal of Supercomputing*, *63*(2), 561–592. doi:10.1007/s11227-012-0831-5

Monfelt, Y., Pilemalm, S., Hallberg, J., & Yngström, L. (2011). The 14-layered framework for including social and organizational aspects in security management. *Information Management & Computer Security*, *19*(2), 124–133. doi:10.1108/09685221111143060

MOOC. (2013). *Mobiles for Development: A Massive Open Online Course for Development.* Open Educational Resources. Retrieved on 01 January 2014, from http://m4d.colfinder.org/node/2372

Morris, E., ... (2004). *System of Systems Interoperability (SOSI): final report. Report No. CMU/SEI-2004-TR-004.* Carnegie Mellon Software Engineering Institute. Retrieved May 31, 2014 from http://www.sei.cmu.edu/reports/04tr004.pdf

Mtebe, J. S. (2013). Exploring the Potential of Clouds to Facilitate the Adoption of Blended Learning in Tanzania. *International Journal of Education and Research*, *1*(8).

Mtega, W. P., Bernard, R., Msungu, A. C., & Sanare, R. (2012). Using mobile phones for teaching and learning purposes in higher learning institutions: The case of Sokoine University of Agriculture in Tanzania. In *Proceedings and report of the 15th UbuntuNet alliance Annual Conference.*

Myers, M. B., Griffith, D. A., Daugherty, P. J., & Lusch, R. F. (2004). Maximizing the human capital equation in logistics: Education, experience, and skills. *Journal of Business Logistics*, *25*(1), 211–232. doi:10.1002/j.2158-1592.2004.tb00175.x

Mykkänen, J., & Tuomainen, M. (2008). An evaluation and selection framework for interoperability standards. *Information and Software Technology*, *50*(3), 176–197. doi:10.1016/j.infsof.2006.12.001

Narasimhan, R., & Kim, S. W. (2001). Information system utilization strategy for supply chain integration. *Journal of Business Logistics*, *22*(2), 51–75. doi:10.1002/j.2158-1592.2001.tb00003.x

National Bureau of Asian Research. (2013). The IP Commission Report: The report on the theft of American Intellectual Propery. Retrieved 18 March, 2014, from http://www.ipcommission.org/report/IP_Commission_Report_052213.pdf

Nielsen, J. (1998). Introduction to web design. In *Proceedings of the SIGCHI on Human Factors in Computing Systems.* Los Angeles, CA: The Association of Computing Machinery.

Nielsen, J. (2000). *Designing Web Usability. Indianapolis, IN: New Riders Publishing. Nielsen, J. & Tahir, M. (2002). Homepage Usability: 50 Websites Deconstructed.* Indianapolis, IN: New Riders Publishing.

NIST. (n.d) Definition of Cloud Computing v 15, csrc.nist.gov/groups/SNS/cloud-computing/cloud-def-v 15.doc

Norris, S. (2004). *Analyzing multimodal interaction: A methodological framework.* London: Routledge.

Novack, R. A., Rinehart, L. M., & Langley, C. J. (1996). A comparative assessment of senior and logistics executives' perceptions of logistics value. *Journal of Business Logistics, 17*(1), 135–178.

Novack, R. A., & Thomas, D. J. (2004). The challenges of implementing the perfect order concept. *Transportation Journal, 43*(1), 5–17.

Novell (1983). Platespin recon. http://www.novell.com/products/recon/

Nuernberg, P., Leggett, J., & McFarland, M. (2012). Cloud as infrastructure at the Texas Digital Library. *Journal of Digital Information, 13*(1).

Nurmi, D. et al.. (2009). The eucalyptus open-source cloud-computing system. In CappelloF.WangC.BuyyaR. (Eds.) *9th IEEE/ACM International Symposium on Cluster Computing and the Grid* (pp. 124-131). Piscataway, NJ: IEEE Computer Society Press.

O'Reilly Media Inc. (2013). *Big Data Now Current Perspectives from O'Reilly Media*. Mumbai: Shroff Publishers & Distributors Private Limited.

Ochara-Muganda, N., & Van Belle, J. (2010). A proposed framework for E-Government knowledge infrastructures for Africa's transition economies. Journal of e-Government Studies and Best Practices, *2010*, 1–9.

Ochara, N. M. (2008). Emergence of the e-Government artifact in an environment of social exclusion in Kenya. *The African Journal of Information Systems, 1*(1), 3.

OCSIA/Detica. (2011). *The cost of cyber crime. A Detica report in partnership with the Office of Cyber Security and Information Assurance in the Cabinet Office*. Retrieved 18 March, 2014, from https://www.baesystemsdetica.com/uploads/press_releases/THE_COST_OF_CYBER_CRIME_SUMMARY_FINAL_14_February_2011.pdf

Oguz, F., & Sengün, A. (2011). Mystery of the unknown: Revisiting tacit knowledge in the organizational literature. *Journal of Knowledge Management, 15*(3), 445–461. doi:10.1108/13673271111137420

Olson, J. R., & Boyer, K. K. (2005). Internet ticketing in a not-for-profit, service organization: Building customer loyalty. *International Journal of Operations & Production Management, 25*(1), 74–92. doi:10.1108/01443570510572259

Om, K., Lee, J., & Chang, J. (2007). Using supply chain management to enhance industry-university collaborations in IT higher education in Korea. *Scientometrics, 71*(3), 455–471. doi:10.1007/s11192-007-1690-3

Open Hybrid Resources (OHR). (2014). Retrieved on, from http://www.redhat.com/solutions/open-hybrid-cloud/cloud-resources/

O'Rourke, C., Fishman, N., & Selkow, W. (2003). *Enterprise architecture using the Zachman framework*. Boston, MA: Course Technology.

OSS. (2014). Plutchak, T. S. (2012). Breaking the barriers of time and space: The dawning of the great age of librarians. *Journal of the Medical Library Association: JMLA, 100*(1), 10. http://www.datamation.com/open-source/60-open-source-apps-you-can-use-in-the-cloud-1.html Retrieved on 3th June 2014

Ostadzadeh, S., & Fereidoon, S. (2011). An Architectural Framework for the Improvement of the Ultra-Large-Scale Systems Interoperability. In ArabniaH.RezaH.DeligiannidisL. (Eds.) *International Conference on Software Engineering Research and Practice* (pp. 212-219). Athens, GA: CSREA Press.

Oztemel, E., & Tekez, E. K. (2009). Interactions of agents in performance based supply chain management. *Journal of Intelligent Manufacturing, 20*(2), 159–167. doi:10.1007/s10845-008-0229-7

Packard, H. (2011). *Power regulator for proliant servers*.

Pagell, M., & Shevchenko, A. (2014). Why research in sustainable supply chain management should have no future. *Journal of Supply Chain Management, 50*(1), 44–55. doi:10.1111/jscm.12037

Parkhill, D. (1966). *The Challenge of the Computer Utility*. US: Addison-Wesley Educational Publishers Inc.

Pautasso, C., Zimmermann, O., & Leymann, F. (2008). Restful web services vs. "big'" web services: making the right architectural decision. In *International conference on World Wide Web* (pp. 805-814). ACM Press.

Pearrow, M. (2000). *Web Site Usability Handbook*. Independence, KY: Charles River Media.

Peck, H. (2005). Drivers of supply chain vulnerability: An integrated framework. *International Journal of Physical Distribution & Logistics Management, 35*(4), 210–232. doi:10.1108/09600030510599904

Peck, H., & Juttner, U. (2000). Strategy and relationships: Defining the interface in supply chain contexts. *International Journal of Logistics Management, 11*(2), 33–44. doi:10.1108/09574090010806146

Perera, C., Zaslavsky, A., Cristen, P., & Georgakopoulos, D. (2014). Sensing as a service model for smart cities supported by Internet of Things. *Transactions on Emerging Telecommunications Technologies, 25*(1), 81–93. doi:10.1002/ett.2704

Peristeras, V., & Tarabanis, K. (2006). The Connection, Communication, Consolidation, Collaboration Interoperability Framework (C4IF) For Information Systems Interoperability. *International Journal of Interoperability in Business Information Systems, 1*(1), 61–72.

Petcu, D. (2013). Multi-Cloud: expectations and current approaches. In *International Workshop on Multi-cloud Applications and Federated Clouds* (pp. 1-6). New York, NY: ACM Press. doi:10.1145/2462326.2462328

Petcu, D., Macariu, G., Panica, S., & Crăciun, C. (2013). Portable cloud applications—from theory to practice. *Future Generation Computer Systems, 29*(6), 1417–1430. doi:10.1016/j.future.2012.01.009

Petrie, C., & Bussler, C. (2003). Service agents and virtual enterprises: A survey. *Internet Computing, 7*(4), 68–78. doi:10.1109/MIC.2003.1215662

Plaszczak, P., & Wellner, R. Jr. (2006). *Grid Computing.* New Delhi: Elesvier.

Plummer, D. C., Bittman, T. J., Austin, T., Cearley, D. W., & Smith, D. M. (2008). *Cloud computing: Defining and describing an emerging phenomenon.* Retrieved from June 24, 2014, http://www.emory.edu/BUSINESS/readings/CloudComputing/Gartner_cloud_computing_defining.pdf

Popa, R. A., Redfield, C. M. S., Zeldovich, N., & Balakrishnan, H. (2012). CryptDB: Processing queries on an encrypted database. *Communications of the ACM, 55*(9), 103–111. doi:10.1145/2330667.2330691

Potdar, V., Sharif, A., & Chang, E. (2009). Wireless sensor networks: A survey. In AwanI.YounasM.HaraT.DurresiA. (Eds.) *International Conference on Advanced Information Networking and Applications Workshops* (pp. 636-641). Piscataway, NJ: IEEE Computer Society Press. doi:10.1109/WAINA.2009.192

Potthast, M., Barrón-Cedeño, A., Stein, B., & Rosso, P. (2010). *An Evaluation Framework for Plagiarism Detection.Proceedings of the 23rd International Conference on Computational Linguistics (COLING)*2010, August 23-27, Beijing, China.

Prasad, M. R., Gyani, J., & Murti, P. R. K. (2012). Mobile cloud computing: Implications and challenges. *Journal of Information Engineering and Applications, 2*(7), 7–16.

Premkumar, G., Ramamurthy, K., & Saunders, C. S. (2005). Information processing view of organizations: An exploratory examination of fit in the context of interorganizational relationships. *Journal of Management Information Systems, 22*(1), 257–294.

Pujari Arun, K. (2004). *Data mining Techniques; New Delhi: Universities Press.* India: Private Limited.

Pujari, A. K. (2003). *Data Mining Techniques; Hyderabad: Universities Press.* India: Private Limited.

Putnik, G., & Sluga, A. (2007). Reconfigurability of manufacturing systems for agility implementation, part I: requirements and principles. In Cunha, P., & Maropoulos, P. (Eds.), Digital Enterprise Technology: Perspectives and Future Challenges (pp. 91-98). New York, NY: Springer Science+Business Media.

Quazi, S. A. (2009). *Principles of Physical Geography.* New Delhi: APH Publishing Corporation.

Quelch, J. A., & Kenny, D. (1994). Extend profits, not product lines. *Harvard Business Review, 72*(5), 153–160.

Rahimi, M. R., Ren, J., Liu, C. H., Vasilakos, A. V., & Venkatasubramanian, N. (2014). Mobile cloud computing: A survey, state of art and future directions. *Mobile Networks and Applications, 19*(2), 133–143. doi:10.1007/s11036-013-0477-4

Rai, A., Patnayakuni, R., & Seth, N. (2006). Firm performance impacts of digitally enabled supply chain integration capabilities. *Management Information Systems Quarterly*, *30*(2), 225–246.

Rajaraman, V. (2014). Cloud computing. *Resonance*, *19*(3), 242–258. doi:10.1007/s12045-014-0030-1

Ramezani, F., Lu, J., & Hussain, F. K. (2014). Task-Based System Load Balancing in Cloud Computing Using Particle Swarm Optimization. *International Journal of Parallel Programming*, *42*(5), 739–754. doi:10.1007/s10766-013-0275-4

Ramgovind, S., Eloff, M. M., & Smith, E. The Management of Security in Cloud Computing"; Information Security for South Africa (ISSA); IEEE; 1-7.2010

Ranjan, R., Buyya, R., & Benatallah, B. (2012). Special section: Software architectures and application development environments for Cloud computing. *Software, Practice & Experience*, *42*(4), 391–394. doi:10.1002/spe.1144

Ranjan, R., Buyya, R., Leitner, P., Haller, A., & Tai, S. (2014). A note on software tools and techniques for monitoring and prediction of cloud services. *Software, Practice & Experience*, *44*(7), 771–775. doi:10.1002/spe.2266

Rao Raja, K. N. (2005). *An Overview of Space and Satellite: Fundamental of Satellite Communication*. New Delhi: Prentice Hall of India.

Rasmussen, C. H., & Jochumsen, H. (2009). The fall and rise of the physical library. In *The 17th BOBCATSSS Symposium*. Retrieved on 01 January 2014, from http://pure.iva.dk/files/30767688/The_Fall_and_Rise_-_Bobcatsss_2009.pdf

Ratten, V. (2014). A US-China comparative study of cloud computing adoption behavior: The role of consumer innovativeness, performance expectations and social influence. *Journal of Entrepreneurship in Emerging Economies*, *6*(1), 53–71. doi:10.1108/JEEE-07-2013-0019

Reese, G. (2010). *Cloud Application Architecture*. Mumbai: Shorff Publishers & Distributors Private Limited.

Reese, G. (2010). *Cloud Application Architectures*. Mumbai: Shroff Publishers and Distributors Private Limited.

Revels, J., Tojib, D., & Tsarenko, Y. (2010). Understanding consumer intention to use mobile services. *Australasian Marketing Journal*, *18*(2), 74–80. doi:10.1016/j.ausmj.2010.02.002

Rhoton, J. (2010). *Cloud Computing Explained: Implementation Hand Book for Enterprises London*. Recursive Press.

Richey, R. G. Jr, Roath, A. S., Whipple, J. M., & Fawcett, S. E. (2010). Exploring a governance theory of supply chain management: Barriers and facilitators to integration. *Journal of Business Logistics*, *31*(1), 237–256. doi:10.1002/j.2158-1592.2010.tb00137.x

Richey, R. G., Tokman, M., & Wheeler, A. R. (2006). A supply chain manager selection methodology: Empirical test and suggested application. *Journal of Business Logistics*, *27*(2), 163–190. doi:10.1002/j.2158-1592.2006.tb00221.x

Rimal, B. P., Jukan, A., Katsaros, D., & Goeleven, Y. (2011). Architectural requirements for cloud computing systems: An enterprise cloud approach. *Journal of Grid Computing*, *9*(1), 3–26. doi:10.1007/s10723-010-9171-y

Rimal, B., Choi, E., & Lumb, I. (2009). A taxonomy and survey of cloud computing systems. In KimJ. (Eds.) *Fifth International Joint Conference on INC, IMS and IDC* (pp. 44-51). Piscataway, NJ: IEEE Computer Society Press. doi:10.1109/NCM.2009.218

Rittinghouse, J. W., & Ransome, J. F. (2010). *Cloud computing: Implementation, management, and security*. Boca Raton: CRC Press.

Rodero, I., Jaramillo, J., Quiroz, A., Parashar, M., Guim, F., & Poole, S. (2010). Energy-efficient application-aware online provisioning for virtualized clouds and data centers. In 2010 International Green Computing Conference (pp. 31–45). IEEE. doi:10.1109/GREENCOMP.2010.5598283

Rosenblum, M. (2004). The reincarnation of virtual machines. *Queue*, *2*(5), 34. doi:10.1145/1016998.1017000

Rosenthal, A., Mork, P., Li, M. H., Stanford, J., Koester, D., & Reynolds, P. (2010). Cloud computing: A new business paradigm for biomedical information sharing. *Journal of Biomedical Informatics*, *43*(2), 342–353.

Roychoudhuri, D., Mohapatra, B., & Yadav, M. (2014, February). Rationalize Your Cloud Model Using Open Source Stack. *CSI Communications Journal, 37*(11), 11–14.

Ruz, C. (2014). Cloud computing key to improving literacy in Africa. Retrieved from http://www.isgtw.org/feature/cloud-computing-key-improving-literacy-africa

Ryan, M. D. (2013). Cloud computing security: The scientific challenge, and a survey of solutions. *Journal of Systems and Software, 86*(9), 2263–2268. doi:10.1016/j.jss.2012.12.025

Saberi, S., Nookabadi, A. S., & Hejazi, S. R. (2012). Applying agent-based system and negotiation mechanism in improvement of inventory management and customer order fulfillment in multi echelon supply chain. *Arabian Journal for Science and Engineering, 37*(3), 851–861. doi:10.1007/s13369-012-0197-2

Sabharwal, N., & Shankar, R. (2013). *Apache Cloudstack Cloud Computing*. Birmingham, UK: Packt Publishing Ltd.

Sacks, H. (1994). *Lectures on conversation*. Oxford: Blackwell.

Sacks, H., Schegloff, E., & Jefferson, G. A. (1974). A simplest systematics for the organization of turn-taking for conversation. *Language, 50*(4), 696–735. doi:10.1353/lan.1974.0010

Sagar, M., Bora, S., Gangwal, A., Gupta, P., Kumar, A., & Agarwal, A. (2013). Factors affecting customer loyalty in cloud computing: A customer defection-centric view to develop a void-in-customer loyalty amplification model. *Global Journal of Flexible Systems Management, 14*(3), 143–156. doi:10.1007/s40171-013-0035-8

Sahin, F., & Robinson, E. P. Jr. (2005). Information sharing and coordination in make-to-order supply chains. *Journal of Operations Management, 23*(6), 579–598. doi:10.1016/j.jom.2004.08.007

Sahoo, J. Mohapatra, S. & Lath, R. (2010). *Virtualization: A Survey on Concepts, Taxonomy and Associated Security Issues* (pp. 222-226).

Sahoo, G., Shabana, M., & Rashmi, R. (2013, November). Applications of Cloud Computing for Agriculture Sector. *CSI Communications Journal, 37*(8), 10–17.

Salih, N. K., & Zang, T. (2012). Survey and comparison for Open and closed sources in cloud computing. *arXiv preprint arXiv:1207.5480*.

Sanchez-Rodrigues, V., Potter, A., & Naim, M. M. (2010). The impact of logistics uncertainty on sustainable transport operations. *International Journal of Physical Distribution & Logistics Management, 40*(1-2), 61–83.

Sanders, N. R., & Premus, R. (2005). Modeling the relationship between firm it capability, collaboration, and performance. *Journal of Business Logistics, 26*(1), 1–23. doi:10.1002/j.2158-1592.2005.tb00192.x

Sanga, C. (2010). *A technique for the evaluation of free and open source e-learning systems*. Doctoral dissertation, University of the Western Cape.

Sanga, C., Lwoga, E. T., & Venter, I. M. (2006). Open Courseware as a Tool for Teaching and Learning in Africa, *Fourth IEEE International Workshop on Technology for Education in Developing Countries*, 2006 (pp. 55-56).

Sarga, L. (2012). Cloud computing: An overview. *Journal of Systems Integration, 4*, 1–12.

Savitskie, K. (2007). Internal and external logistics information technologies: The performance impact in an international setting. *International Journal of Physical Distribution & Logistics Management, 37*(6), 454–468. doi:10.1108/09600030710763378

Saya, S., Pee, L., & Kankanhalli, A. (2010). *The impact of institutional influences on perceived technological characteristics and real options in cloud computing adoption*. Paper presented at the 31st International Conference on Information Systems (ICIS 2010), St. Louis, Missouri.

Scale, M.-S. E. (2010). Assessing the Impact of Cloud Computing and Web Collaboration on the Work of Distance Library Services. *Journal of Library Administration, 50*(7-8), 7–8, 933–950. doi:10.1080/01930826.2010.488995

Scanlon, T., Schroeder, W., Snyder, C., & Spool, J. (1998). Websites that work: Designing with your eyes open. In *Proceedings of the SIGCHI on Human Factors in Computing Systems*. Los Angeles, CA: The Association of Computing Machinery.

Schmarzo, B. (2014). *Big Data Understanding How Data Powers Big Business*. New Delhi: Wiley India Private Limited.

Schramm, T., Nogueira, S., & Jones, D. (2011). Cloud computing and supply chain: A natural fit for the future. Retrieved September 6, 2014, from: http://www.aberdeen.com/aberdeen-library/7470/RA-software-service-cloud.aspx

Seethamraju, R. (2014). Enterprise systems and demand chain management: A cross-sectional field study. *Information Technology Management*, *15*(3), 151–161. doi:10.1007/s10799-014-0178-0

Shacklett, M. (2010). Is supply chain management emerging from the clouds? The short answer is "yes," and now's the time to take a more serious look. *World Trade*, *23*(4), 34–37.

Shadbolt, N., Hall, W., & Berners-Lee, T. (2006). The semantic web revisited. *IEEE Intelligent Systems*, *21*(3), 96–101. doi:10.1109/MIS.2006.62

Shafieezadeh, M., & Sadegheih, A. (2014). Developing an integrated inventory management model for multi-item multi-echelon supply chain. *International Journal of Advanced Manufacturing Technology*, *72*(5-8), 1099–1119. doi:10.1007/s00170-014-5684-z

Sharada, V. N. (2006). *Environment & Agriculture*. New Delhi: Malhotra Publishing House.

Shikharesh, M. (2011, May). Resource Management on Clouds: Handling Uncertainties in Parameters and Polices. *CSI Communications Journal*, *35*(2), 16–17.

Shilton, K. (2012). Participatory personal data: An emerging research challenge for the information sciences. *Journal of the American Society for Information Science and Technology*, *63*(10), 1905–1915. doi:10.1002/asi.22655

Shimba, F. (2010). *Cloud Computing: Strategies for Cloud Computing Adoption*. Retrieved on 08 August 2013, from http://arrow.dit.ie/cgi/viewcontent.cgi?article=1028&context=scschcomdis

Shimba, F. J., Koloseni, D., & Nungu, A. (2014). Challenges and Implications of adoption of cloud services in healthcare in developing countries. In A. Moumtzoglou (Ed.), *Cloud Computing Applications for Quality Health Care Delivery*. Hershey, PA: IGI Global Publishers.

Shokouhi, M., & Si, L. (2011). Federated Search. *Foundations and Trends in Information Retrieval*, *5*(1), 1–102. doi:10.1561/1500000010

Shon, T., Cho, J., Han, K., & Choi, H. (2014). Toward advanced mobile cloud computing for the Internet of Things: Current issues and future direction. *Mobile Networks and Applications*, *19*(3), 404–413. doi:10.1007/s11036-014-0509-8

Shoushtari, K. D. (2013). Redesigning a large supply chain management system to reduce the government administration: A socio-functional systems approach. *Systemic Practice and Action Research*, *26*(2), 195–216. doi:10.1007/s11213-012-9244-x

Shrivastava, V., Zerfos, P., Lee, K.-W., Jamjoom, H., Liu, Y.-H., & Banerjee, S. (2011). Application-aware virtual machine migration in data centers. *In INFOCOM, 2011 Proceedings IEEE, pages 66–70*.

Siddiqui, F., Haleem, A., & Sharma, C. (2012). The impact of supply chain management practices in total quality management practices and flexible system practices context: An empirical study in oil and gas industry. *Global Journal of Flexible Systems Management*, *13*(1), 11–23. doi:10.1007/s40171-012-0002-9

Sife, A., Lwoga, E., & Sanga, C. (2007). New technologies for teaching and learning: Challenges for higher learning institutions in developing countries. *International Journal of Education and Development using ICT*, *3*(2). Retrieved from http://ijedict.dec.uwi.edu/viewarticle.php?id=246

Simchi-Levi, D., Kaminski, P., & Simchi-Levi, E. (2008). *Designing and managing the supply chain: Concepts, strategies, and case studies*. New York, NY: McGraw-Hill/Irwin.

Sindelar, M., Sitaraman, R. K., & Shenoy, P. (2011). Sharing-aware algorithms for virtual machine colocation. *In Proceedings of the 23rd ACM Symposium on Parallelism in Algorithms and Architectures, SPAA '11, pages 367–378, New York, NY, USA. ACM*.

Singh, A., & Wesson, J. (2009). Evaluation Criteria for Assessing the Usability of ERP Systems In *Proceedings of the 2009 Annual Conference of the South African Institute of Computer Scientists and Information Technologists.* Vaal River, South Africa: The Association of Computing Machinery. doi:10.1145/1632149.1632162

Singh, R., & Kumar, S. (2014, November). Big Data Visualization using Cassandra and R; Mumbai. *CSI Communications Journal, 38*(8), 15–21.

Sinkovics, R. R., & Roath, A. S. (2004). Strategic orientation, capabilities, and performance in manufacturer - 3PL relationships. *Journal of Business Logistics, 25*(2), 43–64. doi:10.1002/j.2158-1592.2004.tb00181.x

Soderberg, L., & Bengtsson, L. (2010). Supply chain management maturity and performance in SMEs. *Operations Management Research, 3*(1), 90–97. doi:10.1007/s12063-010-0030-6

Sodhi, B., & Prabhakar, T. V. (2011). Application architecture considerations for cloud platforms, *Communication Systems and Networks (COMSNETS), 2011 Third International Conference on,* 1-4, 4-8 Jan. 2011 doi:10.1109/COMSNETS.2011.5716417

Song, B., Hassan, M. M., & Huh, E. N. (2010, November). *A novel heuristic-based task selection and allocation framework in dynamic collaborative cloud service platform.* In Cloud Computing Technology and Science (CloudCom), 2010 IEEE Second International Conference on (pp. 360-367). IEEE.

Song, Y., Wang, H., Li, Y., Feng, B., & Sun, Y. (2009). Multi-tiered on-demand resource scheduling for vm-based data center. In *Proceedings of the 2009 9th IEEE/ACM International Symposium on Cluster Computing and the Grid,* (pp. 148–155). IEEE Computer Society. doi:10.1109/CCGRID.2009.11

SPECpower (2013). Benchmark results summary of hitachi model no: Ha8000/ss10 (dl2).

Speitkamp, B., & Bichler, M. (2010). A mathematical programming approach for server consolidation problems in virtualized data centers. *Services Computing. IEEE Transactions on, 3*(4), 266–278.

Srikantaiah, S., Kansal, A., & Zhao, F. (2008). Energy aware consolidation for cloud computing. In *Proceedings of the 2008 conference on Power aware computing and systems,* 10. USENIX Association.

Stamper, R. (1996). Signs, Information, Norms and Systems. In Holmqvist, B., Andersen, P., Klein, H. and Posner, R. (Eds.), Signs of Work (pp. 349–397). Berlin, Germany: de Gruyter.

Stein, S., Ware, J., Laboy, J., & Schaffer, H. E. (2013). Improving K-12 pedagogy via a cloud designed for education. *International Journal of Information Management, 33*(1), 235–241. doi:10.1016/j.ijinfomgt.2012.07.009

Stieninger, M., & Nedbal, D. (2014). Characteristics of cloud computing in the business context: A systematic literature review. *Global Journal of Flexible Systems Management, 15*(1), 59–68. doi:10.1007/s40171-013-0055-4

Stock, J. R., Boyer, S. L., & Harmon, T. (2010). Research opportunities in supply chain management. *Journal of the Academy of Marketing Science, 38*(1), 32–41. doi:10.1007/s11747-009-0136-2

Subashini, S., & Kavitha, V. (2010). A survey on security issues in service delivery models of cloud computing. *Journal of Network and Computer Applications.*

Suleman, H. (2012). *Why should African academics care about Open Access?* Retrieved from http://repository.up.ac.za/handle/2263/18808

Sultan, N. (2010). Cloud computing for education: A new dawn? *International Journal of Information Management, 30*(2), 109–116. doi:10.1016/j.ijinfomgt.2009.09.004

Sunitha, C., Kokilam, V. K., & Preethi, M. B. (2013, December). Medical Informatics-Perk up Health Care through Information; Mumbai. *CSI Communications Journal, 37*(9), 7–8.

Swarts, P., & Wachira, E. (2010). ICT in Education Situational Analysis. Tanzania: Global e-Schools and Communities Initiative. Retrieved from http://www.gesci.org/assets/files/Knowledge Centre/Situational Analysis_Tanzania.pdf

Taheri, J., Choon Lee, Y., Zomaya, A. Y., & Siegel, H. J. (2013). A Bee Colony based optimization approach for simultaneous job scheduling and data replication in grid environments. *Computers & Operations Research*, *40*(6), 1564–1578. doi:10.1016/j.cor.2011.11.012

Tang, Q., Gupta, S. K. S., & Varsamopoulos, G. (2008). Energy-efficient thermal aware task scheduling for homogeneous high performance computing data centers: A cyber-physical approach. *IEEE Transactions on Parallel and Distributed Systems*, *19*(11), 1458–1472.

Teddlie, C., & Yu, F. (2007). Mixed methods sampling: A typology with examples. *Journal of Mixed Methods Research*, *1*(1), 77–100. doi:10.1177/2345678906292430

Thakur, I. S. (2006). *Introduction Environmental Biotechnology*. New Delhi: IK International.

Thibodeau, P. (August 03, 2011). Data centers use 2% of u.s. energy, below forecast. *Computer world*.

Thomas, P. Y. (2009). *Cloud Computing: A potential paradigm for practising the scholarship of teaching and learning*. Retrieved May 4, 2014, from http://www.ais.up.ac.za/digi/docs/thomas_paper.pdf

Tilley, S. R., & Parveen, T. (2013). *Software Testing in the Cloud: Perspectives on an Emerging Discipline*. Information Science Reference. doi:10.4018/978-1-4666-2536-5

Tiwari, A. K. (2010). *Infrastructure for Sustainable Rural Development*. New Delhi: Regal Publications.

Torrejón, D.A.R. & Ramos, J.M.M. (2013). *Text Alignment Module in CoReMo 2.1 Plagiarism Detector*. Notebook for Uncovering Plagiarism, Authorship, and Social Software Misuse (PAN) at CLEF.

Truong, D. (2014). *Cloud-based solutions for supply chain management: A post-adoption study*. Paper presented at the ASBBS 21st Annual Conference, Las Vegas, CA.

Truong, D. (2010). How cloud computing enhances competitive advantages: A research model for small businesses. *The Business Review, Cambridge*, *15*(1), 59–65.

Tushman, M. L., & Nadler, D. A. (1978). Information processing as an integrating concept in organizational design. *Academy of Management Review*, *3*(3), 613–624.

Umesh, B. & S, R. C. (2010). Optimal placement algorithms for virtual machines. *arXiv preprint arXiv:1011.5064*.

University Ranking (UR). (2014). Retrieved from http://www.webometrics.info/en/Ranking_africa/Sub_saharan_Africa

Van der Vorst, J. G. A. J., & Beulens, A. J. M. (2002). Identifying sources of uncertainty to generate supply chain redesign strategies. *International Journal of Physical Distribution & Logistics Management*, *32*(6), 409–430. doi:10.1108/09600030210437951

Van, H. N., Tran, F., & Menaud, J.-M. (2010). Performance and power management for cloud infrastructures. *In Cloud Computing (CLOUD), 2010 IEEE 3rd International Conference on, pages 329–336*.

Vaquero, L. M., Rodero-Merino, L., Caceres, J., & Lindner, M. (2009). Caceres J and Lindner M, A Break in the Clouds: Towards a Cloud Definition. *Computer Communication Review*, *39*(1), 50–55. doi:10.1145/1496091.1496100

Vaughan-Nichols, S. J. (2008). Virtualization sparks security concerns. *IEEE computer*, *41*(8), 13-15.

Veen, J. (2000). *The Art & Science of Web Design*. Indianapolis, IN: New Riders Publishing.

Venkatachalam, V., & Franz, M. (2005). Power reduction techniques for microprocessor systems. *ACM Computing Surveys*, *37*(3), 195–237. doi:10.1145/1108956.1108957

Venkatesh, V. (1985). Determinants of Perceived Ease of Use: Integrating Control, Intrinsic Motivation, and Emotion into the Technology Acceptance Model. *Information Systems Research*, *11*(4), 342–365. doi:10.1287/isre.11.4.342.11872

Venkatesh, V., & Davis, F. D. (2000). A theoretical extension of the technology acceptance model: Four longitudinal field studies. *Management Science*, *46*(2), 186–204. doi:10.1287/mnsc.46.2.186.11926

Venkatesh, V., Morris, M. G., Davis, G. B., & Davis, F. D. (2003). User acceptance of information technology: Toward a unified view. *Management Information Systems Quarterly*, *27*(3), 425–478.

Verma, A., Ahuja, P., & Neogi, A. (2008). pmapper: power and migration cost aware application placement in virtualized systems. In Middleware 2008 (pp. 243–264). Springer.

Vickery, S. K., Droge, C., Setia, P., & Sambamurthy, V. (2010). Supply chain information technologies and organizational initiatives: Complementary versus independent effects on agility and firm performance. *International Journal of Production Research*, *48*(23), 7025–7042. doi:10.1080/00207540903348353

Vijayrani, S. (2013, December). Economic Health Records: An Overview. Mumbai. *CSI Communications Journal*, *37*(9), 9–11.

VmWare (2012). Vmware.

VMware. (1983). Capacity planner. http://www.vmware.com/products/capacityplanner/

VMware. (n.d.). Retrieved from http://www.vmware.com/

Vosloo, S. (2009). *The effects of texting on literacy: Modern scourge or opportunity?* Retrieved March 15, 2010, from http://vosloo.net/wp-content/uploads/pubs/texting_and_literacy_apr09_sv.pdf

Vouk, M. A. (2008). Cloud computing: Issues, research and implementations. *Journal of Computing and Information Technology*, *16*(4), 235–246.

Vouk, M. A. (2008). Virtualization of information technology resources. In *Electronic Commerce: A Managerial Perspective 2008* (5th ed.). Prentice-Hall Business Publishing.

Wakefield, J. S., Warren, S. J., & Alsobrook, M. (2011). Learning and teaching as communicative actions: A mixed-methods twitter study. *Knowledge Management & E-Learning: An International Journal*, *3*(4), 563–584.

Walterbusch, M., Martens, B., & Teuteberg, F. (2013). Evaluating cloud computing services from a total cost of ownership perspective. *Management Research Review*, *36*(6), 613–638. doi:10.1108/01409171311325769

Wang, L., Von Laszewski, G., Kunze, M., & Tao, J. (2008). Cloud computing: A Perspective study. *Proc. Grid Computing Environments (GCE) workshop*. doi:10.1007/s00354-008-0081-5

Wang, W., Tolk, A., & Wang, W. (2009). The levels of conceptual interoperability model: Applying systems engineering principles to M&S. In Wainer, G., Shaffer, C., McGraw, R. & Chinni, M. (Eds.), *Spring Simulation Multiconference* (article no.: 168). San Diego, CA: Society for Computer Simulation International.

Wang, C., Cao, N., Li, J., Ren, K., & Lou, W. (2010) *Secure Ranked Keyword Search over Encrypted Cloud Data.Proceedings of the 30th International Conference on Distributed Computing Systems (ICDCS'10)*, Genoa, Italy, June 21-25, 2010. doi:10.1109/ICDCS.2010.34

Wang, E. T. G., Tai, J. C. F., & Wei, H. L. (2006). A virtual integration theory of improved supply-chain performance. *Journal of Management Information Systems*, *23*(2), 41–64. doi:10.2753/MIS0742-1222230203

Wang, K., & Lin, C. L. (2012). The adoption of mobile value-added services: Investigating the influence of IS quality and perceived playfulness. *Managing Service Quality*, *22*(2), 184–208. doi:10.1108/09604521211219007

Wang, M., Chen, Y., & Khan, M. J. (2014). Mobile cloud learning for higher education: A case study of Moodle in the cloud. *International Review of Research in Open and Distance Learning*, *15*(2), 254–267.

Wang, S., Liu, Z., Sun, Q., Zou, H., & Yang, F. (2014). Towards an accurate evaluation of quality of cloud service in service-oriented cloud computing. *Journal of Intelligent Manufacturing*, *25*(2), 283–291. doi:10.1007/s10845-012-0661-6

Wanjiku, R. (2009). East African universities take advantage of Google cloud. *Info World*. Retrieved from http://news.idg.no/cw/art.cfm?id=D3ED873F-1A64-6A71-CE3B759E5A305061

Warden, P. (2012). *Big Data Glossary*. Mumbai: Shroff Publishers & Distributors Private Limited.

Wayne, J., & Timothy, G. (2011). *Guidelines on Security and Privacy in Public Cloud Computing*. Information Technology Laboratory.

Webber, J., Parastatidis, S., & Robinson, I. (2010). *REST in Practice: Hypermedia and Systems Architecture*. Sebastopol, CA: O'Reilly Media, Inc. doi:10.1007/978-3-642-15114-9_3

Weber-Jahnke, J., Peyton, L., & Topaloglou, T. (2012). eHealth system interoperability. *Information Systems Frontiers, 14*(1), 1–3. doi:10.1007/s10796-011-9319-8

WebSphere. I. (1983). Cloudburst. http://www-01.ibm.com/software/webservers/cloudburst/

Wiederhold, G. (1995). Digital libraries, value, and productivity. *Communications of the ACM, 38*(4), 85–96.

Willcocks, L. P., Venters, W., & Whitley, E. A. (2013). Cloud sourcing and innovation: Slow train coming? A composite research study. *Strategic Outsourcing: An International Journal, 6*(2), 184–202. doi:10.1108/SO-04-2013-0004

Winkler, H. (2009). How to improve supply chain flexibility using strategic supply chain networks. *Logistics Research, 1*(1), 15–25. doi:10.1007/s12159-008-0001-6

Wolf, J. (2011). Sustainable supply chain management integration: A qualitative analysis of the German manufacturing industry. *Journal of Business Ethics, 102*(2), 221–235. doi:10.1007/s10551-011-0806-0

Wong, K. (2009). Pictures in the Cloud. *Computer Graphics World, 32*, 42–47.

Wood, T., Shenoy, P. J., Venkataramani, A., & Yousif, M. S. (2007). Black-box and gray-box strategies for virtual machine migration. In NSDI, volume 7, pages 229–242.

Wood, T., Tarasuk-Levin, G., Shenoy, P., Desnoyers, P., Cecchet, E., & Corner, M. D. (2009). Memory buddies: Exploiting page shar- ing for smart colocation in virtualized data centers. *InProceedings of the 2009 ACM SIGPLAN/SIGOPS International Conference on Virtual Execution Environments, VEE '09, pages*31–40*, New York, NY, USA. ACM.*

Wooffitt, R. (2005). *Conversation analysis and discourse analysis: A comparative and critical introduction.* London: Sage.

Wooley, P. (2011). Identifying Cloud Computing Security Risks.

World Wide Worx & Fuseware. (2012). *South African social media landscape 2012 – Executive summary.* Retrieved April 21, 2013, from http://www.worldwideworx.com/wp-content/uploads/2012/10/Exec-Summary-Social-Media-20121.pdf

Wu, Y., Cegielski, C. G., Hazen, B. T., & Hall, D. J. (2013). Cloud computing in support of supply chain information system infrastructure: Understanding when to go to the cloud. *Journal of Supply Chain Management, 49*(3), 25–41. doi:10.1111/j.1745-493x.2012.03287.x

Wyatt, E., Griendling, K., & Mavris, D. (2012). Addressing interoperability in military systems-of-systems architectures. In BeaulieuA. (Ed.) *International Systems Conference* (pp. 1-8). Piscataway, NJ: IEEE Computer Society Press.

Wycisk, C., McKelvey, B., & Hulsmann, M. (2008). Smart parts, supply networks as complex adaptive systems: Analysis and implications. *International Journal of Physical Distribution & Logistics Management, 38*(2), 108–125. doi:10.1108/09600030810861198

Xinping, H. (2010). The Concept of Cloud Library. *Information Studies: Theory & Application, 6*, 009.

Xuan, Z., Nattapong, W., Hao, L., & Xuejie, Z. (2010). Information Security Risk Management Framework for the Cloud Computing Environments. *10th IEEE International Conference on Computer and Information Technology (CIT 2010).*

Xu, J., & Fortes, J. A. B. (2010). Multi-objective virtual machine placement in virtualized data center environments. *InProceedings of the 2010 IEEE/ACM Int'L Conference on Green Computing and Communications & Int'L Conference on Cyber, Physical and Social Computing, GREENCOM-CPSCOM '10, pages*179–188*, Washington, DC, USA. IEEE Computer Society.*

Xun, X. (2012). From cloud computing to cloud manufacturing. *Robotics and Computer-integrated Manufacturing, 28*(1), 75–86. doi:10.1016/j.rcim.2011.07.002

Yang, F., Wu, D., Liang, L., Bi, G., & Wu, D. D. (2011). Supply chain DEA: Production possibility set and performance evaluation model. *Annals of Operations Research, 185*(1), 195–211. doi:10.1007/s10479-008-0511-2

Yang, S. Q. (2012). Move into the Cloud, shall we? *Library HiTechNews, 29*(1), 4–7. doi:10.1108/07419051211223417

Yao, A. C.-C. (1980). New algorithms for bin packing. *Journal of the ACM, 27*(2), 207–227.

Ye, K., Huang, D., Jiang, X., Chen, H., & Wu, S. (2010). Virtual machine based energy-efficient data center architecture for cloud computing: a performance perspective. In *Proceedings of the 2010 IEEE/ACM Int'l Conference on Green Computing and Communications & Int'l Conference on Cyber, Physical and Social Computing* (pp. 171–178). IEEE Computer Society. doi:10.1109/GreenCom-CPSCom.2010.108

Yeo, C. S., & Buyya, R. (2006). A taxonomy of market-based resource management systems for utility-driven cluster computing. *Software, Practice & Experience*, *36*(13), 1381–1419. doi:10.1002/spe.725

Yoo, C. S. (2011). Cloud computing: Architectural and policy implications. *Review of Industrial Organization*, *38*(4), 405–421. doi:10.1007/s11151-011-9295-7

York, NY, USA. ACM .

Yount, W. R. (2006). *Research design and statistical analysis for Christian ministry*. Louisville: NAPCE.

Yousafzai, S. Y., Foxall, G. R., & Pallister, J. G. (2010). Explaining internet banking behavior: Theory of reasoned action, theory of planned behavior, or technology acceptance model? *Journal of Applied Social Psychology*, *40*(5), 1172–1202. doi:10.1111/j.1559-1816.2010.00615.x

Yuan, L., MacNeill, S., & Kraan, W. (2008). Open educational resources—Opportunities and challenges for higher education. Retrieved from http://learn.creativecommons.org/wp-content/uploads/2008/09/oer_briefing_paper.pdf

Yu, J., Sheng, Q. Z., & Han, Y. (2013). Introduction to special issue on cloud and service computing. *Service Oriented Computing and Applications*, *7*(2), 75–76. doi:10.1007/s11761-013-0132-8

Zacharias, N. T. (2012). *Qualitative research methods for second language education: A coursebook*. Newcastle upon Tyne: Cambridge Scholars Publishing.

Zacharia, Z. G., Sanders, N. R., & Fugate, B. S. (2014). Evolving functional perspectives within supply chain management. *Journal of Supply Chain Management*, *50*(1), 73–88. doi:10.1111/jscm.12022

Zhang Qi, Cheng Lu & Boutaba Raouf (2010). Cloud computing: state-of-the-art and research challenges. *Journal of Internet Services and Applications. Springer-Verlag. 1(1), pages 7-18.*

Zhang, L., Chen, Y., Sun, R., Jing, S., & Yang, B. (2008). A task scheduling algorithm based on PSO for grid computing. *International Journal of Computational Intelligence Research*, *4*(1), 37–43. doi:10.5019/j.ijcir.2008.123

Zhang, Q., Cheng, L., & Boutaba, R. (2010). Cloud computing: State-of-the-art and research challenges. *Journal of Internet Services and Applications*, *1*(1), 7–18. doi:10.1007/s13174-010-0007-6

Zhang, X., Shae, Z.-Y., Zheng, S., & Jamjoom, H. (2012). Virtual machine migration in an over-committed cloud. In *Network Operations and Management Symposium (NOMS)*, 2012 *IEEE, pages* 196–203.

Zhao, C., Zhang, S., Liu, Q., Xie, J., & Hu, J. (2009, September). *Independent tasks scheduling based on genetic algorithm in cloud computing*. In Wireless Communications, Networking and Mobile Computing, 2009. WiCom'09. 5th International Conference on (pp. 1-4). IEEE.

Zhao, M., & Figueiredo, R. J. (2007). Experimental study of virtual machine migration in support of reservation of cluster resources. *In Proceedings of the 2Nd International Workshop on Virtualization Technology in Distributed Computing, VTDC '07, pages 5:1–5:8, New*

Zhuge, H. (2011). Semantic linking through spaces for cyber-physical-socio intelligence: A methodology. *Artificial Intelligence*, *175*(5-6), 988–1019. doi:10.1016/j.artint.2010.09.009

Zomaya, A. Y., & Teh, Y. H. (2001). Observations on using genetic algorithms for dynamic load-balancing. Parallel and Distributed Systems. *IEEE Transactions on*, *12*(9), 899–911.

About the Contributors

N. Raghavendra Rao has a doctorate in the area of finance from University of Pune India. He is an advisor to FINAT Consultancy Services India. Dr. Rao has a rare distinction of having experience in the combined areas of Information Technology and Business applications. His rich experience in Industry is matched with a parallel academic experience in Management & IT in Business Schools. He is a visiting Professor to Business Schools in India. He has over two and half decades of experience in the development of application software related to manufacturing, service oriented organizations, financial institutions and business enterprises. He presents papers related to Information technology and Knowledge Management at National and International conferences. He contributes articles on Information Technology to mainstream newspapers and journals. His areas of publications related to research are Mobile Computing, Virtual Technology, and Commerce in Space, Ubiquitous Commerce, Cloud Computing, and Innovation Management.

***

Sourav Kanti Addya is pursuing a Ph.D. in Department of Computer Science Engg at National Institute of Technology, Rourkela, India. He is also a visiting researcher in Department of Computer and Electrical Engineering at San Diego State university, USA. His area of research is cloud computing. His other areas of research are wireless sensor netwoks and network security. He obtained his M. Tech and B. Tech in computer science & Engg form NIT Rourkela, India and West Bengal University of Technology, India respectively. He has 3 years of teaching experience. His technical interests include Algorithm Design, Computer Networks, Optimization techniques, Information security and Web Technologies.

Simon Broome is a published and experienced Prince certified Programme/Senior Project Manager with Cranfield change management accreditation, with considerable experience of managing UK based and offshore Projects. He is currently leading a programme of UK Technology Strategy Board (TSB) sponsored research and development projects at Jaguar Land Rover. Simon has managed a number of large publicly funded, high visibility projects with the European Regional development fund (ERDF) FP7 program and with the UK Technology Strategy Board competition based funded project programme, and has extensive experience (20 years) in leading large multinational software delivery projects with international teams in the Czech republic, America, France, Germany, Brazil, and a number of locations in India, chiefly Bangalore.

Chaka Chaka is a senior lecturer in the Department of Applied Languages, Faculty of Humanities, at the Tshwane University of Technology (Pretoria), South Africa. He previously lectured at three South African universities. His research interests include the following areas: computer-mediated communication; electronic learning (e-learning); computer assisted language learning; mobile learning; mobile assisted language learning; learning and teaching through text and instant messaging; Web 2.0 learning/ Mobile Web 2.0 learning; Web 3.0/Mobile Web 3.0 learning; Semantic Web learning/Mobile Semantic Web learning; online genre and discourse analysis; knowledge management; and learning organization. He has published book chapters related to each of these research areas. One of his latest (2015) published book chapters is: "Digital identity, social presence technologies, and presence learning." In Wright, R. D. (Ed.), *Student-Teacher Interaction in Online Learning Environments* (pp. 181-203). Hershey, PA.: IGI Global (ISBN: 978-1-4666-6462-3). He has also published articles for the *Cutter IT Journal*.

José C. Delgado is an Associate Professor at the Computer Science and Engineering Department of the Instituto Superior Técnico (University of Lisbon), in Lisbon, Portugal, where he earned the Ph.D. degree in 1988. He lectures courses in the areas of Computer Architecture, Information Technology, and Service Engineering. He has performed several management roles in his faculty, namely Director of the Taguspark campus, near Lisbon, and Coordinator of the B.Sc. and M.Sc. in Computer Science and Engineering at that campus. He has been the coordinator of and researcher in several international research projects. As an author, his publications include one book, 20 book chapters and more than 50 papers in international refereed conferences and journals.

Debbie Garside is CEO and Scrum Product Owner of GeoLang's Ascema Solution, protecting critical content across boundaries, which found its origins from within the IPCRESS project collaboration between GeoLang, University of Surrey and Jaguar LandRover. With 25+ years of experience running IT companies, Debbie is an expert in cyber security and natural language. Awarded the first Prince of Wales Innovation Scholarship by University of Wales, Debbie is a Senior Visiting Research Fellow at Glyndwr University. Debbie sits on the advisory board to HPC Wales - £40 million high performance computing network and was an Advisory Board Member to Wikimedia Foundation. An editor of two international (ISO) standards, Debbie chaired a number of BSI/ISO committees as Principle UK Expert and is a named contributor to related internet standards by the Internet Engineering Task Force. Debbie is currently writing her PhD thesis 'Human Visual Perception in Cyber Security' and has patented her Pseudo-Isochromatic CAPTCHA System.

Lee Gillam is a Senior Lecturer in the Department of Computing at the University of Surrey, and Chartered IT Professional Fellow of the British Computer Society (FBCS CITP). Research interests and teaching activities cover Cloud Computing, Information Retrieval and Information Extraction and Ontology Learning, and the Legal, Ethical and Professional dimensions of Computing. He is the Founding Editor-in-Chief of the Springer Journal of Cloud Computing Advances, Systems and Applications (JoCCASA), an editor of a Springer book on Cloud Computing, and has been PI on several Cloud research projects with funding from industry and the UK research councils, most recently for the UK Technology Strategy Board.

K. Hariharanath MBA PhD has 15+ years of experience in IT product design, development and implementation. He has experience in IT products ranging from enterprise suite of products to e-commerce products. His doctoral work is 'Enterprise Application Integration' as a tool for integrating IT infrastructure in companies with the business objective of linking business to Information Technology. All along his career, he has been at the center of teaching on a visiting professor basis at ICFAI, Hyderabad and SSN School of Management, Chennai. His teaching interests are strategic management and IT Business Strategy. He has worked on a consulting assignment in building a new generation business model based on social marketing outlook for a start-up e-commerce company. He is currently working as professor at SSN School of Management and Computer Applications, India.

Mouna Jouini is a PhD student in the Department of Computer Science at the Tunis University in the Higher Institute of Management (ISG). She received her Mastery diploma on computer science applied to management in 2008 from the University of Tunis in the Higher School of Economics and Management of Tunis (ESSECTT) and her master's degree in 2010 from the Tunis University in the Higher Institute of Management (ISG). Her research interest includes software engineering metrics, cloud computing, cyber security and security measurement and quantification. She has published and participated in several international conferences including topics related to the computer science, cloud computing, and cyber security.

Kijpokin Kasemsap received his BEng degree in Mechanical Engineering from King Mongkut's University of Technology Thonburi, his MBA degree from Ramkhamhaeng University, and his DBA degree in Human Resource Management from Suan Sunandha Rajabhat University. He is a Special Lecturer at Faculty of Management Sciences, Suan Sunandha Rajabhat University based in Bangkok, Thailand. He is a Member of International Association of Engineers (IAENG), International Association of Engineers and Scientists (IAEST), International Economics Development and Research Center (IEDRC), International Association of Computer Science and Information Technology (IACSIT), International Foundation for Research and Development (IFRD), and International Innovative Scientific and Research Organization (IISRO). He also serves on the International Advisory Committee (IAC) for International Association of Academicians and Researchers (INAAR). He has numerous original research articles in top international journals, conference proceedings, and book chapters on business management, human resource management, and knowledge management published internationally.

George W. Kibirige is an Assistant Lecturer at the Department of Informatics, Sokoine University of Agriculture, Tanzania. He holds BSc in Information and Communication Technology Management from Mzumbe University and MSc. Computer Science (Information Security) from University of Technology Malaysia, Malaysia. His research interest is in the area of Information Security especially on awareness.

Dilip Kumar is an Assistant Professor in the Department of Computer Science and Engineering, NIT Jamshedpur, INDIA. He has 15 years of teaching experience in undergraduate level in the field of Computer Science and Engineering. He received his B.E in Computer Science and Engineering from BIT Sindri and M. Tech in Computer Science from NIT Rourkela in 2014. He is doing his PhD from National Institute of Technology Jamshedpur in the field of Optimization in Cloud Computing. His technical interests include Cloud Computing, Image Processing, Algorithm and Optimization. He is also member of Computer Society of India and Robotic Society of India.

Tarni Mandal received a Bachelor of Science (Hons.) in Statistics in 1977 followed by a Master of Science in Statistics in 1980 from Bhagalpur University. He received a Master of Science in Mathematics from Ranchi University in 1995 and was awarded his PhD degree from Ranchi University in 2001. He is working at National Institute of Technology, Jamshedpur as Associate Professor in the department of Mathematics. He has more than 30 years of Teaching Experience in undergraduate and graduate levels in the field of Mathematics & Statistics. His research interest includes Operations Research, Statistics, Security and Fractional Functional Programming Problem. He is also a member of ISTE and member of International Academy of Physical Sciences.

Scott Notley graduated from the University of Southampton in 1995 with a MEng in Electronic Engineering and received a Ph.D. from the University of Southampton in 2002. His thesis investigated the application of non-linear signal processing techniques and dynamical modelling to the problem of predicting epileptic seizures from EEG signals. He is currently a research fellow at the University of Manchester where his research interests lie mainly in the areas of signal and image processing with an emphasis on deriving robust quantitative scientific measurements from bio-medical data. Other particular active research areas of interest are pattern recognition, image segmentation, spiking neural networks and computational neuroscience.

Latifa Ben Arfa Rabai is a University associate professor in the Department of Computer Science at the Tunis University in the Higher Institute of Management (ISG). She received the computer science Engineering diploma in 1989 from the sciences faculty of Tunis and the PhD, from The Sciences Faculty of Tunis in 1992. Her research interest includes software engineering trends quantification, quality assessment in education and e-learning, and security measurement and quantification. She has published in information sciences Journal, IEEE Technology and Engineering Education magazine. She has participated in several international conferences covering topics related to the computer science, E-learning, quality assessment in education, cyber security.

Bibhudatta Sahoo obtained his M. Tech. and Ph.D. degrees in Computer Engineering from NIT, Rourkela. He has 24 years of Teaching Experience in undergraduate and graduate levels in the field of Computer Science & Engineering. He is presently Assistant Professor in the Department of Computer Science & Engineering, NIT Rourkela, INDIA. His technical interests include Data Structures & Algorithm Design, Parallel & Distributed Systems, Networks, Computational Machines, Algorithms for VLSI Design, Performance evaluation methods and modelling techniques Distributed computing system, Networking algorithms, and Web engineering. He is member of IEEE and ACM. He was also awarded for National Scholarship for PG study.

Camilius Sanga is an Associate Professor of Informatics in the Department of Informatics at Sokoine University of Agriculture (SUA), Tanzania. He is a head of Department of Informatics in the Faculty of Science, SUA. He has a PhD in Computer Science from University of the Western Cape, South Africa. Also, he holds a MSc. in Computer Science and a BSc. in Computer Science from Osmania University and University of Dar es Salaam respectively. His research interest is in the area of Information and Communication Technology for Development (ICT4D). He has published papers in a number of International journals. He has also published articles in local and International conferences in the field of ICT4D. Furthermore, he has co-authored two books as well as a number of book chapters. Some of the research projects in which Sanga has been involved are: (i) Development of Monitoring and Evaluation system for Projects under Enhancing Pro-poor Innovations in Natural Resources and Agricultural Value-chains (EPINAV) at SUA, (ii) Promoting participation of female students in Science, Technology, Engineering and Mathematics using e-learning and (iii) Farmer Voice Radio (FVR) Project - Building a radio - based, impact driven small farmer extension service system. Currently, he is an assistant project leader for the research titled "The role of mobile phones towards improving coverage of agricultural extension services: a case study of maize value chain". Lastly, he is involved in the project titled "Assessing the impacts of climate variability and change on agricultural systems in Eastern Africa while enhancing the region's capacity to undertake integrated assessment of vulnerabilities to future changes in climate" (2012-2014).

R. Todd Stephens is the Senior Technical Architect for the AT&T Corporation. For the past 32 years, Todd has worked in the Information Technology field including leadership positions at BellSouth, Coca-Cola, Georgia-Pacific and Cingular Wireless. Todd has delivered keynotes, tutorials and educational sessions for a wide variety of technology conferences. Todd holds degrees in Mathematics and Computer Science from Columbus State University, an MBA degree from Georgia State University, and a Ph.D. in Information Systems from Nova Southeastern University. Todd has been awarded twelve U.S. patents in the field of technology and authored/co-authored several books on web-enabled applications, Open Source, Collaboration, and Web 2.0.

Ashok Kumar Turuk is working as an associate professor in Dept. of Computer Science & Engineering at National Institute of Technology, Rourkela, India. He obtained his Ph.D. degree in Computer Science & Engineering from Indian Institute of Technology, Kharagpur, India and his M. Tech and B. Tech form National Institute of Technology, Rourkela, India. He has 18 years of Teaching Experience in undergraduate and graduate levels in the field of computer Science & Engineering. His current research area includes Optical networking, cloud computing, and wireless sensor network. He has handled several technical projects.

Index

Printed in the United States
By Bookmasters